FIT FOR FREEDOM, NOT FOR FRIENDSHIP

D1260392

The Underground Railroad. Oil on canvas painting by Charles T. Webber, 1893. Cincinnati Art Museum, Subscription Fund Purchase.

Fit for Freedom, Not for Friendship

Quakers, African Americans, and the Myth of Racial Justice

by Donna McDaniel
and Vanessa Julye

Quaker Press
OF FRIENDS GENERAL CONFERENCE
Philadelphia, Pennsylvania

Copyright © 2009 Quaker Press of Friends General Conference
All rights reserved
1216 Arch Street 2B
Philadelphia, PA 19107

Printed in the United States of America

Composition and design by David Budmen

Cover photo: Students on the "Joggling board" at Quaker-supported Laing
School, Mt. Pleasant, SC. Courtesy of South Caroliniana Library, University
of South Carolina, Columbia.

ISBN: 978-1-888305-80-7 (paperback)
        978-1-888305-79-1 (hardcover)

Library of Congress Cataloging-in-Publication Data
McDaniel, Donna, 1934–
    Fit for freedom, not for friendship : Quakers, African Americans, and the myth of
racial justice / by Donna McDaniel and Vanessa Julye.
        p. cm.
    Includes bibliographical references and index.
    ISBN 978-1-888305-79-1 (hardcover : alk. paper) — ISBN 978-1-888305-80-7
(pbk. : alk. paper)
    1. Race relations—Religious aspects—Society of Friends—History. 2. Society
of Friends—United States—History. 3. United States—Race relations—History.
I. Julye, Vanessa. II. Title.

BX7748.R3M34 2009
289.6089'96073—dc22

                        2008049334

To order more copies of this publication or other Quaker titles call
1-800-966-4556 or on the world wide web at www.quakerbooks.org

In loving memory of Barbara Hirshkowitz, a wonderful friend, mentor, and editor who left this earth too soon. This book would not have been possible without her hard work and support. And to all those, whose lives, like Barbara's, are a witness to racial justice and equality.

Contents

CONTENTS

Illustrations

ILLUSTRATIONS

Preface

THE HISTORY OF THE RELATIONSHIP between the Religious Society of Friends and Americans of African descent is a difficult and sensitive one to write. Here we want to share our definitions of the subjects we examine, explain our purposes in creating this work, describe how the book is structured, and suggest some of the recurring issues discovered in our examination of this relationship—and in the history of Quakers in general.

Fit for Freedom, Not for Friendship recounts the history of Quaker efforts to achieve racial equity from its beginnings in the New World into the modern era. Our overarching goal is to reveal how insidious, complex, and pervasive racism has been, and continues to be, and to document the spiritual and practical impacts of racial discrimination on the Religious Society of Friends, past and present.

The book is divided into two parts: the first considers the years up to 1900, and the second, the years from the dawn of the twentieth century to about 1980. In a sense this book is a hybrid, for each of its parts is formed largely from a different type of source. Scholarship on the relationship of Quakers and African Americans before 1900 is abundant, and we believe Friends and others would be served best by a work that assembles the dispersed findings and interpretations of the many historians and others who have studied the subject. Accordingly, Part One assembles and synthesizes existing scholarship on the subject in the seventeenth through the nineteenth centuries. In Part One we have from time to time reviewed primary sources, in large part to verify quotations or to attempt to clarify findings of various historians. In contrast, because far fewer scholars have examined the subject in the twentieth century, Part Two is based largely on primary sources—statements from meetings and individual Friends, and articles from Quaker periodicals. From these collected works, we hope to identify a path toward a future we can realize with each other, as an inclusive, nonracist community.

First we must define our terms. We use "Friends" and "Quakers" to denote those who have been, or are, members of the Religious Society of Friends. For most people of European descent, the simple word "Quaker" prompts an image of people of European ancestry. Yet by the late 1800s the Society in the United States included members of Native American, Arabic, Asian, African, African American, and Caribbean African descent. We are acutely aware of the need for inclusive thought and language patterns when we speak of Quakers, and we hope the day will come when it will not be necessary to remind anyone that Quakers include people of many ethnic backgrounds. In the past, the convention in writing was that anyone not specifically identified as "African American" in the text was assumed to be "European American"; readers will note that we do not make that assumption, but identify each person by his or her descent.

The terms used to describe people of African descent in this country continue to change, and in the absence of agreed-upon terminology we chose terms that feel most respectful to us and to the people we surveyed—"African American," and "of African descent." When the immediate origins of people include Africa as well as other parts of the globe, we use the term "people of color." The exceptions to these general rules occur when other terms appear in direct quotations, such as "black power," or when a movement has, historically, described itself in a different manner, such as "the Black Panthers." Accurate descriptions of ancestry during the 1600s and 1700s, however, are sometimes difficult to determine, as enslaved Africans may have been born in Africa and, in later generations, the Caribbean, South America, and North America.

We also faced a difficult choice in the language around enslavement. To call someone a "slave" suggests an inherent identity, an intrinsic status. We chose instead to speak of an "enslaved person," "enslaved people," "enslavement," and "enslavers" because these words more accurately convey the loss of humanity that results from being captured and held in bondage, as well as from the act of enslaving. No one can be said, in any way other than legal, to have owned or to have been owned by another person.

Readers will encounter numerous terms specific to Quakerism. For readers unfamiliar with them, Quaker historian Martha Paxson Grundy has prepared a glossary that appears as an appendix in this volume.

Some complexities in defining membership and rejection of membership, however, should be clarified here. Not only did most early meetings not keep lists of members, but later meetings that did record membership did not routinely identify members by race. At any given time numerous Americans, of both Caucasian and African descent, considered themselves and were considered by others to be Quaker, though they were not actually members. These attenders lived "in the Quaker manner," dressing in plain garments, living simply, and attending meeting regularly. The only aspect of membership attenders were denied was the right to participate in "meeting for worship with attention to business." Similarly, persons disowned by meetings were not allowed to participate in meetings for business, serve on committees, or contribute financially; they were not barred from meeting for worship. Even though African American membership has been and continues to be slim, some African Americans felt sufficient affinity for Quakers to live in the Quaker manner and to attend meeting. Sojourner Truth, Benjamin Banneker, and Robert Purvis are three of the most familiar. Yet they never declared themselves to be Friends, nor were they recorded as Friends, though they are often mistakenly described as such.

Parts One and Two of this book attempt to include actions among Quakers in each region. With respect to the issue of enslavement, critical differences existed between Friends and Friends meetings on a regional level, some perhaps predictable and some surprising. In this connection we have tried to be careful not to assume that what was true for Friends in Philadelphia Yearly Meeting, the most studied and often most populous of all meetings, also was true for other meetings. More documents exist from this meeting than from others, and as a consequence it has been the focus of many scholarly works. We are fortunate that Philadelphia Yearly Meeting had the resources to develop a rich array of committees covering and re-covering seemingly countless concerns, and their minutes are instructive for all of us.

This book is organized in rough chronological order, but each of its chapters considers different issues that often overlap in historical time. Each chapter revolves around a concept and a set of related concepts, and the conceptual discussions are themselves presented as they developed in time and within regions. Chapter One describes the evolution of efforts to rid the Religious Society of Friends of any connection to the enslavement economy, whether trading in Africans, enslaving them, or both. Chapter Two explores the efforts of Quakers generally before 1830 to end enslavement in society at large, either on their own, through their meetings, or through affiliation with non-Quaker organizations, by engaging in such acts as petitioning and lobbying state and federal legislators; publishing antislavery newspapers; participating in national, regional, and local abolition and manumission societies; supporting or opposing colonization and gradual manumission; and boycotting goods made from the products of the enslavement system. Chapter Three deals with the decades between 1830 and 1860, when antislavery groups organized to work for immediate abolition. It analyzes support among Quakers for the immediate emancipation of enslaved people, which for some extended naturally into assisting fugitives from enslavement.

Chapter Four focuses on the efforts among Quakers to aid newly freed people up to the time of the Civil War—financial support in the early years of freedom, legal assistance, job training, restitution for past service, and education in segregated and integrated schools, those Quakers founded for their own children. Chapter Five deals with Quakers and African Americans during and after the Civil War, when one of Friends' principal endeavors was to create, fund, and teach in freedmen's schools. Chapter Six covers the period from 1680 to 1900, and examines the inclusion of African Americans as members in the Society of Friends and the arguments used for or against such inclusion.

In Part Two, Chapters Seven, Eight, and Nine all deal principally with different aspects of the twentieth-century Civil Rights movement. In analyzing the forces that powered discrimination, these facets are often hard to separate from each other, and as a consequence these chapters often describe different dimensions of the same movements. For instance, Chapter Seven explores Friends work specifically in the desegregation of American society, and Chapter Eight considers Friends efforts to realize economic justice for African Americans, including their intense involvement with the question of reparations. Chapter Nine analyzes Quaker responses to the use of violent means in the civil rights struggle and how, from the convergence of the Quaker peace testimony and the passive-resistance wing of the movement, Quakers generated specific nonviolent strategies. Finally, Chapters Ten and Eleven explore the large issue of racial inclusion in the Society of

Friends throughout the twentieth century—in Quaker schools and other institutions and in Quaker meetings—and concludes with views chiefly from African American Friends on the meaning of the Society's overall historical reluctance to integrate itself.

The Epilogue extends beyond 1980 into the current day, demonstrating the persistence of certain issues and trends among modern-day Quakers. Three such recurring issues bear mentioning at the outset.

One issue is the persistent tension between individual and corporate witness when Quaker meetings endeavor to arrive at a "sense of the meeting." Some members may not agree with the sense of the meeting—indeed, in a noncreedal, nonhierarchical organization such as the Religious Society of Friends, one statement rarely encompasses all members. A person who is not able to agree but who does not want to stop the meeting from moving forward may "stand aside" if she or he realizes the meeting is in agreement about God's will on an issue.

Achieving unity can be, and often is, a slow process. Members wait patiently for an "'unfolding' of what 'ought to be,'" as historian Errol Elliott puts it, but he also notes some activist Friends believed waiting for this "unfolding" led to a certain "danger of settling for things as they are." In every era, some Friends have judged the process of reaching unity too slow when measured against the pressing need to achieve racial equity. Frustrated with the direction or pace of corporate decision making, they were openly critical of their meetings and often acted outside them; they were willing to defy meeting leaders, even to risk their membership in their religious community, to carry on such work. While some activists forbore judging fellow Quakers who did not involve themselves in this struggle, others objected to Friends sitting quietly in the meetinghouse, remaining silent about the enslavement and racial injustice surrounding them, even as they held true the notion that "there is that of God in all people." More conservative Friends charged the activists with acting too hastily and on their own accord, unwilling to wait for guidance from the Light Within. In short, each seemed rightly placed to criticize the other of being in some manner unfaithful to Quaker testimonies. For some, attending to inner guidance was motivation to social action; for others, it mandated a separation from the world, which in turn made it difficult to respond to, much less understand, the injustices African Americans faced.

Our work has made clear certain aspects of Quakerism behind the mythology surrounding it. The many individuals who emblemized the "good Quaker"—abolitionists, Underground Railroad activists, Freedom Riders—have come to represent the Society of Friends as a whole. A common assumption is that all Quakers were abolitionists (and sometimes that all abolitionists were Quaker), that all Quakers assisted fugitive slaves, and that all Quakers were involved in civil rights activism because of their beliefs. The entire society has been credited for particular social advances that, in truth, rest properly with individuals bearing their own witness.

A second issue is whether Friends have truly been a "peculiar people" with beliefs and practices that set them apart from society, or have instead tended to mirror the views of society at large. Because many activists believe the Society is singular in its beliefs and actions, they have been particularly critical of those times when Quakers have behaved like other Americans—more concerned about their economic and social status than about justice, more invested in hierarchy than in equality, more apt to take a paternal than fraternal stance in their efforts to assist those who suffer disadvantage in American society. If, as many historians have argued, Quakers over time have shown themselves more likely to share the views of non-Quakers than to adhere to distinct testimonies, then Quakers' share of responsibility for chronic inequality may be judged as no *greater* than that of any other Americans of European descent. Were they "children of their time?" Even if so, can apathy or antagonism to reform be excused in any measure? Does believing that God exists equally in everyone require more of Quakers? Does it demand a greater commitment to achieving racial justice than other denominations demonstrate? Has Quakerism, as one historian suggested, fallen "short of its high calling?"

This second issue relates directly to the third—the historical belief among most European Americans that, while African Americans deserved full and unqualified political equality, they would never realize social equality with European Americans. At the same time meetings and individual Friends sought to secure emancipation, economic equity, voting rights, and integration in schools, housing, and public transportation, they kept African Americans at arm's length in their personal and social lives. Time and again Quaker educators and others warned that integration could lead to social intimacy and thence to intermarriage, an outcome most European American Quakers viewed as wholly undesirable, if not as an outright threat to the Caucasian race. That so little progress has been made in integrating Friends meetings and that integration took so long to effect in Friends schools raises questions about Friends willingness to accept African Americans as social equals. And, that the minority of Friends who have worked for thoroughgoing integration and racial justice is as small today as it has ever been points to the following conclusion: that Quakers have been unwilling to confront their own racism and/or they do not know how to respond to racial issues.

The insularity of the Society of Friends is rooted in its perceived need to preserve its testimonies from corruption by the world. While this inward-looking tendency may have preserved the "purity" of the religion, it makes it far less likely that European American Quakers can appreciate the issues Americans of African descent have confronted since the moment their ancestors were brought forcibly to the New World. The bent of many within the Society against proselytizing has also limited Quaker exposure to people from differing social, economic, ethnic, and racial backgrounds. This lack of knowledge has fostered fear and ignorance about racial relations and has slowed recognition that Quaker testimonies demand political *and* social equality.

One example from our work illustrates the tendency to a certain blindness among Friends to racial issues. African American Quakers chafe at the traditional Quaker use of the word "overseer" and sometimes struggle to have Friends of European descent recognize the pain it causes. In Friends meetings an overseer is a member of the committee responsible for pastoral care. But in the family of one co-author, the term "overseer" refers to Eddie Fields, the man who held in his hands the life of her great, great-grandmother, Leah Warner, and the lives of several other enslaved Africans on the Ruth's Plantation. Quakers of European descent sometimes dismiss this concern because of the term's historical use, but many Friends of African descent find that dismissal invalid and an inadequate response to our concern. The matter exemplifies a behavior that marginalizes African American Quakers.

In the last few years, however, Central Philadelphia Monthly Meeting and several other meetings have come to appreciate and understand the pain the term carries for people of African descent. The monthly meeting realized that the term "overseer" did not accurately reflect the role of the committee. At a 2002 Philadelphia Yearly Meeting "listening session," thirty-eight Friends from twenty meetings determined that the term, in addition to having a close association with the exploitation and enslavement of African Americans in the United States, also implies a hierarchical relationship among Friends. As a consequence Central Philadelphia Monthly Meeting and several other meetings changed the name of the committee from "overseers" to "membership care." "Changing the name," as African American Friend Ernestine Buscemi of Morningside Monthly Meeting in New York City wrote, "would mean that we Quakers are allowing safe places where understanding and love come together, nurturing that of God in everyone."

To the suggestion that looking back is not productive, that Friends time and energy is best spent dealing with the present and working for the future, we counter that there is value in telling this story and, we hope, in provoking thoughtful discussion and action. We hold, as African American intellectual, author, and activist Cornel West has argued, that to learn the truth and to tell the truth is "not just to be informed but to be transformed." As our work progressed, we discovered that to attempt to convey the relationship of Quakers and African Americans accurately required us to place our work within a wider historical context, extending particularly to the history of African Americans in this country—a story that has been, and continues to be, disgracefully neglected. As our eyes have been opened to a history that includes all of our citizens, we are guided by the advice of African American historian Vincent Harding. We need, he argued, to "focus in on trying to move from where we are and where we have been to create a new future. But there is no thought of forgetting the past because, in a sense, we probably could not do that if we wanted to. It is simply creating a new future, but in that process, creating a new past as well, recreating the past, transforming the past and its meaning to us." We accept Harding's admonition, because we believe that only by understanding our past will we be able to create a future in which we are all one.

Authors' Statements

Vanessa Julye

I was introduced to the Religious Society of Friends in my childhood. At that time, even though I felt called to join the religion, I did not do so. It seemed to me that only people of European descent were Quakers, and I feared being isolated, invisible, patronized, and lonely. As an adult, however, I came to see that the principles of the Society of Friends were exemplified in my lifestyle. I experienced that still small voice speaking within me, and I became a Friend because the form of worship and fellowship the society offered was at that time of my life more important than racial isolation. I am one of very few African American Quakers, and I have naturally been drawn into the question of why this is so. I believe that the seeds of this circumstance were planted more than three hundred years ago, that Friends have been plagued by racist attitudes from that time to this day. These attitudes largely account for why our numbers in the Society of Friends have been and continue to be small. I agreed to research and write this book because I thought it would be an important tool in helping me understand why I experience racism within the Religious Society of Friends in the twenty-first century.

When I joined the Society of Friends I believed that Quakers of European descent had a wonderfully special relationship with Friends and non-Friends of African descent. Thus the book provided the opportunity I needed to understand what had happened to this relationship. I learned that the relationship in which I believed had never existed. As a whole community the Religious Society of Friends through the centuries has always reflected the beliefs and cultural practices of mainstream North American society. Over time there have been those courageous few who questioned society's norms, and the behavior that arose from such questioning set them apart—some physically when their religious society disowned them—from the rest of the people in their religious community. I have learned that overall the popular notion of Quaker progressivism is a myth.

Donna McDaniel and I spent many hours talking about the behavior and dreams of Friends over the centuries. When I look back on decisions and behaviors from our past I see many missed opportunities and missteps, but I recognize that speaking out and questioning behavior that has been considered normal is difficult and that not everyone is capable of it. It is a gift. Some Friends possessed that gift and used it. To them I say thank you. However, I do not judge negatively the Friends who were a part of mainstream society. I believe that most were so immersed in their society as it stood at the time that they were not able to step out of it and reflect on how things could be done differently, or even if they should. They were doing what was within them to do, and I am sure if we were able to go back in time they would tell us that.

It has been a long and tough journey for Donna and me as we gathered information, digested it, discussed how to present it, and actually wrote down our thoughts. There were times when we did not agree on what to present, but we have done our best to bring you a complete picture of our history, with its warts alongside its roses.

While writing this book I received a tremendous blessing. That blessing has come in many gifts. I have established a friendship I would not otherwise have had with my coauthor Donna, my friendship with our first editor grew, and I have established new friendships with many people across the country. Many of these Friends opened their homes to Donna and me so that we could physically work together. I have received incredible support from my family, friends, and several meetings, not just my own, as I have worked on this project. Last but not least, I have a better understanding of my history as an African American Friend. It is my hope that reading this book will help others achieve a more balanced understanding of our history, and that we are ready to begin creating our community together.

Donna McDaniel

I am often asked what drew me to work against racism, and though I cannot recall any significant moments in my life that brought me to this work I can think of a few possibilities. The earliest is remembering as a child how uneasy I felt hearing the ugliness of my midwestern relatives' comments about anyone who was not a WASP. Their venom was spread among African Americans, Catholics, and Jews. My mother was the exception. Somehow I knew that she found those words painful to hear, though she rarely spoke up.

It is possible, if not likely, to grow up in North America without ever going to school with a person of color. It was true for me. I attended schools in three states, including one in Virginia, in which no African Americans were enrolled. In the mid-1950s when I went to college, Tufts University had admitted perhaps two African American students, both male, and it is my guess that both were athletes. But in my senior year, two African American women were admitted and my sorority, Sigma Kappa, invited them to be members. When we discussed the national organization's reaction, "What could they do to us?" I asked from my position as local president. What it could and did do was to remove us from membership for a trumped-up reason. But that is another story. In the fifty years since then, I have often wondered if our eagerness to invite these women did not stem more from our desire to be "good liberals" than to become our "sisters'" friends.

I was working overseas through the vital first five years of the Civil Rights movement, and when I returned to Boston, the city was in the midst of the school busing crisis. I lived in a predominantly white suburb of six thousand people where those of us who cared to notice could count on one hand its African American residents. In my early forties I had an experience that I would call pivotal in stirring my desire to work against racism. I volunteered for a "Youth at Risk" program that helped older teens understand that they can take responsibility for their own lives regardless of their circumstances. It was a powerful experience for all of us—professionals, volunteers, and participants. By the end of our time together, I loved these kids, most of them African American, so much that I knew I had to do whatever I could to prevent the awful damage inflicted on human beings by generations of unequal education and opportunities. I also discovered that I could no longer avoid looking at the faces of young African Americans on the streets of Boston—I might miss seeing someone I knew.

It is more than a coincidence that after another ten years I was—and still am—singing in the racially-mixed Boston Community Choir. I have had the blessing of becoming friends with many people of color while rehearsing, sitting around waiting to perform, or (often) enjoying food afterwards. I am blessed by our friendship. I am moved by their faith in God and in a Savior who takes care of them. I know that often when we sing it is what we Friends call "a gathered meeting"—the Spirit is present. And, I have become even more determined to help put an end to the injustices that have happened and continue to happen just because of their color to people I love.

The last part of the journey brought me to this book. When it came time to semi-retire, my plan was to volunteer with a program working effectively to end racism. In asking people familiar with the Boston scene, I "happened" to e-mail my friend Beckey Phipps, who just "happened" to have conceived this book project for the Friends General Conference Religious Education Committee. After I was chosen to be an author, I just "happened" to come in touch with someone, Paul Rasor, who just "happened" to think I would be a good candidate for a full-year's scholarship to live at Pendle Hill near Philadelphia, where he was working and where I would be close to many of the sources of Quaker history. The way it all "happened" with little effort on my part was truly an experience of what we Quakers mean when we say we are "led" to do something and that "way will open." I have no doubt that I am doing what I am meant to be doing at this time of my life. What a gift!

My conviction about the value of this work strengthened beyond measure as our research progressed. To read and tell the truth about the relationship of Quakers and African Americans may not seem a spiritual act, but what I have read has forever touched my soul.

Another blessing of this project has been being able to spend days and weeks at a time with my coauthor. As one who "swims" in the dominant culture, I was not accustomed to seeing things as an African American might, so I had much to learn from Vanessa. As we read and talked together, I had abundant opportunities to notice how pervasive the dominant culture is, how so much of our history is written from that viewpoint, and how easy it is for too many of us not even to think about it. That has changed me as well.

Preparing this book has not been easy work, and it has taken more years than we expected. When I have been weary and when I have paused to listen, I have always heard the words of an African American spiritual I learned with my choir:

> I ain't no ways tired. I've come too far from where I've started from.
> Nobody told me that road would be easy.
> But I don't believe He brought me this far to leave me.

I don't believe He brought me this far to leave me!

Another source of inspiration that reminds me why I am called to work among Friends was Quaker Alison Oldham's keynote address to New England Yearly Meeting in 1984, when I was not yet a Quaker. She asked why Friends should care whether or not our society is racially and culturally integrated. It is a question that could—and should—have been asked at any time in our history and is, I suspect, still asked by many Friends today, though perhaps not aloud. I end with her answer and then a question of my own.

Integration is vital to the Society of Friends, Oldham later wrote, because it is a question of authenticity going *"to the heart of our beliefs about Quakerism."*

> For *if* this faith of Friends that we espouse, this way of seeking for the Spirit of Truth, is indeed authentic, it will be able to speak powerfully to all sorts and conditions of folk, whatever their race, their economic status, or the cultural context through which they see the world.
>
> But if we accept the notion, however subconsciously, that Quakerism really speaks only to certain kinds of people, then it seems to me we have totally denied its religious validity, its universal spirit, and so we will have reduced Quakerism to the status of a social club with a mild religious overlay.

Alison Oldham spoke those words before hundreds of Friends almost twenty-five years ago. In essence, Vanessa and I are calling to Friends to hear those words again. What will it take for Friends in North America to work toward the "authentic" Society of Friends that Oldham has described? What has stopped us from truly addressing this issue among us, and how can we push past those barriers? Finally, twenty-five years from now, will someone else be asking these same questions to yet another gathering of Friends?

Acknowledgments

JUST AS IT TAKES A VILLAGE to raise a child, it has taken a community to produce this book. Dozens and dozens of people supported us over the last seven years, contributing to our work in myriad ways, from Quaker historians who shared their knowledge and ideas freely and frequently to others who were determined that the book would become a reality and offered to help, often in more ways than one—reading the manuscript, checking footnotes, doing research, cooking a meal or helping out with things around the house. Many have been unwavering in their interest and enthusiasm, including those who, like the Boston Community Choir and others whose names we do not know, were holding us in the Light. We could not have persevered without your prayers.

Our thanks go to Quaker historians and curators of the Quaker colleges' historical collections so invaluable to our research including at Haverford: Emma Lapsansky, Ann Upton, and Diana Franzusoff Peterson; at Swarthmore: Christopher Densmore, Patricia O'Donnell, Susanna Morikawa, Charlotte Blandford; at Guilford: Mary Ellen Chijioke and Gwen Gosney Erickson; and at Earlham: Thomas Hamm. Rita Varley and Esther Darlington helped us at Philadelphia Yearly Meeting's library. Other Quaker resources were shared with us by Jane Zavitz-Bond, the Canadian Quaker archives; Marnie Miller-Gutsell, the New England Yearly Meeting archives; and Donald Davis and Jack Sutters, present and former archivists at the American Friends Service Committee collection. Laraine Worby of Framingham (Mass.) Public Library magically produced journal articles via e-mail; the patient staff of Southborough (MA) Public Library dealt pleasantly with much coming and going of Interlibrary loans. The fact that Tufts University's Tisch Library allows alumni to take out books was one of many blessings that eased our way.

Historians Margaret Hope Bacon, Kenneth Carroll, J. William Frost, Martha Paxson Grundy, Deborah Haines and William Kashatus, offered comments and suggestions, as did other readers Paul Lacey, Jane Orion Smith, Paul Rasor, Stephen Angell, Kenneth Sutton, Amharah Powell, Victoria Rhodin, Jean-Marie Prestwidge Barch, Kitsi Watterson, Yvonne Keairns, Neil Froemming, Earl Conn, Carol Coulthurst, Nancy Moore, Bruce Birchard, Janice Domanik, and Liz Kamphausen. Friends and non-Friends who shared their experiences and helpful information on e-mail, by phone, or in person include George and Lillian Willoughby, George Lakey, William Taber, Ginny Coover, Dwight Wilson, Johann Maurer, Phyllis and Richard Taylor, Joan and Ed Broadfield, James English, Steve Braunginn, Barbara Greenler, King Odell, Niyonu Spann, Gordon Browne, Charles Brown III, Thelma Babbitt, the Rev. James Lawson, K [sic] Brown, Elisabeth Leonard, Vinton Deming, Dorothy Treddenick, Jack Snyder, Gail Thomas, Edward Marshall, Gertrude Marshall, and Marian and Nelson Fuson.

Support came from leaders of various yearly meeting groups and individuals working against racism: Helen Garay Toppins and Jeff Hitchcock of New York Yearly Meeting, along with that meeting's White People Working Against Racism Committee and Black Concerns Committee; Pat Schenk and Jane Coe from Baltimore Yearly Meeting; and members of the Working Party on Racism and the Committee on Religious, Social, and Economic Justice of New England Yearly Meeting. Many of those already named were among those Quaker and non-Quaker alike who called to volunteer to do whatever was needed—find a source, get books from the library, create files for the cartons of papers, compile the bibliography, or catch up on gardening and vacuuming—Carole Bundy, Maureen Lopes, Barbara Luetke-Stahlman, Liz Yeats, Kathy Marshall, Sharon Woodruff, and Pamela Strauss. Special thanks go to those who undertook the tedious work of footnote-checking—Tom Conlin, Susannah Garboden, Elin Calver, and Marilyn Manzella. Others generously shared their expertise—Rachel Findley, Jan Hoffman, Chuck Fager, and Marge Abbott and, in the world of publishing, David Chanoff and Ann Jones.

Several people offered us places for our writers' retreats—Miyo Moriuchi and Marian Rebert, Suzanne Day, Takashi and Kitty Mizuno, Phil and Sue Staas, and, at Beacon Hill Friends House, Margaret Hart. Others were hospitable in our travels, Murray and Sylvia Mills, Trayce Peterson, Dinora Uvalle, and Tom Mullen. We are thankful for the support we've received from FGC—interns Angelina Conti and Wren Almitra, the Religious Education Committee and Beckey Phipps, clerk when the idea was initially brought forward, the Committee for Ministry on Racism, FGC staff members Bruce Birchard and Lucy Duncan, who also read the manuscript and provided support in many ways, and the Development staff, including Carrie Glasby for securing grants for the project from the Bequests Granting Group, the Anna H. and Elizabeth M. Chace Fund, The Allen Hilles Fund, Willistown Friends Trust, the Thomas H. and Mary Williams Shoemaker Fund, and Frank and Jean-Marie Prestwidge Barch. Their financial support is most appreciated.

Barbara Mays met the real challenge of arriving in the middle of a project and bringing it all to fruition. We would not be writing these words today if it weren't for her hard work and devotion.

Donna was named the 2001–2002 Henry Cadbury Scholar at Pendle Hill, giving her the gift of proximity to Quaker libraries and the blessing of the support of a spiritual community, students and staff alike, particularly Daniel O. Snyder, B.J. Williams, and John Calder. Both authors received financial support from the Lyman Fund and Obadiah Brown Fund. Donna also had contributions from Salem Quarter of New England Yearly Meeting, and Framingham Friends Meeting, donating both as a meeting and as individuals for various office and travel expenses over the years; the meeting was steadfast in its support, especially the special committee of Richard Lindo, Marilyn Manzella, and Alice Schaefer, Friends always ready with sympathetic ears when it seemed the work had no end!

Vanessa appreciates support from her own monthly meeting, Central Philadelphia, from her ministerial care committee, Yoko Koike Barnes, Chuck Esser and Amy Kietzman, and from Ernie Buscemi. Needed information came from Bob Dockhorn, Howard Mills, and Edward Sargent and computer support from Marvin Barnes. She received financial assistance from the Allen Hilles Fund, the Leeway Foundation, the PYM Bequest Fund, Tyson Memorial Fund, the Good News Association, and the Chace Fund. Vanessa offers special thanks to her family for their love, support, and forgiveness for her absence from family events—her husband, Barry Scott, son Kai Morris, mother Carolyn Julye, and step-daughters Ellen and Maggie Scott.

Donna's special thanks go to dear people who took good care of her, worried when she didn't call, and, albeit reluctantly, understood why she needed to stay home instead of being with them—Helen Bakeman, Gail Grandy, Paula Norton, Pauline Minasian, Joanne Lowry, Bobby and Abe Flexer, John Meyer, Ann Raynolds, Thornton Shepherd, and Sharon Woodruff. Donna's sons, David and Evan, and daughter-in-law, Jess, will ever be proud of the commitment and determination of their septuagenarian mother.

Finally, if you supported us, known or unknown to us, and don't find your name among those on these two pages, please know that you are no less appreciated. Thank you all.

PART ONE

Enslavement, Emancipation, and Movement West

1680–1900

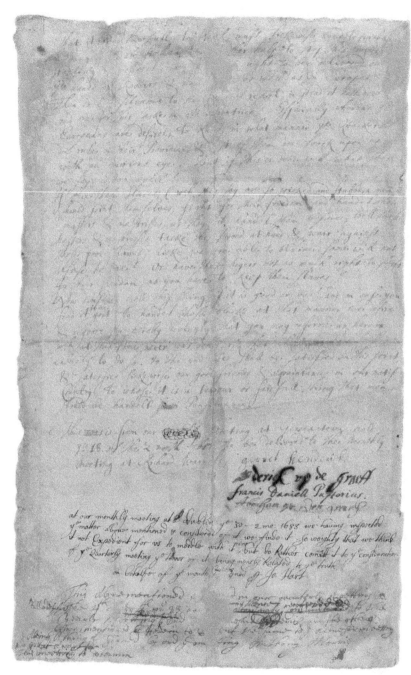

Germantown Friends' protest against slavery, 1688.

CHAPTER ONE

Ending Enslavement among Friends

1688-1787

The buying and selling of men is contrary to the Divine Mind manifest in the consciences of all men.

— *Moses Brown, 1773*

IN THE 1780s, after struggling with the issue for nearly a century, the Religious Society of Friends became the first and only denomination in the American colonies to free itself of enslaving Africans.[1] Though commonly perceived never to have participated in enslavement, some North American Quakers did buy, sell, and enslave people of African descent. Yet their religion seemed to require something different of them. Enslavement violated the Golden Rule, Friends testimonies of equality, peace, and simplicity, as well as the basic tenet that Christ died for all. Friends who believed their religion required them to free themselves of enslavement were, however, in a minority, and their efforts to persuade other Friends of the sin of this practice were frequently met with suspicion and distaste. The issue of enslavement divided meetings and individuals, and before the 1750s it was not unusual for meetings to censure or disown members who were outspoken on the matter.[2]

Ultimately, the ideas that made Friends distinct from all other North American religious groups compelled their early stand against trading in and enslaving people of African descent. By the end of the eighteenth century European American Friends in the North had freed virtually all of the people they had formerly enslaved, even as non-Quakers in the region continued to hold thousands of people in bondage. In the South, where enslavement was such an integral part of the economy and manumission was often prohibited by law, the challenge for Friends wanting to end enslavement came primarily from outside the society. Nevertheless, in the 1780s Friends in Maryland, Virginia, and the Carolinas made enslavement a disownable offense. It took another twenty years of work to be able to fulfill that mandate, very often achieved by transporting those who would be free to the Midwest or, if they volunteered, to Africa or Haiti.

Enslavement among Friends

Despite the absence of a formal creed, Quakers have always relied on other statements—sets of advices, testimonies, and disciplines—to establish what demarcates them as a religious group.[3] Yet the first Friends in the New World arrived with no such principles governing the practice of enslavement.[4] Like others among the earliest European settlers, Quakers initially indentured poor European immigrants to do the monumental work of developing the New World. The supply of indentured servants from Europe was uneven, however, and their sheer numbers insufficient; moreover, their service was limited to a certain number of years.[5] As a consequence, Quakers and other colonists turned to Africans. The growing demand for Africans encouraged the buying and selling of them, an enterprise that was at times extremely lucrative and intensely competitive.[6]

Over the years, scholars have revised the number of Africans transported to the New World. At this point, there is some agreement that from 10 to 11 million living Africans were brought to the Americas between 1600 and 1899 (not counting those who died on the voyage). Only about six percent of these—some 600,000 to 650,000—came to what is now the United States. By 1810, however, the population of people of African descent in the United States had doubled due to the high birth rate. (In the rest of the hemisphere, imports continued to make up for a declining population of enslaved people.)[7]

Quakers of European descent in every yearly meeting benefitted economically from some, if not all, aspects of the enslavement of Africans—transporting, buying, selling, and holding in perpetual servitude. Historian Hugh Thomas believed European American Quaker William Frampton to have been the first to transport Africans to Philadelphia in the 1680s—the same decade in which Quakers founded the colony of Pennsylvania and about three decades after the first

Friends settled in North America.[8] Even in the 1670s, Quaker historian Thomas E. Drake has noted, Friends of European ancestry considered importing Africans and enslaving them "part of the natural order of things."

While the majority of Friends who owned vessels that carried on the trade in Africans in the 1700s were in Rhode Island, some Pennsylvania Friends, including some leaders of Philadelpha Yearly Meeting, also engaged in the trade in the early part of that century and often imported Africans from the West Indies.[9] The European American James Logan, who as William Penn's secretary took care of Penn's financial interests during his employer's long sojourns in England, was a trader and a member of Philadelphia Yearly Meeting's influential Overseers of the Press, the committee that approved or denied members' applications to publish tracts or any other material.[10] Philadelphia Yearly Meeting European American members James Claypoole, William Plumstead, Reese Meredith, John Reynell, Jonathan Dickinson, Francis Richardson, and Isaac Norris I also bought and sold Africans.[11] Dickinson, one of the wealthiest Philadelphia merchants, owned two plantations in the West Indies that his family had acquired in 1655; Norris, an Overseer of the Press in 1711 and clerk of Philadelphia Yearly Meeting from 1711 to 1729, purchased and enslaved more Africans than most of his cohorts.[12]

Newport, Providence, and Bristol, Rhode Island, were among the leading centers of the enslavement trade.[13] Until the Revolution, Newport was responsible for 70 percent of those Africans brought to the New World, but, devastated by the war, the town lost its dominance to Bristol, a bit farther up Narragansett Bay.[14] Newport was also home to the greatest number of wealthy Friends in the northern colonies.[15] By 1772, some 50 percent of the wealthiest Newporters had some connection with the slave trade. Limited data makes it impossible, however, to determine what proportion were Quaker; still, it is clear that a good many were.[16] Among the Newport European American traders was Isaac Howland, a member of Rhode Island Monthly Meeting and later of Dartmouth, Massachusetts, Monthly Meeting, who was captain of the Newport slaver *Dolphin* in 1758.[17] Other Newport Quakers owned part or all of slave-trade vessels. Thomas Hazard, Thomas Robinson and Nicholas Robinson owned shares in the *Dolphin* at various times, and William Redwood Jr. owned shares of vessels involved in four African trade voyages between 1756 and 1758. Abraham Redwood owned the *Martha and Jane,* which he outfitted for at least one slaving voyage.[18] Joseph, Peter, and Edward Wanton all commanded vessels involved in the Africa trade; Edward was captain of the *Sally* on its 1764 voyage, the only one in which European American Moses Brown, not yet a Quaker, was involved.[19] Thomas Richardson, New England Yearly Meeting Clerk for forty-one years (1728–69), held shares in a vessel on one of its voyages to Africa.[20] Unlike Collins and other Quakers involved in this trading activity, Richardson expressed no opposition to the institution in his correspondence, and at one point he helped return a fugitive to a neighbor who enslaved him.[21]

Given both Rhode Island's dominance in this commerce and Quaker dominance of the colony's religious and political life, it seems possible that more Friends were involved in the African trade than have so far been documented.[22] The possibility of wider involvement would seem to be supported as well by the yearly meeting's adverse reaction to any discussion of ending enslavement.[23] In addition, two of Rhode Island's most prominent Quaker families of European descent, the Redwoods and the Hazards, owned slave plantations in the West Indies, where, as Africans were "seasoned" for their new status, conditions were particularly brutal.[24] In 1766 Abraham Redwood was New England's largest holder of enslaved people—238 Africans or people of African descent.[25]

Aside from the commerce in Africans, enslavement among Quakers was not unusual from Georgia and the Carolinas to New England. In Pennsylvania Quakers owned as many as half of all those enslaved in the commonwealth by 1700.[26] Using records of burials and taxable property, historian Gary Nash estimated that about one thousand enslaved people lived in Philadelphia between 1767 and 1775.[27] In 1767 Friends of European ancestry in Philadelphia were overrepresented as enslavers in proportion to their numbers; from burial records, researchers have estimated that about 13 percent of Philadelphia's European population was Quaker, while 17 percent of the enslavers were Friends.[28] European American William Penn enslaved Africans and benefitted from their labor. At one point, complaining about his problems with European indentured servants, Penn wrote that he preferred servants of African descent because "then a man has them while they live."[29] Although Penn's will of 1701 freed his enslaved Africans upon his death and gave one hundred acres to "old Sam," his final will of 1711 included no such provisions. Penn's enslaved people were to pass on to his European American widow Hannah. Nash has suggested that the omission was "probably indicative of [Penn's] deep financial difficulties at the end of his life." In a letter of 6 June 1720, Hannah Penn asked James Logan to sell the enslaved belonging to her husband's estate.[30] Freeing (or manumitting) enslaved people through wills did not become common until about 1740, more than twenty years after Penn's death: in 1740 about one of every three Quakers who enslaved Africans freed them in their wills.[31]

By 1755 there were as many as one enslaved person for every four Euro-American households in Massachusetts, Rhode Island, and Connecticut. Enslaved people lived primarily along the seacoast and in the major cities where the elites—the merchants and political leaders—lived. Their role in the economy of those three states was vital. Far fewer enslaved people were part of the generally less viable agricultural economies in New Hampshire, Vermont, and Maine (then part of Massachusetts).[32]

In New York City, 40 percent of all households owned enslaved people in the 1700s, making the city second only to Charleston, South Carolina, on that measure. Until midcentury, most of the Quakers in New York lived on farms on Long Island or in the Hudson River Valley.[33] In the 1700s "a sizeable percentage of the landowning slaveholders" on Long Island were "prosperous" Quaker farmers, some of whom enslaved as many as eight people of African descent.[34]

Although enslavement permeated every aspect of economic and social life in the South, only about one-fourth of the people of European descent were enslavers even as the number of enslaved people tripled between 1790 and 1830. A small percentage of enslavers held more than five persons in perpetual bondage living on their small farms. Historian Grady McWhiney observed that most planters "lived in rather crude houses and enjoyed few luxuries." Yet any southerner who did not enslave people suffered "the constant pinch of economic competition" from those who did, according to historian C. Vann Woodward; as a consequence many of those who were not enslavers looked to the day when they could be. The fear that freedom for the enslaved would threaten the economic status of poor to middling southerners was pervasive. Many believed that freed African Americans would form a vast labor pool willing to work for less than prevailing wages; not only would this pool of workers depress wage rates generally, but it would create unfair competition for work.[35]

Quakers, particularly those on large plantations, enslaved substantial numbers of people. Twelve percent of the South's enslavers by 1700 were on the tobacco plantations in Virginia, eastern North Carolina, the Western Shore of Maryland, and on the rice and indigo plantations in South Carolina. Typically, thirty to sixty enslaved people labored on any given plantation. Despite their small share of the total population of the South, however, enslavers there had influence "all out of proportion to their numbers," McWhiney said, primarily because they produced the bulk of the region's staple commodities. Though he acknowledged that data on the number of people enslaved by North Carolina Quakers in the colonial period is "noticeably lacking," historian Charles McKiever said that the number of enslaved held by southern Friends along the coast was at one time "quite large." In the Piedmont area of the western Carolinas, Quaker farmers with smaller holdings tended to be migrants from the North who were less inclined to use unfree labor and were the source of much abolitionist agitation as well.[36]

Quaker Perspectives on Enslavement

Friends in the 1700s were likely to view enslavement from one of four perspectives. A majority of Quakers accepted slavery "without much qualm or question." Others were "perplexed, but did nothing." Still others agreed with George Fox, the English founder of the Religious Society of Friends, that slaves should be treated "kindly" and offered a Christian education—a line of thought that did not embrace emancipation. Finally, a "sensitive few" doubted if Christians should be enslaving their fellow men.[37]

By contrast, the greater measure of Friends of European ancestry did not find it "inconsistent with their principles," as one contemporary Maryland Quaker put it, to become enslavers. In Maryland, for example, where three thousand Friends lived by 1775, this attitude was especially prevalent among those who owned tobacco plantations on the Eastern and Western Shores. Tradition has it that, after Yearly Meeting sessions at

West River, Quaker planters on the Western Shore of the colony boarded newly arriving ships "to buy fresh Negroes for their plantations." Manumission records make clear that the prevalence of enslavement differed on Maryland's Eastern and Western Shores. Friends from Third Haven Monthly Meeting on the Eastern Shore began to manumit enslaved people as early as 1685, while manumissions were rarely recorded in meetings on the Western Shore at the same time. Indeed, the concentration of enslavers on the western shore of Maryland, as well as in eastern North Carolina, made it especially difficult for yearly meetings in those areas to reach unity on ending enslavement.[38]

The correlation between economic standing and enslavement among Quakers is clear. Even by the early 1700s, northern trading and commercial interests, including those of Quakers, were more and more intertwined with the enslavement economy of the South. As time went on, "even the best-intentioned Quaker slave owners" could not always see their way clear to "do the thing that was right," as European American Friend John Woolman once put it.[39] Newport Quakers were "as eager as anyone else to reap the profits of the trade"; the rum manufacture made possible by trading in Africans was a boon to Rhode Island's economy and became the chief means of acquiring the cash needed to buy imported finished goods.[40] Meetings—even those that opposed trade in Africans and enslavement—generally hesitated to interfere with the livelihoods of members who depended on the labor of enslaved people, and they recognized that forcing the issue would invite division in their society.[41] In 1715 Isaac Norris I, an active participant in the trade in Africans, warned those who wanted Philadelphia Yearly Meeting to ban trading in Africans that judging Friends who enslaved them could have a "dangerous consequence" for the cohesiveness of their religious society.[42]

Irish Friend William Edmundson said in 1676 that enslavement presented a dilemma to Quakers who believed in the sanctity of property rights on the one hand and in the notion that each person is free to experience his or her own relationship with God on the other. Friends attempts to end participation in all aspects of enslavement was impeded by the domination of yearly meetings by European American Quakers who benefitted from the system. Trading in and enslaving Africans created "a conflict of economic interest and ideology."[43]

From the 1680s into the 1750s, the leadership of Philadelphia Yearly Meeting was dominated by a "surprisingly small group" of Quakers of European descent who moved in the highest commercial, social, and government circles of Pennsylvania and New Jersey.[44] Thirty of the forty-three wealthy and influential leaders of Philadelphia Yearly Meeting—including European Americans James Claypoole, Judge John Eckley, and Thomas Lloyd, president of the Provincial Council—enslaved Africans before 1706. Over the next two decades the proportion of enslavers among meeting leaders declined from 70 percent in 1706 to 59 percent in 1706–30, and to 35 percent between 1731 and 1753. In that last year, sentiments against enslavement began to prevail in the yearly meeting, and the proportion of its leaders who were enslavers dropped to 10 percent between 1754 and 1780.[45] Still, before the 1760s enslavement increased overall in Philadelphia, among Friends and non-Friends, and meeting manumission records show that "few Friends voluntarily complied" with requests for such action.[46]

Historian Jean Soderlund has looked at the issue of enslavement among meeting members from a different perspective—publications issued by the Overseers of the Press. Not all materials Friends published went through the overseers, and they occasionally declined to publish works on topics other than enslavement. Yet the subject of enslavement was especially sensitive. Soderlund determined that from two-thirds to three-fourths of the overseers were enslavers between 1681 and 1751. It is therefore hardly surprising that before 1753 no paper opposing the enslavement of Africans was approved for publication.[47]

The percentage of Philadelphia Yearly Meeting's quarterly and monthly meeting leaders who enslaved Africans was high, according to Soderlund's data. For example, leaders of Chester Quarter tended to hold large farms that depended on the labor of enslaved Africans. Although Chester Friends were prominent in the earlier moves to ban *importation*, their meeting lagged behind others when it came to actually *freeing* those they enslaved.[48] Similarly, in Newport, where most prominent Quakers of European descent bought and enslaved large numbers of Africans, influential Friends "managed to bury the issue temporarily" in 1715. Instead they urged Friends of European descent concerned about the enslavement of Africans to "exercise Christian charity toward each other."[49]

When economic times were good, many Quakers of European ancestry could afford to purchase and enslave Africans and their descendants and did so eagerly, oblivious to antislavery appeals. Some say Friends fervor in arguing against enslavement waxed and waned with the supply of indentured servants. One historian believes that given "a direct choice" between their society's principles and giving up enslaved labor, most Philadelphia Friends of European descent ignored principle.[50] Historian J. William Frost, however, has asserted the opposite of Philadelphia Friends, who, unlike other well-to-do Philadelphians, were ending the practice of enslavement even as the numbers of available indentured servants declined during the French and Indian War (1754–63).[51] To Frost, this demonstrates that Friends had been able to "grow in truth" and had come to understand the moral issue.[52] Still, widespread enslavement among Quakers compelled most meetings to avoid a formal stand that would "reflect discredit" on some of their members who enslaved people.[53]

Quaker Treatment of Enslaved People

For many European American Friends, attention to "right order" did not include freedom for enslaved Africans but only concern about how they should be treated. As early as the 1690s yearly and monthly meetings regularly inquired of their members whether those they enslaved were well cared for, instructed in proper behavior, and given religious training. These queries directly reflect the influence of the ideas of George Fox, who voiced these principles in his 1679 letter, "To Friends In America, Concerning Their Negroes, and Indians":

> All Friends, everywhere, that have Indians or blacks, you are to preach the gospel to them, and other servants, if you be true Christians; for the gospel of salvation was to be preached to every creature under heaven; Christ commands it to his disciples, "Go and teach all nations, baptizing them in the name of the Father, son, and holy ghost."
>
> And also, you must teach and instruct blacks and indians, and others, how that God doth pour out his spirit upon all flesh in these days of the new covenant, and new testament . . . for it will teach them to live soberly, godly, and righteously, and season their words.[54]

Fox was well acquainted with enslavement from his visits to the New World, yet his message to "the children of the Light" did little to give them pause about the practice of enslavement. Fox was clearly a radical who defied the Church of England, as well as the British monarchy, but his radicalism did not embrace racial equality. He never addressed the morality of enslavement, nor did he advise his followers not to engage in it.[55] The closest Fox appears to have come to the concept of manumission occurred in a tract he wrote in 1676 based on a message he had delivered to Friends in Barbados. In *Family Gospel-Order*, Fox suggested that Quakers of European descent could alter the status of African "servants" from enslaved to indentured.[56] "It will doubtless be very acceptable to the Lord, if masters let [their enslaved people] go free after a considerable term of years, if they have served them faithfully," Fox wrote, "and when they are made free, let them not go away empty-handed."[57]

Frost contends that the absence of any statement on Fox's part against the practice "made the condemnation of slavery as an instruction more difficult" for Quakers. Indeed, Friends often appropriated Fox's works to justify enslavement. In 1700 the Overseers of the Press of Philadelphia Yearly Meeting found a way to "use the prestige of Fox to counter the radicals"[58] when they republished Fox's *Family Gospel-Order*. Despite its suggestion of manumission, the work reveals his patriarchal views quite clearly: the master/father had the responsibility for the household and for bringing family members to worship, which is a view not consonant with Quaker egalitarianism.[59] Biographer Larry Ingle has described Fox as "no social egalitarian—he was too much a child of his time to countenance a complete upturning of the social order."[60] Like Fox, William Penn, founder of Pennsylvania—the Quaker "Holy Experiment"—was silent on the issue of enslavement and stood firmly for social hierarchy.[61] "For tho' [God] has made of one Blood, all Nations," Penn asserted, "He has not ranged or dignified them upon the Level, but in a Sort of Subordination and Dependency."[62]

Whether Quaker enslavers who were attuned to Fox's directives were generally kinder to enslaved people than non-Quakers is impossible to know, but several historians believe that, on average, Quaker slaveholding practices were less severe than elsewhere. More recent studies have suggested that these assertions of benevolence are largely fictitious. In his examination of several thousand monthly meeting disownments in 1700s Pennsylvania, historian Jack Marietta found fourteen Friends of European ancestry disowned for assaulting servants; some number of those were probably African American, though the term 'servants' sometimes embraced indentured workers of European descent. One enslaver refused to apologize to his meeting on the grounds that he found nothing wrong with hitting a person of African descent.[63] Soderlund has noted that some Friends tried to instill good behavior not by physical abuse but by holding out freedom as a possible reward—even if that reward was forestalled until the enslaver's death.[64]

One of the few verified instances of maltreatment on the part of a Quaker has been found in the minutes of Dartmouth Monthly Meeting in Massachusetts. In 1711 European American meeting member Abigail Allen was disowned for allowing and even encouraging the whipping an unnamed enslaved man of African descent in a manner that may have contributed to his death. European American historian Elizabeth Cazden has suggested that Allen's European American husband Ebenezer may have been responsible, for he had been disciplined earlier for beating a Native American and then disowned for going to court in a property dispute. Abigail Allen was "apparently not sufficiently remorseful" to escape disownment, although two years later she did convince the meeting that she had become "much troubled" about the beating and was readmitted.[65] Cazden has challenged the conclusion of both Drake and Jones that the Dartmouth meeting's strong reaction indicates that Friends of European descent were turning against enslavement; she found little evidence to link the incident to general objections to slavery in this period.[66]

The notion that northern enslavement was somehow less onerous than southern enslavement has been refuted by some historians. New Englanders were "full participants in the same kind of dehumanizing abuses that have characterized the system in the middle and southern colonies," historian Peter Benes has concluded, especially in the practice of separating parents and children.[67] Historian A. Leon Higginbotham has disputed one assessment of the mildness of enslavement in Pennsylvania. While enslavers "did not brutalize slaves as severely as [those in] the southern colonies did," he noted, after the 1700s "black codes" imposed severe restrictions on African Americans both free and enslaved.[68] Historian Robert K. Fitts has argued that earlier historians of enslavement on the Narrangansett plantations willfully distorted the historical record. Relationships between the enslaver and the enslaved "were not harmonious and the institution of slavery was not mild"; though some planters may have been disposed to kind treatment, "the evidence suggests that this was rare."[69] In his work on New York slavery, historian Shane White noted that it was not necessary to "search very far to find examples of New Yorkers behaving in a cruel and barbarous fashion." He found numerous cases of "deliberate wantonless [sic] torture" that had been brought to public attention by the Quaker-founded New York Manumission Society. These records, with newspaper accounts, coroners' reports, and travelers' journals, make clear that though slavery in New York "may have been small-scale . . . it was also implacable, brutal, and little short of devastating in its impact on the black family."[70]

The 'Sensitive Few': Voices against Enslavement

Quakers who opposed enslavement shared a strong sense of what God singularly demanded of them as Friends, but their opposition often sprang from different motives. Frost has discerned two reform "impulses" among eighteenth-century Friends. One group, which tended to include small farmers who enslaved few people and were wary of the wealthier merchants, believed enslavement "provoked God's wrath." The other reformers, principally "devout and prosperous" Philadelphians, were concerned about "the corruption of Quaker practice" that enslavement entailed.[71]

The Society's traditional peace testimony was also a compelling foundation for Quaker antislavery arguments. Friends opposed to enslavement decried the violence inherent in a system that was founded on and could be sustained only by force. Quakers had long been cautioned against trading in or using the proceeds of violence—"prize goods"—and it logically followed that enslaved Africans and all that they produced fell into this category.[72] Violence potentially loomed, some Friends maintained, in another way: enslaved people might rise up to take their freedom.[73] In 1688 three members of Germantown meeting openly wondered whether the "professors of peace" would "take the sword at hand and war against" their enslaved Africans should they revolt.[74]

Some Friends also held that enslaving Africans was contrary to the testimony of simplicity. Using enslaved labor, they maintained, encouraged idleness and seemed a conscious effort to display wealth for the sake of impressing others. In 1760 New England Yearly Meeting declared that the practice of enslavement "filled the possessors with haughtiness and tyranny, luxury and barbarity, to the unspeakable prejudice of religion and virtue, and the exclusion of that holy spirit of universal love, meekness, and charity.[75] John Woolman expressed concern that children of enslavers of European descent grew up in idleness and experienced "absolute domination over other human beings."[76]

Early Quaker Petitions Against Slavery

The first Quaker voices against the enslavement of Africans were raised in the late 1600s, largely by Friends who had experienced it as an evil in their own lives. In 1676 William Edmundson was the first Friend of European descent in the British Empire to write of his conviction that it was unchristian to enslave Africans. Born in Ireland, Edmundson spent many years traveling to and living in Quaker communities in the British Caribbean and North American colonies where enslavement existed. In Barbados, where he had traveled with George Fox, Edmundson initially expressed concern for Christianizing the enslaved for the sake of their souls, but soon he became impressed by what he viewed as the damaging effect of enslavement on the souls of Quakers. In his letter to Friends in America, Edmundson urged Quakers to consider the oppressive conditions of enslavement and asked how it was possible for them to declare Native American enslavement unlawful yet continue to enslave Africans. His statement was copied into the New England Yearly Meeting's rule book, but there is no evidence that the meeting issued any advice to its members that they take action on the matter. However, as great as Edmundson's concern was, like Fox he advocated only indenture as an alternative to enslavement—in other words, gradual, not immediate, emancipation.[77]

Shocked by finding oppression based on color in the "new world" to which they had come to escape persecution, a group in Germantown

Friends Meeting were the first American colonists to bring the issue of enslavement directly before Friends as a body. In 1688 European Americans Gerrit Hendrics, Derick op den Graeff, Francis Daniel Pastorius, and Abraham op den Graeff of Germantown Meeting appeared before their monthly business meeting at Dublin to ask how Quakers, as Christians, could buy and sell Africans. In their eyes, the practice of enslaving Africans encouraged theft and adultery, raised the possibility of rebellion, gave Pennsylvania and the Religious Society of Friends bad reputations, and defied the Golden Rule.

> We hear that ye most part of such negers are brought hither against their will and consent, and that many of them are stolen. . . . There is a saying that we shall doe to all men like as we will be done ourselves. . . . And those who steal or robb men, and those who buy or purchase them, are they not all alike? . . . To bring men hither, or to rob and sell them against their will, we stand against.

> Pray, what thing in the world can be done worse towards us, than if men should rob or steal us away, and sell us for slaves to strange countries; separating husbands from their wives and children. . . . We contradict and are against this traffic of men-body.

The Germantown letter further asked, "Have these negers not as much right to fight for their freedom, as you have to keep them slaves?"[78]

Finding these queries "so weighty that we think it not expedient for us to meddle with it here," the monthly meeting at Dublin referred them to Philadelphia Quarterly Meeting, which in turn sent them to the yearly meeting. The yearly meeting also termed the queries "too weighty" and deemed it not "proper to give positive judgment in the case, it having so general a relation to many other parts"—meaning that too many Friends of European ancestry profited from the labor of enslaved Africans.[79]

While "the Germantown paper went into the archives and the Germantown Friends lapsed into silence"[80] not to raise an objection again, other Friends of European descent were ready to speak. The appeal described as "the most eloquent early Quaker protest against slavery" was a 1693 petition from the "Keithians," a group of Philadelphia Friends named after their founder, George Keith.[81] Unlike Edmundson, the Keithians believed true Christians would grant immediate manumission or at least help the enslaved to escape—"extremist" views at that time. The Keithian "Exhortation" asserted that "true

Christians" are not "to destroy men's Lives, but to save them, nor to bring any part of Mankind into outward Bondage, Slavery or Misery, nor yet to detain them, or hold them therein, but to ease and deliver the Oppressed and Distressed, and bring into Liberty both inward and outward."[82] Because Keith's group, known as the "Christian Quakers," had broken away from the main body of Friends under acrimonious circumstances, their views were not only less influential than they might have been, but also made some Friends distrustful of abolitionists for years.[83] Nevertheless, Keithians deserve credit for being the first Quakers to declare enslaving Africans a sin and the first to argue that enslaved Africans were "prizes of war." Keith cited Exodus [21:16] to warn that, since enslaved Africans were captured as the result of violence, if not war, they should be considered stolen goods or proceeds of war, which Quakers did not accept. It was an argument that would be used often by the opponents of enslavement in the years to come.[84]

In 1696 several Friends and meetings took up the antislavery argument. Cadwalader Morgan, a leading European American minister of Merion Meeting near Philadelphia, urged the yearly meeting to acknowledge that owning people was wrong. Morgan had been tempted to buy an enslaved African, but as he began to pray doubts arose in his mind, and he came to believe that God would be against enslavement.[85] The same year European Americans William Southeby of Philadelphia Monthly Meeting and Robert Pyle of Concord Monthly Meeting each presented papers condemning enslavement to the yearly meeting. Southeby, born a Catholic in Maryland, was the "first native-born American to condemn slavery."[86] Despite the yearly meeting's failure to respond to the papers from Southeby and Pyle, Chester Meeting, continued to appeal to the yearly meeting to forbid importation for sixteen years.[87] Those protesting enslavement were also influenced by epistles from London Yearly Meeting throughout the 1700s. One in particular advised Friends "in the colonies to be careful to avoid being any way concerned in reaping the unrighteous profits arising from the iniquitous practice of dealing in negroes and other slaves ... in direct violation of the gospel rule, which teachest every one 'to do as they would be done by,' and 'to do good unto all.'"[88]

In 1711, fifteen years after Southeby and Pyle sent their appeals to Philadelphia Yearly Meeting, Chester Quarter asked that meeting to prohibit the purchase of enslaved Africans. The meeting's response to the appeal echoed what Germantown had heard years before—that because "Friends in many other places are concerned in it" speaking formally against enslavement was ill advised.[89] Rather than agreeing to ban enslavement among its members, Philadelphia Yearly Meeting instead asked them only to avoid publicly or privately judging those among them who did enslave Africans. On the other hand unity and community, ideals dear to Quakerism, required those who might defend enslavement not to do so openly.

Friends considered disunity a serious violation of discipline, and meeting disciplines could be changed only if the "sense of the meeting"—a sense of members' unity typically articulated by its clerk—changed. Quaker procedures, Frost has argued, allowed for "growth in the truth," and Friends had to find a way to reach a sense of the meeting that satisfied them individually as Truth. As dissenting Friends awaited the sense of the meeting, they had to take care not to speak their minds about the issue—and not to put those thoughts in print. Thus those who wanted to preserve the status quo could claim that, even though one yearly meeting might unite against enslavement, such a stance was not to be made public until other yearly meetings agreed. "Religious Truth might grow," James observed, "but not in different directions."[90]

Still, Southeby's appeal prompted the Philadelphia Yearly Meeting to pass the question "touching the importing and having negro slaves, and detaining them and their posterity as such" to the London Yearly Meeting, which Friends in the colonies continued to regard as the "mother" meeting. "We thought it rather too weighty to come to a conclusion therein," the yearly meeting's 1712 epistle stated, and it accordingly asked for the London meeting's "counsel and advice."[91] Yet London Friends were not inclined to find a way out for their Philadelphia brethren; rather, the meeting told Quakers in all the colonies to consult each other on the matter and submit a joint opinion "for final judgment." Yearly meetings were thus left to resolve the issue themselves.[92]

Seeing no progress in new appeals sent to the yearly meeting in 1715 and 1716, Southeby published another paper denouncing the enslavement of Africans—and those Quakers who enslaved them. After publishing his works without permission of the Overseers of the Press,

Southeby became the first Quaker to be disowned for his work against enslavement. His defiant action constituted a serious infraction of Quaker discipline.[93] It was one thing to speak out against enslavement and quite another to criticize Friends directly for being enslavers.[94] Southeby was reinstated after he apologized, but when the yearly meeting failed to respond to his expression of concern, in 1718 he again engaged in "disorderly printing" and promptly received another notice of disownment. Whether Southeby was actually disowned at this point is uncertain, because he was a meeting member in good standing when he died in 1722.[95] Still, Southeby's actions may have had some effect: in 1719 Philadelphia Yearly Meeting advised its members "not to buy or sell Indian slaves . . . to avoid giving them occasion of discontent."[96]

In 1716 John Farmer, a recently arrived Englishman of European descent, joined with European American Horsman Mullenix in protesting enslavement at the quarterly meeting at Flushing on Long Island. Frustrated by the fact that Friends there postponed any action against enslavement, Farmer went to New England, where the yearly meeting was also facing uncomfortable questions about enslavement. His paper, "Relateing [sic] to Negroes," was approved by the Nantucket meeting and read before the yearly meeting, but the leaders of the latter meeting warned him not to publish it. Farmer declined to apologize and was disowned.[97]

An infuriated Farmer returned to Philadelphia and read the forbidden works at every opportunity in and outside Quaker meetings. Already angered by Southeby's actions, in 1718 the Philadelphia meetings upheld New England's disownment of Farmer and claimed he had been "led by a wrong spirit" and had acted "contrary to good order used among Friends." In 1720 the Meeting of Ministers and Elders, Philadelphia Monthly and Quarterly Meetings, and then the yearly meeting ratified the disownment.[98] Thus Farmer was the first antislavery Friend whom more than one yearly meeting disowned for his actions against enslavement.

Friends had also raised concerns before other bodies. In 1716 Mullenix had been the first on record to raise the issue of the enslavement of Africans before the New York Quarterly Meeting. Two years later, some members, including William Burling, a prominent European American member of Flushing meeting, asserted that their consciences told them that enslaving Africans was sinful. Although distressed that his questions would provoke conflict among Friends, Burling nevertheless felt compelled to point out that greed caused enslavement and portrayed the evils that enslavement entailed vividly:

> [We] fetch and steal them out of their own Country, where God Allmighty has made them and placed them, and in taking of them murter many, very many, and serve them that we take alive ten times worse; steal Husband from Wife, Wife from Husband; steal the Children from the Parents, bring them here or elsewhere amongst our extraordinary Christians [who] work 'em, whip 'em and starve 'em almost to death, and if the poor Wretch steal a little to satisfy hunger, he is tormented without Mercy.[99]

Whether Burling's work was published at the time is not clear, though it was issued twenty years later as part of abolitionist Benjamin Lay's attack on Philadelphia Yearly Meeting.[100] In 1719, the year after Burling's action, New York Yearly Meeting turned to London for answers, as Philadelphia had six years earlier; again the London Friends provided no guidance.

Edmundson's letter in 1676 and John Farmer's visit in 1717 had prompted concerns about enslavement at New England Yearly Meeting, but twelve years passed before members raised the subject of enslavement by Friends again. Despite his awareness that speaking out could have negative consequences for him, European American elder Elihu Coleman of Nantucket quoted both Fox's advice about freeing the enslaved after a term and the Bible to remind Friends that God did not want them to enslave others. Friends had forgotten their earlier testimony against the violence inherent in enslavement and become "oppressors," Coleman argued. He included the Golden Rule in his paper, "A Testimony against the Unchristian Practice of Making Slaves of Men." As Woolman would after him, Coleman declared that enslaving promoted pride and idleness—"the mother of all vice." He called upon Friends to free those they enslaved, even if doing so would cost them money and status. "Not for all the riches and glory of this world I would not be guilty of So great a Sin," he said, "God will not forgive what is in our power to help."[101]

Coleman's paper was approved first in 1729 by his own meeting, where abolitionism was viewed more favorably earlier than in some others and where there were "very few" enslaved people.[102] A decade before, in 1716, Nantucket Meeting was the first in New England to call upon Friends to treat people of African descent as indentured servants and free them after a term.[103] New England Yearly Meeting approved Coleman's tract for publication, a surprising action in view of the fact that the meeting took place in Newport, home to wealthy Quakers connected with the trade in Africans.[104] The statement was the first such to be approved by any New England Quaker body, but whether Coleman's words had any effect on Friends individually is not clear.

In "The American Defence of the Christian Golden Rule, or an Essay to Prove the Unlawfulness of Making Slaves of Men" (1715), European American Quaker John Hepburn of New Jersey argued that, whatever good it might offer to the masters, enslavement was degrading and miserable for the enslaved.[105] "God hath given to man a Free Will," he wrote, "so that he is Master of his own Choice. . . . It is thus with God and his Creatures, we ought also to do so by our fellow mortals, and therefore we ought not to force and compel our fellow creatures, the Negroes. . . . For when we force their will, this is a manifest Robbery of that noble Gift their bountiful Creator hath given them."[106]

These first protests established a seeming pattern—a decade or more of inactivity followed some statement against enslavement. After Southeby and Farmer were disciplined, no Quaker meeting in Philadelphia addressed the question for another decade. Chester Quarter "quieted down" after 1730 and manumitted enslaved people no earlier than other meetings.[107] The minutes of the New York Yearly Meeting from 1721 to 1745 are missing, but after 1745 they do not again mention enslavement until 1759, when the meeting banned the importation of Africans.[108]

North Carolina Friends also did not act immediately on the first antislavery appeals brought before meetings there. In 1752 European American Friend Thomas Beals preached against enslavement at the New Garden Meeting, but fourteen years passed before that meeting urged Friends to refrain from buying and selling Africans.[109] However, the southern colony of Maryland did move with some speed on the issue of enslavement. In 1762 Maryland Yearly Meeting made it a disownable offense to buy and sell enslaved Africans without the assent of a monthly meeting. Six years later, led by James Berry of Third Haven and other European American antislavery Friends from the Eastern Shore, the yearly meeting agreed to disown anyone still buying or selling enslaved Africans.[110]

An Intensifying Critique

Ultimately, the strident voices of those European American Quakers undeterred by the prospects of disownment forced Friends to confront their own connections to the enslavement of Africans and their descendants. Ralph Sandiford (c. 1693–1733) and Benjamin Lay (1681–1760) —radicals who were among those who put their message "above 'love and unity'" among Friends—were chief among those voices and spoke at a time when Philadelphia's imports of enslaved Africans were again increasing after a serious recession.[111] In 1729 Sandiford and Lay took up the work earlier Friends had begun and pursued it steadily for a quarter of a century.[112]

The writings of Sandiford and Lay reveal the inner struggle of those who, in their desire to be true to their Quaker testimonies, could conclude nothing other than that enslavement was evil and could do nothing other than use their lives to convince people of that truth. Their work, expressed their "moral outrage, internal trauma, and prophetic zeal."[113] Sandiford and Lay faced two choices—either their messages were not truly from God (thus their religion was meaningless) or their meetings were unable or unwilling to understand the evil of enslavement (thus Friends' lives were not witnessing to their oneness with God). The two men chose to trust their own leadings. They were disowned (Sandiford in 1731, Lay in 1738) for openly defying the Philadelphia Yearly Meeting by publishing what Frost termed "searing attacks upon the institution of slavery and upon the ministers and elders who owned men."[114] In "A Brief Examination of the Practice of the Times," Sandiford declared that Friends should be "a burning and a shining light" revealing the evils of enslavement to the rest of the world; they could not continue to participate in "the most arbitrary and tyrannical oppression that hell has invented on this globe."[115] Historian Forrest G. Wood has credited Quakers, in particular Sandiford, Lay, Coleman, and Hepburn, as "the only Christians to speak out consistently against slavery in the colonial era."[116]

Sandiford's meeting certainly considered his behavior outrageous. Lay, whom historian Carter Woodson has described as a "man of desirable class [with] access to the homes of some of the best people," provoked them even further.[117] Lay's zeal seemed to have been fueled by an incident in which he had severely beaten two of his enslaved Africans whom he caught stealing from his store in the West Indies in the 1720s. Deeply disturbed by his own action, he became a staunch opponent of enslavement.[118] Lay traveled extensively, taking his message to Friends in the American colonies and West Indies.[119]

"All slave-keepers," Lay wrote, are "apostates pretending to lay claim to the pure and holy Christian religion." Enslaving others is "a notorious sin" and a practice "so gross and hurtful to religion and destructive to government, beyond what words can set forth or can be declared by men or angels."[120] His writings inflamed meeting leaders, and what angered them most was the lengths to which he went to make certain that Quakers faced their sins. Kashatus has termed Lay's method "one of direct confrontation and he practiced it daily." At meeting after meeting he demonstratively sought attention: at one point he stood in his bare feet in the snow outside the meetinghouse door to show what barefooted enslaved Africans had to endure; at another he temporarily kidnapped Quaker children to convey to their parents how enslaved Africans felt when their children were sold or otherwise taken from them.[121]

Lay's most infamous action to dramatize his cause occurred at the Philadelphia Yearly Meeting Sessions in Burlington in 1738. Under his plain Quaker overcoat he wore a military outfit with a sword and hid a bladder of juice in a book. At the chosen moment, he rose up to chastise "all you Negro masters and especially you who profess 'to do until all men as ye would they should do unto you,'" tossed off his overcoat, and said, "It would be as justifiable in the sight of the Almighty, who beholds and respects all nations and colours of men with an equal regard, if you should thrust a sword through their hearts as I do through this book." He then drew his sword, pierced the book and the bladder, and splattered "blood" on those nearby.[122] His tactics and his writings infuriated Quaker leaders. When he publicly called the slaveholders among Friends "a Parcel of Hypocrites and Deceivers" in *All Slave-Holders that Keep Slaves in Bondage, Apostates* (1738), the Philadelphia

Yearly Meeting took the highly unusual step of instructing its clerk, European American John Kinsey II, to place a notice in local newspapers disassociating Friends from Lay and from his controversial book.[123] In 1808 British historian Thomas Clarkson stated his view that while Lay's "certain eccentricity of character . . . diminished in some degree his usefulness to the cause he had undertaken . . . there can be no question, on the other hand, that his warm and enthusiastic manners awakened the attention of many to the cause and gave them first impressions concerning it, which they never forgot."[124] And Lay's protest took quieter forms as well. Foreshadowing the nineteenth-century movement, he was the first to purchase only goods that were "free made"—that is, not produced by the system of enslaved labor. He lived simply, made his own clothes, and would not accept anything served by enslaved Africans when he visited friends' houses.[125]

While their methods made it possible for most others to disregard their messages as excessive and likely persuaded few, Lay and Sandiford were nonetheless the perfect fit for a time when only stridency appeared capable of pricking the consciences of Friends on the matter of enslavement. Their actions created increasing turmoil among Friends, even among those leaders of Philadelphia Yearly Meeting who might be expected to have been imperturbable. European American Members Isaac Norris and Samuel Preston may have censured the two men in order "to silence anti-slavery critics who trumpeted their hypocrisy to the world," as Nash and Soderlund have argued, but that they "felt discomfort in the practice" is clear in their wills. Both provided for the freedom of those they enslaved.[126]

In large measure Quakers easily dismissed Sandiford and Lay as radical eccentrics whose behavior, James has stated, "demonstrated their lack of devotion to the solidarity of their religious fellowship."[127] Lay was "generally judged insane by his contemporaries." Nevertheless Lay and Sandiford left the ground fertile for John Woolman (1720–72), whom many historians have credited with changing the hearts and minds of many European American Quakers.[128] Woolman went "beyond sheer argument to share the perplexities of both enslaved African and master." His task was "to be sensitive to the will of God, and then be able to lead his people to think God's thoughts after Him."[129] A shopkeeper, farmer and tailor in New Jersey, Woolman had long been convinced that enslavement was wrong, but he waited until 1754 before he asked the Overseers of the Press of Philadelphia Yearly Meeting for permission to publish his antislavery essay, "Some Considerations on the Keeping of Negroes." Circulated extensively with their assent, Woolman's essay was, in Drake's estimation, the single most significant antislavery document published up to that time "in any language anywhere"; it opened the way for the many works that followed. He wrote in part,

> When we remember that all Nations are of one Blood, Gen. iii, 20, that in this World we are but Sojourners, that we are subject to the like Afflictions and Infirmities of Body, the like Disorders and Frailties in Mind, the like Temptations, the same Death, and the same Judgment, and, that the Alwise [*sic*] Being is Judge and Lord over us all, it seems to raise an Idea of a general Brotherhood, and a Disposition easy to be touched with a Feeling of each others Afflictions: But when we forget those Things, and look chiefly at our outward Circumstances, in this and some Ages past . . . our Breasts being apt to be filled with fond Notions of Superiority, there is Danger of erring in our conduct toward them.[130]

When the overseers agreed to print his second and longer version of the same title, Woolman was reluctant to have the meeting fund its publication because enslavers among the meeting members would have donated some of the funds for it. He paid for the printing himself and then charged a small fee on the supposition that enslavers who bought copies would be more likely to attend to the material within. The low-cost copies, printed by European Americans Benjamin Franklin and David Hall, were sent to all the colonies in the Northeast.[131]

Woolman's journal, perhaps the single best-known Quaker publication and a work many students of religion consider a spiritual classic, also laid out his concerns about enslavement. Enslaved Africans, he wrote in 1756, "are the people by whose labour the other inhabitants are in a great measure supported, and many of them in the luxuries of life. These are a people who have made no agreement to serve us, and who have not forfeited their liberty that we know of. These are souls for whom Christ died," Woolman pointed out, "and for our conduct toward them we must answer before that Almighty Being who is no respecter of persons."[132]

Known not for stirring speeches but for quiet, one-on-one conversations, Woolman visited Friends reluctant to free those they enslaved. Wherever he went, he noted, he was usually welcomed with respect; his hosts were anxious to do whatever was right.[133] Soderlund has pointed out that homes and parlors were opened to him because he was known to understand the difficulties his hosts faced. Most of all, he was not confrontational, instead asking Friends to step outside their own self-interest and consider what would be best for mankind. He focused on the sin, not the sinner. Woolman's encounters sometimes wrought an "inward desolation," but he continued these visits unfailingly.[134]

In his visits to Quakers and Quaker meetings up and down the East Coast and in his writings, Woolman laid out the argument that using the "captives of war"—in other words, the spoils of violence—was no different than thievery.[135] Enslavement was linked with avarice, and the focus on material things among many Friends made them more concerned about protecting their estates and goods than about their peace testimony. Enslavers were particularly vulnerable to idleness, sloth, and other evils born of greed.[136] Woolman also pointed out that enslavement tore African families apart when members were sold and fostered adultery when husbands and wives were separated. Like Lay, Woolman refused to benefit from the system. He paid any enslaved person who served him on one of his many visits to a Quaker household, and he offered his host payment for his room and board on the condition that it be given to the people they enslaved.[137]

In 1754 the Philadelphia Yearly Meeting approved the publication of Woolman's antislavery essay, an action that marked an unmistakable shift in the way that meeting viewed enslavement.[138] Woolman's tract triggered the meeting to issue its first antislavery statement, "Concerning the Buying and Keeping of Slaves," also in 1754. "To live in ease and plenty by the toil of those whom violence and cruelty have put in our power, is neither consistent with Christianity nor common justice," the epistle stated, "and we have good reason to believe draws down the displeasure of Heaven; it being a melancholy but true reflection, that where slave-keeping prevails, pure religion and sobriety declines . . . and [it renders] the soul less susceptible of that holy spirit of love, meekness, and charity."[139]

Historians most often credit Woolman's gentle persuasion with turning the tide against enslavement among Quakers, but Barbour and

Frost have stated that there are "many unanswered questions about his significance to his contemporaries." Woolman's own quarterly meeting in Burlington "lagged far behind" other meetings in New Jersey in this regard, they have noted, and in fact the meetings most connected with him delayed action entirely until their yearly meeting at Philadelphia required members to free those they enslaved in 1771.[140]

Still, evidence exists that one or several visits from Woolman made a significant difference in some meetings' positions. Historian Stephen Jay White has called Woolman "the man who most influenced anti-slavery forces in North Carolina."[141] In Newport, where Woolman typically met with the most prominent of the Quakers who enslaved Africans, he was an important influence on that meeting's eventual ban on enslaving Africans.[142] His 1766 visit to Maryland is said to have "provided the spark" that turned some leading Quakers there to his cause.[143] And Woolman's visits in 1746 and his 1757 appeal to Virginia Yearly Meeting "finally" had an effect in 1770, when Quakers there declared they should "be clear of importing or buying negroes or other slaves."[144]

In 1758, as Woolman began to visit Quakers who enslaved Africans, European American Anthony Benezet (1713–84) published a series of pamphlets vividly describing the horrors of the business involved in their enslavement. Born in France in a family persecuted for their Protestantism, Benezet was seventeen when he arrived in Philadelphia in 1731. He joined the Religious Society of Friends and taught in a Quaker school; he is in fact better known for his devotion to educating Philadelphia's African American children than for his antislavery efforts. Although not as widely recognized as John Woolman, Benezet was as prolific a writer, editor, publisher, and distributor of tracts against enslavement.[145]

Benezet was "devoid of worldly ambition, dressed plainly, and liv[ed] a spartan life." The stories he heard from the people of African descent he knew served as the basis for his arguments against enslavement, or "for a touching appeal in one of the almanacs or papers of the day." When Benezet wrote about the evil of enslavement, he knew whereof he wrote, far more than any other Friend working to end enslavement.[146] Benezet termed American enslavement a "mighty evil, which

proceeds from the same corrupt root as War." Regardless of its origin—
"thro inadvertency, or by the example of others"—slavery "sprang from
an unwarrantable desire of gain, a lust for amassing wealth, and in the
pride of their heart, holding an uncontrollable power over their fellow
men."[147] Convinced that a lack of knowledge about enslavement was
the primary reason that religious people, including Quakers, did not act
against it, Benezet, through his pamphlets, began a campaign to make it
otherwise.

Benezet has been called "the first person to delineate fully the
nature and extent of the problem of slavery." His particular effectiveness
is said to have lain in his ability to interpret philosophical arguments
against enslavement in a manner that appealed to ordinary people.
Having worked closely with African Americans from his students to
dock workers, learned of enslavement from people who had been
enslaved, and at the same time being widely read in the works of the
great moral and spiritual thinkers of his time, he could present the most
lucid and convincing of arguments.[148] Frost has written that the influence of both Benezet and Woolman came from combining "the fervor
of Sandiford and Lay with humility before God and deference to the
meeting."[149]

Benezet's works were circulated widely among Quakers and non-
Quakers, including Queen Charlotte of England, John Wesley, and
Thomas Clarkson. Clarkson wrote a history of the abolition of the
British slave trade in 1808 and had a long career as one of the most
influential British abolitionists.[150] Benezet is thus seen as a key figure in
the abolition of enslavement in both the colonies and in England;[151]
Drake has termed him "the foremost propagandist against the slave
trade and the slavery of Africans in the later eighteenth century." After
the American Revolution, Benezet led the Quaker campaign to convince Congress to end the slave trade.[152] Possibly "worn out" by his
antislavery work, Benezet died in 1784, and his funeral procession to
the Philadelphia Friends' Burial Ground has been described as "the
greatest assembly" in the city of people of both African and European
descent of all social standings, educational levels, and religions.[153]

With growth in population by the 1750s, earlier concerns about
insurrection became more pressing.[154] The numbers of enslaved
Africans had dramatically increased—slave populations had more than

doubled in the North and had nearly quadrupled in the South between 1720 and 1750. And such slave revolts as Stono's Rebellion in South Carolina in 1739, when enslaved people killed guards at a warehouse to secure arms they then used to attack enslavers, brought many Quakers to the seemingly inevitable conclusion that force would be required to quell any uprising.[155] In such a climate, southerners of European descent feared that even manumitted people would rise up and retaliate for their former enslavement. Like other Americans of European ancestry, many Quakers sought to limit imports of Africans not out of any altruistic concern for the enslaved but out of fear for their own safety.[156]

The Turning Point

The first corporate appeal to end enslavement among Friends arose from the combination of several forces and was expressed by Philadelphia Yearly Meeting in 1755. One impetus was the movement to restore and refine the "primitive purity" of the society, sparked by the efforts of British reformers in the 1730s.[157] Quakers in the colonies averred that members had become, as Marietta put it, "spiritually dull" and "callous"; European American Quaker reformer John Churchman of Nottingham, Pennsylvania, charged that Friends were "falling away from truth, into pride, highmindedness, and the spirit of the world."[158] Despite proscriptions against marrying outside the sect, these reformers noted, Quakers were marrying non-Quakers in matches made to enhance their affluence, thus corrupting their children by raising them in wealth. Friends of European ancestry were also "buying cheap and selling dear," wrote Benezet; they were "possessed of such an [sic] heap, which might answer the Sober wants of hundreds." And many departed from the testimonies of plain dress and plain speech.[159] The reformers wanted Friends' lives to witness to honesty, simplicity, and asceticism and to provide their children with a "guarded" education. To survive, reformers held, the religious community needed a set of rules for their members' behavior that reflected high ethical standards and uniformity. Members would conform or be disowned, no matter what the costs in membership numbers, and Quakers would once again stand apart from the outside world.[160]

John Woolman, one among this inward-looking group, more point-edly argued that avarice so clouded the view of the enslavers that they could not see the evils of the practice they pursued. And the two fed on each other: avarice and licentiousness led to the desire to enslave Africans, and enslavement "in turn reinforced" avarice, licentiousness, and "a host of cardinal sins—sexual license, indolence, egregious appetites, and conspicuous consumption." "Here," as Marietta summa-rized it, "was a cycle of evil," one that brought divine punishment and suffering in this lifetime.161 Since the 1730s reformers had predicted that misfortunes would afflict their religious community. More and more Friends came to believe that enslavement was one of the worldly behaviors for which God was punishing them.162

Through the efforts of such leaders as Churchman, meetings began to take responsibility for controlling undesirable conduct. The impulse for purification may be seen in the increasing number of Philadelphia Friends who were disowned for breaking the rules of simplicity or nonviolence or for marrying outside the faith. In addition, at this time Friends began to open boarding schools in the country to offer "a totally controlled environment." From the inside, according to Barbour and Frost, a "purified society" was "much more strict, much more divorced from the world, much more consistent." It was extraordinary, Marietta has stated, for a denomination so large and of such importance to undergo such a transformation; Quakers had "re-formed" their "original character." The old spirit of innovation and eccentricity reap-peared and flourished, almost, it seemed, measure for measure with secular society's dislike of Friends.163 Marietta has argued that this inward-turning was essential to the reform movement because Quakers of European descent had first to move away from political concerns "and toward the periphery of American society" in order to appreciate and act according to their sect's founding distinctiveness. The Religious Society of Friends could only survive by returning to its original prin-ciples, aided by a refusal "to compromise with people whose values it disparaged and whose membership it did not court."164

Quaker bodies very much influenced each other through itinerant ministers and the epistles they shared. Friends moved often within the colonies and maintained relationships with those they had known before; they also frequently did business with each other and steadily exchanged letters and news of Quaker matters.[165] By the 1770s the impetus for reform had spread to New York, Virginia, Maryland, North Carolina, and New England (although there, as in New York, Friends of European descent were at first resistant to reform).[166] Though not all of those Friends who opposed enslavement were also absorbed in purifying their religious society, the two groups overlapped enough that each could support the other's cause. As ending Friends' practice of enslavement became an integral part of their "self-conscious drive" for purification, the smaller group found its numbers and influence growing. Still, for many, the primary goal was to purify the meeting, not to end the oppression of enslaved Africans; those who might have had little humanitarian concern for the enslaved now hoped that "purging the Society of sin would pacify an angry God."[167]

The second factor aligning for change in the 1750s was a major turnover in yearly meeting leadership. Soderlund has asserted that the Philadelphia Yearly Meeting effectively "postponed the ban on slaveholding until most weighty slave-owning Friends had either died or left influential positions." After years of domination by mostly conservative Philadelphia and Burlington men who enslaved Africans, control of Philadelphia Yearly Meeting passed to "a more reform-minded and geographically diverse group" between 1738 and 1754.[168] Barbour and Frost have claimed that the death of long-time European American Philadelphia Yearly Meeting clerk John Kinsey II in 1750 "changed the context" for the discussion of enslavement. Kinsey, a wealthy businessman, was not only the clerk of the yearly meeting but at various times served as Speaker of the Pennsylvania Assembly, Attorney General, and Chief Justice of the Supreme Court. Thus he "symbolized the links between politics, wealth and religion." His death opened up powerful positions in the meeting to opponents of enslavement. Although Quakers believe that the source of decisions is the entire body of a meeting, not one individual, Kinsey's death was arguably a pivotal event.[169] Among the new leaders were European American Israel Pemberton Jr., the wealthiest man in the colony and the yearly meeting's clerk, who had been "converted to reform" by English traveling minister Mary Weston, as well as Churchman, Woolman, and Benezet, the last of whom was appointed to the Overseers of the Press. As these and other reformers made their way to meetings from New England to

North Carolina in the 1750s, the move to purify the society spread widely and rapidly.170

The third factor was the 1756 withdrawal of Quakers of European ancestry from the Pennsylvania Assembly, which they had dominated historically. Although their retreat from colonial government has often been attributed to an inability to meet the demands for protection during the Seven Years' War, the political situation was far more complicated. Ostensibly their peace testimony prevented them from supporting any military action, but by 1755, according to James, Quaker office holders "had long since been inured to accepting compromises and had reconciled themselves to all the artful dodging required" of politicians.171 The Pennsylvania House, for example, had approved funds "for the King's use," well aware that they would be used for defense on the frontier. In fact, there was little difference between the Quaker-run Pennsylvania Assembly and other colonial legislatures when it came to their approach to war. For the reformers, the withdrawal affirmed their view that holding public office had come in conflict with Friends testimonies.172

Thus the 1750s became the "crucial decade," for those working against enslavement.173 Finally the larger Quaker body of European ancestry aligned with those who had been raising their voices against enslavement since 1676. The earliest advices of other yearly meetings were against further importation and for kindly treatment of enslaved people; in 1750 Philadelphia Yearly Meeting urged its members to teach those they enslaved how to read and write. Thus while they appeared to make concessions to enslavement's opponents, they essentially left enslavement untouched. It was a way, as James has put it, to "minimize the problem" without truly "tampering with slave labor."174 But in 1755, in what has been labeled a "watershed" session, Philadelphia Yearly Meeting approved a minute banning members from buying or importing an enslaved person.175 A few Friends, the European American John Pemberton among them, not only freed their enslaved people but either paid to free those enslaved by others or hired enslaved people so that they might earn enough to purchase their own freedom.176

But not all Friends were prepared to comply. In 1758 some members of the Philadelphia Yearly Meeting moved to have the minute reversed. Asking for patience, they proclaimed their faith that "the Lord in time to Come, might open a way for the Deliverance of these people." Hearing those words, sitting "silent, with head bowed and tears in his eyes," Woolman suggested that their appeal was motivated not by any interest in Quaker unity but by greed. He warned that if "through a respect to the outward interest of some persons, or through a regard to some friendships which do not stand on an immutable foundation, [we] neglect to do our duty, it may be that by Terrible things in Righteousness God may answer us in this matter."[177]

Woolman's message—focused on the good of the meeting, not on the oppression of the enslaved—was heard. A minute advising, but not requiring, members to free those they enslaved was approved "without spoken dissent."[178] The 1758 meeting stopped short of disowning those involved in trading Africans; rather, it specified that anyone involved in buying or selling them would be removed from positions of authority and from participation in the business meeting. And the meeting vowed to refuse their contributions as "tainted money." Another apparent effect of the 1758 minute involved how monthly meetings handled transgressors, for several meetings began to go beyond half-hearted admonishment of members who enslaved people to expressions of outright disapproval. Between 1758 and 1774 Philadelphia Monthly Meeting, for one, condemned or completely disowned twenty-five of forty-five who disobeyed the minute against trading, even though doing so was more than the minute required.[179] Forrest Wood has asserted, however, that "What was glaringly absent from most of these expressions on the sinfulness of owning slaves was a concern for the suffering of the enslaved. If slavery was an abomination for the slaveholder, what was it for the slave?"[180]

Friends, consciously or not, had found a way to deal with the issue of enslavement by dividing it into steps that meetings took one at a time.[181] Between 1755 and the American Revolution, yearly meetings from New England and Pennsylvania to Maryland and North Carolina went through similar stages. At first, as Philadelphia had done in 1750, meetings issued periodic reminders to those who enslaved Africans to teach reading and writing, "to educate them in the principles of Christianity," and to help them learn a trade or skill in which they might work as free people.[182] Some monthly meetings, such as

Philadelphia, Falls, and Goshen, followed these advices carefully; others such as Gwyned and Radnor in Pennsylvania and Chesterfield in New Jersey were less attentive to them. Meetings then focused on ending the import and sale of Africans but paid little, if any, attention, to ending enslavement itself. Chester Meeting is a case in point: active from the early 1700s in seeking a ban against importation, the meeting was late in coming to oppose enslavement.[183] Shrewsbury Meeting in New Jersey, whom one historian has called a "remarkably independent" quarterly meeting then in Philadelphia Yearly Meeting, decided in 1757 that the monthly meeting should disown an enslaver. The decision was not only in advance of the yearly meeting but was ahead of others working for manumissions; so too were the decisions of Oblong Monthly Meeting and Purchase Monthly and Quarterly Meetings in New York Yearly Meeting.[184]

Focusing on importation often circumvented, at least for a time, more direct criticism of enslavement itself. For example, in Rhode Island, where far more people were enslavers than traders, the yearly meeting found it easier to ban trading. Ship owners could always turn their vessels to other commercial uses, but "a frontal attack" on enslavement itself would have required confiscation of enslaved "property" and thus would have encountered much stronger opposition.[185] Banning trade had serious financial ramifications for those involved in the business and for those to whom enslaved persons had come through bequest. Expectedly then, efforts to achieve this prohibition were not successful until much later in the prolonged struggle over enslavement. As often as the various yearly meetings may have taken a position on participation in the African trade, their advices typically lacked sanctions against violators. Any assumption that their rulings on the slave trade would be, as Frost put it, "essentially self-enforcing as were similar advices" proved wrong. Rather, like a teacher struggling with an unruly class, each new measure a meeting took had to be "more stringent because previous advices had proven insufficient."[186]

The next action yearly meetings took on the issue was to direct members neither to buy or sell enslaved Africans or their descendants nor to accept them as gifts, a ban most yearly meetings had enacted by 1776. Selling was considered the more serious offense because, if enslaved persons were freed after a sale, the monthly meeting would no longer be able to discipline its members who didn't fulfill their responsibilities to educate and support them.[187]

Although many individual Friends had freed those they had once enslaved, most meetings did not become fully involved in the process of banning enslavement entirely—the only action that had any real meaning for the enslaved themselves—until about 1760. After thirty years of avoiding, denying, prolonging, or taking only minimal steps as a community to end Quaker participation in enslavement, the process ultimately took about another twenty years to complete. Meetings began to ban enslavement, often by voicing a softer message "discouraging" the practice and ultimately by declaring it a disownable offense. The date of ultimate censure can be difficult to pinpoint because time often passed between the threat to disown and actual disownment. Recalcitrant Friends of European ancestry were "encouraged" or "cautioned" or perhaps "warned" before they were disowned. They were offered the opportunity to acknowledge their breach of discipline and convince the meeting that they would mend their ways. Indeed, many did apologize. But if an acknowledgment of their wrongdoing was not forthcoming, eventually the meeting discussed disownment and called members together to consider that serious step.[188]

Importance of Traveling Ministers

By the Revolution, as "even the most listless" yearly meetings moved toward ending enslavement, members were commissioned to visit others among them who enslaved Africans and to report on their progress, or lack thereof. Committees sat with fellow meeting members to pray, listen, and help them discern "right action."[189] In addition, Quaker ministers of European ancestry, in "a fairly constant stream," brought concerns about enslavement to even the most isolated of meetings. Many ministers took on the role of the visiting committees; as they traveled up and down the Atlantic coast they sat with Friends in their meetings and homes to hasten the move toward ending enslavement. Some ministers, like David Ferris, followed up their visits with long letters laying out the reasons that those Friends should stop being enslavers. Among the travelers were Ferris, Woolman, Churchman, Pemberton, Norris Jones, Samuel Fothergill, David Scarborough, and a group of European American women including Sarah Harrison, Patience Brayton, Catherine Payton, and Lydia Hoskins, and Irish Friend Mary Peisley.[190]

———•———

The Society of Friends had long considered women to be equal; women traveled as many miles in the ministry as men under the same adverse conditions, many crossing the Atlantic more than once, in the 1700s and 1800s.[191] No evidence suggests that women's counsel was any less valued and attended to than men's. Rebecca Jones, a European American traveling minister from Pennsylvania, spoke to Friends about admitting people of African ancestry as Quakers in the late 1700s. Rebecca Wilson, a British Friend of European ancestry traveling about the same time, urged enslavers to "keep their hands clear from purchasing Negros as believing it never was intended for us to traffick with any part of the Human Species."[192] Patience Brayton of Rhode Island was one of the notable number of ministers against enslavement who had once been enslavers. She and her European American husband, Preserved, had granted liberty to those they enslaved and, her monthly meeting at Swansea, Massachusetts, reported, "thus being afflicted to cleanse her own hands, she became qualified to labor with her brethren and sisters on the account of liberty."[193] Even though her children were young and her husband was weak, in 1771 Brayton traveled in the South for a year; she continued to serve in the traveling ministry for another twenty years, including four years speaking against enslavement in nearly every meeting in Great Britain.[194]

In 1788 Sarah Harrison traveled from her home in Philadelphia through miles of wilderness in Virginia to labor with Quaker enslavers. Like Preserved Brayton, Harrison's European American husband supported her work and, with the help of others in the Quaker community, cared for their ten children. Despite having had little education, Harrison's messages were sufficiently powerful to cause immediate change. After she spoke at a meeting in Blackwater, Virginia, Friends there manumitted fifty people.[195] "A hard laborious opportunity" with one enslaver compelled Harrison to end her visit without a signed manumission paper, but the next morning the man, "having no rest," appeared at her lodging to sign it. On a second visit to a reluctant Friend, Harrison wrote that "at length the power of the Highest softened his hard heart. He gave me his hand and was broken even to weeping."[196]

The importance of patient and personal appeal on the part of such traveling ministers as Brayton, Harrison, and Woolman cannot be overestimated. By all accounts they were crucial in changing the minds of the "ordinary" Friends laboring in their homes and farms and facing a choice that would change their lives, often significantly. If such efforts failed, meetings were compelled to disown members for their continued enslavement of Africans, and they often took years to come to such a conclusion. For one thing, many reasoned, continuing to work with a reluctant Friend as long as possible could be to the advantage of those they enslaved, because the chance of manumission would diminish greatly if the enslaver was no longer a Quaker. For another, the committees confronted any number of rationalizations for enslavement. Some enslavers protested that they could not be faulted because they had inherited those they enslaved; others claimed to have bought them to save them from misfortune or to have sold them because they would not be able to survive in freedom. Harrison had little patience with this argument. "All we have conversed with agree it is not right to hold their fellow-creature in bondage and wish they were all free," Harrison stated in 1788. ". . . But, when any thing is said to promote their freedom, they soon turn and say they are not fit for freedom because they are such poor helpless creatures."[197] In some instances, this last justification arose from a Friend's concern that certain enslaved persons would be physically or financially unable to support themselves in freedom.

Meetings continued their work to enforce the discipline strictly, all the while recognizing that one "cost of reformation" was a loss of members. This concern was critical in view of the fact that births and conversions were insufficient to maintain the size of the Society of Friends. From 1755 to 1776, the Religious Society of Friends in Pennsylvania disowned 3,157 for continuing to enslave Africans; most of these disownments took place after 1760. Using his estimated 13,640 Quakers in Pennsylvania in 1760, Marietta deduced that 21.7 percent of the membership was disowned after that year. Philadelphia Monthly Meeting disowned 17.4 percent of its 1760 membership of 2,250.[198]

By 1774, as an epistle from London Yearly Meeting indicated that year, Quaker compliance with their meetings' ban on holding Africans was improving. The London meeting had been "agreeably informed of the unremitting concern and great labour used by our Friends in the colonies, to obtain the freedom of those poor Africans who are still held in a state of bondage."[199] Philadelphia Yearly Meeting continued to demand that local meetings "testify their disunion" with any member who refused to free enslaved Africans.

Freedom Achieved

No reliable estimate of the number of enslaved people freed by Friends of European ancestry has yet been developed. Turner found it "safe to say" that perhaps between four and five thousand had been manumitted by Pennsylvania enslavers by 1780.[200] Instances of manumission for which actual numbers are identified indicate that North American Friends freed at least 3,500 between 1685 and 1827. By 1782 New England Yearly Meeting reported that it was "clear of that iniquitous practice." By 1787 no member of New York Yearly Meeting was an enslaver. Yearly meetings in Maryland (1792) and Virginia (1794) followed suit. Between 1791 and 1814 members of the Quaker-dominated New York Manumission Society freed 429 enslaved persons either through purchase or "persuasion."[201]

The fact that most states required manumitters to post bond for anyone they freed sometimes discouraged the practice. By posting a bond the manumitter assumed financial responsibility should anyone they released become a burden on the community through sickness, infirmity, or old age. Similar security was required for manumission by will, a common practice among Pennsylvania Friends, until 1766. At times Quaker meetings posted a bond if a manumitter could not.

Manumissions were of different sorts before the 1770s, each reflecting different sentiments about the general desirability of freedom for enslaved people. Freed people sometimes arranged to earn the price of purchase or were freed only upon agreeing to pay back the former owner for the expenses of housing, board, and other services over the years. Some Friends wills stipulated that an enslaved person must serve heirs before their manumission.[202] But by the next decade "Quaker manumissions were very clear and direct—adults freed immediately, children at the age of adulthood (18 for females, 21 for males). Freeing children was not an option. Since children were not adults, it would have been considered abandonment and put the child at risk of re-enslavement." In addition, manumissions were often gradual, requiring the continued labor of young people until they reached a certain age. Quakers freed minors as soon as it was legally possible, "applying the same standards one would use with a white child," which was different from many gradual manumission schemes.[203]

Some Friends went to great lengths to free persons they had formerly enslaved. Having earlier sold a number of enslaved Africans, Joshua Fisher, one of Philadelphia's wealthiest businessmen and a European American Quaker leader in the 1770s, decided to find them, reacquire them, and then free them or their children in the event that the parents were no longer living. He routinely pursued this practice for the last eight years of his life. In one case, he found five children—Glasgow, Paris, Sabina, Moses, and Diana, then in their twenties—bought them and freed them; they chose "Freedom" as their new family name, a practice not uncommon among freed people.[204] Similarly, European American Friends Henry and Elizabeth Drinker of Philadelphia set out in 1756 to find "our black Jude, whom we sold 51 years ago when she was a child." In their diary they wrote, "We were more settled in our minds, and were very sorry we had sold the child to be a slave for life, and knew not what would be her fate." The Drinkers did locate and try to acquire Jude, but her new enslaver resisted their generous offer; later, they learned, she was sold again, this time to a minister. Again they were unsuccessful in purchasing her, but the minister freed her upon his death, and Jude visited the Drinkers to make them aware of her new status.[205] In 1774 European American Friend Warner Mifflin (1745–98), one of the wealthier Quaker planters in Delaware, manumitted more than two hundred Africans he held in bondage and compensated them for their past labor. As a teenager he had been distressed by the fact that he could not answer an enslaved person's query about why one might be enslaved and another free; in his twenties he became a leader of Delaware Friends' efforts to end enslavement. Drake has argued that the commitment of Friends to make recompense to the formerly enslaved "distinguished them from any other group."[206]

Moses Brown, a Baptist of European descent and one of the most prosperous merchants in New England, also manumitted the people he enslaved. In 1764 at least four enslaved people lived in his Rhode Island household, and he enslaved others in concert with his brothers; together the Browns had invested in at least one ship, *Sally*, that brought Africans to the colonies.[207] In 1773, during a time of introspection after his wife's early death, Brown acted upon a vision that God wanted him to free those he enslaved. He also provided a trust fund for their support and offered them the opportunity to work for him for wages. Brown soon became a Friend and not long after retired in order to devote himself to charitable and Quaker causes, including the colony's Quaker-led campaign against the trade in and enslavement of Africans. His special effectiveness was in successfully assuring people like himself that they could prosper without trading "in human lives."[208] Yet some Friends manumitted, even knowing that their livelihood was in jeopardy. European American Quaker Thomas Hazard refused to accept the enslaved Africans his wealthy (and non-Quaker) father offered him for his wedding, thus bearing considerable financial loss on his Rhode Island farm that had depended on their work. Hazard became a key figure in his state's movement against enslavement, particularly in the campaign that culminated in the ban against trading in 1787.[209]

That enslaved people made up a far greater share of total population in the South than in the North made it much more likely that Friends would make use of bound labor on farms and in the trades. For them, manumission made it even more difficult to compete with large plantations. It also had social consequences. As European American Quaker Anna Braithwaite Thomas noted in 1938, Virginia Quakers who freed the people they enslaved "were cut off from the social life of their neighbors and were in general looked on with suspicion and dislike. No wonder that so many of them preferred to leave their homes and their ancestral farms and seek a new life."[210]

Still, manumission did occur in the colonial South, where the number of free people of African descent was minuscule compared to the enslaved population.[211] Feeling "uneasy" as an enslaver, Thomas Newby of North Carolina, a successful European American planter, merchant and elder in his meeting, manumitted those he enslaved in 1777, and after his action ten other North Carolina Friends freed the 134 people they enslaved as well. Three years earlier Newby had become the first Friend in that yearly meeting to speak publicly against enslavement, and he was clearly contemplating manumission at that time. In the same year he queried his meeting for advice and assistance on how to free those he enslaved responsibly, especially in view of the prevalence of traders who seized freed people and sold them into enslavement. Newby's meeting referred his question to 1774 North Carolina Yearly Meeting, which in that year had permitted the publication of European American Quaker Thomas Nicholson's antislavery paper, "Liberty and Property." The yearly meeting instructed those Friends wishing to free an enslaved person to seek permission and advice from their monthly meeting, which in turn was charged with determining whether the freed person could earn his or her own living.[212]

Among major American denominations, the Methodists, Baptists, and Presbyterians had shown "a heartening interest in abolition" for a time, "but [they] had retreated into silence by 1795."[213] By the end of the 1700s other Protestant denominations had stifled any official abolitionist expression; some in fact supported enslavement outright. The Quaker stance against enslavement was singular—no other Christian denomination required its members to end the practice except for a small and relatively obscure group in Delaware and Maryland known as the Nicholites. Followers of European American Joseph Nichols, the Nicholites included both former enslavers and formerly enslaved people; the former began to free the latter in 1766, well before many Friends had. Nicholites would neither dine with enslavers nor admit them as members of their meetings. People of color, "whether slave or free, appear to have been accepted fully and freely at the meetings." Nicholite testimonies were similar to those of Quakers, and by early 1798 sixty-nine people had applied to become members of the Religious Society of Friends.[214]

To end enslavement was a decision with considerable political, economic, and social cost, but by taking one step at a time and honoring Quaker consensus the society avoided the schisms that other denominations would endure over the issue. As Nash and Soderlund have maintained, the fact that the Society of Friends was alone in freeing enslaved people showed that as a body it could choose moral principles over economic interests.[215]

By the end of their first one hundred years in their new land, Friends had come to terms with the immorality of owning other human beings. "It is certainly an unfortunate commentary on the Quakers that they were too often concerned only with themselves and the punishment God might impose on them," Forrest Wood has noted, but "it is an even more unfortunate commentary on all of the other Christian groups of colonial America that they were so far behind the Quakers."[216] Historian Herbert Aptheker concluded differently: the Society of Friends, he had argued, was "scarcely in advance of the majority and moved forward only with the utmost care and difficulty, and in doing so came near wrecking its own existence."[217]

Even if the pace of their move to end enslavement may seem protracted, few historians question Friends leadership on the issue. In the long journey from the pleas of Germantown Friends to the persuasion of Woolman and later reformers, ending enslavement had helped to create a stronger, more distinctive, and more inward-looking Religious Society of Friends. But as the move to end enslavement spread more widely through American society, Friends rediscovered insularity posed a new dilemma for those who were called to be part of that effort: should they stay "in the quiet" and wait for God, or should they join with those non-Quakers urging an end to the enslavement of Africans throughout the country?

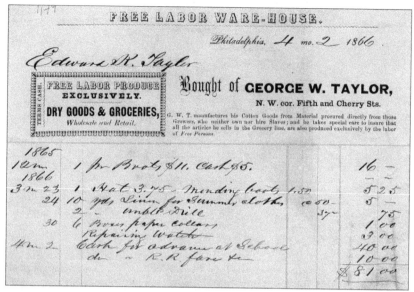

Receipt for Goods bought at Taylor's Free Labor Ware-House, 1866.

Benjamin Lundy, Quaker abolitionst.

CHAPTER TWO

Addressing North American Enslavement

1800-1860

Nothing but a firm conviction of the correctness of our views, the justice of our cause, and the rectitude of our intentions could have sustained us in our undertaking during the earliest stages of this discouraging conflict.

— Benjamin Lundy, 1828

FOR A TIME AFTER THE NEW NATION WAS ESTABLISHED, it appeared that the movement to end enslavement might well prevail. The enslavement economy was becoming less profitable as the tobacco lands in Virginia and Maryland were depleted. Religious revivals were inspiring a generation of fervent reformers who wanted to rid the nation of sin-especially the sin of slavery in a country beset by materialism. Members of other churches were asking the same questions about the morality of enslavement that Friends had dealt with earlier.

But the prospect that emancipation would take place gradually in a foreseeable future would prove to be short-lived. The enslavement trade that had declined because of constraints on shipping during the Revolutionary War was again on the rise.[1] "Unseen but effective forces" were renewing the southern economic dependence on enslavement. Textile machinery lining the banks of New England's rivers signaled the arrival of the industrial revolution and an increased northern dependence on southern cotton. At the same time, the new cotton gin dramatically increased cotton production and the demand for enslaved workers, as did the new sugar cane plantations.[2]

By the early 1800s many European Americans who wanted to end enslavement, including Quakers, were joining societies dedicated to emancipation. Deeply convinced that enslavement had to be prohibited in their new country, both the new groups and the yearly meetings developed a sophisticated lobbying campaign, devoting much effort to petitioning Congress and state legislatures. The fruit of their work, however, was an "abiding resentment" toward Friends among the new country's leaders.[3]

In the early 1800s most Friends held the hope that enslavement could be brought to an end gradually, without violence, and most often with the colonization of the African Americans somewhere else, such as Africa, the Caribbean, or the American West.[4] They believed that relocation would allay the doubts many people had about the ability of people of African descent to live independently, and thus would increase support for emancipation.

A number of opponents believed that the most effective way to end enslavement would be to weaken the institution itself by making it uneconomical for the enslavers. This group, the majority of whom were Friends, was committed to purchasing goods that were not made by the labor of the enslaved. This "free produce" movement was the one effort in which Friends could unite.[5]

Known in the middle 1600s in Britain as radicals whose public defiance of conventional religions and the clergy led to persecution and often imprisonment, by the 1700s Quakers had become respectable, and even wealthy. Their early "explosive, outward-reaching evangelism" was "muted by time," and Quakers had turned inward and become a "settled" people whose lives would witness to their beliefs. As "quietists," Friends' prevailing view was that God's will would be revealed in the silence of meeting for worship,[6] and they began to see other Friends as radicals for their increasingly public advocacy for causes like emancipation.[7]

Campaigning for the End of the Slave Trade

While it might seem that the revolutionary fervor for equality and representation in the 1700s would foster a wider public interest in abolishing enslavement, political leaders focused instead on the war, setting aside other issues—like freedom for African Americans—for the duration. By 1776 any optimism that the spirit of the times would enhance the abolitionists' cause had faded.[8] Quakers, however, set out to head off the revival of the slave trade that was resuming after the war. What they undertook was no small campaign: they submitted petitions, known as "memorials," to the Constitutional Convention and later Congress; produced literature to support their views; lobbied the delegates and Congressmen in public and private meetings; and maintained a visible presence in the gallery. Their methods became "enshrined" as a technique for any group seeking Congressional action on its particular cause and, indeed, continue to be followed to this day.[9]

For people of African descent, the promise of equal rights embedded in Revolutionary rhetoric dissolved almost immediately. The federal Constitution permitted the enslaved to be counted as three-fifths of a person for the purposes of representation in the new Congress, a compromise that not only affirmed the perpetuation of enslavement but greatly strengthened the power of the South in the new union. As European American Quaker whaling merchant William Rotch of New Bedford, Massachusetts, wrote of the Constitution and its "three-fifths rule" in 1787, "It is evident it is founded on *Slavery* and that is on *Blood*, because I understand, some of the southern members utterly refused doing anything unless this horrid part was admitted."[10]

Even before the Revolution, antislavery Friends and others had begun to appeal to colonial governments on behalf of their cause. Among the earliest petitions was one from Virginia in 1771; the colony's assembly approved the petition in 1772, but King George vetoed it.[11] New England Yearly Meeting's Anti-Slavery Committee, newly organized in 1773 by Thomas Hazard, unsuccessfully petitioned the Rhode Island Assembly to end enslavement. The next year, however, the assembly did prohibit further importation of enslaved people, in no small part because of lobbying by European Americans Stephen Hopkins and Moses Brown, two of the most influential men in the colony.[12] Also in 1774, European American William Dillwyn of Burlington Meeting in New Jersey, who had been a pupil of Anthony Benezet, brought before that colony's assembly a petition for emancipation signed by three thousand people. The next year, as the result of appeals from New York Friends, a proposal that would have made it harder to free an enslaved person there was withdrawn.[13]

As antislavery fervor cooled amid the demands of establishing the new nation, Friends continued to agitate. From 1776 to the time the Constitution was ratified in 1787, "Friends became an engine for abolition that no other body, religious or otherwise, matched."[14] Petitions to the federal government began in 1783 when 535 Friends from the Pennsylvania, New Jersey, Delaware, and Western Maryland and Virginia Yearly Meetings signed their names to an antislavery memorial to Congress. Read aloud to the delegates by Warner Mifflin, the petition asked that body to act "as guardians of the common rights of mankind and advocates for liberty." A committee appointed to take up the petition recommended that the trade in Africans be ended, but Congress did not adopt the petition. Despite the outcome, Quaker historian Jay Worrall notes that the petition did provoke "the first bitter floor fight of the U.S. House of Representatives." In addition, Thomas Jefferson, a member of the congressional committee and then at work developing a plan for governing the Western Territory, decided to include an antislavery provision into what eventually became the Northwest Ordinance of 1787.[15]

Exasperated with Friends' persistent petitions, congressmen argued that raising the subject threatened the still-tenuous connection between the North and the South, and thus the new union.[16] Southerners in Congress were especially outraged: European American James Jackson of Georgia called Warner Mifflin a "meddling fanatic" and an "infamous do-gooder of uncertain sanity."[17] "Is the whole morality of the United States confined to the Quakers?" Jackson asked. "Are they the only people whose feelings are to be consulted on this occasion?" He further intimated that Quakers had no standing to protest the institution because they foreswore involvement in the American Revolution: "Did they, by their arms or contributions, establish our independence?"[18] Friends did, however, have their defenders among Northerners. "As for the moral character of the Quakers," European American Congressman Theodore Sedgwick of Massachusetts said, ". . . as a Society, it may be said with truth that they conform their moral conduct to their religious tenets as much as any people in the whole community."[19]

Quakers continued to petition Congress, and the level of rancor about their action increased. A memorial, signed by then president of the Pennsylvania Abolition Society Benjamin Franklin, provoked Jackson to charge Quakers with an impulse for racial mixing, or miscegenation, an assertion that was later common among those who opposed abolition. Quakers, he declared, would be "giving their daughters to negro sons, and receiving the negro daughters for their sons."[20] Still the petitioners were not deterred. In December 1791 various state abolition societies with Quaker connections presented the second Congress with nine petitions to end the trade in Africans. The next year Mifflin, who after Anthony Benezet's death was the most widely known and respected of Quakers working against enslavement, presented another petition, and in 1794 and 1797 Friends and abolition societies submitted more. Southerners buried the nine petitions of 1791 in committee.[21] Although not as successful as their proponents would have wished, these Quaker petitions drew public attention to the issue of enslavement and more significantly prompted wide-ranging, if heated, debates that brought out in the open every argument for and against enslavement and abolition that would be invoked for the next sixty years.[22]

Friends efforts found more success in their home states. In 1774 New England Yearly Meeting's new Anti-Slavery Committee lobbied for laws to "tend to the abolition of Slavery" and to repeal those that in "any way encourage it." The move from working against enslavement in their own society to pressing colonial government on the subject "was the great breakthrough moment."[23] Ten years later, in 1784, Quaker petitions shepherded by Moses Brown and Thomas Hazard supported the effort to enact Rhode Island's gradual manumission law; after another Quaker petition in 1787, the state banned trade in Africans.[24] Joanne Pope Melish argues that "Quaker influence" was critical in the passage of both laws. However, in 1785 state legislators had passed an amendment that severely limited the reach of the law, and it was afterwards generally flouted. Among the most prominent transgressors was Moses Brown's brother John, who was in fact the first person to be prosecuted for defying the national ban.[25]

In 1780, after Benezet and a few other Friends had personally visited every legislator in the state, the Pennsylvania legislature became the first in the new nation to pass a gradual emancipation act. The Quaker petitioners were not successful, however, in bringing about legislation to free children of enslaved parents.[26] Two years later in Virginia, perhaps the most unlikely place, given that more free and enslaved people of African descent lived there than in any other state, four years of Quaker efforts came to fruition when the assembly passed a manumission act. Robert Pleasants, one of the most active advocates, noted that the law allowed "general liberty under certain circumstances to emancipate slaves." Citing this latest success in Virginia, Philadelphia Yearly

Meeting wrote to its counterpart in London to "embrace all opportunities" to discourage enslavement.27

From 1783 to 1795 Virginia Quakers continued to petition their state assembly for laws easing enslavement, including one that declared free African Americans were citizens and made it a crime to enslave their children. One of these petitions influenced the passage of a law in 1795 that allowed African Americans claiming to be free to be heard in court.28 In those years and continuing annually to 1799, Friends in North Carolina also petitioned the state's assembly to protest the re-enslavement of people of African descent whom they had freed, to seek more liberal laws, and to prohibit bringing more enslaved people into the state. The petitions had little real effect.29 More successful were Friends petitions to permit manumission in special cases, including "meritorious service."30

Friends in Maryland did not succeed in influencing the passage of laws against enslavement as rapidly. Baltimore Yearly Meeting, joined by members of Philadelphia Yearly Meeting from Maryland, unsuccessfully petitioned Maryland legislators in 1787 and 1789 for gradual emancipation, but a 1788 petition did help legislate a ban on trading in Africans. A similar effort in the same year to ban the African trade in Pennsylvania was also influential.31

By 1799, Quaker petitioners could offer thanks that Pennsylvania and all the states north of it now banned the trade in Africans at least to some degree, and had passed emancipation laws. Between 1780 and 1804 most northern states enacted gradual manumission laws, which typically freed all those enslaved persons born before a certain date (usually, the date on which the law was enacted), while all those born after that date would be free after a term of service, usually into their late teens or early twenties. And as soon as Congress banned trade in Africans in 1808, Drake notes, Quakers "showered their congressmen" with petitions, including some urging a ban on enslavement in the new western territories.32

Quietism and Gradualism in the Early 1800s

Despite the number of petitions, Quakers who worked to end enslavement in the United States at large were a statistically small portion of their own society. Yearly meetings by and large left the campaign to end enslavement to individual Friends; only New England and North Carolina Yearly Meetings continued to seek an end to the practice as corporate bodies.[33] By the end of the 1700s many Quakers believed that they had done what God required of them by ceasing to buy and sell people and by freeing those they held in bondage; merely belonging to a religious body that had taken a stand against enslavement was, they believed, sufficient atonement for that sin.[34]

Quietism, the idea that God could only "work within and through the human spirit" when all usual activities ceased, or in "the silence of the flesh," inhibited engagement on the broad field of antislavery reform.[35] While the quietists did not shun the world completely, they were still wary of being "contaminated by worldly things."[36] Some Friends found any "vigorous action would be detrimental to religious spirit and solidarity"; those who believed otherwise, they said, gave more importance to their own wills than to their religious community.[37] And so, until 1830 Friends who supported emancipation favored gradual rather than immediate abolition. Like others, they had come to recognize that any successful proposal for gradual emancipation must embrace two features: offering compensation to enslavers for their lost "property," raised either through a national tax or sale of western lands; and identifying a "homeland" where the freed people could live, either within or outside the United States.[38]

European American Friends Elihu Embree, Charles Osborn, and Benjamin Lundy were the bridge linking the anti-enslavement work of such eighteenth-century Quakers as Sandiford, Lay, Woolman, and Benezet to the abolitionism of the 1800s. Though they were not equally radical, the three later Friends intertwined in the same cause and, on occasion, in the same place. The voice of Benjamin Lundy (1789–1839) was the strongest among these early Quaker gradualists. A simple-living Friend from New Jersey like Woolman, Lundy was neither wealthy nor educated. From 1820 to 1830 he spoke against enslavement and organized antislavery societies in nineteen states; he traveled some twenty-five thousand miles, at least five thousand of them on foot, in the course of this campaign.[39] Lundy pursued his abolitionist cause "single-handed and without the shadow of a doubt of his ultimate success."[40] In St. Clairsville, Ohio, in 1815, Lundy founded the

Union Humane Society, the first abolition association west of the Appalachians.[41]

Convinced that unless enslavement ended gradually the country would be torn apart, Lundy outlined his own plan for gradual emancipation in the first issue of his newspaper, *The Genius of Universal Emancipation*, in 1821. He advocated a national ban on trading in Africans, the provision of education for the newly freed, and the use of "moral suasion" with enslavers as the only legitimate path to ending enslavement.[42] Lundy also sought to ban the transportation of enslaved people to another state, to compel free states to receive them on the same footing as European Americans, and to repeal the various "black laws" that restricted the movements and activities of people of African descent in many states.[43]

Lundy published "everything he could find on the subject of slavery and the antislavery struggle" in the *Genius*, which he edited from its founding until his death in 1839. African Americans viewed Lundy as "a great friend and a champion of freedom," but among European Americans he was both "the most admired, and the most thoroughly despised antislavery reformer in America during the 1820s."[44] He is perhaps best known for the influence of his "convincements" on the European American William Lloyd Garrison, whose contact with Lundy stimulated him to found the *Liberator*, the most influential abolitionist newspaper of the nineteenth century. "If I have in any way, however humble, done anything towards calling attention to slavery," Garrison stated in 1863, "I feel that I owe everything in this matter, instrumentally under God, to Benjamin Lundy."[45]

Newspapers such as Lundy's *Genius* were "vehicles of propaganda" that promoted the activities of the various manumission and abolition societies.[46] Of five antislavery papers started before 1826, all of which were published west of the Alleghenies or in the South, four were edited by Quakers.[47] The first incarnation of the *Genius of Universal Emancipation* was the *Manumission Intelligencer*, founded in 1819 by Elihu Embree (1792–1820) and renamed *The Emancipator* in 1820. When Embree died, Lundy assumed control of it and renamed it. *The Emancipator* was the monthly organ of the Tennessee Society for Promoting the Manumission of Slaves, whose constitution Embree helped write; he also asked the Lost Creek Meeting in Jefferson County to approve it. Within two years of its founding in 1814, the Tennessee society had twenty branches and almost five hundred members.[48]

The nation's *first* documented antislavery newspaper was the *Philanthropist*, founded in 1817 and edited and published for one year by European American Quaker Charles Osborn (1775–1850) in Mount Pleasant, Ohio, a predominantly Quaker town that was a center of abolitionist activity in the state and an active Underground Railroad locale.[49] Considered a "fierce, polemical spirit" who called enslavers "monsters in human flesh," Osborn "traveled and preached where there were Quakers" for thirty years and founded manumission societies in many places.[50] Unlike Lundy and Embree, Osborn was not a gradualist. Since about 1808 he had advocated immediate abolition and is believed to have been one of the first Americans, if not the first, to advocate unconditional emancipation.[51] For a time, Lundy and Osborn worked together on the *Philanthropist*.[52] Osborn later left Indiana Yearly Meeting over the issue of enslavement. European American Elisha Bates, a longtime gradualist, bought the *Philanthropist* from Osborn. A highly respected Orthodox Friend and oft-chosen clerk of Ohio Yearly Meeting, Bates continued to present the abolitionists' point of view in the *Philanthropist*.[53] Enslavement was also treated with some frequency in the columns of *The Friend*, the Orthodox newspaper founded in 1827, as well as in the pages of the *Friend, or Advocate of the Truth*, founded by Hicksites and published from 1828 to 1831 or 1832.[54]

Friends and Formal Antislavery Affiliations

From the late 1780s to the 1830s, most Friends who worked against enslavement did so not through their monthly or yearly meetings but through more inclusive organizations created specifically for that purpose.[55] Before 1808 only Maryland, New Jersey, New York, and Pennsylvania had created state antislavery societies, but by 1827 at least 130 such groups had been created in twelve states and the District of Columbia. By 1823 five of the societies were in "slave states."[56]

Quakers played an active role and were often founders of these societies from Rhode Island to North Carolina and west to Indiana, Tennessee, and Michigan.[57] Two-thirds of the founders and fully three-quarters of the most active members of the Pennsylvania Abolition

Society and one-half of the New York Manumission Society were Friends; twelve of the eighteen persons who founded the New York Society in 1785 were Quaker.[58] With the exception of those associations founded in Connecticut and Kentucky, Friends were "the chief organizers and most active supporters" of northern groups.[59]

In the South, abolition and manumission societies were "generally small, ineffective, and gradualist in outlook," but Quaker activity in them was nonetheless profound.[60] In that region, "there was essentially no abolition movement except for Friends."[61] Quakers who had moved from Pennsylvania and North Carolina to Tennessee founded many manumission societies in that state between 1815 and 1822 and gathered for at least eight annual conventions at Lick Creek Meeting House.[62] Eighty percent of manumission societies in North Carolina were Quaker, founded largely by Friends who had come from the North; largely due to Osborn's work, the North Carolina Manumission Society had as many as 1,150 members in at least forty local branches, four of which were female.[63] After the Revolution, most of the antislavery societies were "Quaker fronts" or at least had strong Quaker backing, a fact that both "drew some admiration" and inspired the "contempt normally reserved for blacks themselves" among non-Quakers.[64]

In Rhode Island and Maryland, members of the Providence Society for the Abolition of the Slave Trade, and of the Society for Promoting the Abolition of Slavery and the Relief of Poor Negroes Unlawfully Held in Bondage, founded in Baltimore in 1789, sought to identify illegal kidnappings of free African Americans, filed petitions for their freedom, moved to have kidnappers arrested, and condemned instances of outrageous misconduct on the part of enslavers. European American Quaker Elisha Tyson (1749–1824) was prominent in the Baltimore society. Most widely known for his work to prevent free African Americans from being sold into enslavement, Tyson founded the Protection Society of Maryland in 1818 to enforce legal safeguards for people of African descent. He is credited with having kept more than two thousand free people from this fate between 1799 and his death in 1824.[65]

Friends who organized the Pennsylvania Abolition Society and others who founded similar organizations in their own states "read like a list of the wealthiest members of meetings in Philadelphia, New York, and Providence." In general the wealthier Quaker merchants and professionals, who had once enslaved Africans as house servants, more easily favored abolitionism than did artisans, who were heavily dependent on the work of the enslaved and whose livelihoods were most seriously threatened by the possibility that enslaved people would be freed and begin to work for wages. According to Ingle, such esteemed founders "made reform respectable."[66] Many European American Quaker founders had gained organizational experience by working on meeting committees charged with supporting African Americans.[67] In 1794 Friends began to encourage a loose alliance of abolition societies called "The American Convention for Promoting the Abolition of Slavery, and Improving the Condition of the African Race," but attendance and programs were sporadic; a national antislavery society did not again emerge until 1830.[68]

Almost all early abolition societies supported gradual emancipation. Though not strictly an abolition society, the New York Manumission Society typifies the strategies most abolition societies pursued to bring about the end of enslavement. It worked to outlaw enslavement in the state, monitored compliance with the laws protecting the enslaved, published an array of materials advocating emancipation, endorsed boycotting the products of enslaved labor (known as the "free produce movement"), and opened evening schools for free people of African ancestry. According to historian Leslie Harris, the society "combined a Quaker-based religious impulse with an elite political vision."[69] Yet Shane White observes that at least 27 of its 120 members in 1790 were enslavers, and the society "backed away from confronting the institution" of enslavement "head on in New York."[70] In fact, as Harris notes, some members believed that having a "good" master was one way to achieve the necessary indoctrination of African Americans into the ways of the general society, one of the reasons that the society never required its members to emancipate those they enslaved. Other abolition and manumission societies publicly argued that African Americans could function equally and fully as free people. Moses Brown and his son Obadiah, members of the Providence society, asserted their wish to prove that people of African descent were "of the same species, possessing the same capacities."[71]

Another wave of founding abolition societies began in 1814. Quaker influence was profound in these societies as well, and for the most part they were dedicated both to ending enslavement and to improving the lot of free people of African descent. New England, often considered at the forefront of abolitionism, did not become involved on a noticeable scale until the 1830s and the beginning of the American Anti-Slavery Society.[72] The largest abolition societies before 1830 were in the South, just as the first abolition newspapers were founded in the Midwest.[73] By 1834 manumission societies had all but disappeared, having dissolved over the issue of colonization.[74]

Colonization

Many abolition societies founded before 1830 favored colonization because it answered one of the major questions about abolition—what would the newly freed people do? Where would they live? Finding them another place to live made it much easier to argue for emancipation, and it would calm the fears that many people of European descent felt about a large population of freed people of African descent.[75]

As early as 1715, Quakers had contemplated transporting freed slaves to another location. John Hepburn described it as the "logical" outcome of emancipation. In 1737 even Benjamin Lay, arguably the most outrageous Quaker agitator against enslavement, stated that there was "such a disparity in their Conditions, Colour and Hair" between people of African and European descent that "they can never embody with us."[76] Even Benezet was concerned that the races could never live peaceably together, but thought that Africa would be too difficult an adjustment and suggested instead that land west of the Alleghenies would be "a suitable and beneficial" place in which African Americans might build a "profitable" society with settlers of European descent who chose to live with them.[77]

Friends support for colonization continued into the nineteenth century. In 1805 European American Friend Thomas Brannagan of Philadelphia proposed that the government assist in resettling African Americans and willing European Americans on "a distant island" or in a newly created state in the Louisiana Territory, some two thousand miles away "from white property."[78] In the 1840s, European American Friend Elijah Coffin of Indiana envisioned an independent African nation "in the great American desert [in the west], with blacks forcibly removed to it, if necessary."[79]

Colonization began to gain national attention in 1816 when federal funding for the scheme was sought by European American legislator Charles Fenton Mercer of Virginia, who was motivated by the fear of insurrection, and Robert Finley, the European American director of Princeton Theological Seminary, who created the American Colonization Society (ACS) in 1816. Finley wanted government money to fund large-scale emigration.[80] Between 1818 and 1832, signs of support for federal funding came from at least ten state legislatures and also from leading politicians, philanthropists, and churches. After the American Colonization Society acquired Liberia in 1821, the possibility of large-scale relocation improved considerably. By 1832 there were 105 local colonization societies in the North and 251 in the South.[81]

Some African Americans also supported colonization, principally those who believed they would never achieve racial equality in the United States. "We love this country and its liberties, if we could share an equal right in them," African American Abraham Camp of Illinois wrote, but he and others had "no hope" that such equality would ever be realized.[82] However, most people of African descent actively opposed the movement. When European American Quaker physician William Thornton brought a plan to settle free African Americans in Sierra Leone to Philadelphia's Free African Society in 1787, the society rejected it even though Thornton had garnered some support among Boston and Newport African Americans.[83] "Whereas our ancestors (not of choice) were the first successful cultivators of the wilds of America," the Free African Society of Philadelphia declared later, "we their descendants feel ourselves entitled to participate in the blessings of her luxuriant soil, which their blood and sweat manured."[84] Many also worried giving attention to colonization was detracting from the effort to gain widespread support for emancipation, a concern echoed by key European American abolitionists.[85] In 1817 and 1818 African Americans protested colonization in twenty-two cities, and they continued to express their opposition in their state and national "colored people's conventions" of the 1830s and 1840s.[86] In his 1831 Appeal to the Coloured Citizens of the World, African American David Walker declared that colonization was nothing more than a plan to separate free and enslaved Africans Americans so that the latter could no longer learn from the former "that they are men, as well as other people, and certainly ought and must be free."[87]

In the 1820s Benjamin Lundy was one of those beginning to promote colonization as a means of increasing support for emancipation
among European Americans. But in Lundy's view colonization was
only viable when it promoted emancipation, not when it was limited to
those who were already free. The second key to making emancipation
work was that there would be "no pecuniary sacrifice" or loss of property from those who enslaved. In an 1825 paper—"A Plan for the
Gradual Abolition of Slavery in the United States, without Danger or
Loss to the Citizens of the South"—Lundy detailed his proposal.
Essentially, he would have people freed over a number of years earn
their purchase price by working on land purchased for that purpose.
Then they would move to a colony. The paper detailed the cost of his
whole scheme, from buying land and horses to hoes and food.[88] He
also tried unsuccessfully to find land in Texas and Mexico for free
African Americans, and in 1825 led a group of free African Americans
to Haiti as part of a plan to produce free-labor cotton there.[89]

Margaret Hope Bacon distinguishes between "colonization"—
forced removal advocated by the ACS—and voluntary emigration,
which she terms "resettlement."[90] The latter is what Afro-Indian
Quaker whaling merchant and abolitionist Paul Cuffe (1759–1817) of
Westport, Massachusetts, had in mind when he actively pursued colonization in Sierra Leone beginning in 1810. Cuffe's aim differed
fundamentally from the goals of the American Colonization Society. He
sought, according to Wiggins, not only to create an agricultural economy that would promote "trade in goods rather than humans" for the
benefit of free African Americans who would move there, but also to
develop an international trade between the colony, Great Britain, and
the United States to undercut the economy of the American enslavement system.[91]

Toward this goal, Cuffe established the Friendly Society, a trading
cooperative between the three parties in 1811.[92] By that time Cuffe
had built a transatlantic network of commercial relations with affluent
Friends and others in New Bedford, along the Atlantic coast, and
abroad in his pursuit of philosophical and financial support for coloniz-
ing Sierra Leone. Though he did not gain federal support for his plan,
by 1815 he had managed to overcome most obstacles and set sail with
thirty-eight passengers for Sierra Leone; he paid for the passage of

thirty himself and gave all the prospective settlers a free set of clothing.[93] But Cuffe's health, the demands of his own businesses, and an overwhelming lack of interest in colonization among African Americans undermined the venture; Cuffe died in 1817 before he could undertake a second trip.[94]

Friends from Great Britain and New York were among those who had lent financial support to Cuffe's endeavor. Some of the most committed abolitionists of European descent in New England—William Bassett, James Buffum, and Abby Kelley among them—had initially supported resettlement.[95] In fact, "most American Friends of the early republic shared the general sentiment that both Negroes and whites would be better off, if, on receiving their freedom, former slaves could go somewhere else . . . it did not matter much where, as long as they went to a world of their own color."[96]

———————•———————

Though colonization was more popular than abolitionism among most people of European descent before 1830, many Quakers, with other abolitionists, were increasingly wary of the southern politicians who led the movement and had begun to regard the movement as a plot to remove only free people of African descent.[97] By 1830, the colonization society was "firmly in the grasp of those resisting, not abetting, abolitionism, men whose thoughts on blacks, whether free or slave, easily turned to the topic of innate Negro inferiority and degradation."[98] Thomas Hamm points out that, "one must distinguish between colonizationists who rejoiced at the prospect of expelling all black people, and those . . . who had sadly concluded that massive white prejudice made any other solution impossible."[99] The colonizationists came in the first category.

Some European American Friends—like Abby Kelley and Sarah Grimké, originally endorsed colonization but later rejected it. Others, including Lucretia and James Mott, opposed it from the start.[100] In 1833 European American Quaker John Greenleaf Whittier of Massachusetts wrote in *Justice and Expediency* that of the thousands of people of African descent who had emigrated to Africa in the seventeen-year life of the Colonization Society, the great majority had been free people. In fact, only 613 enslaved people were among those who had left. And at the same time, Whittier noted, the enslaved population of the United States had grown by half a million.[101] Most of those who actually left the United States were southerners whose freedom from enslavement had been granted on the condition that they leave the country.[102] "What has it [colonization] done for amelioration?" Whittier asked. "Amelioration of what? Of sin, of crime unutterable, of a system wrong and outrage horrible in the eyes of God."[103]

Over a period of more than eighty years (1817 to 1899), the American Colonization Society sent 15,386 colonists to Liberia at the cost of $2.8 million, not including those sent at the expense of independent state societies.[104] Persistent criticisms, however, took a toll on the Colonization Society, as did internal disagreements, monumental resettlement problems in Liberia, and financial troubles. The government had not come forward with funding. Garrison had been successful cutting off British support, financial and otherwise.[105] Finally, despite their initial enthusiasm for bringing the Gospel to Africa, the mainstream Protestant churches had not been able to raise any substantial amount. In the end, there were not enough free African Americans who wanted to leave and not enough money to pay for those who did.[106] Colonization came to the fore again among both European and African Americans in the 1850s, but it was not perceived as the remedy it had been in the 1820s."[107]

The Free Produce Movement

From the earliest days of Quaker protest against enslavement, Friends most committed to ending the practice recognized that to use the goods and services of enslaved people was to endorse and promote the system that bound those people. An organized effort to boycott "slave-made" goods began among Quakers on a small scale in the 1700s and burgeoned in the 1800s in the form of "free produce" organizations and "free labor" stores.[108] Among Friends, a boycott of slave-system goods was both moral and, they hoped, a model to be emulated by others. The argument that, according to the peace testimony, enslaved people of African descent were in effect "prize goods"—captured through violent methods—reemerged; Lucretia Mott equated buying the products of enslaved labor with buying stolen goods from a thief.[109]

Another objective of abstaining was to show southerners that forced labor was in the end unprofitable. Absent the profits from enslavement, enslavers would naturally manumit the people they held.[110] Not to be overlooked was another compelling reason for support: for many Quakers, especially those who did not want to be associated with the more activist abolitionists in their religious community, the movement offered a peaceful way to work against enslavement and still remain within the folds of the Religious Society of Friends. The movement gained the support of many national and local abolition societies.[111]

The attempt to avoid slave-produced goods among Quakers of European descent was longstanding. In the eighteenth century, such Friends as Ralph Sandiford and Benjamin Lay had pointedly refused to use the products of enslaved labor. They were joined by traveling ministers Joshua Evans, John Woolman, and others who refused to use services or goods of enslaved people or even to stay in the homes of southern enslavers.[112] In 1811 European American Quaker Elias Hicks of Long Island published—with the approval of New York Yearly Meeting— *Observations on the Slavery of Africans and Their Descendants*, an anti-enslavement treatise that included an argument against using such products.[113] Hicks asked, "What is the difference whether I hold a slave, or purchase the produce of his labour from those who do?" He also tried to counter the contention of those consumers who believed their actions would be too insignificant to affect the overall system. "If we as individuals . . . should imagine that our share in the transaction is so minute, that it cannot perceptibly increase the injury," Hicks wrote, "let us recollect, that, though numbers partaking of a crime may diminish the shame, they cannot diminish the turpitude."[114] Around the same time, Lundy and Osborn, two other avid supporters of free produce, used their antislavery newspapers to urge readers to join the boycott.[115] "A merchant that loads his vessel in the East Indies with the proceeds of slavery does nearly as much at helping forward the slave trade as he that loads his vessel in Africa with slaves," Osborn wrote in the *Philanthropist* in 1817. "They are both twisting the rope at different ends."[116]

———— • ————

Though it was never in any sense a mass movement, between 1796 and the Civil War dozens of free produce associations, some of them exclusively

Quaker, were formed in the East and Midwest. Quakers took the lead. Although the movement never attracted a consistent majority of abolitionists, many Quaker and non-Quaker activists did endorse the boycott.[117] In 1827 some five dozen influential Friends of European ancestry—including James Mott (who married Lucretia Coffin in 1812) and Isaac Hopper, both Hicksites—founded the Free Produce Society of Pennsylvania to solicit supporters, find sources for free labor goods, inform consumers where to purchase such goods, and convince the proliferating antislavery societies to align themselves with the movement.[118] Between 1829 and 1837, with a number of other smaller groups in Philadelphia and eastern Ohio, the Pennsylvania society essentially comprised the free produce movement. In 1837, Hicksites who wanted to work against enslavement exclusively in "Quakers-only" organizations started the Association of Friends for Advocating the Cause of the Slave and Improving the Condition of the Free People of Color. The group promptly issued a letter urging members to consider if they were called by the testimony against enslavement to use only free produce.[119] Twenty thousand Friends foreswearing the products of enslavement would "exert no inconsiderable influence in breaking the yokes and letting the oppressed go free," the Association claimed.[120] In 1839 many of those who had started the first Pennsylvania group founded yet another organization for both Friends and others—the American Free Produce Association. More than one hundred people attended the first annual meeting, including representatives of twenty-three abolition societies as well as William Lloyd Garrison (who later ceased to support the movement).[121] A majority of the officers were Quakers of European descent, including Hicksites James and Lucretia Mott and Orthodox Friends William Bassett of Massachusetts and Abraham Pennock of Philadelphia. Hicksite Friend Lydia White was named to the executive committee.[122] A group of Orthodox Quaker abolitionists formed yet another organization in 1845, eventually renamed the Philadelphia Free Produce Association of Friends. Also that year, New York Monthly Meeting (Orthodox), one of the few Friends meetings that took a stand in the movement, founded the Free Produce Association of Friends of New York Meeting.[123] Second in importance only to the Philadelphia group, the New Yorkers were enthusiastic and looked forward to gaining wide support.[124]

Midwesterners were active, too. In 1846 Friends from smaller organizations in Indiana and Iowa joined to create one of the largest groups, the Western Free Produce Association, and issued an appeal to all officers in the "western" antislavery societies (including Ohio, Indiana, Illinois, and Michigan) to assemble to discuss the movement. The Ohio Yearly Meeting's Free Produce Association's first annual convention at Green Plain, Ohio, attracted over two hundred people, including ministers and government officials, many of them non-Quaker. Still, the group was unable to attract enough investors to create a joint stock company, as it planned.[125] The association did convince the European American Levi Coffin, a Friend best known for his Underground Railroad work, to move to Cincinnati to open a wholesale free produce store and pledged funds to underwrite the venture.[126] But, like other groups, the association experienced "spasmodic attacks of enthusiasm followed by periods of lethargy." One of its member organizations, the Mount Pleasant group of Ohio Yearly Meeting Friends, was "steady and more successful" and did, in 1848, organize the Mount Pleasant Free Produce Company after selling 250 shares at ten dollars each to capitalize it. Membership and customers increased over the next several years, but ultimately the "continued apathy" of Friends doomed the project. In 1857 stockholders had to dissolve the company formally, though it managed to carry on for six more years.[127] This group and the Philadelphia free produce group devoted a great deal of energy and money to sustain the publication of the *Non-Slaveholder*, the only paper devoted exclusively to the free produce movement.[128]

Between 1817 and 1862 the free produce movement fostered the creation of fifty-three stores in the East and Midwest that sold goods made by free people—linen and silk stockings, baked goods and confections made without slave-produced sugar, and such products as sugar, rice, and coffee that had not emerged from the enslavement economy.[129] As early as the 1830s African Americans had also organized groups to promote free produce. In 1830, 230 people signed the constitution of the Colored Men's Free Produce Society of Pennsylvania, and people of African descent in major eastern cities operated free labor grocery stores.[130]

European American Quaker women were often the spark behind the founding of societies—twenty-six were formed in the United States between 1826 and 1856, sometimes organized as separate "female societies"—dedicated to promoting the boycott.[131] The first woman of European descent to speak to a yearly meeting on boycotting was Alice Jackson Lewis of Chester County, who raised the issue at her Philadelphia meeting in 1806. Lewis had forgone the use of enslaved-labor products for years, and she was particularly committed to convincing women to use their power as consumers.[132] In January 1829, the two-year-old Free Produce Society of Pennsylvania started the Female Association for the Promotion and the Manufacture and Use of Free Cotton. Membership grew from thirteen to one hundred women in a few months. Although it was active only for a year, many members went on to join the new Philadelphia Female Anti-Slavery Society, which also supported free produce.[133] Many similar women's groups included a free produce resolution in their constitutions. All three meetings of the Anti-Slavery Convention of American Women—in 1837, 1838, and 1839—appealed to women to join in the boycott.[134] Later, as the abolitionist movement splintered in the 1840s and 1850s, many women abandoned local antislavery societies to work solely for the use of free produce.[135] Lucretia Mott, a leader in both the male and female sectors of the movement, briefly ran, with her husband, a free labor grocery in Philadelphia, as did European American Quaker Sydney Ann Lewis; the more successful store of Lydia White was in business from 1830 to 1846.[136] Many of the free produce societies existed in Quaker strongholds where Friends had been active in forming antislavery societies: western Vermont and New York; Salem, Mt. Pleasant, and Green Plain in Ohio, several counties in Indiana; Chester and Lancaster counties in Pennsylvania; Delaware; Maine; and North Carolina. In some cases, membership in local antislavery groups required the purchase of free-labor goods.[137]

The free produce idea received a great deal of attention from Quaker yearly meetings, but only one—the Indiana Yearly Meeting of Anti-Slavery Friends—made boycotting a part of its required discipline. Indiana Friends first approved taking part in the movement in 1847 and reaffirmed that position in 1853 and 1855.[138] Most other meetings that considered the idea advised rather than required members to participate.[139] At times, the prospects of a successful movement were encouraging. In 1843 the Free Produce Association reported that sales had doubled from the previous year, and more societies were being organized. Friends boarding schools took part in the movement: in 1849 the *Non-Slaveholder* reported that the Friends school in Providence was "almost exclusively supplied with free labor groceries . . . at very little, if any, extra expense." Nine Partners in New York and Haverford Friends School near Philadelphia were doing the same, the newspaper reported, and Westtown, the Quaker boarding school in West Chester, Pennsylvania, was expected to join them shortly.[140] While about fifteen hundred people were members of the various free produce societies at the height of their popularity, as many as five or six thousand other people may have endeavored to buy only free-labor goods.[141] In 1847, the *Non-Slaveholder* put the number far higher, declaring that fully ten thousand Friends, or about ten percent of all Quakers in the United States, were taking part in the movement. In the end, however, acquiring and marketing free-labor goods were formidable challenges, as reports from the first few annual meetings of the Free Produce Association indicated. Supporters were rarely able to raise enough money to identify sources of goods and to purchase them. The higher prices of free-labor goods was a problem for both suppliers and consumers.[142] As dedicated to the cause as many were, they could not afford to be consistent customers, and at most times the demand for goods exceeded the supply.[143] By 1847 Coffin's Cincinnati store had "netted nothing but troubles and losses," and after ten years he was forced to sell out.[144] The free store in New York prolonged its life to 1855 only because a Friend assumed responsibility for its losses. Even the relatively successful store run by European American Friend George W. Taylor of Philadelphia ultimately could not prosper. According to one historian, "no one [was] more faithful in the free produce cause" than Taylor, who strongly believed that the boycott could contribute to ending enslavement.[145]

———————•———————

Along with high prices and a general skepticism about its economic impact, a number of negative opinions doomed the free produce movement. There were those, including Garrison, who thought the movement diverted attention from abolitionism's major goals.[146] The "nonresisters," committed to using only nonviolent means to work against enslavement, suggested that economic coercion might be simply another way of compelling people to do something against their will, albeit without physical force.[147] Elisha Bates maintained that the attempt to hurt the enslavers' livelihood was not Christian, and that, in the end, it was impossible even for Quakers to avoid goods stained by some kind of sin.[148] Both Lucretia Mott and Abby Kelley Foster seemed to agree with Bates. "Unfortunately, free sugar was not always as free from other taints as from that of slavery," Mott admitted, and Foster observed that many goods produced by free labor—for example, textiles made in European mills—were themselves produced in terrible and oppressive conditions.[149] Finally, participating in the free produce movement was a radical shift for consumers, a transition made more difficult by the quality of the goods themselves. As Mott stated, "Free calicoes could seldom be called handsome; free umbrellas were hideous to look upon, and free candies, an abomination."[150]

Even as early as 1837 support had begun to wane. The American Convention for Promoting the Abolition of Slavery and Improving the Condition of the African Race reported at its annual meeting that year that its membership was lethargic about promoting free produce.[151] In 1849 the American Anti-Slavery Society withdrew its support on the grounds that the free produce movement was not advancing abolitionism. By 1854 financial problems compelled the *Non-Slaveholder* to cease publication.[152] On the whole, Quakers persisted in the free produce movement longer than non-Quakers, but by the 1850s support had radically diminished. Many early supporters had grown disillusioned about the movement's effectiveness as a weapon against slavery. Such reformers began to seek "other more spectacular and less exacting fields of anti-slavery."[153] And, as what must have been the "last straw" for many Friends, by the 1850s an increasing number of Quaker meetinghouses in Pennsylvania and Ohio were being closed to free produce gatherings, even gatherings open only to Friends.[154]

With the depression of 1857, the Philadelphia's Free Produce Society's "slender resources" grew more slender still. Among both Quakers and non-Quakers, the boycott "never aroused a surge of emotional enthusiasm." And because the movement was not "sensational or dramatic," supporters were ultimately unable to convince people to endure the hardships entailed in boycotting goods they used so often in their everyday lives.[155] In the end, most of the antislavery measures in which Quakers engaged in the earlier decades of the nineteenth century—colonization, the free produce movement, abolition societies, and petitions to legislators—had done little to trigger a change of heart in enslavers or in the American people generally. As the Pennsylvania Abolition Society lamented in 1817, "Those actively engaged in the cause of the oppressed Africans are very small."[156]

For some Quakers, however, the piecemeal progress toward emancipation was not cause for retreat but, instead, for deeper engagement. After 1830, when Garrison's *Liberator* began to declare its support for immediate emancipation, like-minded Friends pursued more radical measures toward that end, actions that revealed more painfully than ever before the contrasting and contradictory impulses that would continue to trouble Quakers deeply for decades to come.

Portrait of William Still, 1872.

Abby Kelley Foster.

CHAPTER THREE

Quakers and
Immediate Emancipation

What a paradox, that the Society of Friends—the first important Christian group in America to see the evil of slaveholding, and the first to renounce it without regard to cost—the Quakers who had faithfully guarded the antislavery flame in the years when it burned so low, should now divide over the issue of abolition!

— *Thomas E. Drake*

THROUGH THE 1820s, some reformers working for emancipation grew increasingly discontent with what they perceived to be the unacceptably slow pace of the abolition movement. Gradualism, they charged, was a "ruse"-what the Reverend William Goodell termed a "strategy of delay"—that only hurt the abolitionist cause.[1] Such political actions as the 1820 Missouri Compromise, which permitted enslavement in the new state of Missouri and a new "gag" rule on antislavery petitions to Congress, demonstrated forcefully that Southern "slave power" was sufficiently strong to override Northerners' efforts to limit the extension of enslavement.[2] By the 1830s these federal actions helped radicalize many of those committed to emancipation. At the same time, the wider historical setting for the abolition movement as it moved through the 1830s and 1840s reveals a large majority of Americans of European descent increasingly hostile both to African Americans and to those who publicly supported their freedom. Only a small percentage of the country's population supported the abolitionist cause. In the eyes of the radicals, to be against abolitionists was to be for enslavement and so the division was growing.

American abolitionists were further moved toward immediate abolition by events in Great Britain. In 1824 Elizabeth Heyrick (1769–1831), a Quaker of European descent, published the pamphlet *Immediate, Not Gradual Abolition: or, An Inquiry into the Shortest, Safest, and Most*

Effectual Means of Getting Rid of West Indian Slavery. It was said to be the first printed piece in the English-speaking world to advocate immediate abolition. In this brief work Heyrick charged that the enslaver "knew very well that his prey would be secure so long as the abolitionists could be cajoled into a demand for gradual instead of immediate abolition. . . . He knew very well, that the *contemplation of a gradual emancipation would beget a gradual indifference to emancipation itself.*" She charged that support of gradual abolition was a turning away from God, that it was based on self-interest.[3] Most female antislavery societies in England supported Heyrick's views and influenced Britain's Society for the Mitigation and Gradual Abolition of Slavery to drop "gradual abolition" from its title and endorse immediatism instead. Similarly, Heyrick's views inspired female societies in the United States in many ways, including their demands for immediate emancipation.[4] Benjamin Lundy reprinted Heyrick's work in the *Genius for Universal Emancipation* and many European Americans, including William Lloyd Garrison and Friends Lucretia Mott and Angelina Grimké, attributed their belief in immediatism largely to Heyrick's pamphlet.[5]

The first organized commitment to the cause may well have emerged, however, in the community of African Americans in Boston, which in 1826 founded the Massachusetts General Colored Association to work for, among other things, immediate freedom for enslaved people in the South.[6] It was before meetings of this association that David Walker first presented the arguments for immediatism that appeared in print in 1829 in *Walker's Appeal, in Four Articles, Together with a Preamble to the Colored Citizens of the World, but in Particular and Very Expressly to Those of the United States of America*. Walker had been born free in Wilmington, North Carolina, and lived in Charleston when Denmark Vesey, a formerly enslaved West Indian, attempted to organize enslaved people to revolt in 1822. Walker moved to Boston by 1825. Arguing for immediatism on the grounds that enslavement was profoundly unChristian, his *Appeal* advocated enslavement's violent overthrow and predicted divine retribution upon European Americans should enslavers persist.[7]

Walker's Appeal was another trigger for William Lloyd Garrison's ultimate declaration, in the first issue of his *Liberator* in January 1831, that immediate abolition was the only morally acceptable course for the nation.[8] To the gradualist argument that the enslaved were not prepared for independence, Garrison argued that the only way to learn "how to be free was by being free."[9] Several months after the *Liberator* began publication, Garrison issued his "Address Delivered before the Free People of Color," in which he confessed to "feeling ashamed of my own color" because other European Americans continued to hold African Americans in perpetual servitude. "To make atonement, in part, for this conduct," Garrison declared, "I have solemnly dedicated my health, and strength, and life, to your service." Garrison had earlier been part of a small interracial community in Baltimore, where he had lived with and worked for Benjamin Lundy on the *Genius of Universal Emancipation*. Garrison was one of the few abolitionists who maintained throughout his life that achieving emancipation must be an interracial effort,[10] and the *Liberator* is credited with having converted many people to the cause of immediate abolition.[11]

In January 1832 Garrison and both European and African American abolitionists founded the New England Anti-Slavery Society. Parliament passed the Abolition of Slavery Act in 1833, which freed all enslaved people in the British Empire after a five-year apprenticeship and compensated enslavers for their losses. In the same year, energized abolitionists in the United States created the American Anti-Slavery Society. Unlike many of the earlier abolition societies, the post-1830 antislavery societies were committed to immediate emancipation.[12]

Immediatism, however, was taken up only by the radical wing of the antislavery movement. According to historian James Brewer Stewart, most Americans viewed immediate abolitionism as "undiluted fanaticism." Critics were fond of pointing out that Garrison, "our apostle of freedom," offered not "one word of . . . instruction" on how immediate emancipation might be achieved.[13] For the most part, Friends mirrored that popular sentiment, and so were once again confronted with the challenge of standing against enslavement and being faithful to their religious beliefs. While, by this time, all Quakers could be considered *anti-slavery*, only a few chose to be *abolitionists* and align themselves with the new movement of the 1830s.[14]

Some Friends benefited from enslavement, both North and South; some focused their attention on other social problems, and any number were simply apathetic or just didn't want to get involved. Martha Paxson

Grundy believes that, "The fact that all tended to use the same language for not getting actively involved blurs and hides the wide range of motives."[15] But the radical Friends thought it was up to them to do whatever needed to be done to bring God's will to the world by freeing the enslaved people; if they could not convince their Quaker meetings to support immediate abolition, they would act on their own. Historian Jack Marietta claims it was Quakers' impatience not with their own Society, but rather with national leaders' "priorities and postponements" in acting against enslavement, that forced individual Friends to step forward. They did not do so in order to collaborate with others, as some historians have suggested, but to present a point of view contrary to that which prevailed in society at large.[16]

Quakers and the 'Garrisonian' Organization

Although the American Anti-Slavery Society was founded by non-Quakers, Friends accounted for one-third of the sixty-two delegates at its organizing convention in Philadelphia in December 1833.[17] Among them were European American Friends James Mott, Lydia White, Bartholomew Fussell, Isaac Hopper, John Greenleaf Whittier, and Evan Lewis, the last of whom presided over the convention. Philadelphia African American Robert Purvis, who though not a Quaker had numerous connections with Friends, was one of the three African Americans who joined at that time. Convention attendee James Forten, also an African American from Philadelphia, became a manager of the society in 1835.[18] However, fewer than a dozen African Americans were named to the society's board of one hundred persons, and when the society reduced the number of board seats, African American appointments declined more in proportion to their membership than those of European Americans. According to Julie Winch, the presence of African Americans on the society's board was "little more than symbolic."[19] While members of African descent contributed fully fifteen percent of the national society's income, its leadership was almost all of European descent, a fact prompting several historians to conclude that African Americans had little influence on the development of organization policies. Furthermore, the society's agents of African descent were paid only half what European American agents received.[20]

The American Anti-Slavery Society's "Declaration of Sentiments," adopted at this first convention, was a "forthright call to action couched in revolutionary but nonviolent language." It enunciated the group's position that "the slaves ought instantly to be set free, and brought under the protection of law." The declaration further resolved that "in view of the civil and religious privileges of this nation, the guilt of its oppression is unequalled by any other on the face of the earth; and, therefore . . . it is bound to repent instantly, to undo the heavy burdens, and to let the oppressed go free."[21] The society was optimistic that ultimately "every citizen [would] repent of the sin of slavery" and that within two years all African Americans in the upper South would have "complete equality."[22] Though not a religious organization, the society's membership included many African American clergy: European American ministers were "conspicuously underrepresented" in all but a few state societies.[23]

The Declaration of Sentiments also enunciated a commitment to nonviolence. Rather than relying on strategies of "physical resistance," it stated, "Ours shall be such only as the opposition of moral purity to moral corruption—the destruction of error by the potency of truth—the overthrow of prejudice by the power of love—and the abolition of slavery by the spirit of repentance." This part of the declaration held particular meaning for Friends and surely helped draw more of them into the immediatist fold, even though some Quaker and non-Quaker abolitionists warned the South that violence was imminent should enslavement persist.[24]

Abolitionism on the Move

Delegates to the American Anti-Slavery Society convention pledged to create antislavery societies "in every city, town and village in our land." They were to focus especially on converting such influential community leaders as newspaper editors and ministers. By 1836, five hundred local groups existed in the North. Within another two years there were 1,400 local societies with 121,000 members; some estimated twice that number of supporters.[25] Quakers, sometimes working with non-Quakers, organized many of these local groups, and Drake notes that most included some of the "more ardent radical" Friends who "joined without hesitation" even as their meetings viewed their association with such groups unfavorably.26 By the middle 1830s, many societies had been formed in Chester County, Pennsylvania, with Hicksites forming the bulk of the membership.27 Some of the most active abolitionist groups were in Indiana, where hundreds of Friends, many of them migrants from North Carolina, belonged to local affiliates of the American Anti-Slavery Society.28 Though these groups had a share of affluent members, historian Paul Goodman states that most people who joined were "relatively obscure individuals with few resources"—ordinary working people and farmers.29

Women Impact the Movement

As a rule, women were not permitted to be members of the national society, though such women as Lucretia Mott, one of four Quaker women to attend the society's first convention, were permitted to attend and even to address the gathering.30 The Hicksite-founded Clarkson Society and other antislavery groups in Lancaster County, Pennsylvania, were among the exceptions: both men and women were members on apparently equal terms, and in some cases women served on governing boards.31 European American Friend Amy Post was one of the founders of the very active Western New York Anti-Slavery Society in 1843.32 Post was one in a "network of 'ultraist' women" in that area who also worked for women's suffrage and other reforms.33 As many as three-quarters of the leaders of antislavery societies in the Farmington/Rochester area of western New York were Quaker women.34 The general gender exclusion, however, impelled women to form their own groups: while most Indiana antislavery societies were open to men and women, women organized their own societies there as well, the first being in Henry County in 1841.35

Sometimes termed the "nurturer" of other women's abolitionist organizations, the Female Anti-Slavery Society of Philadelphia was formed in 1833 by thirty women of African and European American descent. Of the seventeen Quaker women of European descent at the first meeting, thirteen were Hicksite; Orthodox women also belonged to the society but, after having eighteen Orthodox Quakers in 1835 (and twenty-five Hicksites), either only one or no Orthodox were members for the next fifteen years. By 1836 the female society had a membership of eighty women, almost all of them Quaker.[36] Among the Quaker founders were Esther Moore from Maryland and both Lydia White and Lucretia Coffin Mott (1793–1880) of Philadelphia, all of European descent. A member of a prominent Quaker family on Nantucket, Mott became a staunch advocate of gender equality through the example of the island's women, who often managed family and business affairs while male family members were at sea.[37] While Mott was a student (and later a teacher) at Nine Partners Boarding School in New York State, she came to know James Mott, a European American teacher and, later, fellow abolitionist.[38] She was more militant than a familiar portrait in her Quaker bonnet suggests; historian Carol Faulkner believes this demure image may explain "why history has often dismissed her as gentle and sweet."[39]

Mott seemed to move seamlessly from home to public occasion, from the work of reform to the work of her domestic life.[40] She used no products of enslavement, "refused to curb her political view in meetings . . . and criticized her fellow Quakers for their intolerance."[41] After she became a minister in 1818 at the age of twenty-eight, she traveled and lectured on ending enslavement, activities that impelled the more guarded among her meeting's elders to admonish her during meeting for worship. For her part, Mott charged that Quaker meetings had grown obsessed with obedience and formality and asked rhetorically whether meeting visitors would be able to recognize Friends' traditional testimonies for peace, temperance, and equality. "A deathlike silence reigns," she wrote in 1836. "Our strength seems mainly exerted in holding up to view the necessity of going to meeting and wearing a plain garb." Still, her meeting could not find grounds to disown her, and although she debated leaving the society, she wished not to abandon it to moderates. Speaking in meeting, Mott said, renewed her spirit.[42]

African American founders of the Female Anti-Slavery Society of Philadelphia included Sarah Mapps Douglass (1806–82), who was elected treasurer, and her mother Grace Bustill Douglass (1782–1842), who was elected a vice president.[43] Like her mother and Elizabeth Morey Bustill, her grandmother, Sarah Mapps Douglass was a lifelong activist in the African American community of her native Philadelphia; like her mother, she regularly attended Friends meetings in the city. In addition to serving as treasurer for the Philadelphia Female Anti-Slavery

Society, Sarah Douglass was also at different times recording secretary, librarian, and manager. In 1834, when the female society started a school for African American children, Douglass was a teacher there for nine years.[44] She also established numerous activist and philanthropic organizations in the city, including the Philadelphia Woman's Association (1849) and the Douglass Literacy Circle (1859).[45]

In 1855 Sarah Douglass married the Episcopalian cleric Reverend William Douglass (no relation). Since childhood she had attended Quaker meetings with her mother and siblings, first attending Arch Street Meeting, founded in 1804, and then North Meeting. She also attended the Ninth and Spruce Meeting on Tuesday mornings, the same meeting Lucretia Mott attended.[46] Even though Douglass faithfully attended Quaker meeting all of her life, she never joined the Religious Society of Friends, no doubt because of its racial proscriptions. Being told to sit on the bench "for the black people" at meeting was one of the "often repeated and galling remonstrances" she endured: "galling indeed because I believe they despise us for our colour," Douglass wrote in a letter to her friend William Bassett. She added, "Often times I wept, at other times I felt indignant & queried in my own mind, are these people Christians?"[47]

In the 1830s as many as six of ten people working for immediate abolition were women, and historians have suggested that the abolition movement would not have survived economically or otherwise without them. By 1837 women had formed 139 antislavery societies in the United States, and Quaker women were founders and members of groups throughout the East and Midwest.[48] As an agent for the American Anti-Slavery Society, Abby Kelley toured to "abolitionize" Ohio, Indiana, Upstate New York, and her native New England, where she was particularly unwelcome. Guided by her inner voice, Kelley organized and addressed numerous local conventions—in Utica, New York, she spoke five nights in a row—and sold pamphlets, organized new groups, arranged for the use of lecture halls, and sought funds for the society's work.[49]

As most female antislavery organizations were in small towns,[50] members tended to be European American, although several African American female societies existed in cities.[51] A notable number of the societies were, like Philadelphia's, racially integrated, and Sarah Mapps

Douglass clearly believed that the union was effective. "I wish it was in my power to give you an idea of the enthusiastic affection with which we regard all those dear friends who are advocates of immediate emancipation," she wrote in 1833 to Hicksite Quaker Elizabeth Chandler, an antislavery poet of European descent who wrote for both Lundy's and Garrison's newspapers. With European American Orthodox Friend Laura Haviland, Chandler had founded the Logan Female Anti-Slavery Society in a Quaker meetinghouse in Lewanee County, Michigan, in 1832.[52] Sarah Forten, another African American member of the Philadelphia and the national female groups, declared in a poem published by the 1837 convention that "we are thy sisters. God has truly said that of one blood the nation he has made."[53]

Still, not all female groups welcomed African American women. Only after Garrison chastised the Boston Female Anti-Slavery Society for its exclusivity did that group open its membership to African American women. In New York, African American women found the Ladies' New York City Antislavery Society "not particularly welcoming," according to European American historian Beth Salerno, and created their own antislavery association.[54] When Elizabeth Buffum Chace invited African American women to join the society in Fall River, Massachusetts, European American members welcomed them willingly as visitors but did not extend an invitation to membership.[55] Many leaders of the African American community discerned this trend in the abolitionist community generally. "Instead of realizing what we had hoped for," African American activist Martin Delany stated in 1852, "we find ourselves occupying the very same position in relation to our Anti-Slavery friends as we do in relation to the pro-slavery part of the community—a mere secondary, underling position, in all our relations to them."[56]

——————•——————

Perhaps the single best remembered act of violence against abolitionists was the burning of the new Pennsylvania Hall in 1838. In this period's atmosphere of growing violence, it had become impossible for abolitionists to rent meeting places, so Lundy, the Motts, many Philadelphia Friends, and other abolitionists contributed to a new building providing space for offices, a free produce store, and meetings of various related associations. All of the hall's Board of Managers were Quaker.[57]

The dedication ceremonies for the hall preceded the second Anti-Slavery Convention of American Women in 1838.[58] Some three hundred abolitionists gathered for the occasion.[59] As posters calling attention to the meeting appeared all over the city, word of the gathering spread quickly. So did the news that African Americans were among the guests at the wedding of Angelina Grimké and European American Presbyterian minister and abolitionist Theodore Weld the day before, trumpeted as proof that "social amalgamation" was the abolitionists' goal.[60]

Anticipating trouble, the hall's president asked the mayor for protection. But the mayor blamed the abolitionists for the problem and told them to "avoid unnecessary walking in public with colored people."[61] The request from the hall manager that African American women stay away that evening was read to the assembly by Lucretia Mott, who then suggested that the women of African descent should not "absent themselves." An African American woman from New York replied that it would be "selfish and cowardly" not to come. "Our friends have suffered much for us and shall we fear to suffer a little for ourselves?" she asked.[62]

The fact that people of African and European descent were together was inflammatory enough, but that women speakers addressed mixed audiences of men and women provoked even more outrage and invective. On the second night of the meeting, when Quaker women were to address a mixed-gender audience,[63] a crowd estimated at as many as ten thousand gathered. Many were simply onlookers, drawn by the excitement, but others came with violence on their minds. Inside the speakers—Angelina Grimké, Abby Kelley, and Mott—proceeded with the program,[64] even as rocks crashed against the windows. Grimké took the stage.[65] "What if the mob should burst in upon us, break up our meeting, and commit violence upon our persons?" she asked. "Would this be anything compared to what the slaves endure?"[66] Kelley, still an unknown teacher from Massachusetts, told the women not to fear the rabble-rousers, for the only force that could not be withstood, was "the still small voice within." As the women left the hall that evening, Angelina Grimké suggested that the women of European ancestry join their African American sisters arm-in-arm, as the women of Boston's Female Anti-Slavery Society had done in safety when one of their meetings was stormed by a mob. The display of moral courage by the women in Philadelphia was similarly successful.[67]

The next night (after the women had met there during the day), a mob broke in and burned the empty hall, then started for the homes of the Motts and other delegates. Someone in the crowd thought quickly enough to divert them from the Motts', but the rioters found new targets and burned the Bethel (AME) Church and the Quaker-founded Colored Orphan Asylum nearby.[68] While it is often assumed that the rioters wanted to attack the women of African descent, European American author Anne Boylan offers an alternative explanation: Women of European descent were the real targets because it was their closeness with the African Americans that represented the dreaded mixing of the races.[69]

The following day newspapers, soon echoed by various investigations by officials, blamed the violence on the abolitionists—they had brought it on themselves by their public mixing of the races. A grand jury decided those meeting in the hall had been "injudicious" by associations that were "naturally" offensive to "the nicer feelings of the public."[70] Declaring that the episodes just strengthened their connections, the women found space to continue their convention in a member's schoolhouse and vowed to meet again the next year.[71] The attacks made Kelley feel more strongly about the cause and about prejudice. She felt a "new sense of sisterhood" with the African American women of the Female Anti-Slavery Society—and they with her. Sarah Mapps Douglass wrote Kelley later that their "hearts have been cheered and animated and strengthened by your presence."[72] A different reaction came from a reporter for a West Chester, Pennsylvania, newspaper. He described Kelley as "an enraged woman with a flippant tongue."[73]

Divisions in the Movement

In the late 1830s three issues formed a critical divide between Garrisonian abolitionists and the more "moderate" faction of the movement that broke away from the American Anti-Slavery Society in 1840 to form the American and Foreign Anti-Slavery Society.[74] One issue centered on the morality and efficacy of working through the political system to achieve immediate abolition. For his part, Garrison viewed the entire political apparatus as corrupt and the United States Constitution "null and void" as the product of an "unholy alliance" of the North with enslavers. Garrison charged that the Constitution was "the most bloody and heaven-daring arrangement ever made by men for the continuance and protection of a system of the most atrocious villainy ever exhibited on earth."[75] While the nonresistants' emphasis on moral suasion and nonviolence appealed to the most radical of Friends, the extreme, if not revolutionary position Garrisonians took on the nation's government gave Friends meetings pause.

The second issue splitting the abolitionist movement was the role of the churches and their clergy. Garrisonians' ire had been raised by the general refusal of clerics of all denominations to permit antislavery meetings to take place within their churches or even notices of antislavery events to be read from their pulpits; Quaker meetings were as apt to express these views as any other religious group. Historian David Brion Davis notes that "as a whole churches showed great indifference" to ending enslavement.[76] Some clerics argued that both scripture and law sanctioned enslavement. The American Bible Society, the American Tract Society, and the American Sunday School Union all denounced the American Anti-Slavery Society for spreading "agitations and ill-will" toward other Christians.[77] Many churches drew a firm line between religious dissent and political dissent, and, because abolitionism was a political movement, church leaders maintained that airing its views was inappropriate in a religious sanctuary.[78] Some African American churches shared these views, but to African American Frederick Douglass the fact that the majority of African American clerics opposed promoting abolitionism within their churches signaled their need of "radical reform."[79] And, like the majority of Americans, many churches viewed radical abolitionism as subversive of the nation's political status quo.[80]

Like other abolitionists, the churches generally disapproved of the participation of women in antislavery reform, the third issue of contention between Garrisonians and moderates. After the Grimké sisters presented seventeen antislavery lectures in ten Massachusetts towns in May 1837, Congregationalist clergy from across the state met to compose a pastoral letter declaring that when a woman spoke publicly "she assumes the place and tone of man as a public reformer" and "her character becomes unnatural."[81] Reactions were dramatic: Maria French, a European American Quaker, was physically removed when she preached against enslavement in a Congregational church, and European American Quaker Sarah Gibbons was thrown out into the street from a New York church for the same reason.[82] Members of the Ohio Orthodox Yearly Meeting carried Abby Kelley out of its meeting when she persisted in speaking against slavery.[83] Kelley, who married European American abolitionist Stephen Foster in 1845, learned to deal with the "contents of outhouses" thrown through the windows as she spoke, and she continued to lecture at one church even as a military troop outside tried to drown her out with their drums and fifes.[84] Angelina and Sarah Grimké found it difficult to find places to speak and came to expect that their appearance would produce a barrage of "rotten eggs and stones."[85]

Yet, as European American historians Julie Jeffrey, Katherine Sklar, Beth Salerno, and Julie Winch note, women were doing the lion's share of the work in the movement, in large part through hundreds of female antislavery societies all over the Northeast and Midwest. Moved into the public sphere by their conviction that enslavement was a sin and that their consequent duty as women and mothers was to eradicate it, they planned and managed the many fundraising fairs, recruited members for state and national antislavery societies, circulated petitions, spoke publicly, and donated their own funds to the support of the cause. Never had women been involved in any social movement on such a scale. The female antislavery societies provided the opportunity for "respectable women" to break some of the constraints they endured in their "separate sphere" of the home.[86]

Active female abolitionists for their part saw the clergy as a great hindrance to what European American abolitionist Maria Weston Chapman termed "the vigorous prosecution of our efforts."[87] Abby Kelley minced no words. "The sectarian organizations called Churches," Kelley stated at the 1842 convention of the Massachusetts Anti-Slavery Society, "are combinations of thieves, robbers, adulterers, pirates, and murderers, and as such form the bulwark of American slavery."[88]

Quakers and the Abolitionist Schism

Kelley and the Grimkés stood at the center of the storm that eventually split the abolitionist movement. The specific trigger for the 1839 schism was Kelley's proposed election to the executive committee of the American Anti-Slavery Society, which had permitted women as members but without voting privileges.[89] Those who sided with Lewis Tappan, an influential European American member and substantial donor to the national society, were clear that women should not be among the society's officers. Charles Stuart, a leading Canadian abolitionist of British descent, joined with Tappan because, he wrote, it was "an insane innovation" to think that women could do what is "morally right for a man to do."[90] But the Garrisonian faction, which favored full participation by women, carried the day. An eleven-member board, six of them Hicksite Quakers from New York and Genesee Yearly Meetings, now led the original society.[91] Tappan walked out at the conclusion of the vote, declaring for all to hear that he would never serve on a "promiscuous" committee "in defiance of the Scriptures." That evening, a group of Tappanite supporters, including Friends, met at his home to begin a new organization—the American and Foreign Anti-Slavery Society. Eventually they would also form the Liberty Party, signifying their turn "from propaganda to politics."[92]

Angelina Grimké (1805–79) first stirred hostility among anti-abolitionists and those who opposed women's activity in the movement when she defended Garrison as standing "on holy ground" in an 1835 letter to the *Liberator*. She and her sister Sarah (1792–1873) had been born into an affluent Episcopalian family in Charleston, South Carolina, but as teenagers had grown disillusioned with the church. Having come to know Quakers while in Philadelphia to supervise the treatment of her ailing father, who died in 1819, Sarah Grimké returned to that city in 1821 to find a way to work against enslavement.[93] Angelina, younger by thirteen years, followed her sister's path to attend Quaker meeting in Charleston, and by 1829 went north to join her sister in Philadelphia. There the sisters soon became members of the Orthodox Arch Street Meeting.[94]

Historian Gerda Lerner claims the Grimkés were the only southern women of European descent involved in the abolition movement.[95] Based on her belief that the women of the South held the answer to ending enslavement, Angelina Grimké's crusade began with her 1836 letter, "An Appeal to the Christian Women of the Southern States."[96] "Are you willing to enslave your children?" she asked them in the letter. "You start back with horror and indignation at such a question." She pointed out that while they could not vote or legislate, they were "the wives and mothers, the sisters and daughters of those who do"; they might also "read, pray, speak and act" to persuade men that "slavery is a crime against God and man." A few months afterward, Sarah Grimké issued "An Epistle to the Clergy of the Southern States," which articulated her belief that many southern clergy were receptive to debating enslavement but had been suppressed by the region's political and social milieu. She took strong issue with southern clerics' use of the Bible to justify enslavement, corrected their biblical translations, and gently raised a reality that had hitherto been outside of the enslavement discussion—the sexual relationships of the enslavers with the women they enslaved.[97]

That the Grimké women were southerners made their letters especially sensational. Though Angelina's had no noticeable effect in the South, it encouraged northern women to abolitionist action.[98] Sarah's pamphlet did spark some debate, but officials in southern cities ultimately confiscated copies of both; postmasters in South Carolina burned them. The sisters' appeals placed them solidly in the center of the abolition movement. In 1836 they moved to New York and began to organize "parlor meetings" to raise support for abolitionism; when these meetings outgrew their spaces, the Grimkés began to lecture in more public forums. As agents for the American Anti-Slavery Society, the two traveled New England for eighteen months to solicit members and gather signatures' for the numerous petitions calling for an end of enslavement submitted to state and federal legislatures.[99] In 1838 Angelina spoke before the Massachusetts legislature, the first woman ever invited to do so.[100]

The Grimkés were singular in expressing the notions that skin color, not race, was the basis for enslavement and that gradualism was based on prejudice, not justice.[101] At the first Antislavery Convention of American Women in 1837, Angelina offered a resolution that "the existing of an unnatural prejudice against our colored population is one of the chief pillars of American slavery," and at the second convention in 1838 in Philadelphia she offered a resolution that it was "the duty of abolitionists to identify themselves with these oppressed Americans, by sitting with them in places of worship, by appearing with them in our streets, by giving them our countenance on steam-boats and stages, by visiting with them at their homes and encouraging them to visit us, receiving them as we do our white fellow citizens." The resolution passed, though some convention delegates voted against it on the grounds that it might be "misapprehended" and "injure the abolitionist cause."[102] But some women had reservations about Sarah Grimké's resolution passed the night before. Not only did an unnamed Friend try to have it removed from the convention report, but a few members tried to convince some African American leaders in Philadelphia to make a public statement saying they did not want to socialize with people of European descent. Neither attempt succeeded, but such was the controversy around the subject of social equality.103 Grimké urged forbearance on the part of African American women, because their willingness to "mingle with us whilst we have the prejudice" was the only way "we shall be able to overcome it." Historian Beth Salerno is convinced that Grimké's determination to include African American women was crucial to the organizing work that followed.104

Radicalism and the Yearly Meetings

Even as the seemingly radical positions of Garrisonian abolitionism were broadly disdained both north and south, many individual Quakers stood in the Garrisonian camp. When the board of the American Anti-Slavery Society was reformed after the schism, six of the eleven members were Hicksite Quakers from New York and Genesee Yearly Meetings.105 The relation of Quakers with immediatism brought into starker relief issues that had long confronted the Religious Society of Friends on the issue of enslavement.

Implicit in the notion of divine direction was a rejection of the notion that humans could tell each other how to behave. Gradualists charged that the work of many abolitionist Friends violated the basic Quaker principle that an individual must await divine direction, not "work in their own wills." In 1842 the Hicksite Baltimore Yearly Meeting encouraged members to "be faithful to every clear manifestation of duty which, in the light of truth, may be opened to us" with respect to abolitionism, but warned them not to engage in any activity that relied upon "*political* or other means of a coercive nature."106 Because Friends were to await messages from God, any lecture—particularly by American Anti-Slavery Society agents—was inherently valueless; only Quakers should preach or speak in a meetinghouse, and even then authority rested in the individual recognition of divine will. Opening meetings to others, New England Yearly Meeting once stated, would tend to "draw off the minds of our members from an establishment in the Truth of those principles which have ever been maintained by us."[107] And paying antislavery society agents for a presumed "divine gift" had long been against Quaker testimonies; as several yearly meetings stated, these agents were nothing more than "hireling" ministers, an anathema to most Quakers at the time.[108]

Quaker belief in the primacy of God's will also implied, for some Friends, rejecting any association with non-Quaker groups—that is, with anyone whose work in the service of abolitionism would taint or harm the spirit and solidarity of Quakerism.[109] They sensed danger in either form of engagement with the wider world in antislavery reform—collaboration with abolitionists of other denominations or overt action in the political arena. Maintaining the inward-looking purity of Quakerism probably constituted their chief concern: as an 1835 article in Orthodox publication *The Friend* warned, Quakers should not risk "the integrity of their peculiar testimonies by associating with people of other religious beliefs."[110] Through the early 1840s, for example, the New England, Genesee Hicksite, and Orthodox Philadelphia and New York Yearly Meetings circulated antislavery materials and petitions, but they continued to insist that their work be done alone—as Quakers, not in concert with any "worldly" organizations.[111]

Other Friends dreaded additional potential consequences they perceived in Friends pursuit of radical abolition. After the painful schism into Orthodox and Hicksite branches of the Society of Friends in 1827–28, many Friends feared that further dissension among them would destroy their meetings,[112] and that associating with non-Quakers would "risk the integrity" of the society's "peculiar testimonies."[113] Moreover, the prospect that the radicals would damage the overall reputation of their society was of great moment. In the eyes of the gradualists, Quakers already belonged to an antislavery society by virtue of being Quakers.[114] They also grew increasingly worried about the potential for violence with the heightening prospect of war: should Quakers support or take part in an armed conflict over slavery or maintain their peace testimony no matter how noble the cause?[115] European American Hicksite Quaker Daniel Gerow declared in 1844 that cooperating with non-Quakers in antislavery reform exposed Friends to the "oppressive and unsanctified dispositions" of the world "which, carried out, lead to strife, tumult, commotion, and often to the sword."[116]

In the South, the Garrisonians' pronouncements about immediate emancipation were not only widely viewed as threatening but also made the work of abolitionist Friends living there more difficult. "The extreme attitudes being voiced in the North have closed the doors of usefulness to us in behalf of the slave," declared Virginia Yearly Meeting in an 1836 epistle. "We must now warn all friends against abolitionists." The 1831 insurrection of enslaved people organized by Nat Turner was of course far closer to home for them than for Northerners, and within the next year all the Quaker-supported antislavery societies in the South disappeared—"crushed underground."[117]

From 1836 to 1840 several yearly meetings issued warnings against radicalism.[118] Just as Hicksite Baltimore Meeting had done, Indiana Yearly Meeting cautioned its members in 1841 to stay out of the fray "lest we injure the righteous cause, and suffer loss ourselves."[119] New England Yearly Meeting objected when William Bassett, the Massachusetts abolitionist, referred to enslaved people as "brethren" and "fellow-countrymen" in a letter to Virginia Yearly Meeting and ordered him to remove the offending descriptions. Virginia Friends denounced the new radical movement and also refused to sign a petition seeking the end of enslavement in the nation's capitol.[120]

Even Quakers who supported abolition cautioned that the radicals, by engendering fear and unease in the population generally, were damaging the overall mission to end enslavement. European American Jeremiah Hubbard, one-time clerk of North Carolina Yearly Meeting and an avid colonizationist, complained that the "satire and vituperation" of the immediatists hurt Friends work for that cause.[121] As European American Quaker minister and historian Errol Elliott notes, "Abolition came to be a 'loaded' word, attached to the extremists."[122] Discomfited by the radicals' charge that they were proslavery, moderate Friends were nonetheless unmoved by their appeals,[123] and in 1840, gradualist Friends closed their meetinghouses even to the all-Quaker abolition societies with the pronouncement that "they would tolerate no further agitation."[124]

The radical response to the moderate Quaker critique rebutted the virtues of isolation. If anti-enslavement activities disturbed Quaker unity, then the fault lay within the Society.[125] For the radicals, reform was religion, work they were called to do by God.[126] For a Quaker to remain quiet "while the country seethed" was unconscionable. European

American Jacob Ferris of the Farmington, New York, Quarter, stated in 1843, "It is, to me, absurd that, at this day and age, Friends should talk about keeping to the quiet. Have they not, since the first rise of their society, been agitating the public? Their testimonies are calculated to do so, and, I believe, the agitation has been productive of great good to the world."[127] Lucretia Mott expressed the same view of her denomination in 1860. "I am no advocate of passivity," she wrote that year in the *National Anti-Slavery Standard*. "Quakerism as I understand it does not mean quietism. The early Friends were agitators, disturbers of the peace, and were more obnoxious in their day to charges which are now so freely made than we are."[128] With Mott, Quaker Garrisonians argued that their avid support of antislavery societies reflected their desire not to "mix with the world" but instead to seek witness to their Quaker faith in newer, more concrete ways.[129] Working for immediate abolition fulfilled, rather than betrayed, their Quaker faith.

Radicals also charged that the timidity of many gradualist Friends stemmed from their entanglement in the enslavement economy. Criticizing the Society of Friends "as it is, not as it was," the editor of the radical *Anti-Slavery Bugle* in Salem, Ohio, home to many Hicksites, declared that "Friends had become addicted to wealth and worldly displays . . . [and] gloried in the abolitionist work only to quiet their own uneasy consciences."[130] European American New England abolitionist Parker Pillsbury, who was not Quaker but worked with many Friends in the abolitionist cause, accused Friends of losing "fire" because they were not living according to their beliefs; indeed, he asserted, the very Quakers who cautioned against mixing with non-Friends in reform activities themselves mingled "with the world to a mighty extent in all wealth-getting schemes."[131]

———————— • ————————

Though the Hicksite branch of the Religious Society of Friends has commonly been associated with radical abolitionism, many Orthodox Quakers were also in that camp. While there were theological differences between Hicksite and Orthodox Friends, none of those differences determined how any one Friend might respond to immediatism. Both Hicksites and Orthodox abolitionists contributed and raised funds for local, state, and national antislavery societies and acted on their own in ways sometimes clearly considered radical.[132] An Orthodox statement against enslavement—and there were many—could just as well have been written by a Hicksite.[133] Still, it does appear that Orthodox Friends generally tended to be more "cautious in taking overt and unpopular social and legal positions."[134]

A study of the views of Elias Hicks reveals the difficulty of aligning radical abolition strictly with Hicksites. Hicks was a fervent supporter of the free produce movement and accordingly a severe critic of wealthy urban Friends who benefitted greatly from slave goods.[135] Yet unlike other Hicksite supporters of free labor goods, Hicks was a quietist, urging Quakers to still "our bodies . . . our minds . . . until unruly passions are brought down into submission to the divine will."[136] He also differed from Mott in his belief that Quakers should not align with non-Quakers in reform movements, a view many Orthodox Friends shared.[137] Like Garrisonians generally, Hicks opposed taking part in politics and holding office, and from the early 1820s he had supported immediate abolition, even before Garrison thrust the issue before the public.[138] Mott's radicalism in fact placed her in the minority of Hicksites,[139] and her most severe critics were fellow European American Hicksites—George White and Rachel Hicks among them. The hostility among Hicksites on the issue clearly signifies that radicals were a concern for all gradualist Quakers regardless of their Hicksite or Orthodox affiliation.[140]

The intensifying conflict within the Religious Society of Friends prompted many yearly meetings to become stricter in their disciplines about joining non-Quaker organizations or speaking for abolition. Radicals were faced increasingly with disownment. Thus their choice became withdrawing from abolition societies or from the Religious Society of Friends. Drake labels those who chose to leave the society as "a new generation of Quaker prophets," following in the steps of Southeby and Sandiford, Lay and Woolman, but working *outside* the Society of Friends more than *within* it.[141]

Separations and Disownments

Abolitionists who left churches that failed to stand against enslavement have been termed "comeouters" and were considered extremists both in the larger social world and in their own.[142] And though exceptions did exist, in the Quaker world such extremism typically led to disownment. Some historians have asserted that no disownments were directly linked to one's stand against enslavement, as all Friends were in theory opposed to the practice, but rather for being "out of unity" with other Friends. "Out of unity," in this case, most often meant bringing differences among Friends into public view in some way—by speaking in non-Quaker settings or publishing something deemed not a fruit of the Spirit.[143] Some Friends, including abolitionists Benjamin Lundy and John Greenleaf Whittier, were able "to keep one foot in the Quaker fold and one in the antislavery camp." Even Lucretia Mott "stayed safely within the harbor of the Society of Friends by steering a prudent, wary course."[144] Other Friends, however, were not as prudent, or at least they were not so regarded by their own meetings.

Some mystery attends the disownment by Smithfield, Rhode Island, meeting of Arnold Buffum, a European American abolitionist and one of the most visible and vocal radicals in New England. Buffum had converted to the cause after buying the first issue of the *Liberator* and meeting Garrison.[145] Though numerous sources refer to his disownment, none provide dates for the event, and monthly meeting minutes record no such act.[146] Still, Buffum himself once stated that the Smithfield meeting had disowned him, and his daughter Elizabeth Buffum Chace recalled that the meeting told Buffum the matter might be "amicably settled, if he would give up this abolition lecturing."[147]

In the Quaker world perhaps the most infamous and widely condemned disownments were those that came at the urging of New York Hicksite minister George White, who railed against abolitionists as "sinners and heretics" even as he opposed enslavement. White declared he would "a thousand times rather be a slave and spend my days with slaveholders than to dwell in companionship with abolitionists"; in fact he once praised an enslaved person for returning to the person who had enslaved him.[148]

White took it as his mission to see that Hicksite abolitionists were removed from the society. In 1841 the Hicksite New York Monthly, Quarterly, and Yearly Meetings disowned European Americans Charles Marriott, Isaac Hopper, and Hopper's son-in-law James Gibbons purportedly for allowing publication of an article written against White by the European American Oliver Johnson, associate editor of the

National Anti-Slavery Standard and a non-Quaker.[149] Johnson's article compared one of White's speeches to the "harangue of some unscrupulous demagogue, who supposed his only chance for preferment depend[ed] on the facility with which he could blacken the reputation of his neighbors."[150] The three abolitionists were accused of publishing material "calculated to excite discord and disunity" among Friends.[151] Hopper contested the disownment with great vigor, asserting in the *Standard* that Quaker leaders had "become persecutors, not with fire, halter, and dungeon . . . but with ejectment from religious fellowship, defamation of character, and casting out their names as evil doers." His protest, however, did not succeed.[152]

The disownment of Marriott, Gibbons, and Hopper was highly controversial among Quakers well beyond the borders of New York. The yearly meeting, New York Monthly Meeting, Quaker and abolitionist newspapers, and Hopper himself received letters from all over world, many siding with the three who had been disowned; antislavery newspapers published editorials condemning the action.[153] New York Monthly Meeting historian John Cox argues that the disownments were effected by men who dealt in products of the enslaved "or were allied in business with such, influenced by the pro-slavery tone of the newspapers, and not spiritually awake."[154] Lucretia Mott spoke in her monthly meeting against the disownments, and European Americans Edward Hopper (who had married Anna Mott, the daughter of Lucretia and James Mott), Hopper's daughter Abigail (the wife of the disowned James Gibbons), and Hopper's sons John and Josiah resigned their membership. The disowned Gibbons resigned but not before standing in meeting to read a statement blaming the meeting leaders for, among other things, defaming his "moral character in a most invidious and disgraceful manner" and for not admitting that the men's abolitionist views were the real reason for their disownment.[155] Hopper himself published a long account of his case, but concluded by declaring his unwavering fidelity to Friends principles. Apparently holding no "ill will," Isaac Hopper sat on the facing bench as long as he lived.[156]

The news of the disownments provoked a furor among Quakers and abolitionists. European American author and editor Lydia Maria Child, who was closely associated with numerous Quakers, said of the disownments, "A Society has need to be very rich in moral excellence that they can afford to throw away three such members."[157] At least fifty-two members of the Green Plain, Ohio, Monthly Meeting wrote of their "mortification and astonishment" at the White-led disownments and called upon White to repent.

————•————

A notable number of European American Friends voluntarily separated from their meetings over the issue of abolitionism. Hicksite Rowland Thomas Robinson of Ferrisburgh, Vermont, was one of them.[158] Esther Whinery was another. A teacher from Center Meeting in Indiana, she resigned her membership in 1843 on the grounds that to stay would place her "on the side of the oppressor, and . . . fighting against God."[159] When Elizabeth Sellers resigned from North Darby (Pennsylvania) Monthly Meeting on March 11, 1845, she explained in a five-page letter: "I have always cherished the high principles professed [by Friends]; but, in vainly looking for the action, which would be the legitimate result of the faithful carrying out of these principles, I have been forced to acknowledge that these sublime truths have no abiding place with you, but whilst uttered with the lips, from your hearts are afar off." She spoke of her "deep sorrow" that Jesus' "spirit and example were unheeded" and that "those who were true to convictions of duty and to the higher promptings of their nature, received your severest condemnation."[160]

Though the Grimké sisters at first felt they had found their home in Quakerism, they later found there was "no openness among Friends" on the issue of working against enslavement. Biographer Gerda Lerner says that their "blind loyalty to the Quakers had turned into bitter disappointment." Their reception at meetings was increasingly "chilly" and they were no longer welcome in the homes of Quaker Friends. At the yearly meeting in 1836, presiding elder Jonathan Edwards stopped Sarah as she rose to speak. Sarah elected to use the incident as a "means of releasing" her "from those bonds which almost destroyed my mind."[161] As the sisters expected, Angelina Grimké's 1838 marriage to Theodore Weld provided the pretext for disowning her, and her sister's membership was revoked for attending the ceremony.[162]

In 1841 Abby Kelley resigned from Uxbridge, Massachusetts, Monthly Meeting. She admitted that "the friends' principles had taken deep root in my heart," but she dismissed the "plain language" and dress of Quakers as empty forms and disdained the view among Friends that they must wait to work against enslavement "until the Lord opens the way." That notion was, she declared, "blasphemy. . . . He never shut the way."[163] Greatly troubled by what she saw as Friends "departures from the high ground of truth," Kelley told her meeting that it was her duty "to come out"—that is, to resign from the meeting—"and be separate." Though the meeting delayed in the hope that Kelley might change her mind, it eventually formalized her resignation. In a letter to the *Liberator*, Kelley insisted that she had disowned the Quakers, not they her. Still, she lived the rest of her life in a manner consistent with Quaker ways.[164]

Elizabeth Buffum Chace, daughter of the abolitionist Arnold Buffum, resigned from Providence Monthly Meeting in November 1843. Several historians have reported that Chace resigned because of her father's disownment, but no evidence for the claim is known to exist in her correspondence. Chace wrote that she had been "born and baptized into the Anti-Slavery spirit. Our family were all Abolitionists," not only her parents and sisters but her brothers-in-law, an aunt, and many of her cousins as well.[165] The family's abolitionist views, Chace claimed, "soon put us under the ban of disapproval among Providence Friends."[166] Chace believed that "the prejudice against color, throughout New England, was even stronger than the pro-slavery spirit."[167] Her charge against Friends was harsh: "The Society of Friends in this country was forgetful of its earlier record, and, like the other churches, had submitted to the domination of the slave-holding power.... No belief in Papal infallibility was ever stronger in the Catholic mind, than was the assumption, not expressed in words, that the Society could do no wrong."[168]

———————•———————

The differences over immediatism were sufficiently powerful to cause schism within meetings and to trigger the formation of radical groups throughout the society. The Orthodox Indiana Yearly Meeting had opposed colonization in the 1830s but "mildly discouraged" its members from participating in non-Quaker abolitionist activities.[169] In the 1840s, however, the meeting had become populated by a significant number of radical abolitionists. By 1843 the majority of Orthodox

Quakers lived west of the Appalachians, and they included many who had left the South to escape the culture of enslavement.[170] By that point, Indiana Yearly Meeting, made up of virtually all Friends west of the Scioto River in Ohio, was a "mixing and melting pot of American Quakerism." European Americans Addison Coffin and Levi Coffin, who came from North Carolina, and Charles Osborn, from Tennessee, were all immediatists. In the 1840s Arnold Buffum moved to Indiana to work as an agent for the American Anti-Slavery Society. Buffum's abolitionist message may have been unwelcome in Newport, Rhode Island, but it was well received in Newport, Indiana (now Fountain City), where he lived. Buffum started a newspaper for the Indiana State Anti-Slavery Society, whose membership included some Quakers.[171] Others, worried about "mingling" with non-Friends, organized their own "Friends' Anti-Slavery Society."

Still, like Jeremiah Hubbard and Elijah Coffin, European American leaders among Indiana Friends, the majority of Quakers in that state were gradualists who were critical of the radicals' positions.[172] Some Friends in Indiana disapproved of any assistance to fugitives; some agreed with Miami, Ohio, Quarterly Meeting (of Indiana Yearly Meeting) that fugitives would fare better if they remained with their enslavers.[173] The radicals' attempts to "abolitionize" the yearly meeting in the 1840s were increasingly troublesome, and increased the consternation of moderates.[174] In 1841 the Indiana Yearly Meeting closed all meetinghouses to antislavery lecturers. The conflict grew more intense that same year, when in his "Open Letter to American Friends" Joseph Sturge condemned the conservatism of American Friends and declared that only by joining the American Anti-Slavery Society could they live up to their Quaker testimony.[175]

In 1842, radical Quakers were incensed when the leaders of Indiana Yearly Meeting invited presidential candidate Henry Clay to speak in downtown Richmond while Friends were gathered there for yearly meeting. When the radicals presented Clay with a petition demanding that he immediately free those he enslaved, yearly meeting clerk Elijah Coffin hastened to assure Clay that the yearly meeting itself had "nothing to do" with the petition.[176] Plainly disturbed at having been embarrassed by the radicals in front of several thousand people, gradualists in the yearly meeting declared that a Friend not in unity with the meeting's moderate views could not serve on committees. In addition, the yearly meeting moved to "disqualify for usefulness" eight of the radicals, including Osborn and Levi Coffin. "For pleading the cause of the oppressed," Osborn stated at the meeting, "we ourselves are put in bonds."[177]

Undeterred, the radicals organized the Indiana Yearly Meeting of Anti-Slavery Friends, which drew some two to three thousand of the approximately twenty-five thousand Friends who attended the yearly meeting.[178] Declaring the Indiana Yearly Meeting a proslavery body, twelve monthly meetings in Michigan, Iowa, and Indiana joined the Anti-Slavery Friends. Lacking its radical contingent, Indiana Yearly Meeting raised its collective voice on racial matters only twice in the next twelve years.[179] The antislavery yearly meeting hoped to be supported by London Yearly Meeting, but a delegation London sent in 1845 tried to dissuade them from separation. That attempt, the dissidents said, showed London Friends had "less regard for consistency and truth, than for the forms of order."

Green Plain Monthly Meeting (Ohio) also splintered. When the meeting publicly protested George White's statements against abolitionists, the Indiana Hicksite Yearly Meeting sent a committee "packed with conservatives" to express its displeasure at the meeting's criticism of a minister. In 1843 the yearly meeting dissolved the Green Plain Quarterly Meeting and disowned its members. Claiming to be the true Friends, the radicals thereupon organized themselves as the Congregational Friends Yearly Meeting.[180]

From 1843 to 1848 the Michigan Quarterly Meeting repeatedly asked the Genesee Yearly Meeting to curb the authority of the former meeting's elders, who they believed were denying members the right to speak about the "evils of war, intemperance, slavery, and licentiousness." In 1848 the yearly meeting responded by laying down the quarterly meeting and transferring its meetings to Pelham Quarter. In response, new "Congregational" or "Progressive" yearly meetings were formed in Michigan and upstate New York. The name was changed to the Friends of Human Progress, and the group met at least annually until the 1880s.[181]

In Iowa, a similar controversy the next year prompted a small group to leave the yearly meeting, build a new meetinghouse, and join with the Indiana Yearly Meeting of Anti-Slavery Friends.

Historian Louis Thomas Jones contends that the antislavery Friends in Salem, Iowa, made that town "one of the most hated spots to the Missouri slave-catcher in the southeastern part of the State." A committee from London Yearly Meeting, which had visited Indiana dissidents earlier, also made its way to Iowa but had no more success in mending the separation. The Iowans called it "extraordinary" that the English would judge them "without ever entering into an impartial examination of the causes that led to the difficulty."[182]

For six contentious years, two separate groups in Pennsylvania claimed to be the Hicksite Marlborough Meeting, both attempting to meet in one Chester County meetinghouse at the same time. In 1851, when the dissidents failed to gain recognition from Philadelphia Yearly Meeting, they organized themselves as the Pennsylvania Yearly Meeting of Progressive Friends. Fifty-six Friends invited non-Quakers to join them in a new organization dedicated to the "brotherhood of the human family" and committed to all reforms, including women's rights, abolition, war, capital punishment, and temperance.[183] The Progressives' invitation to prospective members declared its criteria for eligibility:

> We interrogate no man as to his theological belief; we send no Committees to pry into the motives of those who may desire to share the benefits of our Association; but open the door to all who recognize the Equal Brotherhood of the Human Family, without regard to sex, color, or condition, and who acknowledge the duty of defining and illustrating their faith in God, not by assent to a creed, but lives of personal purity, and works of beneficence and charity to mankind.[184]

Early in 1853 many of members of the various Progressive Friends meetings met at Longwood, Pennsylvania; according to Drake, it was more a "convention for reformers" than a Quaker meeting.[185] Not all were Friends: some may have been in the past, others never.[186] One historian describes the new group, also known as the Longwood Progressive Friends, as "the center for the radical abolitionism."[187]

———•———

For some radical Quakers, their belief in abolitionism led them to political action, a movement out of harmony both with Garrison and the basic Quaker practices of working through persuasion to achieve the sense of the meeting and of trusting God, not humans, to lead the way.

Having come to the conclusion that politics offered the only avenue to ending enslavement, some aligned themselves with one or both of two short-lived political parties in the early 1840s.[188] The American and Foreign Anti-Slavery Society and other abolitionists, including Quaker radicals Levi Coffin and Arnold Buffum, created the Liberty Party in 1840, which worked to elect abolitionists to office.[189] The connection with the party became so close in some quarters that in 1847 the Indiana State Anti-Slavery Society meeting timed its adjournment so that some members could attend the party's nominating convention in Buffalo.[190] In 1848 some Liberty Party members and a group of anti-slavery Whigs formed the Free Soil Party, which, though against slavery, did not endorse immediatism; it aimed instead at preventing the expansion of enslavement to new territories.[191] After 1854, however, Midwestern Friends "tended to confine their opposition to slavery to maintaining the traditional testimonies and to supporting the Republican Party." Even though the party's earliest platforms enunciated no commitment to ending enslavement—like the Free Soil Party, it was principally concerned with stopping the spread of enslavement into the territories—many abolitionists became Republicans.[192]

The Underground Railroad: A Quaker Dilemma

In the struggle to end enslavement, another question divided abolitionists, particularly Friends: how to respond to African Americans whose hatred of enslavement was so deep that they "freed themselves," that is, fled enslavement without the legal right to do so. The question was whether their testimonies of peace and integrity precluded Friends, either as a religious body or as individuals, from giving aid to fugitives.

The dilemma for anyone involved with the Underground Railroad became even more difficult with the potentially grave consequences imposed by the Fugitive Slave Law of 1793. In practical terms any enslaver or agent of an enslaver could simply testify that an African American who had been arrested as a suspected fugitive was enslaved by him or her and the person would be remanded to the enslaver. Anyone who harbored an alleged fugitive could be fined five hundred dollars.[193] The situation was eased somewhat because the 1793 law was loosely enforced and because several northern states enacted "personal liberty laws" to contravene it. Unlike the federal law, these state laws granted suspected fugitives a hearing, a jury trial, and access to legal counsel. Written proof of the alleged enslaved status had to be presented and state officials were forbidden to detain alleged fugitives in jail, release alleged escapees to claimants, or offer claimants any assistance.[194] This protection lasted until the state laws were nullified by the more severe Fugitive Slave Act of 1850 which brought even harsher punishment—higher fines and even prison sentences—for anyone, even bystanders, who did not cooperate in seizing runaways.[195] Federal commissioners had the power to compel anyone in any state to do whatever was necessary to enforce the law.[196]

Despite the law, abolitionists in both the South and North actively assisted those enslaved persons who needed their help to escape—though many fled bondage entirely unaided—through what was soon known as the Underground Railroad. In 1869 Unitarian minister and abolitionist Samuel J. May described the Underground Railroad as persons opposed to slavery "scattered throughout all slaveholding states" who knew or had "taken pains to find" others "at convenient distances northward" who felt similarly; these persons were in turn connected to others "still further North" and on "to the very borders of Canada," where enslavement had been illegal since 1834.

———————•———————

One of the most widely held notions about the Underground Railroad is that Friends "ran" it.[197] In fact, the legend of Quaker participation portrays Friends as "people who would always risk life, limb, and fortune, if necessary, for the cause of the helpless slave."[198] Quakers were, in fact, as ambivalent about assisting fugitives as they were about many other aspects of the effort to end enslavement. At any time the proportion of Friends who took active part in the Underground Railroad was small, and recent research documents that Americans of other denominations were as committed as Quakers were.

The legend that the Underground Railroad was primarily a Quaker enterprise appears to have arisen from several sources. First, the early stand of the Religious Society of Friends against enslavement gave its members a reputation as advocates for the enslaved.[199] The fact that many fugitives spent at least some of their time in flight in Philadelphia, its environs, and other areas heavily populated by activist Quakers also contributed to the legend.[200] *Uncle Tom's Cabin* (1852) also played a major role. As the nation's first true best seller, the novel's portrait of the Hallidays, the European American Quaker couple who sheltered the fugitives George and Eliza, was widely influential in the inference of Quaker leadership in the Underground Railroad.[201] Post-Civil War novels and historical accounts of the Underground Railroad enhanced the legend.[202]

As with any myth, some degree of truth undergirds this portrait of Quaker involvement. Aside from the far more plentiful documentation of the roles of individual European American Quakers, many narratives written by fugitives themselves document their belief that Friends were sympathetic and helpful. The renowned African American fugitive, writer, and orator William Wells Brown took his name from the man who aided his 1834 escape, European American Friend Wells Brown of Ohio. "The sight of the broad brim and the plain, Quaker dress, which met me at every turn, increased my sense of freedom and security," Frederick Douglass wrote of the first days after his 1838 escape in New Bedford, Massachusetts. "'I am among the Quakers,' thought I, 'and am safe.'"[203] In 1838, the *Pennsylvania Freeman* quoted the statement of one fugitive that the only advice he was given in escaping was to look for Quaker garb.[204] "Anybody who wanted to go free went from Winton [Virginia] by the hands of Quakers," said another about his father's escape.[205] Fugitive Moses Grandy spoke generally about Friends in his own account:

> During the struggles which have procured for us this justice from our fellow-citizens, we have been in the habit of looking in public places for some well-known abolitionists, and if none that we knew were there, we addressed any person dressed as a Quaker; these classes always took our part against ill usage, and we have to thank them for many a contest in our behalf.[206]

In his seminal study of the legends surrounding the Underground Railroad, Larry Gara determined that "a careful reading of post-Civil War accounts shows the Quaker reputation to have been earned largely by a small number of Friends."[207] Still, Densmore asserts that "the myth of Quaker involvement in the Underground Railroad is built on a substantial foundation of actual Quaker involvement in numbers far in excess of their presence in the general population."[208] According to Kashatus, African American William Still's *Underground Railroad* (1871), a detailed account of his work as secretary of the fugitive-assisting General Vigilance Committee of Pennsylvania Anti-Slavery Society, provides sketches of thirteen Quaker assistants out of the twenty-two he included; the rest, with one possible exception, describe people who worked with Quaker agents.[209] Historian Julie Jeffrey notes Still's observation that fugitives felt safe in areas in which many Friends lived.[210] Kashatus also points out that in Chester County, Pennsylvania, where Friends were about 20 percent of the population in the antebellum period, at least eighty-two of 132 "known" fugitive assistants (or 62 percent) were Quakers; many were couples. Eighty-eight out of a hundred assistants were either Quaker or African American; the role of the latter has been vastly underemphasized in Underground Railroad literature.[211]

Instances of interracial cooperation between Friends and African Americans involved in fugitive assistance are also documented. The North Carolina fugitive Peter Robinson acted with Quaker vessel owners "Fuller and Elliott" to ferry others to the next "station" north. In North Carolina, an enslaved man known as "Hamilton's Saul," rather than escaping himself, worked with Levi and Addison Coffin to send people of African descent who had been kidnapped north.[212] At least five African Americans worked with Levi Coffin when he moved to Indiana.[213] In Delaware, five free African Americans worked for years with one of the most famous "stationmasters," European American Quaker Thomas Garrett, whose consistent work with the enslaved Harriet Tubman is far better known.[214]

Examples abound of both collective and individual action among Friends, often working in less systematic ways with African Americans than did Coffin and Garrett. In 1822 a group of Quakers and African Americans on Nantucket managed to keep the family of Arthur Cooper, who had been enslaved in Virginia but whose wife and children were born free, away from an enslaver's agent named Griffith who pursued them. European American Friend Thomas Macy "put his

Quaker coat and hat on George [Arthur Cooper's name when enslaved] and assisted him and his wife and children out of the window and carried them off to a place of greater safety," which as it happened was the house of local magistrate Alfred Folger. Folger, a Quaker of European descent, then ruled that the Coopers could not be taken from the island. Griffith, disappointed on Nantucket, went to New Bedford in pursuit of another fugitive who had escaped on the same vessel as the Coopers, but there, European American Quakers Thomas Rotch and William W. Swain, through a legal subterfuge, had Griffith jailed in nearby Taunton while they and others helped the fugitive leave New Bedford by vessel.[215]

In 1847, Friends and free African Americans in Cass County, Michigan, similarly protected nine fugitives in an incident known as "the Kentucky Raid." The township of Calvin had become home to many Quakers who left the South in the 1820s and 1830s accompanied by African Americans they had manumitted. Like the Nantucketers, Michigan Friends surrounded a group of armed Kentuckians pursuing fugitives and convinced them to take their case to county court, where the judge ruled that they had no right to remove the people they sought.[216]

In Indiana, the Friends role was "doubtless considerably embroidered by legend," but many Friends of European descent did work closely with African Americans, both free and fugitive. Abolitionists in southwest Ohio, separated from slave states by the Ohio River, recalled that runaways who first went to African Americans would be sent next to Quakers.[217] Levi Coffin (1798–1877), the activist of European descent whom some have called the "president" of the Underground Railroad,[218] exemplifies the relationship of Friends with fugitive and free African Americans. As a seven-year-old in North Carolina, he began to question slavery when he saw enslaved people chained together. Witnessing an enslaved child "torn" away from his screaming mother sealed his commitment to work to end enslavement, he later wrote, "until the end of my days."[219]

Coffin's older European American cousin and mentor Vestal Coffin and his family had been active in helping fugitives make their way to the North.[220] Settling on his conviction that he could no longer live amid the enslavement of the South, Levi Coffin and his European

American wife, the former Catharine White, moved in 1826 to Newport, Indiana. The Coffins' new home was near a settlement of free African Americans who had been brought there by North Carolina Friends. The Coffins joined local African Americans then aiding fugitives traveling north along several well-used routes that converged near Newport.[221] Coffin estimated that an average of one hundred fugitives arrived in Newport each year. He and his wife were among those who were disowned by the Indiana Yearly Meeting in 1842 and helped form the Indiana Yearly Meeting of Anti-Slavery Friends.[222]

After the Coffins moved to Cincinnati in 1847 to open their free produce store, they continued to assist fugitives; they are believed to have donated much of the store's proceeds to provide for them.[223] For twenty years "seldom a week passed without our receiving passengers by this mysterious road," Coffin wrote in his 1880 *Reminiscences*. "We knew not what night or what hour of the night we would be roused from slumber by a gentle rap at the door."[224]

Thomas Garrett (1789–1871) of Wilmington, Delaware, was in many ways the eastern version of Levi Coffin. Born in Upper Darby, Pennsylvania, just west of Philadelphia, he was aware, as a child, of the numerous fugitives who entered Pennsylvania from Delaware. When a free African American who worked in his family was kidnapped in order to be re-enslaved, Garrett chased the kidnappers down and retrieved her.[225] That act was for him a "spiritual awakening," and he thereupon declared that he would "ever devote his life to the active quest for human equality and dignity."[226] His view of his responsibility was simple—"a man's duty is shown to him, and I believe in doing it."[227]

In 1822 Garrett and his wife Rachel (Mendenhall) moved to Wilmington where the family home became the final stop in slave territory for hundreds of fugitives.[228] Between 1825 and 1863, Garrett wrote in a letter to Samuel May that he had helped exactly 2,322 to escape enslavement.[229] Garrett worked closely with Tubman, whom he considered his "heroine," and William Still of the Philadelphia Vigilance Committee.[230] He so angered Maryland authorities that in 1860 they offered a reward of ten thousand dollars for his arrest.[231] In his own state, Garrett and fellow European American Quaker John Hunn were tried in 1848 for aiding the escape of a family.[232] The court levied fines so high as to almost bankrupt both men, but when the court warned them not to "meddle with slaves again," Garrett replied, "I have assisted over 1400 runaways in 25 years on their way to the North, and I now consider the penalty imposed upon me as a license for the remainder of my life." He then announced to the courtroom, "If any know of any slave who needs assistance, send him to me, as I now publicly pledge myself to double my diligence and never neglect an opportunity to assist a slave in obtaining his freedom."[233] Garrett was highly esteemed in the African American community: volunteers guarded his home during the Civil War and carried the coffin at his funeral. Garrett also specified that his African American pallbearers were to "participate in the Quaker service."[234] Lucretia Mott wrote of Garrett's funeral, "Such a concourse of all sects and colors as we never saw—thousands—the street lined for half a mile and nearly as many outside as in."[235]

New Jersey native and Friend Isaac T. Hopper (1771–1852) was perhaps the most durable of fugitive assistants: most accounts of his life note that he was active in that work since 1787, when he was sixteen and a new resident of Philadelphia. He continued to help escaping enslaved people into his eighties. Hopper lived in Philadelphia until 1829 and then moved to New York City, where he worked in concert with African American abolitionist and editor David Ruggles, who was secretary of the New York Vigilance Committee until 1839. Hopper was also later president of this committee. Under his direction it became "the hinge on which the Underground Railroad's operations turned."[236] By his own estimate, Hopper helped one thousand African Americans during his forty-two years in Philadelphia alone. He was also known as an expert in the use of law to thwart fugitive renditions and to assist free African Americans who had been accused of being fugitives. Like Elizabeth Buffum Chace, Hopper's daughter Abigail Hopper Gibbons (1801–93) recalled that the home in which she had grown up "lived and breathed abolitionism." Free African Americans, escaping fugitives, and newly released prisoners were frequent visitors there.[237] In 1835 Isaac Hopper formed the New York Association of Friends for the Relief of Those Held in Slavery, a strictly Quaker organization and one of the earlier societies integrated by gender. His daughter bore major responsibilities in that association. In 1840 he wrote "Tales of Oppression," a series in the the *National Anti-Slavery Standard* relating the stories of fugitives and the treatment of the enslaved.[238]

Their roles are less well documented, but Quaker women were probably as active as Quaker men in assisting fugitives. In addition to such Friends as Lucretia Mott, Abby Kelley Foster, Abby Hopper Gibbons, Amy Post, and Elizabeth Buffum Chace, other Quaker women were centrally involved. The sisters Abigail and Elizabeth Goodwin sheltered fugitives in their home in Salem, New Jersey, and Laura Haviland not only harbored them in her Michigan home but was one of few people who went into the South to accompany fugitives on their journeys north.[239] In fact, Haviland had such a reputation for daring rescues that Tennessee offered a $3,000 reward for her capture. She particularly liked to rescue women fugitives targeted by posses seeking high rewards."[240] In Chester County, Dinah Mendenhall, Abigail Kimber, Lydia Fussell, Mary Pennock, Mary Brosius, Esther Fussell Lewis, and Lewis's daughter Graceanna often sheltered fugitives in their homes.[241]

———•———

Those Quakers who aided fugitives were not only in jeopardy for violating federal law but also by being exposed to the aggressive actions of those who claimed to own fugitives or agents who acted on their behalf. Claimants and their agents were much more likely to pursue fugitives the closer they were to home; thus the areas bordering the Mason-Dixon Line dividing the free and slave states were especially dangerous for both the fugitives and those helping them. And with the passage of the 1850 Fugitive Slave Act, those claimants felt far more empowered in their efforts than they earlier had. In Lancaster County, Pennsylvania, geography, politics, and morality intersected to foment one of the most violent incidents in Underground Railroad history—the Christiana Revolt of 1851.

Standing on the border with Maryland, Lancaster County was often the first free soil fugitives reached. Thus it was an area especially susceptible to the incursion of enslavers' agents. In 1851 European American plantation owner Edward Gorsuch of Maryland rode into the county with a band of men, including his son, Dickinson, and a federal marshal, in search of fugitives he claimed to own. When the Philadelphia Vigilance Committee warned of their imminent arrival in Christiana, the fugitive William Parker, who had lived in the county for twelve years, summoned several other fugitives—including two of the four Gorsuch sought—to the home he rented from his European American Quaker employers, Sarah and William Pownall. Sarah Pownall urged Parker not to use arms but to escape to Canada; instead he and the others stayed in order to confront Gorsuch and his band.242 Upon Gorsuch's arrival at Parker's home the parties exchanged threats, and then shots were fired; Gorsuch was killed and his son and two others were wounded. Local European American Friend Joseph Scarlatt carried the wounded Dickinson Gorsuch to the home of the Pownalls, who cared for him for three weeks. Parker fled to Canada the night of the encounter.243

The Christiana incident demonstrated how the Fugitive Slave Act had pushed resistance to kidnapping and re-enslavement to a distressing point, at least in the minds of many Quakers. Not only African Americans but a notable number of European Americans sympathetic to the plight of fugitives were increasingly willing to resist such efforts forcibly. Despite the marginal involvement of Quakers in the Christiana incident, it fulfilled one of their worst fears—that helping fugitives might place them squarely in a violent situation and thus challenge, or compromise, their peace testimony. *The Friend* advised readers to stay with the "peaceable spirit of Jesus" and to avoid being "improperly influenced by the excitement" surrounding Christiana.244 For Quakers, the questions were whether they should disobey a law they considered morally objectionable, and, if they did, what form that disobedience would take.

Since the reform decade of the 1830s, Friends had been founders and members of "nonresistance societies," the heir to earlier peace societies. The first appears to have been the New England Non-Resistance Society, founded in 1838.245 The society was organized after the American Anti-Slavery Society failed to commit completely to Garrison's nonresistance platform.246 Its membership included New England Friends of European descent who were primarily Orthodox, Abby Kelley and William Bassett among them; the few Friends who joined from outside New England tended to be Hicksite, including Lucretia Mott.247 "The history of mankind is crowded with evidences proving that physical coercion is not adapted to moral regeneration," the society's Declaration of Sentiments, written by William Lloyd

Garrison, declared. History also shows, he wrote, "that the sinful dispositions of men can be subdued only by love; that evil can be exterminated from the earth only by goodness; . . . that there is great security in being gentle, harmless, long-suffering, and abundant in mercy; that it is only the meek who shall inherit the earth, for the violent who resort to the sword are destined to perish with the sword." The society pledged itself against "all wars," and even against all "monuments commemorative of victory over a fallen foe." They were against raising taxes for war or requiring military service. Of particular pertinence to later actions related to the Fugitive Slave Act, the declaration stated, "We cannot sue any man at law, to compel him by force to restore anything which he may have wrongfully taken from us or others; but if he has seized our coat, we shall surrender up our cloak, rather than subject him to punishment."[248]

During the 1834 antiabolition riot in New York City, nonresistant Isaac Hopper was advised to remove antislavery materials from the windows of his bookstore to put off rioters rampaging against those who spoke against enslavement. Hopper responded, "Dost thou think I am such a coward as to forsake my principles, or conceal them, at the bidding of a mob?" he asked. An observer reported that after Hopper stood on the steps of this shop and faced it "calmly and firmly," the crowd ultimately moved on.[249] When nonresistant women abolitionists gathered for a convention in Philadelphia in 1839, they declined proffered police protection on the strength of their confidence "in a higher power."[250]

The nonresistants' criticism of government as "unchristian" was "a radical extension of traditional Quaker pacifism."[251] It was too radical, it seemed, for most Friends, who believed first in obeying the law. Quakers did not play a prominent big role in the organization. Yet the peace testimony that some Friends maintained placed them in the conflict over legal as opposed to God-given rights, particularly during the struggles over the Fugitive Slave Act. In New Bedford, European American Friend Thomas Arnold Greene resigned as president of a local meeting protesting the act when a majority resolved to aid fugitives by physical force if necessary.[252]

Many Friends who may have been inclined to aid fugitives in some way could neither accept violence nor circumvention of nor willful disobedience to civil law. Living by the peace testimony meant that Friends could not bear arms; thus they were at risk of endangering themselves or the fugitives they assisted.253 Some limited their assistance to the strictly legal: Anthony Benezet and Elisha Tyson, for example, helped only African Americans who were legally free. But others were less constrained by law. Isaac Hopper claimed that he never "sought to make a slave discontented, but as long as my life is spared, I will always assist anyone who is trying to escape from slavery, be the laws what they may be."254

The Quaker testimony of integrity also came into play: clandestine aid to fugitives, although integral to the success of the Underground Railroad, "invited making a virtue of falsehood" in the view of some Friends. Friends sought other ways to avoid having to abandon the truth: if they did not believe in such a thing as enslavement, they could truthfully respond "there are no slaves here" to anyone pursuing fugitives.255 An exchange between Friends in Indiana and North Carolina in 1843 and 1844 illustrates how deep the differences were on this issue. As much as North Carolina Friends worked to manumit those they had enslaved, they faced a "moral dilemma" when it came to harboring runaways because of their concerns about integrity. In 1843, the yearly meeting condemned those who gave shelter to fugitives. Indiana Anti-Slavery Friends perceived this action as a rebuke; they were "deeply grieved," they wrote, "to witness such a low, time-serving, man-fearing, popularity-seeking spirit manifested" in the Religious Society of Friends.256

A significant segment of Quakers had no misgivings about assisting fugitives in any way necessary. Some held that in fact the Bible required them to be active in this work and customarily cited Deuteronomy 23:15—"Thou shalt not deliver unto his masters the servant who has escaped from his master unto thee"—or Isaiah 58:6—"Is not this [a way to serve God] to let the oppressed go free and [to] break every yoke?"

The Coming of the War

In 1857, the Anti-Slavery Friends of Indiana laid their meeting down. Nearly all of its remaining members rejoined the Orthodox Yearly Meeting, a move eased when that meeting allowed them to rejoin without the usual "acknowledgement" of wrongdoing expected from Friends who had been disowned.[257] The reconciliation was a sign that both sides knew that the end of enslavement was inevitable.[258] Abolitionist Friends were beginning to believe that their pacifism was counterproductive and actually worked to support a Union that was not ready for emancipation. Jordan notes that in Kansas, where Friends were among the "free soilers" who had moved there to keep it from becoming a slave state, holding to Quaker pacifism in the face of physical attacks against them became an "almost superhuman challenge." In 1859, Quaker Susan B. Anthony responded to one minister's charge of "fanaticism" in the abolition movement: "Read the new [sic] Testament and see if Christ was not an agitator. Who is this among us crying 'peace, peace' when there is no peace!"[259]

In the end, about one percent of the ten million people of European descent in the country in 1840 ever joined the plethora of antislavery societies that were started in the 1830s. Even the fervor to create a perfect society on earth inspired by the revivals of the Second Great Awakening was not enough to turn the tide. The newly evangelized wanted to cleanse people of their sins—intemperance and enslavement being two of them—but, it seems, their desire was not enough to turn abolitionism into the mass movement that temperance became.[260]

By the end of the 1850s, even those abolitionists who believed in the primacy of moral suasion in ending enslavement were no longer united on the question. No longer were as many opposed to the use of force, though many Quakers continued to argue against it.

Union Literary Institute Schoolhouse.

Benezet instructing colored children, from the 1850 New Haven edition of *Historical, poetical and pictorial American Scenes* by John Warner Barber, with the call number AC85.B2333.850h. By permission of the Houghton Library, Harvard University.

CHAPTER FOUR

Friends and Freed People

1700-1860

Today [I] visited the colored school consisting of 120 children who have been in attendance for four weeks past. None of them knew the alphabet when they entered and now of this number 28 can read and nearly all spell easy lessons.... From the interest they manifest I presume they will make full as rapid progress as any children under similar circumstances.

— *Indiana Quaker Elkanah Beard working in Mississippi, 1863*

WHETHER MOVED BY CHRISTIAN CHARITY or by self-interest, many Quakers contributed great amounts of time and energy to aiding freed people in their new lives. In the early national period Quakers came to be recognized as the religious group "most prominent in extending charitable work beyond their own denomination"; Benjamin Quarles notes that by the 1860s Friends were particularly effective in teaching "basic literacy to all ages" among the twenty-two thousand African Americans in Philadelphia.[1] Some yearly, quarterly, and monthly meetings worked to assure that those whom Quakers had manumitted, south and north, received the assistance they needed in freedom. In other cases, when meetings were either unable or unwilling to act corporately to improve the circumstances in which newly freed African Americans lived, Friends worked individually or through numerous groups toward that end.[2]

By 1790 the need for support among people of African descent was great. Though some enslaved people worked in trades on the South's plantations and in its few urban centers, most enslaved people of African descent in the region lacked opportunities to develop skills the American economy needed. In the urban North they struggled to find a place for themselves in an economy that for the most part offered only limited opportunities as unskilled laborers, often employed by the day. In rural regions freed people most often became "cottagers," tenants with a house and a small plot of land to farm. Trying to make new lives with so few resources of their own brought "more risk than opportunity."3 Beyond simple financial support, freed people needed occupational training and schooling, in addition to legal assistance and protection from corrupt or unfair European Americans.4 George Fox had noted the necessity of support in freedom when he cautioned Friends not to permit people they manumitted to "go away empty-handed."5 Yet, just as ending enslavement raised the question of whether some Friends were more intent on cleansing their own souls than on the benefit to those they would free, Friends efforts to assist the newly freed often embodied a paradox. While they may have been willing to accord African Americans a certain measure of political equality, most hesitated to accept them as social equals.

The challenges for both the newly freed and their former enslavers stemmed from different expectations of what freedom would bring. For European Americans, enslavement had been a system not only for procuring labor but also for controlling the behavior of a people who, if free, were generally perceived as threatening. Throughout the colonies certain laws, often called "black codes," restricted the movements of African Americans, limited the increase in their population within a given jurisdiction, sharply curtailed their gatherings, banned them from owning real property, and established separate courts for adjudicating their crimes.6 Moreover, European Americans often doubted the ability of formerly enslaved people to live independently. In 1725–26, for example, the Quaker-dominated Pennsylvania Assembly passed an "Act for Better Regulation of Negroes in This Province" on the grounds that "free Africans are slothful people and often prove burdensome to the neighborhood." A magistrate was authorized to bind out "all slothful black adults."7 To colonists of European descent, "liberation from slavery" was not the same as "freedom to live as one chose, but rather freedom to become a diligent, sober, dependable worker who gratefully accepted his position in colonial society."8

At least some Friends believed that people of African descent had been harmed so much in enslavement that they would never be able to succeed independently unless that damage were somehow undone. Religious conviction compelled some to endeavor to "reform" those who had lived in such oppressive circumstances.9 Such notions may have stemmed, at least in some measure, from class anxiety; European Americans, Quakers and others, sometimes expressed similar concerns about African Americans and new European immigrants alike. "Remarkable and grievous is the Depravity of Manners so observable in our Street," a 1732 Philadelphia Monthly Meeting broadside stated; "sorrowful enough is it to see the great Encrease of Prophaneness and lewdness . . . much owing to the Importation of great Numbers of vicious and scandalous Refuse of other Countries."[10] European American Quaker Herbert Hadley asserts that the philanthropy of Philadelphia Friends aimed to aid the poor showed "little recognition of the need for social change to remove injustices suffered by Negroes."[11]

Freed People and Friends Meetings

For the most part, Quaker meetings took as a corporate obligation the need to go beyond simply manumitting enslaved people; they must also "take good and Christian care" of those they had once enslaved.[12] In 1778 Philadelphia Yearly Meeting instructed Concord Quarter Friends of judgment and experience to advise newly freed people "in respect to their engagements in worldly concern as occasion offers."[13] In 1794 Fairfax, Virginia, Quarterly Meeting reported, "No slaves amongst us, and those few Blacks who have had their freedom secured are provided for as to food and raiment."[14] In 1806 both Baltimore and Philadelphia Yearly Meetings advised members to aid, as best they could, both enslaved and free African Americans.[15]

Some Quakers, at their meeting's behest or on their own, offered legal assistance as needed.[16] From the 1700s to the Civil War, a number of dedicated Quakers not only worked to assist fugitives from capture and return to slavery, but they fought in court and otherwise against the illegal capture and enslavement of free African Americans. Friends had recorded their manumissions carefully, and these accounts often became essential in protecting the legal status of a freed person. In 1761 European American abolitionist David Ferris from Wilmington Meeting in Delaware was apparently the first to practice this careful recording for people freed by members of his meeting.[17] Some Friends often provided job training, perhaps in their own trade, perhaps through an apprenticeship in another occupation, along with the necessary tools or equipment. After being manumitted, Peter Hill (1767–1820) of Burlington, New Jersey, served an apprenticeship with his former enslaver, Friend John Hollinshead, and became a skilled and well-regarded clockmaker. In the South, North Carolina Yearly Meeting endorsed hiring freed people as apprentices in 1817 as the only way to provide them an education, and in 1767 Virginia Yearly Meeting was training enslaved people to be laborers in a free market. Monthly meetings loaned money to African American tradesmen and established apprenticeships for their children.18

To assure that members were taking seriously the urgings or mandates to support those whom they had formerly enslaved, in the late 1770s and early 1780s, monthly and yearly meetings appointed committees to visit freed people to assess their circumstances and offer assistance.19 Friends commonly spoke of "inspecting" homes—not only of African Americans but of all poor people, including the Quaker poor—to gauge the piety that existed within them and the care accorded to children.20 Those visiting committees regularly reported to their meeting the names of members who were inattentive to the needs of newly free people and reminded these members, not always with the desired results, of their obligation.21 Committees generally reported that freed people were in fact "prospering in their new freedom" and did what they could to assist. The Nottingham, Pennsylvania, Friends reported in 1779 that their advice "appeared to have some weight" among African Americans there and that continuing care would be "both acceptable and useful." Members of a New Garden, Pennsylvania, committee reported that most of the freed people in their midst remained living near Friends and had found work. Meetings often expressed particular concern for freed people too old, sick, or disabled to care for themselves.22

Though some Friends visiting committees found African Americans in their areas to be "free and open" to advice and assistance, others did not. Duck Creek Monthly Meeting in Delaware noted that people they had formerly enslaved were not always inclined to receive or follow advice from the mouths of those who had so recently oppressed them.23 A Philadelphia Quarterly Meeting committee also found the formerly enslaved reluctant to seek out their assistance. Thomas Drake argues that the systems African Americans had created "to help one another over rough periods" made it possible to avoid "the paternalistic scrutiny to which Friends generally subjected recipients of their aid."[24] Jean Soderlund charges that Friends "exacted a price" for their financial and other assistance, often by binding children out as apprentices and preparing contracts between free African Americans and their employers. In any assistance they accepted from Quakers, African Americans "discovered that they lost independence in making decisions concerning their own families."[25]

———— • ————

The Religious Society of Friends, however, was the only denomination that held some corporate expectation of compensation to newly freed people for their past service. Such restitution was not the general rule for non-Quakers. In many instances the proposition was inverted: an enslaved person was freed only after remitting a sum to the enslaver to cover the "expense of raising them."[26] In part as a way to avert civil war, some Quaker meetings contemplated compensating enslavers for the enslaved people who had fled. But the more radical Friends considered that "compromising with sin."[27] According to European American Richard Foster, Quakers were alone in believing that "justice demanded exactly the opposite"—that the formerly enslaved were the ones who deserved restitution.[28]

Monthly meeting visiting committees labored long and hard with former enslavers to set compensation that was, as Frost puts it, "neither overpayment nor underpayment but simple justice."[29] In New England in 1782, Friends spoke of wanting to "settle for past services, according to justice and equity." Often asked to help meetings determine what justice required, visiting committees commonly used the wage rates prevailing in that region at that time.[30] In 1761, David Ferris asserted that enslavers should pay each person they had enslaved twelve pounds for each year of their servitude past maturity, while Warner Mifflin of Duck Creek, Delaware, Meeting paid one of the men he had enslaved 270 pounds for every year of past service, in addition to food and clothing. Some, like Rhode Islander Moses Brown, freed those they had enslaved and then hired them as wage laborers.[31] Brown also led other Quakers in a successful campaign to enact legislation making Rhode Island towns responsible for "maintenance of free Negroes" in their jurisdiction.[32] In 1779, European American Thomas Wood provided an annual sum from his father's estate to Caesar, whom his father had freed sixteen years earlier, after a committee of New Garden Meeting in Pennsylvania reported that Caesar should be provided with what "may appear best for him—the negro's benefit—and the reputation of our religious Society." Wood subtracted from that compensation one year during which Caesar had been "nursed in the small-pox."[33] In some places, compensation allotted for the services of deceased freed people was divided among their next of kin. And in some, when former owners did not provide compensation, meetings drew from their own funds.[34]

Some Friends provided compensation for service in the form of land or a dwelling. Sandy Spring, Maryland, Friends gave those they enslaved two-acre plots; one member, European American James Stabler, deeded them land for a Methodist Church as well.[35] About 1700 a Friend from Third Haven Meeting in Maryland gave each person he manumitted a house, fifty acres, and sheep.[36] Another Maryland Friend gave a woman he had enslaved and her two daughters a house, free firewood, and land free of rent for eight years.[37]

Migration and Resettlement

Friends in the South believed that responsible manumission could be accomplished only by the mass movement of people out of the region. To manumit in a region where about half the people were enslaved[38] was not only against the law but flew in the face of pervasive social and cultural mores as well. Friends faced difficult choices: They could acquiesce to the system, thus protecting their own economic interests and abiding by law; they could simply free those they enslaved as a matter of principle and put them "at the mercy of the system"; or they could commit themselves to transcending the system and all of its societal and legal complexities.[39] That last option could well lead to a loss of livelihood and homestead, even bankruptcy, and separation from their community.[40] For many southern Friends of European descent, the choice came down to leaving either their homes or their religious society; eventually hundreds chose to migrate from their region, some as early as 1780.[41]

Though Friends in other states also resettled, the experience of North Carolina Friends was perhaps the most profound. From an early point, the yearly meeting had argued against enslavement. In a 1779 petition to the state assembly protesting legislation that curbed the rights of people of African descent, the yearly meeting declared not only that such acts violated the nation's founding documents but called into question the assembly's authority to govern. "Being fully persuaded that freedom is the natural right of all mankind," the petition stated, "we fully believe [them] to be a contradiction of the Declaration and Bill of Rights on which depends your authority to make laws." North Carolinians generally accused the Quakers of inciting ill feeling and action: in 1791 a grand jury declared that the "great peril and danger" of insurrection was a consequence of Quakers" who "corrupt" the enslaved, turn them against the enslavers, and protect fugitives.[42]

Once North Carolina Friends began to manumit those they enslaved, they encountered several significant impediments. First, until 1830 anyone freed could be seized legally and resold. Second, enslavers who manumitted people were required to post a high bond: in 1830 it stood at one thousand dollars, and only the wealthier enslavers could afford such action.[43] As a consequence of these restrictions, William Gaston, a sympathetic Catholic European American judge, suggested that Friends begin to record ownership of the people they wanted to free in the name of the yearly meeting. Thus, enslaved people could be protected from kidnapping, and the need to post a bond was obviated. The idea of the meeting assuming ownership for this purpose was well received; even some non-Quakers asked Friends to act similarly on their behalf.[44] In 1803 the yearly meeting appointed the former enslavers as guardians, while North Carolina Friends continued to petition the legislature to allow manumission. When granted, those people the yearly meeting held would legally be free.[45]

———————•———————

Even as it followed this course, North Carolina Yearly Meeting became convinced that manumitted people had to be moved from the southern states. In 1808 it established a committee of seven to act as its agents in managing the care of the newly freed and an "African Fund" to help with resettlement costs.[46] By 1814 North Carolina Yearly Meeting technically held 350 enslaved people, almost all of those whom its members then enslaved. To counter the Friends actions, the state's courts offered a reward to anyone bringing in a "Quaker Free Negro," the description for those who had been turned over to the yearly meeting. The meeting hired lawyers to defend those who had been seized. This "cat and mouse game" continued for years. In 1827 North Carolina's Supreme Court declared the Friends tactic illegal on the grounds that because wages were being paid to people of African descent held by the meeting, they must have been freed; therefore Friends had acted illegally.[47]

In the meantime the yearly meeting committee had studied the laws of the new territories to find potential resettlement locations. Ohio, Indiana, and Illinois were deemed to be most suitable.[48] Meeting members devoted most of their time to writing letters, consulting with agents of the various meetings, negotiating with Friends who lived in potential destinations, and appearing in court. Even before the 1827 court ruling, the committee had removed some African Americans to the Midwest, but afterward the committee moved more speedily.[49] By 1828, the Africa Fund contained $13,500.[50] The yearly meeting sent 1,700 formerly enslaved people to various locations in the 1820s and early 1830s; by 1836, the meeting held only 18 people.[51]

Not all of the enslaved people held by North Carolina Yearly Meeting wished to emigrate. In 1826, when 600 were technically the meeting's property, 99 wished to remain in North Carolina, 316 stated their willingness to go to Africa, 15 stated that they would go to another state, and 101 said they were willing to go to the West.[52] When some decided not to leave, at least some Friends stayed behind to protect them, as did about twenty families of Core Sound Meeting in 1825. Stephen Grellet, a French Quaker who traveled widely in North America as a missionary, wrote:

> I felt tenderly for the few members of our Society who continue in this corner. Some of them think it is their religious duty to remain, to protect many of the people of colour, who formerly belonged to those Friends who moved away; and who, unprotected by them, might be reduced again to slavery.[53]

The task of resettlement was a formidable one for North Carolina Quakers; European American Friend Nathan Mendenhall described it as "expensive, troublesome and hard."[54] Friends had to identify and enroll those who wished to move, raise moeny, make certain that each had the proper documents, find means of transport, outfit them with appropriate equipment, utensils, and clothing (often made by Quaker women), and ultimately move them.[55] They also provided religious tracts, Bibles, and school books.[56] In the move of 135 African Americans to the Midwest in 1835, Friends paid most of the costs for 13 wagons and carts and for warm clothing. That trip alone cost $2,490 (about $60,000 in 2007 dollars).[57]

By 1830 the yearly meeting had helped 652 African Americans resettle in the free states, and its expenses grew from between one and two thousand to $13,000.[58] Friends from Rhode Island, Philadelphia, Baltimore, New York, Ohio, Indiana, and London responded to requests for financial assistance, and Philadelphia Yearly Meeting was especially supportive, sending some $7,500 in 1826 and 1827.[59]

The settlers received mixed receptions in their new Midwestern homes. In 1826 Friends in North Carolina learned that some Friends of European ancestry in Indiana there "were resentful toward North Carolina Friends for sending so many blacks there." European American William Parker, who had moved to Indiana from North Carolina, wrote in 1826 that African Americans "are not wanted here. Friends do not want them and they fear they will be brought into difficulties whereby the . . . people do threaten to have it a slave state if blacks do continue to flood in." Persons who had brought African Americans into the state, Parker held, should be willing to move them out. Parker stated that another Friend in the area declared that "he would give $20 to get them out of Wayne County."[60] The clerk of the meeting for sufferings in Indiana wondered privately if, "in view of the attitudes" of European Americans in Indiana, it might perhaps be better to start "a colony for blacks somewhere in the Southwest."[61] Yet European American Friend David White "met with no opposition" when he arrived in Ohio and Indiana from the South with fifty-three African Americans in 1835. Farmers there, he found, were quite willing "to have the coloured people settle on their lands."[62]

Drawn by the prospect of lands free of enslavement, southern Quakers themselves also moved to the Midwest. The trek for Virginians and North Carolinians usually ran over the Appalachians and could last seven weeks or more. If Friends were traveling with people of African descent they were compelled to take more difficult routes to avoid the slave state of Tennessee. A "fringe" of this westward migration spread into Upper Canada. Southerners arriving in the Midwest joined Friends who had already moved there from New England and Pennsylvania. By 1835 Quakers had moved in such numbers that more Friends lived west of the Alleghenies than east. The new settlers had created a yearly meeting in Ohio in 1813 and in Indiana by 1821.[63] By 1843 Ohio Yearly Meeting had 18,000 members and Indiana, 30,000; the two made up 57 percent of all Quakers in the United States.[64] By 1850 the Orthodox Indiana Yearly Meeting was the largest Quaker meeting in the world.[65]

African Americans relocating to the Midwest, probably aware of Friends' efforts to resettle those they had enslaved, often chose to settle near Quaker communities in the belief that doing so would enhance their chances of comfortable existence on the frontier.[66] Nearly all the early settlers of Calvin Township in Cass County in southwestern Michigan were Friends who had migrated from the South in the 1820s and 1830s, and their presence attracted African American settlement there.[67] In the 1840s North Carolina Friends helped freed people settle near Newport, now Fountain City, Indiana, home at that time to well-known abolitionist Friend Levi Coffin.[68] As many as one hundred African American families lived just over the border in Ohio, not far from the Greenville Settlement and its integrated school in Indiana, the Union Literary Institute.[69] Family groups, many of whom were racially mixed, settled by 1830 in Rush County, Indiana, near the Quaker villages of Carthage and Ripley, in what became known as the Beech settlement. By 1835 a group of those settlers moved again to the Roberts settlement in Jackson, Hamilton County, Indiana.[70] Formerly enslaved people threatened with recapture also sought refuge with Friends in Salem, Iowa.[71] A recent study of these African American communities found that the settlers were drawn by the presence of Quakers because of Friends "well-deserved reputation among free blacks as a people who were far more empathetic and tolerant than most other whites."[72]

————— • —————

The westward migration left behind only a handful of Quakers in many southern places. McKiever estimated that sixteen hundred families left the South between 1800 and 1860, most from the Carolinas.[73] By 1861, 83 of the 136 meetings in North Carolina Yearly Meeting had been laid down. Virtually all Quakers left Georgia and South Carolina, and by 1845 so few Friends remained in Virginia that its yearly meeting merged with

Baltimore.[74] Quaker settlements in eastern Tennessee were also greatly diminished.[75] In Maryland the influence of Friends was also lessening as members moved west, and of those who stayed "a disproportionate number had their membership taken away for slaveholding."[76]

One exception to this population trend, however, is documented. In 1846 European Americans Lucas Gillingham and Thomas Wright from Moorestown Meeting in New Jersey began a new and "energetic" meeting in Virginia specifically to create a community in "slave country" to demonstrate that African Americans could prosper as free workers. The two bought three thousand acres for farming and associated businesses with the vision of profitable and "soul-satisfying" work. A dozen or so other Friends from New Jersey soon joined them. At their Woodlawn estate they started a meeting and a school and looked forward to more Friends coming from the North. Their dreams were interrupted, but only temporarily, by the Civil War when most took refuge in their former homes in the North.[77] The Woodlawn Meeting continues to this day as Alexandria Friends Meeting.

Charitable Assistance

Throughout this period, Quaker visiting committees continued to assess the circumstances of free people of African descent. In a detailed forty-three-page report on the lives of African Americans in the city, in 1847 the Meeting for Sufferings of Philadelphia Yearly Meeting (Orthodox) noted the obstacles confronting the bulk of that population. Few had been able to advance beyond menial work, and most lived in "shanties and damp cellars" where they often succumbed to exposure, sickness, or starvation. The meeting blamed "the evil influences of slavery" for these circumstances but nonetheless urged African Americans to take responsibility for their community's problems and "encourage their friends to persevere in their efforts to remove the distress and degradation which prevail among a portion" of them. Still, the report noted, some of "this class of our fellow-citizens" was "steadily advancing" in occupations, education, and "the feeling of self-respect," a fact that "should inspire them with hope and confidence in the future."[78]

By 1821 each yearly and quarterly meeting in the Midwest typically sponsored a "Committee on the Concerns of the People of Color," also known as "the African Committee."[79] Like those in the East and South, these committees helped identify and secure places to settle, helped African Americans find work in their new homes, advised them, and helped support those who were poor.[80] Over time they also opened schools, worked to thwart efforts to kidnap free people, and protested laws that limited the rights or even the presence of African Americans in their states.[81] As the Philadelphia committee had done, the midwestern committees were quick to report that not all free African Americans needed help. "Many of them are in good circumstances in life," Indiana Yearly Meeting minutes noted in 1857, "and fully alive to their interest in procuring an education for their children." Some who had once needed assistance later proved to be "as industrious, moral, and intelligent, and as much interested in the promotion of education and general improvement, as many white citizens."[82]

Indeed, the work of Friends took place amid considerable effort on the part of African Americans to sustain themselves in freedom. Beginning in 1830 and continuing almost every year to the Civil War, free African Americans met in national conventions to organize for abolition, plan political action to improve the lot of free African Americans, and debate issues for the future of people of African ancestry. Historian August Meier has termed the free colored convention movement "the most representative vehicle of thought among the articulate classes," both before the war and during Reconstruction.[83] In 1849, amid the debate over granting the Pennsylvania's African Americans the right to vote, that state's Convention of Colored Citizens of Pennsylvania asserted, "We are not asking the voters of Pennsylvania to elevate us. They cannot do it. All we ask of them is that they 'take their feet from off our necks' that we may stand free and erect."[84] African American activists also published prolifically—in their own and other antislavery newspapers and in books and pamphlets. Between 1827 and 1840, the number of African American newspapers quadrupled. The narratives of fugitives from enslavement, just as often pointed discussions of slavery and the right to freedom as they were tales of escape, were plentiful and highly popular.[85]

Friends were sporadically involved in some organizations initiated and run by African Americans. Moses Brown donated land for the meetinghouse and school of Providence's African Union, and several

Friends worked with African Americans Richard Allen and Absalom Jones to form the Free African Society in Philadelphia in 1787 and to assist in opening at least one school.[86] The Free African Society in that city was closely tied to Quakers. Its incorporation papers specified that the clerk and treasurer be Friends; it appointed visiting committees to "inspect the conduct of fellow city dwellers through house visits"; it adopted the Quaker practice of disownment; and in 1789 it instituted a period of silence to open its meetings. That last innovation, however, provoked Allen, a Methodist minister, to leave the society with a "large number of dissenters." Allen valued some aspects of Quakerism, but he averred that as a religious group Friends "did not seem to speak to the immediate needs of blacks."[87]

Organizing to Aid Freed People

The manumission, abolition, and later antislavery societies in several states worked to enforce state laws passed to protect freed African Americans and to revoke those that circumscribed their rights. The heavily Quaker Pennsylvania Abolition Society helped "upwards of one hundred persons" attain their liberty between 1784 and 1787 and arranged passage and helped find indentures for dozens who had been freed or who had fled to the state.[88] In the 1790s the society helped find work for newly freed people and offered "cash incentives" to help others begin businesses that would employ other African Americans.[89] In 1829, after Cincinnati officials (one of whom was European American Hicksite Friend Benjamin Hopkins) invoked the state law requiring each African American resident to post a prohibitive bond or leave within thirty days, Quakers from Indiana and Ohio Yearly Meetings interceded. As many as two thousand African American residents endured great financial hardship in the rush to sell their property. Several hundred left for Canada, while mobs stoned the houses and destroyed other property of those who remained. The two yearly meetings, according to a report in the *Friend*, raised "a considerable sum" for the relief of those affected by the law and also appealed for help from Philadelphia Yearly Meeting.[90]

Elijah Coffin, clerk of the Orthodox Indiana Yearly Meeting, represented the views of activist Quakers when that state's legislature also debated the imposition of a prohibitively high bond for all African Americans entering the state in 1831. "The negro was a stranger in our land," Coffin declared, "not of his own choice but by oppression and fraud." Ohio Friends called a similar law there "unjust and oppressive." Quakers also protested laws in Indiana and Ohio that prohibited African Americans from testifying in any court case involving people of European descent. Every few years between 1840 and 1858, Indiana and Ohio Friends petitioned their state legislatures to repeal some or all of these discriminatory laws. According to Hamm, one 1850 petition from the Congregational Friends in Dublin, Indiana, urging that the state's constitutional convention extend the franchise to African American males made "some delegates . . . almost apoplectic."[91]

In addition to their work in abolition societies in the 1820s and 1830s, Friends created a variety of benevolent institutions in the interest of assisting freed people. Philadelphia Friends in particular found that their private institutions could accomplish many things "without becoming enmeshed" in the state's secular government.[92] Philadelphia Quaker women founded the Association for the Care of Colored Orphans in 1822 for children with the "dual disadvantage" of being African American and orphaned.[93] In 1854 Orthodox Friends began the Home for the Moral Reform of Destitute Colored Children in that city, whose programs by the late 1800s centered principally on African American youth. The next year a Hicksite women's group organized the Home for the Destitute Colored Children there to provide shelter and education, primarily to boys, who after training went to live in families.[94]

In 1835 European American Quaker Anna Jenkins founded the Providence Shelter for Colored Children in Rhode Island, an organization that persisted under several names until 1949.[95] Delaware's Female Benevolent Society, founded by Friends in 1822, offered "employment to such as might be able to work." The women bought flax, organized spinning classes, and solicited purchasers for the goods their clients produced. They also attended to such health issues as smallpox inoculations.[96] The organizations Friends founded to work for the welfare of African Americans rarely admitted people of African descent as members. These charitable groups operated in a time when the "[ill] feeling against Negroes" was so strong that at least one Philadelphia

Quaker group working among people of African descent "had to wrap its [organizing] efforts in secrecy."[97]

———————•———————

Several other types of Quaker involvement with people of African descent were, in effect, foreign missions. One supported settlements of fugitives in Canada, where enslavement had been illegal since 1834. Among the first arrivals in Canada in the early 1830s were between 150 and 200 people of African descent fleeing the repressive climate in Cincinnati. Friends, particularly in the Midwest, were among those who raised funds to help fund their trip and to purchase land for their settlement, named Wilberforce in honor of William Wilberforce, the British abolitionist.[98] Three thousand people had been expected to move to the settlement from Cincinnati, but in the end less than half that number went, and not all to Wilberforce.[99] Nevertheless, faced with the greater danger that the 1850 Fugitive Slave Act created and the denial of their rights in the Dred Scott case of 1857, African Americans increased their migration to Canada.[100] An estimated fifteen thousand crossed the border in the 1850s.[101]

Of the communities in Ontario (then Canada West) to which they fled, the Dawn settlement near Chatham was the best known. European American Quaker philanthropist James Fuller of Skaneateles, New York, was the primary fund raiser and financier of the settlement. He traveled to his native England to solicit funds to buy land for the settlement and create a manual labor school known as the Dawn Institute.[102] By 1850 Dawn was one of at least seventeen such settlements in Canada.[103] European American Quakers in New York and Genesee Yearly Meeting (Western New York and Upper Canada Hicksite Meetings) raised money and sent goods to help the new settlers, who often arrived with only the clothes on their backs.[104]

Quakers and African American Education

Within the range of their work with African Americans, many Friends recognized that education was the primary, if not the only way that newly freed people might "negotiate the perilous waters between bondage and freedom."[105] The need was great. In the 1840s only one-third of

African Americans in the North could read, and less than one hundred students of African descent were enrolled in American high schools or colleges.[106] Quaker support of the educational needs of African Americans took four principal forms: creating schools specifically for African American children and adults; supporting schools that African Americans themselves founded and operated; admitting African American students to Quaker schools; and, as time went on, creating schools that admitted students regardless of race.

In colonial times most of Philadelphia's schools, Quaker or not, were segregated, but Anthony Benezet began a school in his home in 1750 in which Quaker children were taught during the day and African American students were taught the same subjects in the evening. In 1770 Benezet gained Philadelphia Monthly Meeting's assent to found the Quaker African School.[107] An unidentified Friend left a large part of his fortune to the school, and the bequests of European American Philadelphia Friends Daniel Stanton and Joseph Hilburn allowed the construction of a brick building on Walnut Street. London Friends also contributed, as did African American Thomas Shirley.[108] Benezet undertook most of the work for the school—raising funds, supervising construction, hiring teachers, and assuming teaching responsibilities when staff was short. In 1775, when enrollment had dropped, the meeting allowed six children of European descent from poor families to attend the school, which then had forty African American students. Still, funds for the school eventually ran low; as a consequence Benezet resumed teaching African Americans in his own home.[109] When he died in 1784, he left the rental income from a property he owned to support a school for "negro, mulatto, or Indian children" and to hire and employ a religious-minded person or persons to teach them "to read, write, [do] arithmetic, plain accounts, needle-work, etc." With Benezet's endowment, Quakers and non-Quakers under the oversight of the monthly meeting founded the Benezet School, renamed the School for Black People and Their Descendants (in 1795). A new building on Raspberry Street was opened in 1844, and between that year and 1866 eight thousand children attended. It continued as a school and then as a settlement house until 1917 when it merged with other schools Friends had established for African Americans; as contributions from Friends were "dwindling," the Quaker connection ended in 1935.[110]

Benezet's work in African American education presented a "frontal challenge to the deeply rooted belief in black inferiority."[111] Benezet, with others both Quaker and non-Quaker, believed that any difficulties African Americans might experience in schooling were not inborn but resulted from years of enslavement.[112] "The notion that the blacks are inferior in their capacity is a vulgar prejudice," he wrote, "founded on the pride and ignorance of their lordly masters, who have kept their slaves at such a distance, as to be unable to form a right judgment of them."[113] To doubters, Benezet pointed out that enslaved people had in fact been supporting their enslavers for years.[114] His African American students, he wrote, possessed "as great a variety of talents as amongst a like number of whites."[115]

Benezet's was the only one of sixteen Quaker "charity schools" in Philadelphia specifically for African Americans.[116] The Overseers of the Friends Public School, to which Benezet was named in 1756, had organized these schools to educate children of the poor; they were the forerunners of the city's public school system, instituted in the 1830s. Friends looked to Benezet to handle the thorny task of educating African Americans. His fellow overseers did little more than confirm their support of his work; Kashatus asserts that, like most Philadelphia Quakers, the overseers "were probably grateful to him for accepting the task of educating blacks, something they did not much relish confronting themselves."[117]

African Americans who either belonged to or were closely associated with the Society of Friends also created several schools. The Afro-Indian Quaker Paul Cuffe created the first school in Westport, Massachusetts, in 1797 for all of the village's children.[118] In either 1799 or 1803, Cyrus Bustill, who attended Philadelphia's Arch Street Meeting, opened a school in his home at Third and Green Streets in that city.[119]

In the early years of the Republic, Friends opened other schools for people of African descent through their meetings or other associations. In 1787 the Quaker-led New York Manumission Society opened the African Free School on Mulberry Street in New York City; a decade later 182 students were enrolled there. European American Quaker John Murray, Jr. was the chief financier of its second schoolhouse, built in 1820; in 1846 the free school became one of the city's public schools.[120] Also significant in New York during this period were the efforts of the Charity Society, founded by thirty members of the Jericho and Westbury Monthly Meetings on Long Island in 1794. Described as "An Institution for the Use and Benefit of the Poor Among the Black People," education was to be the focus of this, one of the longest-lasting Quaker charitable organization, that remains to this day.[121] The Society, of which Elias Hicks was a founder, looked forward to the time "when this oppressed [people] . . . will be permitted to enjoy equal privileges of their fellow man," a goal which would be promoted by education. From 1794 through 1868, when New York public schools admitted African Americans, the Charity Society raised money to support schools in several nearby communities, even as attendance fluctuated considerably. After 1868, the Society donated to several Quaker-founded freedmen's schools, including the Schofield and Laing Schools in South Carolina; in the 1900s the Society supported scholarships enabling African Americans to attend local Quaker schools.[122]

———•———

Notable in nineteenth-century Philadelphia was the establishment in 1837 of the Institute for Colored Youth (initially the African Institute). Founded with a bequest from European American Quaker silversmith Richard Humphreys, it was the longest-lived of Quaker schools for African Americans in the city. At a time when African Americans were not admitted to Philadelphia public schools, Humphrey's will left funds specifically to train "descendants of the African race" to work in useful trades and to teach school.[123] The first school was located on a 136-acre farm seven miles from the city. When financial trouble brought an end to classes, students, who were left to do farm work at the facility rebelled, some by running away, others apparently by setting fire to the barn.[124]

The relative merits of manual and intellectual training among African Americans had long been debated within their own community. At free colored conventions and elsewhere, African Americans had argued that vocational training was the most expedient means by which they might escape the service trades and achieve some parity in the American economy. The 1853 national convention criticized education that created individuals who were "literary flowers," but trained for no useful work. Others, however, countered that the sole focus on manual training would foreclose any real possibility of social and economic mobility. Historian Roger Lane is clear that "Blacks were enthusiastic about their own visions of industrial education, but these visions did not involve education in cooking and sewing from the first grade onward, with the implication that their children were doomed to a life in domestic service, incapable from the very beginning of mastering an academic curriculum."[125]

In 1846, the Institute for Colored Youth closed after the students protested the end of the classes. Reopening in South Philadelphia in 1849, it implemented a new model for instruction proposed by a group of African American artisans. The Institute offered day classes in the trades and an evening school for academic subjects, both taught by African American faculty; its Quaker managers also turned over hiring and oversight of the school's operation to the artisan group.[126]

By 1852, when the Institute moved to a new building at Seventh and Lombard Streets, it had added a day school with a full academic curriculum. The revived school's first principal was the later-renowned African American educator Charles L. Reason, and its first teacher was African American Grace A. Mapps, the daughter of David and Grace Mapps of Little Egg Harbor Meeting in New Jersey. Mapps graduated from New York Central College in McGrawville, New York, founded in 1848 and one of the nation's first integrated colleges.[127] In 1853 she became the principal of the Girls' Department at the institute, a position she held until 1864. Sarah Mapps Douglass, who was related to Grace Mapps by marriage, ran the Institute's Preparatory Department from 1852 to 1877.[128]

A second important educational institution started by Quakers in Philadelphia in the 1850s was the Bethany Mission, founded to offer "moral and religious education," as well as provide for the "general elevation of the colored people." Bethany was not sponsored by a Quaker meeting but by individual Friends and others.[129] It was one of the so-called "Sabbath" schools opened by lay people of many denominations in the mid-1800s. "Sabbath" refers to the only day of the week when its students were free to attend. Without teaching a particular denomination's beliefs, its teachers were committed to imparting Christian values to the students.

Although the school was essentially ecumenical, the longest-serving (1860–1935) and most influential superintendent was European American Friend, Marcellus Balderson. The school welcomed both Hicksite and Orthodox teachers, as well as members of Protestant churches. Bethany enrolled as many as four hundred students in the 1870s and 1880s but the numbers began to decline. By the 1930s, as Grundy described it, the school was "an anachronism, a white-run mission to a diminishing black clientele." It was laid down in 1936 after eighty years of serving African Americans and offering Friends a way to contribute to the lives of people of African descent.[130]

A school for African American young women started in Connecticut in 1833 by European American Prudence Crandall (1803–90) left little doubt that prejudice was not only a southern phenomenon. Crandall was born and raised a Quaker and educated at the New England Yearly Meeting Boarding School in Providence, where she could have learned of Friends' earlier anti-enslavement activities. While Crandall had begun attending Baptist services by the time she went to Connecticut, those who knew her said that due to her Quaker upbringing she remained "resolved and tranquil" throughout the trials to come.[131] In the fall of 1832 Crandall opened an academy for young women in Canterbury. When she admitted African American Sarah Harris from nearby Norwich, parents promptly withdrew their daughters. Crandall then decided to create a school only for African American women and sought the assistance of abolitionist William Lloyd Garrison and others in identifying African American families from Boston, New York, and Philadelphia who could afford a private education. In the spring of 1833 twenty young women of African descent arrived at the new boarding school.[132]

Alarmed by the presence of the school's new students, people in the area agreed with the resident who predicted in a letter to the *Norwich Courier* that "New England would become the Liberia of America."[133]The students were shunned by the people of the village (except for the nearby Black Hill Friends Meeting), and Crandall was excoriated at community meetings. Local people began to damage Crandall's building and even dumped manure down the well. Opponents seeking to close the school won the day in May 1834 when the state legislature voted to prohibit the creation of "any school, academy, or literary institution for the instruction or education of colored persons who are not inhabitants of this State."[134] Crandall continued as long as she could with an enrollment as high as twenty, but when citizen mobs attempted to set the school on fire, she felt unable to protect the students and closed the school. She married European American Baptist minister Calvin Phileo, who had supported her through the court proceedings, and moved with him to Illinois, where they ran the Phileo Academy for students of African descent in their home.[135] More than a half-century later, the state of Connecticut publicly apologized to Crandall; the prohibitive law was rescinded in 1838.[136] Albeit a short-lived episode, Crandall's attempt served to reveal the face of racism in the North and gave Quaker women abolitionists their "first hero and martyr."[137]

Friends in the South also involved themselves in the creation of schools for African Americans in their region. In 1782, the year he decided to free the seventy-eight people he enslaved upon his death, Robert Pleasants proposed the creation of a school to educate formerly enslaved people and prepare them for freedom. At his death in 1801, Pleasants left 350 acres of his land near Richmond, Virginia, to these freed people and arranged for a schoolhouse to be built there. Virginia Yearly Meeting arranged for White Oak Swamp Meeting to run the school under a trustee system. The school, called Gravelly Hill, operated until 1824.[138] In the 1830s European American Margaret Crew kept an illegal school for enslaved children at Shrubbery Hill in Hanover County, Virginia, and in 1820 a Quaker couple in Richmond spent time in jail for admitting a few enslaved children into their school.[139] In North Carolina, a number of monthly meetings opened schools for African Americans in the early 1800s; their fates are unclear. In New Garden, the Sunday School started by Levi Coffin and Vestal Coffin was short-lived, closed by European American neighbors who feared the growth of literacy among enslaved people.[140]

In Baltimore, Elisha Tyson and his brother Jesse donated a building on Sharp Street in 1792 for a school for free children of African descent. The school was run by the city's abolition society, whose membership was largely Quaker. Two years later the Baltimore Monthly Meeting opened its own school "for the benefit of Black children of free parents." It must, however, have been short-lived: in 1796 the women's meeting of the monthly meeting minuted that it was "deeply exercised after the neglected situation of the black people," especially with respect to their education. In the absence of a meeting school, several members taught private "mixed schools," according to one 1802 report.[141] In Wilmington, Delaware, Thomas Garrett purchased and donated land for a school for African American children in 1857 and paid for the construction of its building as well. This school was one of two that Friends supported in that city, and Wilmington Friends Meeting was an active backer of one of them.[142] Substantial funding from one Friend underwrote the Normal School for Colored Girls in the District of Columbia in 1851. European American Quaker Johns Hopkins was a trustee, and European American Friend Emily Howland served as an administrator for a short time.[143] In Maryland, Rebecca Morgan Tylor, a woman of European descent in Tuckahoe Neck Meeting, conducted a school for African American children in her home in 1858 despite warnings that it would be closed "if not by fair means [then by] foul."[144]

———————•———————

Midwestern Friends, particularly in Indiana, were also active in the educational efforts. Indiana Quakers appealed to the state to pay for separate schools for African American children; when the state failed to do so, they donated substantial time and money for private schools.[145] Typically Friends there helped pay for books and teachers in schools controlled by African Americans. The Anti-Slavery Friends Yearly Meeting hoped that young Friends might "upon calm reflection" devote "at least three months of their lives to the promotion of education amongst this people." In contrast to most Quaker-run schools for students of African descent in the East, teachers in the Midwest were most often African American, some of them ministers of other faiths.[146]

In 1828, after the Hicksite-Orthodox separation, Indiana Friends created parallel monthly meeting schools and a yearly meeting boarding school for African Americans. By 1851 the Orthodox Indiana Yearly Meeting supported twenty-one day schools.[147] Together with Indiana Yearly Meeting of Anti-Slavery Friends, the two meetings taught more than seven hundred children by 1860.[148] The 1857 African Committee report to the Indiana Hicksite Yearly Meeting described good progress on the children's part and noted that it had begun nine first-day schools "for scriptural instruction" of both children and adults.[149] In 1861 about three hundred students attended Quaker-sponsored schools in the area of Blue River Meeting, near Salem, Indiana, where Friends had helped rebuild a burned African American school and meetinghouse.[150]

In 1838 a bequest of twenty thousand dollars from European American Philadelphia Friend Samuel Emlen, Jr. funded what became the Emlen Institute (also known as Carthagena) in Mercer County, Ohio.[151] Founded by European American Augustus Wattles, who was not a Quaker, the school offered instruction "in school learning and in agriculture and mechanical trades or arts" for "free male orphan children of African or Indian descent." Wattles had acquired the land for the school from African Americans. Supported in part by Emlen's home meeting in Burlington, New Jersey, Emlen Institute remained in operation in Ohio for almost two decades, but it moved to Pennsylvania when people of European descent vehemently opposed the planned settlement near the school of about five hundred freed African Americans from Virginia. In 1857 the Institute moved to Bucks County and eventually to Warminster Township.[152]

Quakers and Integrated Schools

Just as both European and African Americans had debated the relative merits of manual and liberal arts education, they fiercely debated the virtues of integrated education. A significant body of African Americans opposed integration on the grounds that their children received far fewer resources and far less attention in integrated schools; the 1853 Colored National Convention advised segregated education as a way to "catch up in the great race we are running."[153] Conversely, African Americans such as William C. Nell maintained that only through integration could the races come to learn about and respect each other. Nell's fifteen-year campaign to desegregate Boston public schools finally succeeded in 1855.[154] In the 1840s on Nantucket, African American Edward Pompey, secretary of the island's antislavery society and an agent for the *Liberator*, led a successful effort to integrate the town's high school. Some, though not all, Quakers there supported his work. Friend Anna Gardner, the school's European American teacher, was one of the chief supporters of local integration. After seven years of petitioning, boycotting, lawsuits, and debates in both the newspapers and town meetings, Nantucketers elected a new school committee and the schools were integrated.[155] In Bristol, Pennsylvania, in the 1850s and 1860s African American students were admitted and "shared equally the opportunities of" [a] "very successful private school" run by Friends, including the European American sisters Ruth, Anne, Sarah, and Fanny Peirce. A "Miss Buffum" accepted African Americans into her private school in Philadelphia, as did a school run by Pine Street meeting about 1830 and the Darlington Academy in West Chester.[156]

———•———

In the Midwest, Quakers either founded or financed the creation of several integrated schools. In 1837 European American Friends Laura Smith Haviland and Charles Haviland, her husband, created the Raisin Valley Institute in Raisin Township, Michigan, to "educate people of every race." Two other integrated schools were funded by an endowment of forty thousand dollars left by European American Quaker entrepreneur Josiah White in 1850, one east of the Mississippi at Wabash, Indiana,[157] and the other west of the river, at Quakerdale in Iowa. Initially designed to teach girls housework and boys farming, in the first through eighth grades, White's Iowa Manual Labor Institute eventually included a high school curriculum in technical training. Now named Quakerdale, the Iowa program is a not-for profit social service agency for children and families, owned by Iowa Yearly Meeting.[158] The legacy continues in Indiana as White's Residential & Family Services.

Dr. Jesse Harvey admitted African American students to his academy in Harveysburg, Ohio, in 1837 but schooled them in separate classes. Protests from abolitionists compelled him to integrate the school for a time. However, when European American parents withdrew their children, causing financial problems, Harvey re-segregated students, but in separate departments. Nonetheless, the school is considered to have been the first African American school in the Northwest Territory.[159]

In 1845 African Americans and Friends, primarily from the Indiana Yearly Meeting of Anti-Slavery Friends, founded Union Literary Institute in Spartanburg, Indiana.[160] The school was to evidence "no distinction in its management or advantages on account of color, rank or wealth" and to teach "the principles of the Bible as against slavery and war."161 While it was integrated, Union Literary Institute was particularly invested in African American education. The school's director, Samuel Smothers, was African American, as were some of its trustees. Designed for first through eighth graders, the Institute required students to work four hours a day to pay for their room, board, and laundry; they spent evenings in the classroom.162 Of the 230 students in 1849, more than 70 percent were African American. Union Literary became an integrated boarding school in that year, and by 1863 probably all of its students were African American. Enrollment declined after the Civil War when the state's public schools were integrated.163

Integration in Quaker Schools

The willingness to further racial equity by establishing and managing African American and integrated schools was rarely duplicated in the schools Quakers established for their own children.164 One exception was the Friends school in New Bedford, Massachusetts, which by 1810 admitted African American children "on terms of perfect equality," notes European American abolitionist Deborah Weston;165 that school was apparently unique in the yearly meeting. While New England Friends did work to open public schools to children of any race and to organize private schools for African American children and adults, there is no evidence that any other Quaker schools were open to African Americans, even in Rhode Island, home to a large number of both Quakers and Africans Americans. That includes the Yearly Meeting Boarding School (to be named after donor Moses Brown) which re-opened in Providence in 1819 after operating a few years in Portsmouth166 and the numerous local schools run by Friends meetings throughout the 1700 and 1800s (and in a few cases the 1900s, most in Rhode Island, a few in Massachusetts, Maine, and New Hampshire.)167

Some isolated efforts for integration failed. In the 1840s and 1850s, Sarah Grimké and Elizabeth Buffum Chace tried with no success to enroll African American students in Providence and Philadelphia,168 and during the Civil War the yearly meeting school in Providence refused to admit the motherless children of a highly respected African American physician from Boston who was going to New Orleans to do relief work. Despite Chace's urgings that Friends demonstrate their commitment to the freedmen by enrolling these children, the school committee declared that it was not yet time—even though by then Rhode Island's public schools were integrated, as were those in Massachusetts.[169] New England Friends were generous and consistent donors when it came to restoring Quaker education in North Carolina or providing schools for the freed people in the South. Annual donations went, sometimes for decades, to a number of southern schools for African Americans, but the major focus of the New England Yearly Meeting was on freedmen's schools in Washington, D.C., especially in teacher training, and on the Normal Institute at Maryville, Tennessee, for which the meeting bore full responsibility from 1875 to 1905.[170]

African American abolitionist and fugitive Samuel Ringgold Ward, who preached to white and mixed congregations in Upstate New York, noted the general anomaly in Quaker practice when he wrote in 1855, "They will give us good advice. They will aid in giving us a partial education but never in a Quaker school, beside their own children. Whatever they do for us savors of pity, and is done at arm's length."[171] Still, exceptions did exist. While known instances were mostly in the Midwest, students of African descent also occasionally attended Quaker schools in Maryland, New Jersey, Philadelphia, and Virginia.[172] Students of both races attended Uriah Brown's school in Baltimore, next to the East Land Meetinghouse; the school's register for 1801 lists the names of several Friends who paid the tuition for students noted as "Negro."[173] In New Jersey, a Friends school in Lower Alloways Creek in Salem County, New Jersey, had five children of African descent among its student body of fifty-two in 1858. African Americans also attended Hicksite schools in Moorestown, Westfield, Haddonfield, and Chester in the 1840s or 1850s.[174] Among such schools the pattern of accepting the occasional few continued until the Civil War.[175]

In the Midwest, admitting African Americans into Quaker schools appears to have been somewhat more common.[176] Friends in this region "systematically and repeatedly condemned manifestations of racial prejudice" and did not segregate "their schools, their meetinghouses, or their graveyards." An 1850 English visitor noted a "number" of children of African descent in Friends schools in Indiana.[177] Friend Sarah Newby stated that there were "some and often several colored children in attendance" at the school in Carthage, Indiana, near the Beech settlement, and that other Friends covered their tuition if their parents were unable to pay it.[178] By 1852 at least eighty African American children were enrolled in Friends schools in Indiana; twenty-six attended Quaker schools in Indiana Western Yearly Meeting. For students who needed assistance, Friends purchased "many small items, such as books, clothing," and paid their tuition.[179] Dr. Jesse Harvey's decision not to admit African Americans to his Ohio academy, which was not under the care of the yearly meeting, provoked "such intense criticism from local abolitionists" that the school was opened to all, but not even the most radical of Friends in Indiana accused other Friends of purposely keeping the children of the races separate.[180]

Benevolence and Paternalism

Quaker involvement in charitable and educational efforts among African Americans sprang from many impulses. One was the need to reestablish some level of authority in a society from which they had largely withdrawn by the early 1800s. In Pennsylvania, Quakers turned "to true charity" after they removed themselves from the colonial government in the mid-1700s. In creating their own benevolent societies, Sydney James has suggested, Friends saw an opportunity to restore their standing in the community and regain some influence in public affairs.[181] Another historian questions James's interpretation and offers his own: the new work also grew out of Quaker beliefs.[182] Marietta asserts that Friends did not view good works as a way to "ingratiate themselves." If their motive had been to establish an association with "respectable non-Quakers," for example, their abolition societies would not have been as effective.[183]

———————•———————

Related to a possible need to retain authority was the perception, common to American elites and members of the middle classes, that ethnic and racial minorities had somehow to be managed or controlled to avert the possibility of mass disorder, violence, or even class-based revolution. David Brion Davis suggests in this connection a dual motivation among urban Friends in their benevolent work. One was to protect the city from "disease and disorder" so as to preserve the existing social and economic system; the second was to "inculcate the lower classes with various moral and economic virtues," to transform them into obedient, industrious, and efficient laborers.[184] In Indiana, for example, the yearly meeting urged its members to promote "temperance, morality, and religion" among African Americans and "to endeavor to prevent, as far as practicable, their association with persons of dissolute and immoral habits."[185] Historian Michael Katz has argued that Friends were active in public education as a means of exerting social control over people whom they viewed as lesser than they and whose continuing poverty presented a danger to the status quo.[186] The Friends who dominated New York's Manumission Society sought to keep African American children from taking on "the vices their parents acquired in slavery."[187] In Indiana "even the most active members of the Standing Committees considered their efforts a heavy burden and expressed grave reservations about the very people they were attempting to befriend."[188] Such paternalism was a hallmark of all societies dealing with people of African descent.[189] According to Margaret Hope Bacon, all Quaker benevolent activity among African Americans in the antebellum era carried with it "a strong element of condescension."[190]

Such leanings might explain, in part, the attraction of Friends to the instructional program devised by British Quaker Joseph Lancaster in the 1820s. The Lancastrian model was designed to instill the traditional virtues of thrift, obedience, promptness, and competition efficiently and cost-effectively in large groups of students. The system was widely believed to be a "deterrent to crime and other social vices;" it emphasized inner motivation and was based on reward more than punishment.[191] Used in Friends and other schools in England, the Lancastrian model soon spread to the United States and was used in Quaker charity schools when they were first opened to African Americans, including Baltimore's free school built in 1822 by Quaker philanthropist John McKim for children of the poor[192] and the Quaker-led New York Manumission Society's school for people of African ancestry. Public schools in Philadelphia and other cities in New England and the Midwest also adopted the Lancastrian model.[193]

The Orthodox Quaker managers of Philadelphia's Institute for Colored Youth were certainly ambivalent about the capacities of the school's students and staff. On the one hand, they faithfully supported the school financially and lauded its accomplishments in annual reports. Yet they had trouble turning control over to the African American staff and failed to hire any of the school's graduates in their own businesses. Even as they supported new construction and additional staff for the institute in the 1860s, they viewed the school as an "experiment" to test the question of whether students of African descent could succeed in subjects that "required close study, deep thinking and thorough instruction."[194] They had turned over hiring and instruction to African Americans, but they still approved textbooks, library books, and new courses, prepared examinations with the principal, and disciplined errant students. Despite the African Americans' support for drawing and music, the managers, in keeping with the general practice in Quaker schools, refused to permit their instruction. Nash viewed the Quaker effort at the institute as a missed opportunity to promote "black efforts to change the views of a prejudiced society."[195] Yet the Quaker managers seemed unable to envision themselves in such a role.[196]

Such an attitude was apparent in the failure of Friends organizations to consult with leaders of the growing and vibrant African American urban communities, which were developing their own educational and benevolent organizations toward the same ends, about the direction their work should take. This lapse is apparent in the response of African Americans to some efforts Friends made, ostensibly in their behalf. Nash has noted that African Americans "often begrudged the moral guardianship that Friends thought themselves obliged to extend," as Richard Allen indicated when he wrote years before that Quakers did not seem attuned to their "immediate needs." The aims of African Americans may not have differed greatly from European Americans invested in these enterprises: Allen, Cyrus Bustill, and Absalom Jones, among other leaders, consistently stressed the importance of good work habits as key to establishing a secure place in the American economy. Yet Quakers and others for the most part were probably unaware of such similarities, heedless as they were of the need and value of broader racial collaboration. Most African Americans kept contrary views to themselves because "they could hardly afford to express this resentment for Quakers were their best allies in an otherwise indifferent, if not hostile, world."[197]

Another motive undoubtedly existed in this work: the genuine moral compunction to do good works for the sake of equality. Kashatus concluded from his work on Philadelphia that Friends were "much more genuine" than Katz and Davis had suggested. Deeply affected by the difficulties they endured because of their peace testimony, Friends acted out of "their common belief that Christ had admonished all true Christians to care for their less fortunate brothers," he has asserted. Such Quakers felt compelled to do what they could to better the lives of others "simply because they had the means—financial resources, wisdom, experience and connections—to do so." But Kashatus has also stated that Quakers, as others, viewed the work in part as "moral uplift of the poor" and, though "not a matter of condescension," it did reflect "a matter of economic necessity and crime control." Bacon, too, has noted that Quakers generally deserve more credit for the underlying religious and humanitarian motives of their benevolent effort.[198] Historian Carleton Mabee agreed, but in a qualified manner: Friends, he has stated, worked "quietly and steadily, if not very far" in realizing a more just social world.[199] Still, the move from working within their own society to engaging with the rest of the world was "a step of the greatest importance to the future of the organizational life of Friends."[200] The Society of Friends was becoming "a society to do good for all mankind, not solely for its own members."[201]

CALVIN CLARK 1864 to 1886 ALIDA CLARK
Founders of Southland College

Calvin and Alida Clark, Founders of Southland College, 1864–86.

Laing School, Mt. Pleasant, South Carolina, founded about 1866, and supported chiefly by Friends. The teacher at the left is believed to be Robert Purves.

Students at the Laing School, Mt. Pleasant, South Carolina. The teacher at left is believed to be Robert Purvis.

CHAPTER FIVE

The Civil War and Its Failed Reconstruction

If emancipation is only a byproduct of saving the Union, the hate of the colored race will still continue, and the poison of that wickedness will destroy us as a nation.

— Quaker abolitionist Abby Kelley Foster, 1862

FOR QUAKERS, the years preceding the South's secession from the Union were marked by an oppressive fear of war. With the outbreak of hostilities, many Friends lost hope for the peaceful end to enslavement for which they had been praying and working. In the North and South, Friends were harassed for their refusal to support war, yet their spiritual and emotional resources were called upon soon after the fighting began, and Quakers became involved in efforts to provide for the immediate needs of newly freed people. By the end of the war, the steady stream of relief goods and teachers to open schools had become a river, if not a flood. Inadequate and sometimes misguided government assistance, coupled with European Americans' unrealistic expectations of formerly enslaved people, combined to hamper the benevolent postwar efforts of Quakers and others who offered aid. In the end African Americans were left, north and south, to lives tightly circumscribed by persistent racism.

Portents of War

John Brown's 1859 raid on Harper's Ferry is considered by some historians to be the beginning of the Civil War. It exacerbated regional tensions and sharpened the moral dilemma confronting Friends who prayed for a peaceful resolution. Brown had come to believe that force was the only way to "convince and convert" enslavers, and, with financial and moral support from some abolitionists, he set out to create an independent biracial republic as the base for guerilla warfare against enslavers. The raid on the arsenal at Harper's Ferry aimed to procure arms. Brown invited the European American Quaker brothers Barclay and Edwin Coppoc into his troop when it was training in their predominantly Quaker hometown of Springdale, Iowa.[1] Then twenty and twenty-four years old, respectively, the brothers were known for having "developed wayward" early in life; Edwin had been disowned when he "took to dancing" in 1857.[2] Despite their meeting's attempt to dissuade them, the brothers joined Brown.[3] Ten of Brown's company of twenty-two were killed during the raid, including African Americans Dangerfield Newby and Lewis S. Leary. Among the seven captured were Edwin Coppoc and Brown. Barclay and four other men escaped and were never taken.[4] Barclay Coppoc returned to a "warm reception" in Springdale but then left for Canada to avoid arrest.[5] Edwin Coppoc was tried and hanged for his part in the raid. In his last letters he wrote that he did not fear the scaffold, "for I honestly believe I am innocent of any crime justifying punishment."[6] His brother later returned to Springdale, but his meeting made note of his absence from worship and his "practice of bearing arms." After he was extended "the usual care, but with no avail," Barclay Coppoc was disowned in 1860.[7]

Not all, or perhaps even many, Friends supported John Brown's actions. Before the raid, David Gue and two other unidentified European American members of the Coppocs' Springdale Meeting sent an anonymous letter to Secretary of War John Floyd to report on the group's secret training and plans to attack Harper's Ferry, but Floyd put no credence in the warning.[8] The *Friends Review* expressed concern that the raid would make it impossible for southerners to hear "the pleadings of their conscience" against enslavement.[9] Other Friends disagreed with Brown's violent approach but sympathized with his aim. Lucretia Mott, for example, hosted Brown's wife during his trial and offered "what spiritual solace she could."[10] In a letter to Brown while he was in jail, Elizabeth Buffum Chace wrote, "Very many Friends love thee with all their hearts for thy brave efforts on behalf of the poor oppressed; and though we . . . believe it better to reform by moral and not by carnal weapons, yet we openly approve thy intentions, though many Friends would not think it right to take up arms." Brown replied, "May the Lord reward you a thousand times for the kind feeling you express. . . . I always loved my Quaker friends, and I will commend to their kind regard my poor, bereaved, widowed wife."[11]

Abolitionists, who had struggled for decades against enslavement, had to confront the fact that now four hundred thousand more people were enslaved than when they started their movement, and they began to lose faith that "moral suasion" would ever succeed in ending the institution.[12] Even nonresistants were losing patience. "We may as well disband at once, if we never do anything *but talk*." said European American Anne Greene Phillips, wife of well-known Boston abolition- ist Wendell Phillips.[13] Similarly, some Friends, aware that "obstacles to effective Quaker action [against enslavement] seemed insurmountable," as Drake puts it, began to sanction the use of force; at least a few saw the Harper's Ferry raid as a heroic statement against the South and enslavement. Abby Kelley Foster did not hesitate to wish success to any enslaved people who chose to revolt.[14] Even those who did not accept Brown's use of force, including Garrison, were still willing to endorse the right of the enslaved people to revolt.[15] After Brown's raid, Frederick Douglass, who initially supported only nonviolence, began to speak differently. Because force is what made enslavement possible, he declared, force would likely be needed to bring it to an end.[16]

The Peace Testimony in Time of War

As war approached, the peace testimony of the Religious Society of Friends faced a serious challenge. The question of whether war could be justified as the means of ending enslavement was a crucial one and, even as they objected to war in principle, Friends views on this war ranged widely. Some actively supported disunion, the idea that the South leave the Union to be a separate country and take the institution of enslavement with it. Others welcomed the coming conflict as the only way to resolve the issue; the ends would justify the means, even violent means. Still others believed that the war could have no positive outcome; violence begets violence, they held, and one evil cannot be used to end another. Some Friends believed that a forced victory could not be a true one because it would not change southern attitudes and that, rather than bringing justice to the African American, war would only provoke anger and fear among European American southerners.

Some correctly predicted that if the country relied on military power to protect the rights of the newly freed, in the end that power would not be sufficient.[17] The "great object" for Quakers, stated the editor of *The Friend*, "should ever be to convince and convert the slaveholders."[18]

Still, many and perhaps even the majority of Quakers agreed with the view of the Progressive Friends who condemned war as evil, yet still praised it as the destroyer of greater evils.[19] Sarah Grimké, by then no longer a Quaker, called the war "the holiest ever waged." Certainly northern Friends were relieved when the war ended and the Union had won. Quaker abolitionist poet John Greenleaf Whittier was one of many who had prayed for peace before the war—but rejoiced when it was over because it ended enslavement.[20]

Friends had taken their concerns about slavery and the approaching war to the highest levels of government. During the early years of the war, as President Abraham Lincoln struggled to formulate laws that would address slavery and keep peace in the North, European American Friends Sarah and Isaac Harvey of Ohio met with the President to urge immediate emancipation. Longwood Progressive Friends met with Lincoln to urge the same. "God's way of accomplishing the end you have in view may be different from yours," Lincoln told them. "It is my earnest endeavor, seeking light from above, to do my duty in the place to which I have been called."[21]

Reaction to Lincoln's earliest proclamation in September, 1862, which freed all the enslaved people in those Confederate states that did not return to the Union by January 1, 1863, brought this reaction from Whittier: "We may well thank God and congratulate one another on the prospect of the speedy emancipation of the slaves." Other Friends felt differently. Abby Kelley Foster warned that emancipation motivated by the desire to strengthen the Union Army only exacerbated the terrible southern animosity toward people of African descent and castigated abolitionists for seeming more interested in preserving the Union than working for the rights of the enslaved. Many Friends meetings also stated their objection to recruiting formerly enslaved men into the army on the grounds of their being "a peaceable people and unwilling to engage in war."[22]

After the passage of the First Conscription Act in March 1863, a delegation from all Orthodox yearly meetings except Philadelphia visited Secretary of War Edward M. Stanton hoping to persuade him to exempt Quakers from the draft.[23] Although full exemption was denied, a compromise allowed the money paid by Friends for an exemption to go to nonmilitary uses and those who refused to pay to be assigned to noncombatant positions. However, many Friends argued that paying such a fee, set by the government at three hundred dollars, was merely another form of support for war. When Friends persuaded Congress to allow members of "nonresistant" denominations to be assigned substitute jobs, such as in hospitals, Friends also debated whether that alternative service was consistent with the peace testimony, especially since those who recovered could return to the fighting.[24] Southern Friends also sought exemption from the draft.[25]

The yearly meetings uniformly maintained that enlistment was not justifiable, no matter how worthy the cause. In Virginia, Goose Creek Meeting stated in 1861 that its members would "abstain from every act that would give aid" to the war effort. In 1863 members of the Orthodox New York Yearly Meeting explained that its members' refusal to pay war taxes was "not to embarrass government" but was a witness against war. The meeting said it would not "do or say anything calculated, even remotely, to identify our members" with the "unscrupulous" rebels attempting to "rivet the chains of slavery in this land."[26]

Records indicate that many Friends remained faithful to their peace testimony. "A sizeable majority" of the two Philadelphia Yearly Meetings adhered to the testimony.[27] Still, some Quakers were drafted despite their appeals to various officials. The diary of one such Friend, European American Cyrus Pringle of Vermont, recounted his trials trying to convince his superiors that he would not fight. Although some were sympathetic to his stand for a time, in the end he was subjected to abuse, physical and emotional.[28] In Kansas, admitted to the Union as a free state in January 1861, tensions ran high. The lives of Friends who had moved to Kansas to help assure it would keep its free-state status had been so threatened by supporters of slavery that one Quaker pastor suggested "it would have taken superhuman qualities . . . to keep all their young men from participation." Meeting minutes showed that efforts to keep members from the fight "were not entirely successful," but most of the young men in Kansas held true to their Quaker pacifism.[29]

Many non-Quakers declared eligible for service also resisted the draft. Among them were those who were rankled about being compelled to fight to free the enslaved, the very people who would come north after the war and compete with them for work.[30] Hostility toward conscription erupted in draft riots in a number of cities in 1863, the most notable in New York City in July. Quakers were among the targets. A large mob attacked the homes of African Americans and the Quaker-supported Colored Orphan Asylum. At the asylum, 233 children were playing or sick in bed when, according to historian John Cox, "several thousand men, women, and children, armed with clubs, brickbats . . . advanced upon the Institution," broke down its doors, and piled up its furniture to set afire. Nurses and bystanders safely led the children out of the building to a nearby police station.[31] Part of the mob had earlier destroyed the home of Quaker abolitionist Abby Hopper Gibbons, and with it the papers of her father, Isaac Hopper. The New York City mob action was the largest and most destructive riot in U.S. history at that time. Five days of mass disorder had left 120 people dead, while President Lincoln "looked on in horror," hesitating to intervene for fear of further alienating a largely Democratic city already opposed to the war.[32]

Some Friends who were committed to ending enslavement sought to do so by joining the Union army. While most "quietly awaited the unfolding of God's plans," enough joined the Union army to prompt Friends meetings to warn against enlisting.[33] In 1865, the Hicksite Baltimore Yearly Meeting "lamented that so many of our precious young members, and some of more mature age, have been led to join the ranks of the warrior."[34] Arch Street Meeting in Philadelphia disowned eleven young men for serving in the Union forces.[35] In New England, 43 Quaker men had enlisted by 1863; 27 were eventually disowned.[36] According to historian Douglas Harper, "plenty of eager volunteers . . . even among the pacifist Quakers" enlisted from Chester County, Pennsylvania. William Lloyd Garrison noted after a visit to Philadelphia in 1861 that at least one son from nearly every Quaker household was enlisting, much to the concern of his Quaker friends there. A Friend from Michigan doing relief work in Maryland met three European American Quakers, all related to leading Friends, who were serving as officers in the Union Army. The fathers of two were the clerk of New England Yearly Meeting and a minister in the Scipio Monthly Meeting in Upstate New York. The third was James Parnell Jones, who was killed in the war just as his much younger cousin, Quaker philosopher and teacher Rufus Jones, was born.[37]

An exact count of Quaker soldiers in the Civil War will probably never be determined. In her 1991 study of Indiana Friends, historian Jacquelyn S. Nelson discounts "the myth that has been perpetuated by historians for over one hundred years that Quakers, at least in Indiana, refused to fight in the Civil War." After examining local church records, the minutes of Indiana and Western Yearly Meetings, and monthly meeting minutes that were available, Nelson counted 1,212 Indiana Quakers, or about 21 percent of male Quakers in the state between 1861 and 1865 who served in the Union army. Although her research did not capture the full extent of Friends' participation in the conflict, she believes that perhaps as many as 45 percent of male Indiana Quakers might have been in the military.[38] However, Thomas Hamm expresses some doubts about how Nelson identified someone as Quaker. While Hamm does not question the conclusion that many Indiana Friends served in the Union army, he found that Nelson counted some men "who had been disowned decades earlier and who in some cases had joined other churches." Hamm also notes that there are many common last names that may or may not belong to Quaker families and that Nelson may have presumed anyone with one of those names was indeed a Friend.[39]

Recognizing the tensions between two Quaker principles, meetings tended not to disown automatically those who fought, as they had the "Free Quakers" of the Revolutionary War; they offered instead an opportunity to acknowledge wrongdoing and apologize.[40] Of the 1,212 Indiana Quakers Nelson identified as having served, 220 apologized to their meeting for having done so. The apologies of 148 of those were not accepted, so the men were disowned, while 608 avoided disciplinary action.[41] Further, "at least" another 238 Quakers died in the war. George W. Julian, a prominent Indianan of European descent of the late 1800s, claimed that it had been "conceded that in proportion to their number Quakers had more soldiers in the war for the Union than any other religious denomination."[42] *The Friend*, however, labeled such reports "exaggerated," and Rufus Jones said he found the historical evidence for Julian's claim lacking. "Deviations" from the peace testimony of Friends were "more numerous than one would have expected, [but] when all cases are counted . . . the total number appears small.[43] In 1864 the Hicksite Race Street Meeting in Philadelphia asked its members to avoid "harsh condemnation" and welcome home those who served in "a spirit of restoring love."[44] Densmore and Bassett agree that while Friends commitment to pacifism did not waver, "the ability, or perhaps the desire, of the Society to enforce uniformity of behavior through disciplining" did change. "Upholding the Peace Testimony," they say, "was becoming a matter of individual conscience."[45]

While it may seem logical to assume that Quakers who enlisted did so out of commitment to ending enslavement, that assumption does not always hold up on closer examination. While some Friends were spurred by the desire to emancipate the enslaved and to prevent the expansion of enslavement into the territories, this motive was "conspicuously absent" from letters Indiana Quaker soldiers wrote home,[46] and a wider study of the letters of Quaker soldiers asserts that "sentiments of patriotism rather than hatred of slavery were foremost in these soldiers' thought as well as in their letters."[47] That the war was necessary principally to preserve the Union rather than to free the enslaved people of the South was clearly a widespread sentiment that had serious consequences in the postwar era.

Southern Friends faced particular difficulty in holding to the peace testimony. Though they generally tried to keep silent about their opposition to the war, their position was tenuous. They declined to take an oath of allegiance to the Confederacy and refused to pay the Confederacy's "war taxes" on real estate, enslaved people, and other personal property. Some were "severely handled" for refusing to bear arms, and those who chose to pay for substitutes were sometimes "impoverished" in the process. Local officials imposed "distraints"—the taking of an amount of property equivalent to what was owed—on those who refused to serve or pay taxes.[48] Like other southerners, Friends homes were occupied, their food appropriated, and their crops destroyed, first by Confederates and then the Union soldiers. Southern Quakers who refused to serve were treated cruelly and even tortured, some to death. Hundreds of southerners of European descent, most of them Friends, avoided military service by living in the wilderness (either foraging for food or receiving it clandestinely from Quakers). Some young Quaker men were helped to emigrate to the Midwest. Still, apparently a few Friends "were swept away from their conscientious moorings by the wild enthusiasm that accompanied the outbreak of the war" and enlisted.[49]

Relief Activities Among the 'Contraband' and Freed People

From the earliest months of the Civil War, the abrupt transition from total subservience to freedom and responsibility was extremely difficult for many enslaved African Americans; nearly four million people were thrust without support of any kind into the chaotic world of the wartime South.[50] Thousands of southern African Americans wandered through the region in search of lost family members. In 1861, as Union troops entered the South, hundreds sought security and protection behind their lines, forming camps of refugees near Union encampments. By 1862 the Lincoln administration recognized that instead of turning away these fugitives, termed "contrabands" as prizes of war, the wiser strategy was to deploy their labor to serve the Union and thus deprive the Confederacy of desperately needed workers.[51] Many African Americans worked for the army as laborers or farmers until July 1862, when the federal government allowed men of African descent to enlist in the military. Able-bodied men enlisted or were drafted; women, children, and the old, young, and sick—and, indeed, many other refugees—were left essentially to shift for themselves.[52] Dozens of relief associations and northern churches began to send supplies and workers to the growing number of contraband camps.[53]

The war had barely begun when essentially all northern yearly meetings sent delegations south to assess the needs of the freed people. Though "mindful of their refusal to aid the military," Quakers viewed work among the freedmen as "consistent with their beliefs."[54] At least for a time, Friends engaged with members of other churches and the other branches of their own; Orthodox and Hicksite Friends often cooperated on freedmen's work, both in the North and the South.[55] As traveling Friends returned with news of destitution and devastation,

Quaker organizations began to organize their own efforts. In 1863 several groups formed the Western Freedmen's Aid Society with Levi Coffin as the agent. In 1864 alone, Coffin raised more than one hundred thousand dollars, mostly from Quakers, to aid displaced people and open schools.[56] In 1863 Indiana Yearly Meeting (Orthodox) refashioned its Committee on Concerns of People of Color as the Committee on the Freedman and expanded its relief efforts to the refugee camps along the Mississippi.[57] Focusing on Jackson, Mississippi, Ohio Yearly Meeting donated about six thousand dollars in used clothing in 1863. The next year it raised $6,400 and in 1870 another $10,000 from members.[58] Quakers in Indiana, Ohio, Western, and Iowa Yearly Meetings set up a Board of Control to coordinate their efforts, and after 1867 continued their work independently. Yearly meeting committees on African American concerns were growing into "full-scale humanitarian relief agencies."[59] Friends focused on three areas, the most immediate of which was relief for the suffering, followed by attention to spiritual and educational needs.[60]

In 1863 the Indiana Orthodox Yearly Meeting sent two of its members, European Americans Elkanah Beard and his wife, Irena, to the Mississippi Valley to survey the needs of refugees and watch over the distribution of materials soon to arrive. The Beards found more than thirty thousand people without food, shelter, or medical care in just three of the contraband camps in Tennessee and Mississippi. The conditions in the camps were unhealthy and dangerous. "We stood almost baffled by the inroads of disease and death in the crowded camp," Philadelphia European American Friend William Mitchell wrote of his visit to Nashville at the end of the war: "Groups of children were without custodians; they died without notice; and their uncoffined bodies were carried away without attracting attention. We have never conceived such misery as greets us daily."[61] In all, the number of African Americans lost "by disease and death" came to equal the number of European Americans who died in the war itself.[62]

———————•———————

Though Freedmen's Aid Associations were not part of the formal structure of the Society of Friends, Quakers were among the most active of groups in freedmen's relief; for years this work was the predominant interest of many members.[63] Various aid organizations held their annual meetings to coincide with the sessions of the yearly meeting. Freedmen's aid committees and sewing groups existed in virtually every local Quaker meeting in the United States and Britain; Friends from the British Isles were in fact great benefactors of freedmen's relief.[64] Through Levi Coffin's efforts, the London Freedmen's Aid Society shipped duty-free clothes and supplies. Irish Friends also provided "hearty support."[65] Anscombe has stated that there was no lack of British Friends willing to contribute and even "willing to lay aside their affairs, cross the ocean, and labor personally among the Freedmen."[66]

After studying the Washington area, Philadelphia Hicksites concentrated their efforts there.[67] In Philadelphia, two groups formed to offer assistance. The Friends Freedmen's Association was created in 1863 by younger members of some of the oldest and best-known Orthodox Quaker families of European descent who had been active in humanitarian concerns for years—the Copes, Cadburys, Shipleys, Scattergoods, Rhoads, and Garretts among them. The association's earliest efforts were in the area around Yorktown, Virginia, where European American Union General and former Quaker Isaac Jones Wistar had built a community.[68] In 1864 a group of Philadelphia Hicksite women, who had already been aiding freedmen for two years, asked men of their yearly meeting for financial assistance. Their request led to the creation of the Friends Association for the Aid and Elevation of the Freedmen, one of the most active and longest-lived groups.[69] Lucretia Mott was delighted with all the activity. "We are really beginning to do something!" she said, "the Biddles, the Parishes, Whartons, and such like [are] alive to the subject."[70] In addition to providing financial support, many individual Friends and meetings sent material aid by the trunkfuls into the South—medical supplies, money, books, toys, blankets, and clothes. Sewing circles in Philadelphia alone had made twenty thousand garments for the cause by 1864.[71]

Friends were particularly concerned that the freed people not become dependent on aid but take on responsibility for themselves; they often asked the newly freed who were able to do so to pay for supplies and for attending school.[72] At the Southland School in Arkansas, begun by European American Quakers Calvin and Alida Clark in 1864, day students paid a dollar a month and boarders three dollars a week.[73] Teachers on South Carolina's St. Helena Island routinely expected payment in kind for the clothing shipped from the North. The "cost" of a dress was a chicken and half a peck of sweet potatoes for a shirt; but they didn't turn down the child who brought a payment in flowers.[74] African Americans with the means to do so were eager to donate what they could. In Baltimore in 1865, they contributed nineteen thousand dollars toward schools for African Americans created by the Quaker-founded Baltimore Association for the Moral and Educational Improvement of the Coloured People. In the same year African Americans raised money to buy lumber for schoolhouses and to pay the wages of Quaker teachers in Jackson, Mississippi.[75]

All told, hundreds of Quaker men and women went south to distribute supplies in the camps and to nurse and comfort the ill. During the war, European American Cornelia Hancock of Philadelphia worked as a nurse in a Washington, D. C., refugee camp rife with smallpox, tuberculosis, and other health problems. European Americans Tacy and Job Hadley traveled at their own expense to care for the dying in a camp in Cairo, Illinois. The couple wrote home about barracks with no beds and filled with thick smoke from the occupants' stoves.[76] With help from Ohio Friends, the Hadleys started a school at the Cairo camp as well. In 1863 the Boston Education Commission sent Lucy and Sarah Chase, two well-educated young women of European descent from a wealthy family and members of Pleasant Street Meeting in Worcester, Massachusetts, to Craney Island, near Norfolk, with a supply of hospital blankets and shoes. The supplies fell far short of the need. "All the charity of the North could be judiciously expended there; of the absolute poor there were enough to absorb it," they wrote in 1864, and Philadelphia Friends immediately gathered "all things wanted" for the school.[77] In Richmond, Virginia, European American Friends led by John Bacon Crenshaw raised money to open the Friends Orphan Asylum for Colored Children in 1871. And in 1872 the women of European descent in Richmond Meeting opened a shelter for homeless women, mostly those who clustered around the camps.[78]

Quakers and Freedmen's Schools

The need for formal education among newly freed people was universally apparent and viewed as critical to not only improving their lot but, in the eyes of many, to convincing European Americans of their ability. European American Friend Yardley Warner, who founded numerous freedmen's schools in the South, believed that the hostility of European Americans toward the freedmen would decrease with education. "An increase in intelligence among the blacks engages the confidence of the white population, and wins them over to the good work," he wrote.[79]

Even before the Civil War ended, southern African Americans had opened schools themselves, a number in contraband camps. "One of the first acts of the Negroes, when they found themselves free, was to establish schools at their own expense," the American Freedmen's Inquiry Commission stated in 1863. After a tour of the South in the fall of 1865, John Alvord, the European American superintendent of the newly created Freedmen's Bureau, reported the existence in many locations of "a class of schools got up and taught by colored people, rude and imperfect, but still groups of persons, old and young, trying to learn." No southern state supported these schools; during wartime they depended chiefly upon the contributions of northern benevolent organizations.[80]

The scores of Quakers and others who worked in freedmen's assistance gained a measure of public funding and support in March 1865 when the federal government established the Bureau of Refugees, Freedmen, and Abandoned Lands. First approved for just one year, Congress reauthorized it for a second year, and its educational programs ran for a third year. The bureau's mission was to feed and care for the thousands of refugees; to establish and, if necessary, build schools and hospitals; to relocate refugees under the 1862 Homestead Act; to supervise the production of crops and distribution of food and medicine; to find work for the newly freed; and to supervise labor contracts between freed people and their employers. It also provided legal assistance, managed confiscated lands, and generally supported freed people in adapting to their new status.[81] Supplementing and assisting the efforts of groups already developing and working in schools, the Freedmen's Bureau established 4,239 schools between 1865 and 1871.[82] Over those years these schools employed 9,500 teachers and enrolled 274,000 pupils. The bureau also established eleven colleges and universities and sixty-one "normal" schools, or teachers' colleges.[83]

As many as ten thousand northerners went to the South to teach in freedmen's schools.[84] Two-thirds of them were women—an unstated number African American graduates of Oberlin College, the Institute for Colored Youth, and, after 1870, Hampton Institute. About a year after the end of the war, 37 percent of teachers in the South known to the Freedmen's Bureau were African American.[85] By 1871 almost half of the 17 teachers supported by Philadelphia Hicksites were African American, as were a third of those supported by the city's Orthodox association. Moreover, some of the teachers were southerners, including southern Quakers.[86] Almost five hundred Quakers went south to teach: 291 were women, once described as "Gentle Invaders," and most were European Americans in their twenties. For Quaker women, it was unusual to be "teaching among the 'world's people' or at such a considerable distance from their homes," Hamm notes.[87]

In many instances the Freedmen's Bureau and Quakers opened a school together; at other times the bureau asked individual Friends to start a school in a particular location or assume control of one it could no longer maintain.[88] Just a few months after the end of the war, Fairfax Monthly Meeting in Waterford, Virginia, joined with the Bureau and local African Americans to open a school on land sold by a Friend to "the colored people of Waterford and vicinity." Sarah Steer, a young European American Friend who had been educated in Philadelphia, came to teach at the school, and Quakers she had met in that city sent money and supplies to support it.[89] Linda Selleck notes that Freedmen's Bureau officials were impressed by Friends wartime educational efforts: in 1864 alone, for example, teachers sponsored by the Friends Freedmen's Association of Philadelphia taught 3,700 day and evening students and another 21,200 in Sunday schools in Virginia and used Quaker schools as the standard for their own.[90]

By the end of the 1860s Quakers or Quaker associations supported hundreds of freedmen's schools in whole or in part; the most active in freedmen's education were Young Friends.[91] In the immediate postwar period, Quakers contributed funds for freedmen's relief and education "incredibly out of proportion to the numbers."[92] In 1867 the Friends Association for the Aid and Elevation of the Freedmen supported 17 teachers and 1,000 students in 13 schools in South Carolina and Virginia; at the peak of its activity the group supported 25 schools.[93] The conditions of schooling and living were often primitive at best. Classes were held in nearly every place imaginable—in shanty towns and refugee camps and decaying mansions.[94] Often a school was no more than a teacher and a classroom or two.[95] When European American Friend Elizabeth Bond arrived in Young's Point, Louisiana, to teach school in 1864, she found that the school was "a rough log house thirty feet square and so open that the crevices admitted sufficient light without the aid of windows." It was furnished with "undressed plank benches without backs" and heated by a stove rescued from a Mississippi River steamboat. In this room Bond taught 130 students, some as old as forty. Many of the teachers taught all week—children in the daytime, adults at night and on Saturdays, and on the Sabbath in Sunday schools. Some also started orphanages; a few adopted orphans as their own.[96] Aside from teaching basic literacy (and later, spelling, arithmetic, world geography, and some history), Quaker teachers sprinkled their lessons with frequent admonitions about honesty, hard work, and sobriety. European American Quaker Martha Schofield's oft-repeated motto for the students in the school she founded in Aiken, South Carolina, was "be somebody, do something, be thorough."[97]

Most Quakers offered both religious and secular education to the freedmen. Elkanah Beard conducted prayer services and joined with African American ministers to start churches. After 1869, when Southland School established a normal school, Alida Clark sought to train African Americans to teach and to set a "Christian example" among their "despised, oppressed, benighted, and misused" brethren.[98] Students' days there were filled with preaching services, prayer meetings, temperance activities, and academics. At Southland, identified as "a nondenominational Christian academy," Clark worked alongside African American Daniel Drew, who became one of the school's first converts to Quakerism after Indiana Yearly Meeting authorized the Southland meeting in 1873. Clark termed Drew "our main nursing father . . . always ready with a good word, fitly chosen from the clear brook of the spring of life, and how well he 'slings,' and how accurate his aim, is known by the results." To her, Drew was "a chosen vessel of no ordinary qualifications, capable of serving God and his people as few others could."[99] Schofield believed that she was "involved in a great and important work" at her South Carolina school. "I go forth in *perfect trust*," she wrote in 1868, "knowing that if I endeavor to do my duty, the end will be well . . . and that one Eye watches over and protects always." Schofield believed that God was leading her—sometimes even pushing her. "No new thing was ever undertaken in this school until a Power greater than I compelled me to try for it," she told the school's trustees decades later.[100]

———•———

Quakers played significant roles in perhaps the most ambitious of wartime efforts among freed people: the so-called "Port Royal Experiment" on the Sea Islands of South Carolina, which one historian has termed "rehearsal for reconstruction."[101] Just after the war began, a Union fleet sailed into Port Royal Sound in South Carolina and took possession of the area. Most European American residents of the islands fled, while some ten thousand people of African descent whom they had enslaved remained. In March 1862 the federal government appointed European American Boston attorney Edward L. Pierce to create a system of schools and hospitals and establish African Americans as farmers on the cotton plantations they had formerly worked as enslaved people. They were able to buy land at modest prices and were paid one dollar for every four hundred pounds of cotton they produced. Launched to demonstrate that formerly enslaved people were capable of self-sufficiency and would work without the threat of force, the government also recognized that the islands' cotton crop could produce badly needed revenue for the Union.[102] Relief associations, including the Port Royal Relief Committee that a number of Philadelphia Friends had organized, supplemented the federal funding authorized for the Port Royal project.[103]

The first school in the South for freedmen—the Penn School on St. Helena—was the most enduring project to grow out of the Port Royal experiment. Founded in 1862, the school was not a Quaker institution, but Friends had consistent and close connections with it over the years and were a significant source of financial support. Money and supplies came at various times from the Friends Freedmen's Association, the Benezet Society of Germantown, and individual Quakers.[104] Until the mid-twentieth century, a majority of the school's board tended to be Quakers from Philadelphia. The first teachers, European Americans Laura Towne (a Unitarian) and Ellen Murray, went South under the auspices of the Quaker Port Royal Relief Committee and the federal government to provide medical supplies. When they opened a school, Towne and Murray were quickly overwhelmed with students, and within three years the Penn School was sending teachers of African descent into the surrounding areas to open schools of their own.[105] Both Towne, who named the school for Quaker William Penn, and Murray spent forty years there.[106]

Whether the Port Royal experiment succeeded is not clear, and from the start its chances were damaged by greed, political intrigue, and cynicism. "Superintendents" appointed to manage the plantations were often more committed to turning a profit than to improving the lives of the workers. By the end of the war, the people who had come to take part in the project had for the most part returned to the North, and ultimately the government returned the land to its former owners. However, the educational component of the Port Royal Experiment was successful enough to encourage the Freedmen's Bureau to establish schools elsewhere.[107]

One of the most well known of European American Quaker freedmen's teachers was Emily Howland (1827–1929), who went south in 1863 to work in a large contraband camp in Washington, soon known as Freedmen's Village. Howland already had experience teaching southern African Americans: in 1857 she had left the small Upstate New York town of Sherwood to teach African American girls in Washington, D.C. At first working to distribute donated clothing and food at Freedmen's Village, Howland then turned to nursing and ultimately to teaching. Like countless other aid workers, Howland was uneasy with the fact that her own living conditions in the South were superior to those of the people she had come to serve. When Howland proposed to stay in the camp overnight instead, her family and friends, including her close circle of abolitionist women, cautioned her against such a move; she wrote that the notion was "unthinkable, even to the more ardent anti-slavery advocates." In the end, she stayed outside the camp with the cousin of a friend.[108]

In 1866, with support from both the Freedmen's Bureau and the Friends Freedmen's Association, Howland founded Arcadia, an African American farming community in Heathsville in Northumberland County. She bought and initially managed the land for three families from Freedmen's Village, but as more people settled there and earned enough income to buy their own plots, Howland turned over the farm's management to them. She taught in Heathsville's Howland Chapel School until the death of her mother compelled her return home. Though she spent the rest of her life in the North, Howland visited Heathsville often, established another school in Virginia's Westmoreland County, and supported two others created on the Arcadia model. She made regular and generous contributions to several southern African American schools until she died.[109]

When the Freedmen's Committee of Orthodox Indiana Yearly Meeting sent Calvin and Alida Clark (1823–92) to Helena, Arkansas in 1864, they set up an orphanage and school for some eighty needy African American children. Two years later, Charles Bentzoni, European American commander of the Fifty-sixth U.S. Colored Infantry Regiment, donated funds and labor for a new campus for the institutions. Indiana Yearly Meeting acquired more acreage for the school, and the financial support of Friends in the United States and Great Britain helped sustain what became known as Southland School (later Southland College) for the next sixty years.[110]

The Clarks ran Southland for twenty-two years and refused compensation for most of that term of service.[111] Alida Clark's rejection of racial discrimination, particularly the double discrimination against African American women, drew her into increasingly radical positions and strong exhortations to Friends to understand and support their education. Clark aimed to train her best students as teachers "to bring up the next generation of children to make a nation for these people" and envisioned Quaker African American teachers establishing schools and Quaker meetings wherever they settled.[112] By the time the Clarks left, nearly three hundred of Southland's students had become teachers and started schools of their own. Others among the several thousand graduates became doctors, lawyers, and ministers. A former teacher recalled the school as "'a garden spot' for the entire area to which young Friends came for services and adventure and from which many earnest, respectable students launched full and useful careers." The faculty was integrated—living and working together "on terms of friendship and equality."[113]

Friend Martha Schofield (1839–1916) also had a long teaching career among the freed people. Schofield grew up in Bucks County,

Pennsylvania, in an abolitionist family; her "strong spirit-led" mother, Mary Jackson Schofield, was an Orthodox minister who preached against enslavement, sometimes on trips through the upper South. Schofield's mother used only free produce for more than thirty years, and the family home is said to have sheltered fugitives. After moving to Philadelphia, the Schofields became close friends with the Motts and Whittier, with whom Martha Schofield corresponded her whole life.[114]

In 1868 Schofield went to teach on St. Helena Island, but became ill, likely with malaria. Once recovered, she moved one hundred miles inland to the town of Aiken, South Carolina. There she bought a house within Aiken's African American community that also became her first school. Students arrived in such numbers that Schofield soon purchased land with her own money and, with government help, built a school that would grow eventually to a collection of buildings on a 280-acre farm.[115] The curriculum at her Schofield Normal and Industrial School included world literature and world philosophy for prospective teachers, but because so few students were able to stay in school long enough to finish teacher training Schofield added trade programs and industrial training to the school's curriculum.[116]

When one African American declared that students should pay as much as they could for their education, Schofield set school policy accordingly. Students paid fees with produce from their farms and by the products they made in the school's industries. They were also expected to contribute to Schofield's various fund-raising campaigns or to volunteer their labor for construction projects. A model of inventiveness and thrift herself, Schofield had students sort, clean, and mend the clothing that arrived from the North so it could be sold in the school's second-hand store at modest prices. Students also straightened and reused crooked nails that held together boxes sent from the North.[117]

Like Alida Clark, Schofield spent much of her time raising funds, "largely through the power of her pen," and by visiting potential donors. A group of twenty-five Quaker women in Germantown, Pennsylvania, organized as the Pennsylvania Friends Relief Association, faithfully solicited money for many years; one fund-raising venture was the annual Buck Hill Fair, which generated money solely for the school until the late 1930s.[118] The school also received assistance from the Freedmen's Bureau and other government sources. In 1886 the

Philadelphia Hicksite Yearly Meeting refused a request for permanent financial support, but individual Hicksite Friends and monthly meetings supported the school well into the 1890s.[119]

Some of the Schofield school's success may be attributed to the fact that its founder was virtually in sole control of it. She operated without trustees, planned the campus, and determined the curriculum; she also retained responsibility for school discipline and relations with parents. Ultimately, though, Schofield came to depend more and more on government funds, and in 1886 she selected a "group of influential people" from New York, Philadelphia, and South Carolina to serve as trustees—including William Lloyd Garrison Jr., son of the abolitionist, who served a lengthy term as board president. Two of the four Carolinians were African Americans from Aiken. By the time Schofield died in 1916, the faculty was entirely African American.[120]

African Americans in Maryville, Tennessee, within an area ruined and impoverished by the war, initiated another Quaker freedmen's school. Anxious to start a normal school, they asked Friends for assistance and asked European American Yardley Warner, a Quaker from Germantown, Pennsylvania, to help create it. Warner's career in abolitionism and African American education was already well established. In his youth, he wrote in his journal that he "covenanted to give much of my time to the elevation of African Americans"; he had driven wagons transporting fugitives to freedom before the war, had taught in two Quaker schools, had founded the first school for African Americans in Greensboro, North Carolina, just after the end of the war, and became caretaker of a Friends school in Tennessee.[121] Warner began raising funds for the Maryville Friends Normal and Preparatory School in 1872, securing pledges from the local African American community and at one point walking nine hundred miles from Tennessee to seek the aid of New England Friends.[122] African Americans in and around Maryville also provided labor, including making 750,000 bricks, to build the school.[123]

Maryville was one of more than twenty schools for African Americans that Warner is credited with founding in Virginia, North Carolina, Tennessee, Oklahoma, Mississippi, Alabama, and Georgia between 1872 and 1877. In places where public funds to sustain schools did not exist, Warner offered to pay half the expense if the parents sent their children regularly. Committed to creating programs that would then be sustained by their own communities, he removed himself as Maryville's administrator in 1873.[124]

European American Friend Sarah Smiley (1830–1917) put limitless energy into freedman's school projects. She helped start schools in Virginia and built a home to help attract teachers from the North. In the chaotic aftermath of the war, Smiley, who was from Vassalboro, Maine, devoted much of her energy to raising funds for freedmen's programs all over the East Coast, as well as in England and Ireland. Smiley had earlier traveled in the South and in 1865 began work to restore Friends meetings and schools for the Baltimore Association of Friends to Advise and Assist Friends in the South. Within a year of the war's end, Smiley founded a normal school and night schools and brought classes to prisons in northern Virginia and the Washington area. She was especially interested in projects designed to enable women to create goods that would bring income for their families, including sewing schools for mothers and industrial schools that she started around Richmond in 1864. At various times the yearly meetings of New England and New York both sent relief goods for Smiley to distribute. She convinced the federal government to pay the cost of shipping those goods to the South and to permit relief workers free passage by rail.[125]

Though not founded by Quakers, the Christiansburg Institute in Montgomery County, Virginia received a large measure of support from them, specifically from the Friends Freedmen's Association and Germantown Quakers. Founded in 1866, by 1871 it had become the Christiansburg Normal Institute and was among the leading educational facilities for African Americans in Virginia.[126] Although the administrators and board were Quakers of European descent, by 1888 the faculty was entirely African American.[127] In 1884, when contributions to its programs were decreasing, the Friends Freedmen's Association decided to focus its resources on teacher training there, and the institute became the association's one remaining commitment in the South. According to Margaret Hope Bacon, support from the Friends Freedmen's Association was "continual and steadfast" from 1869 to 1934.[128]

The Laing School in Mt. Pleasant, South Carolina, was created and supported by Quakers though it also was not a Quaker school.

Founded by European American Quaker Cornelia Hancock (1840–1927) of New Jersey in 1866, it was initially supported by the Freedmen's Bureau, Philadelphia-area Friends meetings, and the Pennsylvania Abolition Society, the last of which sent money to the school every year and in 1894 took over the administration of its trust fund. Eventually the school was named after European American Friend Henry M. Laing, the treasurer of both the abolition society and the Philadelphia Hicksite freedmen's association.[129]

———————•———————

Predictably, Quaker and other aid workers from the North were not universally welcomed in the South. Many were "socially ostracized," Martha Schofield noted; local people described her students as "pert and impudent" and Schofield herself as "a fanatic" because she chose to live in the African American community. In 1874 the New York Yearly Meeting Friends Aid Association reported, "Our teachers, all young Friends and all members of our Society, leave comfortable homes and social companions to spend a large portion of the year in inhospitable [surroundings], not able to visit any of the white population, and never receiving a kind word from them."[130]

Southerners, angry at the use of federal funds for African American education, reacted violently as well. "Black schools were burned, teachers were publicly ridiculed, whipped, run out of town, and hanged. Thirty-seven schools were burned down in Tennessee in 1869 alone." Disgruntled European American southerners refused to sell needed goods to the northerners and fired at students on their way to school and inside their schoolhouses.[131] During the war, Mississippi camps in which Elkanah Beard worked were raided by bands of guerillas in order to kidnap and re-enslave refugees. In the process, snipers killed or wounded several teachers.[132] Twice teachers had to be sent home. "We have thought best to suspend our schools, dangers seen and unseen crowding around us," wrote Beard in April 1864; nevertheless, he remained in Louisiana, as did his wife, Irena. During the time she taught freedmen in Virginia, Brooklyn European American Quaker Julia Shearman wrote, "I habitually received the polite salutation 'damned Yankee bitch of a nigger school teacher,' with the occasional admonition to take up my abode in the infernal regions." Soon after the end of the war, Friends of the Somerton Meeting in Virginia and newly freed people in the area opened a school in Nansemond County; three months later it was burned down. The day after the fire, African American men told European American Quaker teacher Olive Roberts that they would rebuild the school if she would stay, but records indicate that a new school was probably not erected. Meeting minutes reported in 1867 that "none of the African race are under our immediate care."[133]

In 1870 the Friends Freedmen's Association reported that several teachers had received death threats and were "filled with horror" by what their fellow teachers endured.[134] European American Quaker Alonzo Corliss, a disabled northern man teaching in North Carolina, was attacked by Ku Klux Klansman for "teaching niggers and making them like white men."[135] Schofield was surrounded and threatened by a band of men who vowed to kill her if she did not leave.[136] From her home, Schofield could monitor the campus of her school for arson; on one of her nocturnal walks to check the grounds, she encountered would-be arsonists whom she is said to have dissuaded "by the simple directness of her speech."[137]

Quakers, Freedmen's Assistance, and Reconstruction

Late in 1863, anticipating the eventual success of the Union, Lincoln proposed a two-pronged plan for "reconstructing" the nation. Dismissing the more radical plans of Congress, Lincoln intended to grant amnesty to rebels who declared their loyalty to the Union and wanted to recognize state governments where at least 10 percent of eligible voters took a loyalty oath and where slavery was formally abolished. After Lincoln's assassination, Andrew Johnson enacted a changed plan: he exempted those who owned property worth twenty thousand dollars or more from the oath and established provisional governments in all Confederate states, which were authorized to appoint delegates to state constitutional conventions designed to end slavery. In December 1866 Johnson declared the Union reconstituted, but Congress immediately rebuked the president and claimed for itself the sole right to restore rebel states to the Union.[138]

To those serious about rebuilding the South, the most important step was to secure land for African Americans. "Their very lives were entwined with the land and its cultivation; they lived in a society where respectability was based on ownership of the soil," European American sociologist Vernon Wharton has observed; "to them to be free was to farm their own ground."[139] The government's overall failure to distribute the land necessary for economic independence among formerly enslaved people, according to historian Eric Foner, left them with "an enduring sense of betrayal" by the government.[140] Those who managed to acquire land were often charged high interest rates on loans for farm implements, seed, or land—or even sold nonexistent or marginal agricultural land. With losses from bad crop years during the five years after the war, few could survive.[141] Thus, newly freed African Americans working in agriculture were doomed to a life of sharecropping,[142] or as Wood puts it, "slavery in a new guise."[143]

Several European American Friends bought land and made it available to African Americans at reasonable prices, as Emily Howland did in Virginia.[144] An anonymous donor, thought to be from Massachusetts, bought 135 acres next to Southland School in Helena, Arkansas.[145] In 1867 Yardley Warner purchased 35 acres in Greensboro, North Carolina, with the financial support of the Friends Freedmen's Association and in partnership with his first wife, Hannah. Over the next twenty years, he sold tracts in Warnersville, as it was called, to African Americans according to their ability to pay.[146] The ownership of property, he declared, "would give anchorage to the confused Freedmen, providing them with a sense of security and encouraging them in industry and thrift."[147] Warner viewed the entire Warnersville project as "the means to repel the imputation against the Freedmen, that they are unfit for the liberty which is the rightful boon to every man."[148] Between five and six hundred African Americans lived in their own houses at Warnersville. They established a church and schools; 60 percent of those who graduated school there went on to college and became teachers.[149] Warner shortly turned over management and land sales to one of the African American community's leaders, Harmon Unthank.[150]

Warner himself lived in Warnersville and, according to his son, "was ostracized and regarded as outcast and pariah, by the white population"; his life was threatened more than once. Ultimately, however, opposition to the community faded. In 1869 the local *Greensboro Patriot*, which had been a chief critic of the plan, recorded its "surprise and gratification"

at the exhibition of student work at the school's Christmas night celebration.[151] In 1870 the African American minister R. C. Campbell of
Greensboro noted in a "prayer for the Society of Friends" that Quakers
"stood by us in the hour of our sorrow and distress and difficulty . . .
dear Lord stand by them now, and prosper them in all their efforts. They
helped and taught us when we did not know what to do. Thou help
them and give them good success in all they are doing throughout the
world for the welfare of their fellow men."[152]

The Postwar Western Migration

From early in 1865 some African Americans chose to leave the South
for what they hoped was a more tolerant and economically promising
Midwest,[153] traveling some of the same routes fugitives had almost a
century earlier. Quakers, especially, assisted in this relocation effort. In
Indiana, the Plainfield Quarterly Meeting Committee on Concerns of
People of Color wrote that the African Americans were "in quite destitute circumstances" when they arrived. These resettled people were
eager, Plainfield Friends found, to support themselves and send their
children to schools; by 1867 many had worked hard enough to purchase "comfortable" homes.[154] Threatened by southerners afraid of
losing their labor supply and plagued by disease and unscrupulous deal-
ings, the immigrants, called "Exodusters" in Kansas, arrived at the rate
of almost three hundred a week, most barely clothed and penniless.[155]
Between 1877 and 1879 thousands of people of African descent moved
to Kansas alone.[156]

As news of the Exodusters' plight spread, northerners of both
African and European descent sent money and moral support.
Organizations in Boston and New York held large rallies to raise
funds.[157] In 1879 the Kansas government asked European American
Quaker Elizabeth Comstock (1815–91) to organize the relief effort,
given her experience during the war working in prisons, hospitals, and
camps for freed people.[158] Born in England, Comstock had grown up
in a Quaker community in Canada and moved with her husband, John
Comstock, to Michigan in 1858. Like Laura Haviland, who joined
Comstock in Kansas, she participated actively in the Underground
Railroad. In Kansas, Comstock immediately began a campaign to make

Friends aware of the Exodusters' situation, to raise money, and to recruit volunteers to collect and ship relief goods. Friends freedmen's groups regained some of their "old-time zeal" in 1879 as they gathered goods for Kansas.[159] Comstock worked as well to gain public acceptance for the effort to stem the migration of refugees into Kansas by offering resettlement opportunities in other Midwestern states.[160] Comstock's persuasive speech at a large public meeting in Chicago convinced people in Illinois to help fifty thousand African Americans from Kansas find homes and jobs. A similar event in Nebraska was also successful.[161] Her letters and articles won her praise as well as the charge that she was "a child of the devil." Accused by southerners of lying about their treatment of African Americans, Comstock said: "We endeavor to keep a single eye toward our great Leader, and not be depressed by the one or elated by the other."[162] She has been called one of the "great liberating spiritual forces in the Society, appealing especially to young Friends and calling them to active service."[163]

———————•———————

Quakers in the South, attacked both for being against enslavement and against the war and themselves attempting to survive in a devastated economy, also sought to leave for the Midwest. The possibility of another massive departure was a matter of great concern among Friends in North Carolina, who worried that their meetings would be permanently weakened; Friends meetings in Georgia, South Carolina, and Virginia had already declined from loss of members.[164] Like Addison Coffin, however, many southern Friends of European descent correctly sensed that although the war might end enslavement, it would not resolve the problems between the races.[165] Between the fall of 1865 and spring 1872, fifteen hundred Friends were among the sixteen thousand people of all denominations who left the Carolinas for the Midwest.

Committed to stopping the decline, European American Quaker Francis King of Baltimore urged Friends to stay in the South and rebuild their lives and institutions. In 1865, he and other Orthodox Friends founded the Baltimore Association of Friends to Advise and Assist Southern Friends, which spent more than one hundred thousand dollars to help North Carolina Friends reestablish their monthly meetings, create Quaker libraries, and start schools for their children. Although the Association's focus was on rebuilding the Quaker educational system in the Carolinas, it also opened schools for African Americans and developed a model farm at Springfield, North Carolina, to teach new agricultural methods to all farmers.[166] One "leading citizen" of Raleigh wrote in *Friends Review* in 1869, "The Quakers are doing more to reconstruct the State than all the Legislators we can have. Their silent but Christian work, among whites and blacks, is telling: breaking down prejudice and creating better feeling."[167] Friends from the three Hicksite meetings in Philadelphia similarly formed a committee to raise funds for Virginia Friends whose textile mills and farms were ruined.[168]

The End of Reconstruction

Many historians view Reconstruction as one of the most tragic episodes in American history. To Forrest Wood it was "the great moral failure of the nation."[169] "The tragedy of reconstruction," McWhiney observed, "was that it did not really reconstruct."[170] Essentially, there were no agreed-upon guidelines for what "reconstruction" of the South would mean and what its purpose would be. Nor was administration of the effort clear. The question of which branch of government was to decide appropriate action ultimately overshadowed any discussion of what was to be done. And in the end, President Andrew Johnson set minimal requirements for rejoining the Union for southern states and issued a proclamation forgiving all former Confederate officials.[171]

Exacerbating federal indecision and inaction was the waning of northern interest in the welfare of southern African Americans. The dissolution of both the Freedman's Bureau (1873) and the American Anti-Slavery Society (1870) signaled this diminished concern. At the antislavery group's meeting in New York in 1865, William Lloyd Garrison held that the end of enslavement should mean the end of the national antislavery group, though others favored maintaining it to work for African American suffrage.[172] Nonetheless, in 1870 the society declared that "the equal civil and political rights for African Americans that its members had pledged to secure had been attained," and it thereupon ceased to exist. Some members, one of them the European American Quaker Aaron Powell of Plainfield Meeting in New Jersey, immediately founded the National Reform League to work for integration in schools and public accommodations, but the organization survived only two years.[173] The Philadelphia Female Anti-Slavery Society also dissolved in 1870; as her final word to the organization she had created nearly forty years before, Lucretia Mott stated, "Now, Lord, lettest thou thy servant depart in peace."[174] Finally the freedmen's aid groups of the North, as historian Robert Cruden put it, "folded their tents, satisfied that a good work had been well done" and that the freed African American was now "ready to provide for himself." Yet, such withdrawals utterly "ignored the persistence of racism and racial discrimination in America."[175]

By 1877, Reconstruction ended in a backroom compromise that placed the Republican Party's candidate, Rutherford B. Hayes, in the White House in exchange for the pledge not to interfere in the affairs of the South.[176] The promise of land as compensation for slavery largely evaporated; newfound political rights were circumscribed; "Jim Crow" segregation became a southern institution; northern "carpetbaggers" exploited African Americans for their own profit; and waves of terrorism aimed to keep in place the prewar racial status quo. "By and large . . . the whites were looking for ways to fit the black population into their own plans for America's continued development as a white man's country."[177]

Even before Reconstruction had ended, new "black codes" barred African Americans from renting or buying land, prevented them from leaving their jobs or plantations, and allowed anyone "in idleness" to be arrested and sentenced to plantation labor.[178] Underlying the desire to keep African Americans subordinate was the fear of "amalgamation." Newspapers often claimed that the goal of the amendments and laws passed to assist African Americans in the transition from enslavement to freedom was actually racial mixing. Should African Americans be permitted to exercise their new rights, the editor of *De Bow's Review*, the most widely read newspaper in the South during the war, declared they would "meet us at the marriage altar and in the burial vault."[179] Quaker newspapers were among the few editorializing against discriminatory state laws. In 1863, when Pennsylvania legislators proposed a law to prohibit African Americans from entering Pennsylvania, *The Friend* declared that such an act would be a step back "toward bigotry and prejudices of the dark periods of ignorance and cruelty."[180] Friends involved in Reconstruction concluded that "the [emancipation] proclamation that made the bondsman legally free has not changed the hearts of those who have hitherto ruled in the late slave-holding States."[181]

By 1877, when federal troops were withdrawn from the South, the national government's abandonment was complete.[182] By 1876, the nation's highest court had "effectively destroyed the structures" that had been created to help African Americans achieve freedom, and legislation designed to guarantee full rights to African Americans was "virtually annulled by fraud, force, and legislation."[183] This set the stage for legitimized segregation in such enterprises as hotels, restaurants, and theaters as well as for "Jim Crow," a system of state laws creating, at least in theory, "separate but equal" facilities for Anglo- and African Americans.

Then in 1896, in *Plessy v. Ferguson*, the Supreme Court ruled that political and social equality were different and that laws mandating segregation of the races were "not illegal . . . [nor do they] necessarily imply the inferiority of either race to the other." The court concluded that any meeting as social equals had to be "the result of natural affinities, a mutual appreciation of each other's merits, and a voluntary consent of individuals."[184] In effect, between the court and "Jim Crow," the status quo was preserved by creating patently inferior facilities for African Americans.[185] Almost from the moment African Americans were given the right to vote, southern states put in place poll taxes, literacy tests, and other requirements that severely limited their ability to register. Terror and violence not only kept African Americans from the polls but otherwise severely circumscribed their rights and silenced those who would speak out. The ultimate terrorization was, of course, lynching.

The North's declining interest and the federal government's failure to monitor and enforce equal rights legislation left African Americans in the South in a vulnerable and dangerous situation. Many antebellum plantation owners, who had lost their wealth and their way of life during the war, considered African Americans to be the cause, and they and their supporters pursued unlawful tactics to mete out blame.[186] Formed in 1866, the Ku Klux Klan and several similar groups terrorized and intimidated African Americans, a campaign that marked southern racial relations for the next century.[187] European American Quaker teacher

Margaret Newbold Thorpe noted that the adult students in the school she taught near Yorktown, Virginia, began to come to evening classes armed as Klan activities increased in 1866. European American Friend Martha Lindley did not dare to buy food from people in Clarksville, Tennessee, where she taught at a freedmen's school, because they might have been "glad of the opportunity to have poisoned us." And in Thomasville, North Carolina, threatening letters warned European American Quaker teacher Burnette Brown to leave or suffer unspecified punishment.[188] Sensational newspaper accounts of infractions and insults on the part of African Americans fueled the violence.[189] As historian Henry Litchfield West notes, "The negro was pilloried as the quintessence of all that was brutal and dangerous."[190] Southern governors by their inaction and silence effectively endorsed lynching, and in many instances leading European American members of a given community joined the crowds that gathered around particular hangings. Indeed, historians agree that the intimidation could not have been so widespread unless the surrounding communities had not lent their tacit approval to it.[191] Between 1889 and 1918, 3,224 people—80 percent of them African American—were brutally tortured and killed.[192]

Racial tension was certainly not absent in the North. In Indiana, where the population of African descent had doubled since the war, reports of "mob action" and violence were common in the towns bordering Kentucky, where populations were greater. An 1865 lynching in Evansville revealed persistent racism and discrimination in the Midwest.[193] In Philadelphia, an estimated fifteen thousand African Americans from the South arrived between 1875 and 1895. The migrants, most "untrained and poorly educated," according to the African American intellectual and activist W. E. B. Du Bois, joined the twenty-five thousand people of African descent already living in the city. In part because of the strain this migration placed on state, municipal, and philanthropic organizations, Quakers (among others) tried to stem the tide of migrants heading north.[194] Philadelphia Friends, who managed and operated many charitable associations in the city, suggested that the Friends Freedmen's Association develop more communities like Warnersville in which freed people might live and prosper in the South rather than move to "untried lands" in the North;

their support of freedmen's schools was motivated in part by the desire to assure that African Americans could make a go of it in the South.[195]

Long before federal troops left the South, Friends became "anxious to withdraw from their role as educational benefactors.[196] Just two years after the end of the war, the Quaker Baltimore Association's schools for African Americans in that city became public, and Quaker interest in them faded.[197] By the next year, the Orthodox Friends Freedmen's Association, which saw itself as a temporary organization to meet emergency needs, was planning to turn schools over to states, although their withdrawal was delayed into the 1870s when it became clear that public funding would not be adequate to support them.[198] Principally because Friends were contributing to other causes, association revenues dropped to less than one-quarter of the amount contributed five years before.[199]

———————•———————

After 1870 declining contributions for schools from Friends organizations outside Philadelphia forced some of the schools they sponsored to close. Yet a notable number remained open, some through the end of the century and others for a century or more; they were arguably the most enduring legacy of Quaker involvement in assistance to freed people. Moreover, according to European American Friend Jay Allen of Indiana, who taught in schools for freed people and then became superintendent of North Carolina public schools, the freedmen's schools started and sustained by Friends laid the ground for many southern states' public school systems.[200] These longer-lasting schools shared at least two characteristics—the continuing interest and support of northern Friends, whether individuals, an organization, or a yearly meeting and the presence of a founder (or founders) with a strong personality and even stronger commitment to freedmen's education. In each of these schools, one if not two people devoted nearly all their adult lives to the institution and often remained connected even after their official duties ended. They constantly sought funds from yearly meetings, individual Quakers, the various freedmen's associations, and their family and friends; a few made successful fund-raising trips to England and Ireland. The support of a board of northerners—especially people who were able to contribute financially—was also significant to the longevity of these schools.

Among the long-lived schools was Warner's Maryville school. New England Yearly Meeting assumed responsibility for the school until 1902, when it was sold.[201] Alida and Calvin Clark continued to work at Southland School through 1886 and remained in the community of Helena until Alida's death in March 1892. Eliza, the only one of their three daughters to live to adulthood, also taught at Southland.[202] Another European American Quaker couple, Anna and Henry Wolford, ran Southland in the early 1900s and were able to spark a much-needed "renaissance" in the faltering institution. But an incredible combination of fires, staff conflicts, personal dramas, and unrelenting financial problems unfolded. Unable to bear the thought of closing an institution that had meant so much to them, many committed people in Arkansas and Indiana tried to keep it alive, but in June 1925, after sixty-one years, Southland closed.[203] The Laing School endured longer. Bacon has noted that "crisis followed crisis" at the school, but the Pennsylvania Abolition Society continued to support it after Abby Munro's death in 1913. Although its supporters were hesitant to let the state take over the school because standards were not as high, in 1940 Laing did become a public school.[204] The abolition society continued its support until the 1980s.[205]

The Schofield Normal and Industrial School survived for decades; in 1952 it, too, became a public school. Despite the hostility Schofield and her school initially encountered, the people of Aiken came to accept her and to seek support on community projects.[206] Schofield placed her school in new hands by 1912 but continued to live in her campus home and mix with students.[207] The day before she died, she told her students, "If I had fifty years more to live, I would spend it in teaching colored people."[208]

The Christiansburg Institute also survived. In 1884, when contributions to its programs were decreasing, the Friends Freedmen's Association decided to focus its resources on teaching training there, and the institute became the association's one remaining commitment in the South.[209] The school closed in the 1960s. The Penn School on St. Helena, renamed the Penn Normal, Industrial, and Agricultural School in 1900, remained open until 1948, by which time it was no longer financially viable; its students were transferred to public schools. Over the years Friends continued as active board members and contributors and in 1950 a Quaker couple, Courtney and Elizabeth Siceloff, became the first directors of the newly formed Penn Community Services. Since 1961 the trustees have been southerners and biracial. In the 1950s and '60s, the Center hosted many civil rights groups, including Dr. Martin Luther King Jr., and the planners of the 1963 March on Washington.[210]

Justifying Racial Judgment

The effectiveness of these and other freedmen's schools was arguably limited by a campaign founded on purported evidence of a hierarchy of races that fed what historian Forest Wood has called the "black scare." Even before the Civil War, scientists, academics, politicians, and influential public thinkers engaged in a campaign to combat any move toward equal rights for people of African descent. Sometimes termed "scientific racism," this set of ideas attempted to establish that Caucasian people comprised a different, and higher, species of human than any other race. Personal characteristics were categorized according to race.[211] Prominent among academics was Louis Agassiz, a Swiss anthropologist who taught at Harvard University. "We should beware how we give to the blacks rights, by virtue of which they may endanger the progress of the whites," Agassiz wrote as early as 1863. "Social equality I deem at all times impracticable—a natural impossibility, from the very character of the negro race." The campaign also bolstered the economic and social system that gave both northern and southern commercial interests an inexpensive and easily controlled source of labor. These "scientific" claims were published widely in newspapers and magazines—the new mass media of the day; most editors made no pretense of presenting both sides. As much as abolitionists might point out that any number of well-known scholars refuted scientific racism, the theories of Agassiz and others received widespread publicity and both influenced and condoned public opinion.[212]

When most of the newly freed "could not overcome the overwhelming obstacles in their path to economic security, northerners accused them of being deficient workers and willingly read them out of American society."[213] Wood remarks of the 1870s, "that . . . former supporters of emancipation and impartial suffrage could change so quickly underscored the insidiousness of white racism in America. Four million former slaves had known freedom for barely seven years, during which every conceivable obstacle was thrown in their way, but some of their white 'friends' were already giving up because the freedmen were taking so long to become part of the American mainstream."214

Although Quaker newspapers attacked the wave of propaganda by pointing out the degrading conditions under which the African American population in the South had been living,215 Friends, like others, were not immune to the negativity they encountered at nearly every turn. An article in *Friends Intelligencer* in 1884, for example, described African Americans as "an emotional race" whose condition and behavior were "debased."216 Thomas Hamm has argued that the evidence is "overwhelming . . . that between 1870 and 1920 most American Friends came to embrace the racial attitudes of the larger American society."217

Effects of 'Scientific Racism' on Quaker Schools for African Americans

One consequence of "scientific racism" was a resurgence of interest among European Americans in manual training for African Americans. They were familiar with its success at Hampton Normal & Agricultural Institute in Virginia, widely promoted by Booker T. Washington. A graduate and, later, a teacher at Hampton, Washington became the first principal of Tuskegee Institute (now University) in Alabama in 1881. The Tuskegee curriculum emphasized the development of practical skills over academic studies. Washington believed that only by working steadily and faithfully in agriculture and trades could African Americans "buy southern good will and northern philanthropy," and thereby overcome racism.218 Only after they were accepted by the prevailing society should African Americans pursue "higher" intellectual and artistic education.219

A number of Quaker educators shared enthusiasm for Washington's ideas, which were in keeping with Friends goals for both the freed people and for the southern and eastern European immigrants who were arriving by the tens of thousands—namely to instill habits of thrift, cleanliness, industriousness, and perseverance.220 The philosophy of Armstrong and Washington influenced even some of the best Quaker managers of schools for people of African descent. Martha Schofield sought assistance from Hampton Institute in developing her school's programs. Hampton graduates were also sent to the Penn School to improve both the school and the island's agricultural work[221] and to the Christiansburg Institute to help develop an industrial program.[222]

Support of industrial education often belied a fundamental intellectual disconnect between Quakers and African Americans. Martha Schofield and Yardley Warner, who *sought* the support of the African American communities in the educational enterprises, were rare among school founders. The approach among Quaker educators, who almost uniformly lacked familiarity with and, thus, appreciation of African American culture, was "to make the persons in their programs as much like whites as possible." In this regard Friends were "no better, and no worse than others" who worked in African American education.[223] Yet, in spite of difficulties relating to people with whom so few Friends had any personal acquaintance, Friends commitment to educating the newly freed was at the time "probably the most concentrated, focused and concerted effort American Quakers had ever undertaken."[224]

———— • ————

Not everyone endorsed Washington's philosophy. Fanny Jackson (later Coppin), the influential principal of Philadelphia's Institute for Colored Youth, objected strongly to his view of industrial education. She stood more squarely in the camp of Du Bois, Washington's chief critic, who argued that the focus on vocational education only confirmed the prevailing view that people of African descent were unable to meet European Americans, intellectually and creatively, on their own ground.[225] She held that Washington's views were anti-intellectual and assumed that African Americans were destined to be "common laborers." She wrote, "What the Negro desires today is a Moses who will not lead him to the plow, for he knows the way there, but who will lead him to the point in this country where he can get all of his manhood rights under the Constitution."[226] The institute offered an "uncompromising" curriculum including Latin, physiology, trigonometry, and "enough Greek to read the New Testament"; by the mid-1860s, says historian Linda Perkins, the school "equaled or surpassed many high schools in the nation."[227] Jackson sought to combine a challenging classical education with an awareness of the students' obligations to their race as educated people of African descent.[228] She invited such well-known African Americans as Frederick Douglass and Henry Highland Garnet to take part in a community lecture series and became a popular speaker herself, sharing the commitment to excellence in African American education widely. Jackson did propose the addition of an Industrial Department at Philadelphia's Institute for Colored Youth in 1876, but her motive for doing so was fundamentally different from Washington's: discrimination in employment, she argued, had foreclosed many occupations for African Americans.[229]

The accomplishments of the Institute for Colored Youth were impressive. The industrial program, added to the school's curriculum in 1889, was an immediate success, and the small number of initial offerings quickly expanded to ten trades.[230] The fact that hundreds of people applied for admission to the new program attested its support in the community. While the Quaker managers had been reluctant to spend money on what they considered to be "another experiment," Perkins terms the training "a godsend" to Philadelphia's African Americans—four hundred men and women applied, but only 87 could be admitted; 325 were put on a waiting list.[231] By 1895 five thousand students had been educated at the institute.[232] Still, in 1896 only one of the ninety graduates that year had secured any kind of job.[233]

By the 1890s the managers of the Institute for Colored Youth were "more affluent and 'worldly'" Friends from Philadelphia-area meetings, not the conservative Friends of Arch Street. And despite the presence of three prominent Quaker educators among them, the managers endorsed Washington's program. One of the educators, European American Haverford College professor Francis Gummere, told Jackson the courses were "pitched too high."[234] In 1897 the institute's managers told then Fanny Jackson Coppin that teachers "should guard against the tendency to devote too much time and attention to those studies that lie entirely beyond the future careers of the scholars." Soon afterward she was advised to de-emphasize the classical program; in 1900 the board eliminated history and classics from the curriculum and combined math and science. As a consequence, after thirty-seven years of service, Coppin left, and the managers met with Washington at Tuskegee to choose her successor.[235] In 1902 the Philadelphia building was sold. The school moved to a farm site in Delaware County, twenty-five miles outside the city, and was remodeled after Tuskegee and Hampton with agriculture as its focus.[236] Washington attended the opening; Coppin did not.[237] In 1913 the school became Cheyney State Teacher's College, then Cheyney State College in 1959 and Cheyney University in 1983.[238]

———————•———————

In the 1870s and 1880s, a new generation of Friends, removed from the antebellum era of enslavement and the struggles over abolitionism within their society, began to turn to different causes. The forced and often hostile displacement of Native Americans captured the sympathy of many Quakers who had earlier been active abolitionists.[239] Postwar Friends also devoted increasing energy and resources to evangelism, home and foreign missions, and the temperance crusade. The Orthodox Ohio Yearly Meeting circulated eighty thousand pages of information on temperance, sponsored ninety-five meetings on the subject, and held prayer meetings in 420 saloons.[240]

For a brief time at the end of the century, it seemed that national attention might focus once again on the needs of African Americans. In 1890, after a successful conference on Native American problems, President Rutherford B. Hayes asked European American Quaker Albert Smiley to hold a conference to "consider the condition" of people of African descent. Smiley chaired the initial meeting, considered to be the first to consider "the Negro in America," at Smiley's resort in Lake Mohonk, New York. However, not one of the attendees was African American, an absence that, as historian Ralph Luker notes, made it "easier" for the conference to reach its well-publicized "amicable conclusions."[241] Lyman Abbott, European American editor of the *Christian Union*, responded to criticism of the exclusion with the statement that "a patient is not invited to the consultation of the doctors on his case." A second conference a year later produced many recommendations for improving the education, housing, and opportunities for African Americans, but they were never implemented.[242] The Mohonk conferences, in effect, signaled "the end of an era." The complex relationships of the races in the South would be played out without northern influence for many decades afterward.[243]

ANECDOTES AND MEMOIRS

OF

WILLIAM BOEN,

A COLOURED MAN,

WHO LIVED AND DIED NEAR MOUNT HOLLY, NEW JERSEY.

TO WHICH IS ADDED,

The Testimony of Friends of Mount Holly monthly meeting concerning him.

Philadelphia:
PRINTED BY JOHN RICHARDS,
No. 129 North Third Street.

1834.

Anecdotes and Memoirs of William Boen, title page.

CHAPTER SIX

African American Membership in the Religious Society of Friends

A thorough and deep work of grace is just the same in the heart, no matter the color of the skin.

— Alida Clark, 1871

A T SOUTHLAND SCHOOL IN HELENA, ARKANSAS, Alida Clark made it her life's work not only to educate African Americans but to bring them into the Religious Society of Friends. As the head of Southland, Clark took to heart an 1866 letter from the Indiana (Orthodox) Yearly Meeting to relief workers that spoke of a time when there would be permanent religious meetings among African Americans.[1] Although, strictly speaking, Southland was not a Quaker school but a "nondenominational Christian academy," Clark observed that nearly all of its students "were tinctured at least . . . with Quakerism." The primarily African American monthly meeting started at the school had more than four hundred members at its height. When she sought funding from other Friends for the school she said, "May the good Master be pleased to remind them that at Southland money is needed for educating colored Friends, and for bringing to Jesus the children and youth of former slaves and organizing them into a Friends' meeting."[2]

Clark rarely missed an opportunity to admonish her fellow Quakers about any failure to open meetinghouse doors to African Americans. After fundraising trips to more than four hundred Quaker meetings over one seven-month period in 1879, she professed great puzzlement about why Friends, who were generous with their time and funds in support of schools for African Americans, were so unwilling to invite those students into their religious fellowship.[3] "Think, Friends, of the millions of money expended by Friends toward these people," Clark pointed out, "and yet they must go and unite with some other religious denomination, thus virtually declaring to them that *our profession* is not adapted to them."[4] In contrast to Quaker teachers in other schools for

African Americans, Clark declared that she did not subscribe to the view that "the colored people are too emotional and impressible ever to become Friends."[5]

Southland is a rare example of a Quaker meeting that included African American members after the Civil War.[6] Historian Henry Cadbury concluded after his 1936 study of African American membership that "At no period in history and in no part of America have Negroes ever become in large numbers members of the Society of Friends." In 1948 Bernard Walton, Secretary of Friends General Conference, said that he knew of only seven people of African descent among the 17,000 members of monthly meetings affiliated with his organization.[7] Louis Jones is another historian who has commented on this phenomenon. Writing of Iowa Quakers in 1914, he said he found it "interesting, in view of the long and helpful relation which the Friends of Iowa have borne towards this people, to observe that but very few negroes have ever been taken into membership in the Society of Friends in this State."[8] Historian Stephen Weeks found the scarcity of Quakers of African descent to be "more striking when one recalls the early and constant concern of Quakerism for the colored race, especially for its spiritual welfare." It is "curious," wrote Weeks, that applying for membership would become an often lengthy trial at the same time that Friends were "making such eloquent appeals for the right of liberating slaves." Weeks cites the example of an African American applicant who waited several years in the early 1800s to become a member of his monthly meeting, even though the yearly meeting, North Carolina, had announced that meetings should "attend to the discipline in that respect without distinction of color."[9]

————— • —————

Determining African American membership in the Society of Friends at any point is a difficult task, as few records systematically reveal information about those who have chosen to be Quakers.[10] First, there has not always been a clear distinction between being a member or an attender. Many people participate in the life of the meeting without formally joining. Historian Kenneth Carroll has asserted that there was no such thing as applying for membership until the 1730s and 1740s.[11] In her analysis of early New England Yearly Meeting records Quaker historian Elizabeth Cazden found no comprehensive membership lists until the 1760s when meetings were directed to visit every family and tighten enforcement of the discipline.[12] Meetings often did not keep lists of members unless they happened to divide into two.[13] Among those that did maintain membership lists, Quaker practice by and large has not been to note race in membership records, although some meetings did indicate race in the minutes recording new membership. Quaker minute books did record manumissions and, at one time, African American births and marriages, but such entries did not imply membership in a meeting.[14]

Presented with these problems, Cadbury nonetheless undertook a study of African Americans in the Religious Society of Friends and also sought to identify those who "dressed in Quaker garb," associated closely with Friends, or were Quaker in "everything except official membership." While he was able to verify the names of approximately forty African American Quakers in the 1700s and 1800s, Cadbury's analysis of a substantial number of documents was often inconclusive. Records did not always substantiate the membership of an African American commonly thought of as Quaker. Thus, in large measure, any picture of the experience of African American Friends rests on articles in Friends newspapers, letters, diaries, and, at times, meeting minutes. The count of forty, from Cadbury, does not include all the members of the Southland Meeting, but only the members Cadbury could identify by name; specifically the men who were recorded as ministers. It is also true that that the Southland Monthly Meeting ended with the closing of the school in 1925; with no other Friends meetings in the vicinity to attend, many members found other churches to join.[15] Why there were so few African American Quakers is a disturbing puzzle for many Friends, but scanty African American membership may suggest that Quakers of European descent were, on the whole, unable to separate themselves from the racist attitudes and behaviors of the wider culture.

Special Meetings for African Americans

Although Friends in the North and the South brought people of African descent to meetings for worship, only infrequently were these the Quakers' own scheduled meetings for worship. More commonly, they were separate meetings organized especially for the enslaved but run by Friends of European descent. The meetings had both spiritual and practical purposes—to instill Christian virtues and to help the newly freed prepare for their independent life. Their intent was not, however, to convert the attendees to Quakerism. This is true for meetings for African Americans held sporadically through the 1700s and into the 1800s. In 1700 Philadelphia Monthly Meeting issued a minute expressing William Penn's desire to establish a separate meeting for people of African descent to worship once a month in that city. But it is not clear whether any meetings were held; Cadbury wrote that he had not found any "further references to such actual meetings in any subsequent time."[16]

In 1758, almost sixty years later, North Carolina Yearly Meeting established regular meetings for worship for African Americans at four different locations; Friends attended to make sure that "good order was observed."[17] In 1784 Flushing (New York) Meeting also created regular meetings for people of African descent in four locations.[18] In the 1790s meetings for African Americans were held with some frequency from South Carolina to Nantucket and in Philadelphia and nearby New Jersey and Delaware (both part of Philadelphia Yearly Meeting). Sometimes hundreds attended a meeting, even "1400 to 1500" in Philadelphia in 1853.[19] In Haddonfield, New Jersey, a meeting was established in 1799 that had almost two hundred people of African descent, and other meetings sometimes attracted similar numbers.[20]

Occasionally, traveling Friends ministers held meetings in African American churches, some attracting many people. William Williams reported "a thousand blacks together" attended his candlelight meeting in Baltimore in 1811, and Jesse Kersey spoke of "large number of colored people" at a Philadelphia meeting in 1834.[21] In 1854, Indiana Friends traveling in North Carolina called four special meetings of "free colored people (Baptists)" while they were visiting Rich Square Meeting. Noting that some of the people of African descent at the meetings were "nearly White," William Rees, one of the travelers, reported that the meetings "were orderly, and the people appeared attentive."[22]

Around 1800, Friends in some places came to feel ministry to African Americans was no longer necessary. After traveling through the South seeking African American members, Quaker minister Rebecca Jones determined by 1805 that Friends "upon weighty deliberation were united in the belief that the service to them was over, and they have now several places for worship of their own."[23] The next year Philadelphia Quarterly Meeting held its last meeting for African Americans and their descendants, partly in recognition of the fact that African Americans in the city had established and attended several independent churches.[24]

Quaker Reluctance to Proselytize

Organizing meetings for African Americans was one thing; considering them for membership was quite another. "Excited" discussions about admitting African Americans to the Society of Friends in the 1770s engaged Friends as meetings began to disown members who refused to manumit those they enslaved. While it might seem that those who worked to free the enslaved would look forward to welcoming them into their religious fellowship, Quakers were not necessarily committed to taking that next step. Rarely did Friends of European descent invite people of African descent to learn about their Quaker beliefs, and even more rarely did they try to interest them in becoming members.[25] Nash interprets this lack of interest in sharing to be a sign of Quaker "ambivalence and standoffishness toward black Philadelphia."[26] The mid-1700s was the time of great internal ferment for Friends who were focused on purifying their society. Fearing that the increasing number of members who did not live according to Quaker strictures were damaging both the public's view of Friends and the society's internal spiritual life, their first priority was to become a unified community and rid their society of those who did not live up to its discipline.[27] The Society was becoming stricter, more consistent, and "much more divorced from the world," according to Barbour and Frost.[28] Seeking new members was not consistent with this movement inward; Friends were focused on disciplining their own members, not on adding to their membership rolls.

"The ordinary ideas of charity did not supply a policy" for Quakers, notes James. "Negroes were neither neighbors to be let alone, nor prospective converts, nor children who would outgrow their childhood and be raised into the church."[29] By 1784 the mainstream churches had taken on the prevailing negative attitudes about race and, for the most part, denied people of African descent full church membership and equal participation in church affairs. A few denominations did show more interest in interracial congregations; Christ Church (Episcopal) in Philadelphia and the Moravians were actively seeking African American converts.[30]

———————•———————

In 1796 Quaker John Hunt wrote in his diary that the "spirit of prejudice which had been imbibed on account of colour" may have accounted for the rejection of so many African American membership applications over the last twenty years in Philadelphia Yearly Meeting.[31] Hunt's statement, and others similar to his, undergird the assertion that Friends were fundamentally not concerned for the well-being of the enslaved African.[32] Some historians maintain that they abolished enslavement among themselves to preserve the purity of the Religious Society of Friends, not to restore freedom to people of African descent. The longstanding custom among some branches of Friends not to proselytize for members and the notion that African American religious practice inherently clashed with Quaker practice also inhibited membership. While early Friends often claimed that being a Quaker required no special attitude or training—"only willingness to attend to the Light Within"—their practice with respect to African Americans often contradicted this claim. Perhaps uneasy with such ambiguity, southern Friends soon came to believe "the slaves mysteriously lacking the supposedly universal capacity to adopt Quakerism."[33]

One Friend's opinion of a well-attended Sunday afternoon meeting in the late 1790s at Goose Creek meetinghouse reveals the attitudes that would surely not stir any desire on the part of African Americans to explore Quakerism. In his memoir, European American Henry Hull recounts that he advised those African Americans present to "avoid every evil practice" so that God would bless them. He prayed that they would have "the patience to endure affliction in this world [for] a better world, where they would be freed from servitude and suffering. . . . The poor creatures paid great attention, and sat with unusual quietude."[34]

Philadelphia Friends did make some effort to attract new members in 1782, a venture James describes as a "veritable campaign . . . unprecedented in the eighteenth century." Perceiving that many people were attracted to Quakerism, in that year a Philadelphia committee wrote to Friends in other yearly meetings that it was compiling a list of books for outsiders and urged their brethren everywhere to do so as well. The committee printed pamphlets in French and German and built new meetinghouses in more convenient locations. But these Philadelphia Friends seemed to lack the "zeal of Fox," notes James, and moreover showed no interest in changing some of their more "peculiar" ways to make it easier for new people to feel welcome in Quaker fellowship. The newly convinced had to find their own way in the existing group, and some of those who were drawn to Quakerism were "quietly but firmly discouraged from participation."[35]

Consciously or not, the idea of reaching out for new members appears to have escaped most Quakers. For example, according to historian Martha Paxson Grundy, it seems simply not to have occurred to teachers at Bethany Mission for Colored People. Committed as they were to nurturing their students' moral and spiritual lives and encouraging them to attend church, the Quakers among the teaching staff would not promote attendance at their own meetings. Many other Friends schools for freed people demonstrated the same tendency. Grundy suggests that "Perhaps the gulf of race and class was too wide for the teachers' imaginations to bridge; the question of bringing these new converts to their own churches or meetings may never have entered their minds."[36]

———•———

Disturbed at the objections raised when the question of African American membership came up, Philadelphia European American Friend Joseph Drinker wrote a "Plea for Admission of Colored People to the Society of Friends" in 1795. Drinker observed that, despite their liberal testimonies, Quakers "are the only People I know who make any objections to the Blacks or People of Color joining them in Church Fellowship." His statement may well not have been accurate, but it reveals Drinker's disappointment with the Society of Friends, whose principles, he clearly believed, demanded equal treatment for all the children of God. Their reluctance to admit people of African descent seemed to stem from the view that "if membership . . . was granted, the privilege of intermarriage with the whites could not be withheld, and such mixtures are objectionable." Although Drinker stated his conviction that Christ would not create "one fold for black sheep and another for white,"[37] others could not see beyond the issue of intermarriage. The Quaker "elites" had long been repulsed by the idea of interracial sex and marriage, and to Friends and others, mulattoes were visible but unwelcome manifestations of interracial sex. Historian Alison Hirsch points to the reason European American Quaker James Logan, mayor of Philadelphia in 1723, sent his "Negro boy" south to be sold. Logan said the maturing boy was showing some "inclinations to the wrong Colour," namely to women of other than African descent. Clearly such an "inclination" was unacceptable.[38]

Sarah Smiley, who founded numerous schools for freedmen in the South, was one of the few Friends of the time who remarked on the fact that Quakers committed themselves to ministering to the physical, intellectual, and spiritual needs of the freed people but did not invite them to join the fellowship of Friends meetings. She expressed those views in a letter to the 1867 New York Yearly Meeting, which, according to a report on the reading of her letter in *Friends Review*, created quite a stir. At the same meeting, Friends minister Robert Douglas, also European American, criticized other Friends of European descent for showing no concern that African Americans were joining other churches. According to the same *Friends Review* article, Douglas declared that Friends doctrines "were the best calculated to advance vital Christianity" and should be spread. Douglas's plea impelled the meeting to consider how to make African American membership easier. The "subject obtained a strong hold upon the minds of Friends," a report of the meeting in *Friends Review* stated, but the outcome was familiar: the only decision the meeting could reach was to raise money for African Americans in need.[39] Smiley, for her part, ultimately sought a different spiritual home. She left the Society of Friends in 1873 and became an Episcopalian in 1880.[40]

An 'Obstacle Course'

There is no doubt that people of African descent who might decide to become Friends had "a formidable obstacle course to run."[41] As Sydney James notes, it would have been "logical for [Friends] to take advantage of the domestic tranquility after 1783 to convert outsiders." And those who had been freed by Quakers were an especially likely fit, acquainted as they were, to some degree, with the religion. But, "like so many Friends even until the present day, they showed no such inclination."[42] In addition, many applications from both European and African Americans awaited an expression of their "convincement of the principles of Truth"—a matter subject to the interpretation of any given meeting.[43] When African Americans were accepted at all, a few applicants were accepted readily; but more often Friends acted only after "weighty deliberations."[44] A similarly vague expression—"insufficient knowledge of Friends' principles"—seems to have been the reason that African Americans in the South had been rejected for membership after the Civil War. However, there had been members of African descent in Newbegun Creek, North Carolina, Meeting as early as 1829.[45] In any event, it was rarely recorded that color was the motivating influence in such delays and refusals.

African American Membership: The 1700s

The earliest Quaker of African descent that Cadbury found has no name and only sketchy information about the date—"around 1750"— with a note that he belonged to a meeting in New England. Although he mentions the instance only in a footnote, Cadbury was convinced by two different mentions, one by a Quaker minister from Lynn, the other, Sarah Grimké, who said that the meeting leaders would not affirm the African American's "gift in the ministry." His reply was to the effect that "[If] you will not receive my testimony, then I am authorized to tell you that no testimony bearer shall arise amongst you while the present heads of your meeting are living." Micajah Collins, the minister from Lynn, later said that this "prophecy . . . was strictly fulfilled."[46]

Two of the approximately forty Quakers Cadbury identified were New Englanders. According to the records of Dover (New Hampshire) Monthly Meeting, African American Caesar Sankey and Sarah Sharp, both of Dover, were married on 23 November 1774. While their marriage in the meeting did not necessarily indicate membership, another entry for February 1777 does: Caesar Sankey's disownment in 1777 for "going into the war."[47] In 1780, a woman enslaved by Quaker David Harris was admitted to membership in Smithfield Meeting in Rhode

Island. Pink Harris applied to "come under friends care" in June 1780; she was accepted as a member that September and was eventually man-umitted by Harris.[48]

Just before the American Revolution, Mount Holly Meeting in New Jersey rejected the application of William Boen (1734?–1824), an African American known, it is said, "to walk in the path of truth and righteousness." Born enslaved near Rancocas, New Jersey, Boen encountered the Holy Spirit while he was clearing a hillside for his enslaver during the French and Indian War. Worried about being killed by Native Americans and anxious to be prepared for his fate, he stopped chopping and stood very still. Then, he said, "It seemed as if a flaming sword passed through me. And when it passed over, and I recollected myself (for I stood so, some time) it was showed me how I should be made fit to die." Boen believed that he now had a new "Master," Jesus Christ, and hoped that his enslaver would not order him to do anything against the orders of Christ.[49] At some point after Boen's revelation, his enslaver asked him if he wished to be free. "I didn't say any thing to it," Boen wrote. "I thought he might know I should like to be free." He was manumitted about 1773.

Near the same time, Boen asked to marry a neighbor, a free African American woman named Dinah or Dido, in the manner of Friends. John Woolman, who was Boen's friend, arranged for their marriage in the Mount Holly meeting house, which included a meeting for wor-ship and a certificate signed by all who witnessed. Boen also applied for membership at Mount Holly Meeting, but, while the meeting asked him to be faithful, it ultimately rejected his request. Woolman, disturbed at the delay in responding to Boen, predicted correctly that the meeting would "dwindle and become reduced again" because it was unwilling to see the African American as an equal. Woolman then put forward Boen's name as an elder, but the meeting declined this application as well. Not until forty-three years later, in 1814, did the Mount Holly Meeting approve Boen's longstanding application.[50] Despite his initial rejection, Boen used plain language and dressed in plain, simple, and neutral-colored clothing. Once asked about his appearance, Boen stated, "I am endeavouring to follow the footsteps of Christ." He listened to and followed "*that within* him." He also actively opposed slavery. Weeks before his death he said "he thought he was alone with regard to his testimony against slavery . . . but [he] believed it would grow and increase among Friends."[51]

A New Jersey newspaper published Boen's obituary. "Rare indeed are the instances that we meet with, in which we feel called upon to record the virtues of any of this afflicted race of people," the article read. Boen, however, "was an exemplary member of the Religious Society of Friends; and as he lived, so he died—a rare pattern of a self-denying follower of Jesus Christ."[52] Four years later, on 11 June 1828, Mount Holly Meeting wrote a memorial minute that was read and approved by Burlington Quarterly Meeting in Chesterfield on 25 November of that year. The minute was forwarded to Philadelphia Yearly Meeting of 1829. It stated in part of Boen:

> He made application to become a member of our society; but way not opening in Friends minds, he was not received, but encouraged to continue faithful; which we believe he did, from the account we have of nearly his whole life. . . . By yielding full of obedience to that light, which it was his chiefest joy to follow, he became truly convinced of the necessity of maintaining the various testimonies which we, as a people, have been called upon to bear; and, in some respects, he had to bear a testimony against things in which many of his white brethren indulge, particularly in regard to slavery; refusing to wear, or use in any shape, articles which come through that corrupted channel.[53]

———————•———————

In Philadelphia Yearly Meeting, Abigail Franks, of mixed European, African American, and Native American descent, applied to Birmingham Preparative Meeting in 1781. Ordinarily a monthly meeting would decide on an application, but in this instance the meeting asked a quarterly meeting committee appointed to investigate whether Franks should be rejected because of her "color." Three months later, after some members had visited Franks, the committee reported that "her disposition they apprehended to be worthy of Friends' notice" and noted in addition that "her color appeared to them not darker than some who are esteemed white." Their acceptance of this woman could not be made final, however, until the yearly meeting declared she should be admitted on the "same ground in common" with other applicants. While records do not give the details of the "weighty and edifying deliberations" on the matter, a letter cited described "mountains of opposition" to her admission. Three years after her application, Franks was accepted by the 1784 yearly meeting, which declared that her sincerity was the most important consideration.[54]

In 1790, after lengthy consideration of the proposal, a few radical Friends in Philadelphia Yearly Meeting succeeded in incorporating a statement into the yearly meeting Discipline that "Meetings are at liberty to receive such [convinced persons] into membership, without respect of nation or color." Thus, African American membership became "possible . . . but not common."[55] The first known African American to request membership after the yearly meeting's statement was Cynthia Miers. When she applied to Plainfield (New Jersey) Monthly Meeting to become a member in April 1796, Miers went through a process not unlike Abigail Franks's. Women in the meeting received her application—at that time Friends business was conducted separately for men and women—and informed the men's meeting that "a mulatto woman" had applied for membership. "This being a case of a singular nature amongst us," the women reported, "the meeting thinks it best to proceed very cautiously herein."[56]

The men's meeting appointed an unusually large committee of thirteen of its members to consider the application, a fact likely indicative of the concern about the request.[57] Miers's application also went to the quarterly and yearly meetings, the latter reporting, "We are united in believing our Discipline already established relative to receiving persons into membership is not limited with respect to Nation or Colour."[58] Still, another eight months and three separate meetings for business passed before Miers became a member in December 1796. In July 1799 David and Grace Mapps, two African Americans known widely for their hospitality to traveling Quakers, became members of the Little Egg Harbor Meeting in New Jersey. David Mapps (?–1835?) served as an overseer of the meeting and as a member of its school committee. After Grace died in 1833, David Mapps married Anna Bustill, granddaughter of Cyrus Bustill, one of Philadelphia's prominent African Americans in the late 1700s.[59] Richard Cooper was received into Little Creek Preparative Meeting in Delaware near the turn of the century. His memorial provides no date of his admittance and states only that he became a member "in advanced life." A native of Barbados who had suffered horrendous oppression from early childhood, Cooper became interested in Quakerism because of the female Friend who had enslaved and later freed him. In 1820, as he was dying, Cooper spoke of being thankful for becoming a Friend and stated that he hoped he had "brought no reproach upon the society."[60]

———•———

According to Hiram Hilty, North Carolina Yearly Meeting considered it "startling" when New Garden Quarterly Meeting sought permission to admit African Americans in 1798. A special committee appointed to study the query reported favorably because, it held, the Discipline stood for racial equality. Friends in the Eastern Quarter in North Carolina, concerned about the dwindling number of Friends and the laying down of so many meetings as Friends left for the Midwest, were inclined to open membership to African Americans. Hilty has observed that some there suggested inviting African Americans to their meetings and went "so far as to ask" about accepting them as members. But in 1800 the yearly meeting found it a difficult matter and, after two postponements, rejected possibility of African American membership.[61] In the third year, the Yearly Meeting finally declared the Discipline "fully sufficient in respect to receiving members."[62]

Not only did meetings show considerable hesitation about admitting African Americans, but instances of outright prejudice were certainly a discouragement to others who might be considering membership. In the late 1790s, Joseph Carpenter of New Rochelle, a Friend of European descent who was guardian for three orphaned children descended from enslaved Africans, had been told at meeting that the children must sit in a separate location. Without a word Carpenter moved with his whole family to sit there with the children. Carpenter's action was "a visible reminder that the Society of Friends had fallen short of its egalitarian potential." His action also clearly influenced his meeting, for soon the whole family returned to its accustomed place.[63]

African American Membership: The 1800s

In general the acceptance of African Americans into Quaker fellowship was no more common in the nineteenth century than it had been in the eighteenth. Still, a few notable Friends of African descent did exist. One of the best known was Paul Cuffe, the prominent mariner widely recognized for his "sober demeanor" and sterling character.[64] Cuffe's father, who was freed in 1742, and his mother, a member of the Wampanoag tribe of Massachusetts, "followed" (attended) Dartmouth Monthly Meeting. Though they were not members, they brought their children up according to Quaker principles. Having taught himself reading, writing, mathematics, navigation, and other seafaring skills, Paul Cuffe had shipped aboard a whaling vessel by the time he was fourteen years old. During the Revolution, he and his brother David built a small vessel to smuggle goods through British blockades. Over time, the Cuffe family built more ships and Paul owned shares in up to ten vessels, ran a mercantile business in New Bedford, operated a saw mill and windmill in Dartmouth, and farmed more than one hundred acres in modern-day Westport (carved from Dartmouth in 1787).[65] In 1800 he bought a gristmill and turned its management over to a group of African American partners.[66]

Cuffe attended Quaker meeting for much of his life, used the language of Friends, and dressed in Quaker gray and a wide-brimmed black hat. But he did not become a member of Westport Meeting (New England Yearly Meeting) until 1808, when he was forty-nine years old. Cuffe preached only occasionally; he once "preached a remarkably powerful sermon" at Arch Street Meeting, according to Friend Frances Rhoads.[67] At the time he joined Westport Meeting he was the only member of African descent in New England Yearly Meeting.[68]

Cuffe founded the first school in Westport, which was open to both European and African American children. Many of Cuffe's Quaker colleagues actively opposed enslavement, and Cuffe himself was a lifelong proponent of racial equality. In 1780 he and other Dartmouth men of African descent petitioned the Massachusetts legislature to exempt them from taxation on the grounds that "we are not allowed the Privileges of freemen of the State, having no vote for Influence in the Election with those that tax us"; neither, the petition noted, could they inherit property. His letters relate his frequent encounters with racial prejudice and his commitment to abolition.[69] Cuffe died in 1817; his grave and that of his wife, Alice Pequit Cuffe, are "just outside the back door," of Westport Friends meetinghouse, "apart" from where the Quakers are buried.[70]

Instances of African American membership in the early 1800s could be found in other regions as well. In Indiana, "Bobbie" Peters, freed by his Quaker enslavers and brought to Ohio from Virginia in 1811, was said to be the only African American member of Stillwater Quarterly Meeting, at least through 1936. The meeting cared for him in his declining years and buried him on the Stillwater Friends grounds.[71] In the Midwest, Hamm has stated, evidence of hostility to African American membership is no more abundant than "indications of lack of prejudice."[72] In 1843 the largely Quaker Henry County (Indiana) Female Anti-Slavery Society resolved that "we do not believe that any person who is so prejudiced against color, as to refuse to eat, walk or to sit with colored persons can be a true christian."[73] There is evidence that "at least some Friends" had personal relationships across racial lines, and records show that Quaker graveyards in Indiana and Ohio were not segregated. Still, Hamm notes that the overall number of people of African descent attending regular Midwestern Friends meetings through these decades was not large. He adds that "racism may have been a factor," or not wanting to proselytize.[74]

————•————

By 1841, when English Friend Joseph Sturge made his trips to meetings along the East Coast, he described Philadelphia as a "metropolis of prejudice against colour, of Anti-Abolition feeling among Friends, as well as others," and also noted the scarcity of Quakers of African descent at other stops on his tour. The meeting in New Bedford, Massachusetts, was an exception. "I had the pleasure of witnessing the coloured part of the audience, placed on a level, and sitting promiscuously with the white," Sturge remarked, "the only opportunity I had of making such an observation in the United States; as on ordinary occasions, the coloured people rarely attend Friends' meetings."[75] Some twenty years earlier, the New Bedford meeting had refused membership to African American businessman Nathan Johnson, despite his close association with several meeting members and the fact that his request was presented "very well and properly." The request received "due notice," one meeting member wrote, and was sent to the overseers for decision. Membership rolls indicate that Johnson was never accepted as a member, and no evidence exists that the meeting offered reasons for its rejection.[76] However, by the 1870s another New England African American, Sarah Antone, was on the membership list of New Bedford Meeting.[77] About the same time Sturge made his visit, Sarah Grimké wrote that the application of one elderly African American was rejected despite the fact that his character and convincement of Friends principles were "unquestioned." The meeting identified his color as the reason for the man's rejection; according to one member, the matter was decided privately and, Grimké noted, "elicited no condemnation" from anyone in the meeting.[78]

At a Friends boarding school in New Rochelle, New York, where Susan B. Anthony (then a Quaker) taught in 1838, the "continued prejudice against the colored attenders at meeting" accounted in her view for losses in enrollment; people left the school, she believed, "rather than associate with the Blacks."[79] Even membership did not assure the welcome of a meeting. In a letter to British Friend Elizabeth Pease, Sarah Grimké reported that when an African American Quaker rose to preach in the meetinghouse at Tarrytown, New York, in 1840 "the Friends raised quite a fuss about a colored man sitting in the meetinghouse and some left on account of it."[80] An African American member in a meeting in the South was rare enough to prompt a special notice of his death in an 1850 issue of the *Friends Review*: at least one "responsible Friend" said that Miles Lassiter was the "only coloured member known to him" in North Carolina.[81]

In 1888 the editor of the Hicksite newspaper *Intelligencer and Journal* stated that the only African American Quaker he could name was one whom he had known more than sixty years earlier. One reader said that he, too, knew one African American member but at a similar remove from the time at which he wrote. The editor declared that while nothing in Quaker principles prevented African American membership, "we are conscious how much hesitation and prejudice there might be in applying them to a particular case."[82]

Segregation in Meetinghouses

Though Hamm found no evidence "that Friends in the Midwest ever segregated their few black members and attenders,"[83] that was not always the practice in other regions. According to Cadbury, many meetinghouses had a "special place against the wall, under the stairs, or in the gallery." When one Philadelphia meeting house was enlarged in 1756, the builders were told to allow some "suitable places for African Americans to sit."[84]

Cyrus Bustill, his wife Elizabeth, and his daughter Grace Bustill Douglass, who regularly attended Quaker meeting and lived "in the Quaker manner," were compelled to sit separate from European American Friends. At North Meeting, the first the family attended, they were seated on a back bench apart from those occupied by European American Quakers. After 1804, the year Arch Street Meeting was built, they began to attend there and found themselves again segregated.[85] Grace Douglass was drawn to Quaker fellowship, she once wrote, because "my heart acknowledged the superior eloquence of silence the beauty of sitting down in humility and heart-brokenness to wait the operation of the holy spirit and then to feel its gentle influence distilling like dew upon the soul, and subduing every unholy and wandering thought."[86] Still, neither she, her father, nor her mother ever submitted an application for membership.

Sarah Mapps Douglass (1806–82), the daughter of Grace Bustill Douglass, may well have been the first African American who worshiped within the Religious Society of Friends to share her feelings about the manner of Friends worship and conduct of European American Quakers toward her. She explained her mother's feelings in an 1844 letter to Sarah Grimké:

> While her children were in their infancy she had a great concern to become a member of Friends Society not only because she was fully convinced of the excellence of the principles professed by that society, but because she earnestly desired that her children should receive the guarded education Friends give to theirs. She mentioned her concern to a Friend who said do not apply, you will only have your feelings wounded. Friends will not receive you. Thus admonished, and feeling that prejudice had closed the doors against her, she did not make her concern known to the Society. There was nothing but my Mother's complexion in the way to prevent her being a member, she was highly intelligent & pious; her whole life blameless.[87]

Sarah Douglass and her mother nonetheless continued to attend Quaker meetings but in segregated seating, she told Grimké:

> For several years we were squeezed into a little box under the stairs at Arch Street meeting and after a while we sat upon the back bench.

I do not know who told us to sit there, I only remember that the change was made. When we left Arch Street Meeting and went to North Meeting we sat upon the back bench. When North Meeting was removed to its present location Mother went determined not to sit upon the back bench unless she was told to make her seat there. She was about to seat herself in another part of the house when a Friend beckoned her to the back bench and told her that it was set apart for colored people. There I still sit, *not from choice, as has been asserted,* but because it is appointed for me.[88]

Douglass added that "a friend sat at either end of the bench to prevent white persons from sitting there. . . . I have not been in Arch Street meeting for four years, but my mother goes once a week and frequently she has a whole long bench to herself." Grace Douglass also experienced discrimination at the hands of Philadelphia Friends in other ways. When she attended the funeral of a minister she knew at North Meeting, she was seated in a room by herself. Afterward, while women of European descent rode to the cemetery, Douglass was asked to walk behind the casket with two African American males. Sarah Douglass described similar treatment at New York meeting in 1837, which her mother attended while taking part in a women's antislavery convention that year. "After she had been in Mtg. sometime a Friend came in & sat by her, & asked her who she lived with. Mother said she did not live with any one. The Fd. then said that the colored people sat up stairs 'as Fds. do not like to sit by thy color' & added she had no objection herself to sit by her, but that when she came again she had better sit up stairs. She did not go to the Mtg. again."[89]

News of the segregation made its way to England and stimulated sharp criticism of American Quakers. After visiting Philadelphia Yearly Meeting in 1843, British Friend John Candler had published a letter in the British Friend accusing Quakers of European descent of being prejudiced against African Americans. "Even those we call leading Friends are tainted" by that prejudice, he said. English Friends had also heard of the "Negro pew," thanks to the letter from William Bassett and Sarah Grimké which Elizabeth Pease, the recipient, had printed in part—without using any names—in a pamphlet the same year. British Friends were distressed to hear Arnold Buffum, in London for the 1843 Anti-Slavery Convention, report that some African Americans had been denied membership because of their color. A blanket denial by "P.R." soon appeared in both the Philadelphia and London issues of *The Friend*, claiming that African Americans "sit on the same benches that the whites occupy and often side by side." Referring only to Grace Douglass, Cadbury believed that "P.R." was "evidently mistaken" about membership applications because none had been received.[90] However, as Sarah Mapps Douglass said, Grace Douglass had been advised not to apply for it would be too painful for her.[91] *The Friend* also suggested one reason for the lack of African American members was that Friends' "mode of worship does not suit their dispositions: they are fond of music and excitement," views that, according to historian Ryan Jordan, revealed "the limits of Friends' racial egalitarianism." The denials showed how "subtle and often unspoken" prejudice can be.[92]

Perhaps more motivated by the need to escape criticism than by the need to speak the truth, a four-column article in *The Friend* firmly denied segregation and asserted that African Americans "sit on the same benches that the whites occupy and often side by side."[93] On December 14, 1843, Douglass wrote a letter to the *National Anti-Slavery Standard* saying she had "frequently heard my mother say that very many of our people inclined to Friends' mode of worship" but that the "unchristian conduct kept them out." Some left Quaker meetings because they preferred a church where they would not have to "bear the cross of sitting on the 'black bench.'"[94] The segregated seating caused so many people of African descent to stop attending Friends meetings by 1850 that a Quaker antislavery journal reported that the African American membership of the Society had been dropping steadily for almost fifty years.[95] "Friends only reluctantly opened their religious Society to colored members," Drake has stated, "and they wished no more than other whites of their day and generation to associate with different races on terms of social intimacy" even, apparently, in burial grounds.[96]

For a time African Americans were buried in the Middletown (Pennsylvania) Meeting burial grounds, but in 1703 meeting records reported that "Friends are not satisfied with having negros buried in Friends' burying ground; therefore Robt Heaton and Thomas Stackhouse are appointed to fence off a portion for such uses." In 1738 the same meeting found even the fences to be inadequate separation.

That year the minutes said that "deceased negros [are] forbidden to be buried within the bounds of the graveyard belong to this Meeting." In 1807 in the District of Columbia, however, Friend Jonathan Shoemaker deeded a lot for Friends burials in which both Native and African Americans were interred.[97]

Membership after the Civil War

Despite the great activity in social and educational work among freedmen, Quakers continued to evince little interest in inviting newly freed people and others of African descent into the Quaker fellowship after the Civil War.[98] English and some American Quakers expressed puzzlement over the fact that American Friends seemed blind to the possibility that attracting African American members would help rebuild the denomination in the South. Quakerism seemed logical in part because the Society of Friends was the only denomination to avoid a difficult North-South separation over the issue of enslavement. And, as British Orthodox Friend Stanley Pumphrey reasoned, the Carolinas were "a hopeful field for extension." Traveling in the South after the war, Pumphrey found "a general sentiment among the [African American] people that the Quakers are about right" and that they listened to Friends preaching more closely than others. He was "astonished" at the crowds that traveled over treacherous roads to some spot in the woods for an appointed meeting and "seemed ready to drink in just as long as my strength would hold out to talk to them." Faced with the fact that a thousand freed people had been received into Methodist churches in one year, Pumphrey suggested the yearly meeting consider the reasons for and implications of the fact that such churches were "gathering the fruit instead of ourselves."[99]

Pumphrey's plea went unheeded. Even as the Baltimore Association, working to rebuild Quakerism in the South, held revival meetings that brought in many new converts in the late 1860s, they did not include African Americans in their outreach.[100] Similarly, in 1877 Baltimore (Orthodox) Yearly Meeting, which included many Virginia meetings, created a committee to "bring the unconverted to Christ," but made no effort to invite the newly freed to attend their meetings.[101] Aside from Southland, in Arkansas, postwar African American membership was sparse in the South. Hilty contends that "By and large the prevalent race attitudes of the region gradually found their way into the Religious Society of Friends in North Carolina." African Americans in North Carolina did not become members of Quaker meetings in any noticeable numbers, "nor would they have been welcome in most."[102] Hilty's comments are borne out by the experience of a number of African Americans from Salem who applied for membership in 1869. A committee appointed to meet with them referred them to their nearest monthly meeting. No evidence of a decision appears to exist, but yearly meeting records of 1870 stated that the candidates were "very imperfectly acquainted with the principles of Friends."[103] Still, at least some had become members; the North Carolina Yearly Meeting minutes of 1879 report the "deaths of three colored Friends."[104]

———•———

Some postwar meetings in the South, other than at Southland Institute in Arkansas and at Maryville Institute in Tennessee, accepted African American attenders and members. Jesse McPherson, a minister of Maryville Monthly Meeting, held several meetings for African Americans in 1879. Afterward, according to the Missionary Board of the Tennessee Branch of North Carolina Yearly Meeting, thirty were "received in membership with us" and a room for their meeting and Sunday school had been set up in the Institute building. "They express themselves much gratified with the liberty of serving the Lord directly under the guidance of the Holy Spirit, which priviledge [sic] they regard as peculiar to the Society of Friends" the board reported.[105] Thus, with a meeting membership that reached 450 by 1893, Southland stands alone in bringing a large number of people of African descent into the Society of Friends. Only two years after the school had opened in 1864, 71 students and staff in the school organized a Meeting for Worship and made it known they hoped to become members of the Society of Friends.

After years of delay and even hints that Clark might be acting a bit too hastily, in 1873 the Orthodox Indiana Yearly Meeting recognized Southland as an official monthly meeting with 78 members. Many members were students at the school; others lived nearby.[106] By 1876 all but 9 of the 142 members were of African descent. Always predominantly African American from that time, the meeting grew to more almost 500 members by 1893.[107] "Few friends brought blindfolded into the meeting would have thought themselves among the despised race who, so short a time back, were not accounted a people, but are now the people of God," Clark noted.[108]

———•———

Between 1870 and 1903 a few African American men were recorded ministers of the Southland meeting, which served hundreds of members by the late 1870s. Alida and Calvin Clark petitioned Indiana Orthodox Yearly Meeting to make African American Daniel Drew, one of Southland's first converts to Quakerism, a minister.[109] In 1872, the Missionary Board of Indiana Yearly Meeting appointed him to represent Southland Meeting at the yearly meeting sessions.[110] Drew became a popular evangelist. Later he served as a minister in Oregon Yearly Meeting.

In addition to Drew, others recorded at Southland included ministers Morris Brown, Arthur Crump, and Calvin Kerr—all of whom Cadbury believes were of African descent, as well as Chandler Paschall, who was in the first graduating class of the school. African Americans Monroe Wilburn, George Wilburn, Moses Weaver, Duncan Freeland, Thomas Pollard, and Joseph Coleman, and Arthur Coleman were all in "pastoral work or the ministry," Cadbury determined. Osborn Taylor, who was eight when he appeared at Southland as a refugee, went on to study at Earlham, taught for a time at Southland, and then worked for the federal war department; Taylor became a member of Washington Monthly Meeting.[111]

Ohio Yearly Meeting recorded two African American ministers in the late 1890s, Noah McLean and Cora McLean, who preached and conducted revivals in Toledo and Erie, Pennsylvania, and at yearly meetings in the Midwest and Canada. In Indiana, William Allan (or Allen) (1801–98) was a member of Richland Monthly Meeting (currently known as Carmel) from 1873 and was recorded as a minister in March 1874. Born enslaved in Tennessee and sold twice before he was freed in 1828 under the terms of his enslaver's will, Allan began attending a Friends school at West Grove, Indiana, in 1856.[112] He had been an ordained Methodist minister, but his concern about giving wine to intemperate people at communion led one church official to suggest that he might be more suited to Quakerism. In June 1873 Allan became a member of Richland's meeting, and in April 1874 he transferred to Oak Ridge Monthly Meeting. Allan also lived in Ontario, as a member of Mariposa Monthly Meeting, and Ohio, as a member of Milan Monthly Meeting. He returned to Ontario where he became a member of Yonge Street Monthly Meeting in Newmarket in 1895.[113] Both Allan and the McLeans were credited with contributing to the growth of evangelism in the West Lake Quarter of Canadian Yearly Meeting.[114]

Many Friends knew Allan as a "traveling theological seminary of the Society of Friends." As an Orthodox Friend and evangelist, he preached in Canada, Indiana, Iowa, Michigan, New York, Ohio, and Vermont, usually to full if not overflowing audiences. When Allan conducted a revival in the Friends Meeting House at Moscow in Lexington-Addington, Ontario, the Reverend A. C. Hoffman commented, "It was the largest and most powerful revival ever held in the community, and was conducted by the ex-slave."[115] Allan always traveled with young men who he felt had promise and ability, and he attracted thirty-seven of them to the ministry. He died in 1898 and was buried in the Friends cemetery adjacent to the Hibbert Meeting House in Perth County, Ontario in the family plot of a friend.[116]

When Southland closed in 1925, its monthly meeting was laid down as well.[117] The meeting had once been one of the largest within the Indiana Orthodox Yearly Meeting, but it was never again as vigorous as when Clark and Daniel Drew, its renowned African American minister, were part of it. A few of the school's graduates who left Arkansas found membership in other monthly meetings, and the meeting's recorded ministers seem to have been accepted as evangelists at a number of pastoral meetings in Indiana, Iowa, and Oregon. Although a number of Southland graduates who moved north were able to transfer their membership, the more general fact is that most of the former Southland students were likely to be Quakers in name only as they went out into communities lacking any Friends meetings.[118]

———— • ————

The reluctance to proselytize displayed by many Friends, principally Hicksite and Conservative, has not been characteristic of all branches of Quakerism in the United States. Five Years Meeting in Richmond,

Indiana, led missionary efforts in Kenya, where now there are more Quakers than in the rest of the world combined. European Americans Walter and Emma Malone, leaders of the evangelical movement in the Midwest at the end of the nineteenth century, reached out for new Friends in Cleveland, where they were pastors of the First Friends Church. After Walter Malone made a fortune as a quarry owner, the couple focused on African American ministry by reaching out to Cleveland's community. Between 1884 and 1894 the Malones brought as many as three hundred people of African descent into Quakerism.

All the while, Walter Malone chastised other prosperous Quakers for not attending to the poor, not because they sought to purify the denomination but because they were caught up in the ways of the world. Walter's charge to Friends not to align themselves with the rich was controversial. "I have seen it tried. It is fatal," he told the second National Conference of Friends in 1892. Emma and Walter were both teachers whose vision was that Friends must "come down and take in the poor people and go out after the outcasts . . . with the expectation that we will be a poor, despised people."[119] Well before other Quaker colleges admitted African Americans, the Malones enrolled African Americans in the school they founded in Cleveland, the Christian Workers Training School for Bible Study and Practical Methods of Work. They also defied the custom of the time and welcomed women who wanted to be trained as ministers. By 1907 the school in Cleveland had trained at least sixty-eight women ministers, more than any other school in the country.[120] The school later became Malone College.

Southland Institute founder Alida Clark took the same critical view. In 1871 after attending a racially integrated service at Fisk University, she asked the Friends Executive Board in Philadelphia to "think, Friends, of all the money spent to aid the freed people and yet they must seek out other churches for their spiritual life." Clark envisioned African American meetings spread throughout the South "if only Quakers would 'wake up' and support and encourage blacks in ministry." She could not accept that "the followers of Woolman" should be "the very last to send out ministers, evangelists, & etc., to organize meetings and receive into fellowship these able fellow beings." Clark's effort was always directed toward creating separate meetings for African Americans, yet unlike many Friends she believed that Quakerism must, if necessary, adapt itself to the needs of people of African and American Indian descent:

> I think it is time for the Quakers, the acknowledged friends of the red and the black man, to wake up and arouse themselves everywhere to an aggressive movement. If our system of worship is unsuited to the lowly, let it be altered, but my friends, this, I for one, cannot concede, for I think, as a whole, there is no code so perfectly adapted to the lowly, though ignorant, and the poor.[121]

Quaker Views on African American Religious Practices

For their part, however, many Quakers believed that people of African descent were somehow "unable to appreciate the abstractions and refinements of our [Quaker] spiritual views," visiting European Quaker William Tallack wrote in 1861; such a view clearly belies the assumption that European Americans were intellectually superior. There was, in addition, the idea that the religious practices of people of African descent differed too radically from those Quakers followed. Tallack claimed that African Americans must have "loud prayers, much singing, and colloquial exhortations or else they are apt to go to sleep."[122] But Hamm suggests that Tallack formed his views from listening to Richmond Friends, not from observing African Americans for himself. And, since Tallack's reference to "loud prayers" and "much singing" could also describe the worship of many people of European descent at that time, Hamm's conclusion is clear: "There can be no question that such a view [that African Americans were unable to appreciate Friends' worship] was fundamentally racist."[123] Cadbury also called Friends to hold a wider perspective. "It may be supposed," he wrote, "that Quakerism failed to attract Negroes because of its quietness of worship. We no doubt generalize too easily along that line. . . . Presumably religious temperaments vary without special regard to difference of color."[124]

Many of the Quakers who went South for relief and education work after the Civil War found the "shuffling, clapping, cries, shouts, and groans of an African celebration" difficult to appreciate and, indeed, judged it a vulgar display of paganism with no redeeming religious virtue.[125] Attending a "shout," a traditional African American ceremony, on St. Helena Island, Laura Towne described it as a "savage, heathenish danceout."[126] Camp meetings, however, were also highly emotional experiences; around-the-clock preaching urged sinners of all denominations and races to repent and attracted both European and African Americans, including Quakers, especially in the Midwest. According to one historian, they "induced sensational results": people laughing uproariously, "barking like dogs, falling down as if dead, and experiencing 'the jerks.'"[127]

Some Quaker meetings themselves strayed far from quietism. After the split of 1827, Orthodox Friends became more evangelical, preaching from the Bible and working to save souls. A second division occurred within the Orthodox group and those who were attracted by the preaching of John Gurney, a British Quaker, became even more evangelical and worshipped with "all the apparatus of holiness revivalism—vocal prayer, singing, colloquial preaching."[128] The Gurneyites in the Midwest and, to some extent New York, brought in many converts in the 1880s, although the style of Quaker worship they were choosing would hardly be recognizable to other Friends.[129] Despite similarities between their religious practices and the fact that Gurneyites were the largest group of Friends by the late 1800s, few if any of the converts they made were of African descent.[130] And though missionaries from Friends United Meeting(FUM) developed societies that attracted converts in Japan, Jamaica, the Middle East, South America, and Africa, they made no concerted effort to reach out to people of African descent or other Americans of color in their own country.[131]

African American Attitudes toward Quakerism

Questions about the suitability of European American religious practice to fulfill the spiritual needs of African Americans were raised in both groups. In a letter to his sister in the 1820s, Paul Cuffe's brother John asked, "Why do the collored run after the Whites and joins their churches—and are called brothers and sisters and partake of the same bread and wine and yet are held as slaves and are treated worse than the Dumb Beast of the field." Such churches, he declared, help "to keep Negroes in slavery and whips and kills us and yet calls us Breathern."[132]

Some African Americans voiced particular objections to Quakerism. Richard Allen of Philadelphia and "a large number of dissenters" walked out of a meeting of the city's Free African Society in 1789 when the society adopted Friends practice of opening meetings with a period of silence. The Free African Society's "ties" with the Quakers, who had been active in the group's formation, "had been wearing thin" by 1791. Friends complained that the Free African members were singing psalms in the Quaker schoolhouse where they met, and Allen declared that, while he valued some Quaker qualities, Friends as a religious body "did not seem to speak to the immediate needs of blacks."[133] In the 1840s the African American cleric J. W. C. Pennington, who as a fugitive had been taken in by a Quaker, "W.W.," who then taught him for six months, wrote of Quaker meetings, "My nature was sensitive, and I wanted to hear singing. Sometimes I went and wanted to hear preaching, but I was disappointed."[134] Moreover, that Quakers took so long to free those they enslaved—despite their convictions against the practice—"hardly endeared" freed people to the Religious Society of Friends.[135]

Cadbury's caution against generalizing is borne out; Quakerism was, in fact, attractive to some people of African descent. When the African American James Alford requested membership in the Society of Friends in a meeting near Philadelphia about 1810, one meeting member stated that the "doctrines of the Society of Friends called for perfection" and asked contemptuously, "What does thee know of perfection, James?" Alford replied, "I cannot say much of perfection, but I think I have been convinced of that which if faithfully followed will lead to perfection."[136] In 1843 Sarah Mapps Douglass lamented the fact that Quakers seemed to miss the appeal their beliefs had among African Americans. "Ah, there are many poor stray starving sheep, wandering in this world's wilderness, who would gladly come into your green pastures, and repose them by your still waters, did not prejudice bar the entrance! I am persuaded the Lord has controversy with 'Friends' on this account. Let them see to it."[137]

One African American identified only as "Old Elizabeth" recalled going to a Friends meeting house "in a thinly settled part of the country" with a Quaker and his daughter. "We three composed the meeting," she wrote in 1860. "As we sat there in silence, I felt a remarkable overshadowing of the Divine presence, as much so as I ever experienced anywhere. Toward the close, a few words seemed to be given me, which I expressed, and left the place greatly refreshed in spirit."[138] In 1825 a woman of African descent in North Carolina continued to go to an empty meetinghouse twice a week after the Quakers had migrated west. There she sat in silence, as she had learned to do with Friends.[139]

———•———

In its July 20, 1850, issue, *Friends Review* commented on the paradox in Quakers' views of African Americans:

> It is a remarkable circumstance, that although the members of our religious society have been so long and so extensively known as the advocates of the coloured race, and the discipline established among us presents no impediment to their reception into membership, which is not equally applicable to persons of European origin, still the number of coloured persons found within the society has always been exceedingly small. This circumstance may justly raise the enquiry whether the cause lies with them or with us. Is the religion of Friends unsuited to the coloured race? Or are they kept at a distance by our neglect or repulsive conduct?[140]

Abundant historical evidence reveals that during the time when Quakers had the most natural opportunities to reach out for African American members—whether working side-by-side with people of African descent for the abolition of slavery or teaching them and their children in freedmen's schools, invitations were not offered to them. Whether those invitations were withheld because Friends believed it not appropriate to use their position to promote their own religion or because they did not perceive those with whom they worked with as potential members of the Society of Friends is the question. As Linda Selleck, a pastor within Friends United Meeting, aptly framed it: was the issue a matter of "Quaker spiritual integrity or neglect?"[141] While she doesn't answer that question, Selleck does express disappointment over "a singular missed opportunity": Quakers had earned the trust of the people of African descent in their shared commitment to the Underground Railroad and freedmen's schools, but then, in the case of FUM, turned their missionary efforts overseas.[142]

The conclusion reached in this consideration of African American membership in the Religious Society of Friends in the eighteenth and nineteenth centuries is disturbingly simple. Many Friends did not fully accept people of African descent as "fit" for membership in their society or, for that matter, to be their friends. Many answers have been offered to explain the "remarkable circumstance"; they vary little from one era to another. Underlying them all is the realization that Quakers of European descent have been unable to separate themselves from the attitudes and behaviors of a wider culture based on false notions of differences between races. Those false notions led European American Friends to wonder if African Americans were, in the words of this book's title, "fit for F/friendship." Fit in both senses: for being members of the Society of Friends and for forming close relationships. European American Quakers were all too like most others of European descent, yet Friends, believing that their testimonies required them to reach for a standard higher than that deemed acceptable in society in general, have expected more of themselves.

PART TWO

Twentieth-Century Challenges and Beyond

THE AMERICAN FRIENDS
SERVICE COMMITTEE

PRESENTS

UNDERWOOD & UNDERWOOD

CRYSTAL BIRD

COLORED · YOUNG · DYNAMIC

20 SOUTH TWELFTH STREET
PHILADELPHIA, PA.

RUFUS M. JONES, *Chairman*
WILBUR K. THOMAS, *Executive Secretary*

AFSC Crystal Bird traveling program.

Working for Desegregation

Too often pioneering in racial equality has been left to the few. But in this day of racial crisis every member of the Society of Friends should be concerned that all races have equal opportunity to participate with one another in worship, education, housing, employment and voting, and to join in our fellowship.

— *Five Years Meeting, 1955*

THE URBANIZATION OF AFRICAN AMERICANS brought new challenges to all those with a concern for racial equality and justice. New generations would face the problems created by the country's earlier failure, North and South, to provide equal opportunities to people of African descent and by racism fueled by the too-common belief that African Americans were an inferior people who somehow brought their problems on themselves.

The impetus for Friends involvement in the issues affecting people of African descent was found in their belief that there is that of God in every one and in their testimonies of peace and equality. In whatever way Friends might express those beliefs (i.e. publishing, financial commitment, community building, public activism), their leading—the inspiration to do the work—must arise from the Spirit. Friends needed first to discern God's will by patient listening. Isaac Penington, a seventeenth-century English Friend, wrote of the importance of taking this time:

> Be not hasty, be not forward in judgment; keep back to the life, still waiting for the appearance and openings of the life. A few steps, fetched in the life and power of God, are much safer and sweeter than a hasty progress in the hasty, forward spirit.[1]

Even before the protests of the treatment of people of African descent grew into the Civil Rights movement of the 1950s and 1960s, Quakers had begun to attend to the conditions that severely restricted the lives of African Americans. The work of Friends General Conference (FGC), founded in 1900 as an association of mostly older and smaller Friends groups, included attention to various social reforms such as the treatment of Native Americans, child protection, and education for African Americans. Other national Friends organizations, some Quaker yearly and monthly meetings, and uncounted individual Friends (African American Friends among them) participated in some way on the local or national scene. They were among those working for open housing, desegregated public schools and equal job opportunities, as well as trying to improve the relationships between people of African and European descent. Yet, the number of Friends involved was not large, and those few who were active appealed faithfully to the wider Friends community to join them in the struggle and face the racism within themselves and within the Religious Society of Friends. They were sorely tested throughout the twentieth century.

The 'Great Migration'

By the 1880s, more than 20,000 African Americans had already gone North to find jobs and escape the violence against them. The 1910 U.S. Census showed 27 percent of the nation's African Americans lived in urban areas; by 1920, it was 34 percent.[2] Nearly 800,000 African Americans moved to already overcrowded northern cities during the 1920s and another 400,000 during the Depression.[3] Though the Great Migration was the pivotal event of the new century, it wasn't long before the new arrivals realized that things in the North were similar to what they had left; there were no more or better jobs or housing opportunities, nor were European Americans more willing than they had been to recognize the legal rights that African Americans had been granted after the Civil War.

As in the 1800s, resentments burst out in "race riots," instigated by people of European descent.[4] The summer of 1919, with twenty-five riots, was called the "greatest period of interracial strife the nation ever witnessed."[5] Mobs went on the rampage against African Americans in northern and southern cities, taking over whole areas "for days, flogging, burning, shooting, and torturing at will." In 1923 an entire African American town, Rosewood, Florida, was burned to the ground.[6]

The economic depression that would engulf the whole country in the early 1930s hit people of African descent earlier and harder. By

1934, 17 percent of people of European descent and 38 percent of African Americans were unemployed. Domestic service jobs, filled by many African Americans, were among the first to be lost.[7] These desperate times were relieved only with the passage of some of President Franklin D. Roosevelt's New Deal legislation. It was a new deal for those African Americans who could benefit from job programs, pensions for veterans, and other social and economic reforms.[8]

African Americans *did* experience a freer existence in the North; they could vote and organize for political ends without fear of reprisal. But with the end of the World War II, they increasingly encountered discrimination and segregation guided by "unwritten" rules and diminished economic opportunity.[9] Persistent voting inhibitions, segregation, and intimidation also narrowed the lives and rights of African Americans who remained in the South. These conditions and the African American veterans' sense that the promise of their future had been betrayed would sometimes trigger violent reactions to persistent inequality and would eventually give birth to the Civil Rights movement.

African Americans Organize

As Friends reorganized to deal with the realities of the new century, African American leaders recognized that their community needed to find ways to better the lives of its people, who were faced with continuing violence and the terrible conditions in northern and southern cities. As the number of African American city dwellers grew, so did their interest in civil rights, legal protection, and gaining the political power necessary to realize them.

In 1905 and 1906, African American sociologist, educator, and civil rights activist W.E.B. Du Bois and others took the lead in organizing the "Niagara movement," a group of African American men who met at Niagara, Canada, to mobilize a campaign to promote freedom of speech and the press, universal suffrage, and "the abolition of all caste distinctions based simply on race and color."[10] This conference and two others in 1907 and 1908 led directly to the founding in 1909 of the National Association for the Advancement of Colored People (NAACP), which dedicated itself to ending segregation, lynching and other unlawful acts against African Americans, achieving universal male suffrage and equal education, and improving police protection in the South. By 1921 there were four hundred NAACP branches in the United States.[11] Jane Addams and Helen Marot, both with Quaker backgrounds, were among the NAACP founders, as were Friends Florence Kelley, an associate of Addams (and niece of Sarah Pugh, a member of the historic Philadelphia Female Anti-Slavery Society), and Susan Parrish Wharton. Wharton helped found a Philadelphia settlement house based on W.E.B. Du Bois's philosophy of education and staffed completely by African Americans, which was unusual for such facilities.[12]

A second organization, founded in 1911, the National Urban League (NUL) focused more on African American employment and socioeconomic issues. One of its principal founders was European American Quaker L. Hollingsworth Wood, a lawyer and long-time clerk of the Orthodox New York Yearly Meeting; Wood served as chairman of the League's board from 1915–30. The *Broad Ax*, an African American weekly published in Chicago, noted that "Mr. Wood though a white man is most sympathetic with the Negro's claim for equal opportunity and has an unusual understanding of the Negro's point of view in his efforts to attain the higher things of life."[13] Elizabeth Walton, "a staunch Quaker" who belonged to Spruce Street and then Race Street Meetings in Philadelphia and whose parents had been abolitionists, became one of the organization's "principal leaders."[14] A number of Friends were active in local Urban League chapters.

———•———

Friends organizations also continued to address racial issues. In 1919, responding to the increasing number of lynchings, including one in 1911 in Coatesville, Pennsylvania, the Orthodox Philadelphia Yearly Meeting (Arch Street) appointed a committee to organize protests against the horrendous crimes that were going unpunished.[15] Members reported a good reception when they met with southern state officials to urge them to protect all citizens from such violence.[16] The committee sponsored speakers, distributed information, and issued a statement reminding people of the "more than 65 lynchings in U.S." in 1918. The message sent to Orthodox Friends in Philadelphia spoke of a "sin to be a shameful blot on the fair name of our beloved land" and of lynching's "brutalizing and degrading effect on those who perpetrate the crime and on the thousands who often gather to see their fellowbeing [sic] tortured and killed." It urged Friends to attend a May 1919 conference in New York City organized by NAACP.[17]

AFSC: More Work to Do

In 1917, a small group of leading Friends (Hicksite and Orthodox, adult and youth), who had foreseen a need to provide young Quaker men with alternatives to military service in World War I, met in Philadelphia to create what would become the American Friends Service Committee (AFSC). Among the participants were two of the best-known Quakers of the time, European Americans Rufus Jones and Henry Cadbury. After achieving its original goal of alternative service for conscientious objectors to war, AFSC widened its focus to Quaker peace and social concerns and organized itself into four sections: home or American (domestic peace), foreign (international relief), peace (conferences, peace caravans, work with youth), and interracial (interracial issues and equality). Its interracial section was designed specifically to respond to the persistence of lynching,[18] a terrorist tactic often used by white supremacists, including some members of the Ku Klux Klan.

AFSC's interracial section also broadly concerned itself with employment and housing opportunities, desegregation of public education, and "the quickening of the Quaker conscience with regard to minority groups, particularly Negroes."[19] One of the first things the section did was hire Crystal Bird (1894-1965), an African American native of West Philadelphia who had been on the national board of the YWCA, to speak about "the problems, the needs, and culture of the colored race" at colleges, high schools, churches, and public forums. AFSC believed that Bird's program would be a "splendid means for breaking down prejudice and for building up a constructive understanding on the part of Friends' communities."[20] Bird's interest lay, as she put it, "in having people of other racial groups understand the *humanness* of the Negro wherever he is found."[21] She saw her work as aiming "to lift the curtain that separates the white people and the colored people, to lift the curtain of misunderstanding that is so dividing us." After a year with the interracial section, she worked on the Joint Committee on Race Relations of the Arch and Race Streets Yearly Meetings.[22]

Among those who had urged AFSC to attend to racial issues was L. Hollingsworth Wood of the NUL. In Wood's view the racial divide was the most crucial problem of the new century, and he urged the AFSC's executive board to "get under the burden of this national problem and undertake in a very definite way to find a solution for it." Wood told the board that "existing conditions were so adverse to our colored element that a real hatred of the whites as a race was growing and that unless something was done to ameliorate this condition, it was impossible to see what might happen."[23] AFSC had undertaken an enormous array of programs aimed at eliminating this "condition."

Rufus Jones actively urged Quakers "to transform this present world and these actual human fellows around them to the end that the will of God might become the will of men, and that society here on earth might take on a likeness to the Kingdom of Heaven." In Jones's view, Friends could be effective Christians only if, as a religious society, they took interracial, interclass, or international action.[24] For some Quakers, the movement was transformative: one Friend asserted that while he had been taught only what Quakers *could not* do when he was young, now he was hearing what they *could* do.[25]

Quakers and the Klan

While Philadelphia Friends focused on the random violence against people of African descent, the Ku Klux Klan (KKK) was being revived in the South. By the 1900s chapters had also formed throughout the North, a number of which had Quaker members, particularly in the Midwest. Reinvigorated after the First World War when immigration resumed and African Americans were moving north, as well as by the sensational media depictions of African Americans, the Klan focused on "Americanism," meaning, by its definition, opposition to immigrants, Jews, and Catholics. According to European American Quaker Ben Richmond, the KKK was aligned with the Republican Party and became "a powerful political force" in the Midwest: in 1924, thirty-nine percent of the Klan's nationwide membership was in Indiana, Ohio and

Illinois.[26] In Wayne County, home to the town of Richmond and the Quaker-administrated Earlham College, one-fourth of the adult male Quakers belonged to the Klan at one point, including two Earlham students and another seventy-nine or more former students or alumni.[27]

Quakers, as Hamm puts it, "were not immune to [the Klan's] appeal," but he suspects that the appeal came primarily from the KKK's strong commitment to prohibition, since many Friends were active in the temperance movement. Whether Klan membership would suggest that Friends endorsed the organization's views is not known.[28] Nor is it known if there was any Klan connection with the lynching of Thomas Shipp and Abram Smith, two young African American men in Marion, Indiana, who were hung on August 7, 1930, as a crowd of ten thousand celebrated. As was typical in lynching cases, no one was punished for the crime.[29]

According to European American Quaker activist and author Chuck Fager, the Indiana Klan "played down overt displays of its racism" and functioned "as a kind of Rotary Club with outlandish costumes."[30] In small Midwestern towns, the organization was often the focus of community social life and thus was attractive to European Americans, including Friends. Quaker historians tend to agree that, as Christopher Densmore says, by the 1920s, "at least in the North, the Klan lacked the terrorist impulses of the KKK of the 1860s and 1870s, or the resurrected KKK of the 1950s and 1960s." The northern KKK was "just as racist as its southern forebear," wrote Thomas Hamm, but "much less violent in the Midwest. In Indiana, for example, it was never tied to any lynching."[31]

One Indiana Yearly Meeting Friend who not only joined the Klan but rose in the ranks was Daisy Douglas Barr, who had served several pastorates prior to joining in 1922, including meetings in Lewisville, Muncie and New Castle. She was an effective revivalist, and while at Muncie helped lead the prohibitionist struggle, started a YWCA chapter, and created a refuge for former prostitutes. In 1923 Barr became head of the Women of the KKK in Indiana. After organizing for the Klan, another Quaker, Ira Dawes, left his pastorate in Wabash, Indiana in 1923 to head the KKK's national speaker's bureau in Texas.[32]

Not all Quakers saw the KKK as benign, no matter its commitment to temperance and its patriotic appeal. Some disliked its secretive nature; others its racist activities. The minute about KKK membership approved by the 1922 sessions of Indiana Yearly Meeting was pointed:

> It is important at this time for Friends to recognize that the Ku Klux Klan is a secret and oath-bound order. As a church we want to be fair in our utterance and relations toward all organizations, but we believe that the Ku Klux Klan by hiding behind a mask is un-American, by its antagonism to a church is un-Christian, and by its fostering and fomenting race hatred is unpatriotic, therefore we would advise our members not to join it or in any way assist in its work.[33]

Eight years after the Marion lynching, some Friends expected the yearly meeting to make a statement against the horrendous act. Instead, when it came to the Friends testimony related to interracial matters "a lot of our Friends in Indiana Yearly Meeting are extremely heretical." Willis Beede, administrative secretary of the American Friends Board of Missions in Richmond, described the situation in a letter asking AFSC Clerk Clarence Pickett for help in doing something "constructive." According to Beede's letter, Milton Hadley, a European American Quaker pastor and member of the Ministry of Oversight Committee, wanted the yearly meeting to make a statement about race relations, law enforcement and the treatment of criminals in the state. Hadley was advised by another committee member "to keep his mouth shut;" he received a letter to the same effect. It seemed that Friends from Grant County, where Marion was located, were "bitterly opposed to sending out" a letter that referred to lynching in Marion or anywhere.

Eventually a committee appointed to bring a statement to the yearly meeting produced a letter that, after several revisions, was so general it could apply to any similar situation "in the last fifty years," said Beede. After the letter was approved by the meeting, the clerk was asked to write a cover letter to go with the statement to the governor; he was told he could not mention the word "lynching." The statement called upon Friends "to study the problem of crime and law enforcement, the treatment of criminals, and the problem of better race relations." A committee of three was appointed for the project. Thus Beede was asking for help from Pickett, who found the attitude of the pastors in the yearly meeting (excluding Hadley) "very disturbing" because they didn't seem to realize that the lynching was "but a symptom." Pickett offered several possibilities, including sending a pastor from the meeting to a seminar that would prepare him to travel and help monthly meetings "think more aggressively and clearly on the question of our responsibility on the race question."[34]

---·---

Between 1930 and 1937 there were more than one hundred lynchings.[35] Friends were among those who supported efforts, renewed with President Franklin D. Roosevelt's election in 1932, to pass a federal anti-lynching law. The NAACP organized a new anti-lynching crusade and deliberately sought out women who could donate time to lobby, circulate petitions, and raise funds to keep the campaign going. Many of the women were Quaker. Emily Green Balch, the first Friend to win a Nobel Peace Prize for her role in founding the Women's International League of Peace and Freedom (WILPF) in 1946, brought that organization into the campaign. Quakers Susan Parrish Wharton, Florence Kelley, Marjorie Penny, and Hannah Clothier Hull, WILPF President at the time and former clerk of the Hicksite Philadelphia Yearly Meeting, also supported the effort. The Philadelphia Yearly Meetings' Committee on Race Relations was represented by staff member Helen Bryan and Esther Morton Smith, the only woman to testify at the hearing with reportedly "forceful and vehement testimony" emphasizing Friends support for the legislation.[36] The effort to secure legislation failed, however, due to opposition from the South and lack of support from Roosevelt.

In 1948, the Friends Committee on National Legislation (FCNL), founded five years before to present Quaker views to Congress and the executive branch,[37] testified before Congress in support of a new federal anti-lynching law. At one of the hearings, FCNL's Byron Haworth, a criminal lawyer from North Carolina, said that citizens' rights would not be secure "so long as communities in which lynching occurs are unwilling to apprehend and punish the lynchers." As with other proposals before it, this one did not go far.[38]

'Quickening' Quaker Consciences

As racial tensions began to build, "quickening" Quaker consciences about the issues of racism was to prove one of the most difficult tasks that activists took upon themselves. Friends organizations and individual activists made speeches or invited African Americans to come speak to them, published newsletters, led workshops, brought people of African and European descent together to dialogue, wrote letters full of queries to monthly and yearly meetings, and sat through untold hours of planning meetings. Through it all, they were busy organizing national and regional conferences to bring activists together and to increase their number so that, in the end, the Society of Friends would become a force in ending racism. Wide-ranging topics at conferences included the Friends testimony on equality, race relations, Black Power, the sources of prejudice and the integration of Friends schools.

Results from surveys on race relations taken among Quakers during this period offer a window on their thinking. In 1928 the Board of Home Missions of Five Years Meeting reported on a questionnaire it had sent to "a number of Friends located in many sections of the country." The purpose was to focus chiefly on "any of our own attitudes towards other races which are not Christ-like, and how we may help to remove prejudices from our own hearts and communities." Responses from Friends "in 10 different states . . . from ocean to ocean" were summarized in an article in *The American Friend*. Respondents provided many examples of race prejudice, in Friends schools and colleges, a girls' summer camp, and even in "emphatic opposition" from Friends who did not want people of African descent as visitors or members of their meetings. But the examples are "mostly in the thousand and one little things which happen on the streets and in the markets" or simply in a "lack of interest" in the problems of African Americans. Prejudice against Jews and Germans (because of the recent war) was also reported. Asked about "specific needs or opportunities for Friends to help remove race prejudice," respondents said the first need was for Friends to look at themselves. "I do not say that Friends are MORE prejudiced or indifferent than others but I cannot say that they are appreciably LESS so," wrote one Friend. Other answers focus on paying fair wages, justice, and having "friendly contacts" to get to know people. The third question—how to promote interracial understanding and good-will"— prompted some anecdotes about times when Friends did step out to help African Americans, perhaps hosting someone who had been refused room in a hotel, writing letters to the editor in support of some

African Americans moving into a community who were threatened, or welcoming them to social events over the objections of others. The last survey question was "What are Friends doing?" Answers ranged from visiting various organizations in predominantly African American sections, "guiding" projects for improved housing, sponsoring international conferences, and exchanging visits by pastors or ministers with African American churches.[39]

Gathering to Build Racial Awareness

Friends conferences also heightened awareness of race and racism. Beginning in 1927, AFSC sponsored three annual conferences, one on "the race question" in Washington, and two on interracial peace. "Friends are under a cloud in the South because they have not taken a more outstanding position in regard to the race problem," said one committee member after a visit to Georgia in 1927; in fact, no unity existed among Friends on what action, if any, southern Friends might be taking on the racial problems there.[40]

In 1931 Henry Cadbury, then teaching at Bryn Mawr and Harvard Divinity School and chair of AFSC, asked the AFSC board to assemble Friends "who believe the Society is not meeting in any adequate way the demands of the American racial situation, which situation is a flagrant denial of the spirit and teachings of Jesus." The conference, he hoped, would deepen the sense of responsibility participants felt to change conditions and attitudes and would "search for a technique" to do so. The program for the 1932 event aimed to "revolutionize our present position and extend our activities so that they will more nearly coincide with other principles and early traditions of the Society of Friends."[41]

In 1933, AFSC and the two Committees on Race Relations of the still-divided Philadelphia Yearly Meetings created what they described as "a center where mature-minded men and women come together to study and discuss racial conflict both as a world and as a national problem, and to formulate techniques that will help to create understanding and adjustments." The center, to be known as the Institute on Race Relations and to be open to people of all religions and races, met on the campus of Swarthmore College every summer from 1933 to 1941.[42] In 1944, the Institute became a program of Fisk University, and it continues to this day. In its years in Pennsylvania, half of its students were African Americans drawn from churches, colleges, and the Harlem branch of the YWCA. The first institute in 1933 offered lectures by Johnson and other prominent Friends involved in research and work on racial issues, as well as by W.E.B. Du Bois, then on the faculty of Atlanta University; Walter White, African American secretary of the NAACP; African American professor and author James Weldon Johnson; and Ralph J. Bunche, an African American faculty member at Howard University, who was later a nationally prominent leader in the Civil Rights movement and winner of a Nobel Peace Prize.[43]

Three years later, the same committees from the Philadelphia Yearly Meetings along with Five Years Meeting planned another conference. The purpose of the 1936 conference, called "The Quest for Interracial Understanding," was to help the "Society of Friends prepare itself for intelligent leadership in the cause of racial brotherhood." The closing declaration of the conference affirmed: "We deprecate all forms of race prejudice and beseech our members to take questions of race prejudice which they feel, for advice and solution to the Divine light of the Sprit of God, confident that the honest devotion of our minds to such a guidance will bring to our life the fervor of a Whittier or a Woolman in our own day."[44] Haverford College professor Frank D. Watson, the Friend who chaired the event, followed up the conference with a study guide, *A Quest in Interracial Understanding*.[45]

Racial justice was one of the topics for an international conference of the newly formed Friends World Committee for Consultation (FWCC) at Swarthmore and Haverford Colleges in 1937. The conference's racial justice group set their goal as reaching ". . . a clear understanding of what our modern conception of the Kingdom of God is when applied to race relations." Conference participants wrote a statement admonishing Friends for failing to live up to their testimony, a lack of action that "impoverishes schools, meetings, and communities by cutting the Society off from the enriching experience of sharing in the spiritual life and fellowship of other racial and cultural groups." They advised Quakers to "lay that of God within themselves alongside that in their fellowmen [sic] and in humility and forbearing love . . . cast out fear, remove hypocrisy and banish hate from among themselves and those with whom they work."[46]

———•———

Perhaps the most important series of conferences—important because they were national in scope and because they were intended to be representative of all yearly meetings—were the meetings in the second half of the twentieth century known as the National Conference of Friends on Race Relations (NCFRR). Yearly meetings were invited to send representatives; FWCC's Section of the Americas provided much of the funding. The first conference in 1956 was called to "stimulate individual Friends and Meetings to work directly in the field of race relations and not rely entirely on the work of the AFSC." From 1956 to 1970 as many as two hundred Quakers at a time, of both European and African descent, attended NCFRR gatherings to be educated and inspired by prestigious speakers, to talk about the struggle with racism, discuss the appropriate pace at which activists could expect change, and express concern about a lack of support they felt from the monthly meetings as they worked on a concern that they believed should be shared by all Friends. Monthly meetings were, in fact, much of the focus of the conferences, as attenders were urged to take their concerns and the ideas they had for pursuing their goals home to rouse their meetings to action. The 1963 and 1965 conferences wrote to Friends schools urging them to remedy their lack of African American students. The 1963 conference also had "searching questions" for Friends meetings about their attitudes and actions regarding civil rights.[47]

NCFRR sought to involve more and more Friends; European American committee clerk Marian Fuson wondered how to "make contact with the blank areas on our map of the country where Friends are."[48] It also made a point of inviting members of the pastoral and evangelical branches of Quakerism, especially those involved in peace and social concerns, to their conferences. For the 1969 conference at Earlham College, invitations went to the pastors of each Indiana monthly meeting, who were also asked to bring a member of their meeting with them. The conferences in Wilmington, Ohio, and Richmond, Indiana, did bring Friends from the yearly meetings of Indiana, Iowa, Lake Erie, North Carolina Conservative, Ohio and Ohio Conservative, and Wilmington, as well as Pacific Yearly Meeting.[49] Workshops led by Friends from across the country focused on housing, employment, education, and voting, with special attention to housing, since "just as inhabitants of a community we [all] do affect the racial residential pattern."[50]

Rare among Quaker committees, several African American Friends were active in the NCFRR Continuation Committee, including Barrington Dunbar, George Sawyer, Dwight Spann-Wilson, and Margot Adair, but it often could be discouraging for them. The Society of Friends "is dead," said Dunbar at one point. The Society needs "shaking up," said Sawyer.[51]

Educating for Racial Understanding

In the 1920s AFSC and the Philadelphia Yearly Meetings' Committees on Race Relations began sponsoring more informal events called "Race Relations Sundays" and urged Friends to be especially attuned to the racism in their worship and in discussions with each other.[52] By 1930 this joint program had placed twenty-eight African American speakers in First Day Schools and invited thirty-four African American ministers to preach on the issues of race at meetings.[53]

In 1938 the Community Relations Committee of the two Philadelphia Yearly Meetings embarked on an extensive "Educational Project in Racial Understanding" to involve a hundred Friends in thirty-four monthly meetings. The goals were to educate Friends, since "all too often" attitudes were developed from inaccurate information, and to foster community changes in housing, health care, and recreational facilities. However, James Laird, European American executive director of Philadelphia Yearly Meeting's Meeting on Social Concerns, wrote much later in his review of "Social Concerns for 70 Years" that he could find "no indication" of how the project moved forward in subsequent Community Relations Committee reports. "One may conclude perhaps," Laird wrote, "the members of the project were not clear as to the magnitude of the tasks they had taken on." It would not be the first time that ambitious plans were made and goals set with no apparent concrete results.[54]

Quakers working to improve relationships between the races recognized that work was needed in both the North and the South. In 1945 and again in 1949, each PYM Committee on Race Relations published small pamphlets. "Race Relations and the Society of Friends," by Florence Kite, spoke of "new concern about race relations," given "an acute state of tension and unrest" in the African American population. The second, "A statement on Segregation," was adopted by the two Philadelphia yearly meetings. The small three-page booklet ends with ways that Friends must work to "carry forward our testimony of friendly living among all human beings."[55]

To encourage Friends to work for those religious and democratic ideals, in the 1950s the Philadelphia Yearly Meeting's Committee on Race Relations developed Building Bridges of Understanding, a program aimed at encouraging Quaker meetings, churches, and synagogues to bring European and African Americans together at fellowship weekends, home visits, picnics, and other events in each other's homes.[56] In 1957 Gladys Rawlins, an African American member of PYM's Race Relations Committee, developed a program to combat prejudice in schools. Known as "Green Circle," the highly successful program helped young people appreciate and understand diversity. First used in Philadelphia schools, it rapidly expanded to other areas around the country. After eight years several school districts, YWCAs, and the Girl Scouts of America became sponsors of Green Circle along with the committee.[57]

AFSC began to organize informal interracial and interfaith groups in the region to provide a "rallying point" for people who wanted to take positive steps but were having trouble finding a role to play. As European American meeting clerk Lester Bowles of Augusta, Georgia, said in 1964, "There are so many of both races who feel they cannot join the picket lines; they want to be more active than they are, and *this* they can and would do, if some leadership training could be provided."[58]

———•———

In 1963, noting that "very little real communication" occurred between the races and that what had existed was breaking down, the Peace and Social Order Committee of Friends General Conference developed the Community Friendship Project to demonstrate how effective such communication could be. The project was based on the work of the European American Quaker Rachel Davis DuBois, who had created a particular kind of "frank but friendly" conversation that seemed to open the way to real communication between people of different cultures and different experiences; she and others in the field had used this discussion method successfully since the early 1940s and had also trained others as discussion leaders. Noted psychologist Gordon Allport described the method as a "skillful use of basic psychology," giving people a chance to talk of their memories and share their own cultures and common experiences and thus "strengthen our solidarity with others."[59] During the 1944 FGC conference in Cape May, New Jersey, DuBois had led a five-day "Race Relations Roundtable" demonstrating how a "Neighborhood-Home Festival" can bring people of all kinds together. Other topics included "What a Friends' Meeting Can Do" and "The Moral Basis for Unity" on "developing unity out of the chaos of intergroup relationships."[60]

The FGC Community Friendship Project would similarly train people who could then carry the conversations into the wider community. Offered as a service to local meetings, especially in the South, it was initially arranged through meetings in Atlanta, Augusta, New Orleans, Baltimore, and West Chester, Pennsylvania.[61] Typically, DuBois would be invited to demonstrate the method to members, and then work with community leaders who individual meeting members had invited. DuBois would then schedule training. The goal was to develop a core group of leaders. Often those who were trained were so enthusiastic that they would invite DuBois to come back and work with their own organization. In Atlanta, a Friend on the YWCA staff and another member of the Atlanta meeting brought together parents of seventh graders of European and African descent who were about to attend integrated classes.[62] In Augusta, DuBois was invited back by the meeting to help people in the community who were "dragging their heels in race relationships here."

In 1964 William Taber, a European American member of Ohio Yearly Meeting Conservative, learned DuBois's method and developed a program for training leaders in Richmond, Indiana. Taber, a widely respected author and teacher of Quakerism and spirituality at Pendle Hill, had felt a "distinct leading" to do something about race; he sought the advice of Quaker African American attorney George Sawyer, a leader among Friends in Richmond. DuBois visited Richmond, and Taber worked with Sawyer to set up small mixed-race groups in the summer. Taber later recalled how the "tension dropped out of the voices" of the participants during the session, and he used dialogue method in his later teaching and work with groups.[63]

Young Friends Involvement

As early as the 1920s, the Young Friends Board appointed a Human Relations Commission to encourage students to play a role in building a world in which all men live as brothers by giving time to social service projects.[64] The Young Friends Association, described by Deborah Haines as "part social mixer, part debating or discussion group," attracted Friends, mostly under forty. They held their first general conference in 1895; representatives had been part of the formation of FGC five years later. In 1930, the Young Friends from the Hicksite and the Orthodox yearly meetings had merged (well before their elders reunited). Wanting to play an increasingly visible role in working for better race relations, Young Friends sponsored three conferences on racial issues in 1936, 1937, and 1938. The topics were: "The Answer of Quakerism to Racial Conflict," "Socio-Economic Aspects of Racial Conflict," and "Minority Groups in Our Community: Has Religion a Solution?" Typical conference speakers would be from the NUL, NAACP, or from Friends like L. Hollingsworth Wood and Thomas E. Jones. In the 1936 session organized by and for high schoolers, the speaker was D. Elton Trueblood, a well-respected European American Quaker on the faculty of Earlham College.[65] These wider associations among younger Quakers from local meetings, in which there might be only two or three their own age, prepared them to help nurture the commitment of many of the older Friends who actively led those movements in their monthly and yearly meetings.

A statement from high school students attending the 1944 FGC meeting in Cape May indicates that Young Friends often served as a barometer measuring where their older counterparts stood. Read to the hundreds of adults gathered at Cape May, and later published, the statement of some 250 high schoolers expresses "a need to express our good will towards the young people of all groups, particularly the Negroes of our own country."[66] They added:

> We want those who feel separated from us by race or color to know
> of our realization that racial discrimination, hate and pride will never
> lead to the peace and the kind of world in which we want to live. We

have been thinking of you and have been trying to find ways by which we can show our feeling of kinship with you.

We will strive to carry with us through the coming years respect and appreciation for the Negro and other races, and will endeavor to practice this good will in our daily lives. We want to understand and value your contribution to our common culture. We need your help to do this, as we can not do it alone. Only by individual contact between you and us will this understanding come about.[67]

Printed as a "Message of Friendship from the Young Friends" at the conference, the statement was sent to FGC's member meetings with a list of ideas for "queries and suggestions on race relations" prepared by a committee of high schoolers for First Day Schools and Young Friends groups. Asked to evaluate their workshop experiences at the FGC conference, participants highlighted what they had discussed about race relations, noting, as one did, how valuable it was to have some "steps which we at home can take to solve the race problem...start[ing] with small projects in our own communities." Another wrote, however, that she was "disappointed" with the attitudes of some of the others whose ideas she found "extremely silly," including statements about Japanese Americans who were relocated at the outbreak of the war.[68]

Canadian Young Friends, who often joined their American counterparts for meetings in the late 1940s and 1950s, also gave their attention to issues of race. "Social, economic, and racial relationships" was the topic of one of their weekend meetings in 1957. In 1963 they demonstrated for civil rights at the U.S. Consulate. A few years later their topic at summer camp was equality for minority groups.[69]

In 1969, James Laird wrote that he often found himself "in the unenviable position of trying to be a broker between our deeply committed and impatient young Friends and their equally deeply committed elders. Our young people feel that the tumult of our times does not allow us the luxury of 'business as usual' which older Friends know served us well in the past. . . . We have to try to direct the enthusiasm of the young while convincing them we are able and willing to change our ways." His observation was, he said, that the "intemperance of the young is matched by a lethargy of their elders."[70]

Signs of that impatience would be recognized in the Young Friends' conclusion of the that "the church no longer seems to have the answers" and that there is a "gap between [Friends] professions of belief and their practices." Writing in 1970 about "Religion and the College Generation," Helen Hole, a professor at Earlham College, named racial injustice as one of the "sore points" for the young people who see that meetings might "agree in theory" that injustice must be opposed, but then see that "gap." They are "disquieted by what they feel to be the lack of evidence in Quaker lives of the power of the Christian message," Hole wrote.[71] The 1970 Iowa Yearly Meeting (Conservative) made special note of the good effect of the presence of Young Friends in their report on the meeting's annual sessions. Their "strong concerns and thoughtful questions" often reminded older Friends of the need for "greater effort" in resolving the problems of the day, problems, including racial injustice, that they found "seemingly insoluble."[72]

A 1977 conference grew out of the concerns of Young Friends of Philadelphia Yearly Meeting that "the society of Friends was primarily a white, middle-class society" and their questions on how that "speaks for the present and future of the Society and society at large." Their notices for the conference in their city asked, "What would you say if you were told that there is Racism among Quakers?" At the end of the day, they urged participants to ask, "What can I change?"[73]

At a gathering on racism in Greensboro, North Carolina in 1985, more than three hundred Young Friends representing 34 countries, 57 yearly meetings, and 18 monthly meetings concluded that "where there is racism, there can be no peace" and offered their prayer "that God will direct Friends to find ways to play a central role in helping the people of our nations to [find ways] to abolish the plague of racism from our earth." About two hundred attenders signed the statement signifying their commitment to acting on the message that racism is a "terrible cancer affecting the lives of millions of people throughout the world."[74]

Building Bridges through Cooperative Programs

Friends also developed programs designed specifically to build understanding by bringing European and African American people together. Typically this involved setting up recreational programs, creating community centers or instituting interracial programs at existing ones, sponsoring day care, nursery, or kindergarten programs and weekend work camps.

In the 1920s, the Friends Neighborhood Guild, founded in 1879 to provide such "refining influences" as worship services, youth meetings, a sewing school and temperance meetings for the Northern Liberties section of Philadelphia, turned its attention to racial issues as the neighborhood became predominantly African American. By the 1930s the neighborhood had become, as Frances Bosworth has noted, "an overcrowded, interracial and semi-industrial section." The Guild's annual report noted that the depression left families there without adequate income for rent and that among them "disheartening attempts to find jobs [were] wearing down the fine spirit of men who see their wives and children in want and are powerless to help." In conjunction with other agencies, including AFSC, the Guild provided housing repairs and worked to alleviate "deplorable" sanitary conditions.[75]

The Friends Neighborhood Guild worked in realms other than housing in its Philadelphia neighborhood after the war. In the 1950s it was able to construct a new building for its community center in order to offer a library, new public health clinics and recreation facilities. It also expanded its service area to include a poorer and more ethnically diverse neighborhood.[76] The Guild began to hire professionals to work on the area's "many acute problems."[77] In the mid-1960s it established partnerships with Friends Select and Penn Charter Schools to help underserved young children prepare for school.[78] In 1962 Friends Select offered thirty-one summer scholarships to neighborhood children of all grades; by 1965 the school had made 140 scholarships available. The Guild also helped connect Friends Select with an urban junior high school for a reading program.[79] With Haverford Friends School and funds raised in Quaker meetings and area churches, the Guild created a summer camp for eighty mostly African American children.[80] Through its auspices, neighborhood children were able to attend Pennsylvania State University, Georgetown University, and Swarthmore and Haverford Colleges as well.

———— • ————

In 1938 Helen Fish, a European American Friend in Rochester, New York, moved into a house in the city's impoverished Third Ward to gather children of both African and European descent to talk, read, listen to music, and play. In 1948 Rochester Friends Meeting, with only eight active local members, bought Fish's house as a "corporate witness" to its commitment to the area. Fish lived in an upstairs apartment and continued to work with children in the first-floor meeting room. African American community groups also used the house. Rochester Friends contributed funds to start a playground for children of both races and paid to send a young African American woman to a summer leadership program. In the 1950s the meeting organized weekend work camps to help residents living in overcrowded and deteriorating neighborhoods. When the meeting needed larger quarters in the 1960s, it chose to remain in the inner city, as did a number of members and attenders. In the same decade, the meeting worked to provide reasonable rental housing to African American families and since that time has focused on state prisons, heavily populated by African Americans. A worship group at Attica State Prison eventually brought the meeting some African American members.[81]

In New Jersey, Haddonfield Monthly Meeting addressed the problems of "ghetto Camden" in a six-week "Black-White Relations" course with other community religious groups in 1968. European American Friends formed a "Friends of Black People's Unity Movement" primarily to help other people of European descent understand African American challenges to unfair municipal practices and the "over-response of police." The group provided food, clothing, and legal and medical aid as necessary to the city's African Americans.[82] Nearby Moorestown Meeting took part in an ecumenical community group working on low-cost housing and supporting Wellsprings, an organization that sponsored workshops on racism, and some members were active in the Friends of the Black People's Unity Movement.[83]

———— • ————

Students at Quaker colleges were involved in interracial relations work as well. In the 1960s, Earlham students helped rehabilitate Friendship House, a community center in an almost exclusively African American area of town.[84] Swarthmore students were active in a chapter of Students for a Democratic Society, which ran programs for people at a Chester community center. In the summer of 1964, Swarthmore faculty and students took part in the foundation-supported "Swarthmore-Wade House Study Program"[85] at the Swarthmore meetinghouse. It aimed at heightening the appeal of academic subjects to junior high students with "drama, music, art, field trips, lectures, athletics, discussion—everything except textbooks."[86] The meeting made Whittier House, a building on campus near the meetinghouse, available for informal study and weekend reading.[87] European American Quaker Elizabeth Tolles also found a church building and volunteers for a school readiness program for "several dozen" children from Chester who had not been to kindergarten.[88] And from 1965 to 1967, Swarthmore students and professors acted as counselors and tutors to young people in the community.[89]

Wilmington (Delaware) Friends had an unusual opportunity to work with a group of African American youth who came to the meeting asking for support for a youth club near the meetinghouse after an eighteen-year-old had been killed in a fight in April 1966. What became a six-year project gave meeting members invaluable connections as they worked with young people in their late teens and early twenties that they would never have known otherwise. While there was some uneasiness "on both sides" at first, wrote Elizabeth Cook in *Journal of A Concern: Youth Club—Black Church—Friends Meeting*, "Friends agreed to provide financial support but understood that it was important to the youth—and the success of the club—that the young people be the ones responsible for operating the club." Members shared in helping to fix up and maintain the property they rented for the West Center City Youth Club and learned, as Cook wrote, that "working with young people from a different level of society can be difficult." Some "found the relationship 'an exercise in exasperation,' others described it as 'beautiful,' or 'a great experience of my life' or 'my first, real insight in to inner city life.'" They also learned that, by attempting to "tackle a problem that no one else was willing to deal with, [Friends] discovered the wit, intelligence and waste of young poor Blacks." While the club lost members and eventually disbanded due to the "urban renewal" in the area, meeting members who stayed in touch reported positive effects on the lives of those they had come to know because of the club.[90]

In 1971, Friends in Indianapolis were involved in a plan "designed to bring Quakers and inner-city black citizens onto common ground."

A group, composed of persons who lived in the neighborhood and Quakers who did not,, bought a house downtown to be used as the base for the Neighborhood/Quaker-Black/White Neighborhood Friends Inc. The project would bring people together to work on neighbors' needs: clean-up projects, rat control, improving city services, caring for senior citizens, training, and recreation. While the needs of the residents were being fulfilled, Friends would also satisfy needs of their own, such as erasing prejudice and covert racism, and increasing "sensitivity" to the lives of others unlike their own.[91]

In 1970, Winston-Salem Friends Meeting joined with five nearby churches to cooperate on development projects in the West End community, a decaying area with about three thousand residents,. A nursery school was opened at one of the church halls, using the lawn of the Friends Meeting for outdoor space. Volunteers contributed their time to providing a kindergarten in the community and to a summer program for elementary school children, again using various church facilities and volunteers from three area colleges. For adults, there were medical services and ministry. The hope for the "Downtown Church Center" was that a revitalized neighborhood would eventually empower the community to take responsibility for itself.[92]

Work Camps

Probably the most sustained and intense prewar interracial involvement was the work camp program, which AFSC instituted in 1934. Based on Swiss Quaker Pierre Ceresole's successful work rebuilding villages damaged in World War I, the work camps took place in areas "of economic and social tension," including Indianapolis, Nashville, Chicago, southern California, and New York City. The program was designed to offer participants a chance to "learn first hand some of the basic causes of racial or religious intolerance, economic or social insecurity." Campers had to be at least fifteen years old, and AFSC made a consistent effort to form racially mixed groups, sometimes to the displeasure of people in the receiving community.

The campers paid to participate, and they lived and worked with people of varying ethnic, social, and economic backgrounds. The program was designed to offer participants a chance to "learn first hand some of the basic causes of racial or religious intolerance, economic or social insecurity." With the supervision of trained staff, they worked with community residents, usually building, refurbishing, and repairing homes, schools, and community centers; cleaning up vacant lots; tutoring in schools; or even working on assembly lines.[93] They would live, cook, work together and attend seminars to learn about and discuss the situations they were working in. European American Quaker participant Carol Passmore spent four weekends digging out a new basement room in an African American church in a small town in North Carolina in the 1950s. None of the mixed-race group had ever known someone of another race before, but "after four weekends of digging together and four Saturday evenings of wonderful pot luck meals and social time afterward, David [Richie] knew we would be friends and would understand each other much better. He was right," she said.[94]

———————————•———————————

Most AFSC work camps took on short-term tasks, but a few work camp projects continued for many years. One of the earliest postwar housing efforts helped residents of Indianapolis build cooperative housing. AFSC began a project to reconstruct Flanner House, an African American community and social service center in a "blighted area" near the city center that had been created in 1898 as a daycare center for children of African American female domestics.[95] Every weekend from November through May in 1946 and 1947 a dozen people worked on Flanner House, which still stands today. When nearby housing was condemned, the project expanded to develop self-help housing.

The Mantua Project, conceived and led by European American Friend David Richie, focused on a depressed area of West Philadelphia. Richie had been a camper at the first AFSC project in 1934 at Westmoreland (County) Homesteads, a federally funded community built for unemployed coal miners. In 1939 Richie left his teaching position at a Friends school in Moorestown, New Jersey, to become executive secretary of the Friends Social Order Committee of the two Philadelphia Yearly Meetings and to organize yearly meeting work camps. By 1944 Richie reported that more than four hundred people had participated in Mantua projects in the preceding three years. They cleaned out a littered alley behind a nursery school that had been closed because of an epidemic, brought running water to eight homes that had only two outdoor water faucets, and helped a group of African American families rehabilitate properties they had acquired.[96]

As part of its assault on inequitable housing, the Mantua Project in Philadelphia offered a work camp to bring middle-class people of European descent into contact with the people and problems of urban ghettos.[97] In 1968, despite the turmoil surrounding the assassination of Martin Luther King Jr., David Richie reported a "remarkable total of 1,048 volunteers," some from outside Pennsylvania and about 120 from Friends schools, participating in 72 weekend work camps. Sixty of these volunteers were African American, as were "to a very large extent" the camp leaders. Most volunteers worked on housing, but a number worked with community leaders on such self-help endeavors as thrift shops, neighborhood beautification, a halfway house, rodent control, a medical service, a school and a nursing home.[98] In the evenings, volunteers met to discuss the causes of racism and other issues. In addition, at least thirty area meetings sponsored summer outings for Mantua children beginning in 1968. In that year seven hundred children participated, and by 1971 attendance exceeded one thousand.[99] Neighborhood residents urged that "more adults with skills" come to work there and visit their homes and churches, and the said that they would "welcome more invitations to Meetings for Worship and forums."[100]

"We can go where the need is great, where racial bitterness is at its worst, where lives that have been cramped in dilapidated bandbox shacks, squeezed out in exhausting factory employment, and then discarded as too old at forty-five," Richie wrote in 1944. "We can do the dirtiest job that needs to be done. We can earn the respect and friendship of those that are there." Those who benefited from the work, Richie noted, "were not transformed but they were encouraged." Richie stated that the Mantua work campers had come to know that "the way of brotherhood is right . . . because we have felt the rightness of it in our muscles . . . because we have experienced, to a degree at least, work that is 'love made visible.'"[101]

Work camps continued after World War II. In the 1960s, when the historic Penn Center on St. Helena Island was being converted into a conference center, work campers from Friends United Meeting and

New England Yearly Meeting assisted with the remodeling.[102] During the 1950s and 1960s the center, the only facility in South Carolina where biracial groups could meet without being harassed, hosted many civil rights groups, as well as Dr. Martin Luther King, Jr. and the staff that planned the 1963 March on Washington.[103] In the late 1960s, work-camps organized "Freedom Schools" to educate voters in Haywood and Fayette Counties in Tennessee. The work campers laid "down their lives for what they believed," as they "lived the lives of the threatened blacks and sharing the brutality" directed against them by the police.[104] As time went on, an increasing number of non-Quakers joined the work camps, where Richie noted they often found "a fellowship of kindred seekers, a fellowship of those who have seen with their own eyes a fraction of the unnecessary suffering and poverty that exists all about us."[105]

Integrating Facilities

Individual Quakers and their organizations also tackled de facto segregation in public facilities with visible witness in local communities. In 1930, when few European Americans showed concern about segregation in hotels and restaurants, Margaret Jones of Friends Meeting of Washington challenged the district's prestigious Hotel Willard to accept African Americans who planned to attend a banquet of the World Alliance for Friendship through Churches. When the request was denied, Jones and the meeting's Peace and Race Relations Committee protested directly to the Alliance, which treated Jones rudely and labeled her a troublemaker. Despite being warned that waiters at the Willard would strike and other guests would leave if African Americans were admitted, Jones decided to take Joanna Raynor Houston, an English professor and assistant dean at Howard University, to dinner at the Willard while a friend of Jones's took another African American woman to lunch the next day. Jones reported that, though some guests "looked down upon" the diners, both meals proceeded without incident. Jones's larger concern, however, was the World Alliance's choice to hold functions in segregated facilities. "I say that an organization that sets itself up to create friendship through the churches and then goes all around the most important racial question in the U.S. isn't living up to its name," she wrote.[106]

In 1947, some African American students at Earlham College joined the Richmond, Indiana, NAACP in entering and asking for service at restaurants, theaters, and businesses that refused to admit African Americans. But college president Thomas Jones did not want them to participate. Jones, who had been president of Fisk University for twenty years, found their action "unduly confrontational and coercive" and rejected any "attempts to change local conditions through any means other than discussion."[107]

Six years later, Earlham graduate and African American lawyer George Sawyer decided it was time to desegregate the eating places in the town where he was now practicing. He went down Richmond Indiana's Main Street and entered the first restaurant with his law book in hand. When he was refused, he did not leave. Asked to leave by the manager, who knew him, Sawyer showed him the book on the table told him he had to be served. Otherwise, he said, "I can file a lawsuit and shut you down." By the end of the day, Sawyer had been served in every "whites only" restaurant on the street. Sawyer was also instrumental in the integration of other facilities in his community.[108]

In Wichita, Kansas in 1947, Anna Jane Michener, a European American Quaker and graduate of Friends University in that city, was appointed by the local school board to chair a committee to deal with an NAACP petition protesting the busing of African American children from their neighborhoods to segregated schools taught only by African Americans. Michener's committee found segregation not only in schools but in the city's parks and pools, hospitals, hotels, restaurants, movie theaters, and housing; even the YMCA and YWCA had established racially segregated branches. With consistent pressure by the city's biracial NAACP and National Urban League, the school board eventually developed a modest integration plan.[109]

In 1956 Michener, described by historian Gretchen Eick, as "fearless, energetic, and determined," invited a group of women activists of both African and European descent to her home to discuss working together on racial equity. The group, named the Community Committee on Social Action, worked initially to end restaurant desegregation and was instrumental in the passage of a state law outlawing segregation in restaurants.[110] Joined by numerous community civic and religious organizations, in 1957 the group persuaded the city to create the

Advisory Council on Minority Problems in 1957; Michener was on the council which lobbied officials for fair and low-income housing and, on the state level, to strengthen the Kansas Committee on Civil Rights.[111] Not all Quaker activists met with approval, even within their small community. Friends University graduate Vashti Lewis, an African American woman who had worked with the AFSC as a student, became a leader in the movement for civil rights in Wichita. Lewis received a call from Friends University president Lowell Roberts who warned her that she was giving the school a bad name. "It is not Christ-like to be picketing," he said.[112]

———— • ————

In 1950 European American Friend David Scull, who five years later would chair the FCNL's new Race Relations Committee, worked with others to desegregate restaurants in the District of Columbia. Already a well-known activist, Scull was a friend of African American educator Dr. Mary Church Terrell, who took up the cause that year. Terrell later told FCNL head Raymond Wilson that she contacted Scull because one day she said to herself, "Mary Church Terrell, why don't you do something?" Soon after that phone call, Terrell, with two other African Americans (union official Geneva Brown and Baptist pastor the Rev. W. H. Jernagin) and Scull, entered and were shortly denied service at Thompson's Cafeteria. They immediately filed a complaint with the district's corporate counsel. Their complaint used as precedent an 1872 law that outlawed segregation in the District, which no public officials had been willing to enforce. After three years of working its way to the United States Supreme Court, the complaint, supported by FCNL and other civil rights organizations, was upheld. FCNL, AFSC and the Joint Social Order Committees of the Friends Meetings of Washington then joined in urging district officials to ban discrimination in public accommodations generally and lobbied the district's board of education to desegregate its schools.[113] By 1954 AFSC staff found a "great change in the climate" in Washington, and in September of that year President Dwight D. Eisenhower enforced the Supreme Court order for school desegregation with military presence to protect African American students entering schools in Little Rock, Arkansas. By that year as well, AFSC reported, public recreational facilities, restaurants, and theaters were "open" to all.[114]

The refusal of Rosa Parks to surrender her bus seat to a European American passenger in Montgomery, Alabama, in December 1955 revived prewar efforts to desegregate public transportation. "In a sprit of compassionate love," Philadelphia Yearly Meeting responded to the incident by sending European Americans Clarence Pickett, Dorothy Steere, and George Hardin, all well-known Friends active with AFSC, to Montgomery to bring "Christian greetings" to the city's African and European American leaders and attempt to aid their "search for answers."[115] When the order to desegregate the public schools was defied, as it was in Little Rock, Arkansas, and Jackson, Mississippi, Quaker organizations generally sent similar delegations of "weighty" Friends to talk quietly with beleaguered school administrators, with sympathetic people in the community to marshal their support, and with the families of the students committed enough to send their children each day into such threatening situations.

———————— • ————————

After World War II, federal programs such as the interstate highway system, the G.I. Bill and mortgage guarantees triggered "white flight" to the suburbs, greatly diminishing urban tax bases and exacerbating inner-city housing, schooling, and service problems. African American veterans, who had confronted relatively little racism in Europe, were vocal about the blatant inconsistency between the United States fighting a war against a racist German regime and support at home, open or tacit, for racial segregation. The era was marked by increased agitation surrounding equal rights legislation, increasing violence in the nation's cities, the rise of a vocal African American leadership and the Civil Rights movement.

As before the war, Friends groups sponsored numerous conferences on race questions. Friends meetings in Washington, D.C., and Alexandria, Virginia, sponsored one of the most notable of these postwar meetings in 1949. That conference issued its "Washington Statement" urging the end of discrimination in education, employment and transportation:

> We are living in times that challenge our capacity for growth. Our convictions lead us to approach the opportunities and problems of these times in the light of certain religious principles. It has been the deep-rooted belief of our society that we are all brothers and children before God. We have often found our worship enriched because people of all

races and conditions share our fellowship. Unfortunately, in our American society, practice too often contradicts principle. We welcome, we support, and we urge prompt and friendly lowering of discriminatory barriers.116

The two Washington-area meetings asked Baltimore Yearly Meeting to endorse the statement but, while that body stated its agreement "in principle," it referred the question to its monthly meetings for additional study with a request for a report at the next yearly meeting.117 The 1950 yearly meeting received written responses to the statement from Friends Meeting of Washington, State College (Pennsylvania) Friends Meeting, and Baltimore Monthly Meeting (Stony Run). The last asked the yearly meeting to endorse the Washington statement even as it acknowledged "with humility that because of our ignorance and provincial point of view we have not been able to put this principle into practice." The Stony Run Friends concluded with a plea to others to take rapid steps to align their practices with their Discipline.118 The meeting offered three suggestions about how to do so—to make a friend of "one more colored person" in the next year, to subscribe to an African American newspaper, and to demonstrate the "folly of discrimination" in their contacts with young people.119

In 1955, at the call of the yearly meetings south of the Mason-Dixon Line and AFSC's Southeastern Regional office, about fifty southern Quakers gathered in North Carolina for a regional conference on racial issues. Participants left with "a conviction that we Friends must first set our own house in order." In his report of the meeting, historian Kenneth Carroll wrote that Friends in the South felt "caught in a dilemma as difficult as that which faced Quaker slaveowners of the eighteenth century. It is almost possible to hear Woolman weeping for us, his people." Quakers who attended, Carroll wrote, "frequently felt weak and overwhelmed" by "the magnitude of problems" they faced; they recognized that they must "build bridges" to their African American neighbors but understood at the same time that "the heart of the problem lies within ourselves."120

School Desegregation

School desegregation emerged as a key goal among Quakers in 1951, when Oliver Brown of Topeka, an African American man whose daughter had been refused enrollment at a European American elementary school close to her home, sued the city's board of education with the assistance of the NAACP. It was assumed that the case would end up in the Supreme Court and that it would ultimately rule against segregation, as it did in 1954 in *Brown v. Board of Education.* That year AFSC began its "Southern Program" to work with school boards, officials, teachers and African American community leaders in such cities as Atlanta, Greensboro, Winston-Salem, Nashville and Washington, D.C., to open the way for desegregation.[121]

In the District of Columbia, AFSC inaugurated the "Washington Project," a five-year effort to work with existing community leaders and groups to train teachers and develop materials for integrated schools. The project was a multifaceted one aiming to end segregation of the public schools, recreation areas, accommodations, and housing in the nation's capital. It worked to ensure unbiased newspaper coverage, create new job opportunities, revise the city's housing policies and create in-service police training in anticipation of repercussions from desegregation.

Initially AFSC's Community Relations Committee sought to assemble people "who would not otherwise meet" in Washington in a setting that encouraged them to "talk through problems."[122] But in 1952, feeling that "integration is in sight," the Washington Project shifted from "convincing people" to "preparing the way for carrying out integration." AFSC held individual conferences with district, school and judicial officials, business people, ministers, civic organizations and churches, as well as with "individuals and groups known to be in opposition, with a view to changing their attitudes and opinions." It also set itself up as a "clearing house" and published a newsletter to explain "the deeper story about current issues." As its work progressed the committee identified people who could advise the leaders of various groups on preventing or reducing violent outbreaks should "disturbances" occur.[123]

With school desegregation progressing in Washington, by June 1954 the AFSC's Washington staff was preparing to move to Greensboro, where an AFSC office had been opened in 1947. The AFSC's presence may, in fact, have helped turn that city into a center for supporting desegregation in North Carolina.[124] By 1956, although lower courts

consistently upheld the Supreme Court's ruling, resistance to its decision began to harden. "Something like panic—bred of insecurity and
fear—seized many parts of the South." White Citizens' Council chapters
arose in Louisiana, Alabama, Texas, Arkansas, Florida, Georgia and
Mississippi to wage an assault on the ruling. African Americans who
acted or petitioned on behalf of desegregation were fired from jobs and
refused credit at banks and stores.[125]

Students rioted when African American Autherine Lucy enrolled at
the University of Alabama in 1956, which caused her expulsion.[126] In
response, U.S. Senator Harry Byrd of Virginia called for massive resistance, and 102 southern congressmen signed a "Southern Manifesto"
urging disobedience to the court's 1954 ruling on the grounds that it
was "null and void" as well as unconstitutional. Some states directly outlawed racially integrated schools and withdrew funding from any that
were created; some districts voted to abolish public schools entirely and
to direct public funds to tuition to private, segregated schools.[127] Even
such flagrant defiance of the federal mandate failed to move President
Eisenhower to publicly oppose the manifesto.

———— • ————

In 1957 AFSC began its school desegregation campaign by sending a
Quaker delegation to ask the president "to bring the weight of his office
and leadership on the side of law and order in the South."[128] The AFSC's
southern members observed that "paralysis" and "tension" plagued the
region after the court ruling; liberal forces were simply not prepared or
able to exert any influence, racial relations were "deteriorating," and
African Americans were "frightened and intimidated." AFSC staffers
asked the organization as a whole to commit "every possible resource"
to the South and identified an "urgent" the need for groups in addition
to AFSC to support NAACP petitions calling for integration.[129]

One of the most extensive AFSC school desegregation efforts took
place in Prince Edward County, Virginia, where in 1951 the local school
board built three tarpaper-covered plywood structures to handle extreme
overcrowding at the African American Robert R. Moton High School.
Moton High students lacked desks, and some teachers held classes in a
school bus. In protest 450 students staged a two-week walkout, and
after several of them turned to the NAACP for assistance their grievance

became one of the four local cases in *Brown v. Board of Education.* County school officials strenuously resisted the ruling, and in 1959 its board of supervisors closed the public schools and replaced them with private (although tax-supported) academies not open to African American children. AFSC established a tutoring program for African American students in the expectation that schools would reopen within a year, but instead public schooling was absent for the next five years. AFSC staffer Jean Fairfax, an African American, took the lead in organizing emergency placements that brought some dozens of students to schools, including several Quaker schools, in other states. When the Supreme Court ordered the schools reopened in 1964, Fairfax went from house to house in an effort to convince African American parents that they should send their children to the newly integrated schools.[130]

AFSC's method in Prince Edward County was typical of its work. Staff monitored school closings, challenged them in court, and worked to find people ready to move beyond the idea of "white superiority," to strengthen leadership in the African American community and to enroll volunteers to keep education "in the mind of kids." When officials in Jackson, Mississippi, resisted a court order to integrate, Fairfax organized "Save our Public Schools," which began its work by identifying European American women who could recognize how the exodus of European American children from the public schools would damage their community. Fairfax then brought some of the Mississippi women to Prince Edward County to demonstrate that some people of European descent indeed welcomed integration.[131]

In Greensboro, North Carolina, Friends from local meetings served on committees working to prepare for school desegregation in their communities, even when their local meetings were sometimes reluctant to be involved corporately.[132] The New Garden meeting could not achieve unity on supporting integration.[133] When some New Garden Friends wrote to the local school board pledging to "abide by" plans for desegregating after the 1954 *Brown v. Board of Education* decision, they received threatening phone calls; the "flourishing business" of one of them was "ruined," and he moved from North Carolina as a consequence. After court-ordered desegregation took effect in Yancey County in 1960, North Carolina Friends were among those who supported building new schools closer to the neighborhoods in which African American students lived.[134]

In 1969, European American Quaker Hayes Mizell and other AFSC staff took a bus full of African American parents from Mississippi, Alabama, Georgia, and South Carolina to Washington D.C, because he wanted Attorney General John Mitchell to hear real life stories about the struggle to integrate schools. Although they were told that Mitchell was unavailable, the group stayed in his office and eventually had a few less-than-satisfactory moments with him. In April 1976, Mizell, who as director of AFSC's South Carolina office had monitored desegregation in that state, offered a paper at one AFSC gathering warning that achieving integration did not signify that "all the wrongs have been corrected" or that people in the community would "link arms and walk into the new day of brother/sisterhood." The hard question, he stated, is "after access, what?"[135]

The Challenge of Fair and Open Housing

Friends were perhaps more involved in dealing with housing inequities than in any other aspect of integration. Both before and after World War I, economic inequalities kept African Americans in the cities, in aged and dilapidated housing that often lacked indoor plumbing or adequate light or cooking facilities.[136] In addition, the National Housing Act of 1934 had created the practice of "redlining" when federal agencies asked banks to rank areas of the city by the perceived risk of mortgage lending. "Residential security maps" outlined these prioritized areas in different colors; "type D" neighborhoods, generally occupied by members of racial and ethnic minorities, were outlined in red and deemed the riskiest investments. Banks generally refused to provide mortgages for residents of "type D" neighborhoods, and realtors tended to restrict the movement of African Americans into largely European American urban and suburban areas. The segregation that marked urban schools was, in fact, a direct consequence of housing segregation.

In 1924 the National Association of Real Estate Boards had endorsed a policy that legalized exclusion of certain minorities if a specific percentage of homeowners in a given neighborhood approved the exclusion. In 1938 the Federal Housing Authority also endorsed that policy and included "model covenants" in its housing manual.[137] In the 1950s AFSC was involved in several programs in Santa Clara County,

California, which had some of the most restrictive covenants in the country. There it cooperated with the United Auto Workers in creating an integrated community for automobile industry employees called Sunnyhills, where African Americans occupied about 10 percent of the 112 units. AFSC also challenged housing covenants in Richmond, California, in the local courts.[138]

Friends in many places served on similar commissions to better human relations or create open housing or better integrated schools in their communities. The Human Relations Council in Richmond, Indiana, headed by African American Quaker George Sawyer, was gathering signatures in 1964 for an open housing pledge in that city.[139] Wilmington Meeting in Delaware reported to Philadelphia Yearly Meeting that during 1968 and 1969 it had written to "every realtor in the state supporting the open housing law" and published a letter in the local newspaper as well.[140]

Noting that current housing patterns created what AFSC called "the increasing estrangement of white and Negro Americans," AFSC wanted to join European and African Americans "in a *common* task of overcoming this alienation."[141] One way to work toward that goal was to counteract the claims, or "scare tactics," used to keep African Americans from living where they wanted to live. In 1955 AFSC published *They Say That You Say: The Challenge of Houses and Race*. The fifteen-page booklet attempted to counteract commonly held assumptions. (Eg. "Property values do not necessarily go down when the racial composition of a neighborhood changes." In fact, the booklet asserts "values more often go up." That is, unless the neighborhood itself made it a problem by rushing to sell.[142]

Later, AFSC addressed housing issues in the South as well. Its 1976 *Alabama, 'Kind of Tough Living Here': a report on bad rural housing in all 67 Alabama counties* revealed the condition of rural housing in that state and received wide coverage in the national press, as well as in Alabama. With photographs on almost every page, *The Washington Post* proved its own statement that "words alone cannot describe the unpainted, rotting, flimsy shack with no sanitary facilities," nor could they "photograph the stench of sewage."[143]

The long list of recommendations for action on all levels of government ranged from creating an "Emergency Rural Housing Administration" and providing federal financing for more staff to assure that projects constructed with federal funds were open regardless of race. Finally, the report urged that Congress insist that the Department of Housing and Urban Development function as an "agency for all of America, not just those areas where mortgage bankers are abundant." Groups in other states declared their intention to carry out similar research. AFSC described the publication's "extraordinary reception."[144]

One of the earliest efforts to create fair rental housing was the Citizens Housing Corporation, organized in 1925 in Wilmington, Delaware, with European American Friend George Rhoads as president. The organization's mission was to provide better homes for African Americans living in houses "unfit for human habitation."[145] About ten years later the Corporation reported that those who had purchased shares could feel rewarded not by significant returns on their investment but by knowing that they were "giving self-respecting citizens an opportunity to secure comfortable homes at reasonable cost."[146]

———•———

In 1937, when unemployment spiked among coal miners in southwestern Pennsylvania's Fayette County, AFSC bought the two-hundred-acre Isaiah Craft Farm in Luzerne and organized the "social experiment" known as Penn-Craft. AFSC offered land on which to build a house and loans up to two thousand dollars to those applicants willing to help build their homes and to work in farming and industrial cooperative.[147] Five African American families were among the fifty chosen to settle. Friends strove to ensure ethnic and racial diversity, a high-degree of self-help, and a strong sense of democracy in the new community. Penn-Craft's homesteaders created several cooperative ventures—a store, a clinic, and a library—which they hoped to turn into sources of income. Sixty-five years later about two-thirds of the residents of Penn-Craft were descendants of the original families. The community still exists and for decades has served as a model for other cooperative communities throughout the country.[148]

In the 1950s, groups of Friends in the Philadelphia area joined to create mixed-race, suburban communities like the Cheyney-Westtown Area Housing Group, Tanguy and Bryn Gweled. Needing visibility for another integrated housing project in 1952, European American builder Morris Milgram of Philadelphia asked the AFSC to help him market a medium-priced, integrated, private development. Finding it difficult to attract people, "especially among the majority group," to live in the project, Milgram thought that promoting the project as "Quaker-sponsored" would enhance its appeal. AFSC was uncomfortable sponsoring any private project, but said it would help in other ways such as sending information about the project to its mailing list.[149] Two years later Milgram met with the AFSC again when he faced similar problems attracting buyers of European descent to Concord Park, north of Philadelphia. The project faced a lack of financial support and other "disheartening difficulties," among them the refusal of the Friends Fiduciary Trust and the Race Street Trustees, two Quaker organizations, to provide funding. Milgram noted that individual Friends, rather than "official Quaker bodies ... had been largely responsible for the financial backing of the project." He hoped that AFSC members would visit the homes he had built and spread the word.[150] By 1955, the atmosphere at Concord Park was positive, due to the developer's new policy assuring even representation of families of both European and African descent.[151]

AFSC also lent its support to groups promoting open housing in Philadelphia, Chicago, Los Angeles, and San Francisco. Over some six years, the work brought together members of religious and civic groups and, eventually, realtors to discuss open housing. One goal was to have people sign an "open covenant" declaring that religious and democratic values required equal housing opportunities for all. A listing service for those willing to sell without regard to race and a "home-seekers workshop" that encouraged participation of African American families were all part of what was deemed a "success story." Seventy African American families were able to find homes of their choice in thirteen different communities in the county.[152] The county Human Relations Council that grew out of the discussions became self-supporting after six years and after eighty business, religious and community leaders responded to the Council's call to a conference to talk about the "fears and worries" as well as successes in promoting fair housing.[153]

Friends Suburban Housing

In 1956, a group of Philadelphia Friends organized what was eventually known as Friends Suburban Housing (FSH), a nonprofit cooperative to promote open housing by helping African Americans identify potential properties in the city's suburbs and to encourage Quakers and others in these areas to sell or rent to minorities. European American group chair Clarence Yarrow urged Friends to "ponder the question of whether the privileges we enjoy in our suburban homes are open to our brothers of darker color." He added, "We would be particularly glad to know if you would welcome a responsible family from a minority group as a neighbor (send us a line on a postcard). Would you be interested in joining an area committee to work with us? If you know a Negro or Oriental family who wants a house in the 'burbs' or if you are going to sell your house, call our office."[154]

AFSC lent early support to FSH, but the program was ultimately self-supporting.[155] The group, which eventually included non-Friends, handled project publicity, fundraising and public education. Much of the credit for its success has been given to European American Quaker Margaret Collins of Bryn Mawr, who founded a real estate agency to bring buyers and sellers together and was in the only realtor in the area willing to find homes for African Americans.[156] Collins also stood by her African American clients and offered support during the physical threats and vilification they endured; in one instance, she remained by a client's side when a group of people of European descent "formed a ring and threw cigarette butts at us" when they visited a home for sale.[157] Ultimately, Collins's campaign placed 232 African Americans in previously segregated Philadelphia suburbs twelve years before fair housing became federal law in 1968. Collins successfully sued the Main Line Board of Realtors for refusing her membership. "She was always ready to walk into the lion's mouth," said European American Quaker activist Richard Taylor, who later helped found the Fair Housing Council of Suburban Philadelphia.[158] Richard and Phyllis Taylor were among those who "tested" open housing by being the European American couple welcomed by a landlord or realtor who had illegally declared the same housing "occupied" when the clients were African American.[159]

A sense of integrity moved some members of Wilmington, Deleware, Friends Meeting to take action within their meeting. They discovered that the meeting's Woodlawn Trust, two thousand acres of open land donated to the meeting by clerk William Bancroft in 1918, was not being used as intended for low and moderate-income housing, but in part for expensive housing, bringing de facto segregation into the city's restricted northern suburbs. The meeting group approached Trustee President Philip Rhoads, but Rhoads, a Quaker, refused to meet with them. The concerned Friends then began holding a meeting for worship in front of Rhoads's house across from the Friends School.[160] Appeals to the trustees, most of whom were Quakers, proved fruitless; the Friends group considered legal action against the trust. When they brought the issue to Philadelphia Yearly Meeting's Meeting on Social Concerns in June 1970, the MSC minuted: "The apparent clear divergence of the trustees from the requestor's wishes, from law, and from Christian principles poses a grave problem."[161] According to Jack Snyder, son of concerned members of the group, questions about the trust's nonprofit status were raised with the IRS. As a result, Woodlawn was reclassified as a profit-making real estate trust and its holdings became subject to current and back taxes.[162]

Chicago: A Focal Point

Chicago was the setting of the most inflammatory outbreaks over housing in the country in the 1950s and 1960s. In the late 1940s, Chicago's 57th Street Meeting decided to buy a house near the University of Chicago in the Hyde Park-Kenwood community, which was deteriorating because of "white flight" created by "block-busting" realtors. Like the university, the meeting was determined to stay and maintain the area as a mixed-raced, middle-class neighborhood. Toward that end, members were active in the community group that worked successfully toward having housing covenants declared illegal by the Illinois Supreme Court in 1948.[163] This early commitment prepared members of the meeting for the work that lay ahead, including active support of AFSC's work in the region.

AFSC became directly involved in desegregating housing in 1951 when the newly-rented apartment of an African American man in Cicero, Illinois, was set on fire. When massive opposition in that essentially European American working class suburb of Chicago threatened the lives of the pioneering family, civil rights advocates withdrew, although AFSC considered the setback to be "temporary."[164] AFSC's

Chicago office was known for working quietly to create "interracial harmony and equity." It was staffed by European American Quakers Kale Williams and Bill Moyer and African American Bernard Lafayette, who began his life-long activism at lunch-counter sit-ins in Nashville, Tennessee. European American historian James Ralph notes that the staff created effective education and job programs, even as they responded to "white outbursts over black neighbors."[165] AFSC and the Southern Christian Leadership Conference (SCLC) did things differently than other community organizers, according to Moyer. While others wanted to fire up people to oppose the "enemy," the SCLC and AFSC, Moyer said, "were trying to organize people on the basis of love."[166]

AFSC's long-term integration action plan included working with local community and faith-based councils and with top business executives and municipal officials to raise awareness and gain support.[167] The Cicero experience provided the grounding for the next decade of AFSC's housing work. The model was adapted to other locales, including Philadelphia, Los Angeles, Boston, and San Francisco. While the Cicero of the 1950s was recognized around the world by news photos of mobs throwing bottles at peaceful marchers, change did occur; today many of the same neighborhoods are thoroughly integrated and can be held up as models of peaceful interracial relations.[168]

In 1953, the first African American family moved into Trumbull Park Homes, a low-income public housing project in the South Deering area of Chicago that was then occupied exclusively by European Americans.. The move prompted a hostile reaction from the surrounding community of mostly second-generation European Americans.[169] As AFSC noted, "Mobs have thrown bricks through windows, people have been assaulted on the streets . . . aerial bombs are exploded with frequency, and police protection has been required to keep even an uneasy peace. Publications now appear in the area carrying the most outright racist propaganda."[170] "Forces with selfish interests" kept the frenzy alive for more than two years.[171] In October 1956 AFSC's Clarence Pickett was among those who joined three Chicago Friends to deal with the local situation. They met European American Mayor

Richard J. Daley and people of both races in a community center; area police in attendance explained that their policies would be ineffective in the situations they were facing.[172] After four years in Trumbull Park, efforts continued to keep people informed of neighborhood activity and problems through monthly meetings of citizens and community leaders. A "Walk and Pray" group and a Neighborhood Watch program helped eliminate the need for police patrols.[173]

In Chicago's East Garfield section, Anthony Henry, an African American who did alternative service as a conscientious objector in an AFSC youth program in Chicago,[174] worked with AFSC and others to develop a tenants' organization to demand enforcement of housing codes long ignored by landlords and city officials alike. The "East Garfield Park Union to End Slums" signed the first collective bargaining agreement between organized tenants and a Chicago landlord who had many properties in the area.[175] AFSC's approach, in keeping with Quaker ways, was described by Kale Williams. "We started off by saying that we'd respect the humanity of the landlords, but that nothing would keep us from telling the truth about conditions, and naming the individuals that we felt were responsible," Williams said. The idea was not to scapegoat or create confrontation, but to develop a core of local leaders "to organize people in a neighborhood to deal with their own problems." Rather than adding AFSC staff, local people were trained and paid to run programs. By the late 1960s one thousand tenants from all over the city had organized. Using the East Garfield experience, AFSC helped found a national tenants' rights program in 1969 under Henry's direction. It soon became an independent union with one hundred locals and fifty thousand members.[176]

The 57th Street Meeting and AFSC played a role when Martin Luther King, Jr. chose Chicago for his first northern campaign in 1966. Focusing on open housing, King hoped that a nonviolent and positive campaign would counteract the hopelessness and frustration behind the angry rhetoric of Black Power. SCLC and AFSC joined Albert Raby, the African American leader of the city's Civil Rights movement in the "Chicago Freedom Movement;" a march was planned in southwest Chicago on August 5. For the first time, angry crowds of European Americans stoned King. In the end, the campaign had little impact other than revealing the racism entrenched in Chicago.[177] The 57th

Street Meeting was a base of operations for the 1966 march, as it was later for relief efforts during the riots following King's assassination.[178]

Meeting member Kale Williams, who helped plan the campaign and marched with King, later founded the Leadership Council for Metropolitan Open Communities and served for twenty years as its executive director. The fair housing organization, a direct outgrowth of the movement, was marked by "quiet diplomacy" that proved successful in finding housing for thousands of people who would otherwise have been excluded.[179]

———————•———————

With AFSC and their monthly meetings, Friends worked to end restrictive practices. They helped African Americans to find and to finance better and housing, preferably in an integrated area, and created housing in areas previously segregated by race. They also undertook "hands-on" rehabilitation work.[180]

Philadelphia's Germantown Friends School and Meeting decided not to accept a generous offer of suburban acreage for a new campus but to remain with the meeting in the city and develop ways to support the changing community around them. Germantown Friends Meeting, as well as some individual members and other Friends meetings, invested in neighborhood housing projects for low and moderate-income families. They loaned money to Germantown Homes, Inc. in 1969 for renovations of existing apartments and in 1973 to buy and renovate cooperative housing. With the exception of a portion of the second loan, the money invested was repaid.[181]

One meeting bought a suitable house, sold it at a low cost to a low-income family, and carried the mortgage with no interest. Another meeting purchased and rehabilitated a five-bedroom home and sold it to a low-income family.[182]

Perhaps the largest-scale housing project was Philadelphia Yearly Meeting's continuing work in the Mantua-Belmont project. In response to a petition signed by one hundred neighborhood residents and the meeting's expressed concern for equitable and decent housing, in 1966 the meeting created a Mantua Belmont Joint Committee and Friends Housing, an independent nonprofit corporation dedicated chiefly to raising funds for rehabilitating properties for low-income families.[183]

Fifteen area Friends donated two hundred dollars each to begin the effort, and Friends were actively involved in its support.[184] The corporation acquired nineteen vacant and vandalized houses that ongoing work camps were to convert into fifty-nine living units. Yet the project was still in its formative stages four years later, and some Friends who were skeptical about whether the project would ever take place challenged the yearly meeting's support. Arguing that so many of the residents there had worked so hard for its success that "it would be wrong to give it up now," supporters identified specific ways to cut costs and raise additional capital. The meeting agreed to extend the project and "pledged itself" to confront the Federal Housing Agency "to see why it fails to provide rehabilitation of housing for poor people."[185] Sixty Friends and fourteen monthly meetings helped support the project, and in December 1970 the FHA finally committed the necessary funding.[186] In 1971, construction was underway on six new buildings with three apartments each.[187]

Also in Philadelphia, the long-lived Friends Neighborhood Guild worked with various government agencies and helped organize neighborhood and tenant associations to make certain that urban renewal proposed for the Northern Liberties neighborhood would benefit residents. A self-help housing project—Friends Housing Coop—was developed in conjunction with AFSC.[188] Guild House, a ninety-two-unit apartment building, opened in 1967 to house senior citizens displaced by redevelopment. In 1979 the cooperative completed Guild House West, a residence for elderly and disabled people. Eventually the housing program became a separate endeavor known as the Friends Rehabilitation Program.[189]

The struggle for fair housing was no less contentious in the rural heartland. In the 1960s, when George Sawyer and his family received bomb threats after buying a house in Richmond, Indiana, Sawyer called the mayor and got help from the Earlham community. When some of the college's African American students came with shotguns, he told them the guns would not be needed. The house was watched for several days, and soon Sawyer felt he could safely move his family in. "When you follow the leading of the Spirit, you can't do a bad job," he said.[190] In fact, in his many speeches and articles, Sawyer often told Friends that they should be doing God's work, that simply speaking of "the brotherhood of man" in meeting did not fulfill "our religious duty toward our brothers."191

Promoting Racial Justice in the Courts

AFSC, meetings and individual Quakers tackled still other aspects of racial discrimination. The Friends Suburban Project of Chester (PA) Meeting arose in the sixties from a concern about inequality in the legal system. When an African American man who had been arrested sought help in his upcoming court appearance, several Friends visited Magistrate's Court, the district court in Chester. They discovered that the court conducted arraignments in the cells, operated without a jury or lawyers, and, as European American Friend Vinton Deming notes, was essentially "run by the police." The accused were often held for long periods of time because they could not afford to pay bail. Many African Americans pled guilty because they were ignorant of procedures, a tendency that Friends felt "aggravates problems of disorder."192

Deming and European American Quaker Elisabeth Leonard, soon joined by others, began to monitor the courts. They were arrested after a visit to the jail in Chester, she for sitting on the floor (there were no benches) and he for asking about one of the accused, "Excuse me, shouldn't this guy have a lawyer?" Deming enrolled European American Quaker attorney Allan Hunt in the cause and involved the American Civil Liberties Union, which brought the issue to the attention of the state's attorney general.193 More than two hundred Friends from fifteen monthly meetings were connected with what became the Friends Suburban Project, funded by the yearly meeting. They observed the court to learn "first hand" about discrimination within the local judicial system, attended hearings on conditions in the courts and jails, and raised funds for bail.194 When Concord Monthly Meeting offered some unused and refurbished benches for seating, the city refused the donation on the grounds that they would interfere with the business of the court. Still, the meeting delivered the benches, and when they were refused Friends sat down on them for a meeting for worship outside the courthouse. Finally officials acceded, and the benches were brought in.195 Local officials also filed an injunction against Quakers who attempted to visit people imprisoned there. After another protest, some of these volunteers were themselves jailed for a week and received a standing ovation from other prisoners when they entered the jail's cafeteria.[196]

The work of the Friends Suburban Project seemed not only to change attitudes and practices in the courts but fostered among local Quakers, as one put it, "a great sense of rededication to our struggle against society's oppressive institutions."[197] A number of Friends in the area, including members of Plymouth and Gwynedd Meetings, worked to create bail funds.[198] The Chester action inspired work in other courts including Delaware County's Juvenile Court in nearby Media, which had jurisdiction over young people, many of them African American, who were either truant from school or had run away to escape abusive conditions at home.[199] A small group of Friends in Media became "youth advocates" by taking these young people into their own homes; a few stayed in meetinghouses under the supervision of a resident Friend. They were treated as family members, required to go to school, and taken to ball games and on trips. The program influenced the Juvenile Court itself, which began to look for alternatives for those who needed to be away from their home situation.[200] In the early 1970s, Friends Suburban Project also published a book Deming wrote—*The County Jail: A Handbook for Citizen Action*—and also started the Community Dispute Settlement Program as "an experiment in community mediation." Supported by Philadelphia Yearly Meeting, it was one of the first programs in the country to help individuals resolve disputes without having to go to court.[201]

Federal Action and Civil Rights

Friends Committee on National Legislation played a crucial role in the Leadership Conference on Civil Rights, organized in 1950 by A. Philip Randolph, Roy Wilkins of the NAACP, and Arnold Aronson of the National Jewish Community Relations Advisory Council. Early in the next decade. FCNL's representatives "met almost weekly with other organizations working" for what would become the 1964 Civil Rights Act.[202] According to European American Edward Snyder, then FCNL's legislative secretary and later its executive secretary, its conference room became "the command post" for the many lobbyists working together on the Senate bill.203 Senator Hubert Humphrey and other civil rights activists cited Richard W. Taylor, a European American Friend on sabbatical from Coe College in Iowa who devoted an enormous amount of time to the conference's work, "for using his inexhaustible powers of persuasion and intimate knowledge of the legislative process to increase support for enforceable and comprehensive civil rights legislation."204 After Baltimore European American Friend Helen Baker of Baltimore testified for AFSC and FCNL on the Economic Opportunity Act in 1964, European American Congressman Edith Green of Oregon stated that she knew "of no group that is affiliated with any religious organization that shows anywhere near the interest in legislation that the Friends do on Capitol Hill."205

While civil rights had been an FCNL priority since 1957, in 1968 the the committee increased its staff in order to place highest priority on enforcement, fairness, and funding of civil rights law.206 Stating its intention to serve as "a channel for new voices from the ghetto and rural slums," the committee aimed to inform Congress, influence legislation, and to seek the involvement of African Americans in devising civil rights programs.207 The staff working specifically on civil rights included Edward Anderson, one of the first two African American lobbyists in Washington. Three years later William Lunsford, another African American, began work for FCNL. He and Anderson were the first lobbyists registered with the U.S. Congress to represent a religious organization.208 Lunsford was active in the Campaign for Adequate Welfare Reform Now, a coalition of church and other social reform groups focused on adequate income for the poor. Both men opened valuable connections for FCNL on Capitol Hill, particularly with the Congressional Black Caucus, which became "major allies."209 Many individual Quakers, including African Americans Barrington Dunbar, Jim Fletcher, Ted Robinson and George Sawyer, actively sought political and financial support to create state as well as federal laws banning discrimination in such areas as capital punishment, employment and housing opportunity.210

———————•———————

Despite the record of achievement in racial equity on the part of many meetings and individuals, participation in such activity was not universal among Friends, and it varied greatly from meeting to meeting. The disparity was in part due to the vast differences in meeting size: yearly meetings such as Philadelphia—the largest of all, with seventeen thousand members during the 1960s—had paid staff employed for its individual committees, while smaller yearly meetings depended entirely on volunteers to serve on committees devoted to these issues. Still, sources suggest that few monthly or yearly meetings were fully engaged in a campaign for racial equality. Another few were not engaged at all, and work with racial issues was undertaken in those areas only by individuals or small groups of Friends.

Clarence Yarrow of Friends Suburban Housing posed a question to Friends in 1956 about their own attitudes: "Could my house, or one like it, be bought by a Negro family?" he asked. "If the answer is 'No,' then we have a real burden to lay before the Lord as we sit in the meeting for worship."[211] That some would be compelled to answer in the negative was suggested by the actions of numerous meetings. About 1960, members of one Wisconsin monthly meeting circulated a statement to be signed by those who wished to "indicate their readiness to accept members of minority groups as neighbors," but few Friends appeared to be ready to take that step. In the early 1960s, according to Philadelphia activist Richard Taylor, Quakers in Kansas showed "much reluctance to accept the Negro as a next-door neighbor."[212] When Elisabeth Leonard of the Friends Suburban Project became a "youth advocate," her Swarthmore neighbors responded negatively to the fact that four delinquent or runaway youths lived in her house and attended local schools. Leonard recalled later that she "got hate calls" from those who objected most strenuously.

As Nancy Weiss observes in her history of the Urban League, it is "no doubt true that many social justice Progressives shared to some degree the racial prejudices of their generation."[213] Some critics were not inclined to excuse Quakers on that basis, however. In 1935 Henry Cadbury charged, "Not only do we not have a Quaker testimony as such on today's race problem, but we are more indifferent and more prejudiced than early Friends." Thirty years later PYM's Race Relations Committee concluded that "in the main our movement appears slow in relation to the problem and to the strides in some other religious groups." Still, the record of sustained activity among Quaker meetings and individuals is profound, and the level of introspection directed specifically to racial equity makes clear the awareness among many Friends that they might do more. Many Friends shared European American Elizabeth Powell Bond's belief, stated in 1923 before the Race Street Yearly Meeting: "There is no place in the world where the vital question [of race relations] can be so fittingly taken up as in the Society of Friends.[214]

Children in Friends Neighborhood Guild Swimming Pool.

AFSC Flanner House, Indianapolis Work Camp, 1946.

Working for Economic Justice

What is it we were born to do; for what mission came we into the
world? . . . It is to demonstrate and exhibit a type of religion which
reveals the life of God in the lives of men.
— *Rufus Jones, 1941*

T HE EARLY 1900S brought new political and theological views that
supported a belief in a better life, not just for the privileged but
also for those who were crushed by the rush to industrialization. The
political view manifested in the Progressive movement drew disciples
who worked to end child labor, improve tenement buildings, regulate
big business, and bring the right to vote to women. The theological
view became the "Social Gospel," which taught that one's faith was to
be practiced in daily human concerns, especially caring for one's neighbor and addressing social problems.

Henry Wilbur, the first general secretary of the newly created Friends
General Conference, put "reform" at the center of his concept of
Quakerism and declared that ". . . concerned action by the individual is
the divine plan for leading the race to spiritual light and liberty." The
"concerned action" could be in all areas of a community's need—"spiritual, social, ethical or civic, or all four combined."[1] An Epistle from
Baltimore Yearly Meeting in 1912 illustrated the change that was coming
in the way Friends viewed social problems. "It was desired to bring into
prominence the idea of social service...rather than the thought conveyed
by the word 'philanthropic.'" The distinction is important in that "philanthropy" implies charity, doing something for someone else, while "social
service" implies a "greater involvement" on the part of the donor.[2]

The idea that Christian principles should be applied to social issues
seemed in keeping with Quaker witness over the years. Quakers were
called to act on their social responsibility largely through the influence
of Rufus Jones, considered by many to be the leading Quaker of the
early twentieth century. As the editor of the *American Friend*, teacher
and sought-after speaker, Jones had ample opportunity to spread his

message widely, and Friends received it well. That Jones was a founder and long-time chair of the American Friends Service Committee was a witness to his own practice of the social gospel.[3] Those drawn to the social gospel would soon find themselves challenged by the worsening economic and social condition of African Americans crowding the northern urban ghettos.

True to Rufus Jones's vision, AFSC would come to be the most prominent actor on behalf of Friends in matters of racial justice for the rest of the century. Early work of the Service Committee—to feed the victims of the war in Europe including, eventually, their country's former enemies—gave Friends a new expression of both their pacifism and their philanthropy for those in need. It was an expression that set the stage for later twentieth-century peace and social concerns. It would bring some Friends to engage with the African American community when World War I ended.[4]

Economic Plight of African Americans

Imbalances in the American economic system were not a new concern for Friends; from the beginning of the twentieth century they increasingly recognized that economic inequality lay at the root of many of the country's social problems. In the early 1900s, committees of Philadelphia's Arch Street and Race Street Monthly Meetings both spoke of the need for Christians to ponder "a social order which holds from masses of mankind the means to a self-respecting life."[5] Though economic disadvantage was common to all poor people, Quakers also recognized that race, as well as class, was at issue.

At the turn of the twentieth century the economic prospects of African Americans in the South remained dismal. With virtually no other options beyond sharecropping and domestic service, their severe disadvantage all but negated the possibility of economic advance. Inferior school systems inhibited any move beyond low-wage and menial work. On the whole, the several hundred thousand African Americans who left for the North immediately increased their incomes and experienced a greater range of economic opportunity. During World War I in particular, African Americans found work in factories in which military service and immigration restrictions had curtailed the labor supply. By the end of the war, however, workplace discrimination grew more acute and diminished the promise of economic advance that had brought them North.[6]

Some Friends were aware of the economic difficulty northern African Americans faced before the war. Orthodox Quaker John T. Emlen, a prosperous Philadelphia banker who had taught at Hampton Institute for a year, formed the Armstrong Association in 1908 to survey the services available to Philadelphia's African Americans. It focused on finding employment for new migrants from the South. According to the *Negro Year Book* of 1916, the association was "working in a practical way for the colored people of Philadelphia, and endeavoring from year to year to supplement some of the community needs which are not now being met by other organizations." Named for Hampton's founder, European American General S. T. Armstrong, the association worked to find jobs other than domestic service and helped end the longtime exclusion of African Americans from the building trades.[7] By 1916 the association reported that "in the field of industry, in which the Negro has not been previously employed, we have made material progress" in African American employment.[8]

The stock market crash of October 1929 and the Depression affected millions of Americans but tended to affect African Americans more. Drastically reduced cotton prices impelled many tenant farmers and sharecroppers to move to southern cities already plagued by unemployment. Scarcity of relief programs in the South also drew people north. Black unemployment in northern urban areas nearly doubled that of white urban populations, as struggling European Americans took low-wage jobs in which African Americans had traditionally worked. Trade unions also organized to curb or bar African American employment in various industries, including construction. Largely barred from or discriminated against by the labor movement, many African American families were driven past the brink of economic disaster, yet they received far less public assistance than needy European Americans.[9]

The Economy: A Larger View

The economic collapse of the early 1930s also spurred Friends interest in looking at the larger economic system. As part of this effort, the

Committee on Philanthropic Labor of Philadelphia Yearly Meeting (Hicksite) formed an Economic Order subcommittee. A few years later, the Hicksite meeting created a separate Social Order Committee to cooperate with the corresponding committee of the Orthodox meeting, the Committee on Economic Problems, chaired by European American Quaker Clair Wilcox, an economics professor at Swarthmore College. For ten years, this committee had a number of subcommittees, including Industrial Relations, Community, Economic and Social Research, and a joint subcommittee on the visitation of meetings. Five years later, the Hicksite and Orthodox committees merged into a joint committee.[10]

In the meantime, FGC had formed the Industrial Relations Committee, which soon brought radical proposals to eliminate a money-based economy and share work and wealth. Their ideas were not approved.[11] Neither were those of the Social Order Committee of the Orthodox Arch Street Yearly Meeting, which urged Friends to be open to views that may "appear to be too new or too radical," namely giving serious consideration to modified capitalism in which the government controlled some industries "in the public interest."[12]

In 1941 a new FGC committee, the Economic and Social Services Division, was formed to examine the U.S. socioeconomic system "in the light of Christian ethics" and to "propose such changes as might make it approach more closely to a just and Christian order." Charged with educating Friends so that they could work for a system "more consistent with Christian teaching," the committee began issuing newsletters with facts and arguments on economic issues. In 1948 it led one of the "roundtable" discussions at the annual FGC conference at Cape May. Included in the thirty-two questions on the relationship between economic justice and Christian ethics, which focused the discussion, were: "Would you be willing to dig coal for $1.70 an hour?" and "Is it possible for a good Christian to become exceedingly wealthy or for an exceedingly wealthy man to remain a good Christian?" Another question asked whether corporations should be forced to share some of their high profits with their workers or reduce prices to the consumer or both.[13] Topics in the committee's newsletter, which in 1953 went to almost nine hundred readers, ranged from the unemployment problem and slum clearance to the "frontiers of social security" and whether inflation could be checked by taxation. Some sixty-two newsletters had gone out by 1955, the date of the last minutes on file for the committee.

————— • —————

Racial conflict flared over African American employment in Philadelphia's public transit system in 1944. Working with African American community leaders and individual Friends in the city, AFSC's Race Relations Committee urged the system to hire men of African descent as street car operators; until then, they had had only mainte-nance jobs. By August the group had convinced the rail system to schedule eight African Americans for training runs as conductors, but the action triggered a strike among European American employees. According to AFSC committee secretary Herbert Bergstrom, a European American, the latter had "strong prejudices and emotional feelings against the Negroes and want to keep them 'in their place.'" But because it was wartime, the federal government was allowed to order the strikers back to work and send troops to head off any vio-lence against the African American workers. It was "a shameful disgrace," in Bergstrom's view, that such "severe measures" had been employed to bring about integration. "Very few incidents" of violence or hostility had taken place in this volatile atmosphere, he noted. Bergstrom credited the cooperation of African American leaders and the "long and tireless efforts" of many people to foster better relation-ships between workers of African and European American descent.[14]

World War II and Its Aftermath

When the United States geared up for wartime production in the early forties, African Americans sought assurance that they would not face dis-crimination in the expanded industrial effort. The point was underscored by African American labor leader A. Philip Randolph, who along with African American Friend Bayard Rustin and European American Friend A. J. Muste, threatened to march on Washington in 1941 for the cause.[15] President Franklin D. Roosevelt issued an order declaring a renewed commitment to a "policy of full participation in the defense program by all persons, regardless of race, creed, color, or national origin." At the same time, the Fair Employment Practices Committee was created to handle discrimination grievances in the defense industries.[16] Yet many African Americans continued to be excluded from industries that had federal contracts. By 1944 African Americans still held only slightly more than 8 percent of defense jobs.[17] Those in the military faced much the same situation they had in World War I; their assignments still mirrored the injustices in American society as a whole.

———————•———————

Based on the predictions of economists that "terrific stresses with Negroes, Jews, Japanese-Americans and other minorities" would be expected when veterans of European descent returned to the workforce, AFSC developed a strategy for African American employment. To help educate Philadelphia employers about new regulations after the war, AFSC published "A Step Toward Fair Employment." The publication included succinct information about the new ordinance forbidding employers, agencies, and unions to use information about the race, color, religion, national origin or ancestry in hiring and promoting employees and, among other provisions, banned the use of any such information in employment ads.[18] AFSC also issued *Social and Industrial Peacemaking: A Quaker Program*, which outlined its plans to "eliminate social inequality and racism." Described were its placement service and additional work and study programs like "student-in-cooperatives" and "student-in-agriculture," as well as an economics research unit to study problems and bring its findings to meetings with leaders of management.[19]

In 1945 AFSC conducted a "demonstration project" in Philadelphia to help African Americans trained in technical and professional fields present their qualifications to potential employers. The service went beyond "a conventional employment bureau," because one of its major goals was to change employer attitudes about African Americans. AFSC selected students of African descent "with promise" and not only placed the applicant but offered employers "assistance in techniques that have proved effective" in integrating or promoting workers of color. Similar assistance was also available to people of European descent who wanted to work in a predominately African American business. After nine months, twenty-nine of thirty employers who had been contacted had given a "sympathetic hearing" in interviews; they were still hesitant, however, and afraid of the reaction of their employees or customers. Applicants were placed "only in a few instances," according to Frank Loescher of AFSC. The program, he said, revealed two important things. First, the "job ceiling has not changed very noticeably despite the war" and the city's newly-created Fair Employment Practices regulations. Second, inadequate education and guidance resulted in a shortage of qualified African Americans.[20]

As part of a campaign to integrate staff in department stores, the AFSC visited stores in Philadelphia, met with executives, and conducted a survey that revealed customers would welcome African American salespeople. Loescher was able to report that his personal conversations with at least a dozen business executives in the city indicated that they would welcome a Fair Employment Practices Commission (FEPC); they just didn't want to be the first to take the step. The FEPC brought a "relatively rapid extension" of merit employment, and other employers began to contact AFSC staff for assistance.[21] Another AFSC program provided loans to small African American businesses, and another initiative aimed to open medical school enrollment to African Americans.[22]

AFSC expanded its work nationally during the 1950s. Its merit employment work moved to cities across the country: Chicago, Indianapolis, Dallas, Kansas City, Seattle (with the Urban League), Worcester, Massachusetts; Columbus, Ohio; and Greensboro, North Carolina. AFSC approached companies such as Macy's, International Harvester, Western Electric and Pitney-Bowes. AFSC staff gave workshops on how to apply for jobs and how to work with employers to open up opportunities. European American Thelma Babbitt worked for the AFSC in several of those cities before becoming the program's national director in the early 1960s. The program continued to expand through the mid-sixties.[23]

Raising Awareness among Friends

In 1960, the Board of Peace and Social Concerns of Five Years Meeting, an organization of primarily Gurneyite pastoral meetings (renamed Friends United Meeting in 1960[24]) asked its sister committee at Friends

General Conference to co-sponsor a five-year program of study, self-examination and social action to keep the issue of economic justice at the fore, among both activists and non-activists alike. The board was critical of the inherent inequity of a political system based on raw capitalism:[25]

> So great are the problems and tensions of our times that we are often tempted to seek peace by withdrawing into ourselves and ignoring or disclaiming responsibility for those aspects of the world which make us uncomfortable. But a contentment so easily attained is not the true Peace of God.
>
> We know that peace among nations cannot flourish when selfishness is the primary motivation for national policy and when men feel an insecurity which breeds fear, a hunger out of which grows envy, a sense that others look upon them as less than human which is the most fertile soil for hate.
>
> We cannot do everything but we can do some things . . . and we must begin with ourselves.[26]

Slated to begin in 1960, the five-year program proposed a topic for each year; "our economic order examined from the Christian viewpoint" was to be taken up in 1963–64. The FGC committee discussed the proposal "at length" at a meeting in May 1960. The committee determined that the program was not an appropriate fit, however, because FGC was a service organization for affiliated meetings and had no authority to commit its membership to such an initiative.[27] The choice had to be up to yearly and monthly meetings as well as individual Friends.

In the midst of FUM's five-year study, the 1963 bombing of Sixteenth Street Baptist Church in Birmingham killed four young African American girls. In response FUM called its members' attention to "the deepening crises in race relations all across the land. A revolution in relations between the races is upon us. We can neither stop it nor delay it. Concerned and courageous Christians must participate actively." The meeting asked that Friends "be open" to working for racial justice and to examining "all their contracts, investments, and employment practices."[28]

———————•———————

By the mid-sixties, the federal government had taken three significant actions toward achieving economic justice. The March on Washington in August, 1963, which brought half a million people to the nation's capital to demand economic and social justice, helped persuade federal legislators to pass the Civil Rights Act of 1964, banning discrimination in employment based on race, color, national origin, religion and gender. In 1965 Congress created the Equal Employment Opportunity Commission to mediate complaints and ultimately to enforce the Civil Rights Act.[29] And, in September of that year, President Lyndon B. Johnson issued an executive order requiring every government contractor to practice affirmative action.[30]

The focus of Quaker social action had been moving from race relations to economic justice in the 1960s. To better understand the economic basis of violence, AFSC asked people to recognize that for blacks "born into urban ghetto poverty," the "economic life in America had little to offer," and "there was not much by way of career or rewarding work to be educated for." In 1967 the steering committee of the National Conference of Friends on Race Relations announced that they were finding "a new awareness" about the problems people have been working to overcome. Activist Friends aware of the connection between the economic structure and racism urged Friends to be more conscious of where their funds were invested. In 1968 Philadelphia Yearly Meeting's Meeting for Social Concerns (MSC) visited eight Philadelphia banks to inquire about racial discrimination in their mortgage and lending practices.[31] The next year the yearly meeting created a working group on economic justice.

In 1969 as well, the Meeting for Social Concerns endorsed a seminar, "The American Economic System and How to Humanize It," developed by Richard Taylor. Taylor's focus was on the need for an economic system that would "operate in a more just and humane manner."[32] In 1970 he led weekly seminars on economics for about a dozen Young Friends, many of whom had participated in the 1968 Poor People's Campaign. During the sixteen-week course, the class considered the way power operates in American capitalism and discussed some of the conflicting values: the value to live to be "humane and enlightened," for example, would conflict with to "get, produce, grow, buy and spend as much as you can." Topics also included "The Scandinavian Social Welfare System" and "Cuban History and American Imperialism," as well as the study of nonviolence. The culmination was a discussion, led by European

American Friend George Lakey, on the five stages of nonviolent revolution. Lakey would become one of the founders of the Movement for a New Society, a group organized in 1971 along with European American Quakers Lawrence Scott, George Willoughby, Richard Taylor and others dedicated to bringing about a nonviolent revolution.[33]

In 1972, Philadelphia Yearly Meeting liberated Scott and Willoughby to form a group to study the problems of the "immorality of the profit motive" and the corporate structure of American economic life. To encourage "seeking and study of concerned members of PYM," the working group circulated queries and facilitated discussions in local meetings.[34] They also researched what yearly meetings and other religions were doing about investment and wrote several books, including *Moving Toward a New Society* and *Revolution: A Quaker prescription for a sick society.*[35]

Friends and the Poor People's Campaign

The Southern Christian Leadership Conference (SCLC), formed by civil rights activists in 1957 shortly after the successful Montgomery Bus Boycott, initiated the Poor People's Campaign (PPC) in 1968 to achieve an "economic bill of rights" for poor people of every race. Announcing the campaign plan in December 1967, Martin Luther King, Jr. said SCLC "will lead waves of the nation's poor and disinherited to Washington, D.C. next spring to demand redress of their grievances by the United States government and to secure at least jobs or income for all." The National Welfare Rights League joined SCLC in the campaign.

The idea, suggested by African American activist and NAACP lawyer Marian Wright (Edelman), was to bring "a nonviolent army of the poor" to Washington. The intention was "to build militant nonviolent actions until that government moves against poverty." What SCLC and its supporters wanted to see was specific legislation from Congress authorizing thirty billion dollars to fight poverty by, among other measures, creating a food stamp program, working toward full employment and a guaranteed annual income. In King's view, the campaign against economic inequality was the second phase of the Civil Rights movement; it would build upon first-phase efforts to end segregation.[36]

The AFSC was a major participant because of its relationship with King and Friends like Bayard Rustin and Rachel DuBois, who worked with SCLC. European Americans Bill Moyer and Tony Henry came from the Chicago AFSC office to help recruit participants and plan the event.[37] The committee proposed that every one hundred Friends contribute enough money to send one person from their area to Washington to take part in the campaign, and a number of Friends meetings and individuals did so. To help Friends reflect on the issues of the campaign, the AFSC planned a "crash educational program" with readings and discussion groups. And, wishing to "go beyond simple verbal support," AFSC donated ten thousand dollars to the campaign.[38] Charles Harker, the European American associate secretary of FCNL, was one of the first one hundred leaders to arrive in Washington to lobby for the proposed antipoverty bill. At a visit to the State Department (because the costs of the Vietnam War were believed to be limiting social programs), Harker joined leaders from many organizations to appeal to Secretary of State Dean Rusk on behalf of American poor people from many groups—Native Americans, Puerto Ricans, Mexican-Americans, African Americans, the Euro Americans of Appalachia. The William Penn House, a Quaker center near the Capitol building, provided overnight accommodations for about 1,000 people, supplied more than 2,500 meals, and held 25 meetings during the campaign.[39]

Although Philadelphia Yearly Meeting supported the Poor People's Campaign (one of the first actions of its newly formed Committee on Social Concerns was to donate sixty thousand dollars to the endeavor), not all meetings were behind the effort. Declaring itself "not in sympathy" with the protest, one meeting stated that it feared "the saddest possible thing—these groups of poor people will plod along and soon will be infiltrated and led by the violent and subversive groups. Trouble will break out and many innocent people hurt."[40]

As people gathered in Washington for the campaign, hundreds of Friends were attending an FGC meeting at Cape May. A group of high school Friends there pledged to return to their meetings and communities to work on problems that plagued the everyday lives of so many. "We will actively boycott those economic institutions and specific companies which contribute to the status quo," the working conference's report vowed. They committed themselves to "seek out" those who helped perpetuate the slum, including businesses that offered no training for those who needed jobs. The young people's report concluded, "We believe that all Quakers should act upon these suggestions not simply as members of the Society of Friends but as human beings concerned about the condition of their fellows and in accord with the Inner Light."41

Friends attending the Cape May conference who were interested in the Poor People's Campaign heard that the campaign had not been successful and that the "city" of tents and shacks in "Resurrection City" had been dismantled by the government. Some Friends wanted the entire gathering to close and go to protest. After some consideration, however, they decided the work of the conference, which was aimed at engaging Quakers more firmly in racial issues, was just as important.

As soon as the Cape May conference ended, some 250 Friends went to Washington. They planned to visit congressmen in support of the Campaign's message and then to hold a special meeting for worship and vigil on the Capitol grounds. For that they meeting had obtained a permit for some of the groups. A few Friends, however, planned to commit civil disobedience by going closer than allowed. As that smaller group of thirty-five moved forward, some one hundred feet away they noticed that protesters representing the SCLC had been arrested for taking the same action. Because they wished to "identify themselves fully with the campaign," wrote European American Ross Flanagan, onetime field secretary for New York Yearly Meeting's Peace and Social Action Program, "the Friends couldn't walk away." Flanagan added, "In what seemed a moving of the Spirit, all Friends rose and walked forward in a body, singing, 'No Man is An Island.'" Warned by police to move or be arrested, the twenty-one men and fourteen women sat down. They were charged with unlawful assembly and given sentences from three to ten days in jail, or they were simply suspended.42 One of those arrested was European American AFSC clerk Stephen Cary, who told the court that he violated the permit because it was "intolerable that in this rich country of ours any child anywhere under any circumstances should have to go to bed hungry." The "options for our country are running out," Cary warned.43

The Poor People's Campaign was the last major peaceful demonstration of the Civil Rights movement; after that the leadership seemed to fall to the militant groups. "Law and order" (some considered it "thinly veiled racism") was the campaign slogan for Richard Nixon, who was elected president in the fall of 1968. In appreciation of their role in the March on Washington, the Rev. Andrew Young of SCLC said that "Quakers and the SCLC were perhaps the only two major organizations still committed to non-violence in the struggle."[44] Over the years, the two organizations had joined in many actions together; they "influenced one another . . . borrowed each other's ideas, exchanged staff, and worked together in a number of ambitious programs, including the Poor People's Campaign, to provoke major social changes through nonviolent means." Historian Gerald Jonas notes that AFSC was usually a "silent partner—the way both organizations prefer it." But they shared goals and "same insights into the relation between goals and means."[45]

A Challenge for Quakers: The Urban Crisis

The closing years of the 1960s would be years of turmoil. What had been peaceful demonstrations became violent eruptions by disillusioned African Americans who saw their hope for the future disappearing. Bewildered Friends searched for something they could do, particularly something that would relieve the poverty that fueled so much of the disenchantment with America.

The "urban crisis" was the focus for AFSC's 1967 Avon Institute in New Hampshire, another of the annual retreats that had been sponsored by the regional AFSC Peace Committee since 1952 for its supporters, which included Quakers and non-Quakers. Instead of the discussions most participants expected, thirty-three of the African Americans attending presented a manifesto calling for changes in AFSC's project in the predominantly African American Roxbury section of Boston. They wanted the Roxbury office to be autonomous, with full authority over policy and funding vested in people from the community. They also wanted AFSC to agree to hire African American men to direct all its field offices in ghettos. AFSC did turn the office over to the Roxbury Action Program (RAP) and paid the office expenses for the next two years, which it saw as a moral commitment to the community.

At the 1968 Avon Institute, following King's assassination on April 4, about one hundred African Americans took over one of the buildings and warned "all white people not to approach within fifty feet." They emerged with a demand for "immediate and massive financial aid, with no strings attached, to black liberation groups in urban ghettos." At the institute's closing session, with little dissent, attenders voted to endorse the demands, although that included no actual monetary commitment. Once RAP was reorganized the following year (1969), AFSC received an angry "demand" for $350,000 to finance a major housing rehabilitation project. However, AFSC approved only $25,000 for a feasibility study of such a program.[46] The next year, after several discussions about both Friends responsibility to the African American community and their reservations about donating funds to an unfamiliar non-Quaker group, New England Yearly Meeting's Peace and Social Concerns Committee decided it had gained enough positive information to feel confident in donating $3,000 to RAP without having been asked.[47]

Also in the wake of King's assassination, Philadelphia Yearly Meeting felt "a sense of urgency" and appointed an ad hoc Committee on the Urban Crisis to "examine the total picture" of the situation; they were also asked to consider committees already working on this area and design more efficient use of money and staff.[48] To coordinate work on race and poverty issues, six groups merged into a new group and were authorized to hire an executive director for a Committee on Social Concerns (CSC), later named the Meeting for Social Concerns (MSC). Friends anticipated that the new group and new name, "characterized by openness, flexibility, and wide sharing of concern, commitment and responsibility," would more clearly "lay the weight of social concerns" on all members of the yearly meeting.[49] In addition to its own financial support of the Poor People's Campaign, committee members had visited monthly meetings seeding donations to the PPC and to individual projects designed to improve race relations. "The need is urgent for study and action by individuals, families, Meetings," the committee told meeting clerks. "The time is now, not months hence." To encourage action the committee sent materials to the clerks of each of all ninety-two monthly meetings.[50]

———————•———————

In 1969 Friends United Meeting (FUM) chose to address the issue of racial discrimination by its support of "Project Equality," a group that channeled the purchasing power of religious communities through business firms that did not discriminate in employment or other practices.[51] FUM urged its members in the United States to commit 1 percent of their incomes to "programs of economic development in the inner cities and among the disadvantaged everywhere in America." A National Friends United Meeting Fund for Urban Economic Development would be used "primarily to encourage, and help in the financing of economic enterprises to be owned and operated by members of minority groups, and to attack the problem of housing available to minority group members." The committee developing the program would include African American Friends as well as provide an "active role for young Friends," including conscientious objectors. Friends United Meeting committed itself to a list of actions including an effort to end "a virtual white monopoly" in economic and political affairs. Monthly meetings in FUM were also encouraged to create and raise funds for similar programs in their own areas, perhaps in cooperation with other churches.[52] In the same year, Baltimore's Stony Run Meeting joined FUM's "Project Equality" aimed at bringing fair hiring practices to businesses. The meeting also invested 5 percent of its own assets in "socially significant causes," including an African American-owned bank and companies owning integrated apartment buildings.[53]

When the MSC asked Philadelphia Yearly Meeting to join Project Equality, however, PYM gave "a reluctant no" on the grounds that "a number of Friends were not clear or comfortable about the *means*." Some saw the plan as a boycott and thus coercive; others were concerned about the paperwork and expense during a time of "financial cutback." In addition there was hesitation about the idea of a representative meeting of fifty or sixty people acting without broader support from the monthly meetings themselves, particularly because the activity would have to occur at the local level.[54]

The 'Black Manifesto'

In April 1969, the Interreligious Foundation for Community Organization convened a group of African American leaders to examine ways to improve conditions in urban ghettos. From this meeting emerged the Black Economic Development Conference (BEDC) and its "Black Manifesto." The manifesto laid out "a prophetic version of how we see change and revolution inside the United States" and issued a demand for five hundred million dollars in reparations from "the racist white Christian churches and Jewish synagogues," which it asserted were not only "part and parcel of the system of capitalism" but had also "contributed to our oppression in white America." The manifesto also listed a series of initiatives for which these reparations would be used— among them a "southern land bank" for African American farmers who had been forced off their land and who wished to establish coopera- tives; four publishing houses and four "audio-visual networks" that would present and distribute African American views; a training center to develop communications skills; and a "national black labor strike and defense fund." All of these initiatives aimed "to establish a black power structure outside white society."[55]

Within days of the Detroit meeting, African American civil rights activist James Forman, the author of the manifesto, interrupted the services at Riverside Church in New York City to read the demands. If churches and synagogues failed to make reparations, the manifesto called for African Americans "to seize the offices, telephones, and print- ing apparatus of all church-sponsored agencies and to hold these in trusteeship until our demands are met,"[56] as well as stage sit-ins at selected churches. In the event that these sit-ins were attacked, the manifesto stated, "The principle of self-defense should be applied."

While yearly meetings were examining how they might best respond in such difficult times for African Americans and the inner cities, Philadelphia was the only yearly meeting to have a direct request from the BEDC. The struggle that Philadelphia went through, as well as the challenges faced in New York and New England, may not represent all yearly meetings, but it is fair to say that their discussions about repa- rations evoked the full range of Quaker attitudes, concerns, hesitations and worries in their relationship with increasingly militant African Americans in the late 1960s and into the 1970s.

New York Seeks Economic Development Funds

New York Yearly Meeting faced the question of reparations in 1969 when African American member Barrington Dunbar asked New York

Friends to create a Black Development Fund supported by 1 percent of members' incomes. It was to be "seed money" for African American development projects, among other uses. According to John Daniels, a European American member of the fund committee, a number of meetings and individuals were also inspired to get involved with day-care centers, court watching, and equipping playgrounds. Dunbar was disappointed after the first year, however, because only $19,000 had been raised, not the $120,000 that would have represented the suggested commitment of 1 percent of the income of all Friends in the yearly meeting. That response was "feeble," in Dunbar's view.[57]

After two years the fund had $47,000, which was disbursed in varying amounts to 31 projects in 21 communities in the yearly meeting. The projects supported included a teen center managed by African American youths, a store in a migrant camp, seed money for nonprofit housing in the ghetto and job training for recovering drug addicts. Daniels's own meeting, Albany, was instrumental in a grant at a "critical" moment to open a day-care center. But Daniels was disappointed in the response and the low level of contribution to the fund. Of some 3,700 family and single members of the yearly meeting, only 210 contributions were received in the first year, representing less than 6 percent of the membership; in the second year it dropped to 4 percent, although the gifts were larger. Friends profess that they are concerned, Daniel noted, and then he suggested that in the silence of a meeting for worship they ask the Lord, "How deep is my concern?[58]

New England Focuses on the Crisis

Even before BEDC began its national campaign, in 1967 New England Yearly Meeting had heard an appeal to "examine their consciences and practices for subtle signs of discrimination and prejudice, for blindness in overlooking the degrading aspects of our present social patterns, and for weakness in failing to act on the leadings of the spirit." They were asked to commit themselves to "undertaking to help our brothers find their way to that state of self determination they desire."[59] Monthly meetings were urged "to feel the necessity" of taking some action regarding racial problems, "thus experimentally showing what love can do."[60]

The next year's meeting was marked by awareness of "intensified racial crisis and prevailing poverty." Appeals for Friends to "reorder" their "social and economic priorities" were repeated in 1969 and 1970 in a report from a Workshop on Friends Responsibilities for Victims of Prejudice and Poverty. At the 1970 yearly meeting the keynote, three workshops, three plenary sessions, a special session, and "frequent informal discussions during the week" all focused on the same theme of "reordering priorities."[61]

Returning in 1970 from the Philadelphia Yearly Meeting sessions that were laboring with a request from the local Black Economic Development Council, Daisy Newman, a European American New England Friend, had a message for her yearly meeting: take the initiative toward reparations "without waiting to be coerced." A special yearly meeting committee was created to "look for practicable projects" for "minority" causes and to raise and disburse funds to support them. The meeting made a "firm commitment" to raise one hundred thousand dollars over the next five years to use in ways that would "constructively relieve the hurt of prejudice and poverty." In 1974 a new standing Committee on Prejudice and Poverty (CPP) was created to oversee the fundraising. Friends were urged to "respond thoughtfully to the great needs of our brothers who have no resources." The meetings were also called upon to develop programs on racism.[62]

By 1975, the yearly meeting had met its goal of raising one hundred thousand dollars, and grants had gone to a number of several "self-help" projects, including the Roxbury Action Project and projects in Vermont and New Bedford, Massachusetts. But as elsewhere, Friends interest was waning. Only seven monthly meetings in New England responded to queries on "Prejudice and Poverty," which had been sent with a request that meetings arrange discussions and report back. Skip Schiel, a European American member of the committee, reported that "What had been a concern felt and acted on New England Yearly Meeting-wide" had become the concern of a few members of committees; the yearly meeting's interest "in corporate social action became limited to issuing public statements, requiring nothing of its members."[63] Nevertheless, a certain ebb and flow of concerns about racism, fundraising and educating Friends about poverty and prejudice appear in the minute books through the 1980s and 1990s to the present.[64]

PYM's Long Struggle with Reparations

In the fall of 1969 the local office of the Black Economic Development Conference wrote to Philadelphia Yearly Meeting asking it to endorse the concept of reparations, to lend its moral authority to support the BEDC manifesto in the wider community, and to contribute funds to the requested reparations. The BEDC asked for five hundred thousand dollars by January 1970 and between one and five million dollars over two years for its printing and publishing project.[65] Philadelphia Friends sympathetic to the BEDC request brought the organization's letter to the September session of the yearly meeting. Fifteen hundred Friends attended. The first of many to come, meetings on the issue were the longest and largest ever held by Philadelphia Friends.[66] The local BEDC asked Philadelphia Yearly Meeting for support on the grounds that they were "a people with significant common concerns" and had "a reputation for positive involvement in progressive social movements."[67] Mohammad Kenyatta, head of BEDC for Philadelphia, was invited to speak at the yearly meeting; he spoke and also attended all of the many sessions that followed.[68]

As yearly meeting Clerk Charles E. Brown III recalled that opening session, he wrote:

> We were told about, and experienced, the polarization between the races; we were asked to deal with problem, and with each other, in a loving spirit; we were made aware of the immense struggle, and the immense opportunity that we faced.[69]

Anticipating the September business session, the yearly meeting's Meeting for Social Concerns had prepared a possible four-part response for Friends to discuss. They proposed: (1) to immediately transfer five hundred thousand dollars of the yearly meeting's capital assets to the BEDC; (2) to "catalog" and report on the meeting's financial resources and commit itself to funding five million dollars for black economic development over several years; (3) to develop a skills bank of Friends qualified to assist economic development in the African American community; and (4) to encourage meetings to make their meetinghouses and facilities available to African American projects in their communities.[70] The yearly meeting, however, was unable to reach unity to accept these recommendations. After an October special session in which "tensions ran high," it could only minute its "failure to respond adequately to the legitimate needs of the oppressed and alienated" and acknowledged a "corporate responsibility to place human and material resources at the service" of minority groups. Kenyatta announced publicly that he would fast until the Quakers responded.[71]

Based on available records, it seems many Friends accepted the notion that they, and people of European descent in general, did indeed owe African Americans a debt. Whether the benefits enjoyed by European Americans were expressed in historical terms connected to the enslavement of Africans or in the more contemporary term of "white privilege," few questioned the underlying obligation. Still, according to later MSC minutes, Friends were "shocked" at the proposals. There were many concerns about the recommendations of MSC. One set of questions centered on whether the BEDC truly represented the wider African American community and whether its leadership had the capacity to carry out its plans. Another question was whether the meeting's funds were best used for the BEDC proposal or whether the meeting's funds instead should be funneled to existing Quaker and non-Quaker organizations.

Friends who believed the meeting should accede to the BEDC request as it stood suggested that to do otherwise was inherently racist. "The first task is to get the money, not to question the moral integrity of the victims!" wrote European American Michael Yarrow of the yearly meeting's Friends Peace Committee. He urged Friends not to "fall into the racist trap of asserting that we know who best represents the black community and what projects would be good for the niggers."[72] James Laird said, "The churches would do well to stop talking about love, which seems to mean no more than friendly attitudes, and start talking about justice. And justice in an economic world means hard, cold cash." He suggested Friends lacked sound "justification" for denying control of funds to African Americans. "Are we prepared to say that they lack the wisdom, the maturity, the experience, to make such decisions concerning their own welfare?" Laird asked. "Are whites to be permitted to make errors while Blacks are not?"[73]

———•———

A major concern for many Philadelphia Friends was whether any money the yearly meeting contributed to reparations might end up funding violence in some form. Though they were sympathetic to this fear, Friends supporting the BEDC urged others to be willing to take the organization at its word when it pledged not to use violence. "Can the rich exonerate their callousness by saying of the poor, 'They should have been more gentle in their desperation?'" Laird asked the meeting. "One could argue from these words that the responsibility for violence, if it occurs, will rest with the white churches, including Quakers, who heard a desperate cry for help and then ignored it."[74] The peace testimony, European American Quaker activist Ross Capon pointed out, came naturally to Friends who "grew up in peaceful suburbs, had good educations and time to intellectualize about the inadequacy of gut responses to the desperate conditions they rarely face personally."[75]

A few Friends raised concern about the need for spiritual grounding for any action. They feared, as one said, that "the 'absolutist' nature of the demands was not in keeping with the way that Friends reach spiritual unity and consensus as a basis for action." According to European American Friend Larry Miller, general secretary of FGC, this "spiritual agony" centered on the need "to match the action with a reordering of priorities and changes in life style, consistent with a basically spiritual response." Otherwise, Quakers were aligning themselves with a political movement rather than seeking for right action in the spirit.[76] Finally, as European American Samuel Snipes stated in a letter to Laird, unknown numbers of Quakers suspected that the BEDC was simply attempting to secure donations "from guilt, not concern."[77]

PYM Young Friends were highly visible participants in their yearly meeting's attempt to formulate a response to the Black Manifesto. In a paper drawn up with Michael Yarrow's assistance, Young Friends argued that "simple arithmetic" suggested a "substantial debt" was owed because of all the Friends who had benefitted from enslavement. "Most of the early Quaker fortunes of Philadelphia profited greatly" from the trade and the labor of the enslaved, they noted, even if they did not participate directly after the 1700s. Quaker contributions to various community projects, the group asserted, were "very small compared to the amounts we devote to building new wings on our Meeting Houses, schools, and homes for the elderly."[78] Young Friends in Princeton (New Jersey) Monthly Meeting likened the BEDC goals to those "for which Quakers have been striving for many years." They stated their intention to help meet the BEDC demands and their aim to "persuade the rest of the Society of Friends to do the same." Though they held that only African American leaders should determine how to use the funding, these Young Friends made clear their hope that their own contribution would not support violence.[79]

A Friends 'Manifesto'

In October 1969, European American Friends David Richie, Victor Paschkis, Mary Anderson, and William Shields drew up an alternative to the Black Manifesto to represent their "yearning to do more for our black brothers than we have done, while remaining true to what we believe." While the "Proposed Friends Manifesto" declared its sympathy with the Black Manifesto, it stated their objection to the racial separatism it implied, the possibility of violence in its program and the notion that individuals or churches, not the state, should bear the responsibility for "repairing of past damages." "We say 'no' to [a manifesto] which we understand but cannot approve, but not to sit back and do nothing, but to call for action in line with our beliefs. Belief without action is meaningless; action without belief is deadly."

The Friends Manifesto proposed to raise about half of the BEDC request, but for BEDC purposes only. Funds were to go to children and adults of many disenfranchised groups: "Blacks, Indians, Mexicans." Though the emphasis of the funding program would be education, it would also support a radio and/or television station to "bring home the things now missing in mass communication media regarding the racial injustices." Finally, the group proposed selling a number of unused meetinghouses, taking out mortgages on the remaining active meetinghouses, and selling the "land of Friends cemeteries" as well. The funds raised by those means would be supplemented by an appeal for money to Friends and to Quaker-owned or controlled businesses.[80] In response, Doylestown Monthly Meeting reported that if necessary it would mortgage its meetinghouse to make a contribution of five thousand dollars toward yearly meeting programs in support of African American economic development—but not to go to the BEDC.[81]

After it had held four sessions on the subject, in the spring of 1970, Philadelphia Yearly Meeting appointed a group of Friends "representing divergent points of views" to meet with local BEDC representatives to express a sense of "brotherhood" and to explain and discuss the meeting's "misunderstandings and disagreements" with them, as well as with each other. The group was to report any suggestions arising out of the discussions to the yearly meeting.[82] According to European American Lawrence Scott, the meeting with BEDC clarified how reparations were related to BEDC's plans, and the committee predicted that if the "principle of reparations"—as the Black Manifesto construed them—could be accepted, "a new era of black-white relations could flow."[83] Still, Philadelphia Friends equivocated. One Friend wrote in a letter to the *Friends Journal*: "To collaborate" with such African Americans as Muhammad Kenyattta, he wrote, would be "contrary to the position of George Fox and his associates" and the peace testimony.[84]

1970 Working Party

In an attempt to move forward, Philadelphia Yearly Meeting created the 1970 Working Party, a special group of thirty-five Friends, half of whom were African American, and one non-Quaker who were to consider Friends "involvement in racial and economic injustices in the light of the spiritual meaning of Friends testimonies." It was also to examine the reparations proposal before the meeting, "evaluate ways in which our economic structure affects the lives of all people" and determine how Friends should "reorder" their way of life to avoid those destructive effects. The group was also asked to recommend programs to the representative or yearly meeting "for corporate action in keeping with Friends' testimonies."[85] While the yearly meeting debated reparations, nearly seven hundred Friends from twenty-five monthly meetings offered their expertise to projects in the African American community in and outside of Philadelphia. The Skills Bank developed at the behest of the 1970 Working Party brought forward volunteers in the areas of animal husbandry, art, counseling, engineering, public relations, music, nursing, photography, psychology, youth activities and many other fields.[86]

Months later, BEDC re-issued its call for reparations. Kenyatta wrote that, while he had been "genuinely and deeply moved" by the meetings on the subject, he had concluded that "the Society of Friends as an institution has ceased to hold a special place in my mind as a movement of contemporary merit, as a cutting edge of white Christendom."[87] In fact, he concluded, "no institution and no movement of long standing among people of European descent within this country can remain free from the corruption of privilege until the entire system of privilege is dismantled."[88]

———————•———————

In the middle of the process, yearly meeting clerk Charles Brown realized "that the sensitivity we want, as well as the attitudes of superiority and paternalism which we don't want, are wide-spread in the yearly meeting" and that education on the issues was key to moving forward. What would be needed would be "a cooperative search for the truth," in his view.[89] It was possible, he believed, that the act of simply "asking Friends about themselves" might produce great progress even before any education was initiated. Brown visited as many of the monthly meetings as possible "to try to discover what motivation for this kind of program exists and what the real need is."[90]

The MSC was also interested in learning what Friends were thinking, and many individuals and meetings responded to their invitation to write to them. Most of the letters came from Friends seeking to understand what was happening and searching for guidance in how they might respond, given the tenor of the times. While some supported BEDC's request, other Friends seemed to mirror the prevailing views of many European Americans. One Friend wrote that "Slum conditions are caused by those who live there—the garbage, illegitimacy, and disrepair. Only those who disregard fundamental principles of thrift, industry, morality and self-discipline" find themselves in those circumstances.[91] Like European Americans who lived outside of the cities, the writer from New Garden, Pennsylvania, didn't see much that Friends there could do to help. Perhaps rural areas like that community could plan some event with recreation and a picnic, but then "city residents may not show up," she wrote. "Members of the Meeting have always been free of any feeling of race discrimination but we are now beginning to wonder if our confidence in the industry, honesty, morals and common decency of the colored people was misplaced," wrote another.[92]

The MSC believed that difference in attitudes "seems to be, largely but not completely, between those who have worked and lived closely with members of other minorities and those who have known them only as employees or acquaintances or have had little chance to know them at all."[93] "Until we reach a common sensitivity to the needs that have been expressed, both ours and those of minorities," the MSC concluded, it would be difficult to reach consensus.[94]

Philadelphia Yearly Meeting devoted three special meeting sessions, months of committee work, a year of visits to seventy of the ninety-five monthly meetings—and "great agonizing together"—on the BEDC's request for reparations. Yet in spring 1971 the meeting still was not able to reach unity on the question. One observer wrote, "Neither the members in attendance nor the guests [from BEDC] were able to rise above the level of unfruitful contention." BEDC visitors announced that they planned to stay in the meetinghouse until a decision was reached. Some Friends remained with them in a show of support, but many others were confused, angry, and "bewildered" by this challenge.[95] In the end, the yearly meeting rejected the BEDC request. According to the epistle prepared afterward, the BEDC "accepted gracefully" the meeting's decision, though "with regret."[96]

The Working Party had met nearly every week for eleven months before reporting to the March 1971 yearly meeting. It called for Friends to "look to their possessions, practices, and relationships" to determine "whether the seeds of exploitation and oppression lie in them." All race relations projects at every level of every yearly meeting should be examined, as should every organization that received funds from the yearly meeting.[97] The Working Party also proposed creating an Economic Development Fund for Disadvantaged Minority Groups that would be run initially by a board of managers from the yearly meeting but would, as soon as practicable, be turned over to minority leadership. The fund would derive from the capital assets of the yearly meeting and monthly meetings and from the "earnings of individual Friends." All restricted capital funds of the yearly and monthly meetings should be reviewed to see how the donor's intent might be fulfilled "in light of our present day problems." The Working Party requested $200,000 from the yearly meeting at the outset and an additional $200,000 to be donated by heads of families over the next two years.[98]

When the yearly meeting failed to act on this proposal, a small group of members formed "Friends for Reparations" to collect voluntary contributions. A year later, in May 1972, the group had received nearly $16,000, which it turned over to the BEDC.[99] Though it required a second appeal to members, the group came just $10,000 short of the Working Party's $400,000 goal. The money was disbursed to minority-run businesses, including hard-to-get bonding funds for contractors, organizations developing housing in North Philadelphia and Camden, New Jersey, and various job training programs. The yearly meeting then approved closing the fund, noting that it means "the discontinuance of a project" it had supported since 1969, but that it was "coupled with the likely prospect that other forms of economic assistance to minorities may be proposed in the near future."[100]

Reflecting on the events of surrounding the initial BEDC request, yearly meeting clerk Charles Brown said that the meeting was "led to deal with deep-seated, habitual patterns that were racist, or at least patronizing." The yearly meeting did not "overcome racism. Some of us were led to be more generous in sharing the world's resources. All of us were led to experience the 'seeds of violence' which we carry within us."[101]

Conservative Backlash

Richard Nixon's defeat of Hubert Humphrey in the 1968 presidential race portended what historian Allan J. Matusow has termed "a long-term trend toward conservatism."[102] The "affluent society" of the 1960s had "fostered social optimism and undergirded liberal reform," Matusow has argued, but that optimism withered with the recession of the 1970s.[103]

Friends tried to lessen the impact of the changing political and economic climates. A New York Yearly Meeting Peace Institute workshop on racism noted that the Nixon administration's economic proposals would gut the "social legislation which has been almost the life blood of the big city slums and ghetto areas for nearly a decade" and urged Friends to oppose the proposed legislation.[104] In 1974 FCNL decided to focus on legislation that would end poverty, rather than on programs to assist the poor directly. They lobbied for funding for job training and to help low-income people start small businesses, as well as for an increase in the minimum wage. FCNL staff also worked with the Congressional Black Caucus on their alternative budget, but they found "frustration rampant" among African American legislators who were not being given the data they needed to do their work.[105]

In 1976 the AFSC expressed its concern about the "federal retreat" in affirmative action, housing and community development. All federal programs dealing with these issues required community participation in decision making, but in practice that component had been "wishy-washy, politically underhanded and racist," the committee noted. "We oppose that system which snuffs out the lives of those who have failed or had little chance to succeed in our unjust social and economic order."[106] Also in the mid-1970s, the AFSC's Community Relations Committee decided it would be more fruitful to focus "in a concentrated manner [on] the economic situation" rather than on separate issues such as employment and housing.[107] Its list of priorities in 1978 featured "economic rights" and the situation of farmworkers (only criminal justice and education were judged more pressing).[108]

———————●———————

Individual Friends and meetings did realize some success in their work toward economic equity for African Americans, but as the twentieth century wore on activist Friends expressed increasing frustration at not being able to win wider support in their Quaker community. Friends failed to respond in significant numbers to study groups or lectures offered by people expert in economic matters. Even Quaker-owned firms had been unresponsive to repeated efforts to achieve economic equity. In the eyes of Young Friends, older Friends seemed complacent.

In 1970, Nancy Marlowe Moore, a European American participant in the program for Young Friends at the Seventh National Friends Conference on Race Relations expressed her dismay in a minute to "old Friends":

> You are too comfortable. You can't get up from the easy chair of your middleclass existence. Outside of that existence people are crying for you to come help them escape from the mud that is pulling them down. And all you can do is stand on the edge and intellectualize about how they can pull themselves out. Or you wait for one of them to tell you how to pull them out. But when he tells you, your very ears are so

full of mud that you can't hear him. Your own soul is completely covered with mud that you refuse to see. Why do you pat us on the head
and smile at us when we tell you there isn't much time left? Why don't
you teach us what you've learned? . . . What kind of world is this when
the young have to lead their parents, have to reprimand their parents,
have to provide the conscience for their parents, have to teach their
parents?[109]

Three years earlier, with the country in the thick of the Vietnam
War, those gathering at the 1967 Friends National Conference on Race
Relations in Black Mountain, North Carolina, had expressed their frustration. They could offer "no special Quaker insights clear enough to
set the great movement for human rights on some new course, nor...
say that the Religious Society of Friends is prepared to meet this profoundly troubling challenge." Yet the group recognized the nature of the
problem that Quakers in particular faced:

> Future action must be based on a willingness to work for social
> changes much more far-reaching than we had supposed the correction
> of racial injustice would require. It becomes increasingly clear that our
> existing social-economic-political-legal-military system-the framework
> within which the white establishment operates-simply cannot be
> patched up in such a way as to end exploitation and degradation. We
> must be prepared to discover how much we ourselves, sharing in and
> profiting from the operating of the system, are contributing to the
> power which maintains the very practices we are fighting against.[110]

Bayard Rustin demonstrating in Washington, DC, mid-1940s.

Quakers protesting war in Viet Nam and supporting Poor Peoples Campaign, Washington, DC, June 28, 1968. Photograph © Roland L. Freeman.

CHAPTER NINE

Violence and Nonviolence

We must seek out and remove the seeds of hatred and greed. Instead of self-seeking, we must put sacrifice; instead of domination, cooperation. Fear and suspicion must give place to trust and the spirit of under-standing. . . . Our peace testimony must be inclusive of the whole of life.

— *New England Yearly Meeting Faith and Practice, 1966*

QUAKERS BELIEVE that conflicts are best settled not by force, physical or verbal, but by reaching within for the love that is God. "Appealing to this capacity for love and goodness, in ourselves and in others" is the path to end disputes, not "threatening punishment or retaliation [even] if people act badly," wrote European American Friend Mary Lou Leavitt in her work on the Quaker peace testimony. Friends do not deny there is such a thing as evil, but simply that "there is no effective way to combat evil with weapons which harm or kill those through whom evil is working," she wrote. Friends weapons are "of the spirit"—love, truth-saying, nonviolence, imagination, laughter," all that bring people who are in conflict together to heal, not to destroy, each other.[1] Friends commitment to nonviolent conflict resolution, though often tested, grounded their efforts to address racial strife in the twenti-eth century.

Riots against African Americans had become common in the South in the nineteenth century, but in the twentieth century riots erupted in northern urban areas. After a few relatively peaceful years at the begin-ning of the century, the frequency of riots spiked after both world wars, prompted at least in part by the postwar job anxiety of returning African American and European American veterans. Quakers, like oth-ers of both African and European descent, felt helpless and frightened. In 1917 European Americans went on a rampage through African American sections of Philadelphia and Chester, Pennsylvania; East St. Louis, Illinois; and Houston, Texas, among others. They destroyed and burned homes and businesses, and, often, murdered the residents. When twenty-six cities were hit by violence in 1919, African American writer James Weldon Johnson called it the "Red Summer."[2]

African Americans began to arm themselves against these attacks, which increased the bloodshed of European Americans and African Americans involved in the confrontations. In 1943 violent uprisings against African Americans occurred in ten cities, most notably Beaumont, Texas; New York City, and Detroit. Those three riots alone triggered hundreds of arrests and injuries and the deaths of thirty-four African Americans. Detroit was the most violent and damaging. As elsewhere, federal troops were called in to restore peace.[3] Sensing that Friends simply did not know where or how to begin to mitigate these conflicts, in 1946 AFSC's Community Relations Committee issued the pamphlet, *Some Quaker Approaches to the Race Problem.* "The time is short," it warned, for Quakers and others to take positive action for racial justice in order to prevent "an eruption of force."[4]

As the pace of civil rights activity began to pick up in the 1950s, Friends identified with the nonviolent approach of civil rights leader Martin Luther King, Jr. The centrality of nonviolence to much of the Civil Rights movement resonated clearly with the Friends belief that all forms of violence are "contrary to the spirit and teaching of Christ."[5] Walking with dignity to work instead of riding buses or sitting calmly and silently at a lunch counter to protest segregation struck a chord with Friends. White supremists met peaceful marches with violence, murdered civil rights workers, and killed children in the bombing of a church, but Martin Luther King held true to his commitment. Quakers grew increasingly conflicted, however, when the cries turned to "Black Power," and more-militant calls for separatism came from African Americans convinced that violence was their only route to equality. And when King was assassinated and his call for nonviolence came into question, Quaker participation and support faltered. It was a "cultural confrontation," Philadelphia Friend Vinton Deming, a European American activist, said years later. "Friends just weren't in touch with reality of the times... they were afraid, they felt unsafe."[6] The calls for black separatism grew stronger with time and would become one of the factors in the fragmentation of the Civil Rights movement.

Influence of Gandhian Thought

Some historians credit European American Quaker Richard B. Gregg, who applied the philosophy of Mohandas Gandhi to the pacifist movement in the United States,as the first American to develop a theory of nonviolent civil disobedience and to have a significant influence on both Martin Luther King, Jr. and Bayard Rustin.[7] In his introduction to the first edition of Gregg's book, *The Power of Non-Violence*, Rufus Jones described the book as "a fine blend of *what is* and *what ought to be*."[8] Introducing an abridged version in 1960, King said that Gregg's additional research into this "vital new kind of action" should be of interest to those seeking to achieve equality "in a manner consistent with human dignity."[9]

Another work by Gregg, *Training for Peace: A Program for Peace Workers*, provided one of the bases for the development in the early 1940s of cooperative farms, which he viewed as "a concrete, material way to avoid participating in a system—economic, political, and social—that produced war."[10] In 1941 Lee Stern and other New York Young Friends founded Ahimsa Farm near Cleveland, one of the first cooperative farms, which examined the relevance of the ideas of Gandhi and others to ending segregation and interracial violence in America.[11] About the same time the Young People's Interracial Fellowship in Philadelphia, an organization with Quaker roots that sought "non-violent solutions to social problems," opened Fellowship House as a place where young people of all races and religions could meet and learn how to work for justice and understanding. In 1951 the Fellowship moved to a farm near Pottstown. Renamed Fellowship Farm, the group continues its activities today.[12]

Gandhi's ideas also influenced Bayard Rustin (1912–1987), who was to become a central figure in the Civil Rights movement. Born in West Chester, Pennsylvania, Rustin was exposed to Quakerism by his grandmother, Julia Rustin, who had been brought up as a Friend. Later a member of the African Methodist Episcopal Church, she raised her children to believe in the principles of nonviolence and equality. In 1937 Rustin worked as a volunteer for the AFSC, and in 1941 he became involved in the Fellowship of Reconciliation (FOR), an international pacifist organization founded in England in 1914.

In 1942 the Fellowship of Reconciliation paid Rustin's salary while he and African American James Farmer created the African American-led Congress of Racial Equality (CORE). In the same year Rustin, a conscientious objector, chose prison as a way to protest the war rather than take the alternative of Civilian Public Service. Upon his release in 1945 he became director of FOR's civil rights department and soon after spent six months in India studying Gandhi's movement for Indian independence from the British Empire.

First Freedom Ride: The Journey of Reconciliation

In 1947 the Supreme Court ruled that an African American woman named Irene Morgan had been denied illegally an interstate bus ticket. In support, Rustin led a group of nine African Americans and nine European Americans on the "Journey of Reconciliation," which is generally recognized as the first of many "Freedom Rides." African Americans sat in the front of buses as they traveled throughout the upper South, while European Americans rode in the back. Most of the riders in 1947 ended up imprisoned for as much as three months.[13]

Next, Rustin headed the newly formed Committee against Jim Crow in Military Service (later renamed the League for Non-Violent Civil Disobedience), which helped persuade President Harry Truman to eliminate segregation in the armed forces in 1948.[14] A member of the Fifteenth Street Meeting in New York City, Rustin worked with the Fellowship of Reconciliation until 1952 when he became field director of CORE.[15]

Peaceful Protest

In 1955, African American Rosa Parks refused to leave her seat at the front of a Montgomery, Alabama bus, which put a spotlight on the segregated city transit system. Her determination triggered the Montgomery, Alabama bus boycott, to which, Friends gave direct support. In 1956 New England Yearly Meeting sent a letter "of prayerful support" to the Montgomery Improvement Association, which organized the boycott, and the two Baltimore yearly meetings sent a joint letter of support to King, a key organizer and participant in the protest.[16] The United Philadelphia Yearly Meeting could not reach consensus on preparing such a letter, but it appointed a committee of three "weighty" Friends to visit the city.[17] "We come in humility," said European Americans Clarence Pickett, Dorothy Steere, and George Hardin, "to learn as much as we can from both sides, and to give support and encouragement to the creative potentialities we believe exist in both groups bringing about a solution which does not compromise basic human dignity." Pickett, then AFSC executive secretary emeritus, used a biblical quotation about "the man who talketh with his feet" in addressing a mass meeting with Martin Luther King. Jr., and, according to Hardin, received "an explosive standing ovation."[18]

For Friends who wondered what they and their meetings could do to support the boycott (which eventually would last 381 days), FGC's Peace and Social Concerns Committee advised, "Hold the entire community in affection and prayer; donate through AFSC for the Montgomery Improvement Association; and, "more than anything else, Friends can work to correct racial injustices . . . in their own communities." FGC Friends made additional points: first, "the danger of a self-righteous attitude in regard to the South can never be over-emphasized"; and, second, it is important to be informed about what is happening in the South. Toward that end, they included a recommended reading list.[19] Friends in Muncie, Indiana, participated in a "March of Affirmation and Support" for the boycott organized by the local Ball State University and some Quaker students. More than two hundred people came together in a prayer vigil and silent march "to affirm the cause of human rights and support those persons from here taking part in the March to Montgomery, Alabama."[20]

Quakers and Martin Luther King, Jr.

The relationship between Quakers and King deepened over time. In 1958 King accepted Clarence Pickett's invitation to speak to Quakers gathered at the FGC conference in Cape May, New Jersey. Listening to King speak on "Nonviolence and Racial Justice" was "electrifying," said Larry Miller, FGC general secretary, one of the hundreds of Friends present.[21]

To "deepen King's connection to an international community dedicated to nonviolence," in 1959 AFSC arranged for King and his wife,

Coretta Scott King, to spend four weeks in India with followers of Gandhi in the company of Jim Bristol, AFSC's representative in Delhi. However, the U. S. State Department insisted on controlling the Kings' itinerary, which made the venture a "disappointing and frustrating" one for AFSC. The committee suspected that the government saw the Kings' visit as a series of public relations opportunities to create good will during a time when racial discrimination was damaging the reputation of the United States abroad. Bristol wrote in a letter home that the Kings went through the country "wearing BLINDERS." The trip was orchestrated in such a way that there was little time for serious conversation with Gandhians.[22]

King also connected with Friends in his home town of Atlanta, which was becoming something of a center for the Civil Rights movement. In the late 1950s Atlanta Friends, struggling with differing opinions about whether to locate a permanent meeting house in the city, eventually decided to create a Friends center to house the meeting and to provide space for public gatherings and programs in a city where there were few places for people of African and European descent to meet. Quakers and non-Quakers in the United States and England raised funds for the center. Atlanta Friends Meeting named John Yungblut, a former Episcopalian minister who had become a Quaker activist, and his wife June Yungblut as directors of Quaker House.[23] "Activities that might seem commonplace elsewhere have to be interpreted in the light of the background," said Yungblut. Quaker House was "literally the only public place in Atlanta other than a Negro institution where an inter-racial event could be held."[24]

As racial tensions in the city escalated and discussion turned to whether to close all public schools to avoid integration, the importance of having such a place was clear. King taught a ten-week seminar on nonviolence at Quaker House, and other African American activists, including Vincent and Rosemary Harding and Andrew and Jean Young, took part in programs and small prayer groups. Students and professors from Atlanta's African American colleges came to the center to be trained in nonviolent protest.[25] European American Quakers Staughton and Alice Lynd were involved in the center when Staughton Lynd taught history at Spelman College with Howard Zinn in the early 1960s; Lynd went on to direct the Mississippi "Freedom Schools" in the summer of 1964 and later continued his activism as a prominent labor lawyer and author.[26]

A Quiet Presence: School Desegregation

AFSC's southern members observed that "paralysis" and "tension" plagued the region after the 1954 Supreme Court ruling against segregation in public schools: liberal forces were simply not prepared or able to exert any influence; racial relations were "deteriorating"; and African Americans were "frightened and intimidated." In Baton Rouge AFSC claimed it was the city's "only liberal force," the only organization with a staff member dedicated to school desegregation and the only one that involved the community in its work. Staff there organized counseling for the students who became the first to enter Louisiana State University in 1956.[27]

AFSC "maintained a presence in racially torn communities"[28] such as Little Rock, where the school board's move to desegregate Little Rock Central High School in 1957 spurred the outright defiance of Arkansas Governor Orval Faubus. In September 1958, Faubus responded to a federal court order mandating integration by closing all of the city's high schools rather than comply. AFSC established a group called Education Advisory Services to provide tutoring for students whose schools had been closed. In 1959, when the schools remained closed, European American Thelma Babbitt of New Hampshire, a life member of the NAACP, went to Little Rock to bring together people of African and European descent in the city and thereby help to defuse the hostility. "There was violence," Babbitt noted. "I wondered what a Yankee could do."[29] With Babbitt, who had known no African Americans before she came to Little Rock, the community group organized a race relations forum at Aldersgate, a Methodist camp nearby. Ninety-eight people, one-third of them African American and some of them local Friends, came together to discuss how to remove "the barriers that separate us and create misunderstanding and tension."[30]

While Little Rock struggled with school desegregation, the Little Rock Friends Meeting was, according to its clerk, in "anguish" as the city became "both the fact and symbol of intolerance and injustice." Members of the meeting had worked to develop personal relationships with African Americans and became active in interracial community groups. One member tutored one of the "Little Rock Nine," the label given to the African American students who had tried to enter the then all-European American Central High School in 1957. The monthly meeting sponsored day-long biracial work camps in the summer of 1957 and a World Affairs Seminar for teens of both races with AFSC in 1958. Another seminar for adults and youth groups aimed to analyze the myth that communists were behind the new activism.[31]

Typical of Friends desire to create relationships in even the most difficult of times, the Friends meeting developed an intervisitation program with African American churches in the midst of the violent resistance to school desegregation.. In his series of "Letters from Little Rock," Robert Wixom, clerk of the small, all European-American meeting, wrote of the difficulty of being surrounded by violence. "We in Little Rock have seen prejudice, emotional turmoil and self-perpetuating hatreds and found them ugly indeed. Little Rock Friends join with the impassioned cry of our Negro brothers for justice and dignity....We try to hold before us the approach of Christian love that exalts the good of every individual and converts the wrong doer as it rights the wrong."[32]

Sit-Ins: A New Wave of Nonviolent Protest

The beginning of the sit-in movement is generally considered to have taken place on February 1, 1960, at the F.W. Woolworth's lunch counter in Greensboro, North Carolina, when four African American students from North Carolina Agricultural and Technical College asked to be served. Their sit-in was the first to attract significant national media attention. When they were refused service after sitting silently all that day, they left, only to be replaced by a larger group the next day and on subsequent days. Despite the fact that some of its members supported the nonviolent action, Greensboro's New Garden Friends Meeting was unable to reach corporate unity about it; the meeting did, however, encourage those with a strong concern to express their own views to the store's manager. Aldean Pitts, the meeting's pastor, took "a courageous stand in favor of equal opportunity for all races," but "the sensibilities of some [in the meeting] were offended. . . . As in the case of the slave controversy, the national consensus finally prevailed over regional reluctance" in the meeting.[33] AFSC conducted workshops on nonviolence for the predominantly African American residents and college students working to desegregate downtown hotels and restaurants in Greensboro. The interracial groups attending began meeting informally and ultimately formed themselves into the Greensboro Community Fellowship.[34]

Over the next two weeks, sit-ins occurred in eleven cities. The first violent response to a sit-in occurred in Nashville, Tennessee, when a group of European American teenagers attacked African and European American student protesters there; again, ever larger groups of college students continued the sit-in day after day.[35] Some of the young protestors met at the home of Nashville Friends Meeting founders Marian Darnell Fuson and Nelson Fuson, a professor at Fisk University for forty years. Marian was active in the Friends for Human Justice. The Fusons were driving the students to the protests, as well, and at one point the situation was dangerous enough that they decided it would be better if they drove separately.[36]

In the end, nearly fifty thousand people, both African and European American, took part in sit-ins in seventy-eight cities.[37] Protestors endured obscenities, having cigarettes stubbed out on their skin, and being spat upon, physically threatened or beaten. European American Friend David Hartsough of San Francisco Friends Meeting remembers well the knife that was pointed at his heart. His story so clearly conveys the power of responding to violence with love that it is almost legendary. Like others engaged in nonviolent protest, Hartsough had undergone nonviolence training. Hartsough recalls what happened in 1960 when someone approached him as he sat on a stool in People's Drug Store in Arlington, Virginia:

> The fellow had a switchblade and said, "If you don't get out of this store in two seconds, I will stab this through your heart" (with knife pointed at my heart). I realized I had only two seconds to decide if I really believed in nonviolence. By that time we had had a lot of experience using nonviolence in response to hatred and violence and I said, "Do what you believe is right, but I will still try to love you." His face had been contorted with hatred, but his jaw began to drop, his hand began to fall, and he left the drug store.[38]

Kathie O'Hara, a European American Young Friend from Baltimore
Yearly Meeting, also took part in the lunch counter sit-ins. Through
them she came to understand that "by standing together to maintain
one another's rights" the students were attempting not to hurt the
restaurant owners but to draw them into "a circle which will encom-
pass the entire community in brotherhood."[39]

AFSC staffers in the South felt an obligation to explain the significance of direct nonviolent action at the lunch counters and department
stores to the public in a way that would "support and encourage their
non-violent nature."[40] The AFSC's Community Relations Committee
sought to help people understand the moral issues involved, to "sharpen
insight into the meaning and cost of resistance to integration," and to
foster genuine interracial communication. It also believed it had a role
in helping to "strengthen the morale of the Negro community" and to
find the resources to sustain the struggle.[41]

Young Friends were continuously involved in nonviolent action. By
the middle 1960s, Quaker college students, like others, were heading
south to work on voter registration, Freedom Schools, and desegregation projects with the Student Nonviolent Coordinating Committee
(SNCC), CORE, and other groups. European American David Kendall,
an Indiana Quaker attending Wabash College, spent two months in
Mississippi with SNCC and went to the Democratic National
Convention where the Mississippi Freedom Democratic Party delegates
were denied seats. After a week-long training ("grim and disillusioning,"
Kendall said), he went door-to-door urging African Americans to register. "The main emotion [they had] to overcome was fear, and not
apathy." For the volunteers, "organized police harassment was the
biggest obstacle." Kendall spent eight days in jail over some dubious
charges. In the end, he concluded that the importance of his work was-
n't in the number of new voters registered but in the positive effect it
had on others who then might overcome their fear. He believed "the
most important" fact about the whole Mississippi Summer was that it
showed that "non-violence is a viable alternative" to terrorist tactics.
Kendall ended his account of his experience in *Quaker Life* by asking
Friends what they were doing to work for "racial equality and justice"
in their country.[42] Now a lawyer and a member of Friends Meeting of
Washington, D.C., Kendall says that his experiences in Mississippi have

continued to influence the choices he has made in his legal practice over the years.[43]

————————•————————

Nonviolent demonstrations were not limited to the South. In Chester, Pennsylvania, in 1963 an African American neighborhood association called for a school boycott because of the deplorable conditions in their city schools. During a march they organized that July, the police violence was on a scale "similar to what had occurred in Birmingham."[44] About seventy students from nearby Swarthmore College were among the large numbers of people arrested.[45] An ad hoc group from various committees and members of the Young Friends Movement then met to consider what nonviolent responses Quakers could organize regarding the problems in Chester, "in the Meeting's own backyard." They decided to open a second community center, Chester Friends Project House, and hired Vinton Deming and his wife Carol to staff the center. Initially governed by representatives from the yearly meeting, nearby Friends meetings, and the community, in its second year the center was turned over to community control. It continued to receive support from the yearly meeting.[46]

Individuals or small groups of Friends engaged in peaceful protests rather than participating as a monthly meeting body. A number of Friends were arrested for protesting the conditions in neighborhoods or schools or for supporting school integration. Several went to jail rather than pay bail, refusing privileges not accorded their brothers and sisters of African descent. European American Friend Barbara Greenler remembered several women from Milwaukee Friends Meeting (her meeting at that time) going to jail for protesting in that city or at demonstrations in the South.[47] While the meeting itself might not have taken any formal stand, Greenler estimated that from one-third to one-half of the meeting was actively supporting inner city programs in some way.[48]

Among the New York Yearly Meeting's activists was Lawrence Apsey, an attorney who volunteered with the Lawyers' Constitutional Defense Committee handling civil rights cases in Mississippi. Virginia Apsey and Fay Honey Knopp traveled in Mississippi trying to bring women of African and European descent together and to build support among European American women for civil rights. The Apseys also trained other Friends to lead workshops on nonviolence throughout their yearly meeting.[49]

Quaker Freedom Riders

Individual Friends also took part in the Freedom Rides, which began in the summer of 1961 to protest the fact that federal laws against segregation on public transportation and in public places were being flouted, even with the support of law enforcement officers. Albert Bigelow, a European American from New York Yearly Meeting, took part in the first Freedom Ride, from the District of Columbia to New Orleans, in May that year. At Rock Hill, South Carolina, a European American mob attacked and beat Bigelow and another Freedom Rider.[50] Bayard Rustin was also a Freedom Rider, as was David Fankhauser, a nineteen-year-old European American Quaker student at Central State College in Wilberforce, Ohio, and a graduate of Olney Friends School.

Fankhauser decided to go to Montgomery, Alabama, where he found himself staying in a house with King and the Reverand Ralph Abernathy and taking part in meetings to plan the rides. On May 28, 1961, Fankhauser left on a carefully guarded bus for Jackson, Mississippi, and en route was arrested for sitting in a "colored" waiting room. For the next forty-two days, he and other Freedom Riders on this trip were moved from jail to jail and ultimately to the Parchman Farm, a maximum-security state penitentiary in Mississippi, where guards removed their bedding and window screens, the latter apparently to justify dousing the riders with DDT.[51] Still, Fankhauser's group escaped the worst of the violence endured by some other riders—the wanton beatings and fire bombing of their buses. One of those beaten was African American John Lewis, a leader of SNCC who was later elected U.S. Congressman from Georgia. Speaking at the 2007 annual meeting of the FCNL, Lewis recalled the positive influence that Friends Marian and Nelson Fuson had had on him when he was a student in Nashville learning "the way of love, the way of non-violence, the way of peace."[52]

In 1963 King and others organized a march to the city hall of Birmingham, Alabama, to protest a spate of unsolved bombings in African American neighborhoods, as well as the violence inflicted on

Freedom Riders. It was then that King was arrested and wrote his now-famed "Letter from Birmingham Jail." Having been criticized publicly by eight European American religious leaders who called his activities "unwise and untimely," although he "seldom" took the time to response to critics, King wrote that he was sorry the clerics "deplore the demonstrations" but did not similarly deplore "the conditions that brought" them about. It is, he said, "unfortunate that demonstrations are taking place in Birmingham, but it is even more unfortunate that the city's white power structure left the Negro community with no alternative."[53]

Barbara Moffett, the European American AFSC Community Relations Secretary through nearly the entire civil rights era, saw to it that the committee was the first to publish King's "Letter," smuggled out of the jail, and that another one hundred thousand were printed and distributed.[54] Observing that it offered "Christian solutions to the present social crisis," the Committee on Race Relations of Philadelphia Yearly Meeting sent the letter to all the clergy of Greater Philadelphia.[55] Distributed just before the March on Washington for Jobs and Freedom in August 1963, the letter, many claim, set the tone for a peaceful demonstration.[56]

The March on Washington

The idea for a nonviolent mass protest arose late in 1962, when A. Philip Randolph began discussing the possibility with Bayard Rustin. Originally aimed to protest economic inequality, the events in Birmingham made it more important to mobilize for the passage of federal civil rights legislation; the event was to be a "testimony to the basic principles of human equality and brotherhood." The leaders hoped as many as one hundred thousand people would gather to create a "major interfaith interracial witness." It would be a unified demand for rights—including federal protection, school desegregation, an end to police brutality against protesters, broadened fair labor standards, and a minimum wage increase.[57]

In July, 1963 Rustin was named the chief coordinator for the march. He wrote, printed, and nationally distributed two thousand copies of a manual on how to conduct the event. Drawing between two hundred thousand and five hundred thousand, the March on Washington was the largest political demonstration staged in the United States to that time.[58] Quakers at all levels, from individual to national organizations, supported the March on Washington. PYM's Committee on Race Relations arranged for two busloads of Friends to leave from Philadelphia.[59]

Four Young Friends from Baltimore Yearly Meeting who participated in the event remarked on the absence of anticipated "trouble and violence" and their sense that their "moral responsibilities did not end upon the termination of the march."[60] On the heels of that demonstration, in January 1964 the AFSC proposed a three-year program to train activists in nonviolence. Recognizing the "growing militancy" of many African Americans and other civil rights activists, the committee sensed an increasing "disillusionment with the lack of success of the nominally non-violent demonstrations and an increasing acceptance of violent approaches."[61] Staff hoped that some of the younger movement leaders, who seemed more "open to a fuller application of non-violent philosophies and practices," would then be able to influence the movement in a more peaceful direction. It was also true, however, that while "Quaker literature abounds with statements of commitment to nonviolence," few prominent Quaker leaders marched or took part in nonviolent demonstrations.[62] The Central Committee of Friends General Conference prepared a statement to President Kennedy supporting "both the goals and non-violent principles of the movement." To monthly meetings it wrote, "We are mindful of the many ways in which we, as individuals and as a religious society, have fallen short of our responsibilities and opportunities. We pray that Friends will act upon the best insights of our heritage and seek earnestly for divine guidance."[63]

In 1965 New York Yearly Meeting created the Quaker Project on Community Conflict (QPCC) to provide training and workshops for those who wanted to be involved in the growing movement.[64] In addition to QPCC, the Yearly Meeting's Peace and Social Action Program included an array of projects—workshops on monitoring police relations, the Alternatives to Violence project in prisons, and the Children's Creative Response to Conflict, which brought a conflict resolution curriculum into two Quaker schools and six non-Quaker schools in New York City. In addition, community "Peace Squads," which protected participants in various demonstrations, opened communication with

African American nationalist groups, assisted in the 1968 Poor People's Campaign, and supported Friends in other areas who wished to learn strategies to avert riots.[65]

In 1965 the QPCC responded to a call from Friends in Buffalo Monthly Meeting who were disturbed at the deteriorating relations between the police and the African American community in their city. Ross Flanagan, QPCC program secretary and an expert in nonviolence, went to Buffalo to work with local Friends, members of the police department, African Americans from the community, local churches, city officials, and the area's Community Relations Council. With funding from the Ford Foundation, a series of interviews, workshops, dramatizations by an African American theatre group, and public meetings led the police department to ask the QPCC to develop role playing around racial issues to be used in departmental training, especially to help police "recognize how their behavior can defuse violence." Over 150 police officers and trainees were involved in workshops in June 1968. Although the Buffalo Police did not incorporate the successful training into their regular program due to financial and organizational constraints, a report on the project in a police periodical prompted inquiries to QPCC from several other departments.[66]

Understanding 'Black Power'

As the movement for Black Power became a very real force in much of the country, it was essential for Friends to understand its essence. Otherwise, they might be liable to become "part of the 'white backlash' group," one Friend warned at a 1967 conference on "black rage" at Earlham College.[67] Another friend, Earl Prignitz of Indiana Yearly Meeting, told Friends that "violence is not the real issue. The cause of violence is."[68] Barrington Dunbar urged Friends to "listen in love" and to "understand, encourage, and support" the authority of African Americans to run their own institutions.[69] Many Friends realized Quakers had lessons to learn. Being part of the dominant and privileged Eurocentric culture made them participants, albeit perhaps unwillingly and unconsciously, in the oppression that was driving the call for Black Power. Bayard Rustin minced no words: "There are two Americas—black and white—and nothing has more clearly revealed the divisions between them than the debate currently raging around the slogan of 'black power.'"70 Barrington Dunbar accused Quakers of being part and parcel of the "institutional violence" of American society, a "covert violence—the day to day violence that has been perpetuated by whites on black Americans for over three hundred years." As "allies" in this system, Dunbar charged, Friends were "as guilty of our kind of violence as the militant Black nationalist is of his kind." It was a message to Friends that Dunbar repeated often.71

The message was a difficult one for Friends to absorb and to deliver further. "Merely by being part of an oppressive white culture, Friends today are placed in an indefensible position," one participant at a 1968 Pendle Hill conference argued; another African American attendee called on Quakers to "place your privileged position on the line and recognize that in this nation and all nations things are going to be equal."72 Quakers are finding themselves "in an unaccustomed place— branded as one with the oppressor," European American Quaker Candida Palmer wrote in 1970.73 In a bold and forthright *Quaker Life* article, George Sawyer spoke as "The Stranger Among You," telling Friends that they must tell the "silent, frightened millions" that they do not need to be afraid of their "racist brother. He is wrong." Friends must work to convince those silent millions that "there is no sanity to the ideology of white supremacy" and that "America may well perish if she continues on this perilous path" of exclusion and separation.74 Quaker Kale Williams of the AFSC told Iowa Yearly Meeting (Conservative) in 1968 that Friends needed to recognize "the individual worth and dignity of each person, be he black militant or white segregationist, policeman or rioter, army officer or peasant guerilla, for it is wrong attitudes, not men, which are our enemies."75

———— • ————

In 1966, Ginny Coover, a European American member of Western Yearly Meeting, had moved to Mantua, the predominantly African American neighborhood in Philadelphia, to teach in what was then known as an urban ghetto school. Coover, an Earlham graduate, struggled with what she perceived to be a big gap between what Friends professed to believe and how they lived their lives, especially when it came to the poor and disadvantaged. She learned that "there has been a radical change in black thinking in the past few years, and if Friends are to relate to this radical change in a relevant way we must meet this challenge in an equally radical a way." After Martin Luther King, Jr. was killed, the Young Friends organization sent Coover to travel for six months to meetings, mostly in the Midwest, to try to help Friends understand the rise of Black Power.[76]

Quakers were unsettled to hear of demands for separatism and local control over institutions in African American neighborhoods. In light of the racial unity activist Friends had worked to create, Margaret Hope Bacon wrote, "When we first heard the cry for black separatism we were angry."[77] As a reassurance to Friends, Chuck Fager told them that African Americans did not wish to exclude European Americans from taking part in the struggle; indeed, African American Lincoln Lynch of CORE stated that the organization would "work with anybody, literally anybody, to achieve equality of opportunity, dignity of the individual, and power in the community of Black America." However, he continued, Quakers must understand "that the Negro must lead." African Americans may well have perceived the "friendship" Quakers offered as patronizing, even as "covert condescension"; African American militants saw "their liberal white 'allies' as having little relevance to the power realities" they were facing.[78]

European American Friend Samuel Levering of North Carolina Yearly Meeting reminded Friends in 1969 that dissent often grows out of "basic Christian convictions" and that they should "be in unity with those Christian protestors who follow their consciences, even when as a last resort, under Divine compulsion they break bad laws." Levering advised Friends to be discerning in the ways they chose to express their support for the African American cause and to avoid involving themselves in any project led by someone committed to violence.[79]

An African American Friend explained it this way at PYM's Meeting for Social Concerns in 1969: "I am not a middle-class Negro; I am a black American citizen. I want to be so treated. I want whites to repay to my children what has been taken from them. Whites, not blacks, create violence. You have created it in me. You have moved me to say, 'Give me a piece of the action, or I'll burn it down!'"[80] John A.

Sullivan, a European American Quaker staff member of AFSC, offered a more pointed critique of Quaker attitudes about African American responses to disadvantage, discrimination, and inequity:

> Do *we* in our privileged position counsel *their* enduring longer and more patiently? Have we any right to do that? Do *we* in our privileged position counsel *them* to use our methods and not theirs? Do we draw away from them when they act with violence, hostility, and street language? It's interesting that the latter has such an effect on people; it is clear that for some people their exposure to verbal abuse is a more significant experience than their realization of other people's suffering and needs.[81]

Violence Escalates

Violence escalated in the 1960s. Mobs turned water hoses on peaceful marchers, civil rights volunteers were beaten or murdered, and the bombing of a Birmingham church killed four children. Beginning in 1964, "every week for 60 consecutive weeks, a black church was burned in Mississippi."[82] Michael Yarrow, European American clerk of PYM's Peace Committee, reported in that same year that Freedom House (an Indianola, Mississippi, church that had been used for voter education, a school, and political meetings) was burned after an attempted bombing failed. Police prevented teachers from saving the building or its library. "The house of freedom is in ashes," wrote Yarrow.[83] A number of northern Friends went to rebuild churches in the belief that doing so would constitute a "first step" toward reconciliation and recovery.[84]

New York Friends collected one thousand dollars to send two European American Friends, Ross Flanagan of the yearly meeting Peace Center and Lawrence Scott of Central Philadelphia Monthly Meeting, to learn how the yearly meeting could help in the church rebuilding effort. Flanagan and Scott contacted churches, confirmed the need, and encouraged the development of an interracial, interfaith, committee of concern organized by religious leaders. They pledged to rebuild all the churches, no matter the location, the denomination, or whether parishioners had been associated with civil rights activity. With others, Flanagan and European American Thomas Purdy, then head of Oakwood Friends School, worked with religious leadership in the state to create the interracial, interfaith "Committee of Concern in Mississippi" to raise money for building supplies.[85]

As the church burnings continued into 1965, New York, Baltimore, and Philadelphia Yearly Meetings formed the joint "Friends Mississippi Committee" in part to support the work of Scott, who directed rebuilding projects. Groups of Quaker volunteers, most from Pacific Yearly Meeting, worked with African American congregations.[86] Quakers were also helping churches to obtain fire insurance and replace supplies.[87] By November 1965, Scott reported, twenty-nine churches had been rebuilt and no one had attempted to burn the churches again.[88]

For Scott and other Friends, the reconstruction projects had a deeper meaning. Scott noted:

> By far the most significant achievement has been the project's effect on those Mississippians who have been moved to join in this venture of faith and love. In challenging the rule of violence and establishing new opportunities for the communication of mutual respect and good will between the white and Negro community, Friends are helping to bring about a constructive change in the climate of Mississippi today.

Increasing numbers of Mississippians of European descent were working on the churches, and half of the sixty thousand dollars collected for the projects came from that state. Scott believed that "fundamental" to that participation was that fact that he and his wife Vila were living in Jackson.[89]

———•———

Violence also made headlines more than halfway across the country in 1965 when African Americans rioted for six days in the Watts section of southeast Los Angeles. Thousands were arrested, dozens killed, and many injured. Farther up the Pacific Coast, Friends who were gathered for annual sessions of Oregon Yearly Meeting considered what they would be called to do about the growing violence. They decided they should "prepare to do something positive and not stand idly by." Their statement exemplified the view of Friends who chose not to march or participate in sit-ins but to be a people who made Christ real in lives "filled with faith, hope, and love." A year before, a survey had shown that more than half the pastors in the yearly meeting believed it was up to the government, not individual citizens, to assure African Americans fair job and housing opportunities and integrated schools.[90]

Watts was only the beginning of a season of violence: riots and "racial disturbances" occurred in twenty-three cities in the summer of 1967. The decade also spawned a spate of assassinations—of John F. Kennedy, Malcolm X, Martin Luther King Jr., and Robert F. Kennedy.

Seeking to End the Violence

AFSC and other organizations began serious discussions of how to respond to the increasing violence. Most Friends found the rise of Black Power and separatism and the aggression and the endorsements of violence frightening, difficult to understand, and contrary to their belief that "war and other instruments of violence and oppression ignore the reality" that each person has a "measure of God's Light."[91] And, like other Americans, many were either consciously or subconsciously anxious about the threat violence posed to their own social, economic, and cultural position. Quakers had difficulty discerning how to work for racial equality peaceably as more and more activists in the movement began to believe that violence was the only way to achieve their goals. "Most Meetings facing the present tension are completely bewildered," AFSC staff member Roy McCorkel, a European American Quaker, reported in 1964.[92] "The real significance of 'Black Power' is still widely misunderstood and seen by many Friends as a threat," PYM's Race Relations Committee noted five years later, "not only to their person and possessions but to their pacifist beliefs and testimonies. . . . There is a real need for confrontation, not only Black and White, but between Friend and Friend. The true living of our testimonies requires this."[93] In 1968, the "complexities of violence" was one of the topics for a gathering in Iowa of 148 Young Friends from many yearly meetings. The Friends heard "first-hand experiences with people who know the needs and feelings of a minority of God's people in the USA and a majority in most parts of the world."[94]

—————•—————

For many activist Friends, the first manifestation of Black Power came in the form of demands for local control of entities that may have been started by Friends. In 1968 the board of the Friends Neighborhood Guild in Philadelphia responded by changing its bylaws to make half of its members residents of the Northern Liberties neighborhood.[95] Though another Quaker-run project, Chester Friends Project House, also decided in 1969 to turn its management over to local control, another Chester community house, which was still under a board of Quaker European Americans, was challenged by a group called the Black Commission. Twenty members of the group, including Mohammad Kenyatta of the Black Economic Development Conference, "converged in an orderly manner," according to one newspaper account, and occupied Robert Wade House, which Chester Meeting had opened in a former firehouse in 1961 as a day care center and settlement house. The group challenged the fact that the center's board was European American and included no one from the community it served; as a consequence it demanded the deed to the building and one hundred thousand dollars to operate the center for the next year.[96] The Wade House board allowed that they were guilty of the charge. Declaring that it wanted "no program of ours in the black community [to] have any taint of paternalism or white domination," the board elected an all-African American community board and formed themselves into the Friends of Wade House to help raise money.[97] To the consternation of some Friends who found their action illegal or immoral, Friends declined to challenge the takeover on the grounds that the method was irrelevant in view of the legitimacy of the commission's claim. European American Harry Toland, editor of the local newspaper, endorsed that view in an editorial: "It seems irrelevant to condemn [the BEDC's] method. If we had lived up to our faith in brotherhood and equality and if we had been courageous practitioners of nonviolence, then we might question the methods they are using. But we have not."[98]

Chester Meeting, however, retained the Wade House deed, and as a consequence a group called the Republic of New Africa occupied the Chester Meetinghouse in March 1970 and again demanded the deed as well as funds to run the center and space for their organization. Chester Meeting sent away police who had arrived at the scene and asked the group to leave voluntarily. Though it initially refused, the Republic of New Africa left later that day even as it declared itself occupiers until its demands were met. Days later the meeting agreed to deed the building to the board of the Wade House Neighborhood Community Corporation, a move the Republic of New Africa viewed as a satisfactory outcome of its occupation.[99]

Searching for Explanations: The Kerner Report

In 1968 the Kerner Commission,[100] appointed by President Lyndon Johnson to explain riots in the cities and to recommend how to ensure a peaceful future, warned that the nation was moving toward "two societies, one black, one white—separate and unequal." The report indicted "white society" for isolating and neglecting African Americans and urged legislation to promote racial integration and to put an end to the conditions that create slums, primarily through the creation of jobs, job training programs, and decent housing. President Johnson, however, rejected the recommendations, ignoring the report's warning: "If we are heedless, none of us shall escape the consequences." Less than wo months after the report was issued, Martin Luther King, Jr. was assassinated. Riots in at least 120 American cities ensued.[101]

In a series of meetings held to consider the Kerner Commission Report, Philadelphia Yearly Meeting stated that it was "deeply moved by the sense of urgency expressed in the report." European American meeting clerk Clark K. Brown III wrote to the clerks of all the monthly meetings, "We must either engage in a massive and compassionate national effort to remove the causes of civil disorders—poverty, discrimination, racism and despair—or we are in real danger of having to create a garrison state which constantly erupts into violence and in which racial hatred grows ever deeper."[102] The yearly meeting's Ad Hoc Committee on the Urban Crisis stated, "We are reminded that individual Friends have a deep responsibility to face up to the problems of prejudice and racial violence in ourselves, our Meetings, and our communities. We cannot be content until we begin to change the social order."[103]

Margaret Hope Bacon wrote of Friends responsibility to "interpret the intensity of the anguish which inspire the riots" to the European-American community. Bacon emphasized the "many positive values" of the move for African American independence and suggested that "black empowerment might be a better term for the process in which the Negro community develops its inner strength." From that perspective,

Bacon wrote, empowerment could be seen as "a perfectly natural out-growth of Quaker testimonies," part of Friends work to build people's capacity to "solve their own problems."[104]

Japanese American Friend Magoroh Maruyama advised Quakers that only by learning first hand "what really goes on in the ghetto" could they understand the "resort to violence."[105] But Barrington Dunbar was not hopeful. According to Dunbar, because Friends of European descent had "not experienced the degradation and frustration inherent in the total experience of black people in America," they could not understand African American activism in terms other than "arrogance, violence, and separateness."[106]

Understanding the Black Panthers

As violence became the hallmark of the years after King was killed, the Black Panthers were perceived more and more by European Americans as a threat that had to be controlled. The Black Panther Party emerged shortly after the 1965 assassination of Malcolm X by three members of the Nation of Islam, which Malcolm had broken with to create his own organization the year before.[107] The Panthers put forth a ten-point pro-gram with social, economic, and political goals. It asserted the right of African American and other oppressed peoples to bear arms in self-defense against the police and other enforcement officers. He also called for an end to all "wars of aggression" waged by "the United States rul-ing circle and government "to force its domination upon the oppressed people of the world."[108] The party's demands included full employ-ment, decent housing and education, and free health care; should the nation's economic and political leaders be unwilling to fulfill these needs, the party requested that all resources, including "the technology and means of production," be turned over to their communities so that they might control their own destinies.[109]

———— • ————

At the Peoples Neighborhood Medical Center in Philadelphia, European American Friend and physician Charles Vaclavik was seeing "what love can do" in his work at the medical center. Besides the clinic, he worked with the Black Panthers to develop a neighborhood grocery in a building donated by PYM in 1969. The grocery would be run by members of a street gang who were trained in all aspects of the work.[110] Thirty-three Friends loaned three hundred dollars each to stock and remodel the Pride-in-Community Food Market, a project designed to provide alternative job opportunities for otherwise unemployed young men.[111] Speaking of the project during Philadelphia Yearly Meeting in 1970, Vaclavik expressed his hope that working with the Panthers would decrease the possibility of violence; they were well aware, he said, that he would never condone the use of violence as a response. Vaclavik described the Black Panthers as "so loving that they are willing to die for needed changes," and he worked with them in neighborhood improvement because not to do so would be to "wear blinders."[112] With the help of the yearly meeting's Chace Fund, Vaclavik and other Friends acquired and renovated another building in the neighborhood and outfitted it for a youth center.[113]

In 1970, Arch Street Friends Meeting agreed to use its meetinghouse as a sanctuary for Panthers attending the Revolutionary People's Constitutional Convention in Philadelphia on Labor Day weekend and to allow Friends to act as "observers" at the convention. The Friends Peace Committee also wrote to Philadelphia Mayor James Tate, who had asked the Panthers not to hold the event, to urge him to change his mind and support the convention. Arch Street Meeting and Greene Street Friends School each housed several hundred participants. The Peace Committee organized some 150 volunteers to be a "Friendly Presence" and act as observers in the hope of assuring a peaceful convention at a time when Panthers were being attacked without provocation by the FBI and police.[114]

While at least one of the observers, European American Quaker activist George Willoughby, believed that being a "Friendly presence" served to energize Friends, not all believed that Friends service was appropriate or welcome. Some wondered whether Friends participation was really designed to ease the fears of people of European descent rather than to help the African American community; others held that Friends should have waited for an invitation from the Panthers before offering their help.[115]

As a Quaker organization deeply involved in the Civil Rights movement, AFSC struggled with how to respond to the Panthers and

help Friends see the positive and the "why" of behavior and pronouncements that sounded so very threatening. After conversations
with the Panthers in Philadelphia and in Chicago and lengthy internal
discussions, AFSC was ready make a statement in support of the group.
They asked Friends to understand the utter hopelessness of the people
for whom the Panthers spoke, especially the young African American
man who would "stand up with courage," fight for and defend himself
and his people, and "work for something better than this hell, by any
means necessary."[116] The AFSC urged Friends to look beyond seemingly hostile behavior and pronouncements to what motivated the
group's formation and to the positive elements of its campaign—food
and medical programs for children, working to rid the streets of dope
peddlers, and achieving fair housing and education.[117]

It was a courageous act to stand at the side of Black Panthers and
issue statements in their support in the tense racial climate of late 1960s,
especially for such a highly visible organization as AFSC. When several
Panthers were killed in police attacks against them in Los Angeles,
Chicago, and Philadelphia, AFSC joined with the NAACP and
American Civil Liberties Union in speaking of the "day-to-day arbitrary
use of police powers" and calling for honoring the Panthers' constitutional rights. By 1970 AFSC was joining those who saw evidence that
law enforcement officials were trying to "systematically put [the
Panthers] out of action."[118] FCNL declared its rejection of violence "as
a moral way to change society" and announced its commitment to the
challenge of finding other means of ending injustice.[119]

The relationship of Quaker meetings and individuals to the Black
Panthers illustrates the efforts of Friends to recognize and respond to
inequity even as the threat of violence loomed. A group of New York
Friends was hoping for a public stand from their yearly meeting. "In
this period of intense anger and violent resistance of Black people," a
1970 Peace Institute workshop declared, "Friends should see 'What
Love can do'" in their relationships with such militant groups as the
Panthers. The group of New York Friends advised Quakers to condemn
and protest publicly the repression of the police and courts, provide
legal assistance to the unjustly accused, and support good works of
community groups.[120] In Pennsylvania, Gwynedd Monthly Meeting
expressed "distress" at the attacks on Black Panthers and the significant

number who were the victims of "apparent political murders." Gwynedd Meeting publicly urged government officials to investigate the violence against the Panthers.[121] When Baltimore neighborhoods were destroyed in the rioting after Martin Luther King Jr. was assassinated in 1968, Stony Run Meeting donated food and helped support a Black Panthers' breakfast program.[122]

How Friends should respond to the Panthers' program also arose at a 1970 Wellesley Monthly Meeting in Massachusetts. The meeting invited two Black Panthers to speak about their experiences and what their affiliation meant. Reminding Friends that the dangerous element was not African Americans but "whites who enter black communities to shoot *them* up," the two stated that they had joined the Panthers because of its goal—to defend African Americans, to prevent ongoing oppression, and to see that the promises of the U.S. Constitution were fulfilled. They said that "the Panthers want to do for the poor and the oppressed—black and white—what this country seems unable and unwilling to do. These may be revolutionary statements; they are not violent ones." As European American Friend Elizabeth Gulick notes, "The questions that hung heavily in the air that afternoon but were not spoken were: What can and will Friends do? . . . Does the Society of Friends have a role in all this?"[123]

To Candida Palmer of New England Yearly Meeting, Friends efforts amounted to "token gestures" that demonstrate "no significant change of heart"; understanding "the present anger of young white radicals and black militants" required Friends to reconsider concepts of forgiveness and love in ways that did not carry the "sting of the 'do-gooder'" and the tendency to smother "self-respect and dignity."[124] Barrington Dunbar said the Quaker peace testimony seemed "trite and hollow" to "dispossessed and disadvantaged nonwhites." He likened Friends to "the Pharisee who went to the temple and prayed, 'thank God I am not like other men.' 'Thank God,' we say, 'we are not open advocates of violence like Rap Brown or Stokely Carmichael.'"[125]

Philadelphia Yearly Meeting's Committee on Race Relations credited their study of the 1968 Kerner Commission Report for bringing racism "close to being the number one concern of Friends and other religiously-oriented people."[126] Three years later, their optimism had turned to discouragement. Despite some fifty years of exhortations and appeals, only a few of the most stalwart continued to raise the issues of racial justice at any opportunity.

By 1975, AFSC Boston staff noted in that in the 1950s and 1960s, Friends and others worked for desegregation without being directly affected themselves "because they 'knew' it was 'right,'" but by 1974, the definition of what was "right" was changing. Those who had been committed before now came to understand that desegregation could be inconvenient and could demand "real change in their [own] lives." The staff added that when it was made clear to people that their relationship to the Black community could not be exactly the same as it was [in the fifties and sixties] and their involvement in the decision making process could not be the same, then they felt rejected and were unable to find new "handles" for involvement. [They were not] accustomed to working in such an atmosphere of hostility and isolation. "One senses bewilderment and being caught off balance."[127]

Two quotations from the Friends for Human Justice (formerly the steering committee for the National Conference of Friends on Race Relations), illuminate where Quakers found themselves in the matter of racial justice as Friends turned their attention to the war in Vietnam:

Some Friends who once declared their concern have not continued their interest. This is a time when a rapid decline of interest in and abandonment of civil rights issues has been a national trend.

> In this day when so many are turning their attention to other issues, some even mistakenly asserting that the struggle for civil rights and human justice has been achieved, Friends ought to keep and renew our witness and encourage those who seek to bear testimony.[128]

The Civil Rights movement showed signs of splintering by 1970, and European American supporters began to turn away in large numbers. The work against racism, said AFSC executive secretary Bronson Clark, was producing only minimal results at that time, and little more could be achieved until the war in Vietnam ended and the country's attention could be redirected to issues at home.[129]

Protest at Haverford College, circa 1972.

Earlham College student's car with bumper stickers. circa 1969.

CHAPTER TEN

Integration in Quaker Schools

The leadership in most Quaker schools and colleges today is caught up in the same confusion that bemuses Quakers at large: does Quakerism (or does any traditional religious group) have in these enlightened days some special, fiery good news that is potent enough to warrant taking the risks of becoming a peculiar people once again? Or is it better, more appropriate, to melt into the existing social structures and be good but indistinguishable neighbors?

— *Thomas S. Brown, European American Quaker educator, 1978*

QUAKERS HAD CREATED SCHOOLS for free people of African descent and newly freed African Americans in the eighteenth and nineteenth centuries but, well into the twentieth century, they showed little interest in educating students of color in the schools they had created for their own children. This disinclination was, in part, a function of the Quakerism of earlier centuries when Friends founded schools to retain the purity and the distinctiveness (or sometimes their own branch) of their religious society. Quaker children, Friends maintained, required a "guarded" education where teachers could instill religious values and limit the influence of the secular culture. As the Quaker population began to decrease, Friends faced the choice of opening schools to non-Quaker students or closing for lack of adequate income. Most schools chose the former, but they typically admitted the children of parents attracted to the particular teachings and quality of Quaker education, who-without concerted effots to attract a diverse student body-were virtually always of European descent.[1]

As the twentieth century began, Friends were still committed to funding the few remaining schools in the South for African Americans—Hampton Institute, Christiansburg Institute, and Penn Center among them—but admitting African Americans to their own schools was still not on their agenda. As one English Quaker visiting Philadelphia in 1903 wrote, "In the beautiful city of Brotherly Love . . .

in the schools carried on by Friends today, we were told it would not be convenient to admit a child of partly negro descent."2

As consciousness of racial inequalities began to grow after the First World War, the belief that education was the primary way to create equal opportunities began to strengthen; some Friends were moved to examine admission practices of their own schools. In the 1920s and 1930s, many American colleges continued to maintain quotas on the admission of students of Jewish and Asian descent and largely refused to admit African Americans: a quota for Jewish students at Swarthmore College, for example, remained in place into the 1930s.3 After speaking at dozens of campuses under the sponsorship of the AFSC, Crystal Bird concluded that European American high school and college students in the 1920s, Quaker and non-Quaker alike, tended to regard African Americans as "not quite human" and to believe "that whatever advantages and privileges [they enjoy] are due solely to the magnanimity of white people."4

Henry Cadbury, the well-known European American Quaker theologian, teacher, and activist, was the consistent moving force behind many of the conferences that had the general theme of "interracial education" and were held for Quaker educators as early as 1928. For example, the topic of the 1939 Swarthmore College gathering that he chaired was direct: "Are Friends' schools faithful to Quaker testimonies and are Friends 'prepared to pay the price' of witnessing to them—including racial equality?" Topics for conferences sponsored by Philadelphia Yearly Meeting's Race Relations Committee, the Friends Council on Education, and AFSC and others in the 1930s and 1940s included themes like "Race as A World and National Problem" (for high school students) and featured nationally known speakers, both African and European American.

Cadbury believed Quaker schools should be "be pioneers of thought" and exemplars for the larger Quaker community. "We believe schools can rise higher than the group behind them and drag the Society with them," he wrote. "It is in the schools we must expect to inculcate the Quaker ideals which will influence the future."5 However, the movement toward inclusion was slow. By the early 1930s, even as its Race Relations Committee sponsored conferences on how to arouse Friends "to a deep sense of responsibility regarding the racial situation,"6 neither Philadelphia Yearly Meeting was prepared to integrate each boarding school under its care, Westtown School (Orthodox) or George School (Hicksite).

Some Friends agreed with Cadbury that Friends schools should try to live up to Quaker principles and testimonies, which meant being open to students "on merit alone." They understood that schools might lose some students but believed they might gain other families who shared that moral viewpoint. And they believed it was important to try to work against prejudice.[7] But many spoke of their concerns about whether students and their parents would not be welcoming and might leave. It might be unfair to the students already enrolled to subject them to possible turmoil and bring in people who, as many believed, were intellectually inferior. Others hesitated to subject students of African descent to "all the attention and controversy." And there was the concern about awkward, even unwelcome, social situations. Some even suggested it would be a detriment to resolving the problems by forcing "artificial" relationships.[8] All of these issues played a part along the often discomforting and foggy road to integration in Friends schools.

After some debate in 1933, Westtown School found it "not practical or proper" to admit African Americans at that point, citing the financial impact of a possible decline in enrollment and a fear of interracial socializing.[9] In 1938 and again in 1943 some Westtown students objected to the exclusion. One, Corinne Allen, argued in a letter to the student newspaper that if the school was supposed to be teaching Friends values and the will to work "against society's undesirable influences," not admitting African Americans "betrayed" the Society's principles. But few students shared her view. One student declared the idea of integrating "appalling"; others echoed the notion expressed in society at large that African Americans were intellectually inferior.[10]

In 1935, the George School Committee concluded that the school should not put itself ahead of the parents or the yearly meeting by admitting African Americans. Only "when Philadelphia Quakers welcome Negroes into their fellowship, [should] George School . . . do the same," said longtime European American school head George Walton. To do so in advance of the yearly meeting was not, he argued, in the interest of students of African descent. At George School, Walton stated, such a student "would experience isolation and neglect, and his proper development of personality would be seriously hampered." In 1936, students and many teachers asked for a joint meeting of representatives from different parts of the school community to discuss integration. A year-and-a-half passed before the committee called them together; no report was ever issued.[11]

A 1935 study reported that many Friends supported the idea of "separate but equal" in education and, thus, avoided the question of integration.[12] But in the same decade, two Quaker schools—Oakwood Friends School in Poughkeepsie, New York, sponsored by New York Yearly Meeting (Orthodox), and Media Friends School of Media, Pennslvania, Friends Meeting—took their first steps to integrate. Though Oakwood School trustees initially held that the time was not right, faculty and students began to urge admission of African Americans.[13] In 1933 the Oakwood community and New York Yearly Meeting pronounced themselves "more ready" and accepted two sons of prominent African American YMCA executive Max Yergan; the boys had been rejected by Westtown.[14] At some schools, years passed between that first admission and the next; Oakwood, however, admitted at least one African American student every subsequent year for the next twenty, though never more than three at a time. In 1944 the school reported that rooming arrangements had not been a problem and that the experience has had "far more advantages than disadvantages."[15] In 1953, out of 150 Oakwood students, twelve were African American, and the school decided to admit no more to keep the number "more proportional."[16]

In 1937 the Media Friends School, led by its school trustees, admitted its first student of African descent, a four-year-old boy named Lancess McKnight, Jr. However, the aftermath of this decision revealed reluctance to integrate, this time on the part of the parents. Deliberation about whether t admit McKnight had been long and agonizing and was more an outgrowth of "a spiritual process of continuing revelation, than a revolutionary act."[17] European American school committee member Dorothy Biddle James noted that admitting the boy was "sound educationally" and "the only natural thing to do, in light of Quaker testimony on race."[18] Media teachers, whom the school committee consulted on the admission, had voiced no objection; based on the assumption that parents would also not object, the committee did not inform them.

After all, the committee reasoned, it was not customary to inform parents when a new student of European descent was admitted at midyear, as McKnight was.[19] But when the boy enrolled, parents of thirty-three of the school's ninety-five students withdrew their children.[20]

According to Quaker Paul Furnas, European American chair of the board of trustees in 1938–39 and a school parent, "there would have been fewer losses" in enrollment had one parent of a Media student not convinced others to sign a statement in February 1937 pledging to remove their children if McKnight stayed.[21] Thirty-nine parents stated their regret that the decision was taken "without sufficient consultation" with them. "Not one of us has the slightest prejudice against the Negro race," they maintained, "but on the other hand we believe it unwise and unnecessary to have our children thrown in close daily association with Negro children. Once the door is opened it is inevitable that others will follow."[22]

Two months later the parents of more than thirty of the children still enrolled at the school read a letter at the Media Monthly Meeting saying they were "astonished at the temerity" of the school committee, "which seems not only willing but even determined to destroy so fine a thing" as the school. "Not entirely in agreement among themselves" about the issue, the monthly meeting sent the letter back to the school committee with the recommendation "to act as the way opens." Later the meeting adopted a minute of support for the committee. Said the mother of one student, "We are prepared to rise to a larger expression, and a more costly one, of what it means in this generation to be a society of Friends. To us, I feel, has come the opportunity of *bearing witness to a fresh revelation of truth.*"[23]

Hoping to ease the situation, a group of five "weighty Friends" of European descent—AFSC head Clarence Pickett, Westtown School trustee D. Robert Yarnall, Haverford professor Douglas Steere, Swarthmore professor Patrick Murphy Mailin, and Philadelphia Quaker Edith Cope—met with the parents who signed the 1939 protest. The five may also have been among those who responded to the school's appeal for funds to make up the tuition losses.[24] Additioal financial support of parents from Arch Street Meeting and other Friends guaranteed enough financial backing for the school to continue, and school officials refused the McKnights' offer to withdraw their son "with no hard feelings."[25]

"It is the development of what we believe to be wholesome attitudes in our white children that gives meaning to our policy," said James, "quite as much as believing that the McKnights or any other family should be free to apply to a Friends' school."26 Reflecting on the experience, the Media Friends School Committee noted, "If we have made a mistake, we feel that it lies in the fact that we took too much for granted that our parent group would understand any decision we might make, based upon what we believe to be inherent in the fundamental principles underlying such a school."27

By 1940 the school was on an even financial keel. Its experience with parents informed its response when other African American students applied for admission in 1943.28 Also in the same quarter, Chester Monthly Meeting supported the admissions on the grounds that the school should be "a real expression of our Quaker belief that color of skin should not be the qualification for entrance." Three children of African American descent and three of Japanese descent were admitted. In Media, however, these admissions did not signal a trend. Twenty years later, the number of students of color had dropped from three to zero. The school suggested that the problem was strictly financial. The "economic level of the Negro population of Media means that there is a relatively small population to draw on," the report noted.29

While trustees initiated integration at Media Friends School and teachers supported it, the principal of Germantown Friends School (sponsored by the Orthodox Germantown Meeting) stood in the way of an effort to desegregate there. European American Quaker Headmaster Stanley Yarnall stated that a survey of parents indicated that if Germantown integrated so many children would be withdrawn that the school would be destroyed.30 Thus in 1938, the school committee rejected an application from the African American daughter of two prominent Philadelphia lawyers. The rejected student's aunt, a Quaker, wrote that she had "wept" that "courageous and earnest seeking" for her niece had ended with such a decision.31

"Germantown Friends always had a color line, as all Quaker schools did, but of course we didn't write it down or talk about it, it was simply understood," admitted European American Bill Koons, then a teacher at the school. "What if we'd had the courage to take that gamble?" he asked. "We wouldn't be struggling today, nearly as much, for diversity."

In the end, however, the decision to reject the girl was a "catalyst." European American Quaker Margaret Cary, a Germantown school committee member whose family was one of the "weightiest" in the meeting, was determined to integrate and warned Yarnall that it was only a matter of time.[32] In 1941 Yarnall chose to retire, averting any further confrontation.

At Brooklyn Friends School, European American principal Douglas Grafflin encountered opposition to integration from the school committee of New York Monthly Meeting, which managed the institution. In 1942 Grafflin, a Quaker, proposed admitting an African American child whose father was professor at Columbia University and mother a judge at a nearby court. The committee rejected the application saying it believed its role was not to force Quaker principles onto non-Quaker parents. Grafflin resigned the position he had held for five years, but his resignation apparently stirred the monthly meeting to expand the size of the school committee. Within two years, there were enough new members to bring about "rapid integration."[33]

Aside from these examples, Quaker school integration was minimal before the Second World War. "In spite of their pioneer efforts in Negro education, Friends have not carried their doctrine of race equality to its logical conclusion," European American Quaker Howard Brinton wrote in 1940. "Friends have generally had special schools for whites and Negroes."[34] That situation would continue if Friends opinions were to hold sway. A 1940 poll of Quaker and non-Quaker students at George School revealed that more than half opposed admitting African Americans; thirty-nine said they would leave if such admissions were allowed.[35] And a 1941 survey of private educational institutions (not just Friends schools) in the Northeast undertaken by the Friends Council on Education revealed that all but one of the responding secondary schools found it "impractical" to admit African Americans, even though most had students of Asian descent and all enrolled Jewish and Mexican students.[36]

Rather than documenting momentum toward integration, the 1941 survey also showed that Friends were "separated" from the lives and thoughts of African American youth. Friends secondary school students of European descent believed that "no Negro student would find acceptance by other members of the student body." Although many

Friends agreed that "the question of race discrimination as practiced in many Friends schools is becoming an outstanding cause of concern for our Society," as in other private schools, Friends administrators admitted that they simply lacked the "courage to be pioneers."[37] Almost two-thirds of all the private institutions—elementary schools through universities—did not admit African Americans. With a few exceptions, however, Quaker schools led "all other groups in their refusal to accept their applications."[38]

Into this mix of timidity and outright opposition to moving toward integration, in 1942 the Friends Meeting of Washington "dropped a bombshell," in the words of European American Quaker historian Margaret Haviland, namely a letter asking Philadelphia Yearly Meeting about how they were dealing with "the problem of racial discrimination in Friends' schools." Out of a year of discussion, they discovered that fear of intermarriage and fear that the situation would be too difficult for the few African Americans admitted were the prime reasons Friends were opposed to integration.[39]

The Second World War highlighted the inconsistency inherent in fighting a racist regime abroad while supporting a system of racial segregation at home. Principals, faculty members, students, activist members of local Friends meetings, and, less frequently, school committees spoke out more and more about this paradox. By 1943 Westtown School students' attitudes about integration had changed. A survey conducted by students showed that their classmates favored admitting African Americans by more than two to one, and about the same proportion of the 184 students said that they would live with students of African descent in the dorms. Although fifty students said their parents would object to such a policy, only seventeen said they would withdraw because of it.

In January 1944 the Westtown administration sent letters to 3,700 people in the wider school community of parents, alumni, and benefactors to test the sentiment for integration. The letter, from Westtown General Committee chair D. Robert Yarnall and head of school James F. Walker, both Quakers of European descent, noted that though the school had welcomed students of other races, none of African descent had been accepted and that this fact was "hanging rather heavily on the conscience of some members of the committee, faculty, and student body."[40] The letter also stated, "It seems inconsistent for a Friends school either to exclude or to admit anyone on the basis of race alone," and it expressed the conviction that living up to the Quaker belief that the "Seed of God" is in every person can bring "Christians into conflict in a world divided by class, race, and creed."[41] At a 1943 Westtown faculty meeting, one European American teacher said, "We can talk about practical issues all we like, but until we face the clear testimonial of the Society we have not fulfilled our duty to anybody."[42]

Six hundred of the 3,700 persons contacted responded to the Westtown survey; sixty percent favored integration.[43] However, because the survey fell short of the unity school officials felt they needed, they sought guidance from the Orthodox Philadelphia Yearly Meeting. Though that meeting also could not reach unity, it did record that it would "view with sympathy" steps to end discrimination. That statement was encouragement enough to initiate the process that brought African American Quaker Grace Cunningham to Westtown for her senior year in 1945.[44] Two students withdrew when she arrived. In 1946 the school admitted a non-Quaker African American, but another decade passed before a "sizable" number of African Americans could be counted among Westtown students.[45]

In 1943, the Haverford Friends School committee received an application for an African American student. After consulting an advisory committee and two teachers, the application was turned down because of concern, not about race, but about the good of the child.[46] But three years later after Frances Ferris, European American head of school, shepherded discussions with all parts of the school community on the question, the school admitted its first African American student.[47] The new policy was based on democratic and "religious and moral principles," according to the Haverford Monthly Meeting education committee.[48] A brochure prepared for parents and the wider school community explained that admissions policy would be based on the "intellectual and moral soundness of the applicant," not on race or creed.

In spite of these successful efforts, African American admissions were still controversial among Friends. In October 1943, FGC's education committee, chaired by European American Quaker Hadassah Leeds, focused on the issue in a letter to officials of the schools of meetings affiliated with FGC. Portions of the letter were reprinted in the January

15, 1944 *Friends Intelligencer* editorial, "Friends' Schools and Negroes." There were serious consequences for ignoring the issue, the committee warned:

> There are many indications that the colored races will not long continue to accept the status of inferiority to which they have been subjected. Thus practical consideration combines with the claims of Christian justice to force this issue on our attention. Unless we learn to foster good will, equality of opportunity, and mutual respect, race revolution may be the result.[49]

As citizens of the future, students must be free of "prejudice and race discrimination" because they must be able to work together. A question ends the letter: "Have you given committee and faculty consideration to this problem?"[50]

When FGC's message appeared in the January 1944 issue of *Friends Intelligencer*, letters poured in—primarily from the liberal unprogrammed Friends of European descent who formed the bulk of the weekly newspaper's readership—and revealed the range of attitudes undergirding that reluctance. "Are we *really* keeping alive Friends' most worthy traditions, when through fear, desire for conformity, and need of support for Friends' schools we keep out those who would perhaps receive most . . . and who have certainly a very real contribution to make?" Florence H. Staniels of Passaic, New Jersey, asked. "How can we call ourselves Friends and say our schools are for all when we deliberately shut out the Negro?" William Piepenburg of New York City essentially agreed with Staniels. If Friends school admissions policies were racially discriminatory, he stated, "No greater condemnation of inconsistency may be cited among a group anciently opposed to precisely such injustice."[51]

———————•———————

Among those on the opposite side of the spectrum was Florence Riggs Carpenter of Philadelphia, who deplored the possibility of racial intermarriage. Carpenter reasoned that Friends schools existed not only to provide a better cultural and religious education for Quaker children but also to allow students an opportunity to "associate with children having the same background and environment, so when school days had passed the friendships they had made would continue and often result in marriage." If Quaker children should "choose the Negroes for friends and it culminates in marriage," the parents, not the children, would be to blame, she said. To avoid "such tragedy and calamity" and to protect children of both races, "educated colored people" should keep to themselves socially, "without any feeling of inferiority."[52] Marie Kirkley of Philadelphia also expressed concern about "social intimacy," and note the potential consequences. "Can you contemplate with equanimity the thought of your daughter or son marrying a colored man or girl?" Kirkley asked; "the vast majority" of Friends, she asserted, could not. "Inherently," she further asserted, "such a union would not only be socially unwise, but indeed a biologic retrogression." Like Carpenter, Kirkley believed in segregation; she suggested that teachers of European descent be sent "to inculcate Quaker doctrines among colored people and convert them to the idea of becoming independent Quakers"—that is, within their own schools and meetings.[53]

Friends who responded to the letters from Carpenter and Kirkley were adamant about the necessity of integration. Karl and Helen Klein of Westport, Connecticut, chided Carpenter for "misinterpreting the intention" of Quaker education as if it were to find "suitable associations and friendships for the children." Quaker schools already enrolled Jewish, Chinese, Japanese, and Indian children "without fear of 'nonadvantageous' contacts." Friends should work to be sure that "our actions correspond with the doctrines which we proclaim in the world," the Kleins wrote. In schools that had admitted African Americans "neither heaven nor the social structure nor the school itself has fallen," Louise Mather Ridgway of Norfolk, Virginia, pointed out. "Living with Negroes is actually a great deal more interesting and rich and satisfying than living without them." Lotte F. Jahreiss of Baltimore wrote that keeping Quaker children apart from others creates "sterile habits and helpless distrust" of their fellow men. "The tragedy is not interracial marriage," said another correspondent, "rather it is the bigotry and prejudice of the superstitious."[54]

After World War II, support for integrated Quaker schools grew stronger. Friends Select School in Philadelphia, founded in 1833 and governed by a board of members from each of the city's Quaker meetings, appears to have enrolled African Americans in the first grade with "no problems of any kind" in 1946, though the school had rejected their applications earlier in the decade. The first two African Americans graduates were members of the class of 1958.[55] Two schools originally against integration accepted African Americans for the first time in 1946. McFeely, who had taken the lead on the integration of Friends Central, then went on to play a role in the integration of the George School, which he headed from 1948 to 1966.[56]

Moving cautiously, George School at first admitted only children of African American staff, but in 1946 it admitted Cynthia Crooks, whose father was principal of a Quaker school in Jamaica. Informed of the decision to admit Crooks, forty-one parents wrote to express approval and three, disapproval. School officials worried about Crooks's "isolation" and encouraged others to make her feel welcome but, in the view of European American classmate Gwendolynn Kerr, Crooks was a "victim" of other students' lack of exposure to African Americans and of the school's "overcautious approach to accepting black students."[57] In 1951 the African American diplomat Ralph Bunche, the highest-ranking U.S. representative to the United Nations, made clear his views on the limited integration at George School by refusing to be the commencement speaker.[58]

At Germantown Friends School Burton Fowler, a well-known European American educator who supported integration, had replaced Stanley Yarnall as headmaster. As the number of people in Germantown Meeting who supported integration grew, they inundated the school committee with letters. "We boast a long waiting list of people who are anxious to enter our school," Germantown European American student Janet Rosenwald wrote in the school newsletter, so that if parents opposing integration withdrew their children, they "could easily be replaced by the more broad-minded ones on the waiting list." Rosenwald noted that she had not learned of "any suffering" arising from integration at George, Friends Select, and Westtown Schools. "You may say that this school is not yet ready to accept Negroes," she wrote. "My answer is, if we're not ready now, we never will be."[59] The first African American child at Germantown was admitted to its kindergarten in 1948; the school also hired an African American librarian and assistant teacher.[60] Joan Countryman, who in 1958 would be the first student of African descent to graduate from the school, entered in the third grade and remembered always being the oldest African American during her years in the school. She also recalled that the school was anxious to have more African American students well before it understood how it would need to change its way of doing things before it could reach out. Countryman later returned to Germantown and taught math at for twenty-three years. She then went on to head Lincoln School in Providence, from which she retired in 2005.[61]

FGC, although noting some progress in integration since the war years, reminded Friends schools in 1948 that they should open their enrollment and faculty to people of any race, color, or religion.[62] In the same year, another head of school, European American Friend Richard McFeely of Friends Central School in Wynnewood, a suburb of Philadelphia, asserted that the school had "no valid basis for its present discriminatory policy." The school's board declared that "race, color, religion, national origin, or ancestry" would not be used in choosing among equally acceptable students.[63] By that time too, Greene Street School had accepted its first African American students, and as the demographics of its Germantown neighborhood changed it became the only Quaker school in which students of color were a majority.[64]

———•———

In the 1950s, particularly after the Supreme Court's 1954 decision in *Brown v. Board of Education of Topeka* that "separate but equal" schools were unconstitutional, a number of schools showed noticeable progress toward integration. In the late 1950s, finding itself in a "declining" community with the attendant problems and concerns about safety, Germantown Friends School debated and then turned down the chance to move and build a suburban campus. With the support of Germantown Monthly Meeting, the school decided not to join the "white flight" but to stay and assume some responsibility for bettering its own neighborhood. Among many community initiatives were scholarships for students from Germantown, aid that made a great difference in the racial and economic diversity of the school.[65] It would also turn out that having African American families as neighbors would become one of the "driving forces" in the integration of the school. Another factor was the leadership from the families of the monthly meeting, both of African and European descent, who worked together to make integration a success.[66] By the early 1990s about 20 percent of the Germantown students were students of color.[67] The school also helped to start a Germantown Schools' Community Council, which brought the schools and the surrounding community in the Germantown section of Philadelphia together on various projects.[68]

By the mid-1950s, most Friends schools in the East had admitted at least a few African American students, and in some cases a substantial number had gained admittance. In 1958 Friends Select and Westtown were the two Friends Schools with most African American students.[69] Friends in New England, however, appear to have lagged behind. In 1947 New England Yearly Meeting expressed its concern that Moses Brown and Lincoln School in Providence, Rhode Island, two schools under the yearly meeting's care, should include "children of all races in their school family"; six years later another minute suggested that the schools were then ready to do so. Still, in 1957 the yearly meeting continued to question whether Friends and their schools were "clear of discrimination."[70] Ten years later the meeting created a seventeen-member committee, including heads of the yearly meeting's schools, to further "the meeting's concern to meet the needs of more students from disadvantaged and minority groups" and to raise funds for scholarships. By the 1960s several African Americans had been admitted to Moses Brown School.[71] In the late 1970s, recognizing that more than financial assistance was needed to make students from minority groups "a more integral part of the community," the committee sponsored workshops on promoting integration and sought funds for a "traveling teacher" to serve as a resource on integration for New England Quaker schools. A 1980 minute still noted the yearly meeting's concern with integrating Friends schools.[72] The African American enrollment at Moses Brown was increasing, however, and serious efforts were made to hire African American faculty, according to a teacher who arrived in 1984.[73]

Though integrating Friends School in Baltimore took more than a decade, in the end the school was one of the first two to integrate within the area's independent school spectrum. Aware in the late 1940s that the court would soon rule against desegregated schools, head of school Bliss Forbush, a Quaker of European descent, patiently worked on the integration issue. He noted that the school faced a "moral dilemma: How could a Quaker institution, founded on the principle that 'there is that of God in every one,' refuse to accept children from Baltimore's black families?"[74] But like Yarnall at Germantown, Forbush firmly believed that the school should not integrate until Stony Run, the monthly meeting in Baltimore that operated the school, was itself integrated.

In January 1950, Stony Run agreed that the time had come to open the school, summer camp, and meeting to people of African descent. But when one member of the meeting asked the school to admit African Americans, Forbush continued to insist that the meeting "consider its own practice before requiring a new policy for the school."[75] When Baltimore Yearly Meeting refused to endorse "a simple statement on equal rights" in 1950–51, Forbush took it as a sign that it opposed integration.[76]

A few Catholic schools in Baltimore had started integrating on a limited scale in the late 1940s. In 1951 when the city's Urban League urged their headmasters to change their policies, the Baltimore Friends Meeting Education Committee declared it would admit African Americans only in concert with four or five other of the city's private schools. Students and teachers at Baltimore Friends School showed little sympathy for integration: a survey of one social studies class revealed that twenty of the thirty children said they would leave if the school integrated, and most upper school students opposed such a move.[77] In 1951 Forbush suggested in a memo to the committee that it pick a date to begin integrating one grade at a time, beginning with the nursery school. The committee still demurred.

Even after Forbush proposed to have no new students of color in classes with the current students, in September 1954, the school community was divided on admitting African American students. But by November, the education committee had decided to integrate, though one-fourth of the committee's members preferred a postponement of three to five years. In 1955 six African American children entered the kindergarten. Eighteen students withdrew, but enrollments rose overall as families who were unopposed to racially mixed classes enrolled their children in the school. By 1963, all of the first eight grades of the school included a "small number of black students"; in 1964 enrollment was opened in all grades.[78]

———— • ————

The admission of African American students was even more protracted at Sidwell Friends School in Washington, DC. In no other Friends school did so few block so many who favored integration for so long. Anticipating a Supreme Court move to outlaw school segregation, in the early 1950s, AFSC had developed a five-year plan to support integration in the nation's capital, and the fact that a Friends school there was not integrated left Friends open to the charge of hypocrisy. Thus members of the Washington-area Quaker meetings and many prominent Friends joined AFSC in urging Sidwell to integrate.[79]

European American Thomas Watson Sidwell, who had founded the school in 1883, had told a school assembly in 1897 that "the poorest negro in the land should have every right which the law promises him," but after his death in 1936 the school's board grew conservative.[80] Into the late 1940s, the executive committee of the school, which was not affiliated with any monthly or yearly meeting, had resisted appeals from all quarters to integrate, including those from the influential European American Quaker trustee Hadassah Leeds. The school's longstanding opposition was rooted solely in executive committee chair Austin Stone, also a Quaker of European descent.[81] Stone maintained that open admission policies were "newly fashioned by johnnies-come-lately to the Friendly persuasion who knew nothing of Quaker schools or the Quaker past."[82] Sidwell students who attended gatherings of students from other Quaker schools, however, became aware that their school's policies were gaining "a distressing notoriety." When the equally prestigious National Cathedral's Beauvoir School desegregated in 1952, AFSC and some Sidwell parents and teachers worried that Beauvoir parents who opposed integration there would move their children to Sidwell, thus causing the school to grow even more entrenched in its position.

Just days before the 1954 *Brown v. Board of Education* decision, Leeds wrote Stone that it seemed "wrong to exclude any student who measures up to our standards and for whom we have room in the class for which he applies." Most of the trustees were apparently ready to move ahead if Stone would commit to the change. Stone's response to Leeds revealed not only his view but, no doubt, that of some other Friends:

> I am frankly puzzled as to how some of my friends reach the conclusion that it is unchristian not to admit Negroes to schools where there are both white girls and boys. In the ultimate, I know of no reason why it should be considered unchristian to try and maintain a family relationship on a white basis. Crudely, I would not consider it

unchristian of me if I endeavored to do what I could to prevent my children from marrying Negroes.

I would not think it unchristian to select an environment for my children in which their acquaintances and future husbands and wives are suitable from the standpoint of race as well as morals, etc. In fact, I would feel distinctly guilty if I had not tried to provide my children with the opportunity of associating with other young people whom they might freely invite to our home.

Is my thought in this regard unchristian? I hope not. It was my father's also.[83]

European American Quaker John Putnam Marble, one of Sidwell's trustees was said to "flush almost purple with fury every time he had to hear again Stone's insistence that his racial views were well within the bounds of Friendly principles."[84]

The executive committee's reaffirmation of its position against integration in February 1955 triggered widespread protest. The *Washington Post*'s report on the decision, carried the headline, "In 1955–1956 Friends to Continue Race Ban." Stone received a "deluge" of letters, most "vigorously critical" of the policy. One European American Sidwell parent wrote sarcastically to head of school Robert Lyle, "Why don't you brief your announcement of Feb. 7 as follows: 'No niggers, so enroll at once?'" Parents angry at the trustees' position made plans to poll the school's patrons; Florida Avenue Meeting members asked to meet with the board; and a faculty study committee concluded that a change in Sidwell's policy would be "practicable." Friend James E. Forsythe, a longtime and highly influential European American teacher, urged the trustees to open admissions.[85] But change came only after the board itself changed. By January 1956, through the death and retirement of earlier members, four new trustees had been added and a "large majority" of the board voted to adopt a grade-by-grade integration plan to begin the next fall.[86] The plan assured that progress at Sidwell would be slow: by 1963–64, only seven of the 856 students were African American.[87]

———•———

Integration was not an issue in a number of other Friends schools in the 1950s, however. In September 1952 the Lansdowne Friends School, operated by the Lansdowne, Pennsylvania, Monthly Meeting, reported having enrolled a first-grader of African descent and stated its hope that the admission would stimulate interest among other African American families in the area. By 1956 eleven of the school's 146 students were African American, and, as the school's admission coordinator reported, the school "in no way . . . cater[ed] to an upper income group or one particular sect of people."[88] Media Friends School enrolled African and Asian Americans in 1943 without repercussion though, to the school's surprise, its hiring of African American third-grade teacher Rebecca Mitchell in 1957 inspired another temporary drop in enrollment.[89]

In its 1961 survey, titled "Unfinished Business," the Philadelphia Yearly Meeting Race Relations Committee determined that African American enrollment in Friends schools throughout the Philadelphia area rose between 1954 and 1960. The increase was greatest at Lansdowne School, but it was also substantial at Greene Street and Friends Central. The average increase for all surveyed schools was 2.2 percent.[90] In 1965 Germantown Friends School started its own Community Scholars program to provide partial or full tuition and partial funding of expenses for four to five middle- or upper-school African American students from the neighborhood each year. The program connected the school "more closely" to its predominantly African American immediate community and reached families for whom a private school was unthinkable. Teachers, students, parents, alumni, Germantown meeting, and people in the community worked together to fund the program.[91]

Many Friends schools begun in the fifties and sixties included integration in their founding mission. Most included a statement like that of Virginia Beach Friends School, opened in 1950, declaring their intention to create "a community diverse in religion, race, gender, nationality, age and economic background on every level."[92] Westbury (Long Island) Friends School, opened in 1957, describes itself as a "culturally diverse Friends school for all children." The first African American students enrolled in Westbury in 1963.[93] By 2008, the school had equal numbers of students of African and European descent—49.[94]

Like some other Quaker schools, racial diversity was a founding goal of Cambridge Friends School (CFS) since it opened in 1961 under the care of Friends Meeting at Cambridge, Massachusetts. Purposely located in an area of working and middle-class families, the school participated in the "Bridge," a program to connect the city's "minorities" and independent schools, and reached out to the neighborhood "in a variety of ways," according to European American Quaker Anne Nash,[95] interim CFS head in 1998–99. Nash believes a Quaker school "should mirror life as it should be, not as it is." Thus from its first years, CFS has had some African American students. In 1989 the school reaffirmed its commitment to integration and declared its mission to be providing "anti-racist education" for its students and the wider school community. The school still strives for diversity today. It would like about to have one-third of the students to be children of color and to be able to assure that each child has at least one period on his daily schedule with a teacher of color.[96]

At the end of the 1990s, CFS created a Center for Anti-Racist Education to support the school's efforts and broaden the possibilities for learning and partnerships with others in the community through seminars, internships, lectures, and publications. A series of five-year plans called for more anti-racist training for staff and parent groups and for finding ways to share power and "unpack" the system to give all members of the community equal access within the organization.[97]

The initiative for Detroit Friends School, the only Quaker school in Michigan, came in 1961 from an African American family, the McCrees. After what Dores McCree later described as "the most humiliating day" of her life when her daughter was refused admission to a prestigious private school in the city, she phoned her husband, Wade McCree Jr., a federal judge. Outraged, he shared news of the decision with colleagues, most of them European American. A small group formed to approach the Detroit Friends Meeting, which then had only eight members, about starting a Friends school.[98] In 1963 Detroit Friends School was chartered under the care of Green Pastures Quarter of Lake Erie Yearly Meeting.[99] The board enrolled thirty "founders," who pledged a thousand dollars a year for three years, and "sponsors," who pledged five hundred dollars a year over the same term. Staff members also pledged their support. Detroit Friends Meeting, Ann Arbor Monthly Meeting, and Green Pastures Quarter shared responsibility for the school;[100] now each meeting in the yearly meeting contributes toward the school.

Looking at the school community as a whole, Detroit is "perhaps the most diverse Friends school in the country," according to Quaker Dwight Wilson, its first African American principal.[101] Classwork includes rigorous academics, according to European American Friend Gail Thomas, head of the school from 1991 to 1997. Although most students are not Friends, the parents appreciate the Quaker atmosphere—the values, the worship, the social service. "Any assumptions" that might be made because of their race, "are completely wrong."[102] Housed first in a storefront and temporary buildings, the school broke ground in 1970 for its first permanent building on a lot in the middle of a redevelopment project bordered on one side by a park and an integrated church on another.

When Wilson took over in 2002, the school had 144 students in junior kindergarten through the eighth grade. Sixty-seven percent were African American, 30 percent of European descent, and 3 percent Latino or Asian-American. A former middle-school principal in New York, Wilson said he was "tired of Quaker organizations existing on the reputation of our spiritual ancestors. The Underground Railroad for blacks ended 137 years ago." He sees his school "as an above-ground highway taking a multicultural array of children to the place our ancestors envisioned—America the Beautiful, the one in the Constitution."[103] There are students whose parents earn "six figures" and others whose parents have been or "are currently incarcerated, who are homeless or living apart from parents they've never seen." About 40 percent receive financial aid.[104]

———————•———————

Racial diversity has been an intentional witness of three southern Friends schools. Well aware that they lived in an area where segregation was the norm and that integration provoked "widespread hostility," in 1962 members of Chapel Hill and Durham Friends Meetings in North Carolina purposely started to offer education to students of all colors. In 1995 the board of directors created a special endowment to help make diversity a reality.[105] In 2008 approximately 23 percent of the students were from families who were not of European descent.[106]

The Friends School of Atlanta (FSA), one of the newest Friends schools, was integrated from its opening in 1991. In 2006 students of color made up 48 percent of the school. European American board member Sally MacEwan said the founders from the Atlanta Friends Meeting realized that it had to be diverse from the start; it would not work to say later, "How can I add more black people to my white school?" By seeking diversity in all aspects of the school—faculty, administration, board members, parents and students. FSA hopes to achieve its goal of becoming "a leading example of diversity" in its own city and in the larger educational community.[107]

The Friends School of Wilmington, North Carolina, "actively seeks to enroll students of every race, creed, nationality and social or economic background." Scholarships are available to make attendance possible, regardless of financial circumstances. In a "Commitment to Diversity" section on its website, the school reports that from its beginning in 1995, it has adhered to the "central tenets of the Quaker Faith"—"inclusion, diversity and equality," not only in its student body but on the board and faculty, as well.[108]

Despite the overall trend toward integration, some Friends schools struggled to fully embrace African American students and staff. Though it claimed it would admit an African American applicant "on the same basis as any other child," in 1961 the Buckingham (Pennsylvania) Friends School reported that because it was "operating at a prospective deficit of several thousand dollars, the application on behalf of a Negro child might make our financial status even more precarious and frightening than it is."[109]

Although Moses Brown School in Providence, Rhode Island, has no records of exactly when African American students were first admitted, according to European American school archivist, King Odell, there were a few in the student body sometime in the 1960s. Odell, who has been on the school staff since 1953, said the admissions didn't seem to come from any specific initiative of a particular party at the school (i.e. administration or school committee).[110]

By the 1970s, Moses Brown School was integrating. European American Quaker Rosalind Cobb Wiggins, who taught African American history there in the 1970s and later became a school trustee, charged that of all students at Moses Brown on scholarship, only

African Americans were expected to wait on tables and scrub floors. Wiggins also asserted that racial discrimination existed in grading, but Odell said he had not see any instances where students were treated differently according to their race.[111]

In other Friends schools, according to 1972 Oakwood School graduate Juan Williams, the first generation of African American students at any Quaker school were regarded as "exceptional characters." Williams saw the early integration as more symbolic than real. Only by being able "to shrug off racial slights and focus on our work" were the first attenders able to survive successfully, he said.[112]

———•———

By the turn of the twenty-first century African American students comprised anywhere from 15 to 67 percent of the student bodies at many Friends schools. The highest proportion was at Detroit Friends School. At Philadelphia's Greene Street School more than half of the student body was African American; at the Friends School of Atlanta, 48 percent of students were of African descent in 2008.[113] African American students were from 20 to 36 percent of students at Friends Academy in Locust Valley, New York; Germantown Friends School; Friends Central School in Wynnewood; and Friends Select. And at Sidwell School, once so slow to integrate, 39 percent of the student body was students of color in 2005–06.[114]

Many people associated with Friends schools have come to realize and promote the beneficial effects of integration. "It is my fervent belief that the surest antidote to racism is our realization that we actually need each other," said Germantown Friends School committee member Ayesha Imani, who is of African descent. "We need each other not merely for cultural enrichment, but to see truth and to build institutions based on the truth that we see."[115] Others stress the complexity of the effort. "For many years, people thought that all you had to do to achieve diversity was have students of color and you were there," said George School's former director of admissions Karen Hallowell, of European descent. "But once you step through that door, you realize how much you don't know. At every turn, you realize you didn't know what you were doing, and you don't know what's ahead of you. Working toward diversity is a long journey that never ends."[116]

Integration at Friends Colleges

Over the course of the twentieth century, Quaker colleges and universities have confronted desegregation challenges similar to those of elementary and secondary schools. At least four Quaker institutions for higher learning had admitted students of African descent in the late nineteenth and early twentieth centuries, but such instances are few; others, if any, have not been documented. The first African American student at Earlham College, Osborn Taylor, arrived in 1880.[117] Taylor, who had been enslaved in Arkansas, was encouraged to attend the Indiana school by the Clarks at Southland Institute. According to a college history, Taylor's "presence on campus attracted little attention or comment."[118] From its earliest years Whittier College, founded in 1887 in Whittier, California, had been open to "minorities"—then thought of as American Indian, Mexican American, Japanese American, and Jewish students. The presence of students of color at that time has been described as "occasional." One African American student was recorded as a member of the class of 1889 and one in the class of 1899.[119] From the time Quakers Walter and Emma Malone created Friends Bible Institute in 1892, the school enrolled some African American students and was, therefore, well ahead of any other Quaker college in regard to students of color.[120] In 1902 Wilmington College, founded in 1871 at Wilmington, Ohio, graduated its first African American student, William B. Yoakley. Former college archivist Ina Kelley noted that Yoakley's race was not mentioned in student newspapers and other records. After his graduation, however, there seemed to be a "lull" in the number of African American admissions until after World War II.[121]

———————•———————

A number of Quaker colleges began to integrate after the First World War. Jamaican Osmond C. Pitter was a member of the class of 1926 at Haverford College, and Bryn Mawr (no longer a Quaker-related college) had at least one student of African descent in that decade.[122] Friends University in Wichita, founded in 1898 under the care of Kansas Yearly Meeting, had "an important African American presence on the campus" from 1920 onward, though one school history notes that racial relationships have "not always been tranquil." African

Americans are first pictured in university publications around 1920, and the Federated Women's Clubs of Wichita were providing scholarships for African Americans at that time.[123]

———•———

African Americans admitted to Quaker colleges found themselves at the edge of the community at the least, and often experienced blatant racism. Among the handful of African Americans who attended Earlham College in its early years, were two African American students whose presence was documented only by their "occasional appearances in campus photographs." The first African American to graduate was Quaker Clarence Cunningham, class of 1924. Warned that at Earlham he would "face such racial prejudice as to make it virtually intolerable," Cunningham, the only one of his race in the men's dorm, was assigned a single room. Excluded from campus organizations, he soon learned he was unwelcome at social activities; he was denied the customary seat for seniors at the head of the dining table. A member of the track team, on team trips he stayed in "shabby" facilities and ate in restaurant kitchens. At graduation, unlike his classmates who were to walk in pairs, Cunningham would have walked alone if Earlham President David Edwards, a European American, had not interceded and changed the procession. Despite his treatment, Cunningham later wrote that he was "grateful for the excellence of the academic background" he acquired at the college, and he remained a Friend for the rest of his life.[124]

The new administration of David Edwards at Earlham College and the contributions of Clarence Pickett initiated a "slow change" toward integration. Between 1926 and 1929 African American speakers were invited to the campus. Pickett hosted discussion groups on race relations on Sunday evenings and, in 1929, a group visited students at the Wilberforce University, a historically black university opened by the Methodist Episcopal school in Xenia, Ohio, in 1856 and named after William Wilberforce, the British abolitionist. But Edwards and Pickett left, and William Dennis, the new president, was "not one to encourage anything that smacked of radicalism." When it came to race, he preferred only a "middle of the road" policy. Finding some faculty "a little extreme in [their] preaching racial equality," Dennis limited the number of African American students to be admitted and, while he said there would be no segregation, he also made it clear that "anything that even hinted of inter-racial dating was unacceptable." African American speakers could still be invited, but they would not be allowed to speak about race relations. And Dennis cancelled the eagerly awaited return visit of Wilberforce students that Earlham students had met with, thanks to Pickett, the spring before. Students looking forward to the visit were "outraged," as was the majority of the faculty committee on religious life.[125]

Pickett wrote to Dennis that he personally "felt that it is a tragedy to break off the fellowship which is so extremely valuable to students and which prepares them for the social contacts of the world in which they are about to enter." Dennis's five-page reply focused on his objection to the group's desire to be able to freely discuss race relations, including interracial marriage. It would "stir up a wholly unnecessary contro-versy," he said. He also claimed that the college was "suffering from misconstruction" about race relations "from the unfortunate marriage" of a Jamaican student of East Indian descent and a European American woman at the college. Pickett pointed out in his reply that faculty members would be present and that if the topic of interracial marriage were "suppressed," then it would be discussed "under cover." The truly educational way, he added, would be to "acquaint students with what is really happening" rather than making it "a forbidden subject."[126]

The Wilberforce question divided the community. The board upheld Dennis, including a member who (in spite of having taught at Southland and served on Richmond's Inter-Racial Council) had declared it was the board's "serious obligation . . . to protect our suscep-tible students from their desire to further great causes by outstanding and unwise sacrifice of themselves." Another member described the people who opposed Dennis's policy as "these extraordinary persons who are intent unpon changing the structure of the whole world."[127]

In 1933 Swarthmore College's refusal to admit African American George Francis Arnold, an outstanding student, athlete and class presi-dent in a Philadelphia high school, provoked severe criticism from the city's African American press. With barely a murmur of disagreement, the Swarthmore Board of Managers had turned Arnold down on the grounds that his admission would "raise too many problems and create too many difficulties."[128] Carl Murphy, president of the Afro-American Company of Baltimore, which monitored the acceptance of African Americans at the nation's colleges, would not let Swarthmore's decision rest unchallenged. In a September 1933 letter Murphy asked European American college president Frank Aydelotte to "confirm or deny" that Arnold had been "turned away because he is colored." The company would "hesitate to print a statement that a Quaker and Christian institute, such as yours purports to be, could have such an unchristian and un-American policy," Murphy wrote—unless it were so. If, however, Arnold was excluded because of his race, the company would list Swarthmore to avoid embarrassment to future African American applicants.[129] In his reply to Murphy, Aydelotte wrote that Swarthmore had "no rule against the admission of Negroes, and I am happy to say that the college authorities have followed my suggestion that we should not make any regulation refusing admission to colored students." Arnold's admission application had instead been turned down for social reasons, Aydelotte maintained:

> There are certain social difficulties which are peculiar to this college and which make the admission of a Negro student more difficult than would be the case in another institution. Swarthmore is a co-educational and residential college. The life here is very intimate, and it would consequently be more difficult to make a Negro student comfortable than would be the case in a large institution or in a small one which was not run on such intimate coeducational lines. And you can readily see that it would not be a solution of the problem to admit Negroes to classes if we were not prepared to make them at home socially.[130]

Aydelotte asked Murphy not to quote the letter "in any way whatever" because doing so "would only serve to defeat the efforts of those who are trying to work out a solution which shall be in harmony with the character and traditions of the College."[131] Several other African American newspapers published critical accounts of Arnold's experience with Swarthmore, and one noted the discrepancy between Quaker expressions of belief and their frequent conferences on "racial goodwill and the brotherhood of man" and its treatment of Arnold:

> For a long time this newspaper has had its suspicions concerning the sincerity of purpose of certain Quakers who profess respect for the rights of Negroes. They want to be known as fair and liberal; they desire the public to believe that they are living up to the high standards

set by their glorious ancestors, but they lack the nobility of heart. These modern Quakers are unwilling to maintain the noble traditions of their forefathers.[132]

In a letter to Helen Bryan, an African American member of the Philadelphia Yearly Meeting Race Relations Committee, Aydelotte expressed a reservation similar to the one he had expressed to Murphy. "I do not want to take the whole matter too seriously," he wrote, "but I do rather regret that these newspapers should stiffen the opposition to the eventual admission of a Negro at Swarthmore by charges of 'hypocracy' [sic], which are not justified by the facts."[133] Arnold was admitted subsequently to Dartmouth College, a male-only institution where Swarthmore managers assumed he would be more comfortable.[134]

———•———

By 1941, the Friends Council on Education survey revealed only sixteen African American students were enrolled in eleven Quaker colleges. More concerted efforts to integrate Quaker campuses began about that time. At Swarthmore, founded by Quakers in 1864, as at several other institutions, it took a new head of the college to bring about integration. A open admissions policy was at the top of the agenda for European American John Nason when he became Swarthmore's president in 1940.[135] With support for integration from a "very substantial majority" of the Board of Managers, in 1943 the college enrolled its first African American males, who were members of a navy training unit.[136] The next year a committee of Swarthmore women of European descent expressed its concern about the lack of African American students to the administration and faculty. Thereupon the board told the school's admissions committee "to eliminate no one on basis of race or religion." Two African American women were admitted the next fall and, according to a report by European American Dean Frances Blanshard, "fitted in excellently;" one woman was elected secretary-treasurer of the Student Government Association. Students at Swarthmore raised $1,345 to assist future African American students.[137]

———•———

Toward the end of the war, European American Quaker Cecil Hinshaw, who had been named president of William Penn College (now

University) in Oskaloosa, Iowa, in 1944, endeavored to transform the school into a "truly Christian college" accepting applicants regardless of race or religion. Hinshaw, who had been a professor of religion at Friends University before coming to William Penn, wanted the college to be a "Holy Experiment"—a model witness to Quaker social concerns, including racial equality. According to Hamm, Hinshaw's commitment to diversity "apparently alienated Iowa Friends." In 1949 he was fired, and many faculty and students left with him.[138] By the 1950s and 1960s a history of Whittier College described the school as interracial and stated that at least one African American was a member of its faculty. Whittier developed an exchange program with Fisk University, and sometimes with Howard University, that continued for several decades. "In general," the history notes, "the sprit was one of openness to all."[139]

Founded in 1891 by "Quaker pioneers," the history of George Fox College's first fifty years reported that students in Newburg, Oregon, school were of "the white race, the brown, the red, the black" and that "all have worked together here for the attainment of the truth which makes men free."[140] "American minorities" in the student body increased from four to thirty-four between 1973 and 1980 but then declined. While activists on other campuses became involved in the Civil Rights movement, the college "seemed rather placid" by comparison.[141] In the late 1970s, the university was charged with "institutional racism" by its first African American teacher, Ernest Cathcart, hired in 1977 as head resident and part-time teacher. Cathcart attributed the problem to the scarcity of minority faculty and administrators. He later turned down a full-time position and left. Not until 1990 were there full-time professors of African descent, although there were two African Americans on the college's board.[142]

Desegregation at Guilford College, founded by North Carolina Friends just after the Civil War, came about in an unusual way. In 1961 European American Guilford president Clyde Milner offered the campus as the site for the planned 1967 conference of the Friends World Committee for Consultation, which by its very nature had been integrated since its founding in 1937; Milner was told all Friends would have to be welcome on campus, including representatives from Africa. FWCC would meet at Guilford only "if way should open."[143] Milner carried that message to the October 1961 meeting of the board, and after an intense discussion the trustees agreed to begin integrating the college immediately.[144] The early stages of integration did generate "racial tensions," a college history notes, and by 1967 only a dozen African Americans had been admitted. The next year African American students at Guilford organized themselves into the Brothers and Sisters in Blackness (later called the African American Cultural Society and now the Blacks Unifying Society), which since 1968 had sponsored events to foster unity among African Americans and increase awareness of African American culture and issues.[145]

A radically different college was established by New York Yearly Meeting in 1965 as an experimental international "liberty" college with admission open to all. Located on Long Island, Friends World College had several prominent Quakers as administrators or faculty members, including the president, Morris Mitchell, a retired Columbia University professor who shaped much of the unusual programming[146] and African American Barrington Dunbar, involved in the Black Studies program in which, he said, students could learn "the truth about black people" in America.[147] After continual struggles with accreditation and building sufficient financial aid, in 1991 the college became a distinct program within Long Island University. Now known as the Global College, it continues to offer "an alternative educational path for students considering the world's pressing issues" and maintains the original concept with study centers around the world.[148]

Interracial Dating

Interracial dating was to be the "most divisive, if not inflammatory, racial issue at Earlham."[149] In 1943, European American Earlham President William Dennis had learned that African American student James Turner was dating women of European descent and had asked one to a dance. The woman was called in to speak with a dean; the president himself met with Turner who, apparently fearing for his scholarship, agreed to stop. Many students and some faculty who learned of the episode were "appalled," and a student delegation from the Peace Fellowship described it as "unmerited suppression." These students and three faculty went to Dennis in protest but were told they were agitators making trouble for and dividing the college community.[150]

In the same year, Earlham received a lot of praise—and a lot of criticism—when it welcomed twenty Japanese-American students. Dennis defended the admissions by citing the Declaration of Independence, the Constitution and the Sermon on the Mount, as well as quoting English political philosopher Edmund Burke who refused to indict "an entire people" for the crimes of some. Dennis's defense was particularly interesting given his reaction both to interracial dating between Japanese American Edward Uyesugi and European American Quaker Ruthanna Farlow and other mixed-race relationships to follow. Of Farlow, Dennis told the board that he would take "quiet but efficient methods, through her people if necessary, to end it." He talked to Ruthanna and to her family, but the two married after graduation.[151]

Dennis recommended that Earlham's trustees adopt an official policy to take action against "repeated interracial dating likely to lead to love and marriage." Students lacked the maturity to undertake such a marriage, college officials believed, and Dennis warned that "without maturity, interracial and intercultural contacts become dangerous or impossible."[152] Earlham officials and alums also worried that Indiana and Western Yearly Meetings would respond by limiting the enrollment of African Americans and that donors to the college would also react negatively. One student, disturbed at the college's dating policy, declared that Earlham had "sold its soul for a million dollars."[153] The only trustee to object to the board's policy was European American Quaker Birk Mendenhall, a professor at Ohio State University. Mendenhall asserted that trustees had given in to a conservative faction of the college rather than attend to those in the wider Quaker community who found Dennis's stance unacceptable. The policy was to "bedevil" the college for a decade.[154]

———•———

The greatest controversy at Earlham was to come in the spring of 1952 when two seniors—European American Robert McAllester and Grace Cunningham, the daughter of Earlham's first African American graduate and the first African American to attend Westtown—announced their engagement. Both Quaker, they were seniors and did not plan to marry until after graduation, but Earlham President Thomas E. Jones saw their plan as an "act of defiance," a situation "created deliberately by the couple with a lack of care for the problem of the college." Having summoned Cunningham and McAllester to his office, Jones warned the couple of the "tragedy and suffering" they would encounter and avowed that they would one day be thankful for the college's intervention.[155] As soon as the issue became known on campus, more than four hundred students, by one student's count, held a meeting for worship.[156] Threatened with expulsion if he stayed, McAllester left in the middle of the second semester with Jones's promise that he could return in June to graduate. The two married in Ithaca (New York) Friends Meeting in 1952.[157] One African American student saw the college's decision as a "new low" for social relations at Earlham; another noted the city's close ties to the South meant the community and some alumni had a conservative influence on Jones. On the other hand the more liberal campus community announced that it would have no difficulty enlisting protesters to march on campus. "A number of Quakers would be right beside them," a faculty member at a different Indiana college wrote.[158]

Outside Richmond, the Earlham administration received "blistering criticism" in an African American newspaper in Indianapolis.[159] As word spread around the country, AFSC, the NAACP, and individual Friends expressed their strenuous objection to the college's action. The Berkeley (California) Friends Meeting, to which Cunningham belonged, chided the college for a "poorly advised and punitive measure against the young people" and termed it "extremely regrettable and at variance with the principles of Friends."[160] Dorothy Biddle James from Philadelphia, who had been part of the integration struggle at Media Friends School in the late 1930s, wrote Jones: "I can't help wondering whether it is because all of us have failed to ring true that a too heavy burden falls on you who are on the front. Perhaps if Friends had had the courage to produce a forthright statement, the dilemma at Earlham might not have come to be." In her letter James, a friend of Jones, asked to know Jones's own position on the issue and raised again "the same old question . . . When does the church-related school or college *lead* and when does it wait for the community to be ready?"[161]

In his reply to James, Jones declared that he found a "tide of understanding and good will" in response to his action and believed "more good than bad will come of it." In any event, he stated, Earlham could not allow "direct-actionist pressure groups to make its regulations."[162] Jones left the college presidency in 1958. In 1961 the college offered "some limited counseling of students who get involved in White-Negro romances, which most often develop among the emotionally troubled."[163] After 1965, however, interracial dating was no longer an issue.[164]

The war years brought a growth in student interest in matters of racial justice and equality at Earlham. Students credited the college for having admitted Japanese-American students and asked that it take "a definite Christian stand on racial equality."[165] Dennis, however, opposed the idea and was critical of some faculty who were "a little extreme in preaching racial equality." He was particularly adamant that providing equal opportunity in education should not bring social equality—"our students . . . were not ready for it." In 1945 the admissions policy set a limit of five to ten African American students. But in 1958, with its new European American Quaker president Landrum Bolling, Earlham began to actively seek out African American students.

———•———

The percentage of African American students and staff at many Friends colleges remained low until the latter part of the century. In 1960 only seven of Swarthmore's 937 students were of African descent, three of them natives of Africa. In 1964, a survey by PYM CRR revealed only one of seven Friends colleges had an African American faculty member; six had African American staff; and all had African American students ranging from just 0.5 to 2.5 percent of the total. Secondary schools had from 0 to 5.5 percent African American students and four had African American faculty. Friends schools outside of the Philadelphia area almost all had a policy favoring desegregation but a "very small number" of students and "only a few" made any outreach effort.[166]

Haverford College, founded by Orthodox Quakers in 1833, had admitted a few African Americans in the late 1950s and 1960s. The college ran a vigorous "post-bac" program between 1966 and 1972 that brought graduates of southern colleges to the campus for a year to enhance their preparation for medical, law and graduate schools.[167] But integration did not begin in earnest at Haverford until 1968; by 1972, 10 percent of the student body was African American or Hispanic.[168] In 1960 four of Haverford's 450 students were of African descent, as were one of its faculty of 60 and 33 of its other staff.[169]

Responding to a 1961 Philadelphia Yearly Meeting survey, Earlham College officials stated that, although records did not indicate race, about ten of the college's 870 students were of African descent and were fully integrated in "all normal college life."[170] Indeed, they reported, the college had been integrated "so long that nobody here has had any experience in the matter of 'promoting' integration."[171]

Opening Friends schools to students and teachers of African descent prompted many questions, few answers, and no easy solutions. The dynamics and the difficulties were not unique to any one school nor, indeed, experienced only by Quaker institutions. It did not take long for educators to understand that enrolling a few students of color simply revealed the importance of having more than a few students and the need for faculty of color and for a curriculum—in fact a school culture—that was not Eurocentric. Few suspected how the "simple" act of welcoming African American students would end up requiring everyone and everything in the school to be examined and re-examined through several lenses.

Through the Students' Eyes

While many students at Westtown School were from families with backgrounds similar to the traditional Westonian that made the transition into the school a bit easier, according to "Malik" and "Julien," both African Americans who graduated from Westtown in the middle '70s, for some "the world of Westtown was totally foreign by social class as well as race."[172] One Westtown African American student at that time spoke of feeling uncertain about "how to behave when he was with his 'own people'" and worried that he was losing his identity as a young African American.[173]

According to Juan Williams, a 1972 graduate of Oakwood School, in the beginning integration was more symbolic than real. Being able "to shrug off racial slights and focus on our work" was what gave the earlier African Americans able a chance of succeeding.[174] Williams, who went on to graduate from Haverford College and is now a journalist heard frequently on National Public Radio, said in an address to the 1999 Friends Council on Education National Gathering that at Oakwood he felt "generally embraced by a community that focused on nurturing young people." But at Haverford he "felt marginalized because I was black and working class in a highly competitive and class-conscious school."[175]

The opportunity to be at a prestigious private school was, of course, valuable by any standard, but it also meant that "the initial pressure to get an education and to adjust to unfamiliar surroundings was incredible," "Malik" and "Julien" said of their own experience at Westtown. It was "culture shock."[176] African American students often felt they had to work harder to prove themselves and their race, especially women who thought they had to do better academically in order to be recognized.[177]

Earlham graduate R. Edd Lee, class of 1950, described how it was to be one of a few African Americans on the campus in 1946. "One simply dug in, found a toe-hold and hung on for dear life." But years later in the *Earlhamite* newsletter he mentioned a long list of things he liked to remember: beating Wilmington and being invited to the "Girl Invite Dance"; acting in *King Henry IV*; and calling professors by their first names.[178] Discussions of race were mostly left to sociology and psychology classes; the tendency was to try to live brotherhood instead of talking about it, he said. "A vast majority of students were generally supportive." It was a real "opportunity to grow and be permitted to dream."[179]

Among the African American students at Earlham during the 1960s was Sybil Jordan, one of the five students enrolled in 1959 at Little Rock Central High School when the school reopened after being closed for a year after the "Little Rock Nine" had been admitted.[180] It was Jordan's participation in an AFSC work camp, and her relationship with Thelma Babbitt, one of the AFSC staff in Little Rock during the crisis, that led her to choose Earlham. She graduated in 1966. Her years at Earlham, were "not all sweetness and light," but she felt supported by friends and teachers and did find that "individual worth" was respected at the college. Jordan attributed her ability to find a place for herself at Earlham to her "experiences with the Quaker philosophy beforehand."[181]

George School graduate Julian Bond, the well-known African American civil rights activist, said that he met people at the school "unlike any I'd met before—or since," many of whom remained his friends. Because he first learned nonviolence at the school in the mid-fifties, the sit-ins of the 1960s "seemed natural" to him. Weekend work camps in Philadelphia taught him about "organized efforts to help others face-to face."[182]

————————•————————

An African American Swarthmore graduate assessed his days as a "pioneer" at the college in the late 1950s in a 2002 article in the *Swarthmore College Bulletin.* Maurice Eldridge, class of 1961 and currently vice president for college and community relations and executive assistant to the president, wrote about how his memories of the campus are quite different than that of alumni of European descent. He had been "surprised and disappointed" about the lack of diversity when he arrived in 1957 from an integrated boarding school community at Windsor Mountain School in Windsor, New Hampshire, which was headed by a Swarthmore alumnus.[183]

Eldridge believes that alumni today who criticize the college's efforts toward diversity need to consider what it was like in the 1950s. The college has "come a long way but not without cost to those who helped to integrate it in the 1960s and 1970s." Eldridge arrived as a freshman "not yet ready" to admit there was "racism afoot." He found himself as so many African Americans did, "having to wear identities imposed by others": an expert on jazz; "primarily a sexual being who could score with enviable ease all the time"; and intellectually inferior. Students of African descent carried a "double load: to study and to teach." It made both "that much harder."[184]

When he returned as an administrator, Eldridge said he was "dismayed" that Swarthmore students of color today "experience racism—and, therefore, perceive it even when it was not there."[185] He does believe the college is "consciously" building on the lessons from the past to "develop and sustain a more diverse community" but says "our struggles against racism as a college and as a nation are far from over."[186]

African American Students Voice Concerns

While the benefits to the schools and students of welcoming African American students were many, as their presence grew larger, their increasing numbers empowered those who had not felt able to voice their concerns before. Students of color often felt school leaders did not hear their concerns or keep their promises in such areas as recruiting students and faculty of color and developing a broader, less-Eurocentric curriculum.

In the late 60s, the Swarthmore Afro-American Students Society (SASS) saw the decline in their numbers and began to question whether the college was really committed to enrolling African Americans and to recruiting more African American administrators, and involving African Americans in the college's decision making process.[187] While responses from college authorities were judged by many to be not far apart, there were inevitable misunderstandings and personality clashes.

In 1968, the Swarthmore Afro-American Students Society (SASS) issued a statement critical of the college's efforts:

> White liberal Swarthmore has been content to push for racial justice and black self-determination in Chester, or in Philadelphia, or in Media, rather than in its own backyard. Black Power is good in Chester, but bad on the campus. The racism of outer white society stops at the edge of college property, because . . . the campus community is one big happy racial family.[188]

In January 1969 SASS asked college president Courtney Smith to issue a clear and public acceptance of their demands. Smith replied that he could not let the college "be governed by demands or moved by threats." In response, SASS took over the college Admissions Office. The occupation "set off a frenzy of meetings" on campus and, although students and faculty generally objected to the sit-in, they supported SASS's goals. A resolution seemed in sight.[189]

In the midst of the confrontation, Smith, a much-beloved figure in the college community, died in his office of a heart attack. Some blamed the attack on the stress of the negotiations with SASS. The African American students, as distraught as any, immediately ended their action. It was, a school historian wrote, "the most traumatic week in the history of the College."[190] With the college's sole African American faculty member playing a key negotiating role between SASS and the faculty, within a short time most of the demands were accepted, including the establishment of a Black Cultural Center.[191]

African American students were admitted to Wilmington College in Ohio in the 1950s and by the 1960s there were enough to provoke controversy about the notable absence of students of African descent in fraternities and sororities. Ten years later, several dozen students of color with a list of demands occupied College Hall during the April 1971 inauguration of European American Cecil Hinshaw, the new president.[192] Hinshaw had been championing the idea of a "multicultural campus" since he took over as president in January. But with only 51 African American students among the student body of 953, students of African descent wanted some evidence of Hinshaw's commitment.[193] The Concerned Black Students (CBS) presented eleven demands, including more scholarships and more African Americans in the staff, faculty, and student body. They also sought more black studies in the curriculum and better campus work possibilities for African Americans. The faculty had already agreed to many of the demands, but the students were not satisfied.[194]

The occupation at the inaugural "was controlled and planned," Reginald Broadnax, class of 1972, one of the leaders, said thirty years later. "These were not crazed individuals, but we were serious about what we wanted." The administration sent law enforcement officers away, the inaugural festivities went on as planned (some attended by the occupying students), and, at the end of the day the two sides came to an agreement and left the building with barely a sign they had been there.[195] "We felt it was something we had to do, to express this to the faculty, the other students, the duty—even to ourselves, our parents, and now our children," Broadnax said in 2001.[196]

The number of African American students at Wilmington rose from 5.2 percent in 1970–71 to 7.1 percent in 2000.[197] The first full-time African American faculty member is thought to be Marie H. Buncombe, an associate professor of English and then full professor from 1966–74. In 2000, there were two professors and three administrators of African descent.[198]

Haverford African American students were also skeptical about the college's real commitment to recruiting students and faculty of color. The issue surfaced during the 1960s and into the 1970s. The dismissal of some minority students for academic reasons became a precipitating event. While the college blamed the academic problems on the students, the students saw the problems as part of the difficulty of being minority at the college. In 1972 the Puerto Rican and African American student groups took action with "a series of well-conceived effective maneuvers"—a silent confrontation, speaking out in the dining hall, and boycotting non-academic activities. They made known their demands, steps that would bring the "institutionalization of diversity" to the school. An agreement reached during an all-night session of students, administrators, and faculty at the president's house included more faculty and administrators of color, a summer program for students entering as freshmen, and a review of the curriculum.[199]

In the early days of integration, schools may have opened their classrooms to African Americans, but their curricula remained Eurocentric. At Penn Charter that "curricular quietude" reinforced the invisibility of African Americans.[200] At Westtown, the students "rarely received instruction about anything literary, historical, or spiritual that was not European in origin," wrote "Julien," a Westtown alumnus who later returned to the school as an administrator.[201] As the numbers of African American students grew, so did their requests for a curriculum that recognized their culture, contributions, and issues.

At Haverford College, "increasing diversity in the curriculum proved the most intractable." Although at some colleges students campaigned for a department of Black and/or Hispanic Studies, Haverford students of color wanted to be recognized through courses about African Americans and Hispanics in the United States. Faculty who were not accustomed to being told what they should be teaching raised a number of objections from the impossibility of finding appropriate material, and a fear of "watering down" the course to having to leave out other material. To the objections of some, the college asked each department to submit its plan to a committee so it could be monitored.[202]

In 1976 there was "another confrontation," which resulted in the creation of a position for a Director of Minority Affairs whose job would be devoted to making certain that the college was living up to its commitment to diversity. The students wanted to focus on their studies and activities, not on trying to make the college fulfill its promises to hire more African American faculty and recruit more students.[203]

The Challenge of Recruiting Faculty

In 1945, AFSC established a visiting lecturer program that brought both African American professors to colleges with virtually all European American students and professors of European descent to predominantly

African American colleges. The idea was not to recruit faculty but, as James Fleming, the first African American to hold an executive position in the organization who was heading the lecture program said, to demonstrate that "learning and culture recognize no color lines." For almost seven years African American professors from historically black colleges visited at least twenty-five colleges and a number of public and private secondary schools.[204]

In 1945, sociologist Ira DeA. Reid from Atlanta University went to Haverford as a visitor. His sociology lectures were so well-received that, in an unusual expression of editorial opinion on such a matter, the college newspaper editors offered "An Humble Recommendation" for his appointment:

> Rarely does the [Haverford] News attempt to interfere in a decision such as faculty appointment. But then, rarely do the students of Haverford express themselves so emphatically and unanimously. . . . [One of his addresses prompted] probably the loudest and longest applause accorded to any lecturer here in several years. He is the kind of man we want on our faculty.[205]

Reid had worked for the National Urban League and edited their magazine, served as consultant to many public agencies and commissions, and was a highly respected scholar with a long list of publications. He was hired in 1948 and remained on the sociology faculty until 1966.[206] He began to volunteer for Quaker organizations and in 1950 became a member of Haverford Friends Meeting.[207]

It was challenging enough to recruit African American students; finding faculty was even more difficult. The fact that some candidates of color described their interviews at Haverford as "sordid, paternalistic, and patronizing" would surely have made them less eager to teach there.[208] In 1966 Earlham hired the first African American faculty member, Friend William Cousins, and added African and African American history, literature, and culture to the curriculum. By 1982 the college had eight administrators and thirteen teachers who were African American or Hispanic.[209]

———•———

Since 1985 the George School has required that at least one candidate of color be among finalists for every position at school.[210] Even when potential teachers are found, they realize that salaries at Friends schools are low, especially compared to other private schools, and that chances for advancement may be greater in larger public school systems.[211] In 1974 New England Yearly Meeting offered a small stipend to help Friends schools in New England find teachers of African descent.[212] At Swarthmore, the Minority Scholars in Residence Program, instituted by President David Fraser in the 1980s, was important in attracting minority faculty.[213]

The demands and expectations on the few teachers of color (or even the only one) could be draining or exasperating. "I was not what they were used to," said Swarthmore's first African American professor, Kathryn Morgan. "I was not a white person in black skin. I was a black woman, OK? And they hired me! They wanted me to come!" Morgan had been hired in 1970 to teach one course and returned shortly with a three-year appointment to teach oral history, folklore, and folklife. Morgan said she went to Swarthmore "because I thought the students here needed me—not just the black students. . . . I knew they needed an African American on the faculty."[214] From the first, however, she was discomfited by the image European Americans had, or wished to have, of her. "This is me, and I am going to be like I am," Morgan stated in 1970. "If you want black people who look like white people, who act like white people, get a white person! . . . I didn't not come here to be 'diverse' . . . I'm a human being with a unique body of knowledge to pass on." When Morgan was denied tenure in 1976, professors and students of European and African descent protested. She was granted tenure after a successful legal suit.[215]

Reflections on Integration

European American Nancy Starmer, head of George School since 2000, learned that "like the other desegregation efforts of the time, our decision [to integrate] was fueled by good intentions but [also] by a narrow set of assumptions."[216] According to European American Patricia Macpherson, former dean and president of Bryn Mawr and now at Westtown, whether in secondary school or college, faculty and administrators did not expect that integration would be a problem. No thought was given to the fact there might have to be changes or any "institutional accommodation."

This "business as usual" attitude made it very painful for students who entered a "situation that was really foreign and a set of expectations that often were encoded in such a way that people didn't really understand each other." Somehow they were supposed to be the ones who had to make it work.[217]

Often insight about the difficulties came only when African American students began to speak up, much to the surprise of others in the school community. The issue came to "City Friends" in 1990, when three male African American seniors wrote of their anger about being part of an "experiment" in the school newspaper. They said their presence made the people of European descent feel good, but they felt they were being "shown off" as a "project" and an "experiment that worked." They resented seeing the school get the credit with no recognition of the contribution of the students and their families and others who supported them. The school's attitude, the young men said, was that they "should feel so lucky we even let you come here."[218]

When the number of African American students reached a critical mass at Haverford College, the rest of the community discovered that integration had not been working as smoothly as they had imagined. College officials tended to respond to any dissatisfaction expressed by smiling and saying, "Tell us what you want. We'll try to provide it." While officials thought they were being cooperative and pleasant, what the students heard was that the responsibility was all theirs to explain themselves and their needs.[219] The students believed that their admission was "a matter of Quaker charity and goodwill." Most of the forty minority students admitted in 1969 did not stay long, feeling let down by the college.[220]

"The largest [of the] issues to be addressed," according to Macpherson and Goldman, were the effects racial assumptions had on the "outsiders" who, unnoticed by European Americans, were trying to operate in a world of "white norms" that can punish those who don't understand the unwritten "rules." Successful achievers and assimilators are "anointed," while those who remain outsiders leave, having struggled to articulate their difficulties and most often suffering in silence. It was a while before schools realized why some promising students were leaving—or before they felt responsible for it.[221]

Barrington Dunbar, circa 1970.
New York Yearly Meeting

George Sawyer, circa 1970.
Indiana Yearly Meeting

Mahala Ashley Dickerson, mid-1970s.
Alaska Friends Conference

Toward Integration in the Society of Friends

> Friends like to think of themselves as pioneers in peaceful relationships,
> but do we pioneer here, or do we wait for the pioneering to be done
> by other groups? Are Friends in reasonable agreement as to the impli-
> cations of our testimony on human worth and dignity?
>
> — *AFSC Community Relations Committee, 1954*

QUAKER ACTIVISTS AND INSTITUTIONS in the twentieth century focused
much of their energy on helping other Friends understand racial
issues in the belief that greater knowledge would compel more of them
to work toward the relationships their faith required of them. As their
counterparts had done in the 1700 and 1800s, they raised the issue of
the relationship between individual leadings and the corporate witness
of Friends meetings. Those who felt the need to act wondered whether
the desire of some Friends to listen to the Spirit was a way, conscious or
not, to avoid confronting their own negative feelings about racial issues,
Dunbar noted at a 1986 meeting of the National Conference of
Friends on Race Relations (NCFRR) that the attitude of monthly and
yearly meetings was often, "Let the Race Relations Committee do it."[1]
Meetings that left care for racial justice up to a committee, he argued,
did not understand the role of a monthly meeting as a corporate entity
empowering the individual leadings of its members with respect to creating relationships with African Americans, out of and within the
Religious Society of Friends.

As European American Quaker pastor Errol Elliott asserted, "In the
minds of some Friends there is an urgency that requires immediate and
'direct action,' the quick breakthrough. As they view it, the problem will
not wait! ... Other Friends fear what appears to them to be precipitate
action, having the appearance but not the reality of a solution." Still, he
argued, "Rationalizing and then doing nothing is perhaps the greater

danger for most Friends." The gradualist's patient waiting for an "'unfolding' of what 'ought to be'" could lead to the "danger of settling for things as they are."[2]

As racial tensions began to build after the Second World War, "quickening" Quaker consciences about the issues of racism proved one of the most difficult tasks activists took upon themselves. By that time activists of European descent were joined by a number of African American Quakers in calling out to Friends to commit to ending racism. But the weak Quaker response was discouraging. At one planning meeting for NCFRR in 1969, African American Friends Barrington Dunbar and George Sawyer felt like voices "crying in a white wilderness."[3]

In the view of some activists, efforts to educate other Quakers took vital time away from the real task at hand. "The need for inward growth and renewal of spiritual insight became painfully apparent," the Meeting for Social Concerns of the Philadelphia Yearly Meeting stated after one study in 1969. "With some surprise we found that a sizable proportion of our initial efforts had to be directed inward, rather than directed outward towards the crying needs of the dispossessed."[4]

The general unwillingness of corporate Quaker bodies to bear witness against racism also triggered "awkward questions as to Friends' practices." AFSC's Community Relations Committee pinpointed this issue in a 1954 memo from a discussion on "furthering the testimony of Friends on the equality of all men in the sight of God and one another":[5]

> Where Quaker employers have not hired on a basis of merit, where Quaker schools refuse admission to Negro students, where Friends Meetings fail to welcome attenders of all races, or individual Friends accept too easily the segregated housing patterns of their community, other citizens are quick to notice a seeming departure from Quaker principles.
>
> Friends like to think of themselves as pioneers in peaceful relationships, but do we pioneer here, or do we wait for the pioneering to be done by other groups? Are Friends in reasonable agreement as to the implications of our testimony on human worth and dignity?[6]

In 1955 a consultant from Russell Sage College commissioned to examine AFSC's work confirmed this analysis: "Discriminatory behavior on the part of some Friends' institutions and individuals has served as a continued source of acute embarrassment to the Community

Relations Program. . . . In the House of Friends, outraged community members [had asked], 'How can the Friends dare have a race relations program, when they practice such flagrant discrimination?'"7 Historian Carter Woodson's earlier critique of the Religious Society of Friends was also severe. Comparing Quakers to Moravians in 1943, he asserted, "The Quakers had the same difficulty in translating their profession into action, although they were decidedly the best friends of the Negro in the ante-bellum times. Quakers in certain parts reluctantly admitted Negroes as members, and today Quakers, as a rule, hate Negroes just as others of their race do."8

Ben Richmond, the European American former editor of *Quaker Life*, noted that while the majority of Friends are of African descent, that is the case only because most live in East Africa. "Friends in the U.S.A. often pride ourselves on our diversity," he observed. "The fact is Friends Meetings, whether in Kenya or the U.S., are almost completely homogeneous in terms of race, social class, and education."9 When it came to the question of membership, class-based attitudes gave credence to limiting notions about African Americans. European American Quaker Johan Maurer, former general secretary of FUM, has argued that "long-standing unexamined assumptions" have led many Friends to conclude that people of African descent "would be happier somewhere else."10 Frank Cummings, an Atlanta Friend of European descent, admitted that he once shared this view. European American Friends had "long rationalized that a silent form of worship was not culturally congenial to African Americans." But he came to recognize that this view was fundamentally "racist":

> The reason lies in the barrier the Meeting presents as a white institution. There are a few churches and other small religious groups that have become inclusive to the point of not being white institutions. They have done so primarily by intentionally seeking to do so. It is definitely a matter of intentionality. I do not expect the Meeting to change without openly and intentionally seeking change both within us as individuals and collectively as a Meeting.11

Virginia Friend David Scull was in fundamental accord with Cummings's assessment. "In order to get to the point where race does not matter in anything we do," he stated, "we must first consciously try to counteract its effects in everything we do."12

In 1970 Barbara Norcross, a European American member of Philadelphia Yearly Meeting, who was on the staff of the Friends Suburban Project, posited that Quakers tend to be of one of five types in their responses to social problems such as racism. The "predominant" type was people committed to effecting social change through existing channels and by traditional Quaker methods. A second type declared such methods inadequate and committed themselves to new approaches. A third accepted the existing social structure. And, as had been the case previously, two other types believed Quaker tenets effectively precluded work on social justice: they viewed social problems as alien to the religious life or simply irrelevant, and, in either case, thought that discussion and action on them should not invade Friends meetinghouses.[13]

As PYM's Social Concerns Committee stated in one 1967 minute, "One of the principal sources of tension has been reconciling the urgency of the crisis with the deliberateness of Friends' careful searching for the Light."[14] Reminiscent of earlier Friends, those who counseled that the Quaker way was to follow God's leadings often believed that activists, in their impatience for change, neglected the foundation of Quaker action. European American Beckey Phipps of Fresh Pond Meeting in Cambridge, Massachusetts, discerned a "constant pull between people/Friends who want to 'do' and those who want to 'pray'" and insisted that "our doing must first be grounded in our praying, in our listening for the will of God before we begin to act as God's agents (co-creators) in the world."[15] In Quakerism, prayer is considered to be a form of action, of "doing."

According to European American Friend Thomas Jeavons, former general secretary of PYM, the concern among those who believe that Quakers can reach God only through prayer has been that the Religious Society of Friends is no longer a true "religious body" but has instead become "essentially a collection of political liberals who occasionally sit quietly together."[16] During the PYM debates over BEDC's request, European American Friend Rob Tucker of Philadelphia declared himself "sick up to my ears of the breast-beating, guilt-motivated activism of so many Friends" but no less disgusted by "the failure of so many Friends to understand wherein they are indeed guilty. How many Friends live in Wallingford and pay local taxes to cops who routinely chase strange black people out of the township at sunset, and would they really want this changed?" Tucker wrote to MSC in 1970, adding that both groups in the yearly meeting—"the guilt-motivated and the self-satisfied"—failed to reflect true Christianity. The motivation of the Christian social activist, Tucker argued, can only be love, and to act out of guilt was no better than taking no action.[17]

The tension between individual and corporate witness also constrained Quaker efforts toward social justice.[18] When some among New Garden, North Carolina, Friends felt a concern to proceed as they felt moved in regard to school desegregation, they were "liberated" by their meeting. They pointed out, however, that they had not sought permission to "do their own thing"; rather, they had wanted the meeting to lift up their witness.[19] But some Friends accused those active in the movement of working according to their own will, not out of the sense of a corporate spiritual leading—in Quaker parlance, they were "outrunning their guide." This criticism revealed profound conflict within Quakerism about the place of corporate discernment in pursuing a leading. PYM's Meeting for Social Concerns faced this challenge as it tried to determine how to approach Friends meetings about the request of the Black Economic Development Conference for reparations with hopes of moving them to "action." If the Meeting for Social Concerns was too far ahead of the meeting, the "radical element" could well be ineffective in moving other Friends.[20] They asked of themselves, "How can we handle problems which arise when committee staff and committee members see conditions of which most Friends are not aware and get so far ahead of or so far away from the general membership as to cause polarization and interfere not only with fund-raising, but also with the progress of the yearly meeting in other areas requiring deep unity?"[21] On the other hand, the "lack of commitment on the part of too many Friends" was the source of "anguish" to the yearly meeting's staff.[22] While many activist Friends felt essentially stranded by their meetings, others simply accepted the fact and remained faithful to their personal witness. "As an individual, I should follow the Divine guidance which comes to me," European American Quaker Samuel Levering, then clerk of the Board of Christian Social Concerns of FUM, wrote. "But should I insist that my Meeting, as such, participate, when many members have serious stops about doing so? I do not think so."[23]

PYM's Meeting for Social Concerns ultimately concluded that the only way to realize broad-based support within Quakerism for the work of social justice was "to increase our readiness and ability to hear and to try to understand widely divergent points of view."[24] While maintaining a deep commitment to social action, the 1969 Philadelphia Yearly Meeting also acknowledged the need to be open to members who felt differently:

> The theme that guides us [is] that social involvement is for Friends an inseparable part of our religious life, an extension of worship which transcends Meeting House walls. To walk in the Light is to be sensitive to the miseries and frustrations of mankind, and to feel these is to be called to act. . . . At the same time we can admit varying approaches; we can lovingly encourage each other to find the work and sacrifice for which each is ready.[25]

David Scull expressed a similar sentiment. "Let us make the same effort to enter into the skins of our fellow-members that we would like them to make with respect to those under the burden of discrimination," he stated. "Let us recognize that the most important aspect of any of this work is not where we or they are today, but in what direction we are moving and how fast."[26]

Integration in Quaker Institutions

Discrimination has existed in every phase of Quakers' lives—in Friends schools, meetings, meeting committees, summer camps for children, businesses and social lives, and in support of certain institutions. In 1956 Clarence Yarrow pointed out in *Friends Journal* that "only a few Friends" bought homes in the racially integrated suburban developments in the Philadelphia area that some Friends had helped to create in the 1950s; most remained in their segregated communities without any protest "against the rigid barriers which exclude black people from their midst."[27]

Richard Taylor noted in 1970 that Friends belonged to social clubs and other organizations that refused to admit African Americans and visited resorts in the Poconos, including one run principally by Quakers, which discriminated against African Americans and Jews.[28] In a letter to *Friends Intelligencer* more than twenty-five years earlier,

Victor Paschkis objected to Friends General Conference's having its annual gathering in Cape May, New Jersey, where it has met since 1932. Although townspeople were "fairly liberal toward colored Friends or attenders visiting there," at the annual meeting, the town was "entirely 'southern'" in its treatment of African Americans who actually there. "I do not feel at ease that the FGC patronizes a community with this pattern," Paschkis wrote.[29] Racial injustice in Cape May had prompted concern at FGC's 1932 conference after two African American attendees at the event were denied access to social and recreational activities in the resort town; in response, Young Friends asked FGC's Central Committee to hold the meeting elsewhere. According to European American Sara Houghton's account of the incident, the central committee agreed that discrimination in the New Jersey resort was a serious concern, but it chose nonetheless to continue to hold its meeting there. Houghton stated that her interest in attending the annual event "waned" after that committee's decision.[30]

Quaker-run organizations also showed discriminatory tendencies. Concern about this emerged during the Second World War. From at least the 1950s, Philadelphia Yearly Meeting's Race Relations Committee regularly asked Quaker businesses, hotels, camps, hospitals, and retirement homes to report the number of African Americans among staff and clients. In one survey conducted in 1963, none of the twelve Philadelphia-area Quaker boarding homes for the elderly then had or had ever had an African American resident. No monthly meeting knew of a facility that did. Administrators explained that these homes were for Quakers only, which clearly indicated their perception that all Quakers were of European descent and ignorance of the fact that most did accept non-Quakers. *A Directory of Retirement Homes* issued by Delaware, Montgomery, and Philadelphia Counties in 1955 and 1963 included descriptions of two Quaker facilities (out of five in 1955) specifying admission "for whites only," as did at least a dozen of the other seventy listings that year. By 1963 four of them, including one of the Friends homes, had removed that restriction, and two, a Mennonite home and a Catholic home, specifically stated they were open to all, regardless of race or religion.[31] In 1966 the news that the Friends Home for Children in Secane, Pennsylvania, known as "Friendly Acres," was segregated prompted protests among Friends. The

Philadelphia Community Relations Committee told the home's administrators that they did not want the word "Friend" to be associated with the institution, but the home's administrators warned the committee not to intrude into its affairs.

African American Membership in Friends Meetings

In general, Friends Meetings were slower to integrate than were schools, and bias against African American membership continued for decades. The March 1943 business meeting of a new group of Friends in Atlanta "almost fell apart" over the question of whether African Americans should be allowed, even encouraged, to participate in the meeting. The meeting also was "catapulted into a crisis" four years later when Max Bond, a native of the West Indies and a professor at what is now Clark Atlanta University, wrote to Friends World Committee for Consultation about "the growing alienation of black students there" expressing the hope that Quakers might be able to offer some service. The committee forwarded Bond's letter to Friends in Atlanta, who again confronted the absence of African Americans in their meeting. At a "crowded and anxious meeting" in the space rented by Atlanta Friends at Agnes Scott College, where African Americans would not be welcome, they decided to find a meeting place where they would be. The meeting was refused by "many churches" and ultimately took space at the city's YMCA, where it stayed for about a decade. While many visitors from Atlanta's African American colleges visited the meeting, however, there is no evidence as to whether any joined.[32]

After the Second World War, several Friends organizations demonstrated deeper concern about segregation in meetings. In 1949 Philadelphia Yearly Meeting issued a statement that "every Monthly Meeting should be ready to admit and welcome Negroes into membership and full fellowship" and in 1955, based on that declaration, the Committee on Race Relations surveyed ninety-two monthly meetings to determine how well they were approaching that goal.[33] Of the 85 meetings that responded, nearly 73 percent reported "nonwhites" (defined as "Negroes or Orientals") living in the areas of their meetings, but none reported a nonwhite member. Only 20 of those 85 reported any nonwhite attenders; another 29 reported an occasional nonwhite visitor. Yet of the 33 reporting no nonwhite attenders at meetings, 23 stated that they would welcome people of color.[34] The difficulty lay both in the traditional Quaker tendency not to proselytize and in lack of knowledge. As the clerk of Bristol (Pennsylvania) Monthly Meeting stated in 1970, "Those who wish to speak against racial prejudice simply do not know how."[35]

In 1953, European American Quaker activist Marian Fuson encountered an example of how pervasive discrimination in Friends meetings was. When she arrived at Ashboro Street Friends Church in Greensboro, North Carolina, with two Guilford College students of African descent—one African American, one Ugandan—an usher told the students that he had been "advised not to allow colored people in." When the pastor and Friends who had invited the Fusons to the "Outreach Sunday" service there visited the couple later to explain, Fuson noted, they were "not seeking forgiveness, but saying it was the 'custom of the region.' It took the meeting nine years to face that condition." Fuson admitted that the incident took place in the South, but, she added, "We know there are many 'Souths' all over this country where Quakers are."[36]

A 1961 FWCC survey of seven hundred monthly meetings found that a majority of those who responded—only 190 by the time the results were compiled—felt that ending racial discrimination was "of primary importance," and that some meetings and members were "working creatively to know Negroes as friends and to draw them into their meetings." Most meetings reported doing "little or nothing" corporately to end discrimination in employment, education, housing, and politics, and a majority "did not favor joining any organization which opposed segregation."[37] Many meetings stated that no African Americans lived in their areas, and "a LARGE GROUP [sic]" reported "no local problem."[38] Forty-one percent of respondents stated that Friends should refuse both personally and corporately to participate in any pattern of racial discrimination and segregation; others, however, believed it would be "impossible" to do so, the survey found.

"If Quakers are to engage in work for racial justice," wrote Richard Taylor, they must rid themselves of "a profound and crippling hypocrisy" in their own meetings as well as in businesses, clubs, and other institutions.[39] The fact that such a small percentage of surveyed meetings responded, Taylor noted, demonstrated "less concern for race relations than one would expect from the Society of Friends." A few respondents reported that their meetings "did not dare discuss these problems because differences of viewpoint were so deep and strongly felt."[40] Taylor concluded, "It seems more meetings *rate* race as a primary concern than treat it as such. Many meetings reveal lack of awareness of the problem which is a universal one, not limited to proximity of changing neighborhoods."[41] As the FWCC had noted a quarter of a century earlier, "The commission is humbled by the knowledge that, while Friends' historical testimony on race is fairly well known, no one seems to expect individual members to live up to it."[42]

In 1963, the chair of the NCFRR, Victor Paschkis, came to a similar conclusion after having visited several dozen meetings in New England, upstate New York, and the Midwest. "In almost all Meetings which I visited," he wrote, "there is a lack of complete unity on the 'race issue'; Friends who are aware have thus the double challenge to work both on the issue and with patience and love on the slow members of their meetings."[43] Later surveys replicated these dispiriting findings. After Philadelphia Yearly Meeting's 30 March 1964 "Call to Action" directed meetings to achieve thorough integration in all aspects of their activity,[44] the yearly meeting's Race Relations Committee survey of seventy-three meetings conducted the next year found that less than half of the sixty-seven responding meetings had done anything to make known publicly that their membership was open to all. One-third had some way of worshiping or having fellowship with African Americans, but "in the main," the committee concluded, "our movement appears slow in relation to the problem and to the strides in some other religious groups." The committee noted that one meeting's response to the survey could serve to sum up its findings: "We do not feel that we have done all that we can do. In this area the problems are not pressing right on us from next door and we have probably failed to reach out and help as we might have done in other areas where help was needed."[45]

A 1969 query to Baltimore-area monthly meetings also yielded disappointing results. In that year the yearly meeting's Social Order Committee attempted to survey how "vigorously" meetings were pursuing equal opportunity, however, the survey or questionnaire generated only four responses from about fifty monthly meetings. The committee puzzled over whether the poor response reflected a "lack of significant involvement with the social aspects of Friends' testimony" or the fact that only the more urban meetings concerned themselves with "societal problems." Holding out the hope that the response did not necessarily indicate a lack of "meaningful activity," the committee nonetheless warned that if Friends were unwilling to "face up to the moral and intellectual confrontation, then the only alternative will be violent confrontation."[46]

In a 1970 survey of 48 pastors, 22 of their wives, and 10 teachers and administrators, European American Quaker Richard Foster encountered somewhat similar ideas. While almost all respondents stated the belief that African Americans were not inferior but equal to European Americans, more than half stated that African Americans should "earn their right to equal treatment"; more than half also held the view that "blacks are pushing too hard." Foster concluded, "Many were willing to accept social equality as long as it is on their own terms" and as long as it is accompanied by "a certain life style." Such notions strongly suggested, as one Quaker activist had observed a decade earlier, that "too often the Meeting simply reflected feelings in the community rather than spiritual insight of its own Quaker heritage."[47] Foster's overall assessment was blunt: "These statistics underscore one fact very clearly: as a force for social change the Society of Friends has become impotent."[48]

Concern about evidences of discrimination extended to Quaker committees as well as to the AFSC, the group in the forefront of racial justice work among Friends. In 1970 PYM's Ad Hoc Committee on the Urban Crisis recognized that it had included no African Americans as it studied the BEDC request. The meeting noted that African American Friends "have much to offer to the yearly meeting because of their blackness" and should be involved in all levels of the meeting organization; without their "active counsel and judgment, the yearly meeting would be seriously handicapped."[49] In 1975 African American Tony Henry, then on the staff of the AFSC's Third World Coalition, declared it "striking" that so few people not of European descent served on its various boards, even in cities with large minority populations. Overcoming racism was a struggle in any group within a racist society, Henry allowed, but because racism was so pervasive, the effort to eradicate it could not be "informal, unorganized and haphazard."[50] Others experienced "a lot of discomfort" at how "white" and middle class AFSC was, especially for an organization dedicated to working with people who were disadvantaged by color.51 At about that time Muhammad and Mary Kenyatta had noted similar practices within the AFSC. In a 1974 interview, Mary Kenyatta stated that she had seen little "movement towards building better racial relations" in AFSC, while Muhammad Kenyatta criticized the AFSC's unwillingness to hire people of African descent in its international programs.52

Nevertheless, lack of widespread progress should not obscure the sincerity and effectiveness of efforts on the part of some Friends and Quaker organizations. In 1976 Iowa European American Quaker pastors Steve and Marlene Pedigo started the Chicago Fellowship of Friends in Cabrini-Green, one of Chicago's most troubled public housing projects. Initially distrusted by both African and European Americans, the Pedigos set about getting to know people in the predominantly African American area. Steve Pedigo started pick-up basketball games with neighborhood youth, while Marlene Pedigo introduced herself to the girls who came to watch. Eventually eight or nine boys and several girls began meeting for Bible study at the Pedigos' house. The talk soon turned to Quakers and Quakerism. The group began to worship together, and with support from others, including Friends from many meetings, the Pedigos started a day care program, summer camp, and after-school program. In 1984, with very little money and a lot of volunteer help, the group acquired and renovated a school building where they started a Friends meeting.53

Some of the many benefits of the Fellowship extended to volunteers from the Cabrini Green community or to members of many meetings around the country who went to help for a short time with Bible study or after-school programs. "Going to Cabrini was liberating both culturally and religiously," said Randy Urban, a European American student at the University of Illinois. Urban had visited out of curiosity about people who would "stick their neck out" like the Pedigos; he eventually joined the meeting. Parents of some of the youth who spent time at the Fellowship often came to see what the Pedigos were up to and became interested themselves. Sharon Purifoy Williams, one of those parents, recalls that, "For the first time in my adult life I felt like I was in the place that I needed to be. I was being spiritually fed, not just preached to."54

For a time, the Fellowship gave Chicago Friends who had moved from "changing neighborhoods" to new meetinghouses in the suburbs an opportunity to feel connected to the city they had been escaping, according to David Finke of 57th Street Meeting. "It's true that States of Society reports occasionally show a worry about the comfort and privilege" that many Friends enjoy; the Fellowship of Friends was a way to "repent of if not reverse that pattern," Finke said. However, it was an opportunity short-lived.[55] At first designated as a mission of Friends United Meeting, Chicago Fellowship of Friends was later taken under the care of Western Yearly Meeting. The city's redevelopment of Cabrini-Green displaced most of the low-income residents of the area, and in 2005 the meeting was laid down and the building sold.[56]

The inner-city Chicago Fellowship was rare among Friends meetings. Quaker meetings in other areas, "even with the best of intentions," as Boston Friends said, tended to move from "changing neighborhoods" as African Americans moved in. In the Roxbury section of Boston, Friends had run a summer playground and Bible school at their meetinghouse on Townsend Street, but found that in general the parents of children who participated were not interested in Friends. They had held an evening meeting for worship for adults, but it failed to attract visitors, thus leaving Friends to conclude that "the type of person who can reasonably be expected to join Friends does not now reside in the immediate neighborhood." The meeting came to feel a "growing conviction" that it would be "a help, rather than a hindrance, to the type of work we have been able to do to transfer its meetinghouse to a local organization. In spite of all efforts to remove any suspicion of patronage, we are still looked upon as outsiders," Boston Friends noted, adding "there is every reason to believe that a colored church would be as well or better done by others." The building was sold to an African American Congregationalist church, and the Friends Meeting moved to Cambridge.[57]

Pendle Hill, which since its founding had welcomed residents from all over the world, made a particular effort to reach out to African Americans in the mid-1900s. Annual reports of the 1950s include descriptions of Executive Director Dan Wilson's recruiting trips to various African American colleges, such as Spellman and Paine. Paine's dean, African American Richard Stenhouse, a former Pendle Hill teacher (although not a Quaker), could offer Wilson little encouragement. In his view, "given the revolution against whites going on in Negro society," Pendle Hill's chances of attracting African American students were not good, Stenhouse told Wilson.[58]

In 1984, acting out of concern for dwindling membership and against the traditional reticence of unprogrammed Quakers to proselytize, Philadelphia Yearly Meeting initiated a five-year campaign for members. The *New York Times*, observing that the member drive was "rare," stated that it was the meeting's first such campaign in more than three hundred years. Focusing especially on people of non-European descent, the drive was to be "low key," said European American yearly meeting general secretary Samuel Caldwell. "We do not want to go out thumping our chests or that kind of thing."[59]

Atlanta Meeting also worked concertedly toward inclusion. In the mid-1980s a "very lengthy discussion" arose from what many perceived as the meeting's unfriendly response to African American visitors.[60] By 1999 the meeting founded ORIIARH—"Our Role as Individuals in America's Racial History"—to move the meeting "toward becoming a safer and more welcoming spiritual home for all regardless of color and ethnicity." In a 2000 minute, the meeting asked all its committees and groups to reflect upon and review their own activities and materials in light of the commitment to becoming a "fully diverse institution of true human equality."[61]

As many activist Friends throughout the twentieth century argued, true racial integration within Quakerism had to be the foundation of engagement in the society at large. "In the measure that we become unsegregated from within," Errol Elliott stated before Indiana Yearly Meeting in 1968, "we shall desegregate outwardly."[62] And creating an "institution of true human equality" required a revolution in attitude for many Friends. As he urged AFSC to create a new commission on racial justice in 1940, Thomas E. Jones, then president of Fisk University, advised Friends to leave behind the notion that they were trustees from a "strong race for a weak one" and the tendency to regard African Americans as "wards."[63] Johan Maurer later argued that Friends too often seem to have regarded the world "as a stage upon which we practice philanthropy."[64] Alison Oldham pointed out that what the situation called for most urgently was not benevolence. Quakers, she said, "need to understand why justice may appear far more necessary to oppressed people than kindness or generosity. If I can give you a favor, no matter how lovingly and how sincerely, I can also take it away. The power remains mine."[65] As African American Friend Vera Green noted in 1973, "Sometimes more antagonism is built up by well meaning naive people 'going forth to do good.'"[66]

Views of African American Friends

In its call for greater integration at all levels of the Religious Society of Friends in 1970, PYM's Meeting for Social Concerns urged not only a greater and more sincere effort among European Americans to integrate but also declared it "incumbent upon Black Friends to take the responsibility to speak out in order to interpret to white Friends their feelings and insights as Black people."[67] Several surveys attempted to flesh out those views. In 1973, Friends General Conference asked Vera Green, an African American anthropologist and member of 57th Street Friends Meeting in Chicago, to study "the problems of, and possible approaches for, attracting more Black members."[68] Green interviewed 14 people, 11 of them were African American; 6 of whom were Quaker. Three of the 14 were European American Quakers. The 5 non-Friends did not belong to other churches. All but 2 of the African Americans were or had been students and/or teachers at Quaker schools or colleges. Green sought to determine the "general Black reaction" to Quakerism and why African Americans might or might not wish to "attach themselves to the Society."[69]

Most of the African Americans Green interviewed said they believed that people of color, on the whole, knew "little" about Friends or Quakerism. Those aware of the religion were apt to occupy the same socioeconomic and educational bracket as Friends of European descent and accordingly were likely to feel comfortable in Quaker culture. The African Americans told Green that Quakerism was appealing because of its lack of ceremony, the casual dress of its members, its "understanding towards humanity" and its characteristic patience—though some saw patience as a means by which to remove and excuse oneself from dealing with the racial problems of the time.[70] However, the African American respondents viewed nonviolence as ineffective. Through the turmoil of the 1960s and 1970s, many had come to believe that violence was the only language people of European descent could understand. For African American Quakers, such terms as "peaceful," "passive" and "passive resistance" were too easily associated with submissiveness.[71]

As a result of her study, Green recommended that Quaker contact with the African American community be "lateral"—that is, reaching out to those who would be likely to respond. She advised outreach to educated people from whom a connection with Quakerism might "filter down," and she disapproved of any effort "to involve large numbers of Culture of Poverty-type Blacks in Quakerism as perhaps some might advocate" on the grounds that Friends were not trained for such a "battle."[72]

In 1974 Philadelphia Yearly Meeting asked European American Friend Elizabeth Lehman to interview African Americans, some Quaker, to assess the progress Friends had made in race relations since the meeting's 1964 Call to Action. Four of the eight interviewees noted, in particular, the discomfort evident among European American Quakers even in simple discussions of such matters as job and housing equity. Mercedes Greer, a non-Quaker community activist in West Chester, Pennsylvania, told Lehman that she had been raised to appreciate the historical role of Friends in these areas but was dismayed to find later "these wonderful Friends and Quakers moving back from us; moving back, and hedging, hedging. . . . I think you make—oh, beautiful, beautiful statements. But you're not willing to go all the way."[73] In 2002 Friend Deborah Saunders of Cropwell (New Jersey) Meeting made a similar observation. Some Quakers would not sit beside Saunders in meetings because they feared she "might talk of racial things." Saunders held that she "can't *not* talk about racial matters" and that the reluctance she perceived among her fellow Friends was, in fact, a covert racism.[74] Holly Lawrence stated that when she first became a member of Green Street Meeting in the 1960s, she held out hope that it would "set the example" for Philadelphia by its involvement in social problems. In the end, however, despite numerous committee meetings and reports, Lawrence did not "see too much that has been done." "I felt like a puppet here," she stated. "I felt really focused upon by the people, uncomfortable because they're white." She said it seemed to her that, by "making a special effort," the Friends in her meeting were "still saying, 'you're different.'" Friends of European descent were happy to "hug you" and "pray together, but we'll still go out to our separate neighborhoods," Lawrence stated.[75]

Many interviewees in the 1974 survey, and African Americans both before and afterward, have stated that they were often treated as visitors or invisible guests whom European American Quakers both patronized and ignored. In 2002 Saunders noted, "Friends seem to require a person of color to carry a resume and ask, 'Why are you here?' I have been here for years, and you act like I am a visitor."[76] Lawrence described how deeply insulted she was by the "ignorant and stupid" comments made in meeting by one European American male member "on how pathetic it was for black people to wear blond wigs." She began to attend meeting less frequently, but no one seemed to notice or care enough to contact her.[77] "Many times white Friends have explained to me why African Americans need music, music, music—and lots of emotion—in 'their' worship," Friend Paul Ricketts of Fort Wayne Meeting in Indiana has stated. "When I asked them what color I was, they looked puzzled and humbled. 'But, Paul, *you're* different.' At that moment I became invisible to them as a person of color."[78]

Feelings of isolation and marginalization have also characterized their experience. Tracy Parham of Rahway-Plainfield (New Jersey) Friends Meeting noted that he felt "quite lonely out there, and so do others."[79] In a 1969 article in *Quaker Life*, Quaker George Sawyer labeled himself and other African Americans "the stranger among you"; a stranger, he stated, is "one who does not belong to or is kept from the activities of the group," the group being "White America."[80] Other African American Friends say they have identified a pressure to assimilate and, correspondingly, to leave behind or silence their cultural differences. At an annual gathering of Friends in Ithaca, New York, in 1980 Dwight Spann-Wilson, who was then a member of Ann Arbor (Michigan) Friends Meeting and general secretary of Friends General Conference, described his frustration at the perceived necessity to assimilate into white middle-class culture in order to be a member of the Religious Society of Friends:

> I . . . feel isolated because, as I have traveled hundreds of thousands
> of miles . . . I haven't seen seventy-five black Quakers yet. You can't
> know how it feels to be surrounded almost all the time with faces that

don't look like yours. . . . Sometimes when I'm weak I want to say, "God, why did you send me here?" I don't know. I know I was sent, I know I want to stay, but I wonder why we don't have more blacks. And I feel isolated too because all my life I've been taught that I have to adapt to white society. And sometimes I wonder, "When is somebody going to adapt to me? How come I always have to be the one to make the changes? Why do people never try to understand me?"[81]

Wilson, the first African American general secretary of FGC, believes there were "communication problems" when he held the post, perhaps because he was of another generation, perhaps because he was "openly advocating communication" with the other branches of Quakerism. He said his experience was that Quakers wanted others, like African Americans, "to have leadership ability, but to put it on hold," And he said he has experienced "racist acts" in his working and social relationships with other Friends. But he also remembers how warmly he was welcomed as pastor of Durham (Maine) Friends Meeting and that he "received greater support from FGC than anyone would have a right to expect: "I saw less racism among Friends there than in any other place I can name." He also has taken great pleasure in being able to verify that in 1827 his (four times great-) grandmother married an Ohio Quaker, Charles Ferguson, whose mother was descended from William Penn's family, he wonders if that might have made a difference in the way some old-line Quakers saw him a while ago.[82]

As many European American Quaker activists have also noted, Friends generally seemed disturbingly unaware, if not ignorant, of the essential issues confronting African American members of their own meeting and, as a consequence, have been unwilling to see themselves as part of the problem. George Sawyer has charged that Martin Luther King, Jr. was shot with "a rifle fired by White America," and has challenged European American Quakers to "deny that your own forefinger gave aid, assistance and comfort to the assassin as he lined his sight and pulled the trigger [and] forever silenced the voice of the black prophet of love." Sawyer maintained that most Friends were not aware of what was happening "in the revolution that rages around us" and "within the soul of the Black Man" and that they seemed unable to fathom requests for reparations or any assertion of independence among African

Americans in the management of their circumstances.[83] This distressing lack of awareness has fostered deep misunderstanding of the complexities of the African American situation.

"I feel as though a lot is expected of me and that people often believe that the opinions I voice are opinions of the entire African American population," Claudia Wair of Langley Hill (Virginia) Meeting noted in 1994.[84] Nonetheless, Wair and other African American Quakers also recounted positive experiences with Friends. Wair said that she felt "loved and accepted for who and what I am, that most Friends appreciate the diversity I bring to the meeting and are more than willing to learn about my background. I feel that Friends look beyond the color of my skin to the heart and know I am another soul in meeting for worship—waiting, just as they wait, as all others have done and will do, I trust, long after racism ceases to exist."[85] Amhara Powell, a member of Orange Grove Monthly Meeting in Pasadena, California, noted a sense of comfort as well. "Unprogrammed worship spoke to my condition like no prior religious practice," she said. "I thought of myself as having always been a Quaker without ever having known it." Powell said, "I had sensed early on that on some level, my African American culture might be put at risk not by any religious tenets of Quakerism, but rather by certain of its cultural expectations and assumptions."[86] She discerned no "particular effect on my spiritual life" arising from "the dearth of persons of color in meeting," but she found herself unexpectedly happy when an African American person visited her meeting. "To my great surprise, I threw my arms around her. I felt immediately connected to her . . . as if she were a long-lost friend." She realized that she missed "the presence of African Americans as a regular part of my religious experience," and wondered "if my commitment to Quakerism had come at the price of ethnic isolation. I wondered if my African American spirituality was somehow inherently incompatible with unprogrammed Quaker worship."[87]

Yet numerous African American Quakers have felt, like Powell, a great affinity for Quakerism. Like Sarah Mapps Douglass in the 1800s, Willa Burchett Graves, a Southland Institute graduate, said in 1982 that even as she felt "about half a Quaker [she] preferred quiet religious services to the more boisterous kind."[88] Francine Cheeks, a member of Newton (New Jersey) Meeting, expressed identical sentiments:

> I found myself very comfortable with the beliefs and practices of
> Quakers, including the deep silent worship experience. . . . I believe in
> the transforming power of love and nonviolence over injustice and vio-
> lence, and trust in the power of Spirit to guide me and the collective.
> I am always moved by the power of gathered silence and individual
> witnessing.[89]

For others, including Greg Williams of New Bedford Monthly
Meeting in Massachusetts, a definite connection existed between being
Quaker and acting for social justice:

> I cannot escape from the reality of pain, but I can experience "joy"
> in trying to stop (and at the very least lessen) the impact of social and
> economic injustice on the larger community. As a Friend I am called to
> witness to a living goodness that exists in all women and men. For me
> that often means confronting that which negates a positive life experi-
> ence. I must reflect in the silence of worship, finding strength in my
> spiritual community, and move onward towards an active expression of
> my belief. . . . As a Black, I view the relationship of Christianity to peo-
> ple of color as radical in its expression, serving as a liberating force. An
> important voice in the Black religious community, James Cone, points
> out that "Being black in America has little to do with skin color. To be
> black means that your heart, your soul, your mind and your body are
> where the dispossessed are." . . . This is where I stand as a member of the
> Religious Society of Friends.[90]

In her autobiography, Mahala Ashley Dickerson of Mat-su Monthly
Meeting in Alaska also described the attraction she felt to Quakerism.
"The peace and quiet of it had a special appeal for me in view of my
early childhood years, when I sat for hours and hours in the Baptist
church listening to much noise," she wrote. "I needed quiet contemplation when I tried to worship. To be able to listen also attracted me."[91] A
graduate of Fisk and Howard Universities, Dickerson became the first
African American woman attorney in Alabama. Upon moving from
Washington, D.C., to Indianapolis in 1951, she first attended the
Indianapolis independent Friends meeting, an unprogrammed "fellowship" meeting that met for dinner and worship one evening a month.[92]

After six years in Indiana Dickerson asked to transfer her membership from the Florida Avenue Meeting in Washington to Indianapolis
Monthly Meeting, a pastoral meeting then known as First Friends of

Indianapolis, whose pastor was Errol Elliott. At Elliott's urging Dickerson applied for associate membership for her three sons, all of whom had been attending Quaker schools and wanted to confirm their position as conscientious objectors. The Ministry and Counsel of First Friends failed to act on the transfer for six months, and fifteen members wrote to oppose the action. Among these members and others, one historian of the incident noted, "there began to circulate all manner of libelous stories concerning the character of the Dickerson family," including the claim that she "ran a whorehouse" and "defended prostitutes in her legal practice."[93]

Thirty-nine members of "the Coffee Class," described as "a vigorous young-married group" of the meeting, signed a statement expressing concern that Ministry and Counsel would deny an application "because of race or color."[94] Believing the truth about the Dickersons would prevail, members of the Coffee Class telephoned some of those who insisted that they opposed accepting only Dickerson as a member, not accepting African Americans in general. Other opponents expressed concerns frequently heard in other meetings: accepting members of African descent would cause a drop in property values in the high-priced area surrounding their new church; would turn their neighbors against them when "great hordes of negroes" came to the meeting and might want to live nearby, and would cause the withdrawal of persons of "substantial means" from the meeting, thus injuring it financially. A member walked out of a meeting as letters of support for the Dickersons were read, and a European American couple waived the meeting's budget on the grounds that "a bunch of Socialists were trying to wreck the meeting."[95] About two-thirds of the members "spoke eloquently" in favor of admitting Dickerson and said they believed that it was "the first real test of their Quakerism and what it meant to them." Despite the urgings of her supporters, in December 1959 Dickerson withdrew her application.[96] Eight of her supporters left the meeting and revived an older unprogrammed meeting, Lanthom, which accepted her son Henri's application for membership.[97]

Dickerson moved to Alaska, where she had already passed the bar. There, she stated, "one of my greatest sources of happiness . . . has been attending the very small silent meetings held at various places in Anchorage, Wasilla, Fairbanks, and Palmer."[98] Eager to have a meetinghouse near her, Dickerson donated land for Central Alaskan Friends to construct a meetinghouse next to her 160-acre homestead in Wasilla. Now called Dickerson Friends Center, it has been the site of yearly meeting sessions of the Alaskan Friends Conference. But, to her dismay, Alaska was not the "Quaker paradise" Dickerson had hoped for. Dickerson overheard racist remarks of two Friends whom she had invited to use her indoor pool. "After that," she wrote, "Quakers were no longer welcome in my home but restricted to the meeting house area. I never felt quite the same, as the lack of sensitivity was obvious to me by this racist interchange though it did not matter to the other member. Obviously I am destined to worship alone and I feel that God understands."[99] Years later, however, all parties reconciled.[100]

Nurturing African American Friends

The he struggles that African Americans have faced in Friends meetings have caused some Friends of African descent to go beyond local houses of worship to establish resources to nurture themselves. One of the support systems they have built within the Religious Society of Friends is the Fellowship of Friends of African Descent (FFAD). The organization originated in a 1990 worldwide Gathering of Friends of African Descent, planned by PYM's Racial Concerns Committee. Nearly one hundred adult Friends attended a weekend gathering at Pendle Hill, a Quaker study and retreat center in Wallingford, Pennsylvania. They came from across the United States, the Caribbean, and Africa; eighty-four people were of African descent, the other sixteen were of European descent. Out of that experience and out of a desire that black Quakers get to know each other, FFAD was formed in 1991. Beyond fellowship, FFAD's mission is to publish and respond to the concerns of Friends of African descent within the Religious Society of Friends; to nurture of Friends of African descent, their families and friends; and to address and respond to issues affecting people of African descent in their communities worldwide. Historically there have always been European American Friends also in attendance at FFAD gatherings.

Attended by African American Friend James Fletcher of Atlanta Monthly Meeting, his first Fellowship gathering created within him "a sense of coming home to a place I had been before in some dim memory of my soul":

> As worship proceeded, I felt rising within me a sense of joy and celebration at having been brought here, in this place, at this moment, with this precious group of Friends. . . . Many Friends shared their joy in overcoming the sense of isolation they feel in their home meetings from being "the only one" of African descent.
>
> Even now as I look back on the gathering, I am struck with the special beauty that results when we merge our Quaker experience with the great and ancient beauty of the spiritual traditions and expressions of people of African descent. Throughout the gathering, the feeling grew that we are putty in the hands of something much larger than ourselves, something beyond black and white, and perhaps beyond all words and thoughts.[101]

———————•———————

At its annual Gathering in 1994, Friends General Conference supported a group known as the Friends of Color in Quakerism by offering an opportunity for people of color to come together without European Americans. Participation in the week-long workshop, "Internalized Oppression As It Relates to Racism," was restricted to Friends of African, African American, Cape Verdean, and Hispanic descent. FGC's Advancement and Outreach Committee encouraged the workshop participants to formulate a series of recommendations. FGC honored two: the first, setting aside a room or Center for People of Color at each annual gathering so that Friends of African descent could meet and share information; and, second, developing workshops and plenary sessions that would address racism.

The need for the Center for People of Color proved critical in 1996, when FGC's annual gathering offered an Underground Railroad Game as an evening family activity. While the game's planners believed it would be educational and a way to experience history, members of the African American community at the gathering saw it as a travesty that made light of a time of terrible suffering. That any Quaker could consider turning such an experience into a game (which featured, among other things, "men with guns and dogs" chasing people escaping enslavement) horrified African American Friends. A group formed at a workshop only for people of African descent wrote in protest to the organizers of the gathering, who altered the plan to allow African American Friends to explain their point of view to the children and adults who came to take part in the activity. African American Paul Ricketts said that having to explain "to young children—mostly white children—why the Underground Railroad is not a game to be played but was a life-and-death struggle for thousands of Africans who sought freedom from slavery" was the single "most painful experience yet for me" as a Quaker. The incident remains a sensitive issue among Quakers of both African and European descent. For Ricketts, the 1996 gathering justified separate meetings for African American Friends. "I feel frustrated when I must justify the Friends of Color Center each year to Friends who believe that separatism for any reason is wrong, and when I must explain that the Friends of Color Center provides safe space for us," he stated. "The goal is not to exclude white Quakers, but it is where our souls as people of color can find rest."102

Few African American Friends like the idea of African Americans meeting separately, even on occasion. Alberta C. Rice, a member of Central Philadelphia Monthly Meeting, objected to a monthly worship meeting for people of color on theological grounds. "The Quaker Ministry is composed of all nationalities and no nationality is singled out," she has stated. "So why single out the ministry of a Worship Group for People of Color? As stated in *Faith and Practice*, your faith should not be in the power of man but in your faith in God. . . . There was to be no separatism [so] why are we to have it in meeting for worship?"103 For his part, Ricketts has maintained that focusing on increasing the number of people of color in Quaker meetings is misdirected; Friends instead should work on "trust and building healthy relationships among Quakers and people of color."104

As many Friends and non-Friends have asserted for generations, segregation is damaging to everyone. Ayesha Clark-Halkin, an African American member of Germantown Monthly Meeting, wrote in a 1988 article that true integration would benefit both European and African American Quakers. "The greatest gifts the black community [has] to offer Friends are those of Spirit." And much as early Quakers believed, African Americans' experience with a personal God is "a faith based on life's experience of both triumph and adversity, and not one burdened down by intellectualism":

With each day that we fail to reach out and make our declaration known, we miss still another opportunity to receive the blessing and healing the Spirit of God has in store for both communities. Each holds for the other the possibility of salvation. For one, it is the possibility of the healing of old wounds and the framework of unlimited development; for the other it is the possibility for much needed spiritual quickening and revitalization.[105]

Other Friends at other times have expressed a similar sentiment. European American Young Friend and Earlham graduate Ginny Coover, who had taught at the Mantua project in Philadelphia, told Midwestern Friends in 1968, "It's white people's responsibility to end racism, not black people's, and the reason we need to do that is to improve our own lives."[106] Alison Oldham in essence agreed with Clark-Halkin. "Segregation is impoverishment, for all concerned," Oldham told New England Friends in 1984. "A religious community that actively invites and genuinely welcomes all kinds of people is bound to be wiser and stronger and more authentic than one that doesn't."[107]

Tracy Parham has suggested that Friends need to "start listening again to the charge to love each other spiritually, and live our lives in a true spiritual manner." If Quakers could return to those roots, he has argued, "those inside will feel welcomed, and those of color outside will hopefully find a home here."[108] Johan Maurer has defined what is demanded of Quakers as "radical hospitality," with God at the center beyond the boundaries of race and class and ethnicity.[109] In the words of Quaker Richard Foster, the Society of Friends must "publicly and completely repudiate all belief in the supremacy of any and every race.", Richard Taylor has argued that achieving this repudiation may hinge (as it has throughout the history of American Quakerism) on individuals like John Woolman who insist that Quakers "live up to our profession." These few may not find loving Quaker backing and may "be misunderstood and criticized by Friends," but they will "walk in twos and threes into painful but Spirit-charged confrontations with oppression and injustice. . . . God will not let them rest," Taylor said, "and they will not let the Society of Friends rest."[110]

For those who wonder if it really makes a difference whether Friends are integrated or not, Oldham has a compelling answer: "The question," she says, "is one of authenticity, and goes to the heart of our beliefs about Quakerism. For *if* this faith of Friends that we espouse, this way of seeking for the Spirit of Truth, is indeed authentic, it will be able to speak powerfully to all sorts and conditions of folk, whatever their race, their economic status, or the cultural context through which they see the world." In contrast to that ability to speak to all, some might "accept the notion, however subconsciously, that Quakerism really speaks only to certain kinds of people." She suggests, in that case, "then . . . we have totally denied its religious validity, its universal spirit, and so we will have reduced Quakerism to the status of a social club with a mild religious overlay."[111]

During the height of the Civil Rights movement, George Sawyer called on Quakers to deeply question their actions, or lack thereof, in regards to people of African descent. He encouraged Friends to consider how many times they asked members of their meetings to "stand beside their Negro brethren during a local freedom march or other Civil Rights activity." He wondered if Friends who hesitated to recommend that housing in their own area be open to African American owners were "fearful of our own social position." And if he were here today, Sawyer might still challenge Friends, asking, "How many concerned Quakers buttonhole their fellow members to convince them that race prejudice is a complete denial of God's commandment to love?"[112]

2008 FGC Midwest Gathering of Friends of Color in Quakerism.

Toward an Inclusive Community
by Vanessa Julye

I JOINED THE RELIGIOUS SOCIETY OF FRIENDS because I share its belief that there is that of God in everyone. Thus I was surprised to find that there were times when members of my family and I were not treated as equals within the Society. Friends of African, Asian, Caribbean, Hispanic, Indigenous, Latino/Latina, and Pacific Islander descent have shared with me similar experiences of racism in our religious community. We feel the pain of feeling invisible in and unheard by monthly and yearly meetings and individual European American Friends. The isolation we feel in the Society of Friends stems partly from the fact that until Friends learn as a Society to stop seeing racial difference as a source for judgment we will always look and be treated differently because of our physical characteristics. A few people of color have left our religious community; others are ready to leave. Some of us struggle with the paradox of reaching out to people of color who are not Friends to join a community while we ourselves exert great effort to overcome the barriers we experience with Friends. We want to increase the number of Friends of color within Quakerism, but we do not want them to encounter what we have confronted.

In addition to being judged because of my physical distinctiveness, there have also been times when I have felt accepted within the Religious Society of Friends only because I have adapted to its culture—that is, because I have been compelled to leave my ethnicity and culture outside the meetinghouse door. I perceive the predominant culture of Quaker meetings and communities within this country as middle-class European American, which values higher education, literacy, political activism, political correctness, being quiet, prompt, and orderly, having polite conversations, and avoiding conflict. African American Unitarian minister Mark D. Morrison-Reed supports this experience. He found middle-class status a requisite for "creating a multiracial church."

Joining a church outside the traditional black community was a risk that only few were able to take. They were the few who were already or were in the process of becoming middle class. Financially secure, they depended less upon a community church. They had already begun to see beyond the community and therefore could step out of it. They had broader social, political and cultural commitment and wanted a church that would support these. . . . The black individuals we have attracted are the religiously earnest but uncommitted, who are comfortable in an interracial setting and who believe a liberal religious, non-creedal theology and freedom of conscience is more important than racial solidarity or cultural comfort.[1]

I was raised middle class, but when I joined the Religious Society of Friends I was not financially secure because I was a single mother working in a non-profit organization. I attended private schools all of my life and graduated from college without financial aid from the schools or other organizations. I grew up with the expectation that I would graduate not only from high school, but also from college. My parents taught me, with the assistance of my teachers, classmates and friends, the value of education, the importance of being politically active, prompt, quiet and polite in order to assure financial security in this society. I learned as a young child that I couldn't exhibit characteristics associated with being African American in the middle-class, white environment and succeed.

Being vibrant, spontaneous, creative, sometimes loud, confrontational, forgiving, accepting, sharing everything you have, and being surrounded by persons of varying body shapes combined with the spectrum of light to dark brown skin and straight to kinky hair are, for me, characteristics of African American culture. I am grateful to find many of these characteristics when I participate in the Gatherings sponsored by the Fellowship of Friends of African Descent, and I would appreciate finding more of them in Central Philadelphia Monthly Meeting.

The images reflected within the meetinghouse also play a role in how free and equal I feel. When I walk into a meetinghouse and all of the visual images are European American, as a person of African descent, I feel invisible. As Jean Harris stated, after a year as the only African American student at Pendle Hill, "In the midst of this community-in-process, sometimes I have felt incredibly lonely. I have longed to see a face, like mine, imprinted with Africa. More than that, I have longed for the cultural familiarity of other African Americans and for the visible diversity comprised of other Americans of color that is my world outside of Pendle Hill."2 A meetinghouse is like a home. The images on the wall, in the literature, and on the tables all reflect the members of the family. If my image is not there, that means to me that I am not a member of that family. It is clear to me that in that meeting's world I do not exist.

My parents always told me that, as a member of the African American community, I should give back in any way I could to that community. They told me that, and they were examples. For about five years in the early 1960s, my parents operated a community center for children in Mantua, the African American ghetto in West Philadelphia where I grew up. As a part of my daily life now, I carry the charge of identifying the needs of the African American community so that I will be able to help. Being involved with and reaching out and listening to people in the African American community is not just an aspect of my life; it is also an aspect of my religion.

Like the African American community as a whole, Friends of African descent do not share one unified voice or agenda. Our community is in many ways just as fragmented as European American communities. There are Quaker members and meeting attenders of African descent who express a viewpoint different from mine, and, with one exception, they have been silent about the issue of racism in the Society of Friends. They do not experience race as a barrier in their meeting or in the wider body of Friends, and some are concerned that the work of those of us who do experience racism will fracture the unity they have found among Quakers. One African American told me that she came to meeting for worship to commune with God, not to confront racial problems. For these members and attenders, it is important to feel comfortable in meeting for worship, which will not happen if they make others uncomfortable by focusing on racism. Another told me that racism is not her dilemma to tackle as an African American; because European Americans created it, it is their responsibility to terminate it. Yet another did not choose to deal with issues of racism in meeting because she did not want Friends to restrict their interactions with her to only those times when a need to discuss a racial matter arose.

Our testimony of equality, and how it is followed by me and other members of the Religious Society of Friends, is important. How we carry out that testimony with members of the African American community, Friends and non-Friends, impacts all of us in many ways. Historically, the testimony of equality developed in England not as a testimony of racial equality, but one related to gender and class.

I believe that the Religious Society of Friends is at an important crossroads. Friends of European descent established and have controlled the Society since its inception; we have an opportunity now to examine our past behavior and to change it. It is time for Friends to step away from the status quo and step forward to join the few of us who are working on racial justice. Today we have an opportunity to create a spiritual home where everyone feels free and equal. Now is the time to co-create a religious community that reflects all of us.

Several recent Quaker meetings have heard our plea and are truly seeking to live by our testimony of equality. My husband and I were among fifty Quakers of European, African, and Asian descent gathered for an October 2001 conference titled, "Quakers and Racial Justice" at Pendle Hill. At the end of the conference, we prepared an epistle to the rest of the Society of Friends declaring our profound concern about "the lack of attention to racism and white privilege within the Religious Society of Friends" and our sense of urgency about change:

> We have been called as Friends to act out our consciences and in response to the voices we hear within. We have not listened deeply enough. Our world has cried out to us and as a group we have not heard those voices from without. We cannot continue to participate in the spiritual diminishment of ourselves and those around us. We are called to meet each other as equals. We must take up this testimony with the willingness to follow it to its conclusion. We are called forward now to act as one Society in challenging white privilege and the constant, generations-old diminishment that is the result of racism. To do anything less is, in essence, to disavow our membership in the Religious Society of Friends. We invite you from our hearts to join us from your hearts.[3]

In addition, in 2000 the Ad Hoc Committee on Racism, a small, multiracial group within Friends General Conference, created the Committee for Ministry on Racism as a formal recognition of the importance of dealing with racism at the organizational level. In October 2001 that committee issued its own epistle on the concern:

> We are clear that our best work together is grounded in worship and acknowledge that when we truly center together, we do not know where we will be led. We have been willingly vulnerable to that process and affirm that there is a fundamental relationship to God in what we are doing. We are clear that eradicating racism is a ministry of healing, education and empowerment. It is time to move beyond guilt toward the center of this work, which is God's love.[4]

Friends General Conference program committees have also been taking steps forward in this work. We are told that many monthly meetings are beginning to make their meetings more accessible to Friends of color and are more inviting to people of color who might be seekers. We move toward a time when every Friend will be a willing witness and an agent of change, moving us toward greater racial and ethnic diversity and the eradication of racism within all meetings affiliated with Friends General Conference.

At Pendle Hill's Monday Night Forum in October 2002, African American Quaker historian Emma Lapsansky described a path toward the goal of genuine equity:

> I think that if we . . . can regularly examine ourselves and continue to follow our spiritual Light, can keep an eye on where we've been as well as on where we need to go, can visualize what the future might look like for our descendants, and can keep the faith, and open ourselves to a wide variety of ways and places where we might meet others where they are, not where we have stuck them in our imagination; if we can stay focused on social justice as something that will bring us pleasure, not just a sense of righteousness, and if we can remember that social justice is a bit like housework–no matter how well you do it, it just has to be done again; and perhaps most important, if we can keep our sense of humor, then we have a good chance to be carried over those places where it seems God has abandoned us.[5]

In 2003, after a diversity workshop at Pendle Hill, Melanie Sax, a European American Quaker from Madison Monthly Meeting in Wisconsin wrote an article amplifying what Lapsansky means by being "stuck":

I wanted to stop feeling awkward around people of color. I do not have a full awareness of what it is like to be non-white in this country, but I knew enough that I figured I represented the oppressor to non-whites. . . . I saw how the static, frozen image of guilty white oppressor versus angry victim of color tends to keep everyone stuck playing the same old tune. My shame at being white kept me frozen and held people of color at an arm's length even before I got to know them. We needed a vision that empowered us to move beyond this "stuff." I asked that my heart be opened to the Divine within me. . . .

We do not have to stay stuck and hopeless. We can be empowered to co-create together what happens next to continue bringing forth Light into the world's family.[6]

If African American Friends are to bring other people of color to Quakerism, we need to feel that the Society of Friends is a religion in which we are nurtured and welcomed enough to share it with others. Attracting more Friends of color may mean doing things differently—changing how we all use language, being more flexible about our practices, and being willing to implement new traditions. In a 1999 interview, African American psychologist and workshop facilitator Anita Mendes, a member of Monadnock Monthly Meeting in Jaffrey, New Hampshire, made numerous specific suggestions for change, one of them being constant discussion:

We . . . need to keep talking to each other. When People of Color hear racist things, they could just say, "I didn't get that. Would you tell me more?" We do not have to label people racists. As we continue in conversation, someone of the offending person's color will often become uncomfortable . . . and confront that person. We must not cut each other off. We must stay in dialogue.[7]

What has happened in our past has happened. We cannot change it, and, as Lapsansky noted, being angry at Friends' behaviors and decisions will not help us. What is more important is for us to learn from the past, so that we can create the future many of us envision. It is only possible to change a system once you have a clear understanding of how it operates. In order for us to begin a journey of healing our hurts toward racism, it is important for us to know and understand our individual cultural heritage. We also need to have an honest understanding of how our ancestors contributed to this world and the structure of institutional racism and of how we continue to maintain vestiges of this structure in our behaviors today. Acknowledging the pain and celebrating the accomplishments will help us take one step closer to transforming members of the Religious Society of Friends, and eventually the inhabitants of the world, into peaceful human beings.

The time for healing is now! Let us work to change our pattern of relating with one another into one that honors freedom, equality, and peace. Speak to that of God in each person you meet. Honor their humanity by working to see God inside of them.

Work for systematic change. The structural foundation of racism is collective and precedes all of us. We may not be responsible for its existence, and as individuals we did not create it; however, as individuals we participate in larger social systems. We are the moving parts that allow these systems to run. When we change our beliefs and behaviors, these systems come to a halt. We must become aware of how inequality is orchestrated in our society; we are responsible for what we think and what we do to perpetuate this inequality. Allen Johnson made this point in his 1997 book *The Forest and the Trees*:

> I can decide how to live as a white person in relation to my privileged position as a white person. I can decide whether to laugh or object when I hear racist "humor"; decide what to do about the consequences racism produces for people, whether to be part of the solution or merely part of the problem. I don't feel guilty because my country is racist, because that wasn't my doing. But as a white person who participates in that society, I feel responsible to consider what to do about it. The way to get past the potential for guilt and see how I can make a difference is to realize that the system isn't me and I'm not the system.[8]

In a 1968 article in *Friends Journal*, Barrington Dunbar offered six ways that Friends can demonstrate their love to the wider community through challenging the current system:

1. We need to nurture the Inner Light-the source of the phenomenal power of eighteenth-century Quakers. "Quaker Power" can be as effective as "Black Power" in speeding up revolutionary changes.

2. We need to listen in love to the black people of America and to submit ourselves to the violence of their words and actions if we are to identify truly with their anguish and despair.

3. We need to understand, to encourage, and to support the thrust of black people to achieve self-identity and power by sharing in the control of institutions in the community that affect our welfare and destiny.

4. We must invest our resources–money and skill–to provide incentives for black people to develop and control economic, political, and social structures in the community.

5. We must support the passage of antipoverty legislation leading to programs that will remedy the deplorable economic and social conditions existing in urban settings.

6. We must oppose racial injustice wherever it is practiced: in the neighborhood we live in, in our places of business and in our contacts with the wider community.[9]

I would add that we must oppose racial injustice in the Religious Society of Friends as well.

Stop taking whiteness for granted. Make whiteness visible. Think about what it means to be European American. Acknowledge that whiteness does not symbolize normality and that it is associated with unearned privilege. Begin to think of whiteness in racial and cultural terms. Ask yourself if you live in a predominantly white neighborhood, marry and befriend predominantly European American people, interact predominantly with whites in your profession, and send your children to predominantly European American schools and camps. If your answer is yes, ask yourself why.

Acknowledge and dispel stereotypes about African Americans. Examine information that exists in order to discern these stereotypes. Dredge up the embedded, irrational fears and emotions attached to these images. Let go of those fears and negative feelings, and replace stereotypes with realistic information.

Develop or increase your knowledge of the African American experience in the United States of America by reading our history, watching programs or movies dealing with racial issues, and perhaps taking courses in the subject. Participate in workshops, discussions, conferences, and other activities that promote racial justice.

Widen your circle of friends. Get to know people of African descent. If there are none in your workplace, in your school, or in your meeting, join a group such as the local chapter of the NAACP. Begin attending the meetings of groups that deal with African American issues. Establish a trusting, confiding relationship where you interact with each other outside these settings.

Talk about racism, but know that addressing the issue is highly emotional and difficult. Listen to each other. Be committed to hearing each other accurately. Repeat what you heard being said to be sure you *have* heard it accurately. Be sure to stay with a dispute when it arises until clearness is reached.

Promote racially inclusive collaboration within your community and your meeting. Raise your racial consciousness by educating yourself, your family, your classmates, and your meeting on racial issues. Encourage introspection. Actively work within your community to expand opportunity and access for individuals of African descent. Take action in addressing racial reconciliation at all levels of society and government. Continually adjust your goals and practices to keep pace with changing local needs and racial demographics.

Let us begin to identify and separate the aspects of Quakerism that are not related to the core of our beliefs, the nonessential Eurocentric practices that have become attached to the way we practice our faith. Once they are removed we, people of all racial and ethnic backgrounds working together, can rebuild Quakerism and the world into an equal and peaceful home.

Racial awareness is not static. It is a process. We all are someplace in this process, and everyone benefits when we grow. So get involved.

When I joined the Society of Friends, I wanted to believe that Friends were different. Now that I have a better understanding of our history I see that the Religious Society of Friends is not now and has never been the Blessed Community that I was led to believe existed. This is wonderful news for me. Why? Because it means that we have not lost anything. What we need is ready and waiting for us—a Religious Society of Friends where members honor our testimony of equality and truly see that of God in each person, no matter how deeply it may be buried. I hope you will join me in co-creating that Blessed Community now.

Notes on Resources

Minutes of Yearly Meetings
(Only for minutes used in this publication)

Minutes, Friends United Meeting. Richmond, IN: Friends United Meeting, 1969. Friends Historical Collection, Swarthmore College (SFHL).

Minutes of the Five Years Meeting of the American Yearly Meeting of Friends, Philadelphia, PA. J.C. Winston, 1963; Serial Group 2, SFHL.

Minutes of the Indiana Yearly Meeting of the Religious Society of Friends (Orthodox), Muncie, IN: 1971. Friends Collection, Earlham College.

New England Yearly Meeting Minute Books, Freeport, ME: The Dingley Press, 1947, 1953, 1965, 1966, 1967, 1968, 1970, 1972, 1978, 1980, 1992. Library, Framingham (MA) Friends Meeting.

Proceedings of Baltimore Yearly Meeting of the Religious Society of Friends, Baltimore, MD: 1949, 1950, 1951; Andover-Harvard Theological Library, Harvard Divinity School.

Proceedings of the Yearly Meeting of Friends held in Philadelphia (Orthodox): Philadelphia: Philadelphia Yearly Meeting of Friends, 1924–1955. SFHL.

Proceedings of Philadelphia Yearly Meeting of Friends, Race Street (Hicksite) Philadelphia: Philadelphia Yearly Meeting of Friends, 1924–1955. SFHL.

Proceedings of Philadelphia Yearly Meeting of the Religious Society of Friends, Philadelphia: Philadelphia Yearly Meeting. Minutes, 1968, 1969, 1970. SFHL.

Yearbook of Philadelphia Yearly Meeting of the Religious Society of Friends, Philadelphia: Philadelphia Yearly Meeting. Documents 1964, 1969, 1970. SFHL.

Archives for Unpublished Materials

American Friends Service Committee (AFSC)
Friends Center, Philadelphia, PA
   Minutes from 1927 to present: Interracial Relations Committee,
   Committee on Race Relations (both abbreviated as "CRR" in endnotes)

Andover-Harvard Theological Library
Harvard Divinity School, Cambridge, MA
    Pamphlet collection: AFSC publications

Earlham College Friends Collection
Richmond, IN
    Friends Collection, Earlham College
    Willard Heiss, "A Brief Account of Lanthorn Friends Meeting"
        (paper, February 1960)
    Dorothy Biddle James to Thomas Jones, (1952), Controversial Issues
        Collection, Racial Matters
    "Friends and the 'Suburban Challenge,'" 1969 report
    Letters
    Southland School Records

Haverford College Quaker Collection
Haverford, PA
    Student papers
    Letters
    Dissertation: Richard Foster

Swarthmore College Friends Historical Collection (SFHL)
Swarthmore, PA
    See below.

Swarthmore College Peace Collection
Swarthmore, PA
    Fellowship House, 1947–1967

Unpublished Material in SFHL

Friends General Conference (FGC)
    Minutes, Peace and Social Order Committee, Serial 15/Box 64, 65
    Gathering Cape May, N.J., 1944, Series 17/Box 70
    Minutes, Committee on Education, 1948, Series 11/Box 41
    Vera Green, Report to Advancement Committee, 1973, Series 10/Box 33–40

Friends for Human Justice (FHJ) /
National Friends Committee on Race Relations (NFCRR)
    Series 21 RG2/Phy/758/Box 21
        Programs for Conferences
        Letters

Minutes

Reports

New York Yearly Meeting

Peace and Social Action Program

RG2/NYy/ 607/ Box 3, 4

Philadelphia Yearly Meeting Committee Records

Race Relations Committees

Committee on Race Relations

Arch Street Meeting (Orthodox) 1921–1929

Series 1/Box 1

Committee on the Interests of the Colored Race (Hicksite) 1928–29

Series 1/ Box 1

Joint Committee on Race Relations (JCRR) (for the two PYMs to 1955)

Levittown, Pennsylvania

Report on Levittown, CRR, 1955, PH800/ Series 5/Box 9

Committee on Race Relations 1960–1970 (CRR)

(Named Race Relations Committee in 1940s; also known as Committee on Racial Concerns) (See short history below.)

RG2/PHy800 and PHy/801/Series 5/Box 9

Declaration of Intentions 1956

Series 5/Box 7

Clippings

Letters

"A Quaker Call to Action in Race Relations"

Series 5/ Box 10

Chester Project Report: Series 5/Box 8

Housing, Series 5/Box 9

Minutes, Institute on Race Relations, 1927–1941

Series 5/Box 10

Friends Mississippi Project

Series 5/Box 10, 12

Also: PHy826/Box 1

Schools and Colleges 1937–1968

eries 5/Box 8

1970 Working Party 1970–75 (Serial 1)

Economic Development Fund for Disadvantaged Minority

Groups RG2/Serial 2 /PHy/802

Fund's Board of Managers, RG2/PHy735/Series 7

Minutes of Ad Hoc Committee on the Urban Crisis
RG2/Series 1/PHy758/Box 1
RG2/407/Series 121/ Box 6/1

Survey of monthly meetings' activities and concerns re racism, 1968
RG2/ Series 12//PHy/407/Box 6/11.

Committee on Community Involvement
RG2/PHy/758/ Box 11, 21, 28

Friends Mantua-Belmont Joint Committee And Weekend Work Camps
RG2/PHy/774/Box 1, 2
RG2/PHy/801/Box 7
Minutes RG2/PHy758/Box 10

Meeting for Social Concerns (MSC)
All-Record Group 2 (RG2)
Minutes
PHy758/Box 20, 21
Correspondence
PHy/758/Box 5, 6
Black Economic Development Conference
PHy/758/Series 21/Box 19
Also see PHy 735
Black Manifesto and Local Meetings
Series 5/PHy/758/Box 7
Copy of manifesto
Letters in response from meetings/individuals
Proposed Friends Manifesto
Friends Chester Project
Series 12/PHy/758/Box 12
Friends Suburban Project
Series 12/PHy/758/Box 12
New Jersey Friends Council
Series 21/PHy758/Box 23
Tension Points
Series 20/PHy758/Box 18
Richard Taylor, Economics Course
Series 20/PHy758/Box 18
Friendly Presence
Series 27/PHy/770

Black Panthers
    Series 21/ PHy770/Box 20, 25
    Series 21/PHy758/Box 20
Economic Justice
    Series 16/PHy/758/Box 17
Committee for Economic Responsibility
    Series 17/PHy/758/Box 17
    Also see PHy/730
Friends for Human Justice
    PHy/758/Box 21
New Jersey Friends Council
    Series 21/PHy/758/Box 23
Work Camps
    Series 21/PHy758/Box 26
    Also PHy774

Others in SFHL

Fellowship of Friends of African Descent 1990
    RG2/PHy801/Box 7
Friends Mississippi Project
    RG2/PHy/826 and pamphlet Group 3
Vera Green, Research
    RG 4/025/ Box 4
Presidential Papers (Frank Aydelotte)
    RG6/Series 3

Notes

CHAPTER ONE: Ending Enslavement among Friends: 1688–1787

1. The Religious Society of Friends had essentially freed itself of any members who enslaved Africans by the late 1780s under the prevailing notion that the Bible justified viewing people of African descent as an inferior group that had to be cared for. See Lester Scherer, *Slavery and the Churches of Early America, 1619–1819* (Grand Rapids, MI: Eerdmans, [1973]), 133, 141–44.

2. See Gary Nash and Jean Soderlund, *Freedom By Degrees: Emancipation in Pennsylvania and its Aftermath* (New York: Oxford University Press, 1991), 46, 47 for examples. This work is a comprehensive study that included a great deal about Quakers and enslavement, including tables useful in understanding ownership and manumission by Friends in the larger context of practices in the state.

3. For definitions of these and other terms specific to Quakerism, see Warren Sylvester Smith, *One Explorer's Glossary of Quaker Terms*, ed. Mae Smith Bixby, rev. Deborah Haines (Philadelphia: Quaker Press of Friends General Conference, 2002).

4. Sydney James, *A People among Peoples: Quaker Benevolence in Eighteenth-Century America* (Cambridge, MA: Harvard University Press, 1963), 109; Elaine Forman Crane, *A Dependent People: Newport, Rhode Island, in the Revolutionary Era* (New York: Fordham University Press, 1985), 164.

5. Arthur Zilversmit, *The First Emancipation: The Abolition of Slavery in the North* (Chicago: University of Chicago Press, 1967), 34–36.

6. John Hope Franklin, *From Slavery to Freedom: A History of American Negroes* (New York: Alfred A. Knopf, 1947), 58. A merchant's profits from trading Africans could reach 100 percent; ship captains and lesser traders often profited greatly as well. However, profits were not necessarily assured, as some Philadelphia Friends learned.

7. Peter Kolchin, *American Slavery 1619–1877* (New York: Hill and Wang, 1993), 22–23.

8. Jean Soderlund, *Quakers and Slavery: A Divided Spirit* (Princeton, NJ: Princeton University Press, 1985), 7. Soderlund's work is based on an analysis of ownership and manumission patterns in representative monthly meetings in the Philadelphia area.

9. Hugh Thomas, *The Slave Trade: The Story of the Atlantic Slave Trade, 1440–1870* (Baltimore: The Weant Press, 1988), 298. The fact of Quaker involvement in the trade may, from a twenty-first-century viewpoint, be baffling, but it may be even more so when we learn that Wax concluded that "Virtually all evidence points to the conclusion that until about 1729 selling Negroes in the Philadelphia market was not a profitable form of trade." Wax, "The Negro Slave

Trade in Colonial Pennsylvania," 108. (Philadelphia Yearly Meeting did not ban selling until 1771.)

10. Hugh Barbour and J. William Frost, *The Quakers* (Richmond, IN: Friends United Press, 1994), 348. Drake, *Quakers and Slavery*, 26–27.

11. Thomas, *Slave Trade*, 298. There were two Isaac Norrises, both powerful in their religious and political communities. On Isaac Norris I, see Drake, *Quakers and Slavery*, 26–27.

12. John R. Reis, "The Life and Times of Jonathan Dickinson," Florida History and Antiquities Index web site, http://www.apex-ephemera.com/floridahistory/dickinson2.htm; Jack Marietta, *The Reformation of American Quakerism, 1748–1783* (Philadelphia: University of Pennsylvania Press, 1984), 112.

13. Howard Dodson, *Jubilee: The Emergence of African Culture* (Washington, DC: National Geographic Books, 2002), 22. While Bristol and Newport are less than twenty miles apart, Bristol was not a predominantly Quaker town.

14. Jay Coughtry, *The Notorious Triangle: Rhode Island and the African Slave Trade, 1700–1807* (Philadelphia: Temple University Press, 1981), 25, 20.

15. Arthur J. Worrall, *Quakers in the Colonial Northeast* (Hanover, NH: University Press of New England, 1980), 170; Zora Klain, *Educational Activities of New England Quakers: A Source Book* (Philadelphia: Westbrook Publishing Company, 1928), 35; Thomas, *Slave Trade*, 270; Crane, *Dependent People*, 131.

16. Worrall, *Quakers in the Colonial Northeast*, 154–55; James Garman, professor at Salve Regina University in Newport, as quoted in Paul Davis, "Plantations in the North: The Narragansett Planters," www.projo.com/extra/2006/slavery/day2/3/13/06.

17. Kathryn Grover, *The Fugitive's Gibraltar: Escaping Slaves and Abolitionism in New Bedford, Massachusetts* (Amherst: University of Massachusetts Press, 2001), 44.

18. Coughtry, *Notorious Triangle*, 243, 251, 253; Rosalind Wiggins, notes identifying Quakers in the slave trade, 2000, taken from New England Yearly Meeting records of 1723, 1763, June 1771, and 1776 and Memorials of Deceased Friends of New England Yearly Meeting, 1841. Wiggins identified some thirty other vessel owners who could have been Quaker.

19. Coughtry, *Notorious Triangle*, 253. Worrall, *Quakers in the Colonial Northeast*, 170, has noted that who the "Quaker Wantons" were is sometimes difficult to determine. He identified John and Gideon as Quaker but not their brother Joseph.

20. Thomas, *Slave Trade*, 298.

21. Worrall, *Quakers in the Colonial Northeast*, 76, 154.

22. Ibid., 170. The appendices in Lorenzo Greene, *Negroes in Colonial New England, 1620–1776* (New York: Atheneum, 1968), list the "162 leading slave-holding families in colonial New England," forty-seven of whom are in Rhode Island; among these forty-seven are several Friends.

23. Drake, *Quakers and Slavery*, 31–33. As an example, John Farmer was disowned for publishing his "Epistle Concerning Negroes" without the meeting's permission.

24. Thomas, *Slave Trade*, 270–21; James Horton and Lois Horton, *Hard Road to Freedom: The Story of African America* (New Brunswick, NJ: Rutgers University Press, 2001), 28, have described the "seasoning" in the West Indies.

25. Grover, *Fugitive's Gibraltar*, 44.

26. A. Leon Higginbotham Jr., *In the Matter of Color: Race and the American Legal Process: The Colonial Period* (Oxford, Eng.: Oxford University Press, 1928), 294.

27. Higginbotham, *In the Matter of Color*, 294; Gary B. Nash, "Slaves and Slaveholders in Colonial Philadelphia," in Joe William Trotter and Eric Ledell Smith, eds., *African Americans in Pennsylvania: Shifting Historical Perspectives* (University Park: Pennsylvania Historical Society and Historic Commission and Pennsylvania State University Press, 1997), 44, 51, 62. A much earlier estimate was offered in 1911 by Edward Turner, "Slavery in Colonial Pennsylvania," *Pennsylvania Magazine of History and Biography* 32 (1911): 143, 149, who estimated that at least one thousand people of African descent were in Pennsylvania at the time, though it is not clear how many were free and how many enslaved; Turner found it "almost impossible to obtain satisfactory information as to the number of negroes in colonial Pennsylvania." Nash (62) had noted that records do not reveal the numbers of holders of enslaved Africans in all of colonial Philadelphia's religious groups, though German Lutherans, the second largest denomination, are "to a remarkable degree" absent from the lists of owners of the enslaved. Only 3.3 percent of the Germans can be identified as enslavers. They frequently had indentured servants, most often German.

28. Nash, "Slaves and Slaveholders in Colonial Philadelphia," 44, 51, 61. Still, Pennsylvania had fewer enslaved people than the surrounding areas. According to the 1790 federal census, just more than 2 percent of the commonwealth's population was of African descent, free or enslaved, while in New Jersey their proportion of total population was about 8 percent. In Maryland and Delaware, African Americans were 34 and 22 percent respectively. Christopher Densmore, e-mail to authors, 13 July 2004. Between 1767 and 1775 about one thousand enslaved people lived in Philadelphia, according to an average of various estimates; there were no official city censuses in the colonial era. Nash's estimate for Philadelphia is derived from burial and taxable property data for the period. By the early 1710s one out of every five enslaved persons in the colonies lived in the Northeast; see Zilversmit, *First Emancipation*, 1–6.

29. William Penn, London, to James Harrison, October 1685, quoted/transcribed in *The Absentee Proprietor*, eds. Mary Maples Dunn and Richard S. Dunn, vol. 3 of *The Papers of William Penn* (Philadelphia: University of Pennsylvania Press, 1981–87), 66.

30. Ezra Michener, *A Retrospect of Early Quakerism* (Philadelphia: T. E. Zell, 1860), 337; Gary B. Nash, *Forging Freedom: The Formation of Philadelphia's Black Community, 1720–1840* (Cambridge, MA: Harvard University Press, 1988), 32. Drake, *Quakers and Slavery*, 24, cites a 1720 letter from Hannah Penn to Logan; the original is in Penn Manuscripts 1, 95, Historical Society of Pennsylvania, Philadelphia.

31. On manumission by will, see Gary B. Nash, *First City: Philadelphia and the Forging of Historical Memory* (Philadelphia: University of Pennsylvania Press, 2002), 21.

32. Joanne Pope Melish, *Disowning Slavery: Gradual Emancipation and "Race" in New England, 1780–1860* (Ithaca, NY: Cornell University Press, 1998), 16; Zilversmit, *First Emancipation*, 1–6. In New England, where colonial censuses were compiled, they often included "deliberate exaggeration or understatements" by officials not interested in cooperating with British requests for such data. See Greene, *Negroes in Colonial New England*, 72.

33. Shane White, *Stories of Freedom in Black New York* (Cambridge, MA: Harvard University Press, 2002), 12, 13; Jones, *Quakers in the American Colonies*, xvi, 144–45, 262. By 1790 there were twenty-one thousand enslaved people in the state, and they made up about 8 percent of the total population. See "Slavery in New York," New York Historical Society web site, http://www.slaveryinnewyork.org/about_exhibit.htm.

34. Lynda R. Day, *Making a Way to Freedom: A History of African Americans on Long Island* (1997), cited in Gretchen Haynes, "The Quaker Conflict over Abolitionist Activism: Will of Man, Will of God: Discerning Truth in Abolitionist Activities Center in Westbury Quarterly Meeting, 1830–1860" (Paper, Westbury New York Meeting, n.d.), Westbury Meeting web site, http://www.westburyquakers.org/qt/archive.

35. John Hope Franklin and Alfred A. Moss Jr., *From Slavery to Freedom: A History of African Americans*, 8th ed. (New York: A. A. Knopf, 2003), 139–40; Clayton Cramer, *Black Demographic Data, 1790–1860: A Sourcebook* (Westport, CT: Greenwood Press, 1997), 130; Grady McWhiney, *Southerners and Other Americans* (New York: Basic Books, 1973), 132; C. Vann Woodward, *Tom Watson: Agrarian Rebel* (New York: Macmillan, 1938), 8.

36. Charles McKiever, *Slavery and the Emigration of North Carolina Friends* (Murfreesboro, NC: Johnson Publishing Co., 1970), 9–10; Seth Hinshaw, *The Carolina Quaker Experience* (Greensboro: North Carolina Yearly Meeting, North Carolina Friends Historical Society, 1984), 130.

37. Drake, *Quakers and Slavery*, 9.

38. Saurin Norris, *The Early Friends (or Quakers) in Maryland* (Baltimore: Maryland Historical Society, 1862), 22. The quotation is attributed to a Maryland Quaker. On Quakers boarding ships, see Drake, *Quakers and Slavery*, 65. On differences between Maryland's eastern and western sections, see Kenneth Carroll, "Maryland Quakers and Slavery," *Quaker History* 72, 1 (Spring 1983): 28, 31, 36.

39. Drake, *Quakers and Slavery*, 69.

40. Crane, *Dependent People*, 164 n5; Charles Rappleye, *Sons of Providence: The Brown Brothers, the Slave Trade, and the American Revolution* (New York: Simon and Schuster, 2006), 12.

41. Richard Foster, "Quaker Concern in Race Relations: Then & Now" (Thesis, California Yearly Meeting, 1970), 22.

42. Wax, "Negro Slave Trade," 91; Nash and Soderlund, *Freedom by Degrees*, 62.

43. Nash, "Slaves and Slaveholders in Colonial Pennsylvania," 60.

44. Foster, "Quaker Concern," 35-36. From 1731 to 1753, 94 percent of yearly meeting offices were held by wealthy Philadelphia or Burlington (NJ) Friends who were customarily in high government positions. See Soderlund, *Quakers and Slavery*, 50.

45. Nash and Soderlund, *Freedom by Degrees*, 11; Soderlund, *Quakers and Slavery*, 34-36. Soderlund's data is from probate or tax assessment records that could be found for leaders.

46. Nash, "Slaves and Slaveholders in Colonial Pennsylvania," 60-61.

47. Soderlund, *Quakers and Slavery*, 17, 22, 23, 34-36, 45-46. Soderlund's data pertain only to those for whom records exist. Two of three Overseers of the Press were enslavers between 1681 and 1705, thirteen of seventeen between 1706 and 1730, and six of nine between 1731 and 1751.

48. Soderlund, *Quakers and Slavery*, 48-49 and see tables on 164-66. William Kashatus, *Just over the Line: Chester County and the Underground Railroad* (West Chester, PA: Chester County Historical Society, 2002), Appendix A, lists owners and numbers of enslaved in the county's towns. See also Nash and Soderlund, *Freedom by Degrees*, 46-48, 163.

49. Worrall, *Quakers in the Colonial Northeast*, 156, 159-61.

50. Nash, "Slaves and Slaveholders in Colonial Pennsylvania," 61-62; Soderlund, *Quakers and Slavery*, 10, 138.

51. Frost, e-mail to authors, 23 August 2003.

52. J. William Frost, ed., *The Quaker Origins of Antislavery* (Norwood, PA: Norwood Editions, 1980), 27-28.

53. Drake, *Quakers and Slavery*, 13.

54. *Journal of George Fox*, 8th and bicentenary ed. (London: Friends' Tract Association, 1891), on Quaker Writings web site, http://www.qhpre.org/quakerpages/qwhp/barb.htm.

55. Fox did not use the word "slavery," according to Frost, e-mail to authors, 23 August 2003. At least one study suggests that because enslavement of Africans was a new phenomenon in Fox's time, he may not have understood the full extent of enslavement. See Kenneth L. Carroll, "George Fox and Slavery," *Quaker History* 86, 2 (Fall 1997): 16.

56. J. William Frost, "George Fox's Ambiguous Anti-Slavery Legacy," in *New Light on George Fox: 1624-1691: A Collection of Essays*, ed. Michael Mullett (York, Eng.: Ebor Press, 1991), 71. In one version of his tract Fox suggested a specific duration of thirty years of service, but that number was omitted by an editor preparing his papers for publication in 1694. It is not known whether the emendation came from Fox himself.

57. Frost, "George Fox's Ambiguous Anti-Slavery Legacy," 71.

58. *Ibid.*, 70, 80.

59. The Overseers were "weighty" Friends, close associates of Penn, and one an enslaver. *Ibid.*, 79.

60. Larry Ingle, *First among Friends: George Fox and the Creation of Quakerism* (New York: Oxford University Press, 1994), 236. In Barbados, Friends who followed Fox's advice to teach Christianity and treat the enslaved well suffered negative consequences from other enslavers for doing so. See Marietta, *Reformation of American Quakerism*, 111.

61. Drake, *Quakers and Slavery*, 23.

62. William Penn, *Some Fruits of Solitude* in Richard Dunn and Mary Maples Dunn, eds., *Works I*, 856.

63. Marietta, *Reformation of American Quakerism*, 24.

64. Soderlund, *Quakers and Slavery*, 139 n. 60.

65. Elizabeth Cazden has offered an important corrective on several published accounts of this incident in "Unchristian and Unhuman: The Disownment of Abigail Allen" (forthcoming manuscript) based on extensive study of the monthly meeting minutes and other primary sources.

66. Cazden, "Disownment of Abigail Allen," referred to Drake, *Quakers and Slavery*, 17–18, and Jones, *Quakers in the American Colonies*, 156–57.

67. Peter Benes, "Slavery in Boston Households, 1647–1770," in *Slavery/Antislavery in New England*, ed. Peter Benes (Boston: Boston University, 2005), 15–17.

68. Higginbotham, *In the Matter of Color*, 277, 278, 280.

69. Fitts, *Slave Paradise*, 105–7, 205, 212. In 1774 Thomas Richardson owned four enslaved Africans; Joseph and William Wanton, six, and John Collins, thirteen. See Davis, "Newport Slave Traders."

70. Shane White, *Somewhat More Independent: The End of Slavery in New York City, 1770–1810* (Athens: University of Georgia Press, 1991), 17–20, 87, 114.

71. J. William Frost, "The Origins of the Quaker Crusade: A Review of Recent Literature," *Quaker History* 67, 1 (Spring 1978): 56.

72. Barbour and Frost, *Quakers*, 122.

73. James, *People among Peoples*, 108.

74. Drake, *Quakers and Slavery*, 11–12.

75. Minutes compiled by New England Yearly Meeting Faith and Practice Revision Committee, May 2004. Crane, *Dependent People*, 81, 164, has stated that Newport Quaker merchants intent on profiting on slave trade "showed an unwarrantable desire after the perishing things of the world."

76. Frost, ed., *Quaker Origins of Anti-Slavery*, 69.

77. Minutes of 1719 Philadelphia Yearly Meeting, excerpted in Michener, *Retrospect of Early Quakerism*, 341; on Edmundson, see also Worrall, *Quakers in the Colonial Northeast*, 153–54. Edmundson's letter was also received by Friends in Virginia and Maryland but, as Bliss Forbush has noted in *A History of Baltimore Yearly Meeting of Friends: Three Hundred Years of Quakerism in Maryland, Virginia, the District of Columbia, and Central Pennsylvania* (Sandy Spring, MD: Baltimore Yearly Meeting of Friends), 40, "no one listened." On Edmundson's failure to advocate immediate emancipation, see James, *A People among Peoples*, 105, 109.

78. Gerrit Hendrics et al. "This is from our meeting at Germantown, held ye 18 of the 2 month, 1688, to be delivered to the Monthly Meeting at Richard Worrell's," transcribed in Philip S. Benjamin, *The Philadelphia Quakers in an Industrial Age* (Philadelphia: Temple University Press, 1976), 88. Once thought to be lost, the petition was found in 1844. See also Frost, *Quaker Origins of Anti-Slavery*, 69.

79. At the time, the meeting for business was held at a location solely for that purpose once a month. In modern times, the monthly meeting most often refers to a local meeting which holds weekly meetings for worship as well as its own meeting for business. On the yearly meeting's decision, see Drake, *Quakers and Slavery*, 11–12.

80. Drake, *Quakers and Slavery*, 13.

81. Marietta, *Reformation of American Quakerism*, 112; Frost, "George Fox's Ambiguous Anti-Slavery Legacy," 75.

82. An Exhortation & Caution to Friends Concerning Buying or Keeping of Negroes, Given Forth by our Monethly Meeting In Philadelphia, the 13th day of the 8th Moneth, 1693" (New York : William Bradford, 1693), Microform: Early American imprints, First series, 636.

83. Marietta, *Reformation of American Quakerism*, 112; Frost, "George Fox's Ambiguous Anti-Slavery Legacy," 75.

84. Foster, "Quaker Concern," 15–16. Drake, *Quakers and Slavery*, 14–15. Keith was disowned in 1695 by Philadelphia Yearly Meeting for his theological views. Barbour and Frost, *The Quakers*, 344.

85. James, *People among Peoples*, 110; Drake, *Quakers and Slavery*, 19.

86. Southeby was a prominent Friend very involved in the affairs of Third Haven Meeting in Maryland before he moved to Philadelphia in the late 1690s. While he was recognized for his many humanitarian concerns, he had not spoken out against enslavement until he moved. See Kenneth Carroll, "William Southeby: Early Quaker Antislavery Writer," *Pennsylvania Magazine of History and Biography* 89 (1965): 416, 417. See also Kenneth Carroll, *Three Hundred Years and More of Third Haven Quakerism* (Baltimore, MD: Queen Anne Press, 1984), 38.

87. Drake, *Quakers and Slavery*, 39; see also James, *People among Peoples*, 120.

88. "Epistle LXXXI," London Yearly Meeting, 1758, quoted in *A Collection of the Epistles from the Yearly Meeting of Friends in London, to the Quarterly & Monthly Meetings in Great Britain, Ireland, and Elsewhere, from 1675–1820* (New York, Samuel Wood, 1821) 255–56. The yearly meeting repeated and expanded upon that warning through the 1770s.

89. Drake, *Quakers and Slavery*, 24; Nash and Soderlund, *Freedom by Degrees*, 45–46.

90. Drake, *Quaker Origins of Anti-Slavery*, 27, 28; Drake, *Quakers and Slavery*, 13; Nash and Soderlund, *Freedom by Degrees*, 45–46; James, *People among Peoples*, 117. The Disciplines, more extensive in colonial times, are the written standards governing all elements of Quaker practice from conduct to marriage, and oaths to family visits.

91. Quoted in Michener, *Retrospect of Early Quakerism*, 338–39.

92. Drake, *Quakers and Slavery*, 28–29. "London's cautious statement showed all too clearly that the courageous generation of the Quaker founders had passed," Drake wrote (25). "English Quakers now ought to end controversy, not to provoke it."

93. Drake, *Quakers and Slavery*, 31.

94. James, *People among Peoples*, 123–24.

95. Drake, *Quakers and Slavery*, 29.

96. Minutes of Philadelphia Yearly Meeting, 1719, excerpted in Michener, *Retrospect of Early Quakerism*, 341.

97. James, *People among Peoples*, 123; Drake, *Quakers and Slavery*, 31.

98. Drake, *Quakers and Slavery*, 31–32; Aptheker, "Quakers and Negro Slavery," 340. Quaker historian Christopher Densmore suggests that Farmer could have been disowned not for his views but for holding separate meetings, raising fears among Philadelphia Friends that he was "beginning a separation" as George Keith had done thirty years earlier. Densmore, e-mail to authors, 4 January 2006.

99. Burling's paper is included in Benjamin Lay, *All Slave-Keepers, that Keep the Innocent in Bondage, Apostates Pretending to Lay Claim to the Pure & Holy Christian Religion but Especially in Their Ministers, by Whose Example the Filthy Leprosy and Apostacy is Spread Far and Near* (Philadelphia: by the author, 1738), 40. Drake, *Quakers and Slavery*, 36, 37, 39, 40, 47, wrote that Benjamin Franklin printed Lay's paper as well as Sandiford's and others.

100. Drake, *Quakers and Slavery*, 36–37; Carter G. Woodson, "Anthony Benezet," *Journal of Negro History* 2, 1 (January 1917): 37 n. 1.

101. Drake, "Quaker Antislavery Pioneer," 122–23.

102. Keithian Monthly Meeting "An Exhortation & Caution to Friends Concerning Buying or Keeping of Negroes, Given Forth by our Monethly Meeting In Philadelphia, the 13th day of the 8th Moneth, 1693." Drake, "Quaker Antislavery Pioneer," 126, dates meeting approval of Coleman's paper as 1719; Drake's later *Quakers and Slavery* dates it 1729, one other historians have also cited. The minute of the approval is dated 1729/30, based on the English calendar year."

103. Drake, "Quaker Antislavery Pioneer," 122.

104. Worrall, *Quakers in the Colonial Northeast*, 158; Drake, *Quakers and Slavery*, 38.

105. Frost, *Quaker Origins of Antislavery*, 27–28.

106. John Hepburn, "The American Defence of the Christian Golden Rule, or an Essay to Prove the Unlawfulness of Making Slaves of Men" (1715), microfiche, Early American Imprints, 1st ser., 1678.

107. Soderlund, *Quakers and Slavery*, 163.

108. John Cox, *History of Quakerism in New York* (New York: privately printed, 1930), 54–57.

109. Drake, *Quakers and Slavery*, 32; Hilty, *By Land and by Sea*, 24.

110. Drake, *Quakers and Slavery*, 82; Carroll, *Three Hundred Years*, 38.

111. James, *People among Peoples*, 123.

112. Marietta, *Reformation of American Quakerism*, 112–13. According to Aptheker, Lay had been disowned in his native England but continued to "consider himself a

Quaker." See Herbert Aptheker, "The Quakers and Negro Slavery," *Journal of Negro History* 25, 3 (July 1940): 344.

113. Barbour and Frost, *Quakers*, 122, 178.

114. Frost, *Quaker Origins of Antislavery*, 124.

115. Sandiford quoted in Drake, *Quakers and Slavery*, 40.

116. Forrest G. Wood, *The Arrogance of Faith: Christianity and Race in America from the Colonial Era to the Twentieth Century* (New York: Knopf, 1990), 62.

117. Nash and Soderlund have noted that those who argued against slavery through Ralph Sandiford in the late 1720s were "well-situated men" of the same social status as those whom they chastised. Nash and Soderlund, *Freedom by Degrees*, 47.

118. Woodson, "Anthony Benezet," 38 n. 3; William Kashatus, "Friends Fight for Freedom," *Pennsylvania Heritage* 14, 3 (Summer 1988): 4–9.

119. Lay, *All Slave-Keepers, that Keep the Innocent in Bondage, Apostates Pretending to Lay Claim to the Pure & Holy Christian Religion . . .*, title page and preface.

120. *Ibid.*

121. Kashatus, "Friends Fight for Freedom," 7.

122. Soderlund, *Quakers and Slavery*, 16.

123. Lay, *ibid.* Also see Drake, *Quakers and Slavery*, 221.

124. Thomas Clarkson, *The History of the Rise, Progress, and Accomplishment of the Abolition of the African Slave-Trade by the British Parliament* (London: L. Taylor, 1808), 1: 149–50.

125. Ruth Nuermberger, *The Free Produce Movement: A Quaker Protest against Slavery* (Durham, NC: Duke University Press, 1942) 5; Jean Soderlund, "Radical and Conservative Friends in the Fight Against Slavery," in Eliza Cope Harrison, ed., *For Emancipation and Education: Some Black and Quaker Efforts 1680–1900* (Philadelphia, PA: Awbury Arboretum Association, 1997), 20.

126. Nash and Soderlund, *Freedom by Degrees*, 63.

127. James, *People among Peoples*, 127.

128. Lester Scherer, *Slavery and the Churches*, 71.

129. Foster, "Quaker Concern," 34; Soderlund, *Quakers and Slavery*, 13.

130. Phillips Moulton, ed., *Journal and Major Essays of John Woolman* (New York: Oxford University Press, 1971), 66.

131. Moulton, ed., *John Woolman*, 39.

132. *Ibid.*, 66.

133. Drake, *Quakers and Slavery*, 68–69.

134. Soderlund, *Quakers and Slavery*, 27; Drake, *Quakers and Slavery*, 57.

135. Nuermberger, *Free Produce Movement*, 4.

136. Marietta, *Reformation of American Quakerism*, 101, 103.

137. Frost, "Origins of the Quaker Crusade," 53.

138. Soderlund, *Quakers and Slavery*, 26–27; Drake, *Quakers and Slavery*, 56.

139. Quoted in Michener, *Retrospect of Early Quakerism*, 343. There is some question whether Woolman or his colleague Anthony Benezet wrote the 1754 epistle. Drake, *Quakers and Slavery*, 56, 62, has stated that Woolman was the author, and

has added that "Woolman moved first with Benezet helping at every turn." Frost, "Origins of the Quaker Crusade," 49–50, has dismissed that claim. Soderlund, *Quakers and Slavery*, 26 n. 28, has cited Philadelphia Monthly Meeting records indicating that a committee revised a proposal from Benezet. Barbour and Frost, *Quakers*, 123, have stated that Benezet "probably" wrote the epistle.

140. Barbour and Frost, Quakers, 131; Worrall, *Quakers in the Colonial Northeast*, 160; Drake, *Quakers and Slavery*, 63–64.

141. Woolman made several trips to North Carolina meetings and in 1757 wrote letters outlining his views on enslavement to the New Garden and Cane Creek meetings. See Stephen Jay White, "Friends and the Coming of the Revolution," *The Southern Friend* 4, 1 (Spring 1982): 25.

142. Drake, *Quakers and Slavery*, 68–69.

143. Ken Carroll, "300 Years of Quakerism," Third Haven Meeting web site, http://www.thirdhaven.org/index2.html.

144. Jay Worrall Jr., *The Friendly Virginians: America's First Quakers* (Athens, GA: Iberian, 1994), 186.

145. Nash, *Forging Freedom*, 91; Irv Brendlinger, "Anthony Benezet: True Champion of the Slave," *Wesleyan Theological Journal* 32, 1 (Spring 1997): 5–7, reprinted at Wesley Center web site, http://Wesley.nnu.edu/WesleyanTheology/theorjrnl/31-35.htm. Benezet's letter to Queen Charlotte, written in 1783, is quoted in Clarkson, *The History of the Abolition of the Slave-Trade*, 1:172.

146. Nash, *Forging Freedom*, 31, quoting the work of Benezet's eulogist, Roberts Vaux, *Memoirs of the Life of Anthony Benezet*, 29. "Africans in America," WGBH/PBS Online; www.pbs.org.

147. "Observations on Slavery," in Anthony Benezet, *Serious Considerations on Several Important Subjects* (Philadelphia: Joseph Cruikshank, 1778), 27. The earliest version of the essay was published in 1748.

148. Nancy Slocum Hornick, "Anthony Benezet: Eighteenth Century Social Critic, Educator and Abolitionist" (Ph.D. diss., University of Maryland, 1974), 418–20.

149. Frost, "Origins of the Quaker Crusade," 53.

150. Drake, *Quakers and Slavery*, 92.

151. Scherer, *Slavery and the Churches*, 131, has called Benezet a "one-man abolition society."

152. Drake, *Quakers and Slavery*, 62, 86; see also Roger Bruns, "A Quaker Antislavery Crusade: Anthony Benezet," *Quaker History* 65, 2 (Autumn 1976): 86.

153. Drake, *Quakers and Slavery*, 94; Brendlinger, "Anthony Benezet," 1.

154. Ira Berlin, *Many Thousands Gone: The First Two Centuries of Slavery in North America* (Cambridge, MA, and London: Belknap Press of Harvard University Press, 1998), table 1, 369–71, cites the mainland North American slave population as 70,043 in 1720 and 246,648 in 1750; of that total, 14,081 lived in the North in 1720 and 30,172 in 1750.

155. Barbour and Frost, *Quakers*, 120; Franklin and Moss, *From Slavery to Freedom*, 70.

156. Herbert Aptheker, *American Negro Slave Revolts* (New York: International Publishers, 1969), 369.

157. Thomas Hamm, *The Quakers in America* (New York: Columbia University Press, 2003), 32.

158. Marietta, *Reformation of American Quakerism*, xii, 3; John Churchman, *An Account of the Gospel Labours and Christian Experiences of a Faithful Minister of Christ, John Churchman* (Philadelphia: Joseph Cruikshank, 1779), 119.

159. Marietta, *Reformation of American Quakerism*, 102; Hamm, *The Quakers*, 32.

160. Marietta, *Reformation of American Quakerism*, xii. According to Scherer, *Slavery and the Churches*, 157, at the time of this critique, survival and acquiring new members took precedence in other churches over any concern about enslavement. According to Barbour and Frost, *The Quakers*, 129–30, three-quarters of all disownments in Philadelphia Monthly Meeting between 1750 and 1760 were for marrying non-Quakers. The reformers wanted a "unified family" and would rather disown than try to convert non-Quaker spouses.

161. Marietta, *Reformation of American Quakerism*, 101, 125–28.

162. Soderlund, *Quakers and Slavery*, 30–31.

163. Barbour and Frost, *Quakers*, 129–130; Marietta, *Reformation of American Quakerism*, xiii, 128.

164. Marietta, *Reformation of American Quakerism*, 121–25, 133–135, described some of the many plots by various politicians (including some Friends) to weaken the "Quaker Party" and remove Quakers, who were not particularly popular, from office.

165. Edwin Bronner, "Intercolonial Relationships between American Quakers," *Quaker History* 56, 1 (Spring 1967): 17.

166. Marietta, *Reformation of American Quakerism*, 55; Arthur Worrall and Hugh Barbour, "Building Traditions and Testimonies," in Barbour et al., *Quaker Crosscurrents*, 23.

167. Marietta, *Reformation of American Quakerism*, 275; Nash and Soderlund, *Freedom by Degrees*, 54; Soderlund, *Quakers and Slavery*, 170–71, 177, 186–87.

168. Soderlund, *Quakers and Slavery*, 173, 32.

169. Barbour and Frost, *The Quakers*, 92, 122–23; *Resistance and Obedience to God: Memoirs of David Ferris* (1707–1779), Martha Paxson Grundy, ed. (Philadelphia: Friends General Conference, 2001), xv, xvi.

170. Marietta, *Reformation of American Quakerism*, 43–45; Kenneth Carroll, "A Look at the 'Quaker Revival of 1756'," *Quaker History* 65 (Autumn 1976), 2, 64, 79–80. Carroll presents evidence supporting his contention that by the time Philadelphia Yearly Meeting was most affected by reformers in 1756, there had been a broad reform movement in England, spread by both English and American ministers, that was already taking hold in the Atlantic Quaker community. In Rhode Island the work against enslavement increased; many older Friends who enslaved people had been "dealt with" by that time. See Worrall, *Quakers in the Colonial Northeast*, 162, and Frederick B. Tolles, "An Afterword on Woolman and Slavery," in *John Woolman, Some Considerations on the Keeping of Negroes* (1754; reprint, Northampton, MA: Gehenna Press, 1970).

171. James, *People Among Peoples*, 142; Drake, *Quakers and Slavery*, 55. Marietta and others have provided a more detailed explanation of a complicated political scene involving those whose interests would be served by seeing the province's charter withdrawn and government turned over to the king against those, including most but not all Friends, who feared the consequences of that move for their own status in the colony. See the chapter "Withdrawal from Government" in Marietta, *Reformation of American Quakerism*, 150–68.

172. Marietta, *Reformation of American Quakerism*, 151–52, 122, 163–64. The larger problem was for Friends who refused to pay taxes that were supporting war, who functioned as collectors of those taxes, or who as judges would have to deal with the offenders. See also James, *People among Peoples*, 142–43. The exception to the Quaker legislators' behavior in this matter was refusing to endorse compulsory military service.

173. Soderlund, *Quakers and Slavery*, 8.

174. James, *People among Peoples*, 114–15.

175. Drake, *Quakers and Slavery*, 60–61.

176. Soderlund, *Quakers and Slavery*, 150.

177. Marietta, *Reformation of American Quakerism*, 115. The quotation from Woolman's report on the meeting appears in Amelia Mott Gummere, *Journal and Essays of John Woolman* (New York: Macmillan, 1922), 215–16. See also Drake, *Quakers and Slavery*, 60–61.

178. Gummere, *John Woolman*, 216–17; Foster, "Quaker Concern," 40; Marietta, *Reformation of American Quakerism*, 276.

179. Marietta, *Reformation of American Quakerism*, 115–17.

180. Wood, *Arrogance of Faith*, 286.

181. James, *People among Peoples*, 128.

182. Jean Soderlund, "Black Women in Colonial Pennsylvania" in Trotter and Smith, eds., *African Americans in Pennsylvania*, 84–85.

183. Soderlund, *Quakers and Slavery*, 161, 166; Marietta, *Reformation of American Quakerism*, 114–15, 117.

184. Densmore et al., "Slavery and Abolition in 1830," 66–67; Soderlund, *Quakers and Slavery*, 112, 128.

185. Melish, *Disowning Slavery*, 52–53.

186. Frost, *Quaker Origins of Antislavery*, 123, 27–28. Frost's analysis of why emancipation took as long as it did is particularly lucid and uses as its basis the process of ending enslavement among Philadelphia Friends. See also Soderland, *Quakers and Slavery*, 173–187, on the struggles within individual monthly meetings and Philadelphia Yearly Meeting.

187. Marietta, *Reformation of American Quakerism*, 118.

188. *Ibid.*, 4–10, presents a thorough exposition of the process of disownment in the section, "The Practice of Discipline."

189. Carroll, "Maryland Quakers," 38–39; Marietta, *Reformation of American Quakerism*, 120.

190. More details on the views of the reformers and descriptions of their travels appears in James, *People among Peoples*, chap. 9; see also Rebecca Larson, *Daughters of Light: Quaker Women Preaching and Prophesying in the Colonies and Abroad, 1700–1775* (New York: Knopf, 1999).

191. Marietta, *Reformation of American Quakerism*, 128, cites Mary Mabel Dunn's suggestion that one of the reasons or fruits of the reformation was that within the closed Society of Friends "women could live more comfortably with a social role that was not universally acceptable."

192. Linda Selleck, *Gentle Invaders: Quaker Women Educators and Racial Issues during the Civil War and Reconstruction* (Richmond, IN: Friends United Press, 1995), 21; Larson, *Daughters of Light*, 222; Katherine Smedley, *Martha Schofield and the Re-Education of the South* (New York: Edwin Mellen Press), 10–13. Smedley's book is about Mary Schofield's daughter, Martha, and the school she started in South Carolina. The visits to the South by her mother, a committed abolitionist from Pennsylvania, were cut short by her husband's poor health.

193. Patience Brayton, *A Short Account of the Life and Religious Labours of Patience Brayton, Late of Swansey in the State of Massachusetts: Mostly Selected from Her Own Minutes* (New Bedford, MA: A. Shearman, 1801), iii–iv.

194. *Ibid.*, iii–iv. Brayton also petitioned King George to end trade in Africans and free those held in enslavement; see Drake, *Quakers and Slavery*, 92.

195. Margaret Hope Bacon, *Quiet Rebels: The Story of Quakers in America* (New York: Basic Books, 1969), 77; Selleck, *Gentle Invaders*, 20. According to Selleck, Harrison was credited with freeing two hundred enslaved people.

196. Worrall, *Friendly Virginians*, 230.

197. Harrison quoted in *Friends' Miscellany* 11 (March 1838): 154.

198. Marietta, *Reformation of American Quakerism*, 55, 296 n. 16; Jack Marietta, "A Note on Quaker Membership," *Quaker History* 59, 1(Spring 1970): 40–43. As Marietta noted, no Quaker census other than Philadelphia Monthly Meeting's of 1760 and 1772 exists. He used records of contributions to all meetings in the yearly meeting to estimate yearly meeting membership. J. Reaney Kelly, *Quakers in the Founding of Anne Arundel County, Maryland* (Baltimore: Maryland Historical Society, 1963), 88, noted that while some who were disowned went to other churches, others remained in the Quaker subculture without being able to participate in the business of the community. See also Drake, *Quakers and Slavery*, 79.

199. "Epistle XCVII," 97, London Yearly Meeting, in *Collection of Epistles*, 315.

200. Turner, *Negro in Pennsylvania*, 61.

201. Leslie Harris, *In the Shadow of Slavery: African Americans in New York City, 1626–1863* (Chicago: University of Chicago Press, 2003), 61; Drake, *Quakers and Slavery*, 82–83; Weeks, *Southern Quakers and Slavery*, 213. According to Weeks, by 1785 no members of Virginia Yearly Meeting were enslavers, except for those who were minors or owned by a non-Quaker head of the family. In 1786 the yearly meeting declared that Friends who were overseers of the enslaved were to be considered the same as owners and thus disowned.

202. Turner, *Negro in Pennsylvania*, 60–63; Nash and Soderlund, *Freedom by Degrees*, 87.
203. Christopher Densmore, note to authors, June 2008.
204. Nash and Soderlund, *Freedom by Degrees*, 90.
205. John Woolman, "The Walking Journey," in *John Woolman: American Quaker*, ed. Janet Whitney (Boston: Little Brown, 1942), 349–50.
206. Drake, *Quakers and Slavery*, 75–76.
207. Rappleye, *Sons of Providence*, 56–57. The people enslaved by Moses Brown were Bonno, who was 25 in 1764, Caesar, who was 23, Cudgo, for whom Rappleye gave no age, Pero, 18, from Africa, Prince, 25, and "at least one woman," Eve (or perhaps Peg), who had been given to Brown's daughter, Mary, by her uncle Obadiah Brown. There were also several enslaved people owned by the brothers in common who were not freed. They were Yarrow, 40, Tom, 30, Newport, 21, and a child of one of them. William D. Johnson, *History of Slavery in Rhode Island in the 1894 report of the R.I. Historical Society* (R.I. Historical Society: Providence Standard Printing Co., 1894), 52–53.
208. Hazelton, *Let Freedom Ring*, xix, 31–32, 89; Drake, *Quakers and Slavery*, 79–80; Barbour and Frost, *The Quakers*, 298–299. Brown helped organize the New England Yearly Meeting boarding school and in 1819 revived it on land he donated in Providence after it had failed in Portsmouth. The school today bears his name. He was active in visiting Friends all over New England to help them free those they enslaved. He also brought antislavery petitions to Congress.
209. Thomas Drake, *Quakers and Slavery*, 50.
210. Anna Braithwaite Thomas, comp., *The Story of Baltimore Yearly Meeting from 1632 to 1938* (Baltimore: Weant Press, 1938), 62.
211. See Berlin, *Many Thousands Gone*, 372–73, table 2. Among the population of North Carolina in 1790, for example, were 4,975 free people of African descent and 105,547 enslaved people.
212. Drake, *Quakers and Slavery*, 83.
213. Marietta, *Reformation of American Quakerism*, 123; Donald Mathews, "Religion and Slavery—The Case of the American South" in Christine Bolt and Seymour Drescher, eds., *Anti-Slavery, Religion and Reform: Essays in Memory of Rogert Anstey* (Folkestone, Eng.: W. Dawson; Hamden, CT: Archon Books, 1980), 212–13, 216; Scherer, *Slavery and the Churches*, 64.
214. On the Nicholites, see Kenneth Carroll, *Joseph Nichols and the Nicholites: A Look at the "New Quakers" of Maryland, Delaware, North and South Carolina* (Easton, MD: Easton Publishing Co., 1962), 25, 52, 61–2; Kenneth Carroll, "The Nicholites Become Quakers," *Bulletin of the Friends Historical Association* 47, 1 (Spring 1958): 13–18. Many of the Nicholites who relocated from Delaware to the area around Deep River, NC, also became Quakers. The Nicholite discipline was "too straight" for some, and the deaths of older members were other reasons they thought it would be mutually beneficial to join with Friends, Carroll, *Joseph Nichols and the Nicholites*, 57–58.
215. Nash and Soderlund, *Freedom by Degrees*, 91–92. As Crane, *Dependent People*, 130, notes, some Friends made a different choice. In the 1760s and 1770s in

Newport, for example, a number of Quakers as well as Baptists who were more invested in their social and economic status became Episcopalians. Frost, *Quaker Origins of Antislavery*, 27. Methodists and Baptists divided into northern and southern churches before the Civil War.

216. Wood, *Arrogance of Faith*, 287.

217. Aptheker, "Quakers and Negro Slavery," 362.

CHAPTER TWO: **Addressing North American Enslavement: 1800–1860**

1. Nash, "Slaves and Slave Owners" in Trotter and Smith, 47.

2. Drake, *Quakers and Slavery*, 100–01. Fergus Bordewich, *Bound for Canaan: The Underground Railroad and the War for the Soul of America*, 40–42. The cotton gin, patented in 1794, separated cotton fibers from the seeds more quickly, thus increasing production and the need for more laborers. At the same time, tobacco was becoming an uncertain market, so growers turned to cotton as well as cane sugar which was in demand.

3. William diGiacomantonio, "'For the Gratification of A Volunteering Society': Antislavery and Pressure Group Politics in the First Federal Congress" in *Journal of the Early Republic* 15 (Summer 1995), 194.

4. Recall that during this time Friends were sending memorials against the slave trade and enslavement to Congress (and being turned down), Drake, *Quakers and Slavery*, 93–95.

5. Mabee, *Black Freedom*, 186.

6. Forbush, *History of Baltimore Yearly Meeting*, 49; Grundy, *Resistance and Obedience to God*, xii–xiv.

7. Grundy, *Resistance and Obedience to God*, xii–xiv.

8. Marietta, The *Reformation of American Quakerism*, 122. Nash and Soderlund, *Freedom by Degrees*, 89.

9. diGiacomantonio, "For the Gratification of A Volunteering Society," 169–70, 197.

10. William Rotch, Nantucket, to Moses Brown, Providence, 8 November 1787, Austin Collection of Moses Brown Papers, Archives of New England Yearly Meeting of Society of Friends, Rhode Island Historical Society, Providence.

11. Jay Worrall Jr., *The Friendly Virginians: America's First Quakers* (Athens, GA: Iberian, 1994), 225–26. Worrall stated that Thomas Jefferson initially cited the king's veto as another sign of oppression in the draft of the Declaration of Independence. That section was removed so that Georgia and South Carolina would agree to sign the document.

12. Drake, *Quakers and Slavery*, 88–89. Contrary to the statements in Mack Thompson, *Moses Brown: Reluctant Reformer* (Chapel Hill: University of North Carolina Press, 1962), 176–201. Moses Brown was not the creator of this committee nor even a member, although he was one of the founders of the Providence Society for the Abolition of the Slave Trade in 1789. Minutes of Rhode Island Quarterly Meeting, 1774, 312. In 1835 Moses Brown's nephew was vice-president of a newly founded Providence Anti-Abolition Society. See "Anti-abolition Meeting," *Providence Daily Journal*, Nov. 4, 1835, Brown University Steering Committee on Slavery and Justice web site, http://dl.lib.brown.edu/slaveryandjustice/.

13. Drake, *Quakers and Slavery*, 87.
14. Marietta, *Reformation of American Quakerism*, 276.
15. Drake, *Quakers and Slavery*, 93, citing Philadelphia Yearly Meeting Minutes of 1783; Worrall, *Friendly Virginians*, 237–38.
16. Benjamin Quarles, *Black Abolitionists* (Oxford: Oxford University Press, 1969), 170–77.
17. Mifflin, a Delaware congressman, countered that if his anti-enslavement stand was "fanaticism," then "may the Almighty grant me a double portion," Drake, *Quakers and Slavery*, 107–08. Joseph Ellis, *Founding Brothers*, 97.
18. Worrall, *Friendly Virginians*, 240.
19. *Ibid.*, 104.
20. *Ibid.*, 99.
21. Drake, *Quakers and Slavery*, 107; Worrall, *Friendly Virginians*, 242. The leaders of Philadelphia's African American community began to petition Congress to end the slave trade in 1799 and to "prepare the way for the oppressed to go free." See Julie Winch, *Philadelphia's Black Elite: Activism, Accommodation, and the Struggle for Autonomy, 1787–1848* (Philadelphia : Temple University Press, 1988), 73.
22. Ellis, *Founding Brothers*, 88, 101.
23. Marnie Gutsell-Miller, New England Yearly Meeting archivist, e-mail to authors, 28 March 2007.
24. Drake, *Quakers and Slavery*, 97–98.
25. Melish, *Disowning Slavery*, 71–72; Drake, *Quakers and Slavery*, 97; Rappleye, *Sons of Providence*, 314. John Brown was later elected to Congress.
26. Drake, *Quakers and Slavery*, 86.
27. Worrall, *Friendly Virginians*, 226–27; Ellis, *Founding Brothers*, 95–96.
28. Worrall, *Friendly Virginians*, 227.
29. John Michael Shay, "The Antislavery Movement in North Carolina" (Ph.D. diss., Princeton University, 1971), 224.
30. *Ibid.*, 201–2. Shay described the petitions as "numerous" but offered no exact number.
31. Drake, *Quakers and Slavery*, 89, 95–98.
32. *Ibid.*, 107, 129. Quakers sent petitions to Congress in 1816, 1823, 1836, 1847, and 1849. See Seth Hinshaw and Mary Edith Hinshaw, *Carolina Quakers: Our Heritage, Our Hope* (Greensboro: North Carolina Yearly Meeting, 1972), 135.
33. Thompson, *Moses Brown*, 177.
34. Some northern Friends and non-Quakers opposed abolition "almost as bitterly as did slaveowners." See Hugh Barbour, ed., *Slavery and Theology: Writings of Seven Quaker Reformers, 1800–1870* (Dublin, IN: Prinit Press, 1985), 5. As Marietta cautioned, it would be a "mistake to assume that the social concerns of Friends existed continuously or that they grew steadily since the seventeen century." Rather, "Quaker complacency separated the seventeenth-century leaders from the eighteenth-century reforms and severed the later Friends from the reformist impulse of earlier age." Marietta, *Reformation of American Quakerism*, 97.

35. William Kashatus, *A Virtuous Education: Penn's Vision for Philadelphia Schools* (Wallingford, PA: Pendle Hill, 1997), 173–74.

36. Hamm, *Quakers*, 1–2; Grundy, Introduction to *Resistance and Obedience to God*, xiii.

37. Nuermberger, *The Free Produce Movement*, 114.

38. Ellis, *Founding Brothers*, 100, 106. One historian has stated that compensating enslavers would cost $140 million, about twenty times the federal budget at the time.

39. Vivien Elizabeth Sandlund, "'To Arouse and Awaken the American People': The Ideas And Strategies of The Gradual Emancipationists, 1800–1850" (Ph.D. diss., Emory University, 1995), 3, 178, 181; Jesse Macy, *The Anti-Slavery Crusade: A Chronicle of the Gathering Storm* (New Haven, CT: Yale University Press, 1919), 30. Not a particularly robust man, Lundy nevertheless had, for example, walked from Baltimore to Bennington, VT, and back to urge William Lloyd Garrison to join him.

40. Macy, *Antislavery Crusade*, 32; see also Suzanne R. Wicks, "Benjamin Lundy: Pioneer Quaker Abolitionist, 1789–1839," *Friends Journal* 48, 6 (June 2002): 18–19.

41. Web site: "*Quakers and Slavery*," http://www.drwilliams.org/iDoc/Web-214.htm, 1; William Loren Katz, *Black Pioneers: An Untold Story* (New York: Atheneum, 1999), 31.

42. Barbour, ed., *Slavery and Theology*, 4.

43. For information on the "black laws" see Gwen Erickson, "State Laws and Acts Involving Free Blacks in North Carolina," *The Southern Friend* 24, 1 (Spring 2002): 47–8. Erickson is the curator of *The Friends* Historical Collection at Guilford College. See also Zilversmit, *First Emancipation*, 12–18; Nash, *Forging Freedom*, 35–36; Worrall, *Friendly Virginians*, 287; Litwack, *North of Slavery*, 64–112; Katz, *Black Pioneers*, 26, 27, 84–86, 89, 94, 96, 99–101, 128, 134, 137–39, 142, 147–48; Frank U. Quillin, *The Color Line in Ohio: A History of Race Prejudice in a Typical Northern State* (Ann Arbor, MI: George Wahr, 1913), 31–35. Lundy's Quakerly belief that the right action would be revealed in time did not suit Garrison's vision of how the conversion would come about. Rather, Garrison's approach was to challenge and confront in anticipation of a more dramatic conversion of the whole society—what biographer Henry Mayer described as a "transfiguring moment." Henry Mayer, *All on Fire: William Lloyd Garrison and the Abolition of Slavery* (New York: St. Martin's Press, 1988), 125.

44. Sandlund, "'To Arouse and Awaken,'" 2–3.

45. As quoted in Macy, *Anti-Slavery Crusade*, 33.

46. Drake, *Quakers and Slavery*, 127–28.

47. Asa Earl Martin, "Pioneer Anti-Slavery Press," *Mississippi Valley Historical Review* 2 (March 1916): 17.

48. The society's first newspaper, the *Manumission Intelligencer*, was short-lived because Elihu Embree found he could not keep to a weekly schedule and continue his own business, which was heavily subsidizing the publication. See Jack Mooney, "Elihu Embree and His Antislavery Papers" (Paper, Southeast Colloquium of AEJMC, March 1992), cited in "Elihu Embree: Early Eastern

Tennessee Abolitionism and the Roots of the Abolitionist Press, 1820," Elihu's Antislavery Papers web site, http://elihusantislaverypapers.blogspot.com/.

49. For Osborn, who later lived in Michigan, see transcript of D. Neil Snarr and Associates, *History of Cass County, Michigan* (Chicago: Waterman, Watkins & Co., 1882), 261, transcribed on the Historical Society of Porter County (IN) web site, http://home.comcast.net/~hspc/; Martin, "Pioneer Anti-Slavery Press," 511.

50. Snarr and Associates, *History of Cass County*, 261.

51. *Ibid.*; Weeks, *Southern Quakers and Slavery*, 235. The first publication advocating immediate emancipation is believed to have been George Bourne, *The Book and Slavery Irreconcilable* (Philadelphia: J. M. Sanderson & Co., 1816).

52. Duncan Rea Williams III, "*Quakers and Slavery*," Cyber Williams Niche, http://www.drwilliams.org/iDoc/web-214.htm.

53. Donald Good, "Elisha Bates and Social Reform," *Quaker History* 58, 2 (Autumn 1969): 81–92. Bates was the "most accomplished theologian Orthodox Friends produced in the U.S.," according to Ingle, *First among Friends*, 27, but became "very far in advance" of Friends of his day," as Good wrote, and in 1837, was disowned for some of those views. Good, "Elisha Bates," 82; Christopher Densmore, note to authors, June 2008.

54. In 1844, the *Friends Intelligencer*, another Hicksite paper, began more than a century of publication in Philadelphia. In 1955, *The Friend* and *Friends Intelligencer* merged to become the currently published *Friends Journal*. See Drake, *Quakers and Slavery*, 127; Christopher Densmore, e-mail to authors, 17 March 2007.

55. Drake, *Quakers and Slavery*, 100, 130.

56. The greatest growth was between 1824 and 1827, according to a listing by historian Alice Dana Adams. However, Adams' work ended with 1831. Alice Dana Adams, *The Neglected Period of Anti-Slavery in America, 1808-1831* (Boston and London: Ginn & Co., 1908), 103, 116–18. Kenneth Carroll, "Nicholites and Slavery in Eighteenth-Century Maryland," *Maryland Historical Magazine* 79, 2 (Summer 1984): 130. Carroll cited the existence of three abolition societies in Maryland before 1797. He cited some Nicholite members who later became Quaker, as well as the possibility that other Quakers were active.

57. Drake, *Quakers and Slavery*, 90 n. 19; Nash, *Forging Freedom*, 92; Barbour et al., *Quaker Crosscurrents*, 68–71; Barbara Mallonee, Jane Bonny, and Nicholas Fessenden, *Minute by Minute: A History of the Baltimore Monthly Meeting of Friends, Homewood and Stony Run* (Baltimore: Baltimore Monthly Meeting of Friends, 1992), 166; Grover, *Fugitive's Gibraltar*, 35–36. See also David Brion Davis, *Inhuman Bondage: The Rise and Fall of Slavery in the New World* (New York: Oxford University Press, 2006). Adams, *Neglected Period*, described Friends as "by far the most active opponents of slavery" and the leaders of most abolition societies. Richard Newman, *Transformation of American Abolitionism: Fighting Slavery in the Early Republic* (Chapel Hill: University of North Carolina Press, 2002), 17, described Friends as the "critical base" of abolition societies from Rhode Island to Virginia from the 1750s forward.

58. David Brion Davis, *Inhuman Bondage: The Rise and Fall of Slavery in the New World* (New York: Oxford, 2006), 374–5, n 28; Drake, *Quakers and Slavery*, 90, n.19, 153. Having lapsed during the American Revolution, when Friends were preoccupied with upholding the peace testimony, the society was revived in 1784 as the Pennsylvania Society for Promoting the Abolition of Slavery, the Relief of Free Negroes Unlawfully Held in Bondage, and for Improving the Condition of the African Race; the organization soon shortened its name to the Pennsylvania Abolition Society. Six of the founders of the state abolition society had also been founders of the 1775 group. See Barbour et al., *Quaker Crosscurrents*, 69–71. The Society still meets annually "to distribute its funds, to discuss the status of African Americans in American society today, and to consider whether it should use its voice, as the world's oldest abolition society, to protest fresh abuses to equal rights in its continuing quest for equality," according to an article by Margaret Hope Bacon on the Historical Society of Pennsylvania web site: http://www.hsp.org/default.aspx?id=818

59. Davis, *Inhuman Bondage*, 374–75 n. 28.

60. *Ibid.*, and David Brion Davis, *The Problem of Slavery in the Age of Revolution* (Ithaca, NY: Cornell University Press, 1975), 217.

61. Frost, "Origins of the Quaker Crusade," 54.

62. *Goodspeed's History of Greene Co.* (1887) on Greene County (TN) Genealogy web site, http://www.genealogyforyou.com/usa/tennessee/greene/goodspeed.htm.

63. Shay, "The Antislavery Movement," 214, 410. Shay also found that not only did the leaders of the North Carolina Manumission Society tend to be Friends, but the leaders of the Quaker community tended to be members of the Society. Shay, 424–25.

64. Scherer, *Slavery and the Churches*, 131.

65. Drake, *Quakers and Slavery*, 111; 120–21.

66. H. Larry Ingle, *Quakers in Conflict: The Hicksite Reformation*, 2d ed. (Wallingford, PA: Pendle Hill Publications, 1998), 6. Philadelphia Quakers such as Waln, Coates, Cope, Hicks, Murry, Eddy, and Brown had made their money from the products of enslavement or from shipping, insurance, real estate, banking, and manufacturing. See also Soderlund, "Black Women in Colonial Pennsylvania," 75.

67. J. William Frost, "Years of Separation and Crisis: Philadelphia Yearly Meeting, 1790–1860," in *Friends in the Delaware Valley*, ed. John Moore (Haverford, PA: Friends Historical Association, 1981), 92.

68. Adams, *Neglected Period*, 154; chaps. 14–17 detail the work of the convention. Litwack, *North of Slavery*, 18, mentions the propensity to deliver "moralistic messages."

69. Harris, *In the Shadow of Slavery*, 61; Barbour et al., *Quaker Crosscurrents*, 69–71.

70. White, *Somewhat More Independent*, 80–1, 83. White has questioned the assertion that the New York Manumission Society was responsible for the increase in manumissions in that colony because, in reality, the city was growing so rapidly that the number of manumissions was dwarfed by the increasing new arrivals. Leslie Harris, *In the Shadow of Slavery*, 62, argues that the purpose of the New York

society was not to promote abolition but primarily to protect legally manumitted African Americans who were being illegally enslaved again.

71. Harris, *In the Shadow of Slavery*, 2, 61, 49; James, *People among Peoples*, 293.

72. Worrall, *Quakers in the Colonial Northeast*, 344; Adams, *Neglected Period*, 249–50.

73. Adams, *Neglected Period*, 121; see also Marietta, *Reformation of American Quakerism*, 123.

74. Hinshaw, *Carolina Quaker Experience*, 27.

75. Adams, *Neglected Period*, 139. Henry N. Sherwood, "Early Deportation Projects," *Mississippi Valley Historical Review* 2 (1916): 485. Descriptions of other early deportation projects appears on 490.

76. Benjamin Lay, *All Slave-Keepers that Keep the Innocent in Bondage* (1737; reprint, New York: Arno Press, 1969), 201–2.

77. Drake, *Quakers and Slavery*, 121; Nash, *Forging Freedom*, 184; Winch, *Philadelphia's Black Elite*, 27.

78. Sherwood, "Early Deportation Projects," 495.

79. Thomas Hamm, ed., "On Home Colonization—by Elijah Coffin," *Slavery and Abolition* 5, 2 (September 1984): 164–65.

80. Nash, *Forging Freedom*, 233–34; Douglas Edgerton, "Its Origin Is Not a Little Curious,": A New Look at the American Colonization Society," *Journal of the Early Republic*, 5, 8 (1985), 468–471.

81. Drake, *Quakers and Slavery*, 126.

82. Printed in David Brion Davis, *Antebellum American Culture; An Interpretive Anthology*, 285, who cited Carter G. Woodson, ed., *The Mind of the Negro as Reflected in Letters Written During the Crisis, 1800–1860* (New York: Russell & Russell, 1969), 2–3.

83. Quarles, *Black Abolitionists*, 4. Thornton's presentation had an unexpected consequence. Prompted to consider their position on colonization and whether they believed peoples of European and African descent should live separately, the FAS concluded that they belonged in Philadelphia and would stay to fight for their rights. They may also have taken it as a hopeful sign that that prominent Quakers previously lukewarm about abolition were now participating in the work of a revived PAS, Nash, *Forging Freedom*, 103.

84. Nash, *Forging Freedom*, 238.

85. Litwack, *North of Slavery*, 26–27, cites the 1833 Minutes and Proceedings of the Third Annual Convention for the Improvement of the Free People of Colour in These United States.

86. Quarles, *Black Abolitionists*, 7–8.

87. Ella Forbes, "African American Resistance to Colonization," *Journal of Black Studies* 21, 2 (December 1990, 218).

88. Benjamin Lundy, "A Plan for the Gradual Abolition of Slavery in the United States, without Danger or Loss to the Citizens of the South," Baltimore: Printed by Lundy, 1825, 3, 6–8. Anti-Slavery Literature Project: http://antislavery.eserver.org/tracts/lundyplan/. 13 March 07. Lundy is careful to

give credit for the idea to Johann Georg [sic] Rapp, leader of a utopian community located first at New Harmony, Indiana, and then at Economy, Pennsylvania.

89. Mabee, *Black Freedom*, 193.

90. Margaret Hope Bacon, "Quakers and Colonization," *Quaker History* 95, 1 (Spring 2006): 27.

91. Wiggins, *Cuffe's Logs and Letters*, 45.

92. *Ibid.*, ix, 59, 98.

93. Quarles, *Black Abolitionists*, 125

94. Yet Cuffe's plan may have influenced subsequent ones on the part of prominent African Americans, including two efforts to foster the emigration of free people to Haiti in 1817–18 and 1824. See Charles Shaw, *Topographical and Historical Description of Boston* (Boston: Oliver Spear, 1817), 269–70, and J. Marcus Mitchell, "The Paul Family," *Old-Time New England* 53, 3 (Winter 1973): 73–77; see also Peter P. Hinks, *To Awaken My Afflicted Brethren: David Walker and the Problem of Antebellum Slave Resistance* (University Park: Pennsylvania State University Press, 1997), 75, 101–02.

95. Bacon, "Quakers and Colonization," 31.

96. Drake, *Quakers and Slavery*, 121.

97. Drake, *Quakers and Slavery*, 178, 126; Mark Perry, *Lift Up Thy Voice: The Grimké Family's Journey from Slaveholders to Civil Rights Leaders* (New York: Viking Penguin, 2001), 49.

98. Nash, *Forging Freedom*, 235.

99. Hamm et al., "A Great and Good People."

100. Perry, *Lift Up Thy Voice*, 49. Bacon, "Quakers and Colonization," 37.

101. John Greenleaf Whittier, "Justice and Expediency" in *The Works of John Greenleaf Whittier* (Boston and New York: Houghton, Mifflin, 1892), 15. Whittier took his number from the 1832 Address of the Managers of the Colonization Society.

102. Web site of historian and author Douglas Harper, http://www.slavenorth.com, 29 December 2004.

103. Goodman, *Of One Blood, abolitionism and the origins of racial equality* (Berkeley: University of California Press, 1998), 57.

104. P. J. Staudenraus, *The African Colonization Movement, 1816-1865* (New York: Octagon Books, 1961). Appendix, states that the last ACS report was in 1869 and that these figures appeared on page 28 in the *Liberia Bulletin* 16 (February 1900). Forbes, "African American Resistance," 219, provides the highest estimate—15,386.

105. Hiram Hilty, *Toward Freedom for All: North Carolina Quakers and Slavery* (Richmond, IN: Friends United Press, 1993), 59; Litwack, *North of Slavery*, 28; Henry Mayer, *All on Fire*, 155–57, states that Garrison traveled to England to convince British Friends and others that colonization was not a good idea. His trip was paid for by African American supporters.

106. Wood, *Arrogance of Faith*, 294–95.

107. August Meier, *Negro Thought in America, 1880-1915: Racial Ideologies in the Age of Booker T. Washington*, 2d ed. (New York: Macmillan, 1987), 4; "The

Proceedings of the Convention," cited in Leon Litwack, "The Negro Abolitionist," in *The Antislavery Vanguard: New Essays on the Abolitionists*, ed. Martin Duberman (Princeton, NJ: Princeton University Press, 1965), 153; Katz, *Black Pioneers*, 166–67.

108. Adams, *Neglected Period*, 151–52. For information on the many free produce groups see Nuermberger, *Free Produce Movement*, 39–40, 46, 52–55, 117–18; Mabee, *Black Freedom*, 202–3; Adams, *Neglected Period*, 150; and Kashatus, *Just over the Line*, 41.

109. Mabee, *Black Freedom*, 186.

110. Adams, *Neglected Period*, 151.

111. Mabee, *Black Freedom*, 186–7, 197–98, 201.

112. Drake, *Quakers and Slavery*, 118.

113. Nuermberger, *Free Produce Movement*, 7; Elias Hicks, "Observations on the Slavery of Africans and Their Descendants," in *Slavery and Theology: Writings of Seven Quaker Reformers, 1800–1870*, ed. Hugh Barbour (Dublin, IN: Print Press, 1985), 11, 13–14. Drake, *Quakers and Slavery*, 116, 117; Adams, *Neglected Period*, 65–66.

114. Elias Hicks, *Letters of Elias Hicks* (New York: Isaac T. Hopper, 1834), 16.

115. Drake, *Quakers and Slavery*, 118.

116. Martin, "Pioneer Anti-Slavery Press," 510–28.

117. Mabee, *Black Freedom*, 186, 197–98, 201. Mabee described some of the reasons that abolitionists gave for not supporting the boycott as "flimsy"—for example, the claim that a successful boycott would end up hurting the enslaved people themselves.

118. Emma Lapsansky, "Free Produce, Free People: Philadelphia Quakers and the Environment of Reform, 1800–1854" (lecture, Great Works Symposium on the Underground Railroad, Drexel University, Philadelphia, PA, 17 January 2002). In addition to Mott, the 64 signers included Friends Thomas M'Clintock, Abraham Pennock, and Thomas Shipley; members included Isaac Hopper, Joseph Parrish, and Joseph Parker.

119. Nuermberger, *Free Produce Movement*, 34–35.

120. The Association of Friends for Promoting the Abolition of Slavery and Improving the Condition of the Free People of Color, *An Address to the Members of the Religious Society of Friends, on the Propriety of Abstaining from the Use of the Produce of Slave Labor* (Philadelphia: Merrihew, 1838), 8, 9.

121. Nuermberger, *Free Produce Movement*, 25–26. Mabee, *Black Freedom*, 190–200, 202.

122. Bacon, "By Moral Force Alone," 278, 279.

123. Unlike Philadelphia, however, this was organized during yearly meeting sessions, although it is not clear that it was a formal committee of the yearly meeting.

124. Nuermberger, *Free Produce Movement*, 43, 29, 37; Drake, *Quakers and Slavery*, 171, 173–74.

125. Nuermberger, *Free Produce Movement*, 115; 49–51, 54–56.

126. Mary Ann Yannessa, *Levi Coffin, Quaker: Breaking the Bonds of Slavery in Ohio and Indiana* (Richmond, IN: Friends United Press, 2001), 17–18, 25–26.

127. Nuermberger, *Free Produce Movement*, 13–14, 18–19.

128. The Free Produce Association of Ohio Yearly Meeting was active for about nine years. Nuermberger, 52–55, 105–106, 110 and Drake, *Quakers and Slavery*, 174.

129. Bacon, "By Moral Force Alone, 278; Mabee, *Black Freedom*, 187, 188. True to their commitment, the cake for the wedding of Quaker Angelina Grimké and Theodore Weld, was made from free labor sugar. Stores tended to be where there were concentrations of Quakers—in Philadelphia (several) and elsewhere in that state, especially Chester County; in Wilmington, Delaware; in Bordentown and Egypt, New Jersey; in western New York (four) and New York City; in Maine (two); in Lynn and Boston, Massachusetts; in Indiana; in Cincinnati and Mt. Pleasant, Ohio; and in Salem, Iowa. Nuermberger, *Free Produce Movement*, 119; others are named in Densmore, "Dilemma," 83; see also Adams, *Neglected Period*, 152.

130. Adams, *Neglected Period*, 151; Mabee, *Black Freedom*, 187.

131. Nuermberger, pp. 13–14, 18–19. On pp. 117–118 Bacon, p. 279. Among the places where organizations were found were western Vermont and New York; Salem, Mt. Pleasant, and Green Plain in Ohio, several counties in Indiana; Chester and Lancaster counties in Pennsylvania; Delaware; Maine; and North Carolina. Green Plain's was one example of a female-founded group. Nuermberger lists societies on 39–40, 46, 52–55, Mabee on 202–03, and Adams on 150.

132. Nuermberger, *Free Produce Movement*, 6–7, and Bacon, "By Moral Force Alone," 277.

133. *Genius of Universal Emancipation*, 10, 12, and 16 September 1829, cited in Bacon, "By Moral Force Alone," 278–79; Nuermberger, *Free Produce Movement*, 17.

134. Nuermberger, *Free Produce Movement*, 22, citing *The Proceedings of the 1838 Anti-Slavery Convention of American Women*.

135. Deborah Bingham Van Brockhoven, "Women's Antislavery Petitioning," in *Abolitionist Sisterhood*, 192.

136. Bacon, "By Moral Force Alone," 278; Nuermberger, *Free Produce Movement*, 119.

137. Kashatus, *Just Over the Line*, 41; Bacon, "By Moral Force Alone," 279. Green Plain, Ohio, was one example of a female-founded group.

138. Mabee, *Black Freedom*, 190.

139. Nuermberger, *Free Produce Movement*, 97–98.

140. *Non-Slaveholder*, 1 May 1850, cited in Drake, *Quakers and Slavery*, 174.

141. Nuermberger, *Free Produce Movement*, 115.

142. Ibid., 36–37; 97–98.

143. Kashatus, *Just over the Line*, 40; Nuermberger, *Free Produce Movement*, 114–15.

144. Nuermberger, *Free Produce Movement*, 42; Yannessa, *Levi Coffin*, 28. The Coffins had planned to go to Cincinnati for five years and stayed for thirty.

145. Nuermberger, *Free Produce Movement*, 43, 83; Mabee, *Black Freedom*, 204.

146. Mabee, *Black Freedom*, 200.

147. Ibid., 189–90.

148. Good, "Elisha Bates," 87.
149. Bacon, "By Moral Force Alone," 281.
150. Nuermberger, *Free Produce Movement*, 99.
151. *Ibid.*, 18.
152. Drake, *Quakers and Slavery*, 174.
153. Nuermberger, *Free Produce Movement*, 37–38, 103; Mabee, *Black Freedom*, 186.
154. Drake, *Quakers and Slavery*, 174, citing the *Non-Slaveholder* 5, 1 May 1850, 103–4. Nuermberger, *Free Produce Movement*, 31 n. 4, attributes the voluntary departure of several activists from the Religious Society of Friends to meetings' refusal to allow meetinghouses to be used for meetings of free produce organizations, although those she names, such as Elizabeth Buffum Chace and Abby Kelley, are known to have other reasons for withdrawing as well.
155. Wilkinson, "Philadelphia Free Produce," 311–12.
156. Quarles, *Black Abolitionists*, 13.

CHAPTER THREE: Quakers and Immediate Emancipation

1. David Brion-Davis, *Antebellum American Culture: An Interpretive Anthology* (University Park: Pennsylvania State University Press, 1997), 414.
2. Alice Adams, *Neglected Period*, 210–11.
3. Elizabeth Heyrick, *Immediate, Not Gradual Abolition: or, An Inquiry into the Shortest, Safest, and Most Effectual Means of Getting Rid of West Indian Slavery* (London and Philadelphia, 1824), transcribed on University of North Dakota web site, http://www.und.edu/instruct/akelsch/399/Immediate%20not%20Gradual%20 Abolition.htm. On Heyrick see Goodman, *Of One Blood*, 86, and Carolyn Williams, "Racial Prejudice and Women's Rights" in Yellin and Horne, eds., *Abolitionist Sisterhood*, 161.
4. Beth Salerno, *Sister Societies: Women's Antislavery Organizations in Antebellum America* (Dekalb: University of Northern Illinois University Press, 2005), 19–20. As early as 1825 British Friend Mary Lloyd had written to urge Lucretia Mott their creation.
5. Mayer, *All on Fire*, 70, 231. Williams, "Racial Prejudice and Women's Rights," 161.
6. Horton and Horton, *Hard Road to Freedom*, 127–28.
7. *Walker's Appeal to the Coloured Citizens of the World*, ed. Peter P. Hinks (University Park: Pennsylvania State University Press, 2000), and Peter P. Hinks, *To Awaken My Afflicted Brethren: David Walker and the Problem of Antebellum Slave Resistance* (University Park: Pennsylvania State University Press, 1997).
8. Drake, *Quakers and Slavery*, 137.
9. Martin Duberman, "The Northern Response to Slavery" in Duberman, ed., *Antislavery Vanguard*, 405–6.
10. Mayer, *All on Fire*, 79–80. Garrison's transcribed address appears on the Library of Congress's American Memory web site, http://memory.loc.gov.
11. Duberman, "Northern Response," 405–6.
12. Ironically, the end of enslavement in the West Indies, which took about five years,

created a larger British market from cotton sales to textile manufacturers there. Mayer, *All on Fire*, 153; Brian Ally, "The 1833 Slavery Abolition Act" at web site Cariwave, www.cariwave.com, 7 May 2008.

13. Gilbert Barnes, *The Anti-Slavery Impulse, 1830–1844* (New York: D. Appleton-Century Company, 1933), 101; James Brewer Stewart, *Holy Warriors: The Abolitionists and American Slavery* (New York: Hilll and Wang, 1986), 52.

14. Some would label Friends who did not support abolition as conservative, but a very particular meaning for 'conservative' appeared within Quakerism after a schism in which the new branch was named "Conservative."

15. Martha Paxson Grundy, e-mail to authors, 17 June 2008.

16. Marietta, *Reformation of American Quakerism*, 124–25.

17. Mabee, *Black Freedom*, 8–9, 20. Others were "two or three Unitarians" and twelve "evangelical ministers," according to observations from the Rev. Samuel J. May.

18. Drake, *Quakers and Slavery*, 140; Kashatus, *Just over the Line*, 43. Robert Purvis was the only African American admitted to the Pennsylvania Abolition Society between 1775 and 1859.

19. Winch, *Philadelphia's Black Elite*, 83. Purvis was a well-to-do, active abolitionist with close connections to Quakers. See also Quarles, *Black Abolitionists*, 23–24, and Soderlund, *Quakers and Slavery*, 185.

20. Bordewich, *Bound for Canaan*, 225.

21. Quarles, *Black Abolitionists*, 17. The declaration, delivered by Garrison, is online at the University of Virginia Electronic Text Center web site, http://www.iath.virginia.edu/utc/abolitn/abeswlgct.html.

22. Stewart, *Holy Warriors*, 48–49.

23. Davis, *Problem of Slavery*, 239. The exceptions Davis noted were in Connecticut, Rhode Island, and Kentucky. He also noted that the absence of large numbers of European American clergy was a "striking" difference with Britain.

24. William Lloyd Garrison, *Declaration of the National Anti-Slavery Convention*; web site: Ashbrook Center for Public Affairs, TeachingAmericanHistory.org, 8 May 2008.

25. In Massachusetts alone there were 183 local societies (forty-one of them women's) by 1838. By 1837 eighty-nine antislavery societies had formed in Vermont with more than 5,000 members; the group in Lincoln-Starksboro had 485 members, many of whom were Quakers. Goodman, *Of One Blood*, 124–25; Starksboro data from Vermont History web site: http://www.vermonthistory.org/educate/antisl.htm 3 September 2007. Jordan reported the American Antislavery Society had some 250,000 supporters, Ryan Jordan, *Slavery and the Meetinghouse: the Quakers and the Abolitionist Dilemma, 1820–1865* (Bloomington, IN: Indiana University Press, 2007), ix.

26. Errol T. Elliott, *Quakers on the American Frontier: A History of Westward Migrations, Settlements, and Developments of Friends on the American Continent* (Richmond, IN: Friends United Press, 1969), 90; Scherer, *Slavery and the Churches*, 131. Scherer described the organizations as "Quaker fronts" or with "strong Quaker backing."

27. Kashatus, *Just over the Line*, 43. Unlike the "non-combative" existing Chester County Abolition Society, the Clarkson Society attacked and criticized colonizationists and enslavers and was more aggressive in appealing to the state legislature. Christopher Densmore, "Be Ye Therefore Perfect: Anti-slavery and the Origins of the Yearly Meeting of Progressive Friends in Chester County, Pennsylvania," *Quaker History* 93 (Fall 2004): 30.

28. Hamm, *Quakers in America*, 24.

29. Goodman, *Of One Blood*, 123.

30. Mabee, *Black Freedom*, 24.

31. Densmore, "Before Seneca Falls: Abolition and Women's Rights in Chester County." Talk presented at the Annual Meeting of the Organization of American Historians, Washington, DC, 21 April 2006. Densmore's research revealed that, while in the 1830s other antislavery organizations, including all those on the national level, excluded females, the Clarkson Society's 1833 constitution declared "all persons" were eligible to belong, "without distinction of sex or color," and East Fallowfield, another Chester County organization, welcomed members without attention to gender.

32. Nell Irvin Painter, *Sojourner Truth: A Life, A Symbol* (New York: W. W. Norton, 1996), 118-19.

33. Densmore, "Dilemma," 80-84. There was a "circle of Friends" influencing, supporting, encouraging, sometimes arguing with, and, in a few cases, marrying each other. They stayed in each others' homes, knew each others' children, attended the same meetings, read the same writings, and often appeared on the same platform. At least for a time, they also worshipped in Friends meetings together.

34. Painter, *Sojourner Truth*, 118-19.

35. Herbert L. Heller, *Historic Henry County 1820-1849* (New Castle, IN: *Courier Times*, 1983), 1: 222.

36. Amy Swerdlow, "Abolition's Conservative Sisters: The Ladies New York Anti-Slavery Societies, 1834-1840," in Yellin and Horne, ed., *Abolitionist Sisterhood*, 37.

37. Bacon, *Quiet Rebels*, 104.

38. Margaret Hope Bacon, *Valiant Friend: The Life of Lucretia Mott* (New York: Walker, 1980), 73.

39. Carol Faulkner and Beverly Palmer, "'The Jubilee of Acquiescence and Triumph,' or How History Remembers Lucretia Mott" (Honorary Curator's Lecture, Friends Historical Library, Swarthmore College, 6 April 2005).

40. Bacon, *Valiant Friend*, 76, 100. One editor wrote—"rather unctuously," in Bacon's words—"She is proof that it is possible for woman to widen her sphere without deserting it, or neglecting the duties which appropriately devolve upon her at home." Another observer wrote, "Whenever she was particularly worried or angry, she threw herself into housework"—it seemed to "recharge her batteries for more battles of the mind."

41. Margaret Hope Bacon, *Mothers of Feminism: The Story of Quaker Women in America* (San Francisco: Harper and Row, 1986), 111.

42. Bacon, *Valiant Friend*, 73, 122–23. Abby Kelley Foster, Amy Post, Abby Hopper Gibbons, and Elizabeth Chase Buffum were among disowned female friends Bacon has identified.

43. Soderlund, "Priorities and Power: The Philadelphia Female Anti-Slavery Society" in Yellin and Horne, eds., *Abolitionist Sisterhood*, 69, has suggested that there may have been twelve African American members.

44. Soderlund, "Priorities and Power," 76–77. Soderlund also noted that the female society "cited lack of funds as its excuse to abandon its commitment to the education of African American children," although it had taken in more income in that year than at other times. She also noted that its nine years were not always free of tension between the teacher and the school's managers.

45. University of Central Oklahoma College of Liberal Arts web site, http://www.libarts.ucok.edu/history/faculty/roberson/course/1483/suppl/chpXIII/SarahMappsDouglass.htm

46. Henry Cadbury, "Negro Membership in the Religious Society of Friends," *Journal of Negro History* 21, 2 (April 1936): 151–213.

47. Sarah Douglass to William Bassett, December 1837, included in Sarah M. Grimké to Elizabeth Pease, Anti-slavery Collection, Department of Rare Books and Manuscripts, Boston Public Library; see also Margaret Hope Bacon, "Sarah Mapps Douglass and Racial Prejudice Within the Society of Friends," Friends General Conference web site, http://www.fgcquaker.org/library/racism/smd-bacon.php.

48. Julie Roy Jeffrey, *The Great Silent Army of Abolitionism: Ordinary Women in the Antislavery Movement* (Chapel Hill: University of North Carolina Press, 1998). Jeffrey's work is a full exploration of how important women were to the movement. The figures come from Beth Salerno's lecture at Boston Public Library, 28 March 2006.

49. Sterling, *Ahead of Her Time*, 153, 158.

50. Membership statistics are hard to come by, but an 1838 Massachusetts report showed a total of 183 antislavery societies, 41 of them female, plus another 13 "juvenile" groups likely supervised by women, Jeffrey, *Great Silent Army*, 54.

51. It was women's more traditional work—sewing and baking—that initially prompted many to contribute to antislavery fairs held in many cities and towns, large and small. The fairs became a major source of revenue for abolitionist activity. Salerno mentioned that the goods often carried the abolitionist message with symbols featured on everything from aprons to bibs and that "free" sugar was served with tea. Salerno, "Antislavery Women: The Power and Peril of Organizing Against Slavery," lecture, Boston Public Library, March 2006. See also Jeffrey, *Great Silent Army*, 3, and Barbour et al., *Quaker Crosscurrents*, 183–84.

52. Drake, *Quakers and Slavery*, 148.

53. Goodman, *Of One Blood*, 248.

54. Salerno, *Sister Societies*.

55. Robert L. Hall, "Massachusetts Abolitionists Document the Slavery Experience," in *Courage and Conscience: Black and White Abolitionists in Boston*, ed. Donald

M. Jacobs (Bloomington and Indianapolis: Indiana University Press for the Boston Athenaeum, 1996), 82.

56. Martin Delany, *The Condition, Elevation, Emigration, and Destiny of the Colored People of the United States Politically Considered* (Philadelphia: by the author, 1852), 27.

57. Drake, *Quakers and Slavery*, 156. While many of the donors and managers were Friends, the building, with its marble façade and 3,000 blue plush chairs in the curtained second floor meeting room, would never be mistaken for a Quaker meetinghouse. The description is from Sterling, *Ahead of Her Time*, 62. The building was on the southwest corner of Sixth and Haines Streets, not far from Independence Hall.

58. Drake, *Quakers and Slavery*, 157 and Quarles, *Black Abolitionists*, 28.

59. Sterling, *Ahead of Her Time*, 63.

60. Bacon, "By Moral Force Alone" in *Abolitionist Sisterhood*, 285–289. Angelina Grimké, a "convinced" Quaker, married Theodore Weld, an agent of the AASS who was as committed—and outrageous—as she. She was disowned for "marrying out" of the meeting, as were those who attended the wedding, including her sister, Sarah, and other Quaker guests. Whittier escaped disownment by stepping from the room during the ceremony.

61. Quarles, *Black Abolitionists*, 28.

62. Sterling, *Ahead of Her Time*, 65. Sterling does not identify the speaker. "Law enforcement" at that point, such as it was, consisted of small groups of unarmed constables and/or militia of primarily working-class men of European descent far more interested in abetting the violence against African Americans than in ending it. Nash, *First City: Philadelphia and the Forging of Historical Memory*, 177–178.

63. This was not an official convention event because the delegates had not been able to agree on allowing the women to address a mixed-gender audience and compromised on having the lectures not be an actual convention session. Bacon, "By Moral Force Alone" in *Abolitionist Sisterhood*, 286. Lucretia Mott said of this predicament, "Let us hope that such false notions of delicacy and propriety will not long obtain in this enlightened country."

64. Bacon, "By Moral Force Alone" in *Abolitionist Sisterhood*, 285–289. The estimates of the crowd size actually go as high as 17,000, see Bacon, *Valiant Friend*, 86.

65. Sterling, *Ahead of Her Time*, 64.

66. Salerno, *Sister Societies*, 56.

67. Bacon, *Valiant Friend*, 86.

68. John Greenleaf Whittier, then editor of the *Pennsylvania Freeman*, escaped in disguise with some of his papers, but the books and papers of Benjamin Lundy were lost. Ira V. Brown, "Racism and Sexism: The Case of Pennsylvania Hall," *Phylon* Vol. 37, No. 2 (2nd Qtr. 1976), 131–134. Bacon, "By Moral Force Alone" in *Abolitionist Sisterhood*, 285–287. Fortunately, the children's home was not yet occupied, Cadbury, "Negro Membership in the Society of Friends," fn. 135.

69. Boylan, "Benevolence and Antislavery Activity," in *Abolitionist Sisterhood*, 120.

70. Quarles, *Black Abolitionists*, 38. Brown, "Racism and Sexism," 138–139. Although two men were arrested, no record of their trial could be found in the Philadelphia City Archives, according to Brown, "Racism and Sexism," 133.

71. Bacon, "By Moral Force Alone" in *Abolitionist Sisterhood*, 287. Salerno lecture.

72. Keith Melder, "Abby Kelley and the Process of Liberation" in *Abolitionist Sisterhood*, 237–38.

73. Densmore, "Be Ye," 35.

74. Sean Wilentz, ed., *Major Problems in the Early Republic, 1787–1848: Documents and Essays* (Lexington, MA: D.C. Heath, 1992), 471.

75. William Lloyd Garrison, "On the Constitution and the Union" (29 December 1832), transcribed on Teaching American History web site, http://teachingamerican history.org/library/index.asp?document=570. On the split in the movement see Perry, *Lift Up Thy Voice*, 169.

76. In the late 1700s Baptists, Congregationalists, Presbyterians, and Methodists opposed enslavement, but by the 1830s most churches of these denominations either avoided the issue or supported enslavement. Davis has noted that they were "conspicuously silent." See David Brion-Davis, *Slavery and Human Progress* (New York: Oxford University Press, 1984), 137–38, and Anne C. Loveland, *Southern Evangelicals and the Social Order, 1800–1860* (Baton Rouge: Louisiana State University Press, 1980), 189–90. Methodists in the South "felt bound to protect and defend slavery, even to the point of complete separation" from the North. Episcopalians and Catholics were "apparently neutral." Adams, *Neglected Period*, 98–100, and Ryan Jordan, "Quakers, 'Comeouters,' and the Meaning of Abolitionism in the Antebellum Free States," *Journal of the Early Republic* 24, 4 (Winter 2004): 605, 594.

77. Jordan, "Quakers," 607, 605, 588–89, 594.

78. *Ibid.*, 592.

79. *Ibid.*, 608.

80. *Ibid.*, 588.

81. Mayer, *All on Fire*, 233–35; see also Kathryn Kish Sklar and Thomas Dublin, eds., *Women and Power in American History* (Englewood Cliffs, NJ: Prentice Hall, 1991), 1: 181.

82. Jeffrey, *Great Silent Army*, 151.

83. Dorothy Sterling, *Ahead of Her Time: Abby Kelley Foster and the Politics of Antislavery* (New York: Norton, 1991), 224.

84. Bacon, *Slave Sister*, 62–63.

85. Bacon, *Mothers of Feminism*, 105.

86. Salerno, *Sister Societies*, 55; Emma Jones Lapsansky, "The World the Agitators Made: The Counterculture of Agitation in Philadelphia," in Yellin and Horne, eds., *Abolitionist Sisterhood*, 92.

87. Deborah Gold Hansen, *Strained Sisterhood: Gender and Class in the Boston Female Anti-Slavery Society* (Amherst: University of Massachusetts Press, 1993), 55.

88. Massachusetts Anti-Slavery Society, *Tenth Annual Report* (1842), Appendix, 8.

89. Spartacus Educational web site, http://www.spartacus.schoolnet.co.uk.

90. Robin Winks, "Abolitionism in Canada" in Duberman, 334.

91. Barbour et al, 185. Gibbons, Hopper, Marriott, Joseph Hathaway.

92. Winch, *Black Elite*, 186.

93. Drake, *Quakers and Slavery*, 157.

94. Perry, *Lift Up Thy Voice*.

95. Gerda Lerner, *The Grimké Sisters of South Carolina: Pioneers for Women's Rights and Abolition* (New York: Oxford University Press, 1998).

96. Perry, *Grimké Family*, 131, 133. Predictably, hundreds of copies of the appeal were burned in the South. The mayor of Charleston told Polly Grimké that if her daughter Angelina traveled to Charleston she would be sent back on the same boat.

97. Lerner, *The Grimké Sisters*, 104–7. Among other things Sarah presented her proof to refute the common view that the people of Africa were the people of Ham who had been cursed by Noah and thus were fated to be enslaved.

98. Perry, *Lift Up Thy Voice*, 130. Angelina Grimké, *Appeal to the Christian Women of the South* (New York: American Anti-Slavery Society, 1836), 3, 16–18.

99. Perry, *Lift Up Thy Voice*, 133, 144–147, 156–57.

100. *Ibid.*, 162.

101. *Ibid.*

102. Litwack, *North of Slavery*, 222.

103. *Ibid.*, 222.

104. Salerno, *Sister Societies*, 56.

105. Barbour et al., *Quaker Crosscurrents*, 185.

106. Drake, *Quakers and Slavery*, 149.

107. *Ibid.*, 147.

108. Aptheker, "Quakers and Negro Slavery," 58–60. Aptheker also noted that Lucretia Mott pointed out the inconsistency that allowed Friends to accept hired agents to work with Native Americans while denouncing those who worked for the AASS as "ravenous wolves." The yearly meetings were New England and the Orthodox meetings in Philadelphia and Indiana. See Densmore, "Dilemma," 81.

109. Nuermberger, *Free Produce Movement*, 114.

110. Drake, *Quakers and Slavery*, 145.

111. Drake, *Quakers and Slavery*, 139.

112. Jordan, "Quakers," 583, 601–2.

113. Enoch Lewis, "On Slavery," *The Friend* 8 (1835), 258–59.

114. Drake, *Quakers and Slavery*, 143.

115. *Ibid.*, 134, 136.

116. *Ibid.*, 180.

117. Worrall, *Friendly Virginians*, 348.

118. Quarles, *Black Abolitionists*.

119. Indiana Yearly Meeting for Sufferings, 1841, reported in Edgerton, *Separation in Indiana Yearly Meeting*, 48.

120. Aptheker, "Quakers and Negro Slavery," 358–59.

121. Jordan, "Quakers," 591. Hubbard was considered by some to be Native American. His grandmother was a Cherokee and accounts mention his inheriting physical features from her. Gwen Erickson, reader's comment, 25 August 2003.

122. Elliott, *Quakers on the American Frontier*; Drake, *Quakers and Slavery*, 90.

123. Barbour et al., *Quaker Crosscurrents*, 184.

124. Drake, *Quakers and Slavery*, 161.

125. *Ibid.*, 150.

126. *Ibid.*, 171.

127. Densmore, "Dilemma," 84–85.

128. Bacon, "The Motts and Purvises," *Quaker History* 92, 2 (Fall 2003): 7, and *National Anti-Slavery Standard*, 3 November 1860.

129. Drake, *Quakers and Slavery*, 155.

130. *Ibid.*, 176–77.

131. *Ibid.*, 148, 150.

132. Barbour and Frost, *Quakers*, 193.

133. Drake, *Quakers and Slavery*, 134. Examples of various publications and statements protesting enslavement made by Orthodox Friends, in this case New York Yearly Meeting during the 1830s and 1840s, often at the request of its Farmington Quarter, are included in Densmore, "Dilemma."

134. Lapsansky, "Free Produce, Free People."

135. Ingle, *Quakers in Conflict*, 86, reporting Hicks's preaching about Quakers' need to return to a simpler life. Drake, *Quakers and Slavery*, 117. Drake noted that one of Hicks' chief opponents, Jonathan Evans, used that confusion to declare Hicks "an unbalanced individual."

136. Barbour, *Slavery and Theology*, 6–7; Barbour and Frost, *Quakers*, 193.

137. Barbour, *Slavery and Theology*, 6–7.

138. Densmore, "Dilemma," 81.

139. Hamm, *The Quakers in America*, 44.

140. Hamm et al., "'Great and Good People.'" The 1828 Hicksite/Orthodox split in the Midwest was 80 percent Orthodox, 20 percent Hicksite. Friends there lived "amidst unrelenting racial prejudice" and various measures aimed at keeping people of African descent out.

141. Drake, *Quakers and Slavery*, 160, 154.

142. Jordan, "Quakers," 607.

143. The authors especially thank J. William Frost, e-mail to authors, 30 July 2004, for clarifying these reasons for disownment.

144. Drake, *Quakers and Slavery*, 142, 155–56.

145. Chace, "Anti-Slavery Reminiscences," 114.

146. Marnie Miller-Gutsell, e-mail to authors.

147. Drake, *Quakers and Slavery*, 158; Elizabeth Buffum Chace, "My Anti-Slavery Reminiscences" (1891), in *Two Quaker Sisters from the Original Diaries of Elizabeth Buffum Chace and Lucy Buffum Lovell* (New York: Liveright Publishing Corp., 1937), 122.

148. Hilty, *By Land and By Sea*, 56; Drake, *Quakers and Slavery*, 161.

149. Drake, *Quakers and Slavery*, 161–62; Margaret Hope Bacon, *In the Shadow of William Penn: Central Philadelphia Monthly Meeting of Friends* (Philadelphia: Central Pennsylvania Monthly Meeting, 2001), 29–30.

150. "A Rare Specimen of a Quaker Preacher," *National Anti-Slavery Standard*, 25 March 1841.

151. Drake, *Quakers and Slavery*, 160–62.

152. Bacon, *Lamb's Warrior*, 133. "The spectacle of a little old man fighting for principle against the forces of intolerance stirred sympathy even among those who did not agree" with him. Even some who had been on the committee that disowned him "came to tell him now they bitterly repented."

153. *Ibid.*

154. Cox, *Quakerism in New York*, 101–2. Bacon, *Abby Hopper Gibbons*, 42–43. Hopper wrote later that he was not questioned about the incident in the Quaker manner but "in the manner of a courtroom." He was also not allowed to see the explanation of the disownment written by the Westbury Quarterly Meeting. Bacon, *Lamb's Warrior*, 131–33.

155. Bacon, *Lamb's Warrior*, 135, agrees with Gibbons's view; Bacon has stated that there is "no question" in her mind "that he was disowned because he was an abolitionist."

156. It was not uncommon for Friends who were disowned to continue in this manner, as long as they did not attend the Meeting for Business. Bacon, *Quiet Rebels*, 114. Bacon, *Lamb's Warrior*, 190. Densmore and Bassett, "Quakers, Slavery, and the Civil War" in Barbour et al, 186.

157. Bacon, *Quiet Rebels*, 114.

158. Drake, *Quakers and Slavery*, 147; Elizabeth Moger, "Quakers as Abolitionists: The Robinsons of Rokeby and Charles Marriott," *Quaker History* 92, 2 (Fall 2003): 57.

159. Hamm, "Hicksite Quakers," 567.

160. Elizabeth Sellers, letter of resignation from North Darby Monthly Meeting, 11 March 1845; Minute signed by George Smedley, clerk, of Chester Monthly Meeting, 24 November 1851. Elizabeth Sellers, Papers 1845–1851, MM SC 115, SFHL. It is not clear why the Chester Meeting was the one to respond.

161. Perry, *Lift up Thy Voice*, 128; Lerner, *Grimké Sisters*, 18, 86, 97, 182.

162. Stewart, *Holy Warriors*, 52.

163. Bacon, *Slave Sister*, 69.

164. Sterling, *Ahead of Her Time*, 123. NEYM archivist Marnie Miller-Gutsell reported that the meeting was reluctant to act quickly on her letter for that reason. Mayer, *All on Fire*, stated that Kelley became so impatient with *The Friend* that she gave the letter to Garrison, who published it in the *Liberator*. There is some question about whether Kelley was disowned or left; Elizabeth Buffum Chase wrote that the Uxbridge meeting disowned Kelley for anti-slavery lecturing, "although they did so, ostensibly, on some frivolous charges, which had no real foundation in fact." Elizabeth Buffum Chace, "Anti-Slavery Reminiscences,"

in *Two Quaker Sisters from the Original Diaries of Elizabeth Buffum Chace and Lucy Buffum Lovell* (New York: Liveright Publishing Corp., 1937), 122.

165. Chace, "Anti-Slavery Reminiscences," 113–14.

166. Lucille Salitan and Eve Lewis Perera, eds., *Virtuous Lives: Four Quaker Sisters Remember Family Life, Abolition, and Women's Suffrage* (New York: Continuum, 1994), 114.

167. Drake, *Quakers and Slavery*, 158.

168. Chace, "Anti-Slavery Reminiscences," 122–23.

169. Drake, *Quakers and Slavery*, 163.

170. Hamm, *Transformation of American Quakerism*, 13.

171. Drake, *Quakers and Slavery*, 162–63.

172. *Ibid.*

173. Ryan Jordan, "The Indiana Separation of 1842 and the Limits of Quaker Anti-Slavery," *Quaker History* 49 (Spring 2000): 9.

174. Jordan, "Indiana Separation," 11–12.

175. Drake, *Quakers and Slavery*, 163–64. Sturge was but one of many British Quakers who was familiar with enslavement from traveling in the U.S. and who stimulated interest in and support of the abolitionist cause by British Friends. His open letter to American Friends is published in Sturge, *Visit to the United States*, 149–57.

176. Jordan, "Indiana Separation," 2.

177. Edgerton, *Separation of Indiana Yearly Meeting*, 68.

178. Drake, *Quakers and Slavery*, 165; Jordan, "Indiana Separation," 2; Elliott, *Quakers on the American Frontier*, 92.

179. Jordan, "Indiana Separation," 4, 15–16, 20; Elliot, *Quakers on the American Frontier*, 121–22. Elliott has estimated that there were about fifty Iowan separatists. Hamm et al., "Great and Good People," n. 8, notes that Jordan was incorrect in saying the yearly meeting was silent after the radical Friends left. It did issue a pamphlet and a memorial.

180. Hamm, *Transformation of American Quakerism*; Hamm, "Hicksite Quakers," 567–68; Elliott, *Quakers on the American Frontier*, 92, 175.

181. Densmore, "Dilemma," 86–87; Carlisle Davidson, "A Profile of Hicksite Quakerism in Michigan, 1830–1860," *Quaker History* 59, 2 (Autumn 1970): 111; Densmore, reader's comment, April 2008.

182. Elliott, *Quakers on the American Frontier*, 121–23, 138–39, 144; Louis Thomas Jones, *The Quakers of Iowa* (Iowa City: State Historical Society of Iowa, 1914), 138–39.

183. The ongoing dispute even caused some Friends to call a constable to remove a radical Friend who insisted on speaking in a Meeting for Worship. Christopher Densmore, "Marlborough Friends Meeting and Anti-Slavery: The Separation of 1851 and the Origins of Longwood Meeting" (Lecture, Marlborough Meeting, Chester County, PA, 17 November 2001), 8, 12–13.

184. Quoted in Densmore, "Be Ye Therefore Perfect," 14.

185. *Ibid.*, 13.

186. Drake, *Quakers and Slavery*, 176.

187. Kashatus, *Just over the Line*, 64. Christopher Densmore, "Truth for Authority, Not Authority for Truth": (Lecture, 150th Anniversary Celebration of Longwood Progressive Friends Meetinghouse, 22 May 2005).

188. Williams, "*Quakers and Slavery.*"

189. Jordan, "Indiana Separation," 11–12. Buffum and Levi Coffin were on the executive board of the Liberty Party.

190. Seigel, "Moral Champions," 94; Jordan, "Indiana Separation," 12.

191. Stewart, *Holy Warriors*, 34.

192. Hamm, *Transformation of American Quakerism*, 61–62.

193. Based on Section 2 of Article 4 of the U.S. Constitution, holding that "No Person held to Service or Labour in one State, under the Laws thereof, escaping into another, shall, in consequence of any Law or Regulation therein, be discharged from such Service or Labour, but shall be delivered up on Claim of the Party to whom such Service or Labour may be due."

194. The New York, Ohio, Vermont, Massachusetts, Connecticut, and Pennsylvania legislatures passed personal liberty laws after the 1842 U.S. Supreme Court decision in *Prigg v. Pennsylvania*. The court in this case overturned a York County Court decision finding the claimant, Edward Prigg, who had taken the fugitive Margaret Morgan out of the state in 1837, guilty because his action defied an 1826 Pennsylvania law that made any effort to remove a "negro or mulatto" from the state in order to sell or enslave that person a felony.

195. Lois Horton, lecture on *Hard Road to Freedom*, Annual Meeting of the Chester County Historical Society, Mendenhall, Pennsylvania, 1 May 2002. Also Encarta Encyclopedia.

196. Several spectacular and widely publicized attempts to implement the Fugitive Slave Act, among them the Boston cases of William and Ellen Crafts (1850), Thomas Sims (1851), Shadrach Minkins (1851), and Anthony Burns (1854) demonstrated that the federal government meant to enforce it.

197. Larry Gara, "Friends and the Underground Railroad," *Quaker History* 51, 1 (Spring 1962): 18–19.

198. Larry Gara, *The Liberty Line: The Legend of the Underground Railroad* (Lexington: University of Kentucky Press, 1996), 5–6.

199. Gara, *Liberty Line*, 5–6.

200. Gara, "Friends and the Underground Railroad," 18.

201. Drake, *Quakers and Slavery*, 178–79. The novel was not well received by some Friends who, aside from being reminded of the fact that Friends were not to read novels, found it too sympathetic to the radical abolitionist point of view.

202. Kashatus, *Just over the Line*, 2.

203. Frederick Douglass, *My Bondage and My Freedom* (1855), ed. William L. Andrews (Urbana and Chicago: University of Illinois Press, 1987), 210. Hundreds of fugitive narratives, including those of Robinson, Brown, and Grandy, are online at the University of North Carolina's Documenting the American South web site, http://docsouth.unc.edu/neh.

204. "Fugitive Slaves," *Pennsylvania Freeman*, 19 September 1838.

205. Worrall, *Friendly Virginians*, 389.

206. Moses Grandy, *Narrative of the Life of Moses Grandy; Late a Slave in the United States of America* (London: Gilpin, 1843), 67, available on Documenting the American South web site, http://docsouth.unc.edu/fpn/grandy/grandy/html.

207. Gara, "Friends and the Underground Railroad," 18.

208. Christopher Densmore, e-mail to authors, 20 September 2005.

209. Still expressed his appreciation for those whom he viewed as the most stalwart of the European American abolitionists—Garrett, Mott, and Garrison—when he described their "Christ-like exhibition of love and humanity." Kashatus, *Just over the Line*, 2–3.

210. Jeffrey, *Great Silent Army*, 183–84. Worrall, *Friendly Virginians*, 384–89, stated that many specific strategic locations along the "four Freedom roads" heading north out of Virginia passed near the property of Quakers well known for being sympathetic to fugitives.

211. Kashatus, *Just over the Line*, 59–61; Gara, *Liberty Line*, 9, 18–19; Horton and Horton, *Hard Road to Freedom*, 139, 143, 145; Christopher Densmore, "Dilemma."

212. Bordewich, *Bound for Canaan*, 74.

213. Emma Lou Thornbrough, *The Negro in Indiana before 1900: A Study of a Minority* (Bloomington: Indiana University Press, 1993), 43. Their names were William Bush, William Davidson, Douglas White, James Benson, and Cal Thomas. The Coffin house in Fountain City, Indiana, is open to the public, primarily in the summer. See www.cr.nps.gov/nr/travel/underground/in2.

214. Kashatus, *Just over the Line*, 50.

215. Johnson, "Black-White Relations on Nantucket,"; Grover, *Fugitive's Gibraltar*, 94–97.

216. In 2005 the Michigan Bar Association dedicated a "Legal Milestone" plaque commemorating the story of Quakers and free African Americans. State Bar of Michigan web site, www.michbar.org/news/releases/archives05/Kentucky_raid; Betty DeRamus, "Kentucky Raid epitomizes races pulling together," *Detroit News*, 15 August 2005, http://www.detnews.com/2005/metro/0508/16/B01-280866.htm.

217. Hamm et al., "A Great and Good People," 7.

218. Yanessa, *Levi Coffin*, 36, states that "significant evidence" exists for the claim that those owners of the enslaved and their agents who pursued them into free territory gave Coffin the title.

219. Elliott, *Quakers on the American Frontier*, 88–89. Levi Coffin, *Reminiscences of Levi Coffin, the Reputed President of the Underground Railroad* (Cincinnati, OH: Western Tract Society, [1876]), 126–28.

220. Bordewich, *Bound for Canaan*, 69–72.

221. Lapsansky, "Free Produce, Free People."

222. Yannessa, *Levi Coffin*, 17.

223. Katz, *Black Pioneers*, 52; Yannessa, *Levi Coffin*, 18–19, 42.

224. Katz, *Black Pioneers*, 91. Yannessa, *Levi Coffin*, 33.

225. James A. McGowan, *Station Master on the Underground Railroad: The Life and Letters of Thomas Garrett*, (Jefferson, NC: McFarland and Co., 2005), 25–26.
226. Yannessa, *Levi Coffin*, 36.
227. *Friends in Wilmington, 1738–1938* (Wilmington, DE: Charles L. Story Co., 1938), 79.
228. *Ibid.*, 78.
229. Gara, "Underground Railroad," 6; Kashatus, *Just over the Line*, 10; Thomas Garrett to Samuel May Jr., 24 November 1863, in McGowan, *Station Master*, 151.
230. *Ibid.*
231. Historical Society of Delaware web site, www.hsd.org/DHE_DHE_who_garrett.html. Characteristically, Garrett complained that $10,000 wasn't enough and if it were $20,000 he would turn himself in.
232. John Hunn later lived on St. Helena Island in South Carolina with his wife and daughter. He started a store there. R. C. Smedley, *History of the Underground Railroad in Chester and the Neighboring Counties of Pennsylvania* (1883; reprint, Mechanicsburg, PA: Stackpole Books, 2005), 96. The judge in the trial in Delaware was Roger B. Taney, who later presided at the Dred Scott trial.
233. William C. Kashatus, "Two Stationmasters on the Underground Railroad," *Pennsylvania Heritage* 27 (Fall 2001): 6.
234. Spartacus Educational web site, www.spartacus.schoolnet.co.uk/USASgarrett.htm.
235. Bacon, *Valiant Friend*, 234.
236. Charles L. Blockson, "The Underground Railroad: The Quaker Connection," in Eliza Cope Harrison, ed., *For Emancipation and Education: Some Black and Quaker Efforts*, 38.
237. Bacon, *Lamb's Warrior*, 179; Bacon, *Abby Hopper Gibbons*, 7.
238. Bacon, *Abby Hopper Gibbons*, 40.
239. Bordewich, 369. After the Motts moved to Cheltenham, northeast of Philadelphia, they aided "approximately 400 fugitive slaves" over seven years, Kashatus, "Friends Fight for Freedom," 9.
240. Katz, *Black Pioneers*, 116–17.
241. Susannah Brody, *Constant Struggles: Chester County Biographies, Volume II: The Nineteenth Century* (West Chester, PA: Chester County Historical Society, 2000), 4, 19, 25, 31; Frances Cloud Taylor, *The Trackless Trail: An Exploration of Conductors and their Stations* (West Chester, PA: IP & G Custom Photo Service, 1995), 2.
242. Frances William Browin, "'But We Have No Country,'" *Quaker History* 57, 2 (Autumn 1968): 86. Thomas Slaughter, *Bloody Dawn: The Christiana Riot and Racial Violence in the Antebellum North* (New York: Oxford University Press, 1991), 53–57, 59. While Browin, Slaughter, and others essentially agree on the version of the episode presented here, Slaughter has noted that the record is equivocal on the details of the event.
243. William Parker, "The Freedman's Story," *Atlantic Monthly*, March 1860, quoted in Dorothy Sterling, *Speak Out in Thunder Tones: Letters and Other Writings by Black Northerners, 1787–1865* (Garden City, NY: Doubleday, 1973), 258–61, 263.

244. *The Friend*, 27 September 1851, 16.
245. Hamm, "Hicksite Quakers and the Antebellum Nonresistance Movement," *Church History*, December 1994, 567–568.
246. Bacon, "By Moral Force Alone," 282–83, 286.
247. Hamm et al, "A Great and Good People."
248. William Lloyd Garrison, "New England Non-Resistance Society Declaration of Sentiments" (18–20 September 1838), transcribed on Harmless as Doves Ministries web site, http://www.harmlessasdoves.com/declaration.html.
249. Hamm et al, "A Great and Good People."
250. Bacon, "By Moral Force Alone," 289–91. Mabee, *Black Freedom*, which emphasizes the abolitionists' commitment to ending enslavement by moral persuasion and peaceful means, deserves more attention than it has been given, especially among Quakers, given their Peace Testimony. Mabee described various nonviolent ways of opposing enslavement, especially the use of boycotts of schools, goods made by the enslaved, or public transportation.
251. Hamm, "Hicksite Quakers," 560.
252. Grover, *Fugitive's Gibraltar*, 218–20.
253. Forbush, *History of Baltimore Yearly Meeting*, 62; Bacon, *Lamb's Warrior*, 178; Gara, *Liberty Line*, 81; Drake, *Quakers and Slavery*, 119. When Tyson found six kidnapped African Americans held in a basement, he set three free but left the others because legally they were the enslaver's property.
254. Bacon, *Lamb's Warrior*, 178.
255. Kashatus, "Two Stationmasters," 6–7.
256. Hilty, *Toward Freedom*, 90–91.
257. Thomas D. Hamm, e-mail to authors, 11 July 2005.
258. Jordan, "Indiana Separation," 22–23.
259. Mary Pellauer, *Toward a Feminist Theology: The Religious Thought of Elizabeth C. Stanton, Susan B. Anthony, and Anna Howard Shaw* (Brooklyn, NY: Carlson, 1991), 164–165. For each of these women, Pellauer traces historical contexts, their critical social issue, and religion's role in that issue.
260. According to Davis, there were about 100,000 members in the 1,346 local anti-slavery societies by 1837, when the U.S. population of free people was 9.7 million, making the total around one percent. Davis, *Inhuman Bondage*, 260.

CHAPTER FOUR: Friends and Freed People: 1700–1860

1. Carl Kaestle, *Pillars of the Republic: Common Schools and American Society, 1780-1860* (New York: Hill and Wang, 1983), 37; Quarles, *Black Abolitionists*.
2. Kaestle, *Pillars of the Republic*, 37; James, *People among Peoples*, 213, 291.
3. Nash and Soderlund, *Freedom by Degrees*.
4. Soderlund, *Quakers and Slavery*, 177–78.
5. The quotation appears on page 16 of Fox's letter, reprinted in Frost, *Quaker Origins of Anti-Slavery*, 49. While apparently Fox said nothing to clarify what he meant by "not empty-handed," Drake, *Quakers and Slavery*, 6, 76–77, has argued

that Fox meant to direct Friends to offer some assistance to the persons they manumitted. His advice may have been inspired by Deuteronomy 15:13—"And
when thou sendest him out free from thee, thou shalt not let him go away empty."
See Soderlund, *Quakers and Slavery*, 179.

6. On black codes, see Zilversmit, *First Emancipation*, 12–18; Nash, *Forging
Freedom*, 35–36; Erickson, "State Laws and Acts Involving Free Blacks in North
Carolina," *Southern Friend*, 47–8.

7. The Act was reprinted in 1751 by Benjamin Franklin in his *Pennsylvania Gazette*
with a warning about "frequent complaints" about the freed people.

8. Davis, *Problem of Slavery*, 254.

9. Nash, *Forging Freedom*, 89.

10. Jack Marietta, "The Growth of Quaker Self-Consciousness in Pennsylvania, 1720–
1748," in *Seeking the Light: Essays in Quaker History*, eds. J. William Frost and
John M. Moore (Wallingford, PA: Pendle Hill Publications, 1986), 81.

11. Herbert Hadley, "Diminishing Separation: The Philadelphia Yearly Meetings
Reunite, 1915–1955," in Moore, ed., *Friends in Delaware Valley*, 157.

12. Philadelphia Yearly Meeting query of 1776, in Drake, *Quakers and Slavery*, 77.

13. William Cook Dunlap, *Quaker Education in Baltimore and Virginia Yearly
Meetings* (Philadelphia, 1936), 47.

14. Bronwen Souders and John Souders, *A Rock in a Weary Land: A Shelter in a
Time of Storm: African-American Experience in Waterford, Virginia* (Waterford,
VA: Waterford Foundation, 2003), 10.

15. Drake, *Quakers and Slavery*, 114–15.

16. Soderlund, *Quakers and Slavery*, 177–79. We have found no specific numbers of
monthly or yearly meetings that suggested or required compensation, but
Soderlund has reported on discussions of the question in many of the monthly
meetings she studied. See also Barbour et al., *Quaker Crosscurrents*, 68.

17. Ferris, letter to James Rigby, 7 April 1766, in Grundy, *Resistance and Obedience to
God*, 83; Soderlund, *Quakers and Slavery*, 95–96; James E. Pickard, "A Brief
History of Deer Creek Meeting of the Religious Society of Friends,"
Deer Creek Monthly Meeting web site,
http://www.deercreekfriends.org/dc_history/index.asp?app_id=dc_history.

18. James, *People among Peoples*, 294. The authors thank Ed La Fond of Warrington
(PA) Meeting for telling them about Hill. See: *The Dictionary of American Negro
Biography*, Rayford Logan and Michael Winston, eds, (New York: W.W. Norton &
Co., 1982), 110–11. Hill's wife, Tina Lewis, attended a Quaker-run school for
African Americans in Burlington, New Jersey. One of Hill's clocks is in the
Smithsonian Institution; another at Westtown (Friends) School in West Chester,
Pennsylvania. For photographs of his clocks, see the Smithsonian web site:
http://americanhistory.si.edu/ontime/marking.html.

19. Soderlund, *Quakers and Slavery*, 179.

20. Howard Brinton, *Meeting House and Farm House* (Wallingford, PA: Pendle Hill
Publications, 1972), 15. In fact, the reformation of the 1750s brought "Family

Visits" of all Friends to assure that there was no "backsliding" in adhering to the Discipline. See James, *People among Peoples*, 174.

21. Soderlund, *Quakers and Slavery*, 179.

22. *Ibid.*,182–84; Soderlund, "Black Women in Colonial Pennsylvania," 85–86; Kenneth S.P. Morse, *Baltimore Yearly Meeting, 1672–1830: Gleanings from the records of Friends meetings in Maryland and the adjacent parts of Virginia* (No publisher given, 1961), 23–24; Marietta, *Reformation of American Quakerism*, 120.

23. Soderlund, *Quakers and Slavery*, 184.

24. Drake, *Quakers and Slavery*.

25. Soderlund, *Quakers and Slavery*, 184.

26. Melish, *Disowning Slavery*, 69.

27. Drake, *Quakers and Slavery*, 192.

28. Richard Foster, "Quaker Concern," 46.

29. Drake, *Quakers and Slavery*, 89.

30. Quotation from New England Yearly Meeting in George Selleck, *Quakers in Boston, 1656–1964: Three Centuries of Friends in Boston and Cambridge* (Cambridge, MA: Friends Meeting at Cambridge, 1976), 72. Settlements in New England were completed by 1785. See also Foster, "Quaker Concern," 46.

31. Ferris, Letter to Samuel Field and wife, 21 September, 1767, in Grundy, *Resistance and Obedience to God*, 72. On Brown, see Wiggins, e-mail to authors, August 2003. The information, according to Wiggins, came from the grandson of Cudge who had been enslaved and freed by Brown.

32. Thompson, *Moses Brown*, 182, 103.

33. Michener, *Retrospect of Early Quakerism*, 353–54. Several similar reports are included in Michener's volume of meeting documents.

34. Soderlund, *Quakers and Slavery*, 179.

35. Patricia Andersen, Librarian, Montgomery County (Maryland) Historical Society, e-mail to authors, 20 July 2004. Andersen has cited a chapter on the Sandy Spring "colored settlement" in Everett L. Fly and LaBarbara Wigfall Fly, *Northeastern Montgomery County Black Oral History Study* (Rockville, MD: Montgomery County Department of Housing and Community Development, 1983), 1.

36. Forbush, *History of Baltimore Yearly Meeting*, 41.

37. Soderlund, *Quakers and Slavery*, 179. The Maryland Friends were European American William Dixon and another from East Nottingham Meeting who was not named.

38. Berlin, *Many Thousands Gone*, 372–73.

39. Elliott, *Quakers on the American Frontier*, 51.

40. Drake, *Quakers and Slavery*, 82; Foster, "Quaker Concern," 46.

41. McKiever, *Slavery and the Emigration of North Carolina Friends*, 23, 45.

42. Algie Newlin, ed., "Nereus Mendenhall's Historical Sketch of North Carolina Yearly Meeting," *The Southern Friend* 4, 1 (Spring 1982): 35.

43. Barbour and Frost, *Quakers*, 149. The enslaver also had to file a petition and participate in a hearing before freedom would be granted, McKiever, *Slavery and the*

Emigration of North Carolina Friends, 37. A detailed study of manumissions by North Carolina Friends in one county and the effects on those they attempted to free can be found in Katherine Dungy, "A Friend in Deed: Quakers and Manumission in Perquimans County, North Carolina, 1775–1800," *The Southern Friend* 24, 1 (Spring 2002).

44. Hilty, *Toward Freedom*, 32–33. Eventually Friends were compelled to decline these requests from non-Quakers.

45. Hilty, *By Land and by Sea*, 5–6, 43, 45.

46. Weeks, *Southern Quakers and Slavery*, 224.

47. Hilty, *By Land and by Sea*, 4–5, 44.

48. Weeks, *Southern Quakers and Slavery*, 228.

49. Hilty, *Toward Freedom*, 86.

50. Selleck, *Gentle Invaders*, 130–31.

51. Stephen A. Vincent, *Southern Seed, Northern Soil: African American Farm Communities in the Midwest, 1765–1900* (Bloomington: Indiana University Press, 1999), 33.

52. Hilty, *Toward Freedom*, 69.

53. Cited in Cadbury, "Negro Membership," 165.

54. Mary Coffin Johnson, *Mordecai Morris White* (New York: Frederick H. Hitchcock, 1917), 34–37.

55. *Ibid.*

56. Hilty, *By Land and by Sea*, 62.

57. Thornbrough, *Negro in Indiana*, 35. Measuring Worth.com; http://www.measuring worth.com/calculators/uscompare/result.php#, 7 April 2008.

58. Shay estimated that 680 freed African Americans were sent out from North Carolina between 1814 and 1836. Estimating costs is difficult because contributions made by individuals and funds raised by monthly meetings may not have been included in yearly meeting records. Shay said that more funds came from sources outside the yearly meeting, and the actual number of people and total expenses may have been twice the estimates. Shay, "The Antislavery Movement in North Carolina," 248, n62, 273.

59. Hilty, *Toward Freedom*, 48–49, 84–85. Hamm notes that the allocation from Philadelphia was the last item that yearly meeting approved before the separation of 1827. Hamm, comments, e-mail to authors, August 2003.

60. William Parker to Josiah Parker, 26 July 1826, Friends Collection, Lilly Library, Earlham College; Hamm, e-mail to authors, 25 June 2003.

61. Hilty, *By Land and by Sea*, 64–65.

62. Hilty, *Toward Freedom*, 79.

63. "History of Ohio Valley Yearly Meeting," *Book of Discipline of the Ohio Valley Religious Society of Friends*, 1978, web site of Yellow Springs, Ohio, Friends Meeting, http://www.quakershaker.net/BOD/fifth.html, 1 March 08.

64. McKiever, *Slavery and the Emigration of North Carolina Friends*, 52.

65. Hamm et al., "'A Great and Good People.'"

66. Vincent, *Southern Seed, Northern Soil*, 33–37. Thornbrough, *Negro in Indiana*, 45, 47, cites the "rapid growth" of the African Americans in the three counties—Wayne, Randolph, and Henry—that were heavily Quaker as evidence for this assertion.

67. Howard S. Rogers, *History of Cass County, from 1825 to 1875*, on Google Books web site, http://books.google.com/books?id=0h3mnwahsEAC&pg=PA129&lpg =PA129&dq=rogers+%26+%22history+of+cass+county%22&source=web&ots= ns6LdOLcxV&sig=HcqUqqcbyE02kRHekfTiiT1h2qo; George Hesslink, *Black Neighbors: Negroes in a Northern Rural Community* (New York: Bobbs-Merrill Company, Inc., 1968), 32–40.

68. Elliott, *Quakers on the American Frontier*, 88.

69. Randolph County [Indiana]. "Interim Report, Indiana Historic Sites and Structures Inventory," June 1998, 89, and Thornbrough, *Negro in Indiana*, 49.

70. G. C. Waldrep III, "Meanwhile, Down on the Farm: African-American Settlement in the Nineteenth-Century Midwest," review of Vincent, *Southern Seed, Northern Soil*, on Humanities and Social Sciences web site, www.h-net.msu.edu/reviews. The names of many of the free African American families settling in Indiana were the same as free families in North Carolina. Census research on names has been carried out by Carter G. Woodson, "The Free Negro Heads of Families in the United States in 1830, Together with a Brief Treatment of the Free Negro" (Washington, DC: Association for the Study of Negro Life and History, 1925), 110–13, as cited in Thornbrough, *Negro in Indiana*, 33.

71. Katz, *Black Pioneers*, 126, 132.

72. Vincent, *Southern Seed, Northern Soil*, 27, 31–33. By 1860 newly freed people were living in more than 60 settlements in Indiana, Kansas, Mississippi, Oklahoma, New Mexico, Alabama, and California. For some African American leaders, the self-segregation combined possibilities for economic self-help and "moral uplift with intense pride in race," according to Norman L. Crockett, *The Black Towns* (Lawrence: Regents Press of Kansas, 1979), xi–xiii. Others, Crockett said, worked for the day they could become part of the "mainstream."

73. Charles F. McKiever, *Slavery and the Emigration of North Carolina Friends* (Murfreesboro, NC: Johnson Publishing Co., 1970), 52.

74. Francis Anscombe, *I Have Called You Friends: The Story of Quakerism in North Carolina* (Boston: Christopher Publishing House, 1959), 176, 181.

75. Hamm, *Transformation of American Quakerism*, 13

76. Kelly, *Quakers in Anne Arundel County*, 87–88. In the 1700s many Friends in Maryland's Anne Arundel County left the Society and joined the Church of England.

77. Worrall, *Friendly Virginians*, 354. Two thousand of the acres had originally been owned by George Washington.

78. Philadelphia Orthodox Yearly Meeting for Sufferings, "A Statistical Inquiry into the Condition of the People of Colour in the City and Districts of Philadelphia," (1847), transcribed on Friends Historical Library web site, http://www. Swarthmore./Library/Friends. Some 5,000 households with about 3500 men and 2800 women were surveyed in great detail about jobs, housing,

income, education, churches, benevolent societies, and problems of crime, drinking, and gambling.

79. *Minutes of Indiana Yearly Meeting of Friends (Orthodox)* (Muncie, Indiana: Indiana Yearly Meeting of Friends, 1854), 30.

80. Hamm et al., "'A Great and Good People,'" 12. Poor African Americans were not eligible for the "assistance" given to poor people of European descent, namely, living in a county "poorhouse" where they received food, clothing, and medical care. This was believed to be a more efficient and cheaper way to provide relief, as well as an opportunity to "cure" people of "the bad habits and character defects that were assumed to be the cause of their poverty." See the Poor House Story web site, www.poorhousestory.com.

81. Hamm et al., "'A Great and Good People.'" The committees' work apparently was never done—the Indiana Yearly Meeting Minutes of 1858 note the standing committee's request to be replaced—after it had been working for 20 years. Indiana Yearly Meeting Minutes, 1858, 35.

82. Indiana Yearly Meeting Minutes, 1857, 37.

83. James Oliver Horton, *Free People of Color: Inside the African American Community* (Washington, DC: Smithsonian Institution Press, 1993), 60, and Mabee, *Black Freedom*, 57; Meier, *Negro Thought in America*, 4.

84. Minutes, State Convention of Colored Citizens of Pennsylvania, 1849, in Sterling, *Speak Out*.

85. Richard Newman, Patrick Rael, and Phillip Lapsansky, eds., *Pamphlets of Protest: An Anthology of Early African American Protest Literature, 1790–1860* (New York: Routledge, 2001), 3, 7.

86. James Henretta, "Richard Allen and African-American Identity: A Black Ex-Slave in Early America's White Society Preserves His Cultural Identity by Creating Separate Institutions," in James A. Henretta et al., *America's History*, 3d ed. (1997), reprinted on Early America Review web site, www.earlyamerica.com/review/spring97/allen.html; on Brown, see Hazelton, *Let Freedom Ring*, 223.

87. Carol V. R. George, *Segregated Sabbath: Richard Allen and the Rise of the Independent Black Churches, 1760–1845*, 57. According to George, Allen, who went on to found the African Methodist Episcopal Church, had no "ill feeling" toward Friends, but found that the message of other denominations was more relevant to people of African descent.

88. Nash, *Forging Freedom*, 93–94, 139. The people David Barclay freed were indentured out with the surname Barclay. In 1847 Pennsylvania rescinded the emancipation act provision allowing temporary residence in the state.

89. Margaret Hope Bacon, *History of the Pennsylvania Society for Promoting the Abolition of Slavery* (Philadelphia: Pennsylvania Abolition Society, 1959), 2–12.

90. The information about Hopkins is from Hamm, e-mail to authors, 16 January 2006. Hamm also notes that Hopkins was the first clerk of Indiana Yearly Meeting in 1821. The action was reported in *The Friend*, 29 June 1829, 51; 7 November 1829, 28; and 9 January 1830, 104.

91. Hamm et al., "'A Great and Good People,'" 5, 8.

92. James, *People among Peoples*, 176, 196–97, 214.

93. In 1915 the association relocated to the property of the Cheney Training School for Teachers, and later called the Shelter for Colored Girls and the Shelter for Colored Orphans. In 1965, it became the Friends Shelter for Girls. It served as a home for teenage girls and continued until 1981, when it was converted to an emergency shelter and renamed the Friends Association for the Care and Protection of Children. See background note, inventory of Friends Shelter for Girls Records, Swarthmore College Friends Historical Library web site, http://www.swarthmore.edu/library/friends/ead/4008frsh.xml.

94. In 1922 the home moved to the property of Cheney Training School, and in 1945 its name was changed to Sunnycrest Farm. The proximity to Cheyney's Normal School proved to be especially valuable to the boys, according to the Board of Managers in their 1927 Report of the Home for Destitute Colored Children (Cheyney, PA: Sunny Crest Farm for Colored Children, 1927), 1.

95. R.I. State Home and School Project, www.ric.edu/statehomeandschool/resources Enos.html 28 July 07. Anna Jenkins' name was provided by Rosalind Wiggins, phone call to authors, 24 August 2002.

96. Robert H. Maris, "Friends in Philanthropy" in *Friends in Wilmington*, 60–71.

97. Benjamin, *Philadelphia Quakers*, 126, 128.

98. Accounts differ. Dorland, *Quakers in Canada* refers specifically to Oberlin Friends; others simply identify them as "the Society of Friends."

99. By 1836 the colony had failed. Robin Winks, *The Blacks in Canada: A History* (Montreal and Buffalo, NY: McGill-Queen's University Press, 1997), 156–57.

100. Anthony Cohen, *The Underground Railroad in Montgomery County, Maryland: A History and Driving Guide* (Rockville, MD: Montgomery County Historical Society, 1994) 5, 26.

101. Katz, *Black Pioneers*, 70. In Ontario, home to most of Canada's African Americans, the number dropped from 13,435 in 1871 to 8,900 by 1900. According to Winks, *Blacks in Canada*, 304, estimated numbers were unreliable. For one thing, the census had no clear definition for a person of African descent. See also Mabee, *Black Freedom*, 306. The considerable migration back and forth—many coming to Canada and others returning to the United States for better pay or to be with their families, especially after the Civil War—complicates any estimate of the number of African Americans who moved to Canada. Bordewich, *Bound for Canaan*, 378–79, has suggested that between 20,000 and 23,000 crossed into Canada; in the 1860s people of African descent then living in Canada stated that 35,000 to 40,000 had moved. These estimates are consistent with the 30,000 figure given for the number of people of African ancestry reported to be in Canada at the outbreak of the Civil War in J. C. Hamilton, "Slavery in Canada," in *Magazine of American History* 25 (1892): 233–36.

102. Benjamin Drew, *A North-side View of Slavery: The Refugee; or, The Narratives of the Fugitive Slaves in Canada Related by Themselves* (New York: Negro Universities Press, 1978), 309; Bordewich, *Bound for Canaan*, 264–65.

NOTES FOR PAGES 123–125

103. Benjamin Lundy visited Wilberforce and found there were about 35 families at its largest period and that some had moved on to western Canada. Susanne R. Wicks, "Benjamin Lundy: Pioneer Quaker Abolitionist, 1789–1839," *Friends Journal* (June 2002), online at Tokyo Monthly Meeting web site, http://www2.gol.com/users/quakers/Benjamin_Lundy.htm. However, by 1838 the settlement had declined, and only 18 to 20 families, many destitute, remained. Bordewich, *Bound for Canaan*, 264. Fugitive settlements other than Wilberforce and Dawn included Elgin (initially named Buxton in honor of another British abolitionist), London, Woodstock, St. Thomas, and Brandford.

104. Dorland, *A History of the Society of Friends in Canada*, 297–98. The 1830 minutes of West Lake Monthly Meeting, to which Jane Young belonged, recorded a request for help with its colonization efforts from North Carolina Friends.

105. Nash, *Forging Freedom*, 203.

106. Henry Highland Garnet quoted in Mabee, *Black Freedom*, 145.

107. Charline Howard Conyers, *A Living Legend: the History of Cheyney University, 1837–1905* (Cheyney, PA: Cheyney University Press, 1990), 5.

108. Conyers, *Living Legend*, 4; Worrall, *Friendly Virginians*, 293, reports that in the 1830s Virginia Yearly Meeting received $1,159.82 from London Yearly Meeting to help educate African Americans. See also Nancy Slocum Hornick, "Anthony Benezet and the Africans' School: Toward a Theory of Full Equality," *Pennsylvania Magazine of History and Biography* 99 (October 1975): 410. Hornick also reports that Richard Allen, Absalom Jones, and James Forten were among those who had been students of Benezet.

109. *A Brief Sketch of Schools for Black People and Their Descendants Established by the Religious Society of Friends* (Philadelphia: Friends Book Store, 1867), 9–12, 14.

110. For a detailed account of the school see W. E. B. DuBois, *The Philadelphia Negro* (New York: Lippincott, 1899), 99–100. See also Benjamin, *Philadelphia Quakers*, 189, and Elizabeth Lasch-Quinn, *Black Neighbors: Race and the Limits of Reform in the American Settlement House Movement, 1890–1945* (Chapel Hill: University of North Carolina Press, 1993), 70.

111. Brendlinger, "Anthony Benezet," 5–7.

112. Nash, *Forging Freedom*, 203.

113. Bacon, "The Heritage of Anthony Benezet: Philadelphia Quakers and Black Education," in Harrison, ed., *For Emancipation and Education*, 26. Roberts Vaux, *Memoirs of the Life of Anthony Benezet* (Philadelphia: James P. Parke, 1817), 22.

114. Barbour and Frost, *Quakers*, 146.

115. Vaux, *Memoirs of the Life of Anthony Benezet*, 22.

116. William Kashatus, e-mail to authors, 17 October 2004.

117. Kashatus, *A Virtuous Education: Penn's vision for Philadelphia schools* (Wallingford, PA: Pendle Hill, 1997), 45–46.

118. Wiggins, ed., *Cuffe's Logs and Letters*, 52.

119. Nash, *Forging Freedom*, 204, has the opening date of Bustill's school as 1803, while Kenneth Ives et al., *Black Quakers: Brief Biographies* (Chicago: Progressiv Publishr [sic], 1986), 43, gives it as 1797. Cadbury, "Negro Membership," 52 n., refers to Cyrus Bustill as one of the active members of "the church." Ives states (43) that Bustill, who was trained in his trade by a Quaker, attended meeting in Philadelphia and was buried "by Friends."

120. Sources differ on some of the details of the New York school. Barbour et al., *Quaker Crosscurrents*, 68–70, states that the school opened in 1787 with between forty and sixty students and by 1809 had 182; Cox, *History of Quakerism in New York*, 62, states the school enrolled 182 students in 1797. See also Mott, *Biographical Sketches*, 329.

121. Edith Gaines, *The Charity Society, 1794–1994*, on Westbury Friends Meeting web site at http://www.westburyquakers.org/qt/archive/files/CSIntro.htm. The two monthly meetings were made up of some 450 Friends from meetings in Jericho, Westbury, Matinecock, Cow Neck, Bethpage, and Jerusalem.

122. *Ibid.* At its 200th anniversary, the Society, concerned about the "modest" amount it had available for scholarships for African Americans attending Quaker schools, created a task force to "investigate innovative ways to donate funds to benefit a greater number of needy children."

123. Quarles, *Black Abolitionists*, 109; Linda Marie Perkins, "Fanny Jackson Coppin and the Institute of Colored Youth: A Model of Nineteenth-Century Black Female Educational and Community Leadership, 1837–1902" (Ph.D. diss., University of Illinois at Urbana-Champaign, 1978), 322.

124. Linda Marie Perkins, "Quaker Beneficence and Black Control: The Institute for Colored Youth, 1852–1903," in *New Perspectives on Black Educational History*, eds. Vincent P. Franklin and James D. Anderson (Boston: G. K. Hall, 1978), 20.

125. Roger Lane, *William Dorsey's Philadelphia and Ours* (New York: Oxford University, 1991), 137.

126. Perkins, "Quaker Beneficence," 20–23. The school was on Barclay Street near Sixth. The group organized itself as "the Board of Education Auxiliary to the Guardianship of the Estate of Richard Humphries bequest and legacy for the instruction of colored Boys in trades, literature, and Agriculture." Shortly after the school started, the number of managers was increased to 33, all Quaker and all male. Women were not allowed on the board until 1915. Perkins, *Fanny Jackson Coppin*, 61, 91.

127. Perkins, "Quaker Beneficence," 22; McGraw Central Schools web site, www.mcgrawschools.org/history.

128. Cadbury, "Negro Membership," 27; Roger Lane, "Quakers and the Institute for Colored Youth" in Harrison, 46.

129. Kaestle, 44. Martha Paxson Grundy, "The Bethany Mission for Colored People: Philadelphia Friends and A Sunday School Mission," *Quaker History*, 72.

130. Grundy, "The Bethany Mission," 75–76.

131. "Debate over School for Colored Girls," Prudence Crandall documents, University of Connecticut web site, www.sp.uconn.edu. Susan Strane, *A Whole-Souled*

Woman: Prudence Crandall and the Education of Black Women (New York: W. W. Norton, 1990), 39.

132. Mabee, *Black Freedom*, 148.

133. Letter to the editor of the Norwich (CT) Courier, signed by "Colonizationists," March 27, 1833. "Debate over School for Colored Girls," Prudence Crandall documents, www.sp.uconn.edu. 7/25/2003.

134. Technicality aside, the arguments from the Crandall trials were used in the U.S. Supreme Court's school desegregation decision of 1954, according to the biography of Crandall on the web site of the Connecticut Women's Hall of Fame. 7/25/2003.

135. Elizabeth Yates, *Prudence Crandall: Woman of Courage*, pp. 45–54; 189.

136. Quarles, *Black Abolitionists*, 158. Crandall's Canterbury home and school has been a museum since 1984 and a National Historic Landmark since 1991. "Prudence Crandall Day" is held at the museum every Labor Day weekend. The Prudence Crandall Center for Women serves women in several area towns. www.skyways. lib.ks.us/history/crnadall.html. Crandall is remembered in a roadside marker in Kansas, where she moved after her husband died. The marker says that Connecticut and Kansas honor the lifetime achievements of an educator and champion of human rights.

137. Bacon, *Mothers of Feminism*, 103.

138. Worrall, *Friendly Virginians*, 343–44; Selleck, *Gentle Invaders*, 22.

139. Worrall, *Friendly Virginians*, 293, 379.

140. James, *A People Among Peoples*, 295; Kaestle, *Pillars of the Republic*, 196.

141. Dunlap, *Quaker Education*, 444, 446, 484, 487–88.

142. Quarles, *Black Abolitionists*, 109; see also *Friends in Wilmington*, 38.

143. Mabee, *Black Freedom*, 443. Harriet Beecher Stowe, also a trustee, donated part of the profits of *Uncle Tom's Cabin* to the school.

144. Carroll, "History of Third Haven Meeting."

145. Mabee, *Black Freedom*, 402; Thornbrough, *Negro in Indiana*, 167–68.

146. Hamm et al, "'A Great and Good People,'" 6.

147. *Ibid.*

148. Thornbrough, *Negro in Indiana*, 168.

149. Indiana Yearly Meeting Minutes, 1857, 37. Hiram H. Revels, a U.S. Senator from Mississippi after the Civil War, attended an Indiana Quaker school in the mid-1840s, likely Beech Grove Seminary near Liberty. See Mabee, *Black Freedom*, 147, 402 n. 17.

150. Thornbrough, *Negro in Indiana*, 168.

151. Hamm et al, "'A Great and Good People,'" 6.

152. Records of the Emlen Institution for the Benefit of Children of African and Indian Descent 1765–1956, Haverford College Quaker Collection, www.haverford.edu/ library/special/aids/emlen/12/16/05. The Institution merged into the Friends Fiduciary Corporation in 1978.

153. Convention proceedings quoted in Kathryn Grover, *Make a Way Somehow: African-American Life in a Northern Community, 1790–1865* (Syracuse, NY: Syracuse University Press, 1994), 177.

154. Mabee, *Black Freedom*, 156. A proposal by an 1831 convention of African Americans in Philadelphia to open liberal education colleges for "Young Men of Color" in New Haven, Connecticut, and Canaan, New Hampshire, was unsuccessful because of opposition by residents of both places. See Conyers, *Living Legend*, 9.

155. Frances Ruley Karttunen, *The Other Islanders: People who Pulled Nantucket's Oars* (New Bedford, MA: Spinner Publications, 2005), 84–85; Byers, "Nation of Nantucket," 262–63, 266; Robert Johnson, "Black-White Relationships on Nantucket," *Historic Nantucket* 51, 1 (2003).

156. Aaron Powell, *Reminiscences of the Anti-Slavery and Other Reforms and Reformers* (Westport, CT: Negro Universities Press, 1970, reprinted from 1899 publication by the Caulon Press in New York), 149–50; Margaret Hope Bacon, e-mail to authors, 7 June 2003.

157. Ebenezer Tucker, *History of Randolph County, Indiana, with Illustrations and Biographical Sketches* (Chicago: A. L. Kingman, 1882), 44; Robert M. Taylor Jr. et al., *From Indiana: A New Historical Guide* (Indianapolis: Indiana Historical Society, 1989), 44. Incorporated in 1852 on land given by Josiah White, a Pennsylvania Quaker of European Descent, the Institute in La Fontaine, near Wabash, has become White's Residential and Family Services for orphans or other young people who are wards of the county or state. It is sponsored partially by Indiana Yearly Meeting. White's daughters also added a significant amount, according to Elliott, *Quakers on the American Frontier*, 203.

158. At the writing of this book, the institute is known as Quakerdale. Iowa Yearly Meeting (FUM) appoints nine Trustees, six of whom must be Quakers, but does not finance the agency. Many churches and individual members contribute. E-mail to authors from Donna Lawler, Director of Development, Quakerdale, 20 August 2007. The original benefactor, Josiah White, founded the Lehigh Coal and Navigation Company and was the chief promoter of anthracite coal in Pennsylvania, Jones, *The Quakers of Iowa*, on web Iowa History Project, http://iagenweb.org/history/qoi/QOIPt4Chp3.htm.

159. Hamm et al, "'A Great and Good People.'"

160. Thornbrough, *Negro in Indiana*, 173.

161. Tucker, *History of Randolph County*, 179. Tucker was principal of the school from 1846 to 1856 and from 1872 to 1879.

162. Michael B. Katz, *Reconstructing American Education* (Cambridge, MA: Harvard University Press, 1987), 95; Taylor et al, *From Indiana*, 99.

163. Hamm et al, "'Great and Good People,'" 10.

164. Mabee, *Black Freedom*, 147–48.

165. Grover, *Gibraltar's Rock*, 180.

166. James, *A People Among Peoples*, 293. Robert J. Cottrol, *The Afro-Yankees: Providence's Black community in the antebellum era* (Westport, Conn.: Greenwood Press, 1982) 58–60.

167. Zora Klain, *Educational Activities of New England Quakers* (Philadelphia: Westbrook Publishing Co., 1928). Details on all the Quaker schools are given from pages 34 to 157.

168. Gilbert H. Barnes and Dwight L. Dumond, eds., *Letters of Theodore Dwight Weld, Angelina Grimké and Sarah Grimké, 1822–1844* (1934; reprint, Gloucester, MA: P. Smith, 1965), 855.

169. Chace, *Reminiscences*, 114–15. Cottrol, *Afro-Yankees*, 97.

170. Klain, *Educational Activities of New England Quakers*, 175–186.

171. Quoted in Quarles, *Black Abolitionists*, 72.

172. Marion Manola Thompson Wright, *Education of Negroes in New Jersey* (New York: Teacher's College, Columbia University, 1941), 124.

173. An 1801 register for the school in the possession of David Haines of Hopkinton, MA, shows that Roger Hicks paid for Tom Negro and Moses Negro, that George Palier paid for Jacob Negro, and Dinah Churchman paid for Sam and Stephen, both also with "Negro" as their last names.

174. Wright, *Education of Negroes*, 123–24.

175. Mabee, *Black Freedom*, 147–48.

176. Indiana Yearly Meeting Minutes, 1859, 35; Mabee, *Black Freedom*, 402. Thornbrough, *Negro in Indiana*, 167–68, provides some examples.

177. Hamm et al, "'A Great and Good People,'" 4–6.

178. Vincent, *Southern Seed, Northern Soil*, 196 n. 65.

179. D. Neill Snarr et al, *Claiming Our Past: Quakers in Southwest Ohio and Eastern Tennessee* (Sabina, OH: Gaskins Printing, 1992), 86; *Friends Review*, 27 October 1860, 120–21.

180. Hamm et al, "'A Great and Good People.'"

181. James, *People among Peoples*, 176, 197.

182. Edwin Bronner, "Review of A People Among Peoples: Quaker Benevolence in Eighteenth-Century America," *Quaker History* 52 (Spring 1963), 41–42.

183. Marietta, *Reformation of American Quakerism*, 124–25. Marietta has also questioned Daniel Boorstin's supposition that had Friends remained as leaders in Pennsylvania government they could have had more power to work against enslavement. Their efforts would have continued in a more mainstream mode, uncritical of "the priorities of their countrymen."

184. Davis, *Problem of Slavery*, 242; see also Kaestle, *Pillars of the Republic*, 35.

185. Indiana Yearly Meeting Minutes, 1859, 35.

186. Katz, *Reconstructing American Education*.

187. Kaestle, *Pillars of the Republic*, 39. Similarly, Shane White, *Somewhat More Independent*, 84, argues that the "general desire" of Manumission Society New Yorkers who founded the African Free School was "to order the behavior of New York's lower classes."

188. Vincent, *Southern Seeds, Northern Soil*, 33–34. Hamm et al., "'A Great and Good People,'" agree that "Quaker benevolence was often accompanied by a paternalistic outlook in which African Americans had to be instructed in the virtues of thrift, hard work, and sobriety" but suggest that Friends believed that freed people did not need this advice not because of "any innate racial characteristics, but rather from the ignorance and degradation of slavery."

189. Litwack, *North of Slavery*, 18.
190. Bacon, "Heritage of Anthony Benezet," 27, 28.
191. Forbush, *History of Baltimore Yearly Meeting*, 55. Kaestle, *Pillars of the Republic*, 40–41, wrote that Lancaster's "elaborate plan of instruction" was designed to make it possible to teach large numbers of pupils, as many as 500 at one time. According to Cox, *History of Quakerism in New York*, 175, by 1811 there were 95 Lancastrian schools with 30,000 children (whether this number is for England and/or the U.S. is not clear).
192. For more than 50 years, the McKim school has been a very active community center serving many African American young people. See Baltimore's African American Heritage and Attractions web site, www.baltimore.org/africanamerican/historic-landmarks.htm.
193. Harry Silcox, "Nineteenth-Century Philadelphia Black Militant: Octavius V. Catto (1839–1871)" in Trotter and Smith, 450; Cottrol, *Afro-Yankees*, 58–60; James Brewer Stewart, "What Color Meant in Antebellum New England: The New Haven Negro College and Conflicting History of Race: 1776–1870," on Yale University Law School web site, www.law.yale.edu/outside/pdf; Kaestle, *Common Schools*, 42. When the system was removed from Philadelphia schools in 1828 it was the African American schools that had far fewer teachers (six for 458 students in one school) that suffered most. See Silcox, "Nineteenth-Century Philadelphia Black Militant," 457–58.
194. Perkins, "Quaker Beneficence," 24.
195. Nash, "Slaves and Slaveholders in Colonial Philadelphia," 211.
196. Lane, "Quakers and the Institute for Colored Youth" in Harrison, 51.
197. Nash, *Forging Freedom*, 89–90, 27.
198. Bacon, "Heritage of Anthony Benezet," 27–28. Kashatus, e-mail to authors, 14 October 2004; Benjamin, *Philadelphia Quakers*, 131; Davis, Problems of Slavery, 242.
199. Mabee, *Black Freedom*, 146.
200. James, *People among Peoples*, 215, 315.
201. *Ibid.*, 324.

CHAPTER FIVE: The Civil War and Its Aftermath

1. C. Ray Aurner, ed., *A Topical History of Cedar County, Iowa* (Chicago: S. J. Clark, 1910), 1:431.
2. Elliott, *Quakers on the American Frontier*, 120–21, states that Edwin Coppoc was disowned "for defection from Quaker faith" but does not mention dancing. See Jones, *Quakers on Iowa*, 197.
3. Lapsansky, "Free Produce, Free People."
4. Franklin and Moss, *From Slavery to Freedom*, 216–17, identify the African Americans who were killed as Lewis Sheridan Leary and Dangerfield Newby; John Anthony Copeland and Shields Green, who were captured; and Osborn Perry (or Anderson), who escaped. On the fates of each of them see Sterling, ed., *Speak Out*, 283.

5. Irving Richman, "John Brown Among the Quakers" in Richman, *John Brown Among the Quakers and Other Sketches* (Des Moines: Historical Department of Iowa, [1894]), 51–52. Richman reported that the Coppoc house was surrounded at night to protect Barclay Coppoc against federal agents, which "afforded the unusual spectacle of the close juxtaposition of a musket and a Quaker broad brimmed hat" (54).

6. Aurner, ed., *Topical History of Cedar County*, 431; David S. Reynolds, *John Brown, Abolitionist: The Man Who Killed Slavery, Sparked the Civil War, and Seeded Civil Rights* (New York, Alfred A. Knopf, 2005), 376.

7. Jones, *The Quakers of Iowa*, 196–97. Quaker historians view the Coppocs' participation differently: a century later Drake, *Quakers and Slavery*, 192, put the brothers among "a few hotheads [who] turned to force." Thirty years later, Lapsansky found a parallel to "modern young people who have gone off to support revolutions in third world countries." Lapsansky, "Free Produce, Free People." While the Coppoc brothers' mother, Mary Coppoc Ralley, worked for women's suffrage in the 1870s, she wrote to Susan B. Anthony that she was glad that the revolution she was working for was "bloodless." Bacon, *Mothers of Feminism*, 129.

8. Reynolds, *John Brown*, 304.

9. *Friends Review*, 29 October 1859, 120.

10. On Mott, see Bacon, *Valiant Friend*, 194.

11. Worrall, *Friendly Virginians*, 405.

12. Stewart, *Holy Warriors*, 152–53.

13. Mabee, *Black Freedom*, 5; Stewart, *Holy Warriors*, 153.

14. Mabee, *Black Freedom*, 323, 238.

15. Stewart, *Holy Warriors*, 151, 169–74.

16. Litwack, *North of Slavery*, 250, 266.

17. Drake, *Quakers and Slavery*, 197.

18. *The Friend* (Philadelphia), 33 (1859), 111–112.

19. Drake, *Quakers and Slavery*, 176.

20. Mabee, *Black Freedom*, 342, 358–59.

21. Worrall, *Friendly Virginians*, 420.

22. Ryan P. Jordan, *Slavery and the Meetinghouse: The Quakers and the Abolitionist Dilemma, 1820–1865* (Bloomington: Indiana University Press, 2005), 132, citing *The Friend* of January 1863; Sterling, *Abby Kelley Foster*, 355; John Greenleaf Whittier to William Lloyd Garrison, 24 November 1863, Spartacus Educational web site, http://www.spartacus.schoolnet.co.uk.

23. Christopher Densmore and Thomas Bassett, "Quakers, Slavery, and the Civil War" in Barbour et al., *Quaker Crosscurrents*, 191–92.

24. Mabee, *Black Freedom*, 354–55. Bronner, "Time of Change," 113; Densmore and Bassett, "Quakers, Slavery, and the Civil War" in Barbour et al., 191–92. Similar objections were raised by some Quaker conscientious objectors in World War II.

25. Worrall, *Friendly Virginians*, 422, 340.

26. "Epistle 'To the Meeting for Sufferings of London Yearly Meeting,'" Minutes of the Meeting for Sufferings of New York (Orthodox) Yearly Meeting, 2 September

1863, 186; Minutes of New York (Orthodox) Yearly Meeting, 29 May 1863, cited in Edward Needles Wright, *Conscientious Objectors in the Civil War* (Philadelphia: University of Pennsylvania Press, and London: Oxford University Press, 1931), 197.

27. Edwin B. Bronner, "A Time of Change: Philadelphia Yearly Meeting, 1861–1914," in Moore, ed., *Friends in the Delaware Valley*, 113, 114–15.

28. *The Record of a Quaker Conscience: Cyrus Pringle's Diary*, Quaker Heritage Press web site, www.qhpress.org/quakerpages/qwhp/pringle1.htm.

29. Cecil Currey, "Quakers in 'Bleeding Kansas,'" *Bulletin of The Friends Historical Association* 50, 2 (Autumn 1961): 99, 100.

30. Bacon, *Abby Hopper Gibbons*, 113.

31. Cox, *Quakerism in New York*, 66–68. Bacon, *Abby Hopper Gibbons*, 114, states that the nurses were African American, but that has not been verified. See also Barnet Schecter, *The Devil's Own Work: The Civil War Draft Riots and the Fight to Reconstruct America* (New York: Walker and Co., 2005), 148, 287, which notes that the city paid for the damages, and, because of growing housing segregation, the asylum had to be rebuilt in another part of the city. The rescuers included an Irish street cab driver and three others from the crowd.

32. David Quigley, "Race Relations and Presidential Leadership" (Lecture, Tufts University, Medford, MA, 19 October 2005).

33. Drake, *Quakers and Slavery*, 197, 198.

34. Chuck Fager, "Answers to the Sixth Query of Baltimore Yearly Meeting, 1865," in "Speaking Peace, Living Peace: American Quakers Face the Civil War," Quaker House web site, http://quakerhouse.org.

35. Bacon, *Shadow of William Penn*, 12.

36. Rufus Jones, *The Later Periods of Quakerism* (London: Macmillan, 1921), 737–38.

37. Densmore and Bassett, "Quakers, Slavery, and the Civil War," in Barbour et al., 192, 194, described this encounter but mistakenly stated that Jones was Rufus Jones's older brother. Anne Upton, e-mail to authors, 20 September 2007. For more on Jones, see Maine State Archives web site, http://www.maine.gov/sos/arc/archives/military/civilwar/jones.htm.

38. Jacquelyn Nelson, *Indiana Quakers Confront the Civil War* (Indianapolis: Indiana Historical Society, 1991), 21–22, 25, 34–39. At least 238 of these men died during the war. Some data about Friends military service in other yearly meetings is in Jones, *Later Periods of Quakerism*, 2: 729 and 737–38. According to Nelson, *Indiana Quakers*, 96, many of those disowned had other offenses charged against them.

39. Hamm, e-mail to authors, 21 July 2008.

40. Drake, *Quakers and Slavery*, 197.

41. Nelson, *Indiana Quakers Confront the Civil War*, 30.

42. Nelson, *Indiana Quakers*, 98. Julian quoted in *Ibid.*, 17. Richard L. Zuber, "Conscientious Objectors in the Confederacy: The Quakers in North Carolina," *The Southern Friend* 9, 1 (Spring 1987): 54, refers to the same "myth" of Quaker nonparticipation in the war. He faulted discussions of the topic carried out "in a never-never land of filio-pietistic writing done by amateurs who were primarily

interested in proving that the Civil War Quakers were shining examples of Christian heroism."

43. Jones, *Later Periods of Quakerism* 2:736–37.

44. Bronner, "Time of Change," 114–15, states that researchers agree that in Philadelphia more Hicksites served than Orthodox. See also Nelson, *Indiana Quakers*, 60, 64, 68, 72.

45. Densmore and Bassett, "Quakers, Slavery, and the Civil War" in Barbour et al., 194.

46. Nelson, *Indiana Quakers*, 34–39.

47. Mark A. Schmidt, "Patriotism and Paradox: Quaker Military Service in the Civil War," 18 April 2004, Riggtown History web site, http://courses.wcupa.edu/jones/his480/reports/civilwar.htm.

48. Hinshaw and Hinshaw, *Carolina Quaker Experience*, 152, 155, 158; Wright, *Conscientious Objectors*, 12–13.

49. Zuber, "Conscientious Objectors," 54.

50. Robert Cruden, *The Negro in Reconstruction* (Englewood Cliffs, NJ: Prentice-Hall, [1969]), 99, 92, suggests that this experience has been "too little studied in light of contemporary knowledge of psychology."

51. On the Confiscation Acts see *United States, Statutes at Large, Treaties, and Proclamations of the United States of America* (Boston, 1863), 12: 319, 589–92, transcribed on University of Maryland Freedmen and Southern Society Project web site, http://www.history.umd.edu/Freedmen.

52. Densmore and Bassett, "Quakers, Slavery, and the Civil War" in Barbour et al., 195.

53. Paul Pierce, *The Freedmen's Bureau: A Chapter in the History of Reconstruction* (Iowa City: University of Iowa, 1904), 27.

54. Thomas H. Smith, "Ohio Quakers and the Mississippi Freedmen: 'A Field to Labor,'" *Ohio History* 78, 3 (Summer 1969): 160.

55. In Arkansas, Quakers and the American Missionary Association provided more than half of the state's education budget between 1867 and 1868. The share of the Freedmen's Bureau was 6 percent. See Salemson, "Civil War Writings," 12.

56. Yannessa, *Levi Coffin*, 47, 49–51; Elliott, *Quakers on the American Frontier*, 96. Coffin had earlier been agent for the Contraband Relief Association, organized by Cincinnati business people, some Quakers.

57. Selleck, *Gentle Invaders*, 192. The meeting stated that it would build as many schools as it could finance.

58. Smith, "Ohio Quakers," 162.

59. Selleck, *Gentle Invaders*, 65, 42.

60. Salemson, "Civil War Writings," 11.

61. Selleck, *Gentle Invaders*, 50, 52–53.

62. Anscombe, "Contributions of Quakers," 122.

63. Cruden, *Negro in Reconstruction*, 81.

64. Anscombe, "Quaker Contributions," 277; Henrietta Stratton Jaquette, "'Friends' Association of Philadelphia for the Aid and Elevation of the Freemen," *The Bulletin of The Friends Historical Association* 46, 2 (Autumn 1957): 68–70.

65. Yannessa, *Levi Coffin*, 47, 49–51; Elliott, *Quakers on the American Frontier*. 96.

66. Anscombe, "Contributions of Quakers," 230. Selleck, *Gentle Invaders*, 64, mentions an English couple and their two daughters who came to teach in Virginia and another British woman, her daughter, and a niece, who taught in Virginia and North Carolina. On the Baltimore work, see Forbush, *History of Baltimore Yearly Meeting*, 77.

67. Jaquette, "Friends' Association," 73.

68. Qualls, "Successors of Woolman and Benezet," 92–94, 99.

69. Jaquette, "Friends' Association," 69–70.

70. Benjamin, *Philadelphia Quakers*, 130.

71. Jaquette, "Friends' Association," 68–69.

72. Anscombe, "Contributions of Quakers," 137; Densmore and Bassett, "Quakers, Slavery, and the Civil War" in Barbour et al., 195–96.

73. Thomas C. Kennedy, "Southland College: The Society of Friends and Black Education in Arkansas," *Arkansas Historical Quarterly* 17 (Autumn 1983): 207–38, Arkansas Black History Online web site, http://www.cals.lib.ar.us/butlercenter/abho/docs/.

74. Smedley, *Martha Schofield*, 85.

75. Forbush, *History of Baltimore Yearly Meeting*, 78; Mallonee et al., *Minute by Minute*, 82; Smith, "Ohio Quakers," 163.

76. Selleck, *Gentle Invaders*, 36, 96–97.

77. *Ibid.*, 447; Selleck, *Gentle Invaders*, 71.

78. Worrall, *Friendly Virginians*, 455.

79. Susan Tucker Hatcher, "North Carolina Quakers: The Freedmen's Friends," *Southern Friend* (Spring 1981): 32.

80. Herbert Gutman, "Schools for Freedom," in *Civil Rights since 1787: A Reader on the Black Struggle*, ed. Jonathan Birnbaum and Clarence Taylor (New York: New York University Press, 2000), 110, 113.

81. Cruden, *Negro in Reconstruction*, 119; Forrest G. Wood, *Era of Reconstruction, 1863–1877* (New York: Crowell, 1975), 26–27; Franklin and Moss, *From Slavery to Freedom*, 255–57. See also Judith Colucci Breault, *The World of Emily Howland: Odyssey of a Humanitarian* (Millbrae, CA: Les Femmes Publications, 1976), 91–92.

82. Franklin and Moss, *From Slavery to Freedom*, 257.

83. Data from Salemson, "Civil War Writings," 12, and W. E. Burghardt Du Bois, *Black Reconstruction: An Essay toward A History of the Part Which Black Folk Played in the Attempt to Reconstruct Democracy in America, 1860–1880* (New York: Russell and Russell, 1935), 226–27. According to Du Bois, most of the historically black colleges—Howard, Fisk, and Atlanta among them—were either founded by and/or received some initial funding from the Freedmen's Bureau. According to Cruden, *Negro in Reconstruction*, 61–63, at its height in 1866, there were 760 teachers and 150,000 students with a $3 million budget. The numbers declined after that.

84. Clara Merritt DeBoer, "Blacks and the American Missionary Association," in *Hidden Histories of the United Church of Christ*, ed. Barbara Brown Zikmund (New York: United Church Press, 1984).

85. Gutman, "Schools for Freedom."

86. Souders and Souders, *Rock in a Weary Land*, 44–45.

87. DeBoer, "Blacks and the American Missionary Association"; numbers of Quaker women from Selleck, *Gentle Invaders*, Appendix A, 225–31; Thomas Hamm, "Gentle Invaders: A Review Essay," *Quaker Religious Thought* 20 (February 2001), 19.

88. Smedley, *Martha Schofield*, 73.

89. Souders and Souders, *Rock in a Weary Land*, 44–46.

90. Qualls, "Successors of Woolman and Benezet," 101–3. For student numbers, Selleck, *Gentle Invaders*, 82. One of the key officials was Friend Reuben Tomlinson, who had been active in the earliest reconstruction work in Port Royal in South Carolina, became the bureau's "School Officer" in the Charleston area, and later was the state superintendent of education; he also ran unsuccessfully for governor. Jaquette, "Friends' Association," 76. Benjamin, *Philadelphia Quakers*, 133–34, states that Tomlinson could be called "the only Quaker 'carpetbagger' from Philadelphia" and was skilled in handling race problems diplomatically.

91. Jones, *Later Periods of Quakerism*, 598. Hampton received support early on from both The Friends Freedmen's Association and Pennsylvania Abolition Society; see Bacon, "Heritage of Anthony Benezet," 32.

92. Selleck, *Gentle Invaders*, 76–77.

93. Jaquette, "Friends' Association," 76–77.

94. Selleck, *Gentle Invaders*, 6, 67–68.

95. Jaquette, "Friends' Association," 73.

96. DeBoer, "Blacks and the American Missionary Association."

97. Smedley, *Martha Schofield*, 127.

98. Kennedy, "Southland College," 212; Selleck, *Gentle Invaders*, 203. Indiana Yearly Meeting had begun to actively organize home missions in the 1860s; see Thomas D. Hamm, *Transformation of American Quakerism*, 58.

99. Alida Clark in *The Friend*, 1 August 1883.

100. Smedley, *Martha Schofield*, 86, 221–22.

101. Willie Lee Rose, *Rehearsal for Reconstruction: The Port Royal Experiment* (New York: Oxford University Press, 1976).

102. Rose, *Rehearsal for Reconstruction*, 38.

103. Bacon, "The Heritage of Anthony Benezet" in Harrison, 30. The committee, which became the Pennsylvania Freedmen's Relief Association, supported other efforts as well. The Benezet Committee of Germantown was one of the school's other benefactors.

104. Bacon, "Heritage of Anthony Benezet," 29–32.

105. Monica Maria Tetzlaff, "The Penn School; the Penn Center and Friends," *Friends Journal* 43, 3 (March 1997), 16–19.

106. Selleck, *Gentle Invaders*, 4, 80.

107. Cruden, *Negro in Reconstruction*, 63; Qualls, "Successors of Woolman and Benezet," 89–90; Elizabeth Jacoway, *Yankee Missionaries in the South: The Penn School Experiment* (Baton Rouge: Louisiana State University Press, 1979), 258.

108. The camp moved twice, first to the Lee estate in Arlington, Virginia, and then to Mason's Island; see Breault, *Emily Howland*, 67.
109. Barbour and Frost, *Quakers*, 334–35.
110. Kennedy, "Southland College: The Society of Friends and Black Education in Arkansas," 39.
111. *Ibid.*, 42.
112. Selleck, *Gentle Invaders*, 198–201, 213–14, 220.
113. Kennedy, "Southland College," 50.
114. Selleck, *Gentle Invaders*, 85–86; Smedley, *Martha Schofield*, 11–12.
115. Selleck, *Gentle Invaders*, 89. It was still operating in the early 1900s.
116. Smedley, *Martha Schofield*, 128, 184. Half the cost of one of the new buildings for the program was donated by the sons of Philadelphia Quaker Deborah Fisher Wharton, who had had a long-term interest in African Americans; Mary Patterson, "Martha Schofield," in *Quaker Torch Bearers* (Philadelphia: Friends General Conference, 1943), 127.
117. Patterson, "Martha Schofield," 119, 126.
118. *Ibid.*, 122, 133.
119. Patterson in *Quaker Torch Bearers*, 122, 133. Bacon, "the Heritage of Anthony Benezet" in Harrison, 29. Bacon refers to the Germantown Friends Aid Association (Hicksite), and the Benezet Society (Orthodox). Hamm believes that Hicksite Friends followed Schofield's work with some interest into the 1890s through contributions from individuals and monthly meetings, e-mail to authors, October 2003.
120. Smedley, *Martha Schofield*, 140.
121. Stafford Allen Warner, *Yardley Warner: The Freedman's Friend* (Didcot, Eng.: Wessex Press, 1957), Appendix C. Proceeds of the sale of the Maryville school went to a Freedmen's Fund, still administered by a New England Yearly Meeting committee for the benefit of African Americans. Skip Schiel, e-mail to authors, 25 August 2005.
122. Snarr et al, *Claiming Our Past*, 94.
123. At the invitation of the mayor of Macon (TN), Friends opened a school for indigent white children. "The venture was a wise one, as it tended to remove prejudice against the work of the Quakers for the negroes. In the Lower South the Society was almost unknown, and The Friends experienced opposition of a character not met with in sections where they were well established." Friends also did "extensive work among the poor whites in the mountains of Alabama." Anscombe, "Contributions of Quakers," 246.
124. Snarr et al, *Claiming Our Past*, 94.
125. Selleck, *Gentle Invaders*, 143–44, 146, 148.
126. *Ibid.*, 177.
127. Benjamin, *Philadelphia Quakers*, 140.
128. Bacon in Harrison, "Heritage of Anthony Benezet," 33; Anna Fariello, "Friends and the Christiansburg Institute" (Lecture, Meeting of Quaker Historians, West Chester, PA, 22 June 2002). The school closed in the 1960s.

129. Jaquette, "Friends' Association," 81; Bacon, *History of the Pennsylvania Abolition Society*, 31, 33. The PAS continued its support until the 1980s. Bacon visited in 1980 and heard from graduates how the school had "helped build a strong Africa American community, the ties of which cont'd to this day." Bacon, e-mail to authors, 1 September 2004.

130. Anscombe, "Contributions of Quakers," 202.

131. Selleck, *Gentle Invaders*, 91–94, 134.

132. Horton and Horton, *Hard Road to Freedom*, 183; Salemson, "Civil War Writings," 34, 45–46.

133. Selleck, *Gentle Invaders*, 91, 151–54.

134. Selleck, *Gentle Invaders*, 95.

135. Eric Foner, *Reconstruction: America's Unfinished Revolution 1863-1877* (New York: Harper and Row, 1988), 428.

136. Smedley, *Martha Schofield*, 86.

137. Patterson, "Martha Schofield," 121–22.

138. Cruden, *The Negro in Reconstruction*, 10–19. Wood, *The Era of Reconstruction*, 28–32, 40–45. See also Heather Cox Richardson, *The Death of Reconstruction: Race, Labor, and Politics in the Post-Civil War North, 1865-1900* (Cambridge, MA: Harvard University Press, 2001), 160.

139. Vernon Wharton, *The Negro in Mississippi, 1865-1890* (New York: Harper and Row, [1965]), 59.

140. Eric Foner, *Forever Free, The Story of Emancipation and Reconstruction* (New York: Knopf, 2005), 81.

141. Cruden, *Negro in Reconstruction*, 45. Horton and Horton, *Hard Road to Freedom*, 185; Wood, *Era of Reconstruction*, 75.

142. Crockett, Black Towns, 5.

143. Wood, *Era of Reconstruction*, 75–76.

144. Breault, *Emily Howland*, 81–82.

145. Anscombe, "Contributions of Quakers," 193. The authors suggest that because Southland was a Quaker-organized school supported by Friends from all over the country, it is likely that the donor from Massachusetts was a Friend.

146. Anscombe, "Contributions of Quakers," 200; Hatcher, "North Carolina Quakers," 33–34. According to Benjamin, *Philadelphia Quakers*, 130, based on Friends Freedmen's Association mortgage records, Philadelphia Friends bought 34 acres in Greensboro and made 10-year loans to African American buyers. Benjamin mistakenly uses "Dudley" as Warner's first name.

147. James Woodhams Hood, "The Indefatigable Yardley Warner," *The Southern Friend* 15, 2 (Autumn 1993): 5–6; Warner, *Yardley Warner*, 285–97.

148. Hatcher, "North Carolina Quakers," 32; on Warner's son's work about him, see *ibid.*, 67. Warner taught "for a time" at both Westtown School and the Ohio Yearly Meeting Board School at Mt. Pleasant, Ohio. Hood, "Yardley Warner," 4.

149. *Ibid.*, quoting *Greensboro Patriot*, 7 January 1869; Warner, *Yardley Warner*, 289–92.

150. Hood, "Yardley Warner," 6.

151. Hatcher, "North Carolina Quakers," 34, quoting *Greensboro Patriot*, 7 January 1869.

152. Warner, *Yardley Warner*, 213.

153. Selleck, *Gentle Invaders*, 43.

154. Thornbrough, *Negro in Indiana*, 210-11, 222.

155. Anscombe, "Contributions of Quakers," 252-53.

156. Richardson, *The Death of Reconstruction*, 160.

157. Cruden, *Negro in Reconstruction*, 167; Richardson, *Death of Reconstruction*, 157, 167.

158. *The Friend* (London), 1 October 1880, 269; Jones, *Later Periods of Quakerism*, 616.

159. Jones, *Later Periods of Quakerism*, 616-17; Bronner, "Time of Change," 117-18.

160. Jones, *Later Periods of Quakerism*, 617; C. Hare, comp., *Life and letters of Elizabeth L. Comstock* (London: Headley Brothers, and Philadelphia: J. C. Winston, 1895), 377; *Friends Review* 33, 3 April 1880.

161. Jones, *The Later Periods of Quakerism* (London: Macmillan and Company, 1921), 617, from Elizabeth Comstock, *Life and letters of Elizabeth L. Comstock*, 377. *Friends Review*, 33, 3 April 1880.

162. *The Friend* (London), 2 February 1880, 45.

163. Jones, *The Later Periods*, 598.

164. Anscombe, "Contributions of Quakers," 221. The meetings in those states and in many sections of North Carolina were "depleted and in many cases wiped out of existence," according to Jones, *Later Periods of Quakerism*, 1: 430.

165. Hatcher, "North Carolina Quakers," 28-29.

166. Forbush, *History of Baltimore Yearly Meeting*, Appendix A, vii.

167. Damon D. Hickey, "Pioneers of the New South: The Baltimore Association and North Carolina Friends in Reconstruction," *The Southern Friend* 11, 1 (Spring 1989): 35-36; *Friends Review* 27 March 1869, 476.

168. *Joint Committee to Raise Funds for the Relief of Virginia Friends Who Suffered from the Devastation of Civil War* (Philadelphia, 1864-65), from notebook listing, Philadelphia Yearly Meeting Archives, Society of Friends Historical Library; Worrall, *Friendly Virginians*, 440.

169. Wood, *Era of Reconstruction*, 91; Rose, *Rehearsal for Reconstruction*, 209.

170. Grady McWhiney, *Southerners and Other Americans* (New York: Basic Books, 1973), 129.

171. Wood, *The Era of Reconstruction*, 29.

172. Bacon, *Abby Hopper Gibbons*, 130.

173. James McPherson, *The Struggle for Equality: Abolitionists and the Negro in the Civil War and Reconstruction* (Princeton, NJ: Princeton University Press, 1964), 429-30; Merton L. Dillon, "The Failure of the American Abolitionists," *Journal of Southern History* 25 (1959): 176, has noted, "In spite of all their efforts, the abolitionists . . . failed to create widespread determination in any part of the nation to grant to the freedmen social or political or economic equality."

174. Smedley, *Martha Schofield*, 117.

175. Vincent, *Southern Seed, Northern Soil*, 39; Cruden, *The Negro in Reconstruction*, 114.

176. Richardson, *Death of Reconstruction*, 210.

177. Harding, *Other American Revolution*, 71.
178. Wood, *Era of Reconstruction*, 28–29; Cruden, *Negro in Reconstruction*, 100, 114; Richardson, *Death of Reconstruction*, 166.
179. *Ibid.*, 161. "Progress of Amalgamation," *De Bow's Review* 5 (July 1868), 600. Thornbrough, *Black Reconstructionists*, 15, reports on several murders of African American minor government officials meant to intimidate others from seeking office.
180. *The Friend*, 14 February 1863.
181. Jaquette, "Friends' Association," 75.
182. Harding, *Other American Revolution*, 194. The troops had been sent south after the 1871 passage of the 14th Amendment granting citizenship to all African Americans; see Thornbrough, comp., *Black Reconstructionists*, 16–17.
183. Anscombe, "Contributions of Quakers," 251.
184. About.com: Afroam History web site: \http://afroamhistory.about.com/library/blplessy_v_ferguson.htm, 15 June 2008.
185. Richard K. Taylor, *Friends and the Racial Crisis* (Wallingford, PA: Pendle Hill Publications, 1970), 14.
186. Cruden, *Negro in Reconstruction*, 42; Richardson, *Death of Reconstruction*, 218.
187. Franklin and Moss, *From Slavery to Freedom*, 384. The South was not the only section of the country where African Americans were subjected to threats and intimidation. KKK chapters were founded in New England, New York, Indiana, Illinois, Michigan, and other states. In the 1920s some Midwestern chapters listed Quakers on their membership rolls. In its earliest days, Klan members tended to be embittered veterans of the Confederate army; see Philip Dray, *At the Hands of Persons Unknown: The Lynching of Black America* (New York: Random House, 2002), 14, 41, 47. Hatcher, "North Carolina Quakers," 35, notes that in Burlington, NC, the Klan attacked a handicapped Quaker teacher.
188. Selleck, *Gentle Invaders*, 95–96.
189. Richardson, *The Death of Reconstruction*, 244.
190. Henry Litchfield West, "The Race War in North Carolina," *Forum* 26 (January 1889).
191. Dray, *At Hands of Persons Unknown*, 43–43.
192. Ida Wells-Barnett, *A Red Record: Tabulated Statistics and Alleged Causes of Lynching in the United States, 1892-1893-1894* (Chicago: Donaghue & Henneberry, 1895?). Few records of KKK terrorism were kept until Wells-Barnett, the African American journalist, devoted much of her life to collecting information about and evidence of each incident. The publication of Wells-Bartnett's data launched an international anti-lynching campaign in the 1890s.
193. Thornbrough, *The Negro in Indiana*, 210–11, 222.
194. Cruden, *Negro in Reconstruction*, 114.
195. Benjamin, *Philadelphia Quakers*, 141–43.
196. *Ibid.*, 134.
197. Dean Esslinger, *Friends for Two Hundred Years: A History of Baltimore's Oldest School* (Baltimore: Friends School in cooperation with Museum and Library of Maryland History, Maryland Historical Society, 1983), 157.

198. Benjamin, *Philadelphia Quakers*, 134.
199. Salemson, "Civil War Writings," 13; Jaquette, "Friends' Association," 77–78. The Hicksites were "quicker to abandon the cause than other Friends," according to Benjamin, *Philadelphia Quakers*, 134.
200. Selleck, *Gentle Invaders*, 134.
201. Klain, *Educational Activities of New England Quakers*, 183, 186. The proceeds from the sale of the school were set aside in the "Freedmen's Fund" to provide grants for people of African descent. It is administered by New England Yearly Meeting's Racial, Social, and Economic Justice Committee. Skip Schiel, e-mail to authors, 25 August 2005.
202. Alida Clark noted that after living there for twenty years only "three white women of the Southern land have ever given me a friendly shake of the hand, or any invitation to their homes, or noticed me." Selleck, *Gentle Invaders*, 213.
203. *Ibid.*, 220. The school property gradually reverted to farmland. The only trace, beyond the intangible effects on students' lives, is a scholarship fund initially endowed in 1881 with $25,000 from English Friend Joseph Sturge. Now named after Quaker African American activist George Sawyer's son, Geoffrey, the scholarships for African American students are administered by Friends United Meeting in Richmond, Indiana. See Kennedy, "Southland College: The Society of Friends and Black Education in Arkansas," 61.
204. Bacon, *History of the Pennsylvania Society*, 31, 33.
205. Margaret Hope Bacon, e-mail to authors, 6 September 2004.
206. Smedley, *Martha Schofield*, 238.
207. *Ibid.*, 245–46.
208. Patterson, "Martha Schofield," 134.
209. Bacon, "Heritage of Anthony Benezet," 33. Fariello, "Friends and the Christiansburg Institute."
210. Tetzlaff, "The Penn School," 16–19. Jacoway, *Yankee Missionaries*, 250. See the Center web site: www.penncenter.org.
211. Dray, *At Hands of Persons Unknown*, 93, 96. Cruden, *Negro in Reconstruction*, 117.
212. James McPherson, "A Brief for Equality: The Abolitionist Reply to the Racist Myth, 1860–1865," in Duberman, 159–161. Those who shared Agassiz' view became known as the "American School" of anthropology.
213. Richardson, *Death of Reconstruction*, 154–55, 207–8, 210, 240–41.
214. Wood, *Era of Reconstruction*, 84–85.
215. Qualls, "Successors of Woolman and Benezet," 85–87.
216. Benjamin, *Philadelphia Quakers*, 139.
217. Hamm, "*Gentle Invaders*: A Review Essay," *Quaker Religious Thought* 20 (February 2001): 22.
218. Meier, *Negro Thought in America*, 93.
219. Linda Marie Perkins, "Quaker Beneficence and Black Control: The Institute for Colored Youth 1852–1903," in *New Perspectives on Black Educational History*, ed. Vincent Franklin and James Anderson (Boston: GK Hall, c. 1978), 36.

220. *Ibid.*, 276–77; Lane, *William Dorsey's Philadelphia*, 159.

221. Jacoway, *Yankee Missionaries*, 39–41. Following his suggestion, Towne appointed a board of trustees that included Frissell and European American Quaker Isaac Sharpless, president of Haverford College. Another board member was Francis Reeve Cope Jr., a Philadelphia Quaker whose abolitionist grandfather had been a good friend of Laura Towne and the school.

222. Christiansburg Institute web site, www.christiansburginstitue.org.

223. Bronner, "A Time of Change," 119.

224. Hamm, "Gentle Invaders," 18.

225. Perkins, "Quaker Beneficence," 225, 252.

226. *Ibid.*

227. *Ibid.*, 26; Lane, "Institute for Colored Youth" in Harrison, 45–47.

228. Perkins, "Quaker Beneficence," 225, 252.

229. *Ibid.*, 23, 29. Coppin developed her proposal after a visit in 1876 to the Centennial Exposition in Philadelphia, where she had been so impressed by an exhibit about technical training in Russia that she began a twenty-year campaign to bring industrial education to her school. Coppin, *Reminiscences of School Life*, 23, 25.

230. Coppin, *ibid.*, 21–35.

231. Perkins, "Quaker Beneficence," 38; Silcox, "Delay and Neglect"; Lane, *William Dorsey's Philadelphia*, 147; Linda Marie Perkins, "Quaker Beneficence and Black Control: The Institute for Colored Youth 1852–1903," in *New Perspectives on Black Educational History*, ed. Vincent Franklin and James Anderson (Boston: GK Hall, c 1978), 36.

232. Perkins, *Fanny Jackson Coppin*, 327.

233. Lane, *William Dorsey's Philadelphia*, 161.

234. Perkins, "Quaker Beneficence," 35; Perkins, "Fanny Jackson Coppin," 244.

235. Perkins, "Quaker Beneficence," 37, has stated that Coppin was fired, but other sources state that whether she resigned or was fired is not clear. Perkins has asserted that it seems quite clear that Coppin had already planned to leave after the Industrial Department was created. A teacher training school in West Baltimore, Maryland, now Coppin State University, was named after her in 1926. Coppin University web site, www.coppin.edu.

236. Perkins, "Quaker Beneficence," 38.

237. Coppin died in 1913. In 1938 Cheyney's laboratory school was named after her. Perkins, "Fanny Jackson Coppin," 329.

238. Cheyney University web site: www.cheyney.edu, 06/05/03. While there are varying dates given for the closing of the school and transfer to the state, the dates used here are based on the Records of the State System Of Higher Education in the Pennsylvania State Archives, http://www.phmc.state.pa.us/Bah/DAM/rg/rg57.htm, 14 August 2007.

239. Cruden, *Negro in Reconstruction*, 117. The Baltimore Hicksite Yearly Meeting's Seneca Indian Affairs Committee had opened an orphan's asylum in the 1860s and continued sending funds to schools; see Mallonee et al., *Minute by Minute*, 84.

240. Smith, "Ohio Quakers," 170.
241. Larry E. Burgess, "We'll Discuss It At Mohonk," *Quaker History* 60, 1 (Spring 1971): 14, 21–23; Ralph Luker, *The Social Gospel in Black and White: American Radical Reform, 1885-1912* (Chapel Hill: University of North Carolina Press, 1991), 25, 27.
242. Burgess, "Mohonk," 14, 21–23.
243. Luker, *Social Gospel*, 28.

CHAPTER SIX: African American Membership in the
Religious Society of Friends

1. Selleck, *Gentle Invaders*, 203. Indiana Yearly Meeting had begun to actively organize home missions in the 1860s. Hamm, *Transformation of American Quakerism*, 58.
2. *Ibid.*, 44; Kennedy, "Southland College," 39; Clark quoted in Indiana Yearly Meeting Minutes, 1877, 36.
3. Selleck, *Gentle Invaders*, 202.
4. Alida Clark to Executive Board of Friends, Philadelphia, 1871, published in *Friends Review* 24, 22 (July 1971): 759–60.
5. Selleck, *Gentle Invaders*, 191.
6. Anscombe, "Contributions of Quakers," 21; Indiana Yearly Meeting Minutes, 1872–78.
7. Frank Loescher, *The Protestant church and the Negro: a pattern of segregation* (New York: Association Press, 1948), 76 n. 6.
8. Jones, *Quakers of Iowa*, 202.
9. Stephen Weeks, *Southern Quakers and Slavery*, 223 fn.
10. This text addresses only membership in North America, not in the rest of the world; in Africa, the number of Quakers exceeds that in North America. According to 2001 data, there were about 339,000 Quakers worldwide—157,000 in Africa; 10,000 in Asia-West Pacific; 19,000 in Europe-Middle East; and 153,000 in the Americas. See Friends World Committee for Consultation web site, www.fwccworld.org. On African American Quakers, see Hamm, *Quakers in America*, 172.
11. Kenneth Carroll, telephone interview with authors, 10 December 2005.
12. Elizabeth Cazden, e-mail to authors, 17 February 2007.
13. Brinton, *Meeting House and Farm House*, 13.
14. Cadbury, "Negro Membership," 162, 167.
15. Cadbury, "Negro Membership," 204. Records of the school and the meeting, including membership information, are in Southland Records at the Univ. of Arkansas Special Collections: http://libinfo.uark.edu/SpecialCollections/findin-gaids/southland/southlandaid.html. 23 October 07.
16. Cadbury, "Negro Membership," 153 n. 9.
17. *Ibid.*, 156. The meetings were held at New Begun Creek, Head of Little River, Simon's Creek, and Old Neck.
18. Cadbury, "Negro Membership," 152–159.

19. James, *People Among Peoples*, 233–234. Kenneth Ives, ed., *Black Quakers: Brief Biographies*, 3. Philadelphia Yearly Meeting then, as now, included portions of New Jersey, Delaware, and Maryland, as well as most of Pennsylvania. The New York meetings were held in Westbury, Cow Neck (Manhasset), Matinecock, and Bethpage.

20. Ives, *Black Quakers*, 3.

21. Cadbury, "Negro Membership," 158.

22. Opal Thornburg, ed., "From Indiana to North Carolina in 1854: The Diary of William Rees," *Quaker History* 89, 2 (Autumn 1970), 71.

23. Bacon, *Mothers of Feminism*, 84; Rebecca Jones, *Memorials of Rebecca Jones*, William J. Allinson, compiler (London: Charles Gilpin [1849]), 316.

24. Cadbury, "Negro Membership," 153.

25. James, *People Among Peoples*, 294; Cadbury, "Negro Membership," 155–56.

26. Nash, *Forging Freedom*, 28.

27. Marietta, *The Reformation of American Quakerism*, 1–31.

28. Barbour and Frost, *The Quakers*, 130–131. The authors note that Quakers often chose to disown a Quaker married to a non-Quaker rather than trying to convert the spouse.

29. William Kashatus, e-mail to authors, 17 October 2004.

30. Turner, *The Negro in Pennsylvania*, 44–45. Scherer, *Slavery and the Churches*, 144. The hierarchy refused to ordain African American pastors and segregated seating arrangements were the norm. A few churches formed separate congregations for African Americans and then monitored them closely. Cadbury, "Negro Membership," 167.

31. *Friends' Miscellany* 10 (1837): 273.

32. Scherer, *Slavery and the Churches*, 158.

33. James, *People Among Peoples*, 113.

34. Henry Hull, *Memoir and the Life and Religious Labours of Henry Hull*, (Philadelphia: Friends Book Store, 1873), transcribed on Quaker Heritage Press web site, www.qhpress.org. No dates for his travels are given in this source, but in one entry, Hull mentions George Washington; Cadbury, "Negro Membership," 185.

35. James, *People Among Peoples*, 280.

36. Grundy, "The Bethany Mission for Colored People," *Quaker History*, 64–65.

37. Joseph Drinker, "Plea for Admission of Colored People to the Society of Friends," transcript printed in Thomas Drake, "Joseph Drinker's Plea for Admission of Colored People to the Society of Friends, 1795," *Journal of Negro History* 32, 1 January 1947, 111–12. Drinker's paper is reproduced in this article after a short introduction by Drake. Drinker's brother, Henry, was a recognized leader in the Quaker community; this paper represents one of the few times that Joseph spoke out. He noted that he was not inspired by any particular membership application, but by his wider concern.

38. Alison Duncan Hirsch, "Uncovering 'The Hidden History of Mestizo America' in Elizabeth Drinker's Diary: Interracial Relationships in the Late Eighteenth Century Philadelphia," *Pennsylvania History* 68, (2001) 4, 499, 500.

39. *Friends Review* 29, 22 June 1867, 682.
40. Selleck, *Gentle Invaders*, 159, 163–64. As an Episcopalian, Smiley focused her energies on an organization she founded for home study of the Bible and church history.
41. Quarles, *Black Abolitionists*, 72.
42. James, *People Among Peoples*.
43. Cadbury, "Negro Membership,"172–73.
44. Selleck, *Gentle Invaders*, 174.
45. Weeks, *Southern Quakers and Slavery*, 233 n.
46. Cadbury, "Negro Membership," 181–82 fn. 88.
47. *Ibid.*, 156, 184–85.
48. Cazden cites the Minutes of the Smithfield Monthly Meeting men's and women's meetings for July through September 1780 (Rhode Island Historical Society microfilm #125, 127) and the Providence Monthly Meeting birth and death records, though the date of Harris' death was omitted from the record. (RIHS microfilm 22)
49. William Boen, *Anecdotes and Memoirs of William Boen, a Coloured Man, Who Lived and Died near Mount Holly, New Jersey. To Which Is Added, The Testimony of Friends of Mount Holly Monthly Meeting Concerning Him* (Philadelphia: John Richards, 1834), 6, 16, transcribed on Documenting the American South web site, http://docsouth.unc.edu/neh/boen/boen.html.
50. Cadbury, "Negro Membership," 195–197.
51. Boen, *Anecdotes*, 17.
52. *Ibid.*, 14.
53. *Ibid.*, 16.
54. Cadbury, "Negro Membership," 170–72.
55. Drake, *Quakers and Slavery*, 120–21.
56. Jeffrey Hitchcock's notes on the case of Cynthia Miers appear in "The Plainfield, New Jersey, Meeting House: The Evolution of a Quaker Meeting," Plainfield Friends web site, www.quaker.org/plainfield-nj.
57. *Ibid.*
58. Cadbury, "Negro Membership," 174.
59. *Ibid.*, 186.
60. Ives, *Black Quakers*, 33–35, reprinted from *Friends Miscellany* 1, n.d.
61. Hilty, *Toward Freedom*, 40. That it "was kept alive through three yearly meeting sessions" suggests, Hilty said, that it had "considerable support."
62. *Ibid.*, 177.
63. Densmore and Bassett, "Quakers, Slavery, and the Civil War," in Barbour et al., 189. Carpenter helped integrate the town's public schools. When African-Americans were denied a place in local cemeteries, he donated land for a new one and was buried there in Quaker garb;"his coffin [was] carried by members of the local African-American community."
64. Drake, *Quakers and Slavery*, 124.

65. Lamont D. Thomas, *Paul Cuffe: Black Entrepreneur and Pan-Africanist* (Urbana and Chicago: University of Illinois Press, 1988), 5, 19–21.

66. *Ibid.* Cadbury, "Negro Membership," 199 quotes A.E. Pease, *Diaries of Edward Pease, The Father of English Railways* (London: 1907), 54, saying that "his ship's crew were all black friends."

67. Friends Historical Association, *The Friends' Meeting House, Fourth and Arch Streets. Philadelphia: A Centennial Celebration* (Philadelphia: J. C. Winston, 1904), 93.

68. Wiggins, *Cuffe's Logs and Letters*, 57.

69. Thomas, *Paul Cuffe*, 9, 162.

70. Wiggins, *Cuffe's Logs and Letters*, viii. Deborah Allard-Bernardi, "Recovering History," *The Herald News* online, Fall River, MA, 9 February 2004, www.heraldnews.com 13 February 2004.

71. Cadbury, "Negro Membership," 185. For a time Peters was caretaker of the meeting house at Barnesville, Ohio. The meeting cared for him in his declining years.

72. Hamm et al., "'A Great and Good People,'" data from burial records in Indiana and Ohio; Hamm, "Review of *Gentle Invaders*, #2," 21.

73. Seigel, "Moral Champions and Public Pathfinders," 96.

74. Hamm et al., "'A Great and Good People.'"

75. Joseph Sturge, *A Visit to the United States in 1841* (London: Hamilton, Adams, and Co., 1842), 40, 100.

76. Grover, *Fugitive's Gibraltar*, 102, 135.

77. Hull, *Memoir*, 59–60; Cadbury, "Negro Membership," 186.

78. Cadbury, "Negro Membership," 179.

79. Densmore and Bassett, "Quakers, Slavery, and the Civil War," in Barbour et al, 189. The school was Eunice Kenyon's Quaker Boarding School.

80. Jordan, "Quakers," 597. "The Friend" is not named.

81. Hatcher, "North Carolina Quakers" 33.

82. Cadbury, "Negro Membership," 183–84.

83. Hamm et al., "'A Great and Good People.'"

84. Scherer, *Slavery and the Churches*, 131; Cadbury, "Negro Membership," 168.

85. Bacon, *Sarah Mapps Douglass*, 4–7.

86. *Ibid.*, 6; Sarah Douglass to Sarah Grimké, 2 April 1844, Weld-Grimké Papers, Clements Library, University of Michigan, Ann Arbor.

87. Sarah Mapps Douglass to Sarah Grimké, n.d., Weld-Grimké Papers, Clements Library, University of Michigan, quoted in Dorothy Sterling, ed., *We Are Your Sisters: Black Women in the Nineteenth Century* (New York and London: W. W. Norton & Co., 1984), 130.

88. Sarah Mapps Douglass to Sarah Grimké, 2 April 1844. Weld-Grimké Papers, Clements Library, University of Michigan, as cited in Bacon, *Sarah Mapps Douglass*, 23.

89. Sarah Mapps Douglass to Sarah Grimké, n.d., quoted in Sterling, ed., *We Are Your Sisters*, 130–31.

90. Drake, *Quakers and Slavery*, 178, 180.

91. Sarah Mapps Douglass to Sarah Grimké, n.d., quoted in Sterling, 130.

92. Jordan, "Quakers, 'Comeouters,' and Abolitionists," 598.

93. Drake, *Quakers and Slavery*, 178. "Such criticism cut deeply," said Drake, and the topic upset Friends attending the World Anti-Slavery Convention in London in 1843. The rebuttal in *The Friend* was signed by the otherwise unidentified "P.R."

94. Bacon, *Sarah Mapps Douglass*, 21; Sarah Douglass to Sarah Grimké, 2 April 1844.

95. *The Nonslaveholder*, 2 September 1850, 206.

96. Drake, *Quakers and Slavery*, 120.

97. Theodore W. Bean, *History of Montgomery County, Pennsylvania* (Philadelphia: Everts and Peck, 1884); Records of Middletown Monthly Meeting, 6 March 1703, 1 February 1738, 302; Hamm et al., "'A Great and Good People.'"

98. Hilty, *Toward Freedom*, 108.

99. Stanley Pumphrey, "Address on American Friends," *The Friend* (London), 3 July 1880, 186.

100. Hickey, "Pioneers of the New South," 38.

101. Worrall, *Friendly Virginians*, 468.

102. Hilty, *Toward Freedom*, 108.

103. Hatcher, "North Carolina Quakers," 33, citing the yearly meeting minutes, *The Friend* of January 1870, and the local newspaper.

104. Hatcher, "North Carolina Quakers," 33. The minutes of the yearly meeting did not record the three men's names, according to Gwen Erickson, e-mail to authors, 25 October 2007.

105. Report of the Tennessee Branch of North Carolina Yearly Meeting Missionary Board in North Carolina Yearly Meeting Minutes, 5 November 1879, 29.

106. Selleck, *Gentle Invaders*, 204–5, 208.

107. Cadbury, "Negro Membership," 139–40; Thomas Kennedy, "Southland College," 39, 44.

108. *Christian Worker* 5, 15 February 1874, 59.

109. Kennedy, "Southland College," 44.

110. Hickory Ridge Preparative Meeting began in 1876, twenty miles west of Southland.

111. Cadbury, "Negro Membership," 204–5.

112. *Ibid.*, Negro Membership," 207.

113. Thomas Hamm, e-mail to authors, 28 September 2003.

114. Cadbury, "Negro Membership," 206 n. 145.

115. Jesse M. Walton, *From the Auction Block of Slavery to the Rostrum of Quaker Ministry: The Life of William Allan, The Negro Missionary Preacher of the Society of Friends* (Aurora, Ont.: J. M. Walton, [1938]), 3–8.

116. Fred L. Ryon, "Memoirs of William Allen," *The Canadian Quaker History Journal* 65, 2000, 37–53; Jane Zavitz-Bond, "Hibbert Mtg.," e-mail to authors, May 26, 2004.

117. Selleck, *Gentle Invaders*, 216, 232.

118. Cadbury, "Negro Membership," 204.

119. *Proceedings of the Conference of Friends of America, Held in Indianapolis, Indiana, 1892* (Richmond, IN: Nicholson Manufacturing Company, 1892), 330–333.

120. John Oliver, "Early Evangelical Quakers in the U.S.," *Friends Journal* (March 1997), 15; and Pendle Hill lecture, "Walter and Emma Malone." Also see John Oliver, "Emma Brown Malone: A Mother of Feminism?" *Quaker History* 88 (Spring 1999), 1, 4–21.

121. Selleck, *Gentle Invaders*, 188, 204.

122. Tallack, *Friendly Sketches in America*, 52.

123. Hamm, "Review of *Gentle Invaders*, 21.

124. Cadbury, "Negro Membership," 168.

125. Leon Litwack, *Been in the Storm So Long: The Aftermath of Slavery* (New York: Knopf, 1979), 460.

126. Rupert Sargent Holland, ed., *Letters and Diary of Laura M. Towne Written from the Sea Islands of South Carolina, 1862–1884* (Cambridge, MA: Riverside Press, 1912), 22.

127. *The New Georgia Encyclopedia* web site, www.georgiaencyclopedia.org/nge/Article. 4/18/06.

128. Hamm, "Review of *Gentle Invaders*," 22.

129. In more modern times, the major missionary focus of Evangelical Friends and Friends United Meeting, with a few exceptions, has been to spread the word of Jesus abroad, principally in Africa, Central America and South America. The presence of thousands of Quakers in Kenya is the result of FUM's missionary work. Yet FUM missionaries have made no concerted effort to reach out to people of African descent or other Americans of color in this country.

130. Selleck, *Gentle Invaders*, 180, and Hamm, "Review of *Gentle Invaders*," 21.

131. Bacon, *Mothers of Feminism*, 176–78.

132. John Cuffe to Freelove Slocum, quoted in Grover, *Fugitive's Gibraltar*, 176.

133. Nash, *Forging Freedom*, 101, 109, citing Carol V. R. George, *Segregated Sabbath: Richard Allen and the Rise of the Independent Black Churches, 1760–1845* (1973), 57. Allen went on to found the African Methodist Episcopal Church. Absalom Jones, another student at Benezet's school, founded Philadelphia's St. Thomas Episcopal Church for African Americans. Nash, *Forging Freedom*, 116–119 and Cadbury, "Negro Membership," 154.

134. Quarles, *Black Abolitionists*, 72; Pennington's narrative, *The Fugitive Blacksmith; or, Events in the History of James W. C. Pennington* (London: Charles Gilpin, 1849), is transcribed on Documenting the American South web site, http://docsouth.unc.edu/neh/penning49/penning49.html.

135. Soderlund, *Quakers and Slavery*, 183.

136. Cadbury, "Negro Membership," 181–82.

137. Bacon, *Sarah Mapps Douglass*, 21.

138. "Memoir of Old Elizabeth: A Coloured Woman," in *Six Women's Slaves Narratives* (New York: Oxford University Press, 1988), 18–19.

139. Cadbury, "Negro Membership," 166.

140. *Friends Review,* July 20, 1850, 697.

141. Selleck, *Gentle Invaders,* 185.

142. Selleck, "Author's Response to Thomas Hamm and Shannon Craigo Snell," 25.

CHAPTER SEVEN: Working for Desegregation

1. Isaac Penington, *The Inward Journey of Isaac Penington,* Robert Leach, ed. (Wallingford, PA: Pendle Hill Pamphlet 29, 1943), 28.

2. Nancy J. Weiss, *The National Urban League, 1910-1940* (New York: Oxford University Press, 1974), 93–95.

3. *Ibid.,* 93. The migrants were generally men between twenty and forty-five, but as time went on whole families made the trip to a new home together. Richardson, *The Death of Reconstruction,* 168. PBS, *The Great Migration,* www.pbs.org/wnet/aaworld/reference/articles/great_migration.html 15 February 2008.

4. Franklin and Moss, *From Slavery to Freedom,* 350–51. A case in point: the 1908 riot in Springfield, Illinois. Even the five thousand soldiers dispatched there by the governor could not easily quell the rampage. In the end, two African Americans were lynched, four men of European descent were killed, and seventy were injured. The destruction was great. One hundred people were arrested, fifty indicted, and not one ever punished. Now Southerners could point to Springfield and proclaim that the Northerners were no better than they were after all. They took those incidents in the North as a kind of endorsement of their own behavior. Woodward, *Jim Crow,* 114–15.

5. Franklin and Moss, *From Slavery to Freedom,* 385.

6. C. Vann Woodward, *The Strange Career of Jim Crow,* 114–15.

7. Franklin and Moss, *From Slavery to Freedom,* 385.

8. Cruden, *The Negro in Reconstruction,* 162–63.

9. Vincent Harding, "Come Go with Me to That Land: Visions of Community in the Afro-American Freedom Struggle" (Monday Night Lecture Series, Pendle Hill, Wallingford, PA, 1980).

10. Du Bois, *Dusk of Dawn,* 618.

11. Franklin and Moss, *From Slavery to Freedom,* 352–54.

12. Weiss, *National Urban League,* 41. On Addams, who became an Episcopalian, see Mary White Ovington, *Black and White Sat Down Together: The Reminiscences of an NAACP Founder* (New York: Feminist Press at the City University of New York, 1995), 69.

13. *Ibid.,* 154–55. One of the most active Quakers of his time, Wood also donated his time and money to the Penn School and the New York Colored Mission (sponsors of the Fresh Air program which still exists), served on the boards of Fisk University and Haverford College, and belonged to the Fellowship of Reconciliation and the American Civil Liberties Union. On Wood's life, see Eugene Kinckle Jones, "Phylon Profile III: L. Hollingsworth Wood," *Phylon* 6, 1 (first quarter 1945): 17–21. Jones, an African American, was the first executive secretary of the National Urban League. Perhaps one of Wood's most enduring

contributions was his assistance in procuring the papers of Arthur Schomburg, a Puerto Rican-born New Yorker who as a student loved history but was disturbed at the lack of written documents and histories for people of African descent. The papers he began to collect became the basis for the Division of Negro Literature, History, and Prints at the New York Public Library; the collection, of which he was also curator for a time, was named after him. The Schomburg Center, http:// www.si.umich.edu/CHICO/Harlem/text/aschomburg.html. 27 November 2007.

14. Notices of death in the *Friends Intelligencer* 83 (1926) 296 (Walton) and *New York Times*, 28 August 1975, 36 (Leach); Weiss, *National Urban League*, 19, 51. Leach was also a trustee of Bryn Mawr College; her father T. Wistar Brown, was an active and well-known Philadelphia Friend; her husband, Henry Goddard Leach, was also involved in the NUL. Walton's father was an officer in the African American 54th Massachusetts Regiment, and her mother taught in the South after the Civil War.

15. A 1911 lynching in Coatesville, Pennsylvania, some forty miles from Philadelphia, left people of the surrounding towns and the state incredulous. Yes, lynching was common in the South—but in Coatesville, Pennsylvania? While the northerners were sure they could bring justice to the perpetrators, two trials failed to do so, even with a governor determined to rescue his state's reputation. Benjamin, *Philadelphia Quakers*, 186. Dray, *At the Hands of Persons Unknown*, 178–85.

16. Herbert Hadley, "Diminishing Separate: Philadelphia Yearly Meetings Unite," in Moore, 157–59.

17. Special Committee of Philadelphia Yearly meeting (Orthodox), "Lynching: A Statement by a Committee of the Religious Society of Friends, Fourth and Arch Streets, Philadelphia," 24 April 1919. Careful to point out that the committee had no "official connection" with the New York conference, it nevertheless said it was "in hearty sympathy with it."

18. Margaret Hope Bacon, *Let This Life Speak: The Legacy of Henry Joel Cadbury* (Philadelphia: University of Pennsylvania Press, 1987), 38–39, 82–83.

19. Rufus Rorem and Frank S. Loescher, "Challenge and Opportunity in Race Relations: A Minute for Consideration by the Race Relations Committee of the AFSC," AFSC CRC minutes, 17 October 1951.

20. AFSC Interracial Section, Minutes, 7 July and 21 July 1927.

21. *Ibid.*, 7 July 1927.

22. Later Bird founded the Colored Women's Activities Club for the Democratic National Committee and in 1938 became the first African American woman elected to the Pennsylvania legislature; she represented the majority-white Thirteenth District of Philadelphia. She later served as assistant director of the Pennsylvania Works Progress Administration and was the Office of Civilian Defense's Race Relations Advisor. See AFSC web site. See also "Short History of the Committee on Race Relations," in Finding Aids for Records of Philadelphia Yearly Meeting, SFHL, http://trilogy.brynmawr.edu/speccoll/sw/pymrareln.xml.

23. Minutes of AFSC Executive Board, 22 May 1924, 7.

24. That Jones was a founder and long-time chair of the AFSC was a witness to his practice of the social gospel.

25. Benjamin, *Philadelphia Friends*, 190–91.

26. Dwight W. Hosmer, "Daisy Douglas Barr: From Quaker to Klan "Kluckeress," *Indiana Magazine of History*, June 1991. Ben Richmond, *Quaker Life*, March 1999, 7.

27. Hamm, *Earlham College*, 152.

28. Interview with Hamm, 18 December 2001.

29. CNN.Com/U.S., http://archives.cnn.com/2002/US/05/10/lynching.exhibit/ 24 August 2007.

30. Chuck Fager, e-mail to authors, 12 December 2006. Fager also notes that the Klan in Indiana "came to an abrupt end" when a top leader was convicted of murder.

31. Densmore and Hamm, readers' comments, 8 February 2004.

32. Hosmer, "Daisy Douglas Barr," 187.

33. Richmond, *Quaker Life*, March 1999, 7, citing the minutes of the meeting of Ministry and Oversight, 12 August 1922.

34. Letter from Willis Beede, Administrative Secretary of American Friends Board of Missions, to Clarence Pickett, clerk of AFSC, 29 September 1930; Pickett to Beede, 3 October 1930; Pickett to Isaac Johnson, 11 October 1930. Johnson was one of a few Friends whom Pickett asked to contribute money toward the pastor's training, since AFSC had no funds for that purpose at the time. The letters are in AFSC's Peace Section, Interracial Peace files for 1930. Thomas Hamm provided copies for the authors. Apparently one of the stimuli for the yearly meeting to prepare a statement came from a letter from Philadelphia Yearly Meeting that referred to the lynching and presumably asked if Indiana Friends were going to express their great concern. A copy of that letter has not yet been found in yearly meeting records of either Indiana or Philadelphia.

35. Researchers agree that there is no evidence that the KKK was responsible for the Marion lynchings. Allen Safianow, *Review of Cynthia Carr. Our Town: A Heartland Lynching, a Haunted Town, and the Hidden History of White America* (New York: Crown Publishers, 2006), H-Net Online, http://www.h-net.org/reviews/showrev.cgi?path=108871160756320, 26 August 2008.

36. Mary Jane Brown, *Eradicating This Evil: Women in the American Anti-Lynching Movement, 1892–1940* (New York: Garland Publishing, Inc., 2000), 131, 191–92, 236, 241, 250–51.

37. While FCNL is governed by members of the Religious Society of Friends from around the United States, its network includes tens of thousands of people from many different races, religions, and cultures. FCNL web site: www.fcnl.org 8 June 2007.

38. E. Raymond Wilson, *Uphill For Peace: Quaker Impact on Congress* (Richmond, IN: Friends United Press, 1975), 145, 147. As early as 1871 there was a federal effort to ban lynching; see Dray, *At the Hands of Persons Unknown*, 47.

39. "Friends and Race Relations: Questions for Thought and Discussion," *The American Friend*, 9 February 1928, 89–91. A Gurneyite publication, *The American Friend* is the 1894 combination of *Friends Review* (Philadelphia) and *Christian Worker*. In 1960 it became *Quaker Life*, a publication of Friends United Meeting today.

40. AFSC Interracial Committee Minutes, 30 November 1927. Committee member Agnes L. Tierney, who had visited Georgia, recommended Friends from the North should "go in a very humble state of mind, with no idea of criticism, but rather with a desire to learn." At this time, according to Tom Hamm, southern Friends were primarily in North Carolina with "scattered groups" in Maryland, Virginia, and eastern Tennessee. Hamm, e-mail to authors, 19 July 2004.

41. Program for AFSC Conference on Race Relations, Coulter Street Meetinghouse, Germantown, PA, 8–9 January 1932.

42. Mary Hoxie Jones, "PYM and the AFSC" in Moore, *Friends in the Delaware Valley*, 241. The Institute was inspired by an idea conceived by Fisk University sociology professor Charles S. Johnson (who would later become the first African American president of that college).

43. Institute on Race Relations, papers in PYM CRR files.

44. Minutes of Five Years Meeting, 1935, 108.

45. Frank Watson, *A Quest in Interracial Understanding* (Philadelphia: Sub-Commission on Race Relations and Attitudes of Five Years Meeting and the CRR of Philadelphia Yearly Meetings, 1935), 10, 11, 23, 42, 49, 55, 57.

46. FWCC, *Friends World Conference 1937: Advance Study Outlines*, ed. D. Elton Trueblood (Philadelphia: Friends World Conference Committee, 1936) 30–37, 90, 93.

47. Program for the Fourth National Conference of Friends on Race Relations, June 1963. Fuson papers.

48. Letter to Wanda Harvey at Earlham College from Marian Fuson, April 8, 1969, Fuson papers.

49. List of attenders, Fuson papers and from a copy of Fuson's article sent to *Friends Journal*, March 29, 1969.

50. Program for the Fourth National Conference. Fuson papers.

51. NCFFR Continuation Committee Minutes, March 14–16, 1969, 1–4. Fuson papers.

52. PYM Records. It is not clear if the event took place on just one Sunday in February, as did a Federal Council of Churches program that the PYM Joint Committee on Race Relations supported. "Race Relations Month," *Friends Intelligencer*, 6 February 1932, 304.

53. *Friends Intelligencer* 89, 6, 2 June 1932, 104. The Federal Council of Churches had developed materials used by Friends and others for these meetings.

54. James H. Laird, "Social concerns for Seventy Years, 1900–1970," unpublished paper, April 20, 1970, 7–8. None of the subsequent committee reports mentioned the project. Laird has noted that "one hears no more" of the project in any committee reports he reviewed.

55. Florence L. Kite, *Selected Writings of Florence L. Kite* (Phil: PYMCRR, 1945). Haverford Quaker Collection pamphlets: PYM's "A Statement on Segregation," n.p., n.d. 3pgs.

56. PYM CRR and Social Order Committees, March 1954.

57. However, as of 2006, the Girl Scouts were no longer offering it. Christina Lighbourne, Girl Scouts of America, e-mail to authors, 28 November 2006.

58. Rachel Davis DuBois, Report of Community Friends Project of FGC on visit to Augusta, GA, 10–17 February 1964, 1–3.

59. The method was described fully in a book written by DuBois and Mew-Soong Li, *The Art of Group Conversation: A new breakthrough in social communication* (New York: Association Press, 1963). Allport's comment is in his foreword to that book.

60. Program for "Race Relations Roundtable," 1944 Cape May Conference, FGC Records.

61. FGC, Peace and Social Order Committee Minutes, 7 September 1963, 2.

62. Rachel Davis DuBois, Report of Community Friends Project of FGC on visit to Atlanta, 30 January–3 February 1964, and on return trip, 27 February 1964, unpaginated.

63. Taber interview.

64. Mildred Kearns Hoadley O'Keefe, "Young Friends Movement in the United States (1890–1933)" (Paper, 1987), Young Friends File. Program records of CRC, PYM.

65. Programs, PYM CRR.

66. *Friends Intelligencer*, July 15, 1944, 462.

67. *Ibid.* The statement was printed in a two-page pamphlet, "Message of Friendship from the Young Friends at Friends General Conference, Cape May, N.J., 1944, and mailed with "A Set of Queries and Suggestions on Race Relations."

68. In order, the letters quoted were from Jack Pittenger of Nottingham and Mary Palmer Clarke of Wallingford, both in Pennsylvania.

69. Kyle Joliffe, *Seeking the Blessed Community: A history of Canadian Young Friends, 1875–1996* (Guelph, Ont.: K. Joliffe, Production by TASC, c1997), 58–59, 63–64.

70. Laird, letter of 26 November 1969. PYM MSC.

71. Helen G. Hole, "Religion and the College Generation," *Quaker Life*, April 1970, 6–86 and 7–87.

72. Ardith L. Emmons, "Iowa Yearly Meeting conservative Meets at Interfaith Spiritual Center in Colfax," *Quaker Life*, October 1970, 19–27.

73. Flyer for "Conference on Racism," Religious Education/Young Friends Committee of PYM, conference May 21, 1977. PYM.

74. World Gathering of Young Friends (1985: Greensboro, N.C.), *Visioning a future for Friends: a report of the World Gathering of Young Friends* (London: World Gathering of Young Friends, 1986), 87. The meeting was held at *New Garden* Friends Meeting House and Guilford College, Greensboro, NC, July 19–27, 1985.

75. Friends Neighborhood Guild Annual Report, c 1880.

76. Pamela Haines, "Friends Neighborhood Guild: A Quaker Presence in Philadelphia," *Friends Journal*, May 2006, 16–17.

77. *Ibid.*

78. *PYM News*, June 1965.

79. Friends Council on Education, *The Courier* 26 (Spring 1965): 14–15.

80. *PYM News*, June 1965.

81. Elizabeth Stewart, "Rochester Friends Meeting and Racial Justice for African Americans," an unpublished report prepared by the meeting's historian especially for this book, May 30, 2004.

82. Haddonfield Meeting to PYM Clerk Charles Brown, May 1968, PYM.

83. Jane Cosby, "Wellsprings Ecumenical Center: An Opportunity for Friends," *PYM News*, midsummer 1969.

84. William Taber, interview with authors, 26 March 2003.

85. "Swarthmore-Wade House study program," news release, Swarthmore College news office, 17, June 1964, 1.

86. "Robert Wade House and Chester," *PYM News*, February 1965.

87. "Swarthmore-Wade House study program," 1.

88. "Robert Wade House and Chester."

89. Students for a Democratic Society (U.S.). Economic Research and Action Project, "Summer 1964 project reports: A compendium of reports of 6 summer projects," unpublished reports, 1965. SDS from Swarthmore also worked in Newark and Trenton, New Jersey, and Philadelphia with similarly mixed success.

90. Elizabeth Cook, *Journal of a Concern: Youth Club—Black Church—Friends Meeting*, Wilmington, DE: 1973; unpublished ms, SFHL.

91. Orville R. Woody, "Birth of an Idea," *Quaker Life*, January 1972, 13.

92. Douglas W. Gilbert, "The Growing Edge: Downtown Church Center," *Quaker Life*, May 1970, 14–134. Gilbert, a Methodist minister, coordinated the Downtown Church Center project.

93. Marvin Weisbord, *Some Form of Peace: True Stories of the American Friends Service Committee at Home and Abroad* (New York: Viking Press, 1968), 105–25; on the various work camps see also Anna Curtis, ed., *The Quakers Take Stock* (New York: Island Workshop Press, 1944). See also "Volunteer Work Camps for High School Students" (flyer, 1948), AFSC Archives, and "Summer Work Camps," *Friends Intelligencer*, 7 May 1955, 268.

94. Carol Passmore, "David Richie and Workcamps: 'Work is Love Made Visible'," Religious Education Committee of Friends General Conference, *Lives That Speak: Stories of Twentieth-Century Quakers*, Marnie Clark, ed. (Philadelphia: Quaker Press of Friends General Conference, 2004), 90.

95. "Volunteer Service Projects 1946"; "Volunteer Service Projects 1946–1947"; Sutters, "AFSC's Civil Rights Efforts, 1925–1950," 3. Flanner House celebrated its ninety-ninth anniversary in 1997 and continues to offer services ranging from child care, kindergarten, and support for the elderly and disabled to a computer

lab. Celeste Williams, "Flanner House Full of Stories, Told and Untold, of Black History," *Indianapolis Star*, 20 November 1997.

96. David S. Richie, "Working Together in International Camps," in *Education for a World Society: Promising Practices Today*, eds. Christian Ottomar Arndt and Samuel Everett (New York: Harper, 1951), 106; David S. Richie, "A Testing Laboratory for Post-War Planners," *Friends Intelligencer*, 1 January 1944, 6; Passmore, "David Richie and Work camps," in *Lives That Speak*, 90.

97. Initially the program was under the care of the Social Order Committee but then became an independent subcommittee of the yearly meeting—the Belmont-Mantua Project. "Summer Work Camps," *Friends Intelligencer*, 7 May 1955, 268.

98. Report of the Social Order Committee, PYM Minutes, 1969, 144–45; PYM Minutes, 1970, 19.

99. Report of Work Camp Program, PYM Minutes, 1970, 137.

100. *PYM News*, October/November 1971.

101. Richie, "Testing Laboratory," 6–7.

102. "Summer Work Camps," *Friends Intelligencer*, 7 May 1955, 268.

103. Jacoway, *Yankee Missionaries*, 250.

104. Edith Warner Johnson, "Moments of Truth," *Friends Journal*, May 15, 1970, 304.

105. Richie, "Testing Laboratory," 6–7.

106. Jones, "Letters Home," 30 November 1930.

107. Hamm, *Earlham College*, 204.

108. Frances L. Peacock, "The Opposite of Fear is Love: An Interview with George Sawyer," *Quaker Life*, September 1997, FUM web site: www.fum.org/QL/issues/9709/Sawyer.htm, 5 June 2004. A scholarship fund endowed by the sale of Southland School was later named after Sawyer's son, Geoffrey. The scholarships for African American students are administered by Friends United Meeting.

109. Gretchen Cassel Eick, *Dissent in Wichita: The Civil Rights Movement in the Midwest, 1954–1972* (Urbana: University of Illinois Press, 2001), 29, 37, 55, 56, and 73. Michener, married to a local high school teacher, was also active with the Quaker organization, the National Friends Conference on Race Relations.

110. *Ibid.*, 27; FWCC and the Boards on Peace and Social Concerns of Five Years Meeting and Western Yearly Meeting, *Whose Shoes Can You Walk?* (Indianapolis: John Woolman Press, Inc., 1962), 11.

111. *Ibid.*, 77, 216.

112. *Ibid.* Floyd and Norma Souders, *Friends University, 1898–1973* (Wichita, KS: Friends University, 1974).

113. Wilson, *Uphill for Peace*, 147–48.

114. CRC Minutes, 21 January and 15 April 1953, 6 January 1954.

115. Lawrence McK. Miller, *Witness for Humanity: A Biography of Clarence E. Pickett* (Wallingford, PA: Pendle Hill Publications, 1999), 320.

116. *BYM Proceedings*, 1949, 69.

117. *BYM Proceedings*, 1949, 10.

118. *Ibid.*, 1950, 13.

119. *Ibid.*, 1951, 12.

120. Kenneth L. Carroll, "Southern Quakers and the Race Problem," *Friends Journal*, 7 July 1956, 423–24.

121. AFSC CRC Minutes, 8 May 1951, 3 March 1954, 2 May 1956.

122. AFSC CRC Minutes, 4 December 1951.

123. AFSC CRC Minutes, AFSC, 2 February, 20 May, 7 July, 15 October, 17 December, 1952.

124. Hilty, *New Garden*, 101, 108.

125. Woodward, *Jim Crow*, 150–55.

126. "The Chronology of the Civil Rights Movement," Abbeville Press web site, www.abbeville.com/civilrights/chronology.

127. Woodward, *Jim Crow*, 156–57.

128. AFSC CRC Minutes, 6 February 1957.

129. AFSC CRC Minutes, 1 February and 2 May 1956.

130. Jean Fairfax, talk at Symposium 5 November 2002, "Leadings of the Spirit: Striving for Racial Justice: Celebrating AFSC at 85," presented by AFSC and Pendle Hill at Pendle Hill, 3 to 8 November 2002.

131. *Ibid.*

132. Hilty, *New Garden*, 108.

133. *Ibid.*, 101.

134. *Whose Shoes Can You Walk?* (Philadelphia: AFSC with FWCC, 1962), 12.

135. Finding Aid to the M. Hayes Mizell Papers, 8–9, University of South Carolina web site, http://www.sc.edu/library/socar/mnscrpts/mizellmh.pdf; AFSC, memorandum from education "round up," 14 April 1976.

136. Carter G. Woodson, *A Century of Negro Migration* (New York: Russell and Russell, 1969), 172–74, 179, 186–89.

137. Jonas, *On Doing Good*, 96–97. Report of AFSC Community Relations Round-up, Downington, PA, 7–12 April 1957, 6.

138. Report of AFSC CRC Round-up, Downington, PA, 7–12 April 1957, 6.

139. Press release, Richmond (IN) Human Relations Council, 12 March 1964.

140. Wilmington Monthly meeting reports to MSC, 1968–1970.

141. 1968 PYM Minutes, 137. AFSC, "Housing Opportunities Program of the American Friends Service Committee," May 1963, 1; this ten-page unpublished document provides the rationale for AFSC housing programs and reports on the progress over the last ten years of its "key efforts."

142. AFSC, *They Say That You Say: The Challenge of Houses and Race* (Philadelphia, PA: AFSC, 1955).

143. AFSC, *Alabama, 'Kind of Tough Living Here': a report on bad rural housing in all 67 Alabama counties* (Philadelphia: American Friends Service Committee, 1976), 7–9, 98. AFSC had done the same kind of report in Florida the year before.

144. AFSC CRC Minutes, 4 March 1977.

145. Maris, "Friends in Philanthropy," in *Friends in Wilmington*, 72.

146. *Ibid.*, 73.

147. Cindi Lash, "Penn-Craft Marking 65 Years of Self-Help," *Pittsburgh Post-Gazette*, 18 August 2002, on newspaper's web site, www.post-gazette.com/localnews/20020818penncraft0818p2.asp.

148. AFSC web site: Lash, "Penn-Craft."

149. AFSC CRC Minutes, 18 October 1952.

150. *Ibid.*, 6 October and 3 November 1954.

151. *Ibid.*, 2 February 1955; Jane Reinheimer, report for AFSC CRR on meeting with Milgram, 9 July 1954.

152. AFSC, "Housing Opportunities Program," May 1963, 4–7.

153. *Ibid.*

154. C. H. Yarrow, "White Suburbia," *Friends Journal*, 8 September 1956, 574.

155. AFSC CRC Minutes, 7 March 1956.

156. Margaret Hope Bacon, "Friendly Neighbors," *The Christian Century*, 5 February 1958, 172–73.

157. Diane Mastrull, "Opening Doors for Black Homeowners," *Philadelphia Inquirer*, July 14, 2004, *Philadelphia Inquirer* web site, www.philly.com/mld/inquirer/91453875.

158. Mastrull, "Opening Doors."

159. Interview with Phyllis and Richard Taylor, 18 May 2004.

160. Jack Snyder, e-mail to authors, 21 January 2004. See MSC Minutes, 13 June 1970.

161. MSC Minutes, 13 June 1970.

162. *Ibid.* E-mail of 11 December 2007 from Jack Snyder.

163. Arnold Hirsch, *Making the second ghetto: race and housing in Chicago, 1940–1960* (New York: Cambridge University Press, 1983), 137. George Watson, "Growing in Quakerism with Elizabeth," talk on July 6 at 2007 FGC Gathering, River Falls, Wisconsin.

164. Jonas, *On Doing Good*, 93.

165. James Richard Ralph, Jr., *Northern Protest: Martin Luther King Jr: Chicago and the Civil Rights Movement* (Cambridge: Harvard University Press, 1993) 9, 36, 41, 59.

166. King Center: http://www.thekingcenter.org/mlk/chronology.html, 14 January 2008; Horton and Horton, *Hard Road to Freedom*, 310–11.

167. Wil [sic] Brant, ed., "Memories of 57th Street Meeting on Its 75th Anniversary," (Chicago: 57th Street Meeting of Friends, 2006), 9.

168. Leadership Council for Metropolitan Open Communities web site: http://www.luc.edu/curl/lcmoc/index.html, 28 October 2007.

169. AFSC CRC Minutes, 3 October 1956.

170. AFSC CRC Minutes, AFSC, 1 February 1956.

171. *Ibid.*

172. *Ibid.*, 11 April 1956.

173. AFSC Community Relations Roundup, 7 to 12 April, 1957, Introduction.

174. Margaret Hope Bacon, "Empowering the Traditionally Deprived," *Friends Journal*, 1 April 1970, 191–92.

175. Tony Henry, former AFSC staff, talk at 2002 symposium at Pendle Hill.

176. Jonas, *On Doing Good*, 99–105.

177. King Center: http://www.thekingcenter.org/mlk/chronology.html, 14 January 2008; Horton and Horton, *Hard Road to Freedom*, 310–11.

178. Brant, *Ibid.*

179. Leadership Council for Metropolitan Open Communities, *ibid.* "Fulfilling the Dream," http://cfm40.middlebury.edu/node/17?PHPSESSID=49d8271aa3da9372fabc1da fbf97da, 28 October 2007.

180. AFSC, "Housing Opportunities Program." May 1963, 1.

181. "Schools in the Inner City: Partnership with the Community," Friends Council on Education, *Chronicles of Quaker Education*, Winter 1960, 1.

182. PYM Minutes, 1968, 137.

183. Inventory of Friends Housing, Inc., Report, MSC, 1966; "Rehabilitation in Mantua," *Philadelphia Yearly Meeting News*, 7 February 1971.

184. PYM Minutes, 1968, 136–37.

185. PYM MSC Minutes, 8 November 1969, 1.

186. "Rehabilitation in Mantua."

187. Inventory of Friends Housing; *PYM News*, Midsummer 1971.

188. Haines, "Friends Neighborhood Guild," 14–15.

189. *Ibid.*, 17.

190. Sawyer later moved to Texas, attended divinity school, and became a United Methodist pastor. Peacock, "The Opposite of Fear."

191. George Sawyer, "Conference on Race Is Seeking Solutions," *Quaker Life*, Series VI, 5, May 1965, 150–51.

192. Elisabeth Leonard, Report on Friends Suburban Project, 1970 PYM Minutes, 20.

193. Deming interview.

194. Friends Chester Project Report at MSC, 17 April 1968, in PYM Minutes, 1968, 105; Report of Chester Project and Friends Suburban Project, PYM Minutes, 1970, 149; Deming interview; Ruth Kilpack, ed., "Five Years of Friendly Agitation: Combating Racism in Delaware County: Selections from "The Friendly Agitator" 1969–1974 (Media, PA: Friends Suburban Project, 1975), 19. Mimeographed copy in Philadelphia Yearly Meeting Library. "Five Years" includes selections, the newsletter of the Friends Suburban Project also edited by Ruth Kilpack and published from 1969 to 1974. The Project was one of the few organizations that survived into the mid-1970s, due in part, members said, to the continued support of PYM and to the persistent efforts of an organized group of individuals who believed in its goals. The project engaged two full-time staff members, Charles Walker and Eileen Stief, the latter as director of the Community Dispute Settlement Program. See also Leonard interview.

195. PYM MSC Minutes, 12 September 1970; Betsy [Elisabeth] Leonard, "Court Watching and Waiting," *PYM News*, September 1970.

196. Deming interview. Robert Wade House was named after the Quaker whose home housed the first Friends meeting in the town. "Chester Friends Sponsor Neighborhood House," *Friends Intelligencer*, July 24, 1943, 489.

197. Leonard, "Court Watching," also reported that the Chester court decided to redecorate and include seats, though not the Quaker benches; see also *PYM News*, October 1973.

198. *PYM News*, October 1973.

199. *PYM News*, Fall 1970.

200. Elisabeth Leonard, telephone interview with authors, 27 January, 2007.

201. Jennifer E. Beer, *Peacemaking in Your Neighborhood: Reflections on an Experiment in Community Mediation* (Philadelphia: New Society Publishers, 1986).

202. Friends Committee on National Legislation, *Fifteen Years of Quaker Witness*, 29.

203. *Ibid.*, 29; Edward F. Snyder, *Witness in Washington* (Richmond, IN: Friends United Press, 1994), 117.

204. Wilson, *Uphill for Peace*, 144.

205. *Ibid.*, 143–44. Lobbying for the 1964 Civil Rights Act, in just six months Taylor had 130 meetings with Congressmen or their staff and corresponded with supporters in 28 states; he also took part in fourteen community meetings set up by religious leaders in Iowa who hoped their two senators would influence their colleagues on the bill.

206. *Ibid.*, 346–47.

207. Report from James Dunn, *News Letter of Indiana Yearly Meeting*, Summer 1968, 5.

208. Wilson, *Uphill for Peace*, 149–50.

209. Snyder, *Witness in Washington*, 118–19.

210. Wilson, *Uphill for Peace*, 346–47.

211. Yarrow, "White Suburbia," 574.

212. Richard Taylor, "A Summary of Race Relations Questionnaires" (Paper, 1970), 1. SFHL. The only hint about the sponsor of this 1961 survey is a handwritten notation "FWCC" at the top of the first page. FWCC is the likely source, but the authors could find no references to the survey, which is summarized on a two-page mimeographed paper, in FWCC records or records of FGC or PYM; no newsletter of these organizations around 1961 mentions the survey or the results.

213. Weiss, *National Urban League*, 15–17, 47–48.

214. Mary Hoxie Jones, "The Yearly Meeting and the AFSC," in Moore, *Friends in the Delaware Valley*, 240; PYM (Race Street) Minutes, 1923, 21–22.

CHAPTER EIGHT: Working for Economic Justice

1. Henry Wilbur, *Friendly Fundamentals*, undated pamphlet, 10–11.

2. George Haines, IV, "Trends in Quakerism," *Pennsylvania Magazine of History and Biography*, 66 (July 1942), 89.

3. Hamm, *Quakers in America*, 57–58.

4. Benjamin, *Philadelphia Quakers*, 215.

5. Minutes, Arch Street Social Order Committee, 1919, quoted in Laird, "Social Concerns," 17.

6. Harding, "Come Go with Me." See also Carter G. Woodson, *Century of Negro Migration* and Allen Ballard, *The Education of Black Folk: The Afro-American*

Struggle for Knowledge in White America (1973), cited in Selleck, *Gentle Invaders*, 211. See also Nicholas Lemann, *The Promised Land: The Great Black Migration and How It Changed America* (New York: Alfred A. Knopf, 1991).

7. Benjamin, *Philadelphia Quakers*, 188.

8. Monroe N. Work, *Negro Year Book: An Annual Encyclopedia of the Negro, 1916–1917* (Tuskegee, AL: Negro Year Book Publishing Company, 1916), 10–11.

9. Joe William Trotter, Jr., "From a Raw Deal to a New Deal? 1929–1945," in *To Make Our World Anew: A History of African Americans*, ed. Robert D. G. Kelley and Earl Lewis (New York: Oxford University Press, 2000), 409–44.

10. Explanation from the Finding Aid for the Committee on Economic Problems, SFHL.

11. Deborah Haines, "Friends General Conference—A Brief Historical Overview," *Quaker History* 89, 2 (Fall 2000), 10.

12. Minutes, Arch Street Social Order Committee, 1919, in Laird, "Social Concerns," 17–19.

13. Herbert Fraser, chairman, letter to PYM Friends from the new Economic and Social Section describing the goals and work of the new committee, April 11, 1941, FGC Social Services Division; copies of newsletters from December 1941 to 1955. FGC Records.

14. "The P.T.C. Situation," *Friends Intelligencer*, 26 August 1944.

15. About.com: African-American History, http://afroamhistory.about.com/cs/aphilip randolph/p/aphiliprandolph.htm, 4 May 2008.

16. National Park Service: http://www.nps.gov/archive/elro/glossary/fepc.htm, 10 April 2008.

17. Trotter, "From a Raw Deal to a New Deal," 436–38, 442–44.

18. AFSC, *A Step Toward Fair Employment* (Philadelphia: American Friends Service Committee, 1946), n.p.

19. AFSC, *Social and Industrial Peacemaking: A Quaker Program* (Philadelphia: AFSC, 1946), n.p.

20. "A Step Toward Fair Employment," AFSC, 1946; Frank Loescher, "The Placement Service of the AFSC: A Technique," reprint of article in Occupations, November 1946, 90–93.

21. Clarence Pickett, *For More than Bread: An autobiographical account of twenty-two years' work with the American Friends Service Committee* (Boston: Little, Brown and Co., 1953), 378–80, 382. AFSC attempts to create a state-wide FEPC were persistent but unsuccessful.

22. In 1945 James Fleming became the first African American secretary of Race Relations, a staff position. Minutes, Race Relations Committee 25 October 1945, AFSC Archives.

23. Minutes, AFSC CRC, 18 January, 15 February, 18 May 1951; 6 January 1954; 19 December 1957; 9 April, 7 May 1958; 4 March, 17 November 1959; 20 June 1967; 15 October 1976; 7 July 1979; 29 May 1981; 13 October 1984; 9 February 1985; 8 Mary 1986; AFSC Merit Employment Committee, 11 February 1965.

NOTES FOR PAGES 267–273

24. Thomas D. Hamm, "Friends United Meeting and Its Identity: An Interpretive History," http://avenue.org/quakers/fum-history.pdf.

25. The Five Years Meeting proposal was incorporated into the minutes of the FGC Peace and Social Order Committee, 8 April 1960, 5–6.

26. *Ibid.*

27. *Ibid.*; and committee minutes of 17 May 1960.

28. Five Years Meeting, *Minutes of the Five Years Meeting of the American Yearly Meeting of Friends* (Philadelphia, PA: J.C. Winston, 1963), 95–96.

29. National Archives web site: http://www.archives.gov/education/lessons/civil-rights-act 22 March 08.

30. This background is derived from the Equal Employment Opportunity Commission web site, www.eeoc.gov/abouteeoc/history, and the Civil Rights Coalition for the Twenty-first Century web site, www.civilrights.org.

31. *PYM News,* June 1969.

32. Taylor's proposal included in PYM MSC Minutes, 11/4/70.

33. Economics Seminar in MSC Records.

34. Records of Working Group on Economic Responsibility, 1972–73, MSC files, SFHL.

35. Susanne Gowan, George Lakey, William Moyer, and Richard Taylor, (Philadelphia: New Society Press, [c1976]; Lakey, Moyer, and Taylor, *Revolution: a Quaker prescription for a sick society* (Philadelphia: A Quaker Action Group, 1971).

36. King Encyclopedia at Stanford University: http://www.stanford.edu/group/King/publications/papers/unpub/671204-003_Announcing_Poor_Peoples_campaign.htm, and "Eyes on the Prize," PBS.

37. Minutes, AFSC Report to Philadelphia Yearly Meeting, 1969, 192, AFSC Archives.

38. Charles K. Brown III, letter to clerks of PYM Monthly Meetings, April 1, 1968, 1–2. The report regarding the $10,000 was in a letter written by Young Friends assisted by Michael Yarrow, 1969, in BEDC papers, SFHL

39. Wilson, *Uphill for Peace*, 150.

40. PYM Minutes, MSC, 1968–70.

41. FGC, "Renewal and Revolution: The Report of the Working Conference," June 1968, 14, SFHL.

42. "Witness in Washington," *Friends Journal*, Aug. 1, 1968, 368; Ross Flanagan "Friends Jailed while Supporting Poor People's Campaign at Capitol," *Quaker Life*, ser. 8, 8 August 1968, 240–41.

43. Alison Anderson and Jack Coleman, eds., *The Intrepid Quaker: One Man's Quest for Peace: Memoirs, Speeches, and Writings of Stephen G. Cary* (Wallingford, PA: Pendle Hill Publications, 2003), 104–6.

44. Ross Flanagan, letter to the editor, "Friends Jailed While Supporting Poor People's Campaign at Capitol," *Quaker Life*, series VIII, No. 8, August 1968, 240–41.

45. Gerald Jonas, *On Doing Good* (New York: Scribner's, 1971), 109–10. Quaker William Moyer was also involved in the march; Rachel Davis DuBois worked for

SCLC for several years, and AFSC and SCLC worked together closely in Chicago where African American AFSC staffer Bernard Lafayette helped attract King to the city for the "Chicago Freedom Movement," focusing on housing, in 1965–1966. Stephen Grant Meyer, *As Long As They Don't Move in Next Door: Segregation and Racial Conflict in American Neighborhoods* (Lanham, MD: Rowman and Littlefield Publishing, 2000), 139–40, 189.

46. Jonas, *On Doing Good*, 160–61. With many ups and downs, RAP was successful in creating a significant amount of low-income housing according to its goals of having the residents take responsibility for their own neighborhoods; it exists today offering homebuyer assistance and sponsoring community events. Stewart E. Perry describes RAP's work in *Building a Model Black Community: The Roxbury Action Program* (Cambridge, MA: Center for Community Economic Development, 1978). RAP's prime development was in the Highland Park area of Roxbury, an area with many historic properties.

47. NEYM Peace and Social Concerns Minutes, 11 June, 8 October, 8 November, and 12 November 1970.

48. *PYM News*, May and July 1968.

49. Laird, "Social Concerns," 13; Minutes, MSC Report, 1969, PYM, 133.

50. Minutes, PYM Committee on the Urban Crisis, 8 April 1968, 2, SFHL.

51. FUM, *Minutes of Friends United Meeting* (Richmond, IN: Friends United Meeting, 1969), 45.

52. Five Years Meeting, *Minutes*, 1969, 43–44. The fund was to be given the same priority as an international fund with similar purposes and level of contribution.

53. Mallonee et al, 226–27. Project Equality ended after four years because of "lack of financial support and the sensitivity of the issues raised," according to the meeting's minutes of October 1973. The minutes also report that the meeting's investment portfolio fell in value from $65,000 to $43,000 as the result of those investments.

54. "Representative Meeting Says a Reluctant No to Project Equality," *PYM News*, June 1973.

55. The text of the Black Manifesto appeared in *The New York Review of Books*, 10 July 1969, and appears on the review's web site, www.nybooks.com.

56. Concerned Black Students: http://web.grinnell.edu/CBS/History_BlackManifesto .html 20 June 08.

57. John Daniels, "How Deep Our Concern?" *Quaker Life*, January 1972, 14–15.

58. *Ibid.*

59. NEYM Minutes, 1970, 51–53.

60. Skip Schiel, "How We Have Responded to Racism, In and Among Us: A Chronicle of New England Yearly Meeting Decisions & Actions, 1965–1998," 1.

61. Minute 60, 1970 NEYM Minute Book.

62. Schiel, *ibid.*, 1–2.

63. Schiel, *ibid.*, 3. The request came from the NEYM Peace and Social Concerns Committee. Schiel also reported the lack of interest by Friends schools in taking

advantage of the scholarships for minority and disadvantaged students provided by a separate committee. See Chapter 13. The Committee on Prejudice and Poverty was renamed the Committee on Economic, Social, and Racial Justice in 2003.

64. Schiel, "How We Have Responded," 4, 5.
65. Rev. Vaughn Eason, chairman, Greater Philadelphia BEDC, to James Laird, executive director, MSC, PYM, 25 September 1960, SFHL.
66. Charles K. Brown III, "Pray and Pay Attention," The Twenty-first Michener Annual Quaker Lecture in Florida, 1/20/1991, (Southeastern Yearly Meeting Publications, Melbourne Beach, FL, 1991); *PYM News*, September 1969, 1.
67. Eason letter to Laird.
68. *PYM News*, midsummer 1969, 1.
69. Charles K. Brown III, *Pray and Pay Attention* and *PYM News*, November 1, 1969, 2.
70. Francis G. Brown, general secretary of PYM, MSC, to "Members of the Yearly Meeting," 13 October 1969. Minutes, Meeting for Social Concerns, October 1969, 5, state that "several black Friends" attending the meeting "spoke very openly and tellingly of how racism has cut into their lives."
71. *PYM News*, 1 November 1969; James Laird, "Social Concerns," 14; "Mohammad Kenyatta Speaks to the Philadelphia Yearly Meeting" (notes from lecture, Arch Street Meeting House, Philadelphia, 11 October 1969), SFHL.
72. Michael Yarrow, "Comments on the Black Manifesto and Friends," unpublished paper, undated, c1969.
73. Laird, his response to BEDC request presented to MSC meeting of 18 October 1969.
74. Laird, "Social Concerns," 1.
75. Ross Capon, "Draft statement on Black Economic Development Request," undated paper.
76. Larry Miller to Ross Flanagan, 20 October 1969, SFHL.
77. Samuel Snipes, letter to James Laird, 4 December 1969.
78. Letter by Young Friends with Yarrow, 1969.
79. "Young Friends Response to the Black Manifesto," Princeton (NJ) Monthly Meeting, c1969, SFHL.
80. David Richie, Victor Paschkis, Mary Anderson, and William Shields, "A Proposed Friends Manifesto," unpublished paper, October 1969, 1–2. MSC Papers, SFHL.
81. Minute 41, PYM, 1970, 42, SFHL.
82. *Ibid.*, 45.
83. *PYM News*, August 1970.
84. Joseph Cope, "Contrary to George Fox," *Friends Journal*, 1 September 1970, 461.
85. Minutes, PYM, 1970, 43–44.
86. "Yearly Meeting Skills Bank," *PYM News*, Spring 1971, 1.
87. Muhammad Kenyatta to Meeting for Sharing, 15 April 1970, in *PYM News*, June 1970, reprinted as "The Saving Remnant," *Friends Journal*, 15 June 1970, 352.
88. Kenyatta, *ibid.*

89. Letter from Charles Brown to Richard Taylor. No date but indications are it would be from January 1970.
90. *Ibid.*
91. PYM Ec Dev Fund Serial 1 Box 1. BEDC Fund from PYM from 7/1/71 to 10/31/76.
92. *Ibid.*
93. *Ibid.*
94. PYM, MSC Letter to Members of the Yearly Meeting, 30 December 1969, 1.
95. W. Russell Johnson, "The Courage to Say 'No': Philadelphia Yearly Meeting," *Friends Journal*, 15 May 1971, 306–7.
96. *Ibid.* The yearly meeting's reply was delivered by a group of appointed Friends. The hope was that "the visit will be an opportunity for dialogue and understanding." *PYM News*, May 1971.
97. *PYM News*, September 1970; Preliminary Report, 1970 Working Party, PYM, 3 March 1971, SFHL.
98. Preliminary Report, 1970 Working Party.
99. *PYM News*, May 1972.
100. *PYM News*, November 1972, February 1977; Preliminary Report, 1970 Working Party, PYM, December 1976.
101. Brown, *Pray and Pay Attention*, 25.
102. Allen J. Matusow, *The Unraveling of America: A History of Liberalism in the 1960s* (New York: Harper and Row, 1984), 439.
103. *Ibid.*
104. "Statement from the Topic Group on Race Relations," Peace and Social Action Institute, New York Yearly Meeting, 13–15 April 1973, 1, SFHL.
105. Snyder, *Witness for Peace*, 168–78.
106. Minutes, CRC, AFSC, 15 October 1976.
107. *Ibid.*, AFSC, 4 April 1975.
108. *Ibid.*, AFSC, 5 April 1978.
109. Nancy Marlowe Moore, "Minute from a Young Friend to old Friends," 8 August 1970, Minutes of PYM MSC, 1.
110. "Black Power, White Power, Shared Power," NCFRR.

CHAPTER NINE: **Violence and Nonviolence**

1. Mary Lou Leavitt, *Quaker Peace Testimony*, Pamphlets on Line on Philadelphia Yearly Meeting web site, http://www.pym.org/pm/comments.php?id=1117_0_178_0_C 15 December 2007.
2. Horton and Horton, *Hard Road to Freedom*, 224.
3. Ruth A. Miner, "America's Emotional Revolution," *Friends Journal*, 1 May 1968, 219–20.
4. AFSC, *Some Quaker Approaches to the Race Problem* (Philadelphia: American Friends Service Committee, 1946).
5. Hamm, *Quakers in America*, 163.
6. Vinton Deming, phone interview, 23 January 2007.

7. Wikipedia contributors, "Richard Gregg," *Wikipedia, The Free Encyclopedia*, http://en.wikipedia.org/w/index.php?title=Richard_Gregg&oldid=239446753 (accessed 24 September 2008).

8. Rufus Jones, "Introduction to First Edition" of Richard B. Gregg, *The Power of Non-Violence* (New York: Fellowship Publications, 1944 edition), 7.

9. Martin Luther King, Jr., "Foreword" to Richard Gregg, *The Power of Nonviolence*, abridged by M.M. Temple, 1960, on Jesus Radicals web site: www.jesusradicals.com/library/gregg.php 16 December 2007.

10. Applebaum, "Material Pacifism," citing Richard B. Gregg, *The Value of Voluntary Simplicity* (Wallingford, PA: Pendle Hill, 1936), and Richard B. Gregg, *Training for Peace: A Program for Peace Workers* (Philadelphia: Lippincott, 1937).

11. Barbour et al., *Quaker Crosscurrents*, 252.

12. Fellowship Farm web site, http://www.fellowshipfarm.org/ffhist.htm, 25 March 2008.

13. Bayard Rustin, interview with Ed Edwin, 12 September 1985, in Columbia University Oral History Collection, cited on the History Matters web site, www.historymatters.gmu.edu; Daniel Levine, *Bayard Rustin and the Civil Rights Movement* (New Brunswick, NJ: Rutgers University Press, 2000), 64. Rustin's article, "Twenty-two Days on a Chain Gang" was published in the *New York Post* and is reprinted in *Down the Line: The Collected Writings of Bayard Rustin* (Chicago: Quadrangle Books, 1971).

14. Walter Naegle, "Bayard Rustin (1912–1987)," on "Brother Outsider: The Life of Bayard Rustin" web site, www.rustin.org. Naegle was Bayard Rustin's partner from 1977 until Rustin's death in 1987 and is executor and archivist of the Bayard Rustin Estate.

15. Buzz Haughton, "Bayard Rustin, Civil Rights Leader" on Quaker Info web site: http://www.quakerinfo.com/quak_br.shtml, 14 June 2008.

16. FGC Peace and Social Order Committee, Memo, 28 May 1951.

17. John D'Emilio, *The Lost Prophet: the life and times of Bayard Rustin* (New York: Free Press, c2003), 268–69.

18. Lawrence McK. Miller, *Witness for Humanity: A Biography of Clarence E. Pickett* (Wallingford, PA: Pendle Hill, 1999), 320. Clarence Pickett, like other people in the same position at AFSC, was also active on the national level, holding positions like the chair of the newly created American Council on Race Relations in 1944. Having met Eleanor Roosevelt who was interested in the work AFSC was doing with homesteads for coal miners, Pickett was invited to a highly unusual meeting with African Americans at the White House and soon developed a close working relationship with the First Lady, which gave him opportunities to present the Quaker point of view on many topics. Mrs. Roosevelt allotted some of the earnings from broadcasts to AFSC. A few years after Pickett left his AFSC post, he became the chairman of Friends General Conference, a volunteer position. Miller, *Witness for Humanity*, 136, 150, 316.

19. FGC Peace and Social Order Committee, Memo of 28 May 1951.

20. "In Muncie March," photograph and information on the march in "What Some Friends Are Doing," *Quaker Life*, May 1965, 151.

21. Miller, *Witness for Humanity*, 318, 328. A pamphlet and an audio CD of Martin Luther King's 1958 Cape May address were published in 2008 by Quaker Press of FGC.

22. D'Emilio, *The Lost Prophet*, 268-69.

23. Janet Boyte Ferguson and Janet Adams Rinard, *As Way Opened, A History of Atlanta Friends Meeting, 1943-1997* (Atlanta, GA: Atlanta Friends Meeting, c1999), 2, 5, 21-27. "Ironically," the authors pointed out, "this same group . . . accepted the presence of a Japanese student . . ., even though U.S. was at war with Japan. Members Phern and John Stanley proposed the idea.

24. Yungblut made the comment at the Third National Friends Conference on Race Relations in 1961, according to David Scull, "Tender Tension in the Edible Portion with Handles On," a summary of 1961 NFCRR, 6.

25. Ferguson and Rinard, *As Way Opened*, 31, 45, 77, 162, 174; Minutes AFSC 1957.

26. *Ibid.* 35, 45. By 1989, the Atlanta group had outgrown Quaker House and began to build their current meetinghouse just outside the city in Decatur.

27. AFSC CRC Minutes, 7 November 1956.

28. Sara Alderman Murphy, *Breaking the Silence: Little Rock's Women's Emergency Committee to Open Our Schools, 1958-1963* (Fayetteville: University of Arkansas Press, 1997), 215; 145. *Ibid.*, 215, 219, 220-21. A number of the Aldersgate attendees were members of the Women's Emergency Committee to Open Our Schools, a group formed in 1956 that grew into a powerful force for schools and better government in the city.

29. Thelma Babbitt, interview with authors, March 2002. Many Philadelphia Friends contributed to AFSC's work in Little Rock, which spurred segregationists to throw rocks through the windows of AFSC's local office.

30. Their suspicions that their movements were being watched and reported on were later confirmed when Governor Orval Faubus's papers were made public. See Murphy, *Breaking the Silence*, 215, 218-19.

31. Robert Wixom, "Letter from Little Rock," *Friends World News*, No. 57 (April 1959), 8-9. Wixom wrote a series of these articles giving readers a closer view of the crisis over desegregation in their city.

32. Wixom, *ibid.* and "Letter from Little Rock: Concerns of Little Rock Monthly Meeting," *Friends Journal*, 17 May 1958, 313-14.

33. Hilty, *New Garden*, 101-2.

34. AFSC Southern Programs Committee Minutes, 25 May 1963, 3.

35. Jessica McElrath, "Lunch Counter Sit-Ins," About.com: http://afroamhistory.about.com /od/sitins/a/sitins.htm 20 June 2008; For a rich biography of the leading personalities involved on both sides of the Nashville sit-ins, see David Halberstam, *The Children* (Random House Publishing Group: New York, 1999, Fawcett Edition).

36. Marian and Nelson Fuson, interview with authors, 20 June 2002.

37. About.com: African American History, http: afroamhistory.about.com/od/sitins/ a/sitins.htm. 16 December 2007.

38. E-mail from David Hartsough to authors, 2 September 2008.

39. Kathie G. O'Hara, "An Open Letter," *Baltimore Young Friends Newsletter* 2, 12 (10 December 1960), n.p.

40. Minutes, CRC, 15 March 1960.

41. Minutes, AFSC CRC Round-up, 28 February–4 March 1960.

42. David Kendall, "Prophetic Young Friend Writes of Mississippi," *Quaker Life*, February 1965, 44–45.

43. Telephone interview with Barbara Mays, 1 August 2008.

44. Vinton Deming, telephone interview with authors, 23 January 2007.

45. "Student Concern for Social Justice Takes Many Forms," *Swarthmore College Bulletin*, Alumni Issue, December 1964, 21.

46. Deming interview.

47. Authors; phone conversation with Barbara Greenler, 21 April 2004.

48. Conversation with Greenler.

49. *Ibid.*, 291–94; Liz Yeats, "Fay Honey Knopp/ Lighting Dark Corners" in *Lives That Speak*, 43–44.

50. Bigelow was earlier captain of the *Golden Rule*, one of the two boats that protested against nuclear tests in the late 1950s. Barbour et al., *Quaker Crosscurrents*, 291, 294.

51. David Fankhauser, e-mail to authors, 10 May 2004. Fankhauser describes his imprisonment in detail with photographs on http://biology.clc.uc.edu/Fankhuaser/ Society/freedom_rides/Freedom_Ride_DBF. Fankhauser, now a biology and chemistry professor at the University of Cincinnati, spent his last two years of college at Earlham. He did not recall any particular civil rights actions taking place while he was at Earlham.

52. John Lewis, keynote at FCNL Annual Meeting, November 2007, audio on www.fcnl.org.

53. Martin Luther King, Jr., "Letter from Birmingham Jail," 15 April 1963, The Martin Luther King, Jr. Research and Education Institute, Stanford University. www.stanford.edu/group/King/popular_requests/frequentdocs/birmingham.pdf.

54. Jack Sutters, "AFSC in History: Martin Luther King, Jr.," AFSC web site, http://www.afsc.org/about/hist/king.htm.

55. Report, Committee on Race Relations, to Philadelphia Yearly Meeting, Advisory Committee Reports 1964, 168–69.

56. Sutters, "AFSC in History."

57. Flyer for the March on Washington, PYM CRR. Estimate of number of marchers from web site for the march.

58. Flyer for March on Washington.

59. CRR Report to PYM, 1964 Advance Committee Reports, 168–69.

60. Anne and Elizabeth Geiger, "We Shall Overcome . . . Young Friends at the March for Jobs and Freedom," and Randy Webb, "We'll Walk Hand in Hand . . ."

Baltimore Young Friends Newsletter 5, 2 (23 September 1963), unpaginated. Quaker activist George Watson, a European American, recalled later in a talk before the 2007 FGC Gathering in River Falls, Wisconsin, that there was a large group of Young Friends from Shenandoah (Meeting) who felt it was like a big family picnic. Watson also recalled that there was not a scrap of litter, for which he credited "good organizing" by Bayard Rustin.

61. Minutes, Executive Committee of AFSC CRC, 9 January 1964.
62. Taylor, *Friends and the Racial Crisis*, 32–33.
63. Minutes, FGC Peace and Social Order Committee, 7 September 1963, 3.
64. In 1980 the committee became the Friends Committee on Black Concerns; it continues its work today.
65. Barbour et al., *Quaker Crosscurrents*, 291, 297–98.
66. *Ibid.*, 295–96.
67. Minutes, NCFRR Continuation Committee, November 1968, 9.
68. Earl J. Prignitz, "Made in America!" *Quaker Life*, no. 8, 8 (July 1968): 202–04. Prignitz was also editor of the *Penn Adult* and *Penn Teacher*, publications for First Day Schools at FUM.
69. Barrington Dunbar, "Black Power's Challenge to Quaker Power," *Friends Journal*, 15 September 1968, 460.
70. *Ibid.*
71. James Fletcher and Carleton Mabee, (eds.). *A Quaker Speaks From the Black Experience: the life and selected writings of Barrington Dunbar* (New York: New York Yearly Meeting of the Religious Society of Friends, 1979), 33–34.
72. Ruth A. Miner, "America's Emotional Revolution," *Friends Journal*, 1 May 1968, 219–20.
73. Candida Palmer, "Another Dimension to Forgiveness," *Friends Journal*, 1 September 1970, 455.
74. Sawyer, "The Stranger Among You," *Quaker Life*, October 1969, 5–289, 290, 291, 292.
75. Robert Berquist, "Iowa Conservative Faces Problems of our Times," *Quaker Life* ser. 8, 10 (October 1968): 307. Video interviews with Kale Williams about his years of work on urban housing, particularly in Chicago, can be found on the Chicago Freedom Movement web site: http://cfm40.middlebury.edu/node/195?PHPSESSID=303de936f2155c969a708032a84c0aa6 25 March 2008.
76. Ginny Coover, "Life in the Ghetto: Out of Suburbia into the Ghetto," *Quaker Life*, ser. 8, 12, December 1968, 385–87.
77. Margaret Hope Bacon, "The Voices of Change," *Friends Journal*, 15 October 1971, 522.
78. Fager, *White Reflections on Black Power*, 83, 89.
79. Samuel Levering, "Dissent and Protest: A Quaker View," *Quaker Life* ser. 10, 1 (January 1969): 11–13. Levering, a Virginian, also represented his yearly meeting on the board of AFSC.
80. Minutes, Meeting for Social Concerns, September 1969, 5.

81. John A. Sullivan, *Dilemmas for Quakerism in Action* (Philadelphia: American Friends Service Committee, 1974), 70.

82. Rev. Ed King, World Wide Faith News Archives, http://www.wfn.org/2001/11/msg00137.html.

83. Michael Yarrow, "The Burning of a Dream," *Friends Journal*, 1 April 1965, 165; *PYM News*, 1 October 1964, 2.

84. *Friends Journal*, 15 March 1965, 140. The two New York Friends were "released" by their meeting, meaning they were freed from other responsibilities to work on the meeting's behalf and would receive some financial and moral support.

85. Nancy Sorel, Lloyd and Margaret Bailey, Barbour, Bassett, Fleck, Seeger, Sexton, Simkin, Singsen, Sorel, Wagner, Watson, and Wheeler, "Peace and Social Concerns: The Last Forty Years, 1955–1995," in Barbour et al., 292–93.

86. *Friends Journal*, 15 March 1965, 140.

87. "Friends Aid in Church Reconstruction," The News: Quaker Style, 15 August 1965, 5, in Friends Mississippi Project, SFHL.

88. *PYM News*, November 1965. Just about thirty years later, in 1996, Quakers were among those who went once again to rebuild burned-out churches after a wave of fires. See Martha Honey, "Rebuilding Burned Church is a First Step: Alabama Small Town Has Two of Everything, One Black, One White," *National Catholic Reporter*, 32 and 37, 23 August 1996. Honey had helped rebuild churches at Quaker work camps in the mid-sixties in Mississippi and Alabama. The mayor of one town in the 1990s called her and others "outside agitators" who "caused a lot of friction among the races."

89. *Friends Journal, Ibid.*

90. Ralph Beebe, *A garden of the Lord: A history of Oregon Yearly Meeting of Friends Church* (Newberg, OR: The Barclay Press, c1968), 111.

91. *PYM Faith and Practice* (Philadelphia: PYM, 1997), 85.

92. McCorkel was speaking to the Pendle Hill Board of Managers on 18 April 1964. Minutes, Pendle Hill Board of Managers, 1959–1969, 4.

93. Minutes, PYM, 1969, 143.

94. Cited in William Griggs, "National Youth Conference Report: Where Are You?" *Quaker Life*, ser. 8, 8, August 1968, p. 239. Speakers included an AME pastor from Iowa and a representative of the Delta Ministry in Mississippi.

95. Frances Bosworth, "The Story of the Friends Neighborhood Guild," www.friendsneighborhoodguild.org/entry 29 November 2006.

96. Francis X. Geary, "Blacks Invade Quaker Center in Chester, Demand Deed, Funds to Run It," *The Bulletin*, 12 June 1969, unpaginated. Kenyatta, who left the group in Chester when he found their tactics approaching violence, had also gone to a Mass at a Catholic Church in May to ask for reparations.

97. PYM MSC Minutes, 16 August 1969; 3–4, and 11 April 1970, 1.

98. Harry G. Toland, "In Chester, a Yule Story Plus an Empty Stocking," *The Bulletin*, 21 December 1970, RG 2, ser. 12, SFHL. In a letter to the editor of the *Delaware County Times*, 8 September 1969, Quaker John Wills of Cheyney objected on

both moral and legal grounds, as well as on his belief that the services the center, which had run well, were now disrupted and should continue under the same leadership. Those who endorsed the takeover were "supporting conspirators."

99. Minutes, Meeting for Social Concerns, 11 April 1970, 1.

100. Officially named the National Advisory Commission on Civil Disorders.

101. Laird, "Social Concerns," 12. At that time, Laird, a former Presbyterian minister, was working for AFSC.

102. Charles K. Brown III to clerks of Philadelphia Yearly Meeting Monthly Meetings, 1 April 1968, 1.

103. *PYM News*, June 1968.

104. Margaret Hope Bacon, "Quakers and Black Empowerment," *Friends Journal*, 15 March 1968, 130.

105. Magaroh Maruijama, "The Logic of the Ghetto," *Friends Journal*, 15 October 1968, 518–20.

106. Fletcher and Mabee, eds., *A Quaker Speaks From the Black Experience*, 33–34.

107. Edith Warner Johnson, "Moments of Truth," *Friends Journal*, May 15, 1970, 304.

108. See the Black Panther Party web site, www.blackpanther.org, for the text of this ten-point program.

109. CRC of AFSC, "Draft of Proposed 'WHY: The AFSC and the Black Panthers'," March 1970, 1.

110. Minutes, PYM, 1970, 12; Report of the Meeting for Social Concerns, Minutes, PYM, 1970, Advanced Documents, 127. The building was donated for community use by a Friend to honor his father whose clothing store had been at that location. *PYM News*, September 1970.

111. "Chain Reaction in North Philadelphia," *PYM News*, January 1971.

112. Minutes, PYM, 1970, 12, 22. In 1973, when financial problems at the clinic continued, the meeting decided that Vlaclavick's work was important enough that they cancelled his loans. *PYM News*, October 1974.

113. Edith Warner Johnson, "Moments of Truth," *Friends Journal*, 15 May 1970, 304.

114. Minutes, MSC, 1970, SHFL. Greg Barnes, e-mail to authors, 4 August 2003. The "Friendly presence" included Brown, Capon, Deming, Flanagan, Elisabeth Leonard, Frank Loescher, Larry Scott, Lyle Tatum, Charles Walker, and Lillian and George Willoughby.

115. Barnes e-mail. 4 August 2003.

116. Minutes and associated materials regarding AFSC's relationship to the Black Panthers can be found primarily in the files for the CRC in 1970.

117. The Black Panther Party celebrated its fortieth anniversary in 2006. For its history see Curtis Stephen, "Life of A Party: The Black Panthers Mark 40 Years," *The Crisis*, September/October 2006, 30–37.

118. CRC of AFSC, Minutes, 9 January 1970, 9, 11, 13–5, and *WHY???!!!*, I, No. 2, March 1970, AFSC in-house newsletter.

119. Indiana Yearly Meeting, *News Letter*, Summer 1968, 1, citing guidelines adopted by FCNL in January 1968.

120. "Recommendations of Black Development Workshop" to the plenary of NYYM Peace Institute, 26 April 1970.

121. CRC of AFSC, Minutes, 9 January 1970, 11.

122. Mallonee, et al, *Minute by Minute*, 220.

123. Elizabeth Gulick, "What the Black Panthers are Trying to Tell Us," *Friends Journal*, 15 June 1970, 352–53.

124. Palmer, "Another Dimension," 455.

125. Barrington Dunbar, "Black Power's Challenge to Quaker Power," *Friends Journal*, 15 September 1968, 460.

126. CRR Report, PYM Minutes, 1969, 143.

127. AFSC staff, memo re situation in Boston, 9 January 1975.

128. Friends for Human Justice, "Report to the Committee to Evaluate FHJ," November 1975, 1–2. Fuson papers.

129. Gerald Jonas, *On Doing Good*, 165.

CHAPTER TEN: **Integration in Quaker Schools**

1. In some schools, Westtown for one, there was an intermediate step—admitting the children who had only one Quaker parent, which occurred there in 1920.

2. Quote from unidentified source in "Color Trends Among Friends in the 'Forties,'" *Friends Intelligencer*, 14 June 1947, 309–10.

3. Lawrence M. Schall, "Swarthmore College: The Evolution of an Institutional Mission" (Ph.D. diss., University of Pennsylvania, 2003), 112.

4. "Lifting the Curtain: Crystal Bird Fauset," American Friends Service Committee web site, http://www.afsc.org/about/hist/2003/crystal_bird_fauset.htm.

5. Henry Cadbury, notes on 28 April 1939 conference at Swarthmore sponsored by Race Relations, Religious Education, and Educational Committees of the PYMs, 3. Program in Conferences folder.

6. "Purpose of the Conference" from program for Conference on Race Relations, 8–9 January 1932, sponsored by AFSC. Programs, Records of Committee on Race Relations, Philadelphia Yearly Meetings, SFHL.

7. Principal sources are the 10 February 1943, minutes of the School Committee of Haverford Friends School, Miriam Jones Brown, *Friends School, Haverford, 1885–1985* (Exton, PA: Schiffer Publications, c1985), 68–70, and Richard McFeely's statement in Clayton L. Farraday, *Friends Central School, 1845–1984* (Philadelphia: Friends' Central School, 1984), 87. While Haverford Friends School is adjacent to Haverford College, there is not institutional connection between the two. Farraday was head of Friends Central School.

8. *Ibid.* It would be "cruel to admit a few Negroes and a danger to the school to admit many," said one Westtown student in a survey there. Said another: "If all races are equal, all would have been born one color." Seth Hedderick, "Consistency in Thought and Action," unpublished paper for Haverford College course, n.d., 13.

9. Seth Hedderick, "Consistency in Religious Thought and Action," 8.

10. Hedderick, "Consistency in Thought," 9–10.
11. Kingdon Swayne, *George School: the history of a Quaker community* (Philadelphia: Philadelphia Yearly Meeting, c. 1992), 60.
12. Watson, *A Quest in Interracial Understanding*, 27–29.
13. William J. Reagan, *A Venture in Quaker Education at Oakwood School* (Poughkeepsie, NY: Oakwood School, 1968), 67–68. Reagan (104) identified Oakwood student David Johnson as the first African American enrolled at Haverford College, though college records state that the first student of color was admitted in 1926, almost ten years before Oakwood allowed its first African American student.
14. The Yergan boys are mentioned in Minutes, Executive Committee of the Board of Managers, Oakwood School, 1921–36, 20 September 1933 and 22 February and 24 September 1934.
15. The Oakwood report is included in F. L. K., "Schools' Race Policy Discussed," *Friends Intelligencer*, 29 April 1944, 286. The author is most likely Florence L. Kite, a member of Philadelphia Yearly Meeting's Committee on Race Relations.
16. Oakwood School Minutes, Executive Committee of Board of Mangers, 1921–1936, report of 24 September 1934; 1947–1952, reports of 24 May 1951, 21 November 1952 and 9 July 1953.
17. Sue Gold, "Bearing Witness to a Fresh Revelation of Truth: The Desegregation of Media Friends School in 1937" in *Schooled in Diversity: Readings on Racial Diversity in Friends Schools*, eds. Pat Macpherson, Irene McHenry, and Sarah Sweeney-Denham (Philadelphia: Friends Council on Education, 2001), 65. The "Schooled in Diversity" project is a collaboration of alumni and teachers at two Quaker schools formed to apply the lessons of their research to the issues that arise in the search for diversity. The interviews with alumni "give voice to the unheard, silent, tongue-tied" and "visibility" to those who were invisible, Macpherson wrote in a 2003 unpublished paper, "Big Designs, Small Stitches," 9.
18. Hedderick, "Consistency in Thought," 9, citing a 6 December 1937, letter from James in the Haverford College Quaker Collection.
19. Gold, "Bearing Witness," 66.
20. Vincent Pinto and Frederick W. Echelmeyer, eds., *A Century of Love and Learning: Media Friends School, 1876–1976* (Media, PA: Joint Centennial Committee of Media Friends School and Media Monthly Meeting, 1976), 15–18.
21. Conference Report, CRR and Friends Council on Education (FCE), PYM, April 1944, SFHL.
22. Gold, "Bearing Witness," 66.
23. *Ibid.*, 69. Italics are Gold's.
24. Pinto and Echelmeyer, eds., *Century of Love and Learning*, 15–20.
25. Gold, "Bearing Witness," 67.
26. *Ibid.*, 69.
27. *Ibid.*, 66–67.

28. Some Friends Believed integration would attract people who supported that goal as it did for the Reverend Max Adams and Eleanor Adams who enrolled their daughters, Joan and Jane, for just that reason. Years later Joan Adams (Mondale) said of Media's action: "You lived your ideals and brotherhood."

29. Pinto and Echelmeyer, eds., *Century of Love and Learning*, 15-20, 40-41.

30. Bill Koons, "'If One Could Choose a School for One's Child:' A Desegregation Story about Germantown Friends School" (paper, n.d.), 2-3.

31. Koons, "Desegregation Story," 2.

32. *Ibid.*, 1, 3.

33. Mary Ellen Chijioke, interview with authors, 19 April 2002, e-mail to authors, 15 August 2006.

34. Howard Brinton, *Quaker Education in Theory and Practice* (Wallingford, PA: Pendle Hill Pamphlet # 9, 1940), 90.

35. Swayne, *George School*, 60.

36. FCE, "Enrollment of Negro Students in Private Schools and Colleges of New England, New York, New Jersey, and Pennsylvania" (Paper, FCE, 1941), 5.

37. *Ibid.*

38. Thomas Jones and Esther Jones, Report from Interracial Relations Committee, *Friends World News*, 12, Spring 1944, 8. Thomas Jones, president of the historically black college, Fisk University, was serving as a consultant on relations to FWCC, Section of the Americas.

39. Margaret Morris Haviland, "Westtown's Integration: 'A Natural and Fruitful Enlargement of Our Lives'," *Quaker History* 95, 2 (Fall 2006), 25-26.

40. The letter was printed in *Friends Intelligencer*, 15 January 1944.

41. *Friends Intelligencer*, 15 January 1944.

42. Haviland, "Westtown's Integration," 27-28.

43. Ingrid Viguera, "The Admittance of 'Negroes' to Westtown" (Paper, Westtown Friends School, n.d.), 1.

44. Grace Cunningham hoped to attend Earlham College and had been accepted already for her senior year at Oakwood but preferred Westtown; see Hedderick, "Consistency in Thought," 15.

45. Hedderick, "Consistency in Thought," 16. According to Hedderick, one of those who withdrew was ill and the other was from the South. However, Haviland questioned his belief that it was a southerner because she found no mention of it in any of the board's minutes and, in fact, she found that northerners were the ones who objected more strongly. Haviland, e-mail to authors, 8 December 2003.

46. Brown, *Friends School, Haverford, 1885-1985*, 70.

47. *Ibid.*

48. *Ibid.*, 68-70. While Haverford is adjacent to Haverford College, there is not institutional connection between the two.

49. Editorial, *Friends Intelligencer*, 15 January 1944, 39.

50. *Ibid.*

51. The Open Forum," *Friends Intelligencer*, 12 February 1944, 109.

52. *Ibid.*, 4 March 1944, 156.

53. *Ibid.*, 197–99.

54. *Ibid.*, 156, 198–99.

55. Survey of PYM Schools, 1958, PYM CRR.

56. Hedderick, "Consistency in Thought," 17. Farraday, *Friends' Central School*, 87–88.

57. Swayne, *George School*, 61.

58. Bunche's son had been turned down by Sidwell. See article in the Spring 2001 issue of the Sidwell school magazine; Jane Coe, e-mail to authors, 19 March 2004.

59. Koons, "Desegregation Story," 3–4; Janet Rosenwald, *The Pastorian*, March 1947.

60. Patricia Macpherson, interview with authors, 5 November 2003, *Germantown Meeting News* 71, 2, March 1961. Koons's paper gives the date as 1948. Also Koons reported that the admissions committee had not kept records that would document any similar decisions earlier.

61. Joan and Rachel Countryman, "Navigating Diversity" in *Stories of Change, in Community, Second International Congress on Quaker Education*, 1997, ed. Pat McPherson, (Philadelphia: Friends Council on Education 1997), 77–78.

62. Minutes, Committee on Education, Friends General Conference, Cape May, NJ, 29 June 1948, SFHL.

63. Minutes, Friends Central School Board of Trustees, 20 April 1948, SFHL.

64. Started in 1855, Greene Street school shares property with its parent, the Hicksite Greene Street Meeting, the historic home of a congregation that supported the Underground Railroad and welcomed abolitionist Lucretia Mott. According to Edward Marshall, head of the school in 2006, e-mail to authors, 25 August 2006, the exact date on which African American students were first admitted cannot be pinpointed.

65. "Schools in the Inner City: Partnership with the Community," *Chronicles of Quaker Education*, Winter '00. http://friendscouncil.org/web/newsletters/Chro winter-00.html. 3 November 2003.

66. Macpherson, "Action Research Inside/Outside Quaker Education: An Introduction," in, Daryl Ford, *Schooled in Diversity: Action Research: Student and African-American Alumni Collaboration for School Change* (Philadelphia: Friends Council on Education, 2005–2006), 14.

67. Eric Askew, Gillian Grannnum, J. Kwame Gray, and Charles Minor III, "Demands for Changes, 1991" in Macpherson et al, 75. The authors are students from Germantown School's class of 1991.

68. Susan Goodman, *Germantown Crier* 1, no. 3, September 1949, 22.

69. Reinheimer Report, 1.

70. Minute 37, Minute Book, New England Yearly Meeting, 1947, 33; minute 56, *ibid.*, 1953.

71. King Odell, archivist, Moses Brown School, interview with authors, 2 February 2007; Minute 27, Minute Book, New England Yearly Meeting, 1967.

72. Minute 23, 1978, and minute 41, 1980, Minute Books, New England Yearly Meeting.

73. James English, Moses Brown teacher, phone interview with authors, 19 January 2007.
74. Dean R. Esslinger, *Friends for Two Hundred Years: A History of Baltimore's Oldest School* (Baltimore: Friends School, 1983), 148, 156.
75. Mallonee, Bonny, and Fessenden, *Minute by Minute*, 215, 217.
76. Bliss Forbush, "Integration in Baltimore Friends School," *Friends Intelligencer* 112, 1 (1 January 1955), 7–8.
77. Esslinger, *Friends for Two Hundred Years*, 165.
78. *Ibid.*, 161, 165, 207.
79. Minutes, MSC, Philadelphia Yearly Meeting, August and and 4 December 1951, 17 December 1952.
80. William R. MacKaye and Mary Anne MacKaye, *Mr. Sidwell's School: A Centennial History, 1883–1983* (Washington, DC: Sidwell Friends School, 1983), 62, 115.
81. From a long-time Quaker family, Hadassah Leeds (later Holcombe) was also cofounder of the Friends Council on Education and served on the boards of Swarthmore, Antioch, and Haverford Colleges and of George and Sidwell Schools.
82. MacKaye and MacKaye, *Mr. Sidwell's School*, 168.
83. *Ibid.*, 168–69; If African Americans were admitted, Stone told Leeds, he would resign. Leeds' response: "If thee should resign from the Board because a measure which thee does not approve be adopted, it would seem to me unworthy action from one whose principles are so high. It would appear as more of a disservice to thyself than to the school." When the time came, Stone did resign, but returned later, *ibid.*, 171–73.
84. *Ibid.*, 167.
85. *Ibid.*, 170–72.
86. Jane Meleney Coe, e-mail to authors, 19 March 2004.
87. MacKaye and MacKaye, *Mr. Sidwell's School*.
88. Reported by Nancy Werner, the schools' Admissions/Development Coordinator, in an e-mail dated 18 November 2003. Werner studied school records in preparation for the school's centennial in 2002.
89. Pinto and Echelmeyer, eds., *Century of Love and Learning*, 21–22.
90. "Unfinished Business," 1961 PYM CRR survey.
91. Rita Goldman, "When the Rubber Meets the Road" in Macpherson et al., *Schooled in Diversity*, 45; "Germantown Friends Community Scholarships Program," http://www.nais.org/search/idea.
92. Virginia Beach School web site: http://www.friends-school.org/homespun/vbfs/index.php?id=diversity
93. Palmer, Noel, *Westbury Friends School, The First Forty Years, 1957-1997, Birth and Survival* (S.l.: s.n., c. 1997), 26, 39.
94. Web site: Long Island private schools: http://www.longislandschools.com/private-schools/westbury-friends-school.html. 9 September 2008.
95. Nash, "Embracing Diversity" in *Schooled in Diversity*, Macpherson et al, 19.
96. *Ibid.*, 19–21.

97. *Ibid.*, 21.
98. Gail Thomas, interview with authors, 24 October 2003. Detroit Friends Meeting, which dates back to 1924, met at the school from around 1966–1971, Margaret Walden, clerk, e-mail to authors, 12 December 2007.
99. Jeanne Rocwell, "A Permanent Home for Detroit Friends School," *Friends Journal*, 15 January 1970, 54; *Detroit Free Press*, 27 October 2002. Information on the meeting and the parents' reaction is from Thomas interview. Eleven members of the school's board of twenty-one people were to be Quaker
100. "Bright Spot in Detroit," *Friends Journal*, October 1967, 515–16.
101. Dwight Wilson, e-mail (25 May 2004) and phone interviews with the authors, 25 and 27 May 2004.
102. Conversation with Gail Thomas, 24 October 2003. Most of the families are middle and upper class, said Thomas, although there are numbers who need financial aid. Retaining students has become a problem, she said, because of competition among private schools for African American students.
103. *Detroit Free Press*, 27 October 2002.
104. Wilson interview.
105. Carolina Friends School web site, www.cfsnc.org/aboutcfs/basicinfo.htm. 3 March 2003; personal conversation with Pam Fitzpatrick, former teacher, 1 November 2003.
106. *Ibid.*, 24 August 2008.
107. Friends School of Atlanta, Fact Sheet, web site, www.friendsschoolatlanta.org, 23 August 2006.
108. Friends School of Wilmington web site, www.fsow.org 30 August 2006.
109. Buckingham Friends School to Philadelphia Yearly Meeting, 1961.
110. King Odell, archivist, Moses Brown School, interview, 2 February 2007.
111. Rosalind Cobb Wiggins, telephone interview with authors, 25 November 2003; King Odell, interview.
112. Juan Williams, "Who Needs Integration?" Can Quaker education cope with the hip-hop challenge?" Transcript of address to the 1999 FCE National Gathering. Williams, a journalist appearing frequently on National Public Radio, was one of the authors of the acclaimed TV series "Eyes on the Prize."
113. Fact sheet, Friends School of Atlanta, Aug. 23, 2006; Edward Marshall, interview with authors, 5 December 2003.
114. Friends School of Atlanta web site: http://www.friendsschoolatlanta.org/about_us/faq.aspx, 10 September 2008. Peace and Social Action Plan Committee (PASAP), "Diversity at Friends Academy: A Brief and Incomplete Overview," 1. Unpublished paper, c. 1996, 2. Germantown Friends School web site:http://www.germantownfriends.org/RelId/623131/ISvars/default/Fast_Facts.htm, 10 September 2008. Friends Central web site: http://www.friendscentral.org/who/about/diversity.asp?bhcp=1, 10 September 2008. Sidwell web site: www.sidwelll.edu/aboutsfs 10 September 2008. Sandi Seltzer, Director of Public Relations and Publications, Moses Brown School, interview with authors, 2 February 2007.

115. Ayesha Imani, "We Cannot See Clearly or Completely Until We See Togther: A Letter to a Meeting about its School Committee Composition" in Macpherson, *Schooled in Diversity*, 71–72.

116. *Ibid.*, 39.

117. Hamm, *Earlham College*, 151. Miller, *Witness for Humanity*, 98–99.

118. Hamm, *Earlham College*, 46. Just why he went back to Southland to graduate is not clear, but Hamm suggested he may have been enrolled in the preparatory school on the Earlham campus and chose to complete his degree in Arkansas. Hamm, e-mail to authors, December 2001.

119. Charles William Cooper, *Whittier: independent college in California, founded by Quakers, 1877* (Los Angeles: Ward Ritchie Press, 1967), 377–78.

120. Oliver, "Early Evangelical Quakers," 15.

121. Wilmington College had earlier rejected the admission application of Calvin B. Gilliam, an African American who had been educated at Spiceland, one of the Quaker communities in which schools admitted students of African descent if there were no other schools for them in the area. Gilliam was rejected reportedly because of his color. Ina Kelley, letter to authors, 31 March 2003.

122. Gregory Kannerstein, ed., *The Spirit and the Intellect: Haverford College, 1833–1983* (Haverford, PA: Haverford College, 1983), 11.

123. Earl Holmes, "Friends University" (Paper, Friends University, Wichita, KS, n.d.)

124. Clarence M. Cunningham, "Being Black at Earlham in the Early 'Twenties,'" *The Earlhamite*, 100, 2 (Spring 1979), 1–2; Hamm, *Earlham College*, 152. Fifty years later the college dedicated the new Clarence Cunningham Cultural Center in his honor. *The Earlhamite*, July 1979, 7.

125. Hamm, *Earlham College*, 153.

126. Miller, *Witness to Humanity*, 105–6. The students who married were Harold Ballysingh and Marion Cowperthwaite; Harold because a lawyer in Jamaica. Their daughter went to Westtown.

127. Hamm, *Earlham College*, 154.

128. Richard Walton, *Swarthmore College: An Informal History* (Swarthmore, PA: Swarthmore College, c1986), 84.

129. Letter from Carl Murphy, president of the Afro-American Company of Baltimore, to Swarthmore President Frank Aydelotte, 14 September 1933. From Records of the Office of the President of Swarthmore College, Frank Aydelotte papers, 1905–1956. RG6/Do7, SFHL.

130. Letter from Aydelotte to Murphy, 22 September 1933. Ayedelotte was the first Swarthmore president who was not a Quaker, "although he attended meeting at Swarthmore Monthly Meeting and was "in accord with its principles" according to the Biographical and Historical Notes in his Presidential Papers, 4.

131. *Ibid.*

132. Clipping from the *Philadelphia Tribune*, undated, under the headline "Hypocritical 'Friends.'" PYM CRR.

133. Letter to Helen Bryan, September 1933. Aydelotte Records. PYM CRR 1932–1941.

134. Walton, *Swarthmore College*, 84.
135. *Ibid.*
136. *Swarthmore College Bulletin*, "A Wartime Journey," September 202, college site: http://www.swarthmore.edu/news/history/index5.html. From 1943 to 1946, more than 900 men were on campus in the U.S. Navy's V-5 and V-12 for short-term programs. Among them were 49 Chinese naval officers who were there for nine months, primarily to learn English. Some others were African American.
137. "Schools' Race Policy Discussed," *Friends Intelligencer*, 29 April 1944, 286.
138. Hamm, *Earlham College*; see also "Holy Experiment," *Time*, 4 April 1949, which states that eight professors left with Hinshaw at the time of his firing.
139. Charles William Cooper, *Whittier: Independent College in California, Founded by Quakers*, 377–78.
140. Veldon J. Diment, *The first fifty years: a record of the first fifty years in the life of Pacific College* (Newberg, OR: by authority of the Board of managers, 1941), 26. (Later re-named George Fox.) No class or team photos show anyone who is noticeably African American. The school was small when the book was written.
141. Ralph K. Beebe, *A heritage to honor, a future to fulfill: George Fox College, 1891–1991*, 104. Similarly, there were no African Americans in photos of the 1960s in Beebe's history either. However, there were students of African descent in basketball team photos for 1977–78 and an apparently African American homecoming queen in 1987 (106, 125).
142. *Ibid.*, 107.
143. Erickson, e-mail to authors, 3 June 2002.
144. Gordon Browne, "And Your Neighbor as Yourself," *Quaker Life*, 6 March 1999.
145. Alexander Stoesen, *Guilford College: On the Strength of 150 Years* (Greensboro: Board of Trustees, Guilford College, c1987), 99.
146. Barbour et al, *Quaker Crosscurrents*, 284–87. Long Island University web site, http://www.brooklyn.liu.edu/globalcollege/worldwide.html, 10 September 2008.
147. Barrington Dunbar, "Blacks and Whites in a Friendly College," *Friends Journal*, 15 May 1971, 293–94.
148. Long Island University web site.
149. Hamm, *Earlham College*, 205.
150. *Ibid.*, 176.
151. *Ibid.* Edward and his brother Newton were among those who came to Earlham in 1942 as a result of the activities of the Japanese American Student Relocation Council (JASRC). A special collection in Earlham's Lilly Library is dedicated in the memory of Dr. Edward T. Uyesugi and other American citizens of Japanese heritage whose families were forced to relocate into internment camps during World War II. Among other things it provides materials that explore the contribution of those of Japanese ancestry to the United States.
152. *Ibid.*, 205.
153. *Ibid.*
154. *Ibid.*, 176.

155. *Ibid.* McAllester was on the faculty of William Penn University when Cecil Hinshaw was president and was among those who left the school when Hinshaw left.
156. Letter to Richmond *Palladium-Item*, 23 April 1952.
157. Hamm, *Earlham College*, 207.
158. *Ibid.*, 208.
159. *Ibid.*, 207.
160. Letter from Berkeley Friends Meeting to Thomas Jones, n.d.
161. Dorothy Biddle James to Thomas Jones, [1952], Controversial Issues Collection, Racial Matters File, Earlham College.
162. Thomas Jones to Dorothy Biddle James, 22 May 1952, Controversial Issues Collection, Racial Matters File, Earlham College.
163. Survey, PYM CRR, 1961.
164. Hamm, *History of Earlham*, 256.
165. *Ibid.*, 175.
166. Survey of Schools and Colleges, PYM CRR, 1964.
167. Kannerstein, *The Spirit and the Intellect*, 11.
168. *Ibid.*
169. One full professor was Hispanic Manuel J. Asensio. The other was African American Quaker Ira DeA. Reid, hired after he was a visiting lecturer in 1945. Kannerstein, *The Spirit and the Intellect*, 49, 115.
170. PYM CRR, 1961.
171. *Ibid.*
172. "Malik" and "Julien," "Seen and Not Heard" in Ford, 2.
173. *Ibid.*
174. Juan Williams, "Who Needs Integration? Can Quaker education cope with the hip-hop challenge?" Transcript of address at FCE conference in 1999, 6–7. Williams was also one of the authors of the acclaimed PBS series, "Eyes on the Prize."
175. *Ibid.*
176. "Malik" and "Julien," "Seen and not Heard," in Ford, 55.
177. Pamela Williams, "Where the Waters Part: Divergence in the Westtown Community" in Macpherson, et al, 128.
178. R. Edd Lee, "Cornfields, conservatism and urban life styles," *The Earlhamite*, 1979, 2–3.
179. *Ibid.*
180. Hamm, *Earlham College*, 258; Susan Altman, *Encyclopedia of African-American Heritage*, 2d ed. (New York: Facts on File, 2000), 97.
181. Sybil Jordan Stevenson, "From Little Rock to Earlham," *The Earlhamite*, Spring 1979, 5–6.
182. Swayne, *George School*, 62.
183. Maurice Eldridge, "Diversity then and Now," *Swarthmore College Bulletin*, June 2002, www.swarthmore.edu/bulletin/june02/diversity. 9/26/06. Eldridge has been in the vice president's post since 1989.

184. When Eldridge received anonymous hate mail, Dean William Prentice "scoured the hand-written registration cards" to find the culprit. The person was expelled. Eldridge took a year off and returned "determined to make it on my own terms."

185. *Ibid.*

186. *Ibid.*

187. Walton, *Swarthmore College*, 85.

188. *Ibid.*

189. *Ibid.*, 86.

190. *Ibid.*, 83. Among Courtney Smith's accomplishments was to begin to seek out African American faculty. Also "Background" for Courtney C. Smith Papers, 1953–1969 at SFHL.

191. Walton, *Swarthmore College*, 87, 91. Swarthmore alumnus James Michener (class of 1929) donated $100,000 for the center and for a black studies program. The previous June, Smith had announced his resignation effective the fall of 1969 to become head of the Markle Foundation.

192. Wilmington Yearly Meeting of the Religious Society of Friends. Wilmington College Study Committee, *Partners in education: Wilmington College and Wilmington Yearly Meeting of Friends* (Wilmington, OH: Wilmington Yearly Meeting, 1992), 36.

193. *Ibid.*

194. Concerned Black Students still exists, according to a college brochure, "Is the Wilmington Experience for You?"

195. Wilmington Yearly Meeting, *Partners in Education*, 124.

196. Randy Sarvis, "Black students Occupy College Hall," *The Link*, Spring/Summer 2001, 12–13.

197. *Ibid.*

198. *Ibid.* and Kelley, letter to authors, 31 March 2003. A unique offering of Wilmington gave inmates at a state correctional institution the opportunity to earn B.A. and B.S. degrees from Wilmington—until state funding dried up in the 1990s. Since 1968 the college has offered courses at two correctional institutions. The courses at Warren and Lebanon Correctional Institutions consist of a series of certificate programs in business administration. "Course Offerings at Warren and Lebanon," brochure, 2003–2004. See also Wilmington Yearly Meeting, *Partners in Education*, 36.

199. Gregory Kannerstein, ed., *The Spirit and the Intellect: Haverford College, 1833–1983* (Haverford, PA: Haverford College, 1983), 112.

200. Darryl J. Ford and Cheryl Irving, "Voices in Penn Charter's Diversity History" in Macpherson et al, 111.

201. "Malik" and "Julien," "Seen and Not Heard," 58.

202. Kannerstein, "*The Spirit and the Intellect*," 116.

203. *Ibid.*, 114.

204. AFSC, "A Short History of the Visiting Lectureship Program of the AFSC," 1952, Also unpublished report and correspondence in the Visiting Lectureship files.

Fleming had worked with the Fair Employment Committee for Middle Atlantic States which ordered the hiring of African American trolley and subway operators in Philadelphia, the move that precipitated the strike in 1944.

205. Minutes, AFSC CRR, 25 October 1945.

206. *Ibid.*

207. Ives, *Black Quakers*, 82.

208. Minutes, AFSC CRR, 25 October 1945, and "Visiting Lectureship for Schools and Colleges: A New approach to Interracial Understanding" (Paper, AFSC, 1948).

209. Hamm, *Earlham College*, 258.

210. Hallowell, "George School's Journey" in Macpherson et al, 42.

211. Interview with Gail Thomas.

212. Wiggins, phone conversation, 25 November 2003.

213. The program invited minority scholars to be on campus either just before or after they receive a Ph.D. to finish doctoral work or do postdoctoral research—and teach. Since there were not always vacancies to match the candidates, in the 1990s, President Alfred Bloom hired good new faculty of color "off budget" until there was a regular vacancy in a department. Thus the numbers moved from 11 to 14 percent.

214. Laura Markowitz, "Disturbing the Peace of Racism: An Oral History of the Oral Historian Kathryn Morgan," www.swarthmore.edu/bulletin/archive/00/sept00/morgan. 22 August 2006. In 2000, a $100,000 scholarship in Morgan's name was donated by Eugene M. Lang, an alumnus and founder of the "I Have A Dream" Foundation. Morgan stipulated that preference for the award be given to students with an interest in Black Studies. www.swarthmore.edu/home/news/media/release/00/morgan, 22 August 2006.

215. *Ibid.*

216. Nancy Starmer, "Reconciling Diversity and Community" in Macpherson et al, 8.

217. Earl Harrison, "Governing Change" in *Stories of Change*, 43.

218. Pat MacPherson and Rita Goldman, "City Neighborhood, City Friends Meeting, and City Friends School" in Ford, *Action Research*, 28, 34–35. Note: In this volume, pseudonyms are used for the schools, as well as students, "to protect alumni and school privacy." It also helps "shift the focus from individuals to patterns." From introduction to Part One of Ford.

219. Kannerstein, *The Spirit and the Intellect*, 112.

220. Williams, *Who Needs Integration?*

221. Macpherson and Goldman, "City Neighborhood" in Macpherson et al, 26–27.

CHAPTER ELEVEN: Toward Integration in the Society of Friends

1. Minutes, National Council of Friends for Race Relations, November 1968, 8.

2. Elliott, *Openings for Life and Thought* (N.p., 1988) 351, 354.

3. Minutes, National Conference of Friends on Race Relations, 1969.

4. Minutes, Philadelphia Yearly Meeting, 1969, 130.

5. Minutes, AFSC CRC 6 January 1954 in a proposal for an "Examination by American Friends of their ideals and practices in Race Relations."

6. Minutes, Community Relations Committee, AFSC, 6 January 1954.

7. Minutes AFSC CRC 31 May 1955 and 1 February 1956. Report prepared for the CRC by Robert Johnson of Russell Sage College entitled "In the House of Friends."

8. Carter G. Woodson, "Review of Records of the Moravians," *Journal of Negro History* 28, 3 (July 1943): 362.

9. Ben Richmond, Introduction, *Quaker Life*, March 1999.

10. Johan Maurer, e-mail to authors, 25 February 2004. Maurer is former general secretary of Friends United Meeting and at one time pastor of Reedwood Friends Church in Portland, Oregon.

11. Frank Cummings, "The Intention for an Inclusive Meeting," *Atlanta Friends Meeting Newsletter*, March 1999.

12. David Scull, "The Community of Peoples" in Friends World Committee on Consultation, *No Time But This Present* (Birmingham, England: Friends World Committee on Consultation, 1965), 143. Scull was active in integration of schools in Prince Edward County.

13. Barbara Norcross described her conclusions about the different types of Friends involvement in social concerns at a meeting of PYM's Social Concerns as recorded in the minutes of 10 January 1970.

14. Laird, *Seventy Years*, 14; Minutes, Philadelphia Yearly Meeting, 1969.

15. Beckey Phipps, reader's comments. 28 June 07.

16. Thomas H. Jeavons, "General Reflections: Quakers-Church or Political Party?" *PYM News*, March/April 2006, Philadelphia Yearly Meeting web site, www.pym.org. Jeavons was general secretary of Philadelphia Yearly Meeting from 1997 to 2006.

17. Rob Tucker, letter to "Elizabeth Lehman, thence to Faith Peterkin, Larry Scott, Ty Cunningham, and to called meeting. 9 mo. 10," 2 September 1970, 1. Tucker, a Philadelphia teacher and counselor, was a frequent contributor to the journal, *Quaker Religious Thought*, but not as a member of any of the committees active in the issue, according to Charles Brown, PYM clerk at the time.

18. Errol T. Elliott, *Openings for Life and Thought* (N.p., 1988), 33.

19. Hilty, *New Garden*, 101.

20. Minutes, Meeting for Social Concerns, Philadelphia Yearly Meeting, 17 May 1969.

21. Report, Meeting for Social Concerns Retreat, January 1970, 1.

22. Minutes, Meeting for Social Concerns, 13 December 1969.

23. Samuel Levering, "Dissent and Protest: A Quaker View," *Quaker Life* ser. 10, 1 (January 1969): 11–13.

24. MSC Minutes for retreat of January 21–23, 1970, 2.

25. Minutes, Philadelphia Yearly Meeting, 1969, 133.

26. Scull, "Community of Peoples," 5.

27. C. H. Yarrow, "White Suburbia," *Friends Journal*, 8 September 1956, 574.

28. Richard Taylor, "A Summary," 1.

29. *Friends Intelligencer*, 5 August 1944, 517.

30. *Ibid.*, 2 September 1944.

31. The Health and Welfare Council of Delaware, Montgomery, and Philadelphia Counties, *Directory of Services for the Aged*, rev. ed., eds. John Hill and Cecelia Strauss (Philadelphia: Health and Welfare Council, 1995), 129–30.
32. Ferguson and Rinard, *As Way Opened*, 7–8.
33. Martha Gordon,"Brothers and Equals," *Friends Journal*, 25 February 1956, 118–20.
34. *Ibid.*, 118–19.
35. Response from Bristol Monthly Meeting to PYM Ad Hoc Committee on the Urban Crisis's survey of monthly meetings' activities and concerns re racism, 1968. RG2/407/Ser12, Box 6/11, SFHL.
36. Marian Fuson to Fred Newkirk, Long Beach, CA, 19 October 1968.
37. Taylor,"Summary," 1.
38. *Ibid.*, 1–2.
39. Taylor, *Friends and the Racial Crisis*, 25–28.
40. *Ibid.*, 1.
41. *Ibid.*, 2.
42. Report, Friends World Committee on Consultation, 1937, 90–93.
43. National Conference of Friends on Race Relations, *Newsletter* 2, 1, April 1963, 2–3.
44. Information sheet, Philadelphia Yearly Meeting, "A Quaker Call to Action in Race Relations," SFHL.
45. Survey, Race Relations Committee, Philadelphia Yearly Meeting, 1965.
46. Social Order Committee, "Friends and the 'Suburban Challenge'" (Report, Philadelphia Yearly Meeting 1969), SFHL.
47. Foster is best known as the author of *Celebration of Discipline: The Path to Spiritual Growth* (San Francisco: Harper and Row, 1978). Foster, "Quaker Concern,"114–23.
48. Foster,"Quaker Concern," 141.
49. Minutes, Final Ad Hoc Committee, 18 March 1970.
50. Minutes of AFSC Board of Directors Tony Henry, 24 April 1976. Staff review for AFSC's Third World Coalition (staff members from other countries and ethnicities) by Tony Henry who visited AFSC's regions to learn how AFSC relates to the Third World Coalition and to Third World people in general.
51. *Ibid.*
52. "Seeing Ourselves," *PYM News*, September 1974.
53. Hamm, *Quakers in America*, 173, described it as "almost entirely African American." Gloria Riley, "Chicago Fellowship of Friends," *Quaker Life*, May 2001; Marlene Morrison Pedigo, *New Church in the City: The Work of the Chicago Fellowship of Friends* (Richmond, IN: Friends United Press, 1988), 78, 82; Marlene Morrison Pedigo, "Marlene and Steve Pedigo: Growing into Urban Ministry," in *Lives that Speak: Stories of Twentieth-Century Quakers*, ed. Marnie Clark (Philadelphia: Friends General Conference, 2004), 63–71, 82; Selleck, *Gentle Invaders*, 221; Gloria Riley,"Chicago Fellowship of Friends," *Quaker Life*, May 2001, Friends United Meeting web site, http://www.fum.orrg/QL/issues/0105/news.htm.

54. Greg Porter, "Branches on the Vine: The Chicago Fellowship of Friends," *Quaker Life*, June 2000, Friends United Meeting web site: http://www.fum.org/QL/issues/0006/Branches%20on%20the%20Vine.htm 12 April 2002.

55. David Finke, "Introducing Chicago area Quakers," Remarks to FWCC Section of the Americas Annual Meeting, Zion, Illinois, 18 March 2000, web site: Street Corner Society, http://www.strecorsoc.org/docs/chicago.html, 10 December 2003; "Missions," *The Iowa Friend* 57, 3 (March 2002), 2; Hamm, *Quakers in America*, 173, described the Fellowship as "almost entirely African American;" Marlene Pedigo, e-mail to authors, 22 January 2007.

56. E-mail announcement from Robert Garris, "Chicago Fellowship of Friends News," Paul Ricketts, e-mail to authors, 22 June 2005.

57. George Selleck, *Quakers in Boston, 1656–1964: three centuries of Friends in Boston and Cambridge* (Cambridge, MA: Friends Meeting at Cambridge, 1976), 171–72.

58. "The Spirit of Pendle Hill as experienced by Dan Wilson During the Fifties and Sixties," 1994 Annual Reports, p, 360. According to the PH history, the center's "social witness side floundered" after this, 31.

59. "Quakers in Rare Drive for Members," *New York Times*, 8 December 1984, 20.

60. Ferguson and Rinard, *As Way Opened*, 165.

61. Minute from "Our Role as Individuals in America's Racial History," Report, *Atlanta Friends Minute on Making a Welcome Spiritual Home for All*, September 1999.

62. Errol T. Elliott, "The Quaker Conscience under Test" (Lecture, Indiana Yearly Meeting, 1968), 15.

63. Thomas E. Jones to AFSC, 1940.

64. Maurer e-mail.

65. Oldham, Keynote NEYM, 10.

66. Vera Green, Report to Friends General Conference Advancement Committee, 1973, 6. The minutes of the conference's Central Committee for 1973 and 1974 have no reference to Green or the study.

67. Minutes, Final Ad Hoc Committee, 18 March 1970.

68. Green report.

69. *Ibid.*, 5

70. *Ibid.*

71. *Ibid.*

72. *Ibid.*, 6

73. "Seeing Ourselves," 2.

74. Deborah Saunders, "My Journey as an African American Quaker" (Lecture, Pendle Hill Monday Night Forum, 18 November 2002).

75. "Seeing Ourselves," 2–3.

76. Saunders, "My Journey."

77. "Seeing Ourselves," 2, 4.

78. Paul Ricketts, "A Call for Racial Justice among Friends," *Friends Journal*, July 1997, 17–18.

79. Friends General Conference, *Seeking Racial & Economic Diversity: Welcoming People of Color* (Philadelphia: Friends General Conference, n.d.), 1.

80. George Sawyer: "The Stranger Among You," *Quaker Life* ser. 10, 10 (October 1969): 9.

81. Dwight Spann-Wilson, *Quaker and Black: Answering the Call of My Twin Roots* (Philadelphia: Friends General Conference, 1980), 11–12.

82. Letter from Wilson, 27 May 2004.

83. "Editorial: Differing Opinions Held by Friends," *Quaker Life*, ser. 11, 1 (January 1970).

84. Claudia Y. Wair, "Different Trees," *Friends Journal*, August 1994, 6, 7.

85. Wair, "Different Trees," 7.

86. Amhara Powell. "Discovering Fellowship Among African American Friends," *Friends Bulletin* 74, 1 (January 2003): 3–4.

87. *Ibid.*

88. Willa Burchett Graves quoted in Kennedy, "Southland College: Society of Friends and Black Education," 64 fn27, Kennedy interview with Willa Burchett Graves, 18 February 1982, W. Helena, Arkansas, 112.

89. Francine E. Cheeks, "My Spiritual Journey," *Friends Journal*, December 2004, 16.

90. Greg Williams, "An Open Letter To New England Yearly Meeting" (Memorandum, 12 August 1983), New England Yearly Meeting Records, RIHS.

91. Mahala Dickerson, "Negro Lawyer in the South," *Friends Intelligencer* 107, 47, 25 November 1950, 687–89, and *ibid.*, 107, 48, 2 December 1950, 707–8, describes her experiences practicing law in Montgomery, AL, with African American clients oppressed by a court and criminal justice system. See also Mahala Dickerson, *Delayed Justice For Sale: An Autobiography* (Anchorage, AK: Al-Acres, 1998). Wayne Carter, e-mails to authors, 8 and 13 February 2004.

92. Willard Heiss, "A Brief Account of Lanthorn Friends Meeting" (Paper, February 1960), Friends Collection, Earlham College Library. Heiss was a founding member of the meeting, according to Thomas Hamm, e-mail to authors, 4 December 2006.

93. Heiss, "Brief Account."

94. *Ibid.*

95. *Ibid.*

96. Dickerson, *Delayed Justice*, 145–46.

97. Carter e-mails note that Ministry and Counsel, the committee that receives applications for membership, could not reach agreement on whether to recommend membership. Another committee said it would not be ready to report until they had a chance to talk with her, but by then Dickerson had decided to stay in Alaska.

98. Dickerson, *Delayed Justice*, 146–47.

99. *Ibid.*, 88, 147.

100. Charlotte Basham, phone conversation with Barbara Mays, 10 November 2008.

101. James A. Fletcher II, "Gathering of Friends of African Descent: 'Coming Home: Where Tradition and Spirit Meet,'" *Friends Journal*, February 1991, 24. See Fellowship of Friends of African Descent web site, http://www.fellowshipof friendsofafricandescent.org/.

102. Ricketts, "A Call for Racial Justice," 17–18.
103. Alberta C. Rice, "Why Do We Need a Worship Group for People of Color?" *Central Philadelphia Monthly Meeting Newsletter*, September 2000, 3–4.
104. Ricketts, "Call for Racial Justice," 17–18.
105. Ayesha Clark-Halkin, "Blacks and Quakers: Have We Anything to Declare?" *Friends Journal*, June 1988, 6–8.
106. Ginny Coover, "Life in the Ghetto: Out of Suburbia into the Ghetto," *Quaker Life*, ser. 8, 12 (December 1968): 385–87; Ginny Coover, interview with authors, 20 May 2004.
107. Oldham, NEYM Keynote, 8.
108. Friends General Conference, *Seeking Racial & Economic Diversity*.
109. Maurer e-mail.
110. Taylor, *Friends and the Racial Crisis*, 35–36.
111. Oldham, NEYM Keynote, 7.
112. Sawyer, "Conference on Race Is Seeking Solutions" *Quaker Life*, May 1965, 150–51. The "Conference" was the 1965 NCFRR at Earlham. In his comments, he cited an example when the clerk of a Social Concerns Committee exhibited that fear when he and his family were moving into a home.

EPILOGUE: **Toward an Inclusive Commuity**

1. Mark D. Morrison-Reed, *Black Pioneers in a White Denomination* (Boston: Skinner House Books, 1984), 205, 162, 210.
2. Jean Harris & Mary Helgesen, "Diversity: A Challenge for Pendle Hill, *Jean's Story,*" *Perspective*, June 1994, 2.
3. Epistle from the Quakers & Racial Justice Conference, October 12–14, 2001, Quakers and Racial Justice Conference at Pendle Hill.
4. Epistle from Friends General Conference, Committee for Ministry on Racism, 27 October 2001. http://www.fgcquaker.org/cmr/epistle.html.
5. Transcript of the Pendle Hill Monday Night Forum 2002–2003, *Racial Justice: Speak Truth to Power, Racial Justice: How Do Friends Get There From Here?*, Emma Lapsansky, 21 October 2002.
6. Melanie Sax, *Madison Friends Meeting Newsletter*.
7. Interview with Anita Mendes-Lopes by Marsha Holliday, "Nurturing People of Color," *FGConnections* (Winter 1999), 2.
8. Allan G. Johnson, *The Forest and the Trees: Sociology as Life, Practice and Promise*, Temple University Press, Philadelphia (1997), 16.
9. Barrington Dunbar, "Black Power's Challenge to Quaker Power" *Friends Journal*, 15 September 1968, 460.

Glossary

advices: Wisdom culled from epistles and minutes; advices were written and circulated by yearly meetings to their subordinate meetings for edification and encouragement. Traditionally the advices are companions to the queries, both seeking to build up the church in faithful living consistent with Friends testimonies.

Conservative Friends: A small branch of Friends in North America currently organized into three yearly meetings. Today the term tends to be used to describe Friends who are traditional in worship and methods of meeting activities, with orthodox doctrine.

Disciplines: Compilations of advices, queries, and statements of faith and experience, as well as guidance in conducting church business; these are gathered by each yearly meeting into a book of Discipline. More recently this is called a book of Faith and Practice, offering and containing descriptions of testimonies, individual statements of faith, queries, and procedures for marriages, funerals, and meeting for business.

Disownment: A meeting's action making clear that an individual's behavior does not uphold Friends witness in some regard and that the individual is no longer "owned" as a member. Such a person might still worship with Friends but traditionally could not attend meetings for church governance. A disowned Friend could appeal the monthly meeting's decision to the quarterly meeting. He or she would be welcomed back into the meeting upon acknowledging and condemning the behavior to the satisfaction of the group.

Epistle: A letter, such as the epistles from Paul and others in the New Testament, from an individual Friend or body of Friends to one or more other groups of Friends. Traditionally, these letters contained loving greetings, encouragement, advice, or admonitions, and often were circulated widely among Friends. Important material was excerpted as advices for inclusion in what became books of discipline.

George Fox: Fox (1624–1691) traveled across England during the Reformation preaching the immanent presence of Christ and gathering like-minded people into what became the Religious Society of Friends.

'guarded' education: The form of schooling that Friends thought would benefit their children and aid them in becoming useful adult Friends; Friends tried to separate their children from non-Quakers, inculcate Quaker behaviors, and stress science and "useful" things rather than classical education.

Hicksite-Orthodox separation: A schism among Friends in North America in 1827–28. The Orthodox branch hoped to move Friends towards a more orthodox Protestant, Bible-based theology. The Hicksites (a name chosen pejoratively by the Orthodox) resisted what they saw as an effort to concentrate power in the hands of Orthodox elders. Most monthly, quarterly, and yearly meetings split, with considerable acrimony and pain.

inner voice: The Divine Presence within the human heart which, if attended to, gives comfort, guidance, and strength. Friends experience of this is referred to with many images, such as the Inward Light, Light Within, Inward Christ, or Holy Spirit.

labouring among Friends: The work of a few Friends, often appointed by their meeting, with other Friends, in an effort to bring them to a new understanding or changed behavior. Prayer, listening, persuasion, discussion, example, and repeated visits would probably be used for this purpose.

Leading: An inner conviction to carry out a specific act (large or small) under a sense of divine guidance. A Friend may submit a larger leading to the meeting for testing by corporate discernment.

Light of God: Reference, The Gosepl of John in the Christian Bible, 1:1–9; see "inner voice."

meeting of ministers and elders: A regular event (gatherings of ministers and elders for the purpose of worship, meeting business, and fellowship), and the group of people named to participate in such gatherings.

Minute: Statement of an item of business approved by those in attendance at a meeting. In Friends meetings for business (meetings for church governance that traditionally were called meetings for discipline) the clerk (presiding officer) lays an agenda item before the body. After it is prayerfully considered, if there is unity (see "sense of the meeting") the clerk records it. This is read back to the group and edited until it meets Friends' approval. Then the clerk brings up the next item. The entire document is referred to as the "minutes"; each item that the clerk writes is an individual minute.

monthly meeting or "meeting": An event, an organizational structure, and also a group of people. Friends gathered once a month at monthly meeting to discern matters of local church discipline or governance. Today it is often called meeting for business or monthly meeting for worship with attention to business. The term "meeting" by itself could mean a number of things, depending on context. It could be the meeting for worship, held once or twice a week; or the group of people who were members of the local congregation; or the local organization (either a preparative, monthly, indulged, or some other type depending on its size, age, and degree of responsibility).

plain dress: Traditionally Friends wore distinctive clothing that tended to be a generation behind the fashion of the rest of the populace, without the gaudy colors, frills, laces, and extremes of fashion. Friends could easily be identified by their dress. This began to phase out in the last third of the nineteenth century and was pretty well extinct by the middle of the twentieth. Today a few (often younger) Friends have adopted Mennonite or Amish dress.

plain speech: Simplicity and integrity were at the core the plain speech of early Friends. As part of their witness to simplicity, Friends used the second person singular to everyone ("thee" and "thou" rather than the plural "you" to a single individual). They also eschewed use of pagan names for days of the week and months, numbering them, instead (e.g., First Day for Sunday, First Month for January).

quarterly meeting: Term used for an event, organizational structure, and/or the people who attend the same. Quarterly meetings were made up of a number of monthly meetings in a geographical area, that met four times a year to discuss issues of concern to the larger body. Quarterly meetings receive monthly meeting responses to the queries, adjudicate occasional disputes on appeal, and provide an opportunity for fellowship and worship. Quarterly meetings also served as intermediaries between the yearly and monthly meetings, exchanging messages, information, and decisions.

Queries: Questions to be responded to by individuals and meetings, generally consisting of open-ended explorations of individual or corporate Friends' faith and practice. Queries began as an effort to get specific information about practices around slave-holding and other spiritual and community issues at the end of the eighteenth century. Not long into the nineteenth century they had become codified, with responses to a set of queries expected to be given by each monthly meeting regularly to the respective quarterly meeting; the quarterly meeting then forwarded a summary of monthly meeting responses to the yearly meeting. Today's practice around queries varies widely, but they are often open-ended questions through which to explore individual and corporate faithfulness.

Quietism: As embraced by Friends for much of the eighteenth century, it supported the belief that thoughts and emotions are unreliable guides to God's will, and that one must be utterly still inwardly in order to prepare to receive Divine guidance. When carried to an extreme, the practice inhibited ministry.

Religious Society of Friends: A formal name of the Quaker movement, which began in mid-seventeenth-century England. This title is used especially in Europe and North America today; also known (at first pejoratively) as Quakers or (more recently in some areas) as the Friends Church.

right action: The sense that an activity is in accord with Divine will. Also right order, the procedures that have been found by experience to best facilitate corporate activities as Friends seek to find and carry out God's will.

sense of the meeting: Rather than vote in their meetings for business (church governance), Friends seek to come into unity on an understanding of God's will for the group at that time on the issue being addressed. When the members present discern clearness on God's will for that time and issue, the decision is minuted and approved.

testimonies: Originally Friends understood themselves to be a people called by God to demonstrate what the "Kingdom of God" is like, to live under the direct leadership of Christ, known inwardly. Early testimonies grew out of the Christian scripture, much of which Friends knew by memory—and what Friends felt as the direct experience of Christ Within. Specific testimonies (peace, simplicity, integrity, equality, community) are intended to witness to Friends understanding of God's intention.

traveling minute: A minute approved by the meeting (monthly, quarterly, and/or yearly) that was copied and signed and given to a Friend who intended to travel in the ministry among other Friends. Such minutes indicated approval of the ministry of the bearer, that she or he was in good standing, and that the meeting gave its approval to the journey. Usually the clerk or a member of each meeting being visited would endorse the minute, expressing some sense of how the traveler's ministry had been received. The process provided accountability and a sense of community.

visiting committees: Particularly in the eighteenth and nineteenth centuries, monthly, quarterly, or yearly meetings appointed small committees to visit families or subordinate meetings to encourage and admonish. At times of stress these were used to try to see that Friends principles (as defined by the larger body) were being upheld.

yearly meeting: Like "meeting," the term refers to an event, in this case one held annually, and an organization or institution, in this case of Friends meetings in a geographical area. It also refers those people who are members of the body. Traditionally matters of behavior or practice would work their way up from the local to the quarterly meeting and then to the yearly meeting for final decision, at which point the decision would be sent back out to all the subordinate meetings. The yearly meeting was also the highest body to which an individual could appeal disownment. Today yearly meetings differ widely in their governing role over local meetings.

Selected Bibliography

We include here books or sections of books by and/or about Quakers that have been useful in writing this book. See www.fitforfreedom.org for a full bibliography including magazine and journal articles, lectures, unpublished papers, and general works.

Anscombe, Francis Charles. *I Have Called You Friends: The Story of Quakerism in North Carolina.* Boston: Christopher Publishing House, 1959.

Bacon, Margaret Hope. *Abby Hopper Gibbons: Prison Reformer and Social Activist.* New York: State of University of New York Press, 2000.

Bacon, Margaret Hope. *Central Philadelphia Monthly Meeting of Friends: In the Shadow of William Penn.* Philadelphia: Central Philadelphia Monthly Meeting, 2001.

Bacon, Margaret Hope. *I Speak for My Slave Sister: The Life of Abby Kelley Foster.* New York: Crowell, 1974.

Bacon, Margaret Hope. *History of the Pennsylvania Society for Promoting the Abolition of Slavery; the Relief of Negroes Unlawfully held in Bondage; and for Improving the Condition of the African Race.* Philadelphia: Pennsylvania Abolition Society, 1959.

Bacon, Margaret Hope. *Lamb's Warrior: The Life of Isaac T. Hopper.* New York: Thomas Y. Crowell Company, 1970.

Bacon, Margaret Hope. *Let This Life Speak: The Legacy of Henry Joel Cadbury.* Philadelphia: University of Pennsylvania Press, 1987.

Bacon, Margaret Hope. *Mothers of Feminism: The Story of Quaker Women in America.* Philadelphia, PA: Friends General Conference, 1986.

Bacon, Margaret Hope. *The Quiet Rebels: The Story of Quakers in America.* New York: Basic Books, Inc., 1969.

Bacon, Margaret Hope. *Sarah Mapps Douglass: Faithful Attender of Quaker Meetings, View from the Back Bench.* Philadelphia, PA: Quaker Press of Friends General Conference, 2003.

Bacon, Margaret Hope. *Valiant Friend: The Life of Lucretia Mott*. Philadelphia, PA: Friends General Conference, 2nd edition, 1999.

Barbour, Hugh. *Slavery and Theology: Writings of Seven Quaker Reformers 1800-1970*. Dublin, IN: Prinit Press, 1985. [sic: Prinit]

Barbour, Hugh, Christopher Densmore, Elizabeth Moger, Nancy Sorel, Alson Van Wager and Arthur Worrall. *Quaker Crosscurrents: Three Hundred Years of Friends in the New York Yearly Meetings*. Syracuse: Syracuse University Press, 1995.

Barbour, Hugh and J. William Frost. *The Quakers*. Richmond: Friends United Press, 1994.

Bassett, William. in *Society of Friends in the United States: Their View of the Anti-Slavery Question, and Treatment of the People of Colour*. 3 August 1839, Darlington, Eng: J. Wilson, 1840.

Beebe, Ralph. *A Garden of the Lord: A History of Oregon Yearly Meeting of the Friends Church*. Newberg, OR: The Barclay Press, c. 1968.

Beebe, Ralph. *A Heritage to Honor, A Future to Fulfill: George Fox College. 1891-1991*, Newberg, OR: The Barclay Press, c. 1968.

Benjamin, Philip S. *The Philadelphia Quakers in the Industrial Age: 1865-1920*. Ann Arbor, Michigan: University of Michigan Press, 1971.

Benezet, Anthony. *Observations on Inslaving, Importing and Purchasing of Negroes*. Germantown, PA: Christopher Sower, 1760.

Benezet, Anthony. *Serious considerations on several important subjects*. Philadelphia: Joseph Cruikshank, 1778.

Berquist, Robert, David Rhodes and Carolyn Smith Treadway. *Scattergood Friends School, 1890-1990*. West Branch, IA: Scattergood Friends School, 1990.

Boen, William. *Anecdotes and Memoirs of William Boen, a Coloured Man, Who Lived and Died near Mount Holly, New Jersey, To Which Is Added, The Testimony of Friends of Mount Holly Monthly Meeting Concerning Him*. Philadelphia: John Richards, 1834.

Brayton, Patience. *A Short Account of the Life and Religious Labours of Patience Brayton, Late of Swansey in the State of Massachusetts: Mostly Selected from her own Minutes*. New Bedford, MA: A. Shearman, 1801.

(A) brief sketch of schools for black people and their descendants established by the Religious Society of Friends, in 1770. Philadelphia: Friends Book Store, 1867.

Breault, Judith Colucci. *The World of Emily Holland: Odyssey of a Humanitarian*. Millbrae, CA: Les Femmes Publications, 1976.

Brinton, Howard. *Meeting House & Farm House*. Wallingford, PA: Pendle Hill Pamphlet # 185, 1972.

Brinton, Howard. *Quaker Education in Theory and Practice*. Wallingford, PA: Pendle Hill, Pamphlet 39, 1940.

Brown, Charles, III. *Pray and Pay Attention, or how to enjoy meeting for business!* Orlando, FL: Southeastern Yearly Meeting of the Religious Society of Friends, 1991.

Brown, Miriam Jones. *Friends School, Haverford, 1885-1985*. Exton, PA: Schiffer Publications, c. 1985.

Candler John. *A Friendly Mission: Letters from Americas, 1853-1854*. Indianapolis: Indiana Historical Society, 1951.

Carroll, Kenneth. *Three Hundred Years and More of Third Haven Quakerism*. Easton, MD: Queen Anne Press, 1984.

Ceplair, Larry, ed. *The Public Years of Sarah & Angelina Grimké*. New York: Columbia University Press, c. 1989.

Chace, Elizabeth Buffum. "My Anti-Slavery Reminiscences" (1891) in *Two Quaker Sisters from the Original Diaries of Elizabeth Buffum Chace and Lucy Buffum Lovell*. New York: Liveright Publishing Corp., 1937.

John Churchman. *An Account of the Gospel Labours and Christian Experiences of a Faithful Minister of Christ, John Churchman*. Philadelphia: Joseph Cruikshank, 1779.

Coffin, Elijah. *Slavery and Abolition*. London: F. Cass, 1980.

Comstock, Elizabeth. *Life and letters of Elizabeth L. Comstock*. Philadelphia: J.C. Winston, 1895.

Cooper, Charles William. *Whittier: independent college in California, founded by Quakers, 1877*. Los Angeles: Ward Ritchie Press, 1967.

Coppin, Fanny Jackson. "Reminiscences" in *Charline Howard Conyers, A Living Legend: the history of Cheyney University, 1837-1905*. Ann Arbor, Michigan University, 1975.

Cox, John, Jr. *Quakerism in the City of New York*. New York: (Privately printed), 1930.

Curtis, Anna, ed. *The Quakers Take Stock.* New York: Island Workshop Press, 1944.

D'Emilio, John. *The Lost Prophet: the life and times of Bayard Rustin.* New York: Free Press, c. 2003.

Dickerson, Mahala. *Delayed Justice For Sale: An Autobiography.* Anchorage, AK: Al-Acres, 1998.

Diment, Veldon. *The first fifty years: a record of the first fifty years in the life of Pacific College.* Newberg, OR: by authority of the Board of Managers, 1941.

Dorland, Arthur. *The Quakers in Canada: A History.* Toronto: The Ryerson Press, 1968.

Drake, Thomas. *Quakers and Slavery in America.* New Haven, CT: Yale University Press, 1950; reprinted with permission by Peter Smith, Gloucester, MA, 1965.

Dunlap, William Cook. *Quaker Education in Baltimore and Virginia Yearly Meetings with an Account of Certain Meetings of Delaware and the Eastern Shore Affiliated with Philadelphia.* Lancaster, PA: Science Press Printing, 1936.

Edgerton, Walter. *A History of the Separation of Indiana Yearly Meeting.* Cincinnati: A. Pugh, 1856.

Ellis, Ellwood. *Early Friends in Grant County, Indiana (1825–1913).* Willard Heiss, ed. Indianapolis: Indiana Quaker Records, 1961.

Elliott, Errol. *Quakers on the American Frontier: A History of the Westward Migrations, Settlements, and Developments of Friends on the American Continent.* Richmond, IN: Friends United Press, 1969.

Esslinger, Dean. *Friends for Two Hundred Years: A History of Baltimore's Oldest School.* Baltimore: Friends School in cooperation with Museum and Library of Maryland History, Maryland Historical Society, 1983.

Fager, Charles. *A Man Who Made A Difference: The Life of David H. Scull.* McLean, VA: Langley Hill Friends Meeting, 1985.

Farraday, Clayton L. *Friends Central School, 1845–1984.* Philadelphia: Friends' Central School, 1984.

FCNL. *The Friends Committee on National Legislation Story: Fifteen Years of Quaker Witness.* Washington: FCNL, 1958.

Ferguson, Janet Boyte, and Janet Adams Rinard. *As Way Opened, A History of Atlanta Friends Meeting, 1943–1997.* Atlanta, GA: Atlanta Friends Meeting, c. 1999.

James Fletcher and Carleton Mabee, eds. *A Quaker Speaks From the Black Experience: the life and selected writings of Barrington Dunbar.* New York: New York Yearly Meeting, 1979.

Forbush, Bliss. *A History of Baltimore Yearly Meeting of Friends: Three Hundred Years of Quakerism in Maryland, Virginia, the District of Columbia, and Central Pennsylvania.* Sandy Spring, MD: Baltimore Yearly Meeting of Friends, 1972.

Forbush, Bliss. *Moses Sheppard, Quaker Philanthropist of Baltimore.* Philadelphia, PA: Lippincott Company, 1968.

Ford, Daryl, ed. *Schooled in Diversity: Action Research: Student and African-American Alumni Collaboration for School Change.* Philadelphia: Friends Council on Education, 2005–2006.

Frost, J. William. *The Quaker Origins of Anti-Slavery.* Norwood, PA: Norwood Editions, 1980.

Frost, J. William, and John M. Moore, eds. *Seeking the Light: Essays in Quaker History.* Wallingford, PA.: Pendle Hill Publications, 1986.

Gara, Larry. *The Liberty Line: The Legend of the Underground Railroad.* Lexington, KY: University Press of Kentucky, 1961.

Gerow (also Gerau), Daniel. *Some Thoughts on Slavery, Addressed to the Professors of Christianity, and more Particularly to Those of the Society of Friends.* New York, Baker & Crane, 1844.

Grimké, Angelina. *Appeal to the Christian Women of the South.* New York: Arno Press, 1969.

Grundy, Martha. *Resistance and Obedience to God: Memoirs of David Ferris (1707–1779).* Philadelphia: Friends General Conference, 2001.

Hamm, Thomas. *Earlham College: a history, 1847–1997.* Bloomington: Indiana University Press, c. 1997.

Hamm, Thomas. *The Quakers in America.* New York: Columbia University Press, 2003.

Hamm, Thomas. *The Transformation of American Quakerism: Orthodox Friends, 1800–1907.* Bloomington: Indiana University Press, 1988.

Harrison, Eliza Cope, ed. *For Emancipation and Education: Some Black and Quaker Efforts, 1680–1900.* Philadelphia, PA: Awbury Arboretum Association, 1997.

Hazelton, Robert Morton. *Let Freedom Ring! A Biography of Moses Brown.* Jackson Heights, New York: New Voices Publishing, 1957.

Heiss, Willard. *Early Friends in Grant County, Indiana (1825–1913).* Ellwood O. Ellis, ed. Indianapolis: Indiana Quaker Records, 1961.

Henshaw, Nathan, ed. "Early Settlement of Friends in Kansas," in *The Newman Collection on Kansas Friends.* Earlham, IN: Earlham School of Religion, 1966.

Hickey, Damon. *Sojourners No More: The Quakers in the New South, 1865–1920.* Greensboro, NC: North Carolina Friends Historical Society, North Carolina Yearly Meeting of Friends, 1997.

Hilty, Hiram. *By Land and By Sea: Quakers Confront Slavery and Its Aftermath in North Carolina.* Greensboro, NC: North Carolina Friends Historical Society and North Carolina Yearly Meeting, 1984.

Hilty, Hiram. *New Garden Friends Meeting, The Christian People Called Quakers.* NC Friends Historical Society, NCYM, New Garden Meeting, 1983.

Hilty, Hiram. *Toward Freedom for All: NC Quakers and Slavery.* Richmond, IN: Friends United Press, 1993.

Hinshaw, Seth. *The Carolina Quaker Experience.* Greensboro. N.C: North Carolina Friends Historical Society, 1984.

Hinshaw, Seth, and Mary Edith Hinshaw. *Carolina Quakers: Our Heritage, Our Hope.* Greensboro, NC: North Carolina Yearly Meeting, c. 1972.

Holland, Rupert Sargent, ed. *Letters and Diary of Laura M. Towne.* New York, Negro Universities Press, 1969.

Hull, Henry. *Memoir of the Life and Religious Labours of Henry Hull.* Philadelphia: Friends' Book Store, 1873. Also available on www.qhpress.org.

Ingle, H. Larry. *Quakers in Conflict: The Hicksite Reformation.* Wallingford, Pennsylvania: Pendle Hill Publications, 1998.

Ives, Kenneth. *Black Quakers: Brief Biographies.* Chicago: Progresive Publishr, 1995. [sic]

Jacoway, Elizabeth. *Yankee Missionaries in the South: The Penn School Experiment.* Baton Rouge: Louisiana State University Press, c. 1980.

James, Sydney. *A People Among Peoples: Quaker Benevolence in Eighteenth-Century America.* Cambridge: Harvard University Press, 1963.

Joliffe, Kyle. *Seeking the Blessed Community: A history of Canadian Young Friends, 1875–1996.* Guelph, Ont: K. Jolliffe, production by TASC, c. 1997.

Jonas, Gerald. *On Doing Good.* New York: Scribner's, 1971.

Jones, Louis Thomas. *The Quakers of Iowa.* Iowa City: The State Historical Society of Iowa, 1914.

Jones, R. Bruce. *The History of Green Street Monthly Meeting of Friends of Philadelphia, and of the Meetings under Its Care at Fair Hill, Frankford, and Girard Avenue.* Philadelphia: Green Street Meeting, 1988.

Jones, Rebecca. *Memorial of Rebecca Jones, 1739–1817.* Compiled by William J. Allinson. Philadelphia: Longstreth, c. 1849.

Jones, Rufus. *The Later Periods of Quakerism.* London: Macmillan and Company, 1921.

Jones, Rufus. *The Quakers in the American Colonies.* New York: Russell and Russell, 1962.

Kannerstein, Gregory, ed. *The Spirit and the Intellect: Haverford College, 1833–1983.* Haverford, PA: Haverford College, 1983.

Kashatus, William. *A Virtuous Education: Penn's Vision for Philadelphia Schools.* Wallingford, PA: Pendle Hill, 1997.

Kashatus, William. *Just Over the Line: Chester Country and the Underground Railroad.* University Park: Pennsylvania State University Press, 2002.

Kelly, J. Reaney. *Quakers in the Founding of Anne Arundel County, Maryland.* Baltimore: The Maryland Historical Society, 1963.

Kilpack, Ruth, ed. *Five Years of Friendly Agitation: Combating Racism in Delaware County: Selections from 'The Friendly Agitator,' 1969–1974.* Media, PA: Friends Suburban Project, 1975.

Klain, Zora, ed. *Educational Activities of New England Quakers: A Source Book.* Philadelphia: Westbrook Publishing Company, 1928.

Kohrman, Allan. *New England Yearly Meeting of Friends, 1994–1995.* Worcester, MA: New England Yearly Meeting, 1995.

Larson, Rebecca. *Daughters of Light: Quaker Women Preaching and Prophesying in the Colonies and Abroad, 1700–1775.* Chapel Hill, NC: The University of North Carolina Press, 1999.

Lerner, Gerda. *The Grimké Sisters of South Carolina: Pioneers in Women's Rights and Abolition.* Chapel Hill: University of North Carolina Press, c. 2004.

Letchworth, Rachel. *Yesterday, Today—and Tomorrow? Friends Council on Education, 1931-1981.* Philadelphia: Friends Council on Education, 1981.

Levine, Daniel. *Bayard Rustin and the Civil Rights Movement.* New Brunswick, NJ: Rutgers University Press, 2000.

Lundy, Benjamin. *The Life Travels and Opinions of Benjamin Lundy.* Thomas Earle, ed. New York: Augustus M. Kelley, 1971

Mabee, Carleton. *Black Freedom: The Nonviolent Abolitionists From 1830 Through The Civil War.* London: The Macmillan Company, 1970.

MacKaye, William, and Mary Anne MacKaye. *Mr. Sidwell's School: A Centennial History, 1883-1983.* Washington, DC: Sidwell Friends School, 1983.

Macpherson, Pat, Irene McHenry, and Sarah Sweeney-Denham, eds. *Schooled in Diversity: Readings on Racial Diversity in Friends Schools.* Philadelphia: Friends Council on Education, 2001.

Mallonee, Barbara, Jane Bonny, and Nicholas Fessenden. *Minute by Minute: A History of the Baltimore Monthly Meetings of Friends; Homewood and Stony Run.* Baltimore, MD: Baltimore Monthly Meetings of Friends.

Maris, Robert H. "Friends in Philanthropy," in *Friends in Wilmington, 1738-1938.* Wilmington, DE: C. L. Story Company, 1938.

Marietta, Jack D. *The Reformation of American Quakerism, 1748-1783.* Philadelphia: University of Pennsylvania Press, 1984.

Mather, Eleanore Price. *Pendle Hill: A Quaker Experiment in Education and Community.* Wallingford, PA: Pendle Hill Publications, 1980.

McGowan, James A. *Station Master on the Underground Railroad: The Life and Letters of Thomas Garrett.* Jefferson, NC: McFarland and Co., 2005.

McDaniel, Ethel. *Contribution of the Society of Friends to Education in Indiana 1939.* Indianapolis: Indiana Historical Society, 1939.

McKiever, Charles Fitzgerald. *Slavery and the Emigration of North Carolina Friends.* Murfreesboro, NC: Johnson Publishing Company, 1970.

Miller, Lawrence McK. *Witness for Humanity: A Biography of Clarence E. Pickett.* Wallingford, PA: Pendle Hill, 1999.

Michener, Ezra. *A Retrospect of Early Quakerism, Being Extracts from the Records of Philadelphia Yearly Meeting and the Meetings Composing It.* Philadelphia: T. Ellwood Zell, 1860, reprinted by Cool Spring Publishing Co., Washington, D.C., 1991.

Moore, J. Floyd. *Friends in the Carolinas.* Greensboro: N.C. Friends Historical Society, North Carolina of Yearly Meeting of Friends, 1997.

Moore, John M., ed. *Friends in the Delaware Valley: Philadelphia Yearly Meeting, 1681-1981.* Haverford, PA: Friends Historical Association, 1981.

Mordell, Albert. *Quaker Militant: John Greenleaf Whittier.* Boston and NY: Houghton Mifflin, 1933.

Morse, Kenneth S.P. *Baltimore Yearly Meeting, 1672-1830, Gleanings from the records of Friends meetings in Maryland and the adjacent parts of Virginia.* N.p., 1961.

Mullett, Michael, ed. *New Light on George Fox, 1624-1691: A Collection of Essays.* York, England: The Ebor Press, 1991.

Nash, Gary and Jean Soderlund. *Freedom by Degrees: Emancipation in Pennsylvania and its Aftermath.* New York: Oxford University Press, 1991.

Needles, Edward. *Pennsylvania Society for Promoting the Abolition of Slavery, An historical memoir of the Pennsylvania Society for Promoting the Abolition of Slavery, the relief of free negroes unlawfully held in bondage, and for improving the condition of the African race.* Philadelphia: Merrihew and Thompson, 1848.

New York Yearly Meeting (Orthodox). "Address of the Yearly Meeting of the Religious Society of Friends, to the professors of Christianity in the United States." New York: R. Craighead, 1852.

Nelson, Jacquelyn S. *Indiana Quakers Confront the Civil War.* Indianapolis, IN: Indiana Historical Society, 1991.

Norris, J. Saurin. *The Early Friends (Or Quakers) in Maryland.* Baltimore, MD: Printed for the Maryland Historical Society by John D. Toy, 1862.

Nuermberger, Ruth. *The Free Produce Movement: A Quaker Protest Against Slavery.* Durham, N.C: Duke University Press, 1942.

Patterson, Mary. "Martha Schofield," in *Quaker Torch Bearers.* Philadelphia: Friends General Conference, 1943.

Pedigo, Marlene Morrison. *New Church in the City: The Work of the Chicago Fellowship of Friends.* Richmond, IN: Friends United Press, 1988.

Penn, William. *Works*. Richard Dunn and Mary Maples Dunn, eds. I: 856. Philadelphia: University of Pennsylvania Press, 1981.

Perkins, Linda. *Fanny Jackson Coppin and the Institute of Colored Youth, 1865–1902*. New York: Garland Publishing, Inc., 1987.

Perry, Mark. *Lift Up Thy Voice: The Grimké's Journey from Slaveholders to Civil Rights Leaders*. New York: Penguin, 2001.

Pickett, Clarence. *For More than Bread: An autobiographical account of twenty-two years' work with the American Friends Service Committee*. Boston: Little, Brown and Co., 1953.

Powell, Aaron. *Personal Reminiscences of the Anti-Slavery and Other Reforms and Reformers*. Westport, CT: Negro Universities Press, 1970, reprinted from 1899 publication by the Caulon Press in New York.

Quaker Torch Bearers. Philadelphia: Friends General Conference, 1943.

Rappleye, Charles. *Sons of Providence: The Brown Brothers, the Slave Trade, and the American Revolution*. New York: Simon and Schuster, 2006.

Reagan, William. *A Venture in Quaker Education at Oakwood School*. Poughkeepsie, NY: Oakwood School, 1968.

Religious Education Committee of Friends General Conference, Marnie Clark, ed. *Lives That Speak: Stories of Twentieth-Century Quakers*. Philadelphia: Quaker Press of Friends General Conference, 2004.

Salitan, Lucille and Eve Perera, eds. *Virtuous Lives: Four Quaker Sisters Remember Family Life, Abolitionism, and Women's Suffrage*. New York: Continuum, 1994.

Selleck, Linda. *Gentle Invaders: Quaker Women Educators and Racial Issues During the Civil War and Reconstruction*. Richmond, IN: Friends United Press, 1995.

Selleck, George. *Quakers In Boston, 1656–1964: Three Centuries Of Friends In Boston And Cambridge*. Cambridge, MA: Friends Meeting at Cambridge, 1976.

Shoemaker, John S. *Life of Elisha Tyson: The Philanthropist, By a Citizen of Baltimore*. Baltimore, MD: B Lundy, 1825.

Smedley, Katherine. *Martha Schofield and the Re-Education of the South, 1839–1916*. New York: Edwin Mellen Press, 1987.

Smedley, Robert C. *History of the Underground Railroad in Chester and the neighboring Counties of Pennsylvania.* Lancaster, PA: Office of the Journal, 1883.

D. Neil Snarr and associates. *Claiming our past: Quakers in Southwest Ohio and Eastern Tennessee.* Sabina, OH: Gaskins Printing, 1992.

Snyder, Edward F., Wilmer A. Cooper, Stephen L. Klineberg, Joseph Volk and Don Reeves. Tom Mullen, ed. *Fifty Years of Friendly Persuasion.* Richmond, IN: Friends United Press, c1994.

Soderlund, Jean. Quakers and Slavery: A Divided Spirit. Princeton, N.J.: Princeton University Press, c. 1985.

Spann-Wilson, Dwight (also Wilson, Dwight). *Quaker and Black: Answering the Call of My Twin Roots.* Philadelphia: Friends General Conference, 1980.

Sterling, Dorothy. *Ahead of Her Time: Abby Kelley and the Politics of Anti-Slavery.* New York: W.W. Norton, 1991.

Stoesen, Alexander. *Guilford College: On the Strength of 150 Years.* Greensboro, N.C.: Board of Trustees, Guilford College, 1987.

Strane, Susan. *A Whole-Souled Woman: Prudence Crandall and the Education of Black Women.* New York: W.W. Norton, 1990.

Sturge, Joseph. *A Visit to the United States in 1841.* Special Collections, SC. Boston: Dexter S. King, 1842. Also on Explorian web site: http://explorian .net/index.html1106-1199.

Swayne, Kingdon. *George School: the history of a Quaker community.* Philadelphia: Philadelphia Yearly Meeting, c. 1992.

Taber, William, Jr. *The Eye of Faith: A History of Ohio Yearly Meeting Conservative.* Barnesville, Ohio: Representative Meeting of Ohio Yearly Meeting, Religious Society of Friends, c. 1985.

Tallack, William. *Friendly Sketches in America.* London: A.W. Bennett, 1861.

Taylor, Richard K. *Friends and the Racial Crisis.* Wallingford, PA: Pendle Hill Publications, 1970.

Thomas, Anna Braithwaite. *The Story of Baltimore Yearly Meeting from 1672 to 1938.* Baltimore: The Weant Press, Inc., c. 1938.

Thomas, Lamont. *Paul Cuffe: Black Entrepreneur and Pan-Africanist.* Urbana and Chicago: University of Illinois Press, 1988.

Tolles, Frederick B. *Quakers and the Atlantic Culture*. New York: Macmillan Company, 1960.

Tolles, Frederick B. *Meeting House and Counting House: The Quaker Merchants of Colonial Philadelphia, 1682-1763*. New York: W. W. Norton and Company, 1948.

Towne, Laura Matilda. *Letters and Diary of Laura M. Towne, Written from the Sea Islands of South Carolina, 1862-1901*. New York: Negro Universities Press, 1969.

Vaux, Roberts [sic Roberts]. *Memoirs of the Life of Anthony Benezet*. Philadelphia: James P. Parke, 1817.

Vining, Elizabeth Gray. *The Virginia Exiles*. New York: Lippincott Company, 1955.

Walton, Jesse. *From the Auction Block of Slavery to the Rostrum of Quaker Ministry: The Life of William Allan, The Negro Missionary Preacher of the Society of Friends*. Aurora, Ont.: J. M. Walton, 1938.

Walton, Richard. *Swarthmore College: An Informal History*. Swarthmore, PA: Swarthmore College, c. 1986.

Warner, Stafford Allen. *Yardley Warner: The Freedman's Friend*. Didcot, Eng: Wessex Press, 1957.

Weeks, Stephen B. *Southern Quakers and Slavery*. Baltimore: John Hopkins University Press, 1957.

Whittier, John Greenleaf. "Justice and Expediency," in *The Works of John Greenleaf Whittier*. Boston and New York: Houghton, Mifflin, 1892.

Wiggins, Rosalind, ed. *Captain Paul Cuffe's Logs and Letters, 1808-1917: A Black Quaker's 'Voice from within the Veil.'* Washington, D.C.: Howard University Press, 1996.

Wilmington Yearly Meeting of the Religious Society of Friends. *Partners in education: Wilmington College and Wilmington Yearly Meeting of Friends*. Wilmington, OH: Wilmington Yearly Meeting, 1992.

Wilson, E. Raymond. *Uphill for Peace: Quaker impact on Congress*. Richmond, IN: Friends United Press, 1975.

Woolman, John. *Some Considerations on the Keeping of Negroes*. Northampton, MA: Gehenna Press, 1754.

Woolman, John. *Walking Humbly with God.* Nashville: Upper Room Books, 2000.

Worrall, Arthur J. *Quakers in the Colonial Northeast.* Hanover, N.H.: University Press of New England, 1980.

Worrall, Jay, Jr. *The Friendly Virginians: America's First Quakers.* Athens, GA: Iberian, c. 1994.

Wyman, Lillie Buffum Chace and Arthur Crawford Wyman. *Elizabeth Buffum Chace, 1806-1899, Her Life and Its Environment.* Boston: W.B. Clarke Co., 1914.

Yannessa, Mary Ann. *Levi Coffin, Quaker: Breaking the Bonds of Slavery in Ohio and Indiana.* Richmond, IN: Friends United Press, 2001.

Contributing Historians

The authors are grateful for the years of research, study, analysis, and writing represented by the African American and Quaker historians and authors below (not mutually exclusive), whose body of work has been invaluable to this project.

African American

Charles Blockson
Martin Delany
Mahala Dickerson
W.E.B. DuBois
John Hope Franklin
Lorenzo Greene
Vincent Harding
A. Leon Higginbotham
Darlene Hine
James Oliver Horton
Lois Horton
Emma Lapsansky
Nell Irvin Painter
Linda Marie Perkins
Benjamin Quarles
William Still
Carter Woodson

Quakers

Francis Anscombe
Margaret Hope Bacon
Hugh Barbour
Howard Brinton
Edwin Bronner
Henry Cadbury
Kenneth Carroll
Elizabeth Cazden
John Cox , Jr.
Christopher Densmore
Thomas Drake
Walter Edgerton
Errol Elliott
Charles Fager
Bliss Forbush
J. William Frost
Larry Gara
Martha Paxson Grundy
Thomas Hamm
Willard Heiss
Damon Hickey

Hiram Hilty
Mary Edith Hinshaw
Seth Hinshaw
H. Larry Ingle
Kenneth Ives
Sydney James
Kyle Jolliffe
William Kashatus
Emma Lapsansky
Jack Marietta
Ezra Michener
Elizabeth Moger
J. Floyd Moore
John Moore
John Oliver
Linda Selleck
Frederick Tolles
Rosalind Wiggins
Arthur Worrall
Jay Worrall

Index

INDEX

INDEX

Brown, Clark K., III, 312

Brown, Geneva, 238

Brown, John, 49, 141–43, 142, 451n4

Brown, Morris, 200

Brown, Moses: African Union and, 120–21; enslaved people and, 55, 416n207; on enslavement, 3; manumissions and, 39–40; petitions, 49; prohibition on importation of enslaved people, 47; Providence Society for the Abolition of the Slave Trade, 417n11; on restitution, 113; school creation and, 133, 416n208; slave trade involvement, 6

Brown, Obadiah, 55, 416n207

Brown, Oliver, 240–41

Brown, T. Wistar, 470n14

Brown, Thomas S., 319

Brown, Uriah, 134

Brown v. Board of Education, 241, 243, 331, 334

Bryan, Helen, 219, 345

Bryn Mawr, 341, 358

Buckingham (PA) Friends School, 339

Buffalo Monthly Meeting, 305

Buffum, Arnold, 89, 92, 93, 96, 196

Buffum, James, 59

Building Bridges of Understanding, 225

Bunche, Ralph J., 222, 330

Buncombe, Marie H., 355

Bureau of Refugees, Freedmen, and Abandoned Lands, 153

Burling, William, 19–20

Burlington Quarterly Meeting, 189

Bustill, Anna, 190

Bustill, Cyrus, 125, 137, 190, 195, 447n119

Bustill, Elizabeth Morey, 75, 195

Byrd, Harry, 242

C

Cadbury, Henry: on African American ministers, 200; on African Americans and Quakerism, 181–82, 187, 194–95, 197, 203; AFSC conferences, 221; alternative service, 215; caution against generalizing, 205; on interracial education, 320–21; on Iowa Quakers, 180; on Quaker racial attitudes, 257; on Southland Meeting, 180

Caesar, 114, 416n207

Cairo (IL), 152

Caldwell, Samuel, 374

"Call to Action" (1964), 370

Cambridge Friends School (CFS), 336–37

Camp, Abraham, 57

camp meetings, 204

Campaign for Adequate Welfare Reform Now, 256

Campbell, R.C., 165

Canadian Yearly Meeting, 201

Canadian Young Friends, 228

Candler, John, 196

Cane Creek Meeting (NC), 412n141

Capon, Ross, 281

Carpenter, Joseph, 191, 465n63

Carroll, Kenneth, 180, 240

Carthagena Institute, 131

Cary, Margaret, 325

Cary, Stephen, 272

Cass County (MI), 100

Cathcart, Ernest, 346

Cazden, Elizabeth, 13, 181

cemeteries, segregated, 197–98

Center for Anti-Racist Education, 337

Center for People of Color, 383

Central Committee (of FGC), 304

Central Philadelphia Monthly Meeting, 384, 390

Ceresole, Pierre, 233

Chace, Elizabeth Buffum: activity in Underground Railroad, 103; anti-slavery organizations and, 77; on father's (Arnold Buffum) disownment, 89; John Brown and, 142; on Kelley, 434n164; school integration efforts of, 133–34; separation from Quakers, 92, 426n153, 429n42

Chandler, Elizabeth, 77

Chapel Hill Friends Meeting, 338

Chapman, Maria Weston, 81

charity schools, 125

Chase, Lucy, 152

Chase, Sarah, 152

Cheeks, Francine, 379

Cheney Training School for Teachers, 445n93, 445n94

Chester County, Pennsylvania, 74, 99, 103, 146, 291, 301

Chester Friends Project House, 301, 311

Chester (PA) Meeting, 17, 34, 254, 311–12; 324

Chester Quarter, 10, 17–18, 21

Cheyney University (formerly Cheyney State Teachers College), 177

Cheyney-Westtown Area Housing Group, 246

Chicago (IL), 247, 249–54, 372

Chicago Fellowship of Friends, 372, 373

Chicago Freedom Movement, 251, 481–82n45

Christian Union, 177

Christian Workers Training School for Bible Study and Practical Methods of Work, 202

Christiana Revolt of 1851, 103–4

Christiansburg Institute, 161, 172, 175, 319

church burnings, 308–9, 489n88

Churchman, John, 29, 30, 31, 35

Cicero (IL), 249

Cincinnati, Ohio, 63

Citizens Housing Corporation (Wilmingrton, DE), 246

Civil Rights Act of 1964, 255, 269, 479n205

civil rights, and federal action, 255–58

Civil rights legislation, 255–58

Civil War, 141–77; end of reconstruction, 167–73; Freedmen's Schools, 152–63; John Brown's raid on Harper's Ferry, 141–43; justification of racial judgment, 173–74; peace testimony during, 143–49; postwar western migration, 165–67; Quaker nonsupport of, 414n171, 414n172, 453–54n42;

Index

Lynd, Alice, 296
Lynd, Staughton, 296

M

Mabee, Carleton, 138
MacEwan, Sally, 339
Macpherson, Patricia, 358–59
Macy, Thomas, 99–100
Madison (WI) Monthly Meeting, 393
Mailin, Patrick Murphy, 323
Malcolm X, 310, 313
Malone, Emma, 202, 341
Malone, Walter, 202, 341
Malone College, 202
Mantua Belmont Joint Committee and Friends Housing, 252
Mantua Project, 234
Mantua-Belmont housing project, 252–53
Manumission Intelligencer, 52, 419n47
manumission law, 49–50
manumissions: of children, 38–39; Fox on, 12; numbers of, 38, 403n3, 403n9; recording of, 111; social consequences of, 40; in South, 40–41
Mapps, David, 127, 190
Mapps, Grace, 127, 190
Marble, John Putnam, 335
March on Washington, 236, 268–69, 303–5, 481–82n45
Marietta, Jack: on disownments, 37; on Friends' view of good works, 135; on Quaker attitudes toward abolition, 72, 418n33; on Quaker treatment of enslaved people, 13; on Quakers in government, 450n183; on reform movement, 29, 30
Marot, Helen, 214
Marriott, Charles, 89–90
Marshall, Edward, 494n64
Maruyama, Magoroh, 313
Maryland: antislavery societies in, 53, 54; enslaved population in, 8; enslavement as disownable offense, 4; petitions to state government, 8–9; Quaker perspectives on enslavement, 8–9; Quaker school integration in, 134; Quakers after migration, 119; reform movement and, 31; Woolman's influence in, 27
Maryland Yearly Meeting, 21–22, 38
Maryville (TN), 134
Maryville Friends Normal and Preparatory School (later Institute), 160, 172, 199
Massachusetts Anti-Slavery Society, 81
Massachusetts General Colored Association, 70
Massachusetts legislature, 83
Mat-su Monthly Meeting, 380
Matusow, Allan J., 286
Maurer, Johan, 363, 374, 385
May, Samuel J., 97, 101
McAllester, Robert, 348–49
McCorkel, Roy, 310

McCree, Dores, 337
McCree, Wade, Jr., 337
McFeely, Richard, 330, 331
McKiever, Charles, 8, 118
McKim, John, 136, 451n192
McKnight, Lancess, Jr., 322, 323–24
McLean, Cora, 200–201
McLean, Noah, 200–201
McPherson, Jesse, 199
Media (PA) Friends Meeting, 322
Media Friends School, 322–24, 336, 493n28
Meeting for Social Concerns (MSC, PYM): economic justice, 269; formation of, 274; integration, 362; Laird and, 224; reparations, 279, 284–85; on role of African American Friends, 375; Woodlawn Trust and, 249
Meeting for Sufferings of Philadelphia Yearly Meeting (Orthodox), 119
memorials. *See* petitions
Mendenhall, Birk, 348
Mendenhall, Dinah, 103
Mendenhall, Nathan, 116
Mendes, Anita, 394
"Message of Friendship from the Young Friends," 228
Methodists, 41, 431n76
Miami (Ohio) Quarterly Meeting, 93
Michener, Anna Jane, 237–38
Michener, James, 500n191
Michigan, 63, 100
Michigan Quarterly Meeting, 94
Middletown Meeting (PA), 197
Midwest: free produce movement in, 63; integration in Quaker schools, 134–35; migration to, 165–67; Quaker migration to, 166–67
Miers, Cynthia, 190
Mifflin, Warner, 39, 48–49, 113
migration of freed people, 114–19, 442n58, 443n70, 443n72
migration of Quakers, 117–18
Milgram, Morris, 246–47
Miller, Larry, 281, 295
Milner, Clyde, 346
Milwaukee (WI) Friends Meeting, 301
Missionary Board of Indiana Yearly Meeting, 200
Mississippi, schools in, 160
Mississippi Freedom Democratic Party, 300
Mississippi Freedom Schools, 296
Mississippi Summer, 300–301
Mitchell, John, 244
Mitchell, Morris, 347
Mitchell, Rebecca, 336
Mitchell, William, 150
Mizell, Hayes, 244
Moffett, Barbara, 303
Monadnock (NY) Monthly Meeting, 394
Montgomery (AL) bus boycott, 239, 270, 294–95
Montgomery Improvement Association, 294–95

CPSIA information can be obtained
at www.ICGtesting.com
Printed in the USA
FSHW022125101121
86058FS